Praise for *God's Word in Human Words*

"This is a fine survey of the issues that historical criticism raises for an evangelical understanding of Scripture and a useful survey of options in approaching those issues."
—**John Goldingay**, David Allan Hubbard Professor of Old Testament,
Fuller Theological Seminary

"Finally, a fresh, creative, carefully nuanced approach to biblical criticism from an evangelical! Sparks skillfully makes his case for a 'believing criticism' by carefully assessing the current available alternatives. In the process, he offers a useful survey of, and response to, typical hot-button issues. His thorough, methodical work stakes out for many thoughtful evangelicals a credible, theologically based, devout place to stand in integrating critical work and faith. I highly recommend it."
—**Robert L. Hubbard Jr.**, professor of biblical literature,
North Park Theological Seminary

"This important volume provides a bridge between critical scholarship and traditional views on Scripture. Sparks's aim is to present a reasoned and sometimes impassioned insider look at evangelical approaches to biblical scholarship. In the process of surveying the flash points created by modern critical scholarship, he champions 'practical realism' as an approach that provides a more productive middle ground between traditionalist views of authorship and dating of the text, which depend on harmonization or forced interpretations, and the antirealists of postmodern scholarship, who disregard historical context or the original audience. Both evangelicals and nonevangelicals will benefit from this very frank discussion of the history and possible future for biblical scholarship."
—**Victor H. Matthews**, associate dean, College of Humanities
and Public Affairs, Missouri State University

"Sparks issues an irenic invitation to reconcile academic consensus with evangelical conviction in ways that respect and inform both. His plea for his fellow evangelicals to take historical criticism much more seriously features impressive and honest arguments for mainstream critical stances toward Old and New Testament texts, informative tours of fields from hermeneutics to Assyriology to patristic and Reformation theology, and a bold proposal to affirm biblical inerrancy in terms of perfect divine accommodation to human error. May it encourage and shape the fruitful conversation we evangelicals absolutely need to have."

—**Telford Work**, assistant professor of theology, Westmont College

"Kent Sparks asks hard questions. In this volume he provides answers that he believes satisfy intellectually as well as spiritually. His erudition is evident on every page, whether summarizing the epistemological heritage of the Enlightenment, the historical-critical methods as applied to Assyriology, the constructive features of Barthian hermeneutics, or the ways in which the church has 'trumped Scripture.' Of course, not all will agree with his version of 'practical realism' and how it relates to biblical hermeneutics, but few can deny that that he has advanced the conversation in a way that is helpful and healthy."

—**Bill T. Arnold**, professor of Old Testament and Semitic languages, Asbury Theological Seminary

"What do we mean when we say our Bible—written by prophets, chroniclers, sages, evangelists, and apostles—is the word of God? In this book, Kenton Sparks engages that very question, emphatically affirming both the methodology and results of historical and modern biblical criticism *and* the authority of Scripture. He distinguishes divine inerrancy from the finite and fallible human vessels through whom God chose to reveal God's Word. The biblical text manifests significant theological diversity that is best addressed by recognizing the distinct genres of human and divine discourse; God accommodates his message to the finite and fallen perspectives of his human audience. While some readers will be uncomfortable with Sparks's characterization of conservative evangelical scholarship and his conclusions regarding the historicity of biblical narratives, this is a valuable window into the 'progressive evangelical' approach to the nature of Scripture."

—**Elaine A. Phillips**, professor of biblical and theological studies, Gordon College

GOD'S WORD
IN HUMAN
WORDS

GOD'S WORD IN HUMAN WORDS

An Evangelical Appropriation of Critical Biblical Scholarship

KENTON L. SPARKS

a division of Baker Publishing Group
Grand Rapids, Michigan

© 2008 by Kenton L. Sparks

Published by Baker Academic
a division of Baker Publishing Group
P.O. Box 6287, Grand Rapids, MI 49516-6287
www.bakeracademic.com

Printed in the United States of America

All rights reserved. No part of this publication may be reproduced, stored in a retrieval system, or transmitted in any form or by any means—for example, electronic, photocopy, recording—without the prior written permission of the publisher. The only exception is brief quotations in printed reviews.

Library of Congress Cataloging-in-Publication Data

Sparks, Kenton L.
    God's word in human words : an evangelical appropriation of critical biblical scholarship / Kenton L. Sparks.
       p. cm.
    Includes bibliographical references and indexes.
    ISBN 978-0-8010-2701-7 (pbk.)
    1. Bible—Criticism, interpretation, etc.—History. 2. Evangelicalism. I. Title.
BS500.S597 2008
220.601—dc22
                                                                                         2007037586

Scripture quotations labeled RSV are from the Revised Standard Version of the Bible, copyright 1952 [2nd edition, 1971] by the Division of Christian Education of the National Council of the Churches of Christ in the United States of America. Used by permission. All rights reserved.

Scripture quotations labeled NIV are from the HOLY BIBLE, NEW INTERNATIONAL VERSION®. NIV®. Copyright © 1973, 1978, 1984 by International Bible Society. Used by permission of Zondervan. All rights reserved.

Scripture quotations labeled NRSV are from the New Revised Standard Version of the Bible, copyright © 1989, by the Division of Christian Education of the National Council of the Churches of Christ in the United States of America. Used by permission. All rights reserved.

Scripture quotations labeled KJV are from the King James Version of the Bible.

To my father,
who taught me that God is big enough for our questions

Contents

Preface 11
Abbreviations 15
Introduction 17

1. Epistemology and Hermeneutics 25
2. Historical Criticism and Assyriology 57
3. The Problem of Biblical Criticism 73
4. "Traditional" Responses to Biblical Criticism 133
5. Constructive Responses to Biblical Criticism 171
6. The Genres of Human Discourse 205
7. The Genres of Divine Discourse 229
8. The Context of the Whole and Biblical Interpretation 261
9. Negotiating the Context of the Whole 279
10. Biblical Criticism and Christian Theology 329

Conclusions: Biblical Criticism and Christian Institutions 357
Bibliography 375
Scripture and Ancient Sources Index 395
Author Index 401
Subject Index 409

Preface

I RECALL THE MOMENT well. I was 14. It was a hot summer evening in the woodlands of Georgia, where I was attending yet another week of Christian service camp. While sitting on a tree stump during the "quiet time" hour, I read these words from Exodus 6:3: "I appeared to Abraham, to Isaac, and to Jacob as God Almighty, but by my name the LORD I did not make myself known to them." Instinctively, I flipped back through the book of Genesis, ready to observe the black-and-white evidence for this, yet another mystery from Scripture. But what I found was not mystery but rather mystery upon mystery. While Exodus clearly said that the patriarchs did not know the divine name, numerous texts from Genesis seemed to confirm that they surely did know that God was "the LORD." Although I did not realize it at the time, this was my first bout with historical criticism, or at least with the kinds of data that give rise to historical criticism.

It would be some thirteen years before an answer for this conundrum was inadvertently presented to me, in a set of study notes from the hand of the evangelical scholar Kenneth Kitchen. It was Kitchen's purpose to explain why the prevailing notion in biblical scholarship, that Genesis and Exodus were composed from several different sources, was completely wrong. The theory was not entirely new to me. I had heard this theory before from my graduate professor at the University of North Carolina, John Van Seters. Van Seters explained that there were two major sources in Genesis and Exodus, one in which the divine name was known to humanity more or less from the beginning of history, and another in which the divine name was revealed to humanity only at the time of Moses. When these two narratives were combined, he said, this produced the odd effect that I noticed on that old tree stump as a teenager. Of course, I did not believe Van Seters. He was not any sort of evangelical Christian, and I had been warned about the deceptive and beguiling ways of the biblical critics. Paradoxically, it was Kitchen himself— not Van Seters—who convinced me that the critics were right.

I have read numerous books by Kitchen, and though he is a fine Egyptologist, it is my experience that he generally does a poor job of presenting the views of critical biblical scholarship. But in the study notes to which I refer here, Kitchen's presentation was adequately clear. Indeed, by the time he had fully explained the critical theory of sources in the Pentateuch, I could hardly believe how reasonable and sensible the theory seemed. So I turned to the next page of Kitchen's notes with great anticipation, looking forward to a robust and convincing rebuttal of the critical deception. Then came the moment of disappointment. Having already shown me the earth from an orbiting spaceship, Kitchen then proceeded to argue that the earth was flat. For the first time it began to dawn on me that the critical arguments regarding the Pentateuch were far better, and carried much more explanatory power, than the flimsy broom that Kitchen was using to sweep them away. At that moment I began to doubt that evangelical scholars were really giving me the whole story when it came to the Bible and biblical scholarship.

Looking back on these events some years later, I can only say with regret that my early suspicions have often been confirmed. Though I can point to thoughtful evangelicals who have admitted that the critical arguments are often good (a pioneer in this regard was the late Ray Dillard of Westminster Theological Seminary), these scholars have been few and far between. Only now are we witnessing the emergence of a new generation of evangelical scholars who are willing to admit that the standard critical arguments are often much better than the ill-advised apologetic that evangelicals have aimed at them. If one cares at all about the truth, then this is a welcome development.

I count myself a member of this new generation of evangelical scholars, and the present volume is a modest contribution to their work. Its purpose is to provide resources that I have found helpful during my own intellectual pilgrimage, as I have tried to navigate the sometimes precarious path that takes both faith and critical thinking seriously. The path is precarious because, as Scripture has warned us, those who teach in the church will be especially culpable for their errors. So here, as in other ways, I work out my salvation with fear and trembling. But when I fearfully exercise my duty as a teacher, it means that I must make good judgments about the kinds of dangers that can arise when I err in my work. For the old-school evangelicals, the chief danger to be feared has been that our teaching might explicitly or implicitly undermine the authority of Scripture, and this is a concern that I very much share. But there are other threats to the gospel that this generation of scholars has not taken seriously. Chief among them is the possibility that their version of the Christian faith might harbor false ideas and beliefs that, because they are mistaken, serve as barriers to faith for those who see our evangelical errors. As one example, evangelicals often fail to recognize the possibility that, by arguing strenuously for the strict historicity of Genesis 1, they are more or less shutting their church doors to countless scientists and scholars who might otherwise have come to faith. In essence, the old-school evangelicals have been so sure that they are right that they no longer consider seriously the possibility that they are *too* conservative; "conservative," not in the sense of theological orthodoxy, but in the sense that they are unable to really think critically about whether their traditions are intellectually adequate and spiritually healthy.

The new generation of evangelicals is generally more comfortable than the last with raising serious questions about the evangelical tradition, especially when mounting evidence suggests that certain aspects of that tradition are symptomatic of an intellectual "scandal" (as one prominent evangelical expressed it).[1] But let me be clear on this point. By saying this, I am not denying that our faith should involve a kind of scandal. For I would affirm with the apostle Paul that the truest power of God is revealed most vividly in the scandal of the cross. My chief concern is that we should avoid a grave theological error, which uses the *legitimate scandal of faith* as a basis for our *illegitimate intellectual scandals*. If the fear of God is to play a role in our Christian thinking and teaching—and I affirm that it should—then let us realize that our intellectual and doctrinal errors can be of many types and head in many directions. Very conservative evangelicals are right to be vigilant in their defense of biblical authority. But, as I hope to show, biblical authority is a complex matter, and it is only one of many theological matters that require our thoughtful vigilance.

As I make my case for this and some of the other positions that I will take in this book, one of my objectives along the way is to demonstrate that my viewpoints are not wholly new but, in important respects, stand in continuity with the long-standing traditions of Christian theology and with important strands of the evangelical tradition. Doing so reflects my firm conviction that whole-cloth theological innovation can never pass the canons of orthodoxy. One way of demonstrating this connection with the past is to cite authors from those traditions (whether ancient fathers like Augustine or evangelicals like James Orr) whose views comport with mine to some extent. Now, my citations are necessarily selective, and one could as easily find quotations from Augustine and Orr that disagree with my conclusions in various ways. But of course the main point is not that my views will or should suit any particular author all of the time; the rather more modest point is that many of the things that I say resonate with things that other Christians, with unquestionable faith pedigrees, have already said. This does not mean that I will ignore contrary voices in my discussion, however. For as a rule much of this book is given to an engagement with those viewpoints that I find wanting in whole or part.

Since I plan to quote, I might as well begin now. Although I often disagree with the viewpoints of Alexander Campbell, namesake of the Campbellites, there is at least one instance where I find that his wisdom is dead on. In his first reply to Robert Owen in the famous Campbell-Owen debate, Campbell declared: "I know, indeed, that there is no circumstance in which any person can be placed more unfavorable to his conviction, than that which puts him in a public assembly

---

1. Mark Noll, *The Scandal of the Evangelical Mind* (Grand Rapids: Eerdmans, 1994).

upon the proof of his principles. The mind is then on the alert to find proofs for the system which has been already adopted, and is not disposed to such an investigation as might issue in conviction. Arguments and proofs are rather parried than weighed; and triumph rather than conviction is anxiously sought for."[2] Campbell's point is clear enough: even in matters of faith, all of us should be prepared to accept the fact that we can be wrong. This is true of you as a reader, but I know that it is also quite true of me as a writer. So, while I do hope to make some points that readers will find helpful, I am painfully aware that my own views are always a work in progress.

Before I begin my discussion in earnest, I have a long list of accrued debts that I can only confess but never repay. First on the list are my valued colleagues at Eastern University: Steve Boyer, Eric Flett, Chris Hall, Betsy Morgan, Dwight Peterson, Margaret Peterson, Mary Stewart Van Leeuwen, Randy Colton, and especially Phil Cary, Carl Mosser, and Ray Van Leeuwen. I should mention as well my research assistant, Greg Klimowitz, who gave me a student's perspective on the manuscript. Others who have read the manuscript, or discussed with me its substance, include John Goldingay (Fuller Theological Seminary), Peter Enns (Westminster Theological Seminary), Leo Sandgren (University of Florida), Jim Kinney (Baker Academic), and an anonymous (but insightful) reader acquired by Baker Academic on my behalf. Whether those listed here actually agree with my conclusions is another matter, but there is no question that I have benefited from their expertise.

As is always the case at the end of a project, I am very thankful for the support, encouragement, and patience of my wife, Cheryl, and of my two daughters, Emily and Cara Ellen. Among other things, Cheryl read and commented on certain parts of the manuscript and made it possible for me to put in some extra time in the office, especially toward the end of the project. As for the girls, the joy that they give us makes every labor of work a little less laborious.

I am very pleased that this book affords an opportunity to modestly express my deep gratitude to my father, Morris Sparks, to whom this book is rightfully dedicated. In many talks over the years, he has always taught me that critical thinking and faith in God go together. I knew long ago that he was right about this, but I had no idea just how right he was.

Soli Deo Gloria!

---

2. Alexander Campbell and Robert Owen, *Debate on the Evidences of Christianity* (London: R. Groombridge, 1839), 14.

Abbreviations

AB	Anchor Bible
ABD	*Anchor Bible Dictionary.* Edited by D. N. Freedman. 6 vols. New York: Doubleday, 1992.
ANET	*Ancient Near Eastern Texts Relating to the Old Testament.* Edited by J. B. Pritchard. 3rd ed. Princeton: Princeton University Press, 1969.
ANF	Ante-Nicene Fathers
ATSHB	Kenton L. Sparks, *Ancient Texts for the Study of the Hebrew Bible: A Guide to the Background Literature.* Peabody, MA: Hendrickson, 2005.
BibInt	*Biblical Interpretation*
BZAW	Beihefte zur Zeitschrift für die alttestamentliche Wissenschaft
CBQ	*Catholic Biblical Quarterly*
CNT	Commentaire du Nouveau Testament
COS	*The Context of Scripture.* Edited by W. W. Hallo. 3 vols. Leiden: Brill, 1997–2002.
DtrH	Deuteronomistic History
E	Elohistic source
EKKNT	Evangelisch-katholischer Kommentar zum Neuen Testament
ICC	International Critical Commentary
Int	*Interpretation*
J	Yahwist
JAOS	*Journal of the American Oriental Society*
JBL	*Journal of Biblical Literature*
JETS	*Journal of the Evangelical Theological Society*
JHI	*Journal of the History of Ideas*
JNES	*Journal of Near Eastern Studies*

JSNT	*Journal for the Study of the New Testament*
JSOT	*Journal for the Study of the Old Testament*
JSOTSup	Journal for the Study of the Old Testament: Supplement Series
KJV	King James Version
LKL	Lagash King List
LXX	Septuagint
MT	Masoretic Text
NAC	New American Commentary
NCB	New Century Bible
NEchtB	Neue Echter Bibel
NICNT	New International Commentary on the New Testament
NICOT	New International Commentary on the Old Testament
NIV	New International Version
NPNF	*Nicene and Post-Nicene Fathers*
NRSV	New Revised Standard Version
ODCC	*Oxford Dictionary of the Christian Church.* Edited by F. L. Cross and E. A. Livingstone. 3rd ed. Oxford: Oxford University Press, 1997.
OTL	Old Testament Library
OTP	*The Old Testament Pseudepigrapha.* Edited by James H. Charlesworth. 2 vols. Garden City, NY: Doubleday, 1983–1985.
OTS	*Old Testament Studies*
P	Priestly source
RSV	Revised Standard Version
SBLDS	Society of Biblical Literature Dissertation Series
SBLMS	Society of Biblical Literature Monograph Series
SHS	Scripture and Hermeneutics Series
SJT	*Scottish Journal of Theology*
SKL	Sumerian King List
SP	Samaritan Pentateuch
TOTC	Tyndale Old Testament Commentaries
VT	*Vetus Testamentum*
WBC	Word Biblical Commentary
WTJ	*Westminster Theological Journal*
ZAW	*Zeitschrift für die alttestamentliche Wissenschaft*
ZBK	Zürcher Bibelkommentare

Introduction

Aᴌʟ ᴏꜰ ᴜs believe that the earth orbits the sun, and in this idea we find nothing deceptive, theologically dangerous, or heretical. Yet it is instructive to recall that this was not always so. When Galileo first joined Copernicus in intimating that the earth was not at the center of the universe, he was soundly rebuked by church authorities—Catholic and Protestant alike—who averred that Scripture, church tradition, and common sense clearly taught that the astronomer was wrong. Some of Galileo's detractors even refused to consider the evidence by looking through his telescope.[1] The astronomer was eventually put on trial in a church proceeding, during which church authorities insisted that he recant his views. Galileo eventually yielded to their demands, but we can surmise that his words of repentance did not convince the gray matter in his head.

The significance of this moment in church history is elucidated by an instructive question. Were Galileo's views really *dangerous*? We are tempted perhaps to insist that his ideas were true and hence could not be dangerous, but there is clear evidence that Galileo's views—and the similar views of Copernicus—indeed spawned grave theological doubts in the minds of some people. This was a natural consequence of the fact that the church could not easily absorb the insights of Galileo and Copernicus when standard Christian doctrine contradicted their new astronomical insights on so many levels. From this we can reasonably conclude that even the truth can be dangerous and harmful to the church if this truth is not properly assimilated to the world of Scripture and faith. That is, in some measure we might say that "true facts" when wrongly understood turn out to imply all sorts of "false facts." Yet it hardly seems possible to conclude that the church's proper

---

1. For the whole story, see: Giorgio de Santillana, *The Crime of Galileo* (Chicago: University of Chicago Press, 1955); Maurice A. Finocchiaro, *Retrying Galileo, 1633–1992* (Berkeley: University of California Press, 2005); Jerome J. Langford, *Galileo, Science, and the Church*, rev. ed. (Ann Arbor: University of Michigan Press, 1971).

response to new theories and insights, whether of Galileo or of someone else, is to ignore or deny them. Rather, what is sorely needed in every age—for the sake of believers and unbelievers alike—is a church that knows how to thoughtfully consider and assimilate the fruits of academic endeavors to its faith in Christ. In broad strokes, my aim in this volume is to help shape the intellectual contours of the church so that it can perform this scholastic duty better. However, my pursuit of this objective is prompted not by general concerns but rather by a more specific problem faced by the modern church.

The Church's Problem with Historical Criticism

My chief interest here is not in the astronomical views of Galileo and Copernicus. I am interested instead in considering another kind of scholarship that some corners of the church have found dangerous and unhealthy, namely, that approach to biblical scholarship that goes by names like "historical criticism," "higher criticism," or "biblical criticism." Just as Galileo invited us to turn a critical eye toward the cosmos, so modern biblical scholars bid us to reflect critically upon our assumptions about the nature of Scripture and about how it should be read properly. Such a critical exercise should be a vital element in our study of Scripture because we are so apt, as finite and fallible human beings, to commit interpretive errors when we read the Bible. In many corners of the church, however, historical criticism has not been so helpful. Why not?

In order to answer this question in a preliminary way, let us briefly consider a few instances in which the church's traditional readings of the Bible have differed from the critical conclusions offered by most modern biblical scholars. We will consider three examples from the Old Testament and three from the New Testament (see table 1).

For instance if we inspect our first example more closely (the Pentateuch), it becomes rather clear that the differences between the traditional and the historical-critical readings are striking. Church tradition has assumed that the Pentateuch is an historically accurate document written by Moses during the second millennium BCE. Modern scholars, on the other hand, are very skeptical about the historical value of the Pentateuch, and they attribute these five biblical books to several authors working well after Moses would have lived. At this juncture we needn't debate the relative merits of these traditional and critical viewpoints; it is enough to appreciate why biblical criticism appears so different from—and threatening to—the traditional approach.

Over the years there have been three basic responses to the tension between traditional views of Scripture and modern biblical scholarship. First, in some circles, the embracing of biblical criticism has had the effect of desacralizing the Bible. According to this view, the results of biblical scholarship provide "sure evidence" that Scripture is a thoroughly human product rather than a divinely

Table 1

Text	Traditional Reading	Modern Scholarship
The Pentateuch (Genesis–Deuteronomy)	This historically accurate narrative was written by Moses during the 2nd millennium BCE	Myth, legend, and other ancient traditions have been written or assembled by several authors who lived long after Moses
Isaiah	Written by the prophet Isaiah in the 8th century BCE	Written by several prophets over a period of several hundred years
Daniel	Written by the prophet Daniel during the 6th century BCE	A pseudonymous work written in the name of Daniel by a scribe (or scribes) living during the 2nd century BCE
The Four Gospels (Matthew–John)	The four Gospels present historically compatible pictures of Jesus's life	The Gospels provide four different, sometimes quite different, portraits of Jesus's life. Moreover, some of these Gospel traditions are fictional rather than purely historical literature.
Pastoral Epistles (1–2 Timothy, Titus)	Written by Paul during the 1st century CE	Pseudonymously attributed to Paul by another author during the 2nd century CE
Revelation	Predicts that the parousia (second coming) of Christ will come at some unknown point in the future	Wrongly predicts that the parousia of Christ would come during the Roman period

inspired book. Thus divested of its authority, the Bible becomes just another of many religious texts for scholars to study, dissect, and critique. Although this response might strike us as thoroughly irreligious, there are interpretive communities within Judaism and Christianity that embrace this skeptical posture toward the Bible. Because of its tendency to secularize the Bible, I prefer to call this response to biblical criticism the *secular* response.

Second, at the other end of the spectrum, we find the *traditional* response. Included in this camp are Jews and Christians—as well as many evangelicals—who have rejected the standard results of biblical scholarship because they believe that these results, if true, would represent a serious threat to biblical authority. Traditionalists normally argue that theories of biblical criticism are wrong because they rest on poor scholarship or, worse, upon the naive, naturalistic assumptions of the Enlightenment. Although the traditional and secular responses are obviously poles apart in their perspectives on biblical authority, it is worth noting that the two views agree on an important point: biblical criticism seems to strike a blow against the Bible's authority. They disagree only on whether biblical criticism's judgments about the Bible are correct (the secular view) or incorrect (the traditional view).

Between these two perspectives—but quite different from both—one finds various efforts to forge a tertium quid option, in which traditional faith and critical scholarship are somehow integrated into a healthy whole. This program has yielded mixed results, as we will see in chapter 5. But the underlying impulse of tertium quid scholarship is its dual confidence in the divine origins of Scripture and in the usefulness of modern biblical scholarship. In view of this dual commitment, let us call this third response to biblical criticism the *constructive* response. So the three responses to modern biblical criticism may be neatly contrasted like this: the *secular* response (which rejects biblical authority on the basis of biblical criticism), the *traditional* response (which rejects the results of biblical criticism to protect biblical authority), and the *constructive* response (which attempts to integrate biblical criticism to the faith). Because of its twofold commitment to faith and scholarship, the constructive response is sometimes referred to as *believing criticism*, which is a label I like to use.

The theological tradition in which I live and serve is American evangelicalism, a modern sociological and religious movement whose roots lie in the Christian fundamentalism of America's nineteenth and twentieth centuries. Although it is fairly accurate to describe its view of the Bible as "traditional," there are strong tendencies within progressive evangelicalism to seek out a "third way" that integrates faith with modern scholarship. This move is in some respects new to the American scene, but it has been a fixture in British evangelicalism for some time. Consider these words of F. F. Bruce, written in 1947: "In such critical *cruces*, for example, as the codification of the Pentateuch, the composition of Isaiah, the date of Daniel, the sources of the Gospels, or the authenticity of the Pastoral Epistles, each of us is free to hold and proclaim the conclusions to which all the available evidence points."[2]

It is fascinating to compare this comment, which reflects no anxiety about critical conclusions concerning the book of Isaiah, with the comments recently offered by Richard Schultz, an American evangelical, on the same issue: "The gates have been opened wide, and applications of historical-critical methods and conclusions are flooding evangelical biblical studies. Such irrigation can foster growth initially, but ultimately it may cause destruction."[3]

The different temperaments toward critical scholarship that we see in Bruce and Schultz epitomize what Schultz correctly sees as a new and serious tension that is emerging within evangelical circles, as traditionalists labor to protect evangelical hermeneutics from historical criticism, while other evangelicals invite modern historical criticism to the table of debate. Let me say quite clearly that the concerns of those who are suspicious of biblical criticism are not unfounded. Historical criticism has been around for only a few centuries, yet it seems clear enough that its work has often undermined the perception of Scripture's authority, leaving many destructive effects in its wake: believers have lost their faith, churches and seminaries have abandoned creedal orthodoxy, and unbelievers have found reasons to doubt the authenticity of the Christian

---

2. F. F. Bruce, "The Tyndale Fellowship for Biblical Research," *Evangelical Quarterly* 19 (1947): 58–59.
3. Richard L. Schultz, "How Many Isaiahs Were There and What Does It Matter?" in *Evangelicals and Scripture: Tradition, Authority, and Hermeneutics*, ed. Vincent E. Bacote, Laura C. Miguélez, and Dennis L. Okholm (Downers Grove, IL: InterVarsity, 2004), 150–70.

message.[4] One could easily speak of "the death of Scripture."[5] These negative assessments of historical criticism are not evangelical alone but appear as well in many nonevangelical Christian communities, as we will see. So it seems to me—and to many others—that historical criticism has often been a dangerous and destructive force in the life of the church.

The Paradox of Biblical Criticism

So we face a curious paradox. If biblical criticism leads to false and destructive results, and if it is indeed as intellectually bankrupt as some conservative theologians aver, then why have so many thoughtful believers entered university graduate programs with a vibrant devotion to God only to emerge on the other side of their studies with a dead or failing faith, and with the firm conviction that historical criticism easily bests the traditional viewpoint? Do Christian graduate students succumb to the deceptive power of university professors? Are they easily swayed to sacrifice their faith on the altar of academic respectability? Is hubris so endemic to academic inquiry that most graduate students—even Christian graduate students—arrogantly use critical scholarship to escape God's claim on their lives? Perhaps. But even if these questions direct our attention to important issues, there are other questions worth asking, questions that traditionalists sometimes overlook. Is it possible that the persuasive power of historical criticism rests especially in its correctness? Could it be that historical criticism—like the astronomy of Galileo—has been destructive not because it is false, but because the church has often misunderstood its implications? If so, then we may eventually have to face a tragic paradox: the church's wholesale rejection of historical criticism has begotten the irreverent use of Scripture by skeptics, thus destroying the faith of some believers while keeping unbelievers away from the faith. If this is indeed what has happened and is happening, then nothing less is needed than the church's careful reevaluation of its relationship to historical-critical readings of Scripture. That reevaluation is my agenda here.

Given this agenda, I would like to remind the reader where I am coming from. I am an evangelical, committed fully to the Bible as God's authoritative Word, to the doctrines of historic creedal orthodoxy, to the unique significance of the death, resurrection, and ascension of Jesus Christ, and to the hope of his return. I would go even further than this by confessing my profound appreciation for the

---

4. Roy A. Harrisville and Walter Sundberg, *The Bible in Modern Culture: Theology and Historical-Critical Method from Spinoza to Käsemann* (Grand Rapids: Eerdmans, 1995); Walter Sundberg, "The Social Effect of Biblical Criticism," in *Renewing Biblical Interpretation*, ed. Craig G. Bartholomew, Colin Greene, and Karl Möller, SHS 1 (Grand Rapids: Zondervan, 2000), 66–81; James A. Sanders, *Canon and Community: A Guide to Canonical Criticism* (Philadelphia: Fortress, 1984).

5. Robert Morgan and John Barton, *Biblical Interpretation*, Oxford Bible Series (Oxford: Oxford University Press, 1988), 44–61.

evangelical tradition, for its emphasis on Christian living, its practical commitment to evangelism and missions, and also its doctrinal commitment to the inerrancy of God's Word. So I would not be writing this book, with evangelical readers in mind, were it not for the profound spiritual vitality that marks the character and mission of evangelicalism. At the same time, as I have just mentioned, few would deny that considerable tensions are now emerging within the evangelical fold. In many respects these tensions can be traced back to the problem that I wish to consider here, the problem of modern biblical criticism.

Historical Criticism: An Example

I have so far assumed that readers have some familiarity with the spirit and practice of historical criticism, but it cannot hurt before moving on to be more specific about it. I would like to do so by providing a very old but straightforward example of historical criticism, which dates from the fifteenth century.

During the latter part of the Middle Ages, papal authority in the Christian West was partially secured by an appeal to the Donation of Constantine. This document purported to be an imperial edict of Constantine (fourth century CE), in which he donated all of the Western Roman Empire to the authority of the pope. At about the same time, however, scholars of the Middle Ages were becoming increasingly interested in the study of technical philology. Scholars studying the languages of ancient texts began to notice that human languages have a history. Latin of the first century was different from Latin of the sixth century, and so forth. As a result, texts could be dated on the basis of their grammar, vocabulary, and dialect; one could even demonstrate that supposedly ancient texts were actually forgeries, falsely written in the name of some famous person. Such was the case when the Renaissance humanist Lorenzo Valla (c. 1406–1457) deduced that the Donation of Constantine was a forgery.[6] Valla had a fine enough sense of Latin's historical development to discern that the text could not have been written during the fourth-century reign of Constantine but was instead a much later forgery.

Valla's work is often cited as one of the earliest instances of historical criticism.[7] As the example shows, historical criticism is really, at its heart, nothing other than an interpretive method that appreciates the historically contingent nature of human discourse. That is, when it comes to interpreting verbal discourse, that discourse is a product of—hence dependent upon—the changing currents and tides of language, religious belief, social structure, cultural values, and political realities. Now in this case it will not surprise us that the Reformers, particularly Martin Luther, loved Valla's critical impulse. For the work of Valla embodied what

---

6. "Donation of Constantine (*Constitutum* or *Donatio Constantini*)," *ODCC* 499; "Valla, Lorenzo," *ODCC* 1677–78.

7. Carlo Ginzburg, "Lorenzo Valla on the 'Donation of Constantine,'" chap. 2 in *History, Rhetoric, and Proof* (Hanover: University Press of New England, 1999), 54–70.

would become standard practice for the Reformers: radical historical criticism. Historical research was the primary method used by the Reformers to expose much of the Roman Church's doctrine and power base as medieval accretions rather than biblical teaching. So far so good for conscientious Protestants—but the other shoe was still to fall. Though these early Protestants were accustomed to thinking that good historical scholarship was on their side, their heirs were not really prepared for the way that historical-critical scholarship would eventually affect the reading of the Bible itself.

Conclusions

We live in the era of historical consciousness, which emerged during the Renaissance and Reformation and then reached full bloom during and after the Enlightenment. As a result, all of us are historical critics of a sort, or at least believers in many ideas that were produced by historical criticism. So while we should for good reason be cautious about embracing everything that passes as "historical and critical," perhaps it is reasonable to consider the merits of historical criticism more carefully. But let me be clear from the outset. I have no desire to bring the methods and results of historical criticism directly into our local churches, or to have its critical conclusions carelessly preached from pulpits or taught in Sunday school classes. Nor do I wish to defend historical criticism at all cost, as if modern biblical scholarship is in all respects healthy and helpful. It is clear to me—and to many others—that certain kinds of biblical criticism reflect neither of these qualities. No, my objective in this book is more modest. There are at present two major impulses within the evangelical tradition regarding biblical criticism. One of these accepts the criticism as a legitimate way to study Scripture, and the other more or less rejects the criticism. I write to suggest that one of these paths is healthier than the other, and also to suggest how that path can be fruitfully traveled by Christians. In the end, it is for the reader to judge whether and to what extent my conclusions are sensible and right.

Let me conclude by returning to the example of Galileo. The church eventually realized that his astronomy was correct and integrated his new insights into its worldview. This had the positive effect of rendering Galileo's ideas theologically safe. My purpose in this volume is similar. I would like us to consider the possibility that historical criticism—in spite of its potential faults and negative import—might offer a relatively accurate portrait of Scripture that will be of theological value once the church correctly understands its insights. Here is how I will proceed. In the chapter that follows I will consider various epistemological and hermeneutical issues that are to my mind prerequisite to our discussion of historical criticism. I do not believe that one can understand or evaluate historical criticism apart from this background. Chapter 2 will discuss historical criticism per se, followed in turn by a discussion of biblical criticism in chapter 3. In chapters 4 and 5 I will outline a variety of Christian responses to historical criticism before I attempt to forge a healthier set of solutions in chapters 6 through 9. In chapter 10 I will test these solutions by applying them to a set of specific problems raised by historical criticism. My deliberations will then end with prospective comments in the concluding chapter. Among other things, in this concluding chapter I will give special attention to how the subject of biblical criticism ought to be managed in the life of the local church and in the curricula of Christian institutions of higher learning. The ultimate goal of this agenda is to fashion a Christian response to modern biblical criticism that is intellectually satisfying as well as theologically and spiritually healthy.

1

Epistemology and Hermeneutics

I PROPOSE TO BEGIN with the problem of interpretation. Not with biblical interpretation only, but with interpretation in the widest possible sense, in terms of its history and philosophy. Some friends and colleagues who have read this manuscript have suggested that this part of my discussion ought to be presented later in the book, or even left out altogether. Their arguments in this direction have been uniform: that evangelical readers might be put off by some of the points that I make here; that they might as a result either put the book down or, barring that, continue reading with suspicion toward all that I say. Indeed, this advice reflects a concern that I have, and because of it I have toyed with all sorts of rhetorical options. But in the end I have decided that what we are about to discuss fits precisely here in our deliberations together. The reason for this is straightforward. I believe that the rise of modern biblical criticism, and the various responses to it that dot the intellectual landscape, cannot be understood very well apart from the history of interpretation sketched in this chapter. If this is so, if what we are about to discuss is truly prerequisite and prolegomenon to all else that will be said, then we have little choice but to tackle the matter right now—even if doing so is less than ideal.

Epistemology and hermeneutics are two closely related fields of academic study. Epistemology is the branch of philosophy that studies human knowledge. It attempts to answer fundamental questions like: What is knowledge? How do we acquire it? How do we know (or can we know) that what we believe is true? As for hermeneutics, this field of study originated with a methodological focus on how to interpret texts, but during the nineteenth century it quickly transitioned from a focus on *method* to a focus on the *event* of understanding itself. Hermeneutics in this modern sense has to do with understanding the conditions that make interpretation and knowledge possible. Its interests are not only in interpreting texts, like the Bible, but also in the interpretation of human experiences, from the phenomena that pass before our eyes to the very thoughts that pass through our heads. In other words, very little in life escapes the interest of hermeneutics. To be human is to interpret. Or, to put it in the brash words of Jacques Derrida, "In the beginning is hermeneutics."[1]

Although the history of Western epistemology and hermeneutics is complex, I would like to offer a brief historical overview of developments in these fields over the past few centuries. In doing so, I will refer to the major periods of development in this history as the *premodern*, *modern*, and *postmodern* periods. The differences between these three periods hinge, in many respects, on the concept of *tradition*. "Tradition" comes from the Latin term *traditio*, meaning that which is transmitted or "handed on." In scholarly parlance, it is "the recurrence of the same structures of conduct and patterns of belief over several generations."[2] In every society, whether ancient or modern, "primitive" or "advanced," most of what passes as knowledge comes from tradition. Individuals tend to receive their view of the world passively, as they grow up in and are acculturated to their native family and society. Knowledge in such cases is not something that one discovers so much as something that happens to us in culture and experience. As Michael Polanyi has expressed it, most of our knowledge is "tacit" knowledge—knowledge that we have unconsciously inherited from experience and tradition.[3] Although tradition is for this reason an essential source of knowledge in every culture, this does not mean that all societies are equally disposed toward tradition. While simple (or "primitive") societies tend to accept tradition without much reflection, in some cultures tradition is questioned pretty rigorously. Our quest to appreciate the history of Western epistemology and hermeneutics, and its import for our discussion, will have to attend carefully to how each era responded to tradition.

The Premodern Period

The historical period that interests me presently runs from the early church to the dawn of the Renaissance, that is, from the first to the fourteenth century. Historians of interpretation sometimes refer to this period as the "precritical" period, but I prefer "premodern" for reasons that will become clear. How did premodern scholars respond to tradition? It is commonly asserted that the modes

---

1. Jacques Derrida, *Writing and Difference*, trans. Alan Bass (Chicago: University of Chicago Press, 1978), 67.
2. Edward Shils, "Tradition," *Comparative Studies in Society and History* 13 (1971): 123.
3. Michael Polanyi, *The Tacit Dimension* (Garden City, NY: Anchor Books, 1967).

of inquiry that prevailed during this period were very traditional, that people tended simply to embrace whatever tradition said. Now to some extent this is how it was, particularly respecting religion. The church's authority on matters of faith was generally accepted without serious question. Consequently, while scholars from Augustine to Aquinas raised all sorts of critical questions about theological and philosophical issues, these questions tended to assume the church's Rule of Faith and so moved within its orbit. This traditional posture foreclosed certain questions and options, even for brilliant and critical thinkers like Aquinas.[4] Of course, some scholars openly challenged church dogmas, but they usually reaped trouble for their effort. Heretics were generally removed from their posts, exiled, or sometimes executed.

I suspect that premodern scholars sometimes submitted to the authority of church tradition more out of duty than intellectual conviction, but this response to tradition needn't imply an exercise in duplicity, in which scholars merely pretended to accept church doctrine. Even when their minds suggested alternatives to tradition, premodern scholars tended to follow the church's judgment because they were profoundly aware of the great gulf that separated divine knowledge from human knowledge. The early fathers believed that God was ultimately mysterious and incomprehensible, so that his revelation in Christ and in the Bible was an accommodation or condescension to our level.[5] God spoke to us in baby talk, as it were, because human beings are simply unable to understand anything as God understands it.[6] So premodern scholars were theoretically and theologically committed to humility in matters of interpretation and human knowledge. In general, they thought it better to trust the judgments of tradition more than the impulses of their private individual judgments. Whether they always lived out this humility is another matter, but they were certainly aware of the limitations of human knowledge.

Premodern methods of interpreting Scripture reflect this concept of divine mystery. Biblical interpretation in this early period was deeply influenced by Greek philosophy, especially by Platonism and Platonic exegesis. One result is that early Christians found multiple levels of meaning in Scripture, not only its literal sense but also its figurative senses, that is, its allegorical, tropological (moral), and anagogical (eschatological) meanings. These mysterious figurative senses of Scripture were not discernible to everyone, but only to those with the necessary theological and spiritual qualifications.[7] Contrary to a common modern miscon-

---

4. *Summa Theologica*, pt. 2.2, q. 10, art. 7 (= *The Summa Theologica*, 5 vols. [Allen, TX: Christian Classics, 1981], 3:1212).

5. Christopher A. Hall, *Learning Theology with the Church Fathers* (Downers Grove, IL: InterVarsity, 2002), 43–81; John Chrysostom, *On the Incomprehensible Nature of God*, trans. Paul W. Harkins, Fathers of the Church 72 (Washington, DC: Catholic University of America Press, 1984).

6. For a discussion of this feature in patristic theology, see chapter 7 of the present volume and Stephen D. Benin, *The Footprints of God: Divine Accommodation in Jewish and Christian Thought* (Albany: State University of New York Press, 1993).

7. See Origen, *Against Celsus* 4.71 (*ANF* 4:529); Origen, *On First Principles* preface, 4.8–17 (*ANF* 4:355–66); Augustine, *On Christian Doctrine* 2.7; 2.41; 3.5 (*NPNF* 1 2:538–39, 555, 559).

ception, this multilevel hermeneutic did not involve ignoring the intentions of the biblical author. For the ancients, God himself was the author of Scripture, of both its literal and figurative senses. So biblical allegories were no less "intended" than the literal sense of Scripture.

As I said, allegories reflected the mystery of Scripture and so enhanced the perception that the Bible was a divine book. But the utility of allegory for early Christians went beyond this. One of the chief difficulties faced by early Christians involved the apparent conflicts and contradictions in the Bible, especially the tensions between the Old and New Testaments. How could God command us to love our enemies in the New Testament when, in the Old Testament, he was praised for dashing Babylonian infants against rocks (Ps. 138:8–9)? For Augustine and the other early fathers, Old Testament texts like this did not have literal or plain meanings at all. They were allegories from the ground up. In this particular case Augustine believed that the "infants" of Babylon were not literal children but rather the "vices" of the Babylonians.[8] Even Jerome, who was much less prone to allegories, resorted to them when necessary. Upon reading the account in 1 Kings 1:1–4, in which the aged and decrepit David was warmed by placing a beautiful young lady in his bed, Jerome concluded that this story could not be historical. After all, David had many wives who could have provided this support. For him to turn aside after this young woman would have been wholly immoral. From this Jerome surmised that in 1 Kings we have instead an allegorical tale, in which David was warmed not by a literal woman named Abishag but by "Lady Wisdom" (cf. Prov. 4:5–9).[9] Patristic exegesis employed this method extensively, for it was the primary means for resolving the ostensible contradictions in Scripture. Gregory the Great expressed it this way: "Undoubtedly the words of the literal text, when they do not agree with each other, show that something else is to be sought in them. It is as if they said to us, 'When you see us apparently embarrassed and contradictory, look within us for that which is coherent and consistent.'"[10]

While just about everyone in the early church allegorized Scripture, tolerance for allegories varied from scholar to scholar and place to place. Allegories were all the rage in North Africa and the Christian West (e.g., Augustine, Gregory the Great), but scholars in the Christian East, such as Theodore of Mopsuestia and Theodoret of Cyrus, were suspicious of these figurative meanings.[11] In theory they allowed for allegories, but only when these seemed genuinely compatible with Scripture's plain meaning, which they preferred. So there were great differences in the hermeneutical temperaments of Christian scholars in the East and West. Nevertheless, they shared at least one important quality: they deeply respected the Christian tradition.

---

8. Augustine, *Expositions on the Book of Psalms* (*NPNF* 1 8:632).
9. Jerome, "To Nepotian," 52.2–3, in *Letters* (*NPNF* 2 6:89–90).
10. Gregory the Great, "Moralia in Job," in William Yarchin, *History of Biblical Interpretation* (Peabody, MA: Hendrickson, 2004), 89.
11. See the comments of Theodore and Theodoret in Yarchin, *History of Biblical Interpretation*, 76–85.

Premodern commitment to the church and its traditions began to unravel during the modern era, but this more skeptical view of traditional authority did not appear out of thin air. Two premodern developments paved the way for this new view of tradition, both of them suitably represented by the work of Thomas Aquinas. Aquinas was an avid student of Greek philosophy and discovered that the works of Aristotle were chock-full of valuable philosophical insights. His great work, *Summa Theologica*, was an effort to enhance traditional Christian theology by joining it with Aristotle's insights. Naturally, it was important for Aquinas to explain the philosophical success of this pagan philosopher, to explain how one without Christ could uncover so many truths that were compatible with Scripture. Aquinas's answer to this question was straightforward: because God created the natural world and also human reason, it followed that all rational pursuits of truth would lead inexorably to conclusions that were compatible with those taught by the church and in the Bible. Scholars in the modern period would eventually understand this to mean that philosophical reflection could be safely and profitably unmoored from traditional theological assumptions. Aquinas is often blamed for this development, but as a philosophical move it was utterly foreign to his thinking.[12] Nevertheless, it is true that these developments eventually led to conclusions that flew in the face of traditional Christian dogmas.

The other premodern development that prepared the way for modern thinking was the rise of technical philology. Scholars were able to notice that languages have histories and, hence, that texts could be dated to some extent by their linguistic characteristics. Such was the case when Aquinas realized that *De Spiritu et Anima* ("On the Spirit and Soul") was composed not by Augustine, as the text alleged, but rather in the time of Aquinas himself (12th century).[13] Scholars gradually realized that the import of these philological observations went far beyond language. Culture itself was an evolving reality, and many important things—including theological traditions and even the Bible itself—were inextricably tied to the changing tides of culture. So philology was pointing the way to historical consciousness, and because of that, to historical criticism.

One result of this historical impulse was that medieval scholarship became increasingly interested in the Bible's literal and historical meanings, and increasingly uncomfortable with traditional allegorical interpretations. Aquinas especially worked to resolve the conflict between the new and old methods.[14] He reasoned that the divine and human meanings of Scripture did not wholly correspond because of the great difference between God and humans. While the words of the Bible were signs through which both God and the human author could speak, for God the things about which Scripture spoke could also serve as signs. The phenomenon could be illustrated like this: Moses spoke for God when he referred

---

12. See my comments on Aquinas in chapter 9.

13. Thomas Aquinas, *Quaestiones de Anima*, q. 12, ad. 1 (= *Questions on the Soul*, trans. James H. Robb [Milwaukee: Marquette University Press, 1984], 158–59).

14. Aquinas, *Summa Theologica* 1:7–9 (= *Summa Theologica*, pt. 1, q. 1, art. 10).

to the literal place called Mount Sinai, yet for God that mountain allegorically signified the law (as we see in Gal. 4:21–31). So the plain sense of Scripture was from both God and the human author, and this plain sense in turn provided the foundation or basis for God's divine discourse, for his allegorical (as well as tropological and anagogical) messages. One result of Aquinas's approach was that the literal or plain meaning of the biblical text gained special privilege toward the end of the premodern period. Another result is that the divine and human levels of biblical discourse were theoretically separated, so that the Bible could bear a "fuller sense" (*sensus plenior*) than its human author intended. Modern scholars would eventually do away with this fuller sense, leaving as important only the human author's intention, as understood in its historical context.

To summarize, we may say that premodern scholars generally trusted tradition and worked within the theological boundaries established by church authority. They lived in the "Age of Faith." At the same time, particularly toward the end of the period, premodern scholars became increasingly aware that tradition is far more historically contingent than first strikes the eye. The recognition that tradition changes in response to the vagaries of historical and cultural circumstances engendered a profoundly new mode of thinking, which set the stage for the rise of modern interpretation.

The Modern Period

The chief characteristic of the modern age is that it went beyond the premodern critique of tradition to a full-blown suspicion of tradition. As I have noted already, the seeds of suspicion were already being sown during the premodern period, but we shall not go far wrong if we locate the real taproot of suspicion in the Renaissance, a period beginning in the late fourteenth century and ending in the sixteenth century, during which the political, literary, artistic, and philosophical resources from ancient Greece and Rome were recovered and studied by scholars in the West.[15] Exposure to these classical texts made Renaissance scholars more aware of the radical changes that transpire in matters of religion and culture during the course of history. This awareness of historical change—commonly referred to as *historical consciousness*—prompted Renaissance scholars to consider new options, as they questioned the reliability and correctness of the ideas and traditions inherited from the monastic and scholastic traditions of the Middle Ages. As a result, it became increasingly clear that in many cases the scientific and philosophical reflection of the ancient Greeks and Romans surpassed by far the traditions of the Christian Middle Ages. This being the case, it was only a matter of time before intellectuals in the West began to critique not only medieval science and philosophy but also the church itself.

---

15. James Michael Weiss, "Renaissance," in *The Oxford Encyclopedia of the Reformation*, ed. H. J. Hillerbrand, 4 vols. (New York: Oxford University Press, 1996), 3:418–21.

During the Renaissance, critical eyes were increasingly focused on the flaws and corruption present in the church's leadership and practices. This critical stance eventually culminated in a new religious movement, the Reformation. The Reformers—men like Luther, Calvin, and Zwingli—believed that the flaws and failures in the Roman Church implicitly raised questions about the validity of the church's claim to be the infallible institution of God. Eventually, these dissenters rejected the authority of the pope and the Roman Church altogether, claiming instead that two theological points were unassailably true: (1) the proper authority for Christian theology and practice was not the word of the church but "Scripture alone" (*sola scriptura*), and (2) according to that Scripture, human beings are saved by "faith alone" (*sola fide*), apart from the works and rituals prescribed by church tradition. Just as Renaissance scholars hurdled the Middle Ages to retrieve the "pristine" traditions of Greece and Rome, so the Reformers hurdled centuries of church tradition in order to retrieve what they viewed as the original and uncorrupted apostolic tradition in Scripture. This confident use of Scripture to trump church tradition was grounded in one of the most basic assumptions of the Reformation project, namely, that the expression of truth in Scripture is perspicuous, not only because its words are clearly expressed and easy to understand but also because the Holy Spirit illumines Christian readers of the Bible. It followed that sound biblical interpretation did not require the help of a Catholic bishop or priest. Hence the three foundational beliefs of the Reformation were *sola scriptura*, *sola fide*, and a perspicuous Bible. Reformation theology was critical of many things, even recognizing and struggling with the textual problems in Scripture. But in the end, it did not doubt the authority and correctness of Scripture, nor did it doubt our human ability to understand Scripture *with God's help*.[16] Consequently, the Reformers tended to overlook the fact that their theology was itself an interpretation of Scripture that might be wrong. They believed that they were merely reading precisely and only what Scripture plainly said (which is why they generally rejected allegorical interpretations).[17] We might question these confident claims as sleight of hand, but it was the only path to take if one wanted theology without errors. That was precisely what the Reformers needed to trump the authority of the Catholic Church.

---

16. Luther said that "no man perceives one iota of what is in the Scriptures unless he has the Spirit of God. All men have a darkened heart, so that even if they can recite everything in Scripture, and know how to quote it, yet they apprehend and truly understand nothing of it." See Martin Luther, *Luther's Works*, ed. Jaroslav Pelikan and Helmut T. Lehman, 55 vols. (St. Louis: Concordia; Philadelphia: Fortress, 1955–1976), 33:28.

17. As Calvin expressed it, "the true meaning of Scripture is the natural and obvious meaning." Luther goes still further in "The Bondage of the Will," averring that everything in Scripture is quite clear, once the obscurities of language are accounted for. It seems to me, however, that Luther contradicts himself on this point. In another place he muses that even the biblical writers did not fully understand what they wrote down in Scripture. See John Calvin, *Commentaries on the Epistles of Paul to the Galatians and Ephesians*, trans. William Pringle (Edinburgh: Calvin Translation Society, 1854), 136; Luther, *Luther's Works*, 33:24–28; cf. *Luther's Works*, 54:9, for the contrary view.

The Reformation's confidence in human interpretation rested in part on its high view of humanity's rational capacity. As Luther put it, "man alone is endowed with the glorious light of reason and intellect. Human beings' ability to devise so many noble arts and skills, their wisdom, dexterity, and ingenuity, all derived from this light, or from the Word who was the light of men."[18] At the same time, in spite of their sometimes overconfident rhetoric, Reformation scholars inherited and even advanced the old Christian belief—inherited especially from Augustine—that human beings are fallen and possess quite limited rational and perceptual capacities. We are unable to understand even our own minds, still less the minds of others and of God. "Now if it is true that I cannot fully express the thoughts of my heart," said Luther, "how many thousand times less will it be possible for me to understand or express the Word or conversation in which God engages within His divine being."[19] "All our faculties," he said, "are leprous, indeed dull and utterly dead."[20] It is fairly easy to detect the tension in Reformation thought. On the one hand, human beings bear God's image and so possess irrefutable abilities to comprehend reality; on the other hand, human beings are so desperately wicked, and their hearts and minds so darkened, that they have no access whatsoever to what counts most: God's true and saving Word. This paradoxical commitment to the dignity and darkness of human reason was not so different from the premodern views of men like Augustine, but the Reformers did not stop there.

Many theological and political issues fueled the Reformation, but none of these were as important as soteriology. How is one saved? And how can one know that one is saved? The Reformation answer to the first question was, of course, "by faith in Christ." But it is the second question that interests me presently. "How can I know that I am saved?" The traditional Augustinian answer to this question was straightforward: you can't. But neither Calvin nor Luther was satisfied with this answer. They were anxious to provide a theological understanding of salvation that would allay our anxieties about the final judgment and the threat of eternal damnation. Although they accomplished this in different ways, both could offer Christians an indubitable confidence that they were saved. Luther taught that believers could be certain because God keeps his promises,[21] whereas Calvin believed that certainty stemmed from the Spirit's testimony that God had saved them.[22] I will not pursue this any further. I mention these things mainly because the Reformation anxiety about eternal destiny, and the solution it found

---

18. *Luther's Works*, 22:30.
19. Ibid., 22:11.
20. Ibid., 22:66.
21. Ibid., 26:387.
22. Werner Krusche, *Das Wirken des Heiligen Geistes nach Calvin* (Göttingen: Vandenhoeck & Ruprecht, 1957), especially 212–16. For the relevant primary texts, see John Calvin, *Institutes of the Christian Religion*, trans. Henry Beveridge, 2 vols. (London: J. Clarke, 1949), 1:474–78, as well as his commentaries on Rom. 1:4; 1 Cor. 1:6; 2:12; and Eph. 1:4.

in indubitable salvation, was the direct ancestor of more general modern anxieties about the validity of human knowledge.

The intellectual spirit of the Renaissance (fourteenth through sixteenth centuries) and Reformation (sixteenth century) eventually culminated in the Enlightenment, that eighteenth-century intellectual movement that marked the true beginnings of the modern age. If there is one philosopher whom we might credit for the rise of the Enlightenment, it would be René Descartes (1596–1650).[23] Descartes observed that our traditions and sense experiences often mislead us, so that the things about which we feel quite certain sometimes turn out to be wrong. A salient example is provided in the area of cosmology, where for most of human history our finite perceptions of the earth caused us to believe that its surface was essentially flat. If tradition and perception mislead us so, mused Descartes, then how can we ever achieve certainty in our pursuit of knowledge? This question encapsulates the so-called "Cartesian anxiety." Descartes' solution for this conundrum was "methodological doubt." Good philosophy should begin from scratch by doubting everything in order to ascertain what is certainly true. Once tried and tested, these indubitable truths could in turn provide the foundations for constructing true and certain perceptions of reality. In his search for such basic truths in *The Meditations*, Descartes discovered that a great many things that we take for granted cannot be proved with any certainty. The only exception, so he thought, was a basic and indubitable truth that could not be doubted: *Cogito ergo sum*, "I think, therefore I am." From this basic truth, Descartes went on to prove to his own satisfaction many other things, including the existence of God and of created reality. In essence, Descartes' epistemology was a strong foundationalism, which began with a few basic incorrigible truths and then proceeded to build upon this foundation a supposedly incorrigible understanding of reality.

For the most part, the Enlightenment as a movement shared the Cartesian assumption that a careful and deliberate search for truth could and would yield certain knowledge, especially in matters of science. But many Enlightenment scholars doubted that this confidence was suited to religious questions. They doubted, for instance, that the validity of religious beliefs in the existence of God or in the divine origins of Scripture could be proved. Among the continental rationalists (who like Descartes believed that truth comes to us intuitively through reason) and the British empiricists (who believed that truth comes to us solely through experience), the existence of God was increasingly questioned, and Scripture was more and more viewed as a merely human book, to be interpreted—like any other book—as a product of its ancient historical context. During this period historical biblical criticism emerged as a decisive presence in the intellectual landscape, in the work of men like Baruch Spinoza (1632–1677), Richard Simon (1638–1712), Hermann Reimarus (1694–1768), J. S. Semler

---

23. His classic works may be found in René Descartes, *Discourse on Method and The Meditations*, trans. F. E. Sutcliffe (New York: Penguin, 1968).

(1725–1791), J. G. Herder (1744–1803), and J. G. Eichhorn (1752–1827), among others. Most of these biblical critics were Protestant scholars. This was in part because Protestants—especially German Protestants—enjoyed greater academic freedom than their Catholic and Anglican counterparts, whose scholarship was more closely scrutinized by the church. But it was also because the Protestant tradition was by nature a thoroughly critical tradition, which made it fairly natural for Protestant scholars to turn their critical sights from the church to the Bible. Religious skeptics of course added their voices to this critical perspective. What these scholars discovered is that the Bible, when approached critically as an historical document, seemed to contain the same sorts of tensions and contradictions that appear in other ancient documents. So the Bible was tradition. For modern thinkers who were suspicious of tradition, this meant trouble for biblical authority.

The Bible's authority was further undermined by two very different and almost contradictory Enlightenment tendencies regarding history. On the one hand, Enlightenment-era scholars became increasingly confident that they could reconstruct human history to a high degree of certainty. Their confidence stemmed especially from G. W. F. Hegel's idea that human cultures develop along the same, unilinear lines from one stage to the next.[24] This theory made it seem easy to produce a history of past events and even modestly to predict the future flow of history. One result of this development was that truth was no longer conceived in religious terms but in historical terms. *Historicism* is a term often used to describe this view, which believes that truth is closely bundled up with a correct account of what has happened, is happening, and will happen in history.[25] In the English-speaking world, this Enlightenment-era tendency is no better illustrated than by the influential Scottish historian Thomas Carlyle (1795–1881).[26] Carlyle believed that there were in fact two basic genres of writing, "Reality" (meaning history) and "Fiction." He invited his readers to realize "how impressive the smallest historical *fact* may become, as contrasted with the grandest *fictitious event*"; indeed, Carlyle went as far as saying that fiction "partakes of the nature of *lying*."[27] This Enlightenment tendency toward historicism tended to undermine biblical authority, since scholars of that era increasingly believed that the biblical narratives, or parts of them, were more fictional than historical.

The other Enlightenment tendency respecting history is exemplified in the work of Gotthold Lessing (1729–1781), who claimed that "the accidental truths

---

24. For Hegel's philosophy see below.

25. The standard critique of historicism came from the hand of Karl Popper. See *The Open Society and Its Enemies*, 2 vols. (London: Routledge, 1945); and *The Poverty of Historicism* (1957; repr. London: Routledge, 1993).

26. For the pertinent essay see Thomas Carlyle, "Biography," in *Critical and Miscellaneous Essays*, ed. H. D. Traill, 5 vols., Works of Thomas Carlyle 26–30 (New York: Scribner's, 1904), 3:44–61. For a discussion see Walter E. Houghton, *The Victorian Frame of Mind, 1830–1870* (New Haven: Yale University Press, 1957), 128–36.

27. Carlyle, "Biography," 49, 54.

of history can never become the proof of necessary truths of reason."[28] This might strike us as a lot of fancy jargon, but the idea itself is fairly simple. Lessing was asserting that truths derived from the exercise of pure reason are of a higher order than knowledge achieved through the senses (such as historical knowledge). This was true in part because historical knowledge, based as it is on questionable testimony, cannot offer us unqualified certainty. But it was also true because historical facts do not come packaged with rational truth. So, even if Jesus did rise from the dead, that historical fact in itself could never serve as the basis for securing rationally verified knowledge of the resurrection's religious significance. "Lessing's Ditch" is the name commonly given to this Enlightenment chasm between historical events and rational inquiry. Insofar as Christianity and other religions are founded on historical claims, Lessing's Ditch has had the effect of rendering those claims irrelevant for modern thinkers.

The aforementioned developments spawned many tensions and conflicts in the Enlightenment era, as traditional Christians worked hard to defend the Bible and faith against the critical onslaught. But scholars committed to the Enlightenment were very determined in their effort to dismantle religious faith. What propelled their rabid critique of religion, especially of the Christian religion? European history leading up to the Enlightenment featured a litany of religiously motivated persecutions and wars, especially the Thirty Years' War (1618–1648). Even the Protestant hero John Calvin is remembered in history for his role in the conviction and execution (by burning at the stake) of the heretic Michael Servetus.[29] These macrolevel difficulties during the sixteenth and seventeenth centuries were still reflected at microlevels during the eighteenth-century Enlightenment, as many political and educational institutions in Europe continued to persecute scholars who raised serious intellectual questions about the authority of religious tradition. Consequently, while we may wish to recall the Enlightenment as an intellectually arrogant retreat from God and biblical authority, and this it may have been, we should recall again and again—lest we forget—that the Enlightenment's rejection of dogmatic religion was fueled in no small part by the dark and oppressive side of faith. This is precisely why intellectual freedom and religious toleration were among the most cherished of the Enlightenment virtues.[30]

Their religious doubts aside, Enlightenment philosophers were profoundly confident in human reason's ability to distinguish fact from fancy and thereby to arrive at indubitable truth. But the first chinks in this armor of epistemological confidence appeared already during the Enlightenment itself in the work of David Hume (1711–1776). Hume agreed with the Cartesian assumption that

---

28. Gotthold E. Lessing, *Theological Writings*, trans. Henry Chadwick (Stanford: Stanford University Press, 1957), 53.

29. J. Friedman, "Servetus, Michael," in *The Oxford Encyclopedia of the Reformation*, ed. Hans J. Hillerbrand, 4 vols. (New York: Oxford University Press, 1996), 4:48–49.

30. Peter Gay, *The Enlightenment: An Interpretation*, 2 vols. (New York: Norton, 1966–1969), 2:398–407.

true knowledge should be indubitable and certain, but he noted that our rational inferences about reality can never really be proved.[31] There is no way, for instance, to be certain even about something as basic as patterns of cause and effect. I might see one billiard ball strike another and infer that this collision caused the second ball to roll across the billiard table, *but I do not see the cause/effect itself.* Perhaps, said Hume, what we call "cause and effect" is not a reality in the external world at all; perhaps it is merely a perception grounded in our habit of thinking. Hence, according to Hume, while we might postulate that our cause-effect inferences give us access to an external world that exists, we can by no means prove it. There is a layer of interpretation that separates us from the things we observe. We have access only to our perceptions of things, not to the things themselves. Now Hume's point may strike us as naive and even silly, but in the history of philosophy it was important: if facts must be proved indubitably to count as knowledge, as Descartes demanded, then much of our "knowledge" is not knowledge at all.

The classic reply to Hume's skepticism was from Immanuel Kant, and I will consider him in a moment. But his was not the only important response. Another is found in the Common Sense philosophy of Thomas Reid (1710–1796).[32] Reid did not buy Hume's idealism, which assumed that our understanding of things is not direct and immediate but rather through the mediation of ideas—through representation. While Kant and many others responded to Hume from *within* this idealist framework, Reid headed in an entirely different direction. According to Reid, God has so constituted the human mind that we are able to perceive the world directly. Our commonsense knowledge of things is therefore immediate and dependable. Reid freely admits that this assertion cannot be proved; it is simply the most compelling account of human knowledge because all of us—even the most skeptical—can get by only by trusting deeply in our faculties of perception and rationality. Therefore, unlike most of his philosophical peers, he was not really interested in a Cartesian search for incorrigible truth, which focused on *proving* the interpretive connection between sense data and the world behind it. Reid's approach essentially eliminates that gap by replacing it with an immediate access to the world through perception (for example, I infer from the "feeling" of hardness that an object is hard). His brand of epistemology deeply influenced the early evangelical tradition, in both its Wesleyan and Reformed permutations,[33] and it is still visible in some modern evangelical epistemologies. But the appeal of Reid's

---

31. David Hume, *A Treatise on Human Nature* (repr. London: Collins, 1962).

32. Thomas Reid, *Essays on the Intellectual Powers of Man*, ed. D. R. Brookes and K. Haakonssen (University Park: Pennsylvania State University Press, 2002); Reid, *Thomas Reid's Inquiry and Essays*, ed. K. Lehrer and R. E. Beanblossom (Indianapolis: Bobbs-Merrill, 1975). For discussions of Reid's work, see Keith Lehrer, *Thomas Reid* (London: Routledge, 1989); Nicholas Wolterstorff, *Thomas Reid and the Story of Epistemology* (Cambridge: Cambridge University Press, 2001).

33. James E. Hamilton, "Epistemology and Theology in American Methodism," *Wesleyan Theological Journal* 10 (1975): 70–79; Hamilton, "Academic Orthodoxy and the Arminianizing of American Theology," *Wesleyan Theological Journal* 9 (1974): 52–59; Tim McConnel, "The Old Princeton Apologetics: Common Sense or Reformed?" *JETS* 46 (December 2003): 647–72; Leland H. Scott, "The Message of Early American

philosophy to very conservative evangelicals stems largely from a misunderstanding of his "common sense" approach. For as Wolterstorff has pointed out, Reid did not believe that "common sense" yielded incorrigible knowledge; he believed instead that the knowledge it yielded was generally dependable and trustworthy.[34] I will come back to Reid's philosophy before long. At this point I would only say that any good epistemology will need to explain why common sense seems to work so well; but it will also need to contend with the fact that common sense is that innate capacity by which we infer that the earth is flat.

As I have said, Immanuel Kant (1724–1804) responded to Hume differently. Kant was more optimistic than Hume about our human capacity to get things right, but he agreed with Hume that we need to give attention to the role that the human mind plays in our observation of reality. Kant explored this question in his *Critique of Pure Reason*, in which he concluded that our perceptions of reality are possible only because we come to the world already equipped with a set of fixed *ideas* about how things work—a philosophical approach that is fittingly called *idealism*.[35] For Kant, and for many thinkers after him, idealism constitutes a two-edged epistemological sword.[36] On the one hand, the mind's categories provide the essential rational patterns that allow us to successfully interpret the world of our experience. On the other hand, by their very nature, these ideal patterns have the effect of shaping the world to our point of view, so that we never see reality as it actually is. Consequently, in Kant's view, human beings cannot perceive the *Ding-an-sich*, the "thing-in-itself."

Kant's other major work, *Critique of Practical Reason*, is equally important for its effect on the development of theology and biblical criticism.[37] Here Kant made room for religious faith but also eliminated its conceptual claim to "special revelation." He believed that we make sense of the phenomenal world (the world of the five senses) through the exercise of our rational categories. He referred to this exercise as "scientific reason." He noted, however, that scientific reason cannot be applied to the "noumenal world" of God, ethics, immortality, and faith. We simply cannot see God or morals. From this experience Kant concluded that our rational categories are really of two types, one suitable for observing the phenomenal world ("scientific reason") and the other suited for postulating the content of the noumenal world ("practical reason"). Kant's approach therefore implies the

---

Methodism," in *The History of American Methodism*, ed. Emory Stevens Bucke, 3 vols. (New York: Abingdon, 1964), 1:291–359.

34. Wolterstorff, *Thomas Reid*, 185–214.

35. These basic preconceived (a priori) ideas, which Kant called "categories," included concepts of Quantity (e.g., unity, plurality, totality, etc.), Quality (e.g., reality, negation, limitation), Relation (e.g., inherence and subsistence, causality and dependence, community), and Modality (e.g., possibility-impossibility, existence-nonexistence, necessity-contingency). For the details see Immanuel Kant, *Critique of Pure Reason*, trans. N. K. Smith (New York: St. Martin's, 1965).

36. Other important idealist thinkers included J. G. Fichte, F. W. J. Schelling, and G. W. F. Hegel.

37. Immanuel Kant, *Critique of Practical Reason*, trans. and ed. Mary Gregor (Cambridge: Cambridge University Press, 1997).

existence of God as an object of faith, but it also implies that God never "crosses over" from the noumenal world into our phenomenal experience. There is no room left in Kant's religion for miracles or for revealed words from God, such as the Bible or the incarnation. Truth be known, the Bible and Christ's incarnation are nothing other than human exercises in practical reason.

It fell to Friedrich Schleiermacher (1769-1834) to offer a theological response to Kant's philosophy, and his response was rich with implications for interpretation.[38] Among other things, Schleiermacher's most important task was to overcome the thick wall that Kant had erected between God (the noumenal world) and the world we live in (the phenomenal world). Schleiermacher's solution was essentially to collapse these two worlds into a monistic whole, so that humanity could enjoy direct access to God.[39] Direct access to God was possible because, according to Schleiermacher, all human beings possess a precognitive awareness of God. This dormant or vague *God-consciousness* could be increasingly brought into conscious thought by the disciplines of academic inquiry and study. A kind of dialectic therefore emerges from this model of human knowledge. Knowledge of reality through the academic disciplines enhances our knowledge of God, and our resulting knowledge of God in turn enhances our understanding of the disciplines. At its heart, then, the goal of Schleiermacher's project was to discern a universal basis for all interpretation. Being universal in scope, its effect was to eliminate the uniqueness of biblical revelation, since the Bible became merely one of many instances in which God-consciousness appears in human beings.

Central to Schleiermacher's theory of interpretation was the concept of the *hermeneutical circle*, that paradox of interpretation by which we understand the parts only in light of the whole, but the whole only in light of the parts. This sets up a kind of dialectic between words and sentences, sentences and paragraphs, paragraphs and written texts, written texts and contexts, contexts and God, in which the meaning and significance of each element depends on its dynamic relationship to all of the other elements. When textual interpretation is understood in this way, it becomes clear that "meanings" per se do not simply reside in texts. Rather, meanings are inferred by human beings as we try to make sense of the text in light of its parts and whole, and in light of the larger context within which it was composed and read. Theoretically, this sets up not only a hermeneutical circle but also a kind of hermeneutical spiral, in which our readings of a text can become increasingly better (as we better grasp the parts and whole) without ever finally arriving at perfection. I will come back to this concept frequently in our discussion, primarily because just about all interpreters—including most

---

38. Friedrich Schleiermacher, *The Christian Faith* (New York: Harper & Row, 1963). For discussion see Jens Zimmermann, *Recovering Theological Hermeneutics: An Incarnational-Trinitarian Theory of Interpretation* (Grand Rapids: Baker Academic, 2004), 144-59.

39. Schleiermacher denied that his theology amounted to pantheism, but it seems to me that this is essentially where his theology came down.

evangelicals—find that the hermeneutical circle provides a good metaphor for describing how interpretation works.[40]

If Schleiermacher provided a theological response to Kant, then the philosophical response was from G. W. F. Hegel.[41] As we have seen, Kant imagined that all human beings see the world with a set of lenses—his "categories"—that are essentially alike. Hegel disagreed. He pointed out that human beings often reach different judgments and conclusions on matters of interpretation precisely because our ideas about the world are formed and shaped by our cultural background, which he called the *Zeitgeist* ("spirit of the age"). As a result, Hegel struck a second blow to the human apparatus for seeing the world. Not only is our perspective of the world shaped by basic patterns of rationality (so Kant), but these patterns of rationality are in turn shaped by our various cultural experiences (so Hegel). Hegel believed that human culture was evolving and developing in a positive direction, in a process that would eventually end in a pure and perfect philosophy that could unite the spiritual and material dimensions of reality into a single perceptual whole. This perfect philosophy was, unsurprisingly, his own.[42] Though later postmodern philosophers would disagree with this teleological portrait of history, it was Hegel's philosophy that set the stage for the rise of postmodernism.

The Postmodern Period

Though I speak here of the postmodern *age*, this nomenclature can be misleading. One of the misconceptions in much contemporary thinking is that most scholars are nowadays postmodernists, but this is not true. Many scholars still work within a paradigm of epistemic optimism, with philosophies that are nearly Cartesian in terms of the results if not the methods and theory.[43] For these scholars indubitable and incorrigible truths are still real possibilities. But these optimists cannot be clearly understood unless we stand them next to the postmodernists.

The history of ideas is never simple or straightforward, but few would deny that one of the important fathers of postmodernism was the German philosopher Friedrich Nietzsche (1844–1900). Central to his philosophy was the concept of the "will to power," that our putative claims to objectivity are expressions of our subjective will, tools that mask our pursuit of power over

---

40. For an evangelical example, see Grant R. Osborne, *The Hermeneutical Spiral* (Downers Grove, IL: InterVarsity, 1991).
41. G. W. F. Hegel, *Phenomenology of Spirit*, trans. A. V. Miller (Oxford: Oxford University Press, 1977).
42. Hegel is particularly interesting because his form of idealism comes close to a realist notion of the *Ding-an-sich*. But Hegel's key twist is that individual humans cannot see the *Ding-an-sich*, but the whole goal of history is for Spirit (*Geist*/Idea) to come back to itself and know itself for the first time, fully and transparently. Hegel calls this "absolute knowledge," and it happens only at the end of history.
43. See, for example, Roderick M. Chisholm, *Theory of Knowledge*, 3rd ed. (Englewood Cliffs, NJ: Prentice-Hall, 1989).

others.[44] Through this manipulative power—expressed most clearly in our use of language, *especially our religious language*—we can assert our view of the world against other views that impede our access to the things that we desire: freedom, money, status, sex, and many other things. Nietzsche expressed it this way: "Everything hitherto called 'truth' is recognized as the most harmful, malicious, most subterranean form of the lie; the holy pretext of 'improving' mankind as the cunning to *suck out* life itself and to make it anemic. Morality is *vampirism*."[45]

Nietzsche recognized that the philosophies of Kant, and especially of Hegel, had more profound implications for epistemology than either of the earlier philosophers had realized. If all views of the world are shaped by human rationality, as Kant argued, and if rationality itself is in turn formed and informed by our cultural traditions, as Hegel suggested, then there is no reason to suppose that human beings can ever be objective observers of reality. We live and breathe in our cultural traditions as a fish swims in water. As a result, the modern ideal of an objective interpreter, whose viewpoint is unobstructed by tradition, turns out to be an impossibility. The knowing subject of Descartes, who sees the objective world aright, is gone, replaced by the culturally embedded knower, whose views, perceptions, and notions of "truth" depend profoundly on the social discourse and cultural fabric of his community. Human reason never was, and never could be, an exercise that discovers disembodied, ahistorical, decontextualized truths. Our truth claims, and even our reason itself, are contingent upon our cultural heritage. Hence, in certain respects, postmodernism brings us full circle in the history of epistemology, for it claims that the modernist attempt to escape tradition was destined from the beginning to fail because all human beings—Descartes included—are radically formed by, and unavoidably participate in, an ideological tradition. Postmodernism is, at the heart, a reaffirmation of the significance and importance of tradition in human life. Whether this should lead to epistemic pessimism or to a reaffirmation of tradition's epistemic value is the matter to which we now turn.

Two schools of postmodernism have risen in the wake of modernism's demise, the *antirealists* and the *practical realists*. Let us consider each in turn. According to the antirealists, who take their cue from Nietzsche, "reality" is nothing other than an invention of human culture. There is no "real world" behind our perceptions because the concepts of "real" and "world" are themselves linguistic products of culturally conditioned viewpoints. Hence the label *antirealists*. To be sure, most antirealists would concede that there is "something out there" behind our perceptions (they are *ontological realists*), but when it comes to our knowledge of that something, they are *epistemological antirealists* because, in their view, all truth

---

44. Friedrich Nietzsche, *The Will to Power*, trans. Walter Kaufman and R. J. Hollingdale (New York: Vintage, 1967).

45. Friedrich Nietzsche, *Ecce Homo*, trans. R. J. Hollingdale (London: Penguin, 1992), 103.

claims lie embedded within a matrix of cultural fiction. Interpretation, whatever it is, does not recover "the truth" but creates it. This means, for instance, that the book you presently hold is something quite other than you think it to be, and that the intentions you attribute to me by reading its words are quite other than I intend. Perhaps the point becomes yet clearer if I add that, according to antirealists, in the final analysis this book and my intentions in it are not fully grasped even by me—after all, I also have unintended meanings. Obviously, if this antirealist account of things is right, it will have profound implications for how we understand the reading of any text, including Scripture.

Although it will seem at first that this opens the door for an "anything goes" philosophy, antirealists rarely play it out this way. Many antirealists believe that "justice" is the proper objective of good philosophical reflection.[46] Because reality is a matter of invention and imagination, human beings are free to invent and reinvent our images of reality in ways that serve our purposes, especially our ethical purposes. For instance, if a text like the Bible has been interpreted by Christians or Jews as a means to oppress unbelievers, antirealists strongly believe that they should—in fact, must—offer new interpretations of the text so that it no longer serves this oppressive religious agenda. One way of doing this, called "deconstruction," uses interpretation to divest the tradition of its authority. Deconstruction highlights the incoherence and hidden contradictions within the oppressive tradition, thus revealing that the tradition's "authority" is nothing other than a fictional construct (hence, "*de*-construction"). Deconstruction is possible because, according to antirealists, all human literature and systems of thought invariably exclude, reduce, obscure, or neglect important elements of experience because they are subject to the vagaries of the finite linguistic and cultural traditions in which we live. Another antirealist tactic for handling oppressive traditions does not attack the authority directly but rather uses the authority of the tradition against itself. Textual authorities in the tradition, such as the Bible, are (re)interpreted so that their message better suits the ethical tastes of antirealists. When this is done, the antirealist does not much care whether the new reading would suit the wishes and intentions of the ancient biblical author. We are free to interpret texts in any way that we wish, not only because it is impossible to recover the intentions of the biblical authors but also because reality is itself an invention. That is, for most antirealists, the modern interest in historical criticism—in attempting to understand texts in relation to their original context—is not only impossible but also uninteresting.

Because justice is an ideal that is never achieved, it is the ongoing task of deconstruction to challenge human systems of reference so that institutionalized injustices are constantly challenged and undone. Hence the task of deconstruction

---

46. This tendency among left-wing postmodernists appears to have been inspired largely by the well-known philosopher Emmanuel Levinas (see Zimmermann, *Recovering Theological Hermeneutics*, 187–229). For a good introduction to the ethical dimensions of deconstruction, see Jacques Derrida, *Deconstruction in a Nutshell: A Conversation with Jacques Derrida*, ed. John D. Caputo (New York: Fordham University Press, 1997).

is never satisfied and is always oriented toward the future. Well-known representatives of this antirealist school would include Michael Foucault and Richard Rorty.[47] Jacques Derrida is sometimes associated with this school of thought as well, but philosophical developments late in his life may suggest that he was leaning in the other postmodern direction.[48]

As the name implies, the other wing of postmodernism, which I call *practical realism*, heads in a very different direction. Practical realism is a "soft" postmodernism, which represents a kind of mediating position between the epistemic optimism of Cartesian realism and the pessimism of antirealism. But it does not get there by simple moderation, as if one had mixed hot and cold water to get something lukewarm. It arrives at this position by disagreeing strongly with the one point on which the Cartesian realists and postmodern antirealists most agree. Both Cartesian and antirealist philosophers assume that, when it comes to epistemology, tradition is a problem; it blinds us to the truth. The two views differ mainly on matters of epistemic success. Cartesian realists assume that we can escape tradition in our objective quest for indubitable truth, whereas antirealists believe that human viewpoints are always traditional and hence do not permit objective quests. It is precisely on this point—on the matter of tradition—that practical realists take a very different path. For practical realists, tradition does not blind us to truth. It is instead the imperfect but useful way that humans grasp, discover, and perpetuate truth. That this is so is reflected in our everyday experience. Two people cannot really converse unless they begin with a common set of expectations regarding language, culture, and belief. Apart from this common ground, they would be able to converse no more than two people who speak entirely different languages. Hence preunderstanding—a common, shared tradition—is an essential ingredient of communication with others and for interpretation in general.

It is not terribly difficult to see where this line of thought leads us. If practical realism has it right that tradition is the path of understanding but also a road sign that partly misleads, then the epistemic result will be neither pure fancy nor belief emancipated from human error. Human beings enjoy a modest and *adequate* capacity to understand and successfully live in the world. But we understand things always partially and always, in some respects, wrongly. This means, of course, that human knowledge moves on a continuum that runs from "better" to "worse" rather than on a Boolean switch that toggles between "perfect" and "wrong." Our view of things is approximate and useful rather than utterly precise. It is as though we see everything through a warped mirror, whose warp—sometimes more, sometimes less—depends upon the relative influences of finitude and faulty tradition on our perspective. In this account of things, good perception and misperception cohere

---

47. For introductions to the thought and work of Foucault and Rorty, see Gary Gutting, *Foucault: A Very Short Introduction* (Oxford: Oxford University Press, 2005); and Alan Malachowski, *Richard Rorty* (Princeton: Princeton University Press, 2002).

48. For the similarities between Augustine and Derrida, see John D. Caputo, *Philosophy and Theology* (Nashville: Abingdon, 2006), 51–74.

in one sight experience. So we needn't choose between the perfect knowledge of Cartesian realism or the imaginary knowledge of antirealism. "Perfect" human knowledge is an illusion, which mistakenly confuses good and useful knowledge with perfect, God-like knowledge.[49]

Implicit in this practical realist account of epistemology is an account of human language and textual meaning. If human thoughts and ideas do not perfectly mirror reality, still less will this be true of our words. Words are not the bearers of full meaning so much as the specific clues by which we infer meanings when we read or hear verbal discourse. Inference is always necessary because meaning does not inhere in the discourse itself but rather in the way that the discourse suits certain contexts and situations. To the extent that this context is unknown or misunderstood (and it always is in some degree), to that same extent the discourse itself will be misunderstood. That is, according to practical realists, we are able to understand verbal discourse very truly—but always partially and to some extent even wrongly.

How do practical realists prove their twofold assertion that the real world exists and that we can get it right? Being postmodernists, they don't. They simply observe that all of us, whether realists or antirealists, live with an everyday sense that we not only get things wrong but also get many things right. Practical realism offers a better account of this experience than either antirealism or Cartesian realism. Antirealism does not explain the unavoidable work-a-day assumption that we get things right, and Cartesian realism—which promises indubitable truth—cannot avoid the fact that our "certainties" often turn out to be wrong.

Advocates of practical realism are of varied philosophical stripe and would include the likes of Hans-Georg Gadamer, Alisdair MacIntyre, Michael Polanyi, Paul Ricoeur, Charles Taylor, T. F. Torrance, and (I believe) Nicholas Wolterstorff.[50] I do not mean to suggest that these scholars see things in precisely the same way. On matters of faith and philosophical detail they differ at important points (especially in the case of Taylor). But all of them—including the evangelicals

---

49. For a misguided attempt to show that knowledge can be completely true and also partial, see Paul D. Feinberg, "A Response to Adequacy of Language and Accommodation," in *Hermeneutics, Inerrancy, and the Bible: Papers from ICBI Summit II*, ed. Earl D. Radmacher and Robert D. Preus (Grand Rapids: Zondervan, 1984), 379–90.

50. For representative works see Hans-Georg Gadamer, *Truth and Method*, trans. Joel Weisenheimer and Donald G. Marshall, 2nd rev. ed. (New York: Continuum, 1989); Alisdair C. MacIntyre, *Whose Justice? Which Rationality?* (Notre Dame: University of Notre Dame Press, 1988); Michael Polanyi, *Knowing and Being* (Chicago: University of Chicago Press, 1969); Charles Taylor, "Overcoming Epistemology," in *After Philosophy: End or Transformation?* ed. Kenneth Baynes, James Bohman, and Thomas McCarthy (Cambridge: Massachusetts Institute of Technology Press, 1987), 464–88; T. F. Torrance, *Reality and Scientific Theology* (Edinburgh: Scottish Academic Press, 1982); Torrance, *Theological Science* (Oxford: Oxford University Press, 1969); Paul Ricoeur, *The Rule of Metaphor: The Creation of Meaning in Language*, trans. Robert Czerny (1977; repr. New York: Routledge, 2003); Ricoeur, *Interpretation Theory: Discourse and the Surplus of Meaning* (Fort Worth: Texas Christian University Press, 1976); Nicholas Wolterstorff, *Thomas Reid and the Story of Epistemology* (Cambridge: Cambridge University Press, 2001).

listed (Torrance and Wolterstorff)—agree that even the best instances of human knowledge are good and adequate but also finite and imperfect.

At this juncture I should emphasize one point. Many who stand in the Cartesian philosophical tradition—and this includes many evangelicals—equate reading a text with nothing other than trying to understand its author's intention.[51] But for practical realists, and for postmodernists in general, the idea that reading should attend only to the author's "intended meaning" is theoretically naive.[52] Authors certainly do have intended meanings, and a practical realist would say that readers can *potentially* (though not necessarily!) understand that meaning to an adequate extent. But postmodernists would point out that it is equally true that: (1) authors have unintended meanings, (2) authors can sometimes write something other than what they are thinking or intending, and (3) readers can legitimately ask all sorts of questions that have little or nothing to do with the author's intention. We could ask, for instance, what we might learn from Paul's Letters about Greek grammar or about the psychology of religious people. The apostle did not have these kinds of questions or issues in mind when he wrote his letters, but there is no reason at all why we cannot bring these questions to his texts. For these reasons, though practical realists can fully agree with the traditional evangelical interest in the intended meanings of the biblical authors, they do not believe that we can fully recover those meanings, nor do they believe that we can be incorrigibly certain that our readings of those meanings are correct, nor do they believe that the author's intentions are the only thing of interest when it comes to reading and interpreting a text. The thirst to have certain and incorrigible judgments about these things is a modern, Cartesian thirst that postmodernism wants to put behind us.

Speaking of modernism, I should like to backtrack at this point to something I noted in the beginning of this section. I pointed out that there remain scholars in this so-called postmodern era who are essentially modern, whose epistemic optimism outstrips not only the pessimism of antirealism but even the guarded optimism of practical realism. I would like to look at these scholars in closer detail by focusing only on those evangelical theorists who fit this category. These theorists are essentially of two types, which I will attempt to describe in terms of their respective claims and their respective critiques of postmodernism. It seems right to say that these approaches were partially or largely inspired by the Common Sense realism of Thomas Reid.[53] But I do not believe that Reid would have shared in the extremes of their epistemic optimism. Reid's thought was much more nuanced, and much closer to practical realism than to any sort of modern realism.

---

51. See, for example, Walter C. Kaiser Jr., "The Single Intent of Scripture," in *Rightly Divided: Readings in Biblical Hermeneutics*, ed. Roy B. Zuck (Grand Rapids: Kregel, 1996), 158–70.

52. As even some evangelicals have noted. See Philip B. Payne, "The Fallacy of Equating Meaning with the Human Author's Intention," *JETS* 20 (1977): 243–52.

53. Hamilton, "Epistemology and Theology"; Hamilton, "Academic Orthodoxy"; McConnel, "Old Princeton Apologetics"; Scott, "Message of Early American Methodism."

The first approach, called *presuppositionalism*, is most closely associated with the philosophy of Cornelius Van Til.[54] Presuppositionalists essentially radicalize the postmodern claim that all interpretation is contextual, concluding in fact that *we must know everything (the whole context) in order to know anything (that which we are interpreting)*. The rationale for this conclusion is as follows. Each thing is understood in relation to other things, which are in turn understood only in relation to still other things. So, to the extent that other things remain unknown to us, something about the thing in question also remains unknown. Now given that nothing is more important than God, it can only be the case that those who do not know God—those who are not Christians—are missing the most important elements of interpretation. So their interpretations cannot be good. In essence, presuppositionalists believe that correct interpretation requires a belief in God.

But there is more. Presuppositionalists not only assert that Christian beliefs are essential for good hermeneutics. They also adamantly deny that these beliefs can be acquired through *general hermeneutics*. Faith in Christ is not something that we can achieve ourselves through the usual path of understanding; it is a gift, bestowed upon select individuals through a supernatural intervention by God. These facts, taken together, lead the presuppositionalist to an inevitable conclusion: If we need Christian beliefs to interpret things correctly, and if these beliefs cannot be acquired through an everyday general hermeneutic, then the only healthy way to interpret anything is via a *special hermeneutic* that presupposes the truth of Christian belief. To put this in the technical terminology of epistemology, presuppositionalists are strong Cartesian foundationalists, for whom the basic beliefs necessary to reach incorrigible truth are gifts of grace available only to genuine Christians. It follows that only Christians (to whom God has granted these basic beliefs) can employ the special hermeneutic necessary to interpret the Bible correctly. Moreover, insofar as Christians fail to operate as presuppositionalists, they will likewise fail as interpreters. Hence, in the final analysis, correct interpretations are available only to Christian presuppositionalists.[55]

Variants of this presuppositional approach appear in the work of other evangelical theorists, most notably Richard Lints.[56] Lints admits, along with postmodernism, that "humans (Christian and non-Christian) are inevitably influenced by their own culture, tradition, experience."[57] He goes on to say that this pessimistic

---

54. Cornelius Van Til, *A Christian Theory of Knowledge* (Philadelphia: Presbyterian & Reformed Publishing, 1969).

55. Van Til's epistemology seems to equivocate. On the one hand he claims that correct thinking amounts to thinking "God's thoughts after him"; on the other hand, he admits that any human attempt to see things as God sees them is "analogical" (see *Christian Theory of Knowledge*, 16). If Van Til wishes to maintain his argument (that to know anything one must know everything), then he cannot have it both ways. Either we think God's thoughts after him (because, in essence, God tells us everything) or we think analogically, in which case we really do not think *God's thoughts* but something that approximates them.

56. Richard Lints, *The Fabric of Theology: A Prolegomenon to Evangelical Theology* (Grand Rapids: Eerdmans, 1993).

57. Ibid., 27.

conclusion is based on "genuine biblical theology." Yet Lints wants something more. He very much yearns for the "speech of God," for "His very voice."[58] The only way to achieve this, he suggests, is to "overcome" our "unreflective biases" and "cultural filters." But how shall we do so? Here Lints parts ways slightly with Van Til's presuppositionalism. While Van Til prefers to credit God with the miracle of successful interpretation, Lints prefers a volitional model, in which individual Christians choose to examine and set aside our cultural biases in order to read the Scriptures without distortion.[59] If we do this, he believes that we will hear the unadorned voice of God.

I will not respond to Van Til or Lints in any detail at this juncture. I would only point out that, when it comes to interpreting biblical texts, Christians get a great many things wrong and profit quite frequently from the scholarship of non-Christians. So whatever advantages faith gives to our interpretations, it seems quite doubtful that Christians enjoy an absolute corner on biblical interpretation, or on truth in general.

The other optimistic evangelical epistemology is suitably described as the "propositional school." Its chief representatives are William Lane Craig and J. P. Moreland.[60] Because these philosophers are "modest" rather than "strong" (Cartesian) foundationalists, they no longer presume that all knowledge must clear the bar of indubitable certainty. But they do have a deep confidence in human perception and rationality, and believe that our knowledge really is incorrigible and indubitable in some instances. It seems hard to doubt, for instance, that "1 + 1 = 2," or that "all *a* is not *non-a*," or that "I perceive a red fire truck." This line of thought accentuates the so-called correspondence theory of truth, in which our ideas and linguistic expressions are true to the extent that they perfectly mirror reality.

Given what we have said so far in this chapter, one objection to propositionalism will involve the matter of context. If context is as important in interpretation as postmodernists (and even evangelical presuppositionalists) say it is, and if the truest context of interpretation is really too large for human beings to fathom, then how do propositionalists overcome this contextual difficulty? Propositionalists believe that reality can be conceptually atomized into a practically infinite set of discrete, true propositions (hence the name "propositionalist"). Because each proposition stands on its own two feet, the contextual problem is eliminated. True propositions can be expressed linguistically, but they are not identical to sentences. For instance, "Grass is green," "Gras ist grün," and "L'herbe est verte" are three different ways of expressing the same proposition. But the proposition's truth valence does not depend at all on whether any human being notices it or speaks of it. The grass

---

58. Ibid., 58–59.

59. Ibid., 82–86. See also discussion of Lints in James K. A. Smith, *The Fall of Interpretation: Philosophical Foundations for a Creational Hermeneutic* (Downers Grove, IL: InterVarsity, 2000), 49–56.

60. William Lane Craig and J. P. Moreland, *Philosophical Foundations for a Christian Worldview* (Downers Grove, IL: InterVarsity, 2003). For an excellent summary of this viewpoint, see J. P. Moreland, "Truth, Contemporary Philosophy, and the Postmodern Turn," *JETS* 48 (2005): 77–88.

simply *is* green. So the propositionalist metaphysic assumes that objective reality and propositional truths about it are fully independent of human perception. Yet these theorists are also very optimistic about the epistemic prospects of human perception, not only in terms of our capacity to grasp propositional truth but also in terms of our ability to communicate that truth through verbal discourse. Sentences like "the grass is green" have the capacity to bear perfect, incorrigibly true propositions.

But how can these propositionalist claims be maintained in the face of the powerful postmodern claim that all human perspectives are influenced by tradition and so are subjective rather than objective? According to propositionalists, this postmodern critique of propositional truth confuses "psychological objectivity" with "rational objectivity." While psychological objectivity is rarely possible, rational objectivity is something that all human beings can enjoy. Moreland expressed it this way:

> Rational objectivity is the state of having accurate epistemic access to the thing itself.... The important thing here is that bias does not stand between a knowing subject and an intentional object nor does it eliminate a person's ability to assess the reasons for something. Bias may make it more difficult, but not impossible. If bias made rational objectivity impossible, then no teacher—including the postmodernist herself—could responsibly teach any view the teacher believed on any subject! Nor could the teacher teach opposing viewpoints, because she would be biased against them![61]

So, according to Moreland, the biases of cultural tradition merely impede but do not really prevent our ability to understand truth. This is proved, he suggests, by the fact that those who claim to reject objective truth must carry on as if it exists. That is, the correspondence theory of truth is assumed even by the postmodernists who deny it.

My formal response to evangelical propositionalism is still to come, but at this point I would note that its critique of postmodernism applies only to the antirealist wing of postmodernism. Practical realists are also postmodern, but they would not deny that an objective world exists, nor that our beliefs might correspond to it in some respect or measure. Given that this is so, and that propositionalists like Moreland claim to be only modestly foundational, one wonders how different the two approaches finally are in actual practice.

Hermeneutics, Epistemology, and the Christian Tradition

Enough of technical hermeneutics and its history. The question that remains for us to consider is how thoughtful Christians should evaluate this epistemological

---

61. Moreland, "Truth," 82.

discussion. Should we be premodernists, modernists, postmodernists, or something else altogether? Though we might wish things were otherwise, the question cannot be answered merely by asking what Christians believe about these matters. As we have seen, even among evangelicals there is a debate—a fairly vigorous debate—about whether or to what extent human beings can see things as they really are. I would like to pursue this matter further by considering the first few chapters of the book of Genesis. But before I do, a few comments about the use of Scripture, and about that phenomenon often called "prooftexting," are in order.

Like anyone else who takes the Bible seriously, I want to support my theological arguments by drawing upon and citing Scripture. This is a well-worn practice that needs no defense. But the quotation of Scripture, especially small portions of it, can often be criticized as prooftexting. Defined colloquially, to prooftext is to misuse the text, to remove it from its proper biblical context, or theological context, so that the text is made to speak a word that it does not speak, or is taken as the *final* word on some matter when it is not. Most of us would agree, for instance, that one is prooftexting who demands silence from women in the church because "it is disgraceful for a woman to speak in the church" (1 Cor. 14:35). I suspect that we would offer the same critique of anyone who challenged the doctrine of original sin by citing the words of the psalmist in Psalm 71:6: "From birth I have relied on God." At the same time, none would call it prooftexting to condemn terrorism by citing, "Thou shalt not kill," or to take as God's final word, "Do not commit adultery." In each of these cases, we are agreeing that the assumed context behind the quotations is either sufficiently clear, so as to allay the charge of prooftexting, or insufficiently examined, so as to invite the charge. It is in the space between these extremes, in that space where we disagree on the larger context in which a quoted biblical text should be understood, that the question of prooftexting is likely to arise. It does not matter whether the contextual disagreement regards the biblical book in question, the Bible as a whole, or the theological traditions of the church. It matters only that the reader and writer have different takes on the text because of the different contexts that they bring to its interpretation.

In the arguments that follow, it is my responsibility to make good judgments about when a text can simply be quoted (because I suspect that you, the reader, will agree with me about its context) and when my reading must be defended in detail by clarifying the context as I see it. I will try, of course, to make the best judgments that I can in this regard. At the same time, I beg a bit of indulgence from the reader, for the discharge of my duty in this instance is far from foolproof. I cannot provide a detailed exegesis of every biblical text that I cite, so there will undoubtedly be instances in which I give less evidence for my reading of Scripture than readers might want. Where this is so, and when I seem to take a text out of context, or to do some injustice to it, I ask that readers thoughtfully consider whether my arguments as a whole are really weakened by those discrete instances of logical or rhetorical failure. All arguments have their weak points; I hope that in this case the stronger arguments prove to be more numerous and coherent than the weaker ones. With these comments behind us, let us turn our attention at last to the first few chapters of Genesis.

In many respects these early chapters of Scripture provide an essential preface for the entire biblical canon. This is not merely because of their location at its beginning but also because these chapters address many familiar and important theological themes, such as creation, fall, judgment, grace, and redemption. Though it is not always recognized, these texts also address matters relevant to our discussion of epistemology.[62] Genesis introduces us to the first human couple, Adam and Eve, and to their story, which Christians have long believed is foundational for our understanding of human nature and of the human predicament. Among other things, we discover from Genesis that even in their sinless and pristine state, these first bearers of the divine image were *finite* beings. They did not know all that God knows (see Gen. 3:5, 22), nor did they understand even what was before their very eyes (i.e., they did not know that they were naked). Encapsulated in this brief portrait of unblemished humanity is the profound distinction between an *infinite creator* who knows all and *finite creatures* who do not. According to Genesis, the couple's dissatisfaction with this difference eventually led to their downfall.

If we may judge from the narrative itself, humanity's primeval innocence was interrupted almost at once by the wise and crafty serpent, which appeared on the scene as a creature knowing less than God but more than human beings. Drawing upon this knowledge, he tempted the human couple with a chance to acquire divine knowledge: "You will be like God, knowing good and evil." Eve and Adam quickly succumbed to the temptation, and, according to Scripture, this error became the fount of all that ails humanity. Genesis depicts human beings as both *finite* and *fallen*, and respecting the fall, it pins at least part of the blame on our misplaced desire to know what God knows.

Now Genesis is certainly not a philosophical text in the formal sense, but it seems to me that its creation-fall sequence has definite implications for hermeneutics and epistemology. Primary among them is the way that Genesis defines the finite horizon of the human perspective. Our view of things is not God's. He "sees" things that we simply *cannot* see, hidden verities that are, as the psalmist says, "too wonderful" for us (Ps. 131:2). The biblical economy also restricts the proper domain of human knowledge. There are things that we could know—such as the knowledge of good and evil—that we should not know. For instance, while a married man might wish to know what adultery is like, that knowledge is not intended for him; it breaches the divine limits placed on human curiosity and inquiry.

Other aspects of finitude are subtler still. Even respecting the things that God allows us and wishes us to observe and experience, finitude has a limiting or circumscribing effect on our pursuit of knowledge. Naturally it prevents us from seeing all of the facts, but it also prevents us from understanding all of the facts

---

62. As James Smith has accentuated in *Fall of Interpretation*.

that we see. Adam and Eve "saw" each other naked, for instance, but they did not realize that they were naked. Moreover, finitude implies not only that we do not know things but also that *we do not know when we do not know*. Consequently, it would be quite impossible for us to do what Descartes attempted to do, namely, to avoid holding any mistaken opinions and beliefs. The ancients did not choose to believe in a flat earth; this mistaken false idea was simply inferred from the obvious fact that, so far as they could see, the earth looked flat. In a similar way, our reservoir of cultural and personal knowledge is chock-full of mistaken ideas and impressions that were tacitly formed in us through unconscious processes, processes that are generally and adequately reliable, but never perfect. So finitude would seem to imply not only that our ideas and beliefs about the world are limited but also that they are in some respects distorted. Only an infinite being—God himself—is able to perceive reality without distortion. As for us, "we see through a glass, darkly" (KJV), said Paul in 1 Corinthians 13:12, "as in a mirror" (NIV). And as the apostle also said, "My conscience is clear, but that does not make me innocent. It is the Lord who judges me" (1 Cor. 4:4 NIV). This is undoubtedly why God takes notice of our finitude in his assessment of human behavior: "The times of ignorance God overlooked" (Acts 17:30 RSV).

If our epistemological success is limited by finitude, then our fallenness limits it in more profound, and sometimes even sinister, ways.[63] Because we have a natural desire to indulge guiltlessly in our vices, we are fairly resistant to learning or assimilating new perspectives that might imply that our sins are out of bounds. Nowhere is this better expressed than in the biblical metaphor, "having eyes, they do not see; having ears, they do not hear" (cf. Isa. 43:8; Mark 8:18). Obviously, human finitude and fallenness are considerable obstacles on the path to truth. For this reason, a thoughtful Christian appraisal of hermeneutics and epistemology will need to consider these features of the human disposition.

Were this the whole of the Christian story, Christians would have good reasons to embrace a pretty pessimistic epistemology. But Scripture and Christian tradition give us all sorts of reasons for believing that human beings do know things about reality. Genesis tells us that we are finite and fallen, but it also describes us as a beautiful creation of God—as the grandest product of his creative acts. We are "very good" creatures who bear the divine image (Gen. 1:27–28) and the capacity to recognize and do good things (like caring for our children). While Adam's transgression has marred our humanity and, in the language of the New Testament, made us "slaves to sin," Scripture clearly conveys that this tragic failure did not rob us of the divine image: "For in the image of God has God made man" (Gen. 9:6 NIV; cf. James 3:9). One of the reasons that we bear God's image is implicit in Scripture from beginning to end. Because humanity bears the divine image, human beings provide the richest source of metaphors for conveying truths

---

63. For a more robust discussion of this matter than I can offer here, see Marguerite Schuster, *The Fall and Sin: What We Have Become as Sinners* (Grand Rapids: Eerdmans, 2004).

about the divine nature. God created us to be illustrations of himself. According to Scripture, God is a "father," "husband," "king," and "righteous judge." He is "gracious," "kind," "patient," "angry," and "jealous." God "sees" and "hears," and even changes his mind. To be sure, all of these images are metaphors rather than rigidly literal portraits of the divine nature. Nevertheless, these images bring us closer to an understanding of God and his attributes because they were placed within us to serve such a purpose. As Augustine pointed out, the fact that we share God's image speaks well of our ability to succeed as interpreters of the cosmos that God has created.[64] God has made the cosmos to be seen, and he created us to see it.

The theological assertion that we bear God's image also has important implications for our assessment of tradition. I mentioned above that tradition presents a curious problem. Although tradition offers us distorted images of reality that need to be critically examined, it is impossible for us to examine critically all of the traditions that we inherit. Under these circumstances, what gives us warrant to trust the many unexamined and potentially fallacious traditions that we inherit from our forebears? Here is the answer: If we are indeed bearers of the divine image and endowed with good faculties of perception, then this will imply that our interpretations of reality, while imperfect, tend nonetheless to be reliable and useful. Consequently, although tradition is always influenced by human finitude and fallenness, much of what we call "tradition" is good, true, and healthy because it was created and perpetuated by human beings who bear God's image. This means that tradition does not need to be cynically and endlessly interrogated in the manner that Cartesian philosophy suggests. Tradition needs to be closely examined only when we can see compelling reasons for doing so.

When all is said and done, it seems to me that a biblical account of human knowledge goes something like this. God has given human beings the innate but limited capacity *to see*, to understand reality through interpretation. This means that we have good reasons not only for trusting tradition (what our forebears saw) but also for trusting our own perceptions (what we see). Nevertheless, because all human interpretations—even the best ones—are distorted to some extent by the finitude and fallenness of our faculties, the knowledge we acquire through tradition and perception is always partial and always in need of critical appraisal, insofar as this is reasonable and possible.

But let us return now to the question that originally prompted this discussion. How should thoughtful Christians assess the epistemological options represented by premodern, modern, and postmodern modes of inquiry? Shall we be Cartesian realists, or antirealists, or practical realists, or something else altogether? Evangelicals are nowadays somewhat sharply divided on this question. There are those such as I have mentioned already—scholars like Craig, Moreland, and Lints—who wish to maintain a very optimistic account of human knowledge. On this account, human perception provides unmediated access to the world of

---

64. See the discussion of Augustine in Zimmermann, *Recovering Theological Hermeneutics*, 43–44.

our experience. The result is not necessarily indubitable and incorrigible knowledge in every case, but such an outcome is certainly possible according to these scholars. On the other hand, many other evangelicals—particularly those whose expertise is in theology and the humanities—would prefer to temper this epistemic optimism. Though they would not go so far as embracing antirealism (although a few come close to that!), these scholars would generally identify with some form of practical realism, with an epistemology that admits our capacity to get at and understand truth without shielding human perception from either the limits of finitude or the effects of fallenness. These seem to be the two options on the table at this point.

Now I have natural sympathies with the optimistic school. Who can doubt that "1 + 1 = 2," that "*a* is not *non-a*," or that "grass is green"? These conclusions are so obvious, and so above suspicion, that one is tempted to believe that human beings sometimes enjoy indubitable certainties. And perhaps we do. But scholars who are more skeptical will argue that mathematical and logical operations like "1 + 1 = 2" appear to be special cases, having to do with things native to the mind rather than with the external world. Our perception that the "grass is green," while undeniable as an experience that we have, can be wrong and hence cannot serve as an incorrigible witness to reality itself. Moreover, these instances of apparent perceptual certainty do not exactly correspond to many of the claims that we make in everyday life. When we say that "such-and-such caused the rise in prices," or "so-and-so is a nice fellow," or "she does this or that because she was mistreated as a child," or "God is like this or that," we are dealing with very complex matters that no human being could fully understand. Our explanations and descriptions of such things might not be wholly wrong, but they will always be simpler than the reality we seek to explain. This reductionistic tendency stems in part from the fact that we simply cannot know all of the factors involved, and in part because our appraisal of what we do understand will fail to some extent. If Luther was right when he said that we cannot understand even our own hearts, how much less can we expect to understand God, other humans, and the complexities of the created order?

It is fairly easy to see where I am heading on the question of epistemology. The biblical account of things, with its dual emphasis on both the value and limits of human perception, seems much closer to postmodern practical realism than to any of the other options. Practical realism is the only contemporary approach to epistemology and hermeneutics that admits our capacity *to know* without falling into the illusion that we have access to error-free, God-like knowledge. The close relationship between practical realism and Christianity on this point is further confirmed by the fact that similar appraisals of human perception appear in the theologies of both premodern (Augustine) and early modern Christians (Calvin, Luther). To be sure, if practical realists are correct, these earlier Christians did not fully understand the implications of their somewhat paradoxical commitment to both epistemic optimism and pessimism. The Reformers especially tended to be far too optimistic about their capacity to get things right. Nevertheless, it is not difficult to spot a close resemblance between the epistemological ideas expressed in the Bible, Augustine, Calvin, Luther, and postmodern versions of practical realism.

At this point I should like to direct readers to the recent monograph of Jens Zimmermann.[65] His book is apropos for our discussion because it highlights, in far more detail than I have here, the theoretical similarities between older Christian theologies and practical realism. More specifically, Zimmermann demonstrates that the proverbial godfather of practical realism—Hans-Georg Gadamer—was deeply influenced by Christian ideas. Gadamer himself admits as much, especially his debt to Augustine and Luther. So, though Gadamer wants to describe his own orientation as "nontheistic," Zimmermann's study reveals that Gadamer's progress in epistemology and hermeneutics would have been impossible apart from what he borrowed from Christian theology, particularly from its doctrine of the incarnation. Only the incarnation allows the transcendence of God to enter the immanence of human history. It was precisely this close connection between transcendence and immanence, albeit in a nontheistic form, that allowed Gadamer to ground the immanence of experience in the stability of transcendence. It is no wonder that many contemporary evangelical philosophers have profited by studying and embracing some form of practical realism. As an account of human knowledge, practical realism stands much closer to the premodern Christian traditions than does the optimistic Cartesian-like realism that dominates so much evangelical thinking.[66]

Now a final word of caution is in order. My conclusions so far could be taken to imply that premodern and especially modern modes of inquiry were (or are) founded on mostly bankrupt epistemologies, and that everything believed or said before the likes of Gadamer was sheer fancy. I do not believe this at all. One can surely build a house on the assumption that the earth is flat. It is only when one sends a rocket to the moon that the flat-earth assumption fails. Similarly, as accounts of human knowledge, premodern and modern epistemologies worked very well precisely because both assumed that human beings get things right—and we certainly do get a great many things right. These older epistemologies sometimes fell short, however, as proper accounts of how and why human beings get things wrong. Premodern and modern Christian epistemologies, as well as modern atheistic epistemologies, failed to account adequately for the consequences of sin and finitude in human knowledge. This is where some type of practical realism, even in its nontheistic forms, improves upon its epistemic competitors.

One implication of practical realism's account of human knowledge is that the *experience of certainty* ("I am certain") does not translate into incorrigible, epistemic

---

65. Zimmermann, *Recovering Theological Hermeneutics*.
66. In this vein of thought, note the comments of John D. Caputo: "Pre-modern can communicate with the postmodern, which stands to reason if both are free from the kind of antagonism between faith and reason that grew up in and was so badly exacerbated by and in modernity" (*Philosophy and Theology* [Nashville: Abingdon, 2006], 59).

certainty ("therefore, I cannot be wrong"). We can be quite certain and quite wrong at the same time. Given that the Reformation in general, and evangelicalism in particular, have tightly hitched their wagons to epistemic certainty—especially to the certainty of salvation—it is only fair that I should address this implication of my approach. What is "certainty" if it does not yield incorrigible, epistemic certainty? I believe that a useful explanation of our experience with certainty, which would suit practical realism, appears in John Henry Newman's monograph, *A Grammar of Assent*.[67] According to Newman, although our rational capacity can advance logically toward certainty, the concrete evidence and experiences of life never offer all that we need to get there. Even in the best scenarios, the evidence only converges but never quite arrives at what we might call "proof." It is a faculty of the human mind (which Newman calls the "Illative Sense") that allows us to close the proof gap from high probability to certainty, so that we can give full and unqualified assent to truths that are not fully proven. In this account of human knowledge, we can be truly certain, but not certainly right. Nevertheless, in the final analysis, certainty works for us because it is almost always right—not perfectly right, but adequately right.

I am not qualified to provide a full-blown critique of Newman's sophisticated thesis, which goes far beyond what I have mentioned here. But his basic point regarding certainty seems very sensible and plausible. Certainty is an essential element in our engagement with the world. It is not foolproof, but it serves us quite well.

Conclusions

Though we have covered significant historical and theoretical ground in this chapter, the most important implications of this survey are few and straightforward. First, there is nothing unseemly or tragic about the limited perceptual horizon that God has granted to human beings. Our finite capacities are good aspects of God's created order, in both its original (prelapsarian) and subsequent (postlapsarian) permutations. We are doubly blessed by these finite capacities, for they allow us not only to interpret adequately but also to notice and appreciate the profound difference between the divine and human viewpoints. Our mediated interpretations of reality contrast sharply with our Creator's immediate knowledge of things. It is a difference that powerfully reveals to us the genuine majesty of God. The grave error of modern humanity, says Lesslie Newbigin, is its Cartesian demand for this god-like grasp on the truth. But this is an empty pursuit that ultimately paves the way for Nietzsche's nihilistic antirealism.[68] If human knowledge must be incorrigible and indubitable to count *as* knowledge, then we will never have it.

---

67. John Henry Newman, *A Grammar of Assent* (Garden City, NY: Doubleday, 1955).
68. Lesslie Newbigin, *Proper Confidence: Faith, Doubt, and Certainty in Christian Discipleship* (Grand Rapids: Eerdmans, 1995): 29–44.

A second and somewhat narrower implication of our discussion regards the interpretation of texts. Interpreters are thoroughly shaped by their respective communities and so tend to employ exegetical methods that are current within those communities. Early interpreters of Scripture expected to find both plain and figural (especially allegorical) meanings in the text because that is how interpretation was done in their day. For the same reason modern interpreters were interested only, or mainly, in recovering the historical facts, and in understanding the true intentions of Scripture's human authors. Postmodern interpreters then moved beyond this, either by adding other dimensions of meaning to the equation (practical realism) or by ignoring the author's intentions altogether (antirealism). Whether some of these approaches are better than others is beside the point. My interest is merely to show that all individuals interpret Scripture according to the methods practiced by their interpretive communities. If this is really how interpretation works, then we can expect that it will be true not only of Augustine, Aquinas, and Calvin but also of Jesus, Paul, and Luke.

The two preceding points suggest a third. If we find ourselves satisfied with the quite adequate communication experienced in our everyday life, and if that discourse serves us tolerably well, then why should we expect or even demand—as many conservative evangelicals do—an inerrant Bible? One answer might be that God authored the Bible and that we simply expect more from God than from human beings: God does not err, therefore the Bible contains no errors. On one level, I believe that this reasoning is sound. Yet I do not believe that we can so easily overlook that God has chosen to speak to human audiences through human authors in everyday human language. Is it therefore possible that God has selected to speak to human beings through *adequate* rather than *inerrant* words, and is it further possible that he did so because human beings are *adequate* rather than *inerrant* readers? Might it be the very height of divine wisdom, of *inerrant* wisdom, for God to speak to us from an *adequate* human horizon rather than from his divine, inerrant viewpoint? Before we presuppose what kind of discourse God must offer us, perhaps we should carefully consider the discourse itself to see what he has done in Scripture.

When all is said and done, I will strongly support a doctrine of inerrancy when it comes to Scripture; but I will further suggest that this doctrine, as traditionally understood, differs significantly from the doctrine as it has come to be understood by those evangelicals who stand more or less firmly within the Cartesian tradition. In my opinion, this tradition leads one into an epistemological cul-de-sac, which demands of the Bible something that it is not so that our human interpretations of Scripture can be turned into infallible "verbal idols."[69] Practical realism—which accentuates the validity and adequacy of human discourse—offers a viable exit from this cul-de-sac and is, in my opinion, an essential element in the church's healthy response to biblical criticism.

---

69. I borrow this term from Kevin Vanhoozer's insightful book, *Is There a Meaning in This Text?* (Grand Rapids: Zondervan, 1998), 459.

2

Historical Criticism and Assyriology

Modern approaches to the study of the Hebrew Bible and of the New Testament are legion, but the vast majority of these approaches fit comfortably into what I have called "historical criticism." Historical criticism is a hermeneutic (interpretive theory) that embraces three basic assumptions. First, it assumes that the Bible, like our everyday conversation, is understood best in light of its contemporary situation (in its ancient *historical* context). So biblical critics give careful attention to identifying and reconstructing the historical, cultural, linguistic, political, and religious world that produced the biblical text. The second assumption is that our modern attempts to reconstruct this ancient context should proceed on the basis of *historical analogy*. We should assume that the patterns of life and history that prevail in our own day and time help us understand how life would have unfolded in antiquity. Many (but not all) historical critics therefore assume that the great miracles of the Bible either did not happen at all or, at least, cannot be proved on the basis of analogy, since miracles are by nature unusual rather than normal events. I will consider this difficulty later on. Third, as the name implies, historical criticism assumes that biblical interpretation should be carried out with a *critical* disposition that does not assume that traditional or accepted perspectives on the Bible are correct. The need for such a critical perspective should be obvious: just because some human view or theory about the Bible has been believed, or is believed, does not ensure its correctness.

Unsurprisingly, one result of this threefold critical posture is that many traditional beliefs about the Bible, and interpretations of the Bible, have been rejected in favor of new perspectives on the text. This has given historical criticism a bad name in many religious communities—both Christian and Jewish—as modern critics have challenged cherished theological views. Of course, the perception that historical criticism has been dangerous to faith is not a groundless illusion. Large swaths of the church have been almost decimated by it. By beginning with matters of religion and faith, however, we are perhaps prejudicing the case against historical criticism too quickly.

Historical criticism of the Bible is in reality only one species of a larger historical-critical phenomenon that most of us already embrace. Since the Enlightenment, nearly every discipline of the humanities, arts, and sciences has undergone a kind of revolution in which its scholars have learned to reevaluate critically the dominant views and theories in their respective disciplines. Advances in our understanding of literature, language, history, and science all attest to the positive results of these historical-critical endeavors. Perhaps we can appreciate the positive benefits of historical criticism better by examining how this critical turn has contributed to the origins and development of a modern discipline that is closely related to—but distinct from—the study of the Bible. In order to do this, I would invite us to consider the discipline of Assyriology, which specializes in studying the history and languages of ancient Mesopotamia. As disciplines go, it is a very challenging field of study, which can be mastered only by men and women with unusual intellectual gifts and with a healthy work ethic. The importance of these two traits is best exemplified in Assyriology's first and greatest feat: the deciphering of Mesopotamia's ancient cuneiform languages.

The Origins of Assyriology

Etched on the rock face of Mount Bisitun in western Iran is a long inscription, written in a script that modern scholars call "cuneiform" ("wedge shaped").[1] The inscription was left behind by Darius, a king of ancient Persia. Darius's inscription is some 100 meters above the ground, looking down upon the road that ran between the ancient cities of Ecbatana and Babylon. The inscription includes a picture of various kings bowing down to Darius as well as a text, recorded in three languages, in which Darius describes how the god Ahuramazda helped him seize the throne from a fellow named Gaumata. The obvious purpose of the text was to memorialize Darius's rise to power and to accentuate the legitimacy of his claim to the throne. Darius insured that his propaganda would survive by ordering that the ledge beneath it be knocked out after the inscription was completed. This strategy to preserve the text obviously succeeded.

---

1. See J. C. Greenfield and B. Porten, *The Bisitun Inscription of Darius the Great, Aramaic Version* (London: Lund Humphries, 1982); R. Schmitt, *The Bisitun Inscriptions of Darius the Great, Old Persian Text* (London: Lund Humphries, 1991); E. von Voightlander, *The Bisitun Inscription of Darius the Great, Babylonian Version* (London: Lund Humphries, 1978); see also *ATSHB*, 398–400.

Although Darius's text stood on that rock face of Bisitun for centuries, it was not until the nineteenth century that anyone seriously attempted to decipher the three long-dead languages in which it was inscribed.[2] Numerous people were involved in this effort, but a young British officer, Sir Henry C. Rawlinson, is famous for scaling the rock face and for taking squeezes and making copies of the text so that it could be deciphered. The act of making these copies was heroic in itself, since Rawlinson had to remain in uncomfortable positions for many hours, perched precariously upon long ladders. Nevertheless, this logistical feat pales in comparison with the daunting intellectual task of actually deciphering the scripts.

How does one decipher an unknown script? Essentially, one begins with known languages and then uses them to move ever closer to deciphering the ancient and unknown tongue. In the case of the Bisitun inscription, Rawlinson recognized that one of the languages in the inscription seemed to have relatively few characters, suggesting that the script was alphabetical. Using his knowledge of modern Farsi (i.e., Persian), Rawlinson was able to deduce that the alphabetic language was none other than Old Persian. With this knowledge in hand, he was able to decipher this portion of the text with relative ease, as well as those portions of the text written in the second language, which turned out to be Elamite. Of course, a person of average intellectual frame could not have accomplished this feat. But Rawlinson, like the others involved in deciphering the texts, was a *Sprachgenie*, a true genius in matters of language. Nevertheless, even for a genius, deciphering the third and last language from Bisitun presented special problems.

The third language—which modern scholars came to know as Akkadian—was inherently more difficult to decipher because the script employed several hundred different cuneiform signs, some of which could convey more than one phonetic or ideographic value. To the uninitiated, it looks like chicken scratches. Nevertheless, Rawlinson and several other scholars were finally able to translate the language. This linguistic feat was so great that many leading scholars of the day, such as J.-E. Renan in France and G. C. Lewis in England, did not believe it. The matter was put to a test in 1855 at the suggestion of W. H. Fox-Talbot, when four scholars—Fox-Talbot, Rawlinson, E. Hincks, and J. Oppert—presented the Royal Asiatic Society with their independent translations of a previously untranslated Akkadian text. A committee of the society compared the translations and found that they agreed tolerably well. Assyriology was born.

At about the same time that Akkadian was being deciphered, numerous cuneiform texts in that language were being unearthed from sites in Mesopotamia. Scholars soon discovered that some of these texts—here we speak of the Neo-Assyrian royal annals—bore the names of characters and places from the Bible

---

2. For a discussion of the deciphering of Akkadian, see Henry C. Rawlinson, *The Persian Cuneiform Inscription at Behistun Decyphered and Translated* (London: J. W. Parker, 1847); R. W. Rogers, *A History of Babylonia and Assyria*, 6th ed. (New York: Abingdon, 1915).

(such as Hezekiah, Judah, and Israel) and also referred to biblical events (such as Assyria's conquest of Samaria and siege of Jerusalem). Archaeologists also discovered a creation story (*Enuma Elish*) and a flood story (tablet 11 of the Gilgamesh Epic) that were older than, and uncomfortably similar to, the biblical creation and flood stories in Genesis. The public announcement of this link between Mesopotamia and the Hebrew Bible naturally infused Assyriology with religious interest and caused biblical studies to take on a new, comparative dimension.

Assyriology has been unswerving in its commitment to the historical-critical method and so provides a good window into the nature and benefits of historical criticism. Unfortunately, we may peer through this window only by wading through a somewhat detailed analysis of several Mesopotamian texts. Whether a given reader will find this survey of texts tedious and difficult, I cannot say. But even one who finds the details tedious can still gain something from the discussion. One purpose of this survey is to illustrate the sheer complexity of the ancient data and the extent of expertise needed to interpret it. So I can only encourage readers who do not presently harbor a robust interest in Mesopotamian literature (and I suppose that this will describe many readers of this book) to give careful attention to the brief but somewhat arcane discussion that follows. Perhaps it will help a bit if we begin our deliberations with that most famous of all ancient Mesopotamian texts, the Gilgamesh Epic.

The Gilgamesh Epic

The stories of Gilgamesh were the most popular in ancient Mesopotamia and are arguably, next to the various flood stories, the Mesopotamian texts most familiar to modern readers.[3] The popularity of Gilgamesh stems, no doubt, from the fact that its primary theme resonates with all of us: the search for immortality. Readers familiar with Gilgamesh will know that Gilgamesh first pursued immortality through fame as a great warrior and king, but the death of his close friend, Enkidu, reminded him that mortal fame was not enough. In a last-ditch effort to save himself, Gilgamesh sought help from the only man who had ever achieved immortality: Ut-Napishtim, the flood hero (the Mesopotamian Noah). Unfortunately, Gilgamesh soon learned that Ut-Napishtim was granted immortality in the unique circumstance of the great flood. Because Gilgamesh could never duplicate this experience, he recognized that his search for immortality had ended in disappointment. So, at its heart, the Epic of Gilgamesh is a tragic story about the brevity and transience of mortal life.

Early on in their interpretations of the Gilgamesh Epic—long before they had the sources to prove it—Assyriologists like Marcus Jastrow realized that this

---

3. Texts and translations: A. R. George, *The Babylonian Gilgamesh Epic: Introduction, Critical Edition, and Cuneiform Texts*, 2 vols. (Oxford: Oxford University Press, 2003); *ANET*, 44–52, 72–99; *COS*, 1.132:458–60; 1.171:550–52. For discussion see *ATSHB*, 275–78.

long text was probably not written by a single author at one point in time but was instead the product of a rather long and complicated literary process. Scholars noticed that the various stories about Gilgamesh seemed like separate episodes rather than parts of a single narrative plot, and they also noted that the tales fell into two distinct groups: those focused on Gilgamesh as a death-defying hero, and those in which Gilgamesh grimly faced his death. There were also certain tensions in the story, such as the reappearance in tablet 12 of Enkidu, the long-dead friend of Gilgamesh. Eventually, these initial historical-critical suspicions about the text's history were confirmed by the discovery of other texts and versions of the Gilgamesh Epic. The following is what we learned from these texts.

Although the final "canonical" form of the Gilgamesh Epic includes twelve carefully structured tablets, it is now clear that the traditio-historical process that created the epic was quite complex.[4] Gilgamesh was a king in ancient Uruk sometime between 2800 and 2500 BCE. At some point—we are not certain when, but no later than 2150 BCE—poets writing in the Sumerian language (not in Akkadian) began to express the king's fame in heroic tales of his exploits. We might suppose that a rather long interval passed between the king's death and the heroic legends about him, but we know from other Mesopotamian texts that poetic legends of this sort were sometimes composed even during the king's his own lifetime.[5] This makes it difficult to determine precisely when the Gilgamesh traditions first appeared. At any rate, by 2150 the kings of the Third Dynasty of Ur were particularly taken with Gilgamesh and claimed him as their ancestor. This prompted Ur's court poets to compose and recite various Gilgamesh tales at royal banquets. From this early period, modern scholars know of at least five separate Sumerian compositions that treated the life of Gilgamesh. Most of these stories were eventually rolled into the later epic version of Gilgamesh's life, which was written in Akkadian. Although other Sumerian stories were also incorporated into the Akkadian epic ("Inanna's Descent into the Underworld"; the flood story), during the Sumerian period these tales had no direct relationship to Gilgamesh.

The first known attempt to integrate thematically the older poetic stories into a single epic is a fragmentary Akkadian text from the Old Babylonian period (c. eighteenth century BCE). The details of how this was done are not entirely clear. What is clear is that the thematic concern of this epic version was derived from older Sumerian stories that addressed the deaths of Enkidu and Gilgamesh, and Gilgamesh's confrontation with mortality.[6] This mortality theme was then systematically applied to the various traditions, causing the author(s) to take many liberties with the older stories. For instance, in the Akkadian epic the story of "Gilgamesh and Huwawa" was transformed from a Sumerian tale in which

---

4. Jeffrey H. Tigay, *The Evolution of the Gilgamesh Epic* (Philadelphia: University of Pennsylvania Press, 1982).
5. See the discussion of the Epic of Zimrilim in *ATSHB*, 286–87.
6. Hope Nash Wolff, "Gilgamesh, Enkidu, and the Heroic Life," *JAOS* 89 (1969): 392–98.

Gilgamesh sought fame by felling the famous trees of the Cedar Mountain into a quest to achieve immortality by killing the beast Huwawa.

While the Old Babylonian epic represented an obvious step forward in the development of the Gilgamesh traditions, the standard epic tradition, dating from circa 1250 BCE and current in the first millennium, introduced other changes. The most significant modification introduced was the addition of a prologue and epilogue, which framed the epic so that the heroic value of Gilgamesh's deeds became less important than the wisdom he acquired through these experiences. Other important changes included the incorporation of the flood story (tablet 11) and, somewhat later, the addition of traditions paralleling the Sumerian story of "Gilgamesh, Enkidu, and the Netherworld" (tablet 12). Although it has not been proved that tablet 12 is a later addition to the standard version, two features make this likely: (1) Enkidu, the friend of Gilgamesh who died in tablet 7, is suddenly alive again, and (2) the style of the text is a literal rendering from the Sumerian version rather than a creative adaptation, such as appears elsewhere in the Akkadian epic. Our latest copy of Gilgamesh is a fragmentary text from Seleucid-era Uruk, but this includes an episode that is not covered in the standard version.

What can we learn about historical criticism from our survey of the interpretation of the Gilgamesh Epic? Above all, we see that historical critics are sensitive to the realities that give rise to ancient texts. They recognize that many ancient stories are of a fictional sort, even if the characters in the stories—in this case, Gilgamesh—turn out to be historical figures. They also recognize that the writing of ancient texts can be much more complicated than it appears at first blush. Even when scholars had only a single epic about Gilgamesh before them, they were able to deduce from its features that the text was the product of a long and complex literary process. This deduction was subsequently confirmed by the discovery of older texts that became part of the epic version. Critics know as well that all texts are products of tradition. As texts pass through the successive hands of many generations, critics expect that their content and arrangement will sometimes change to reflect the concerns of each generation of readers. This process is vividly illustrated in the epic version of Gilgamesh, which transformed the earliest Sumerian stories about Gilgamesh's heroic exploits into a philosophical treatise on human mortality.

And one other point before we go on. Skeptics of historical criticism often disparage the critics because they "claim to know everything about everything." Now to be sure, there are certainly "know-it-all" critics who exude this arrogance. But if one looks again at our survey of the Gilgamesh Epic, one finds that the critics have often admitted when the data at hand do not permit a reasonable hypothesis. Critics do not know precisely when Gilgamesh lived, nor do they know precisely how much time elapsed before tales were written about the king. There are also many unanswered questions about how, precisely, to interpret certain passages in the epic. Nevertheless, it is clear enough that the data permit only certain kinds of hypotheses about the development and significance of this ancient text. The hypothesis that the Gilgamesh Epic was composed by a single author living during one historical milieu is not on the list of scholarly options, nor should it be.

Mesopotamian Histories: The Assyrian Annals and Babylonian Chronicles

Although Assyriologists have categorized the Gilgamesh tales and many other Mesopotamian texts as fiction, they are well aware that some Mesopotamian texts give us genuine history. The two best-known genres of Mesopotamian historiography are the Assyrian annals and the Babylonian Chronicles. Scholars use these texts not only to reconstruct the history of Mesopotamia but also as windows into the history of Israel and ancient Palestine. For this reason these texts are important for students of the Hebrew Bible. Because the Assyrian annals and Babylonian Chronicles differ in important ways, let us consider each historical genre in turn.

The Neo-Assyrian annals come from the first millennium BCE, when Assyrians from the upper Tigris River were rapidly expanding their empire to control all parts of the Near East.[7] Assyrian kings memorialized their colonial successes by composing histories of their conquests and of other noteworthy accomplishments. The histories were arranged to provide year-by-year accounts of the king's deeds and for this reason are called "annals" (cf. Latin *annus*, "year"). The annals were composed by combining temporary records from recent years with older information gleaned from earlier copies of the annals. Generally speaking, the annals were inscribed in two different kinds of places, and these locations help us understand the purpose of the texts. First, the annals were composed on the walls and floors of temples and palaces, where literate servants, scholars, and priests of the royal courts and temples could read them. Second, the annals were buried beneath the walls of new construction projects. The intended readers in this second case were the gods (who could manage reading a buried text) and future kings, who would find the texts during the refurbishment of buildings and temples. We can deduce from the "publication" of these texts that the king wished above all to win the favor of the gods and of the literati from the royal courts and priestly guilds. Promoting satisfaction in these audiences was a constant concern for ancient kings, since many kings died in coup attempts hatched by disgruntled or dissatisfied subjects from the royal and priestly classes. Given the propagandistic purposes of the annals, we must ask whether the authors of the annals were concerned about getting history right. Even a cursory reading of the annals reveals that their depictions of the king are invariably flattering, so that they rarely mention his failures and setbacks. Historical evidence confirms

---

7. Texts and translations: D. D. Luckenbill, *Ancient Records of Assyria and Babylon*, 2 vols. (Chicago: University of Chicago Press, 1926–1927); *ANET*, 274–301; *COS*, 2.113:261–72. For discussion see *ATSHB*, 364–68.

that this positive assessment was sometimes achieved by "cooking the books." In 853 BCE, for instance, Shalmaneser III of Assyria conquered regions in northern Syria and then headed south down the Orontes River toward the Syrian heartland and Israel. He was confronted in the Battle of Qarqar by a formidable coalition of nations that included, among others, Hadadezer of Damascus and Ahab of Israel. Although the coalition successfully repulsed the Assyrian invasion, Shalmaneser's annalist recorded this battle as a great victory for Assyria.[8] This sort of scribal fiction was rarely necessary because Assyrian victories were far more common than setbacks, but such fictions do appear in the annals.

Fiction also plays a role in those sections of the annals that scholars call "royal apologies," such as the "Esarhaddon Apology" that appears in one section of King Esarhaddon's historical prism from Nineveh.[9] This composition responded to two objections that were being raised against Esarhaddon's dynasty. First, the text explained how Esarhaddon became the legitimate crown prince when he was not the oldest son of Sennacherib; and second, it averred in the strongest possible terms that Esarhaddon played no role in the coup attempt that led to the murder of his father. Esarhaddon blamed his bellicose brothers for this patricide, as they fought vainly for a throne that neither their father nor the gods would give them. Modern scholars suspect that Esarhaddon was not so innocent in these matters as he would have us believe. At any rate, the propagandistic shape of the annals—and of the royal apologies they contain—is clear. Because propaganda tends to tell only half of the story, scholars are cautious when they use the Assyrian annals as sources for writing modern histories of ancient Mesopotamia.

Now, for purposes of comparison, let us consider not only the annals but also the Babylonian Chronicle Series.[10] This series comprises a number of tablets that cover Babylonian history from the eighth to the third century BCE, in other words, from the advent of the Neo-Babylonian dynasty down to the Hellenistic period. The tablets are connected to one another using "catch lines" to show how to place them in the proper order. Were all of the texts in our possession, we would have a continuous narrative of Babylonian history during the period in question, but there are substantial breaks in our preserved copies of the series. In terms of outlook, phraseology, and structure, the chronicle genre has a peculiar character that distinguishes it markedly from the annalistic tradition of the Assyrians.

The chronicles are selective and do not provide a record of each year but rather, on average, of about one year in three. The entries in the text are arranged in segments by year, with each segment marked off by dividing lines and a regnal date

---

8. *ANET*, 278–79.

9. Hayim Tadmor, "Autobiographical Apology in the Royal Assyrian Literature," in *History, Historiography, and Interpretation: Studies in Biblical and Cuneiform Literatures*, ed. Hayim Tadmor and Moshe Weinfeld (Jerusalem: Magnes, 1983), 36–57.

10. Texts and translations: A. K. Grayson, *Assyrian and Babylonian Chronicles* (Locust Valley, NY: J. J. Augustin, 1975), 8–28, 69–124; *ANET*, 301–7 (partial); *COS*, 1.137:467–68 (partial). For discussion see *ATSHB*, 369–71.

formula, such as, "The nth year of PN" (where PN = "personal/king's name"). The end of each king's reign is also marked with a formula of sorts: "For n years PN1 ruled in Babylon. PN2 ascended the throne in Babylon." The authors consulted written source material while compiling the chronicles, as is confirmed by the confession in chronicle 1 that source materials were not always available: "the battle which Nabu-nasir waged against Borsippa is not written." Modern scholars have deduced that the primary historical sources used by the authors of the series were Babylonian astronomical diaries. This conclusion is based on the fact that the diaries provide a chronological list of information like that found in the Chronicle Series, and on the fact that the chronicles and diaries use similar phraseology.

The Babylonian Chronicles are concerned with a number of different topics, especially with kingship and the process of royal succession. Their compilers were also interested in occasions when gods (in statue form) failed to attend religious festivals, when gods were abducted from their temples, when military activities took place, and when coup attempts either threatened or altered an orderly monarchic succession. Although the subject matter is in many respects similar to the Assyrian annals, the chronicles are narrated in the third person and are dispassionate from a political point of view, interested not only in Babylonian kingship but also in the politics of neighboring states that affected Babylon. Both Babylonian victories and military defeats are included in the texts. Judged from a modern perspective, the Chronicles seem to reflect a genuine intellectual interest in the history of Babylon itself. For this reason, modern scholars generally trust the Babylonian Chronicle Series as a source for good historical information.

Why is the evenhanded history of the Babylonian Chronicles so different from the propagandistic and one-sided Assyrian annals? The ideological differences between the annals and chronicles are a result of the different constituencies who sponsored the texts. While the annals were composed under the sponsorship of the Assyrian king as part of the state's official propagandistic effort, the chronicles were produced by private (or at least nonofficial) scribal activities unfettered by influences from the Babylonian court.[11] This difference in context gave rise to two distinct genres and interests, one in promoting the Assyrian state (the annals) and the other in discovering the history of Babylon (the chronicles).

What do we learn from the annals and chronicles about the historical-critical method? First, regarding the annals, we notice that Assyriologists are cautious about using them as historical sources, even though the texts purport to be royal histories. This caution seems justified because the texts are obviously propagandistic compositions in which the annalists deliberately misrepresented the facts in order to make history serve the king's purposes. This being so, the annals should

---

11. J. A. Brinkman, "The Babylonian Chronicle Revisited," in *Lingering over Words: Studies in Ancient Near Eastern Literature in Honor of William L. Moran*, ed. Tzvi Abusch, John Huehnergard, and Piotr Steinkeller, Harvard Semitic Studies 37 (Atlanta: Scholars Press, 1990), 73–104.

always be interpreted by reading between the lines and against the grain, and by examining other types of sources that might confirm or cast doubt on the annalistic accounts. This reading strategy is not a bias against the annals; rather, it correctly recognizes the bias *in* the annals. Second, we learn that the critics are not at all opposed to trusting the histories of ancient writers when this is warranted. Assyriologists generally trust the Babylonian Chronicles because of their dispassionate tone, balanced perspective, and the fact that the texts seem to have been based on very good sources, namely, the Babylonian astronomical diaries. In sum, when modern scholars use ancient works of history to write modern histories, their disposition toward the ancient sources naturally depends upon the genre and nature of those sources. This means that modern scholars will not trust the Assyrian annals quite so readily as the Babylonian Chronicles.

One word of caution, however. Even when texts like the Babylonian Chronicles seem to be trustworthy for historical purposes, modern scholars never expect them to provide faultless portraits of the past. Histories are always works of inquiry, and inquiry is necessary only because the authors of the Chronicles were finite human beings, who applied their finite intellects to still older sources that were also products of—you guessed it—finite human beings. Consequently, although human inquiry may indeed produce a relatively good account of the past, this history will never be hermetically sealed from the finitude of the human perspective that produced it. Far from providing us with perfect access to the past, historical narratives are perhaps the clearest examples of human finitude, since in them we depend on older written sources for our information about the past.

The Uruk Prophecy

This interesting text is one of several similar exemplars from the ancient world, so let us examine it closely. As the title partly suggests, the text is a prophecy that predicts great things for the Mesopotamian city of Uruk.[12] Its author presented the "future" as a sequence of eleven kings, some good and some bad, who are introduced anonymously and schematically in this fashion: "A king will arise, and he will [or will not] grant justice to the land." The last two kings in the sequence, kings ten and eleven, seem to provide the key to the text's interpretation.[13] The prophet foretells that the tenth king would renovate Uruk's temples and retrieve the statue of Uruk's protective goddess from

---

12. Text and translation: Hermann Hunger and Stephen A. Kaufman, "A New Akkadian Prophecy Text," *JAOS* 95 (1975): 371–75; Tremper Longman III, *Fictional Akkadian Autobiography: A Generic and Comparative Study* (Winona Lake, IN: Eisenbrauns, 1991), 237–38. For discussion see *ATSHB*, 243.

13. Paul-Alain Beaulieu, "The Historical Background of the Uruk Prophecy," in *The Tablet and the Scroll: Near Eastern Studies in Honor of William W. Hallo*, ed. Mark E. Cohen, Daniel C. Snell, and David B. Weisberg (Bethesda, MD: CDL, 1993), 41–52; Hunger and Kaufman, "New Akkadian Prophecy Text."

Babylon, and that the eleventh king would forever rule the world and "exercise dominion like the gods."

Although the text sports all the trappings of a genuine prophecy, Assyriologists—who embrace the historical-critical method—doubt that this is what it is. First, scholars have noticed that the prophecy about the tenth king fits the life of the Babylonian king Nebuchadnezzar II (604–562 BCE) so closely that it must have been written *after* the events in Nebuchadnezzar's life had already occurred. Scholars refer to this pseudoprophetic phenomenon using the Latin phrase *vaticinium ex eventu*, which means "prophecy after the event." This skeptical judgment is reinforced by a second observation about the text, which concerns the prophecies about the eleventh king. Although these prophecies clearly predicted that a grand and glorious eschatological kingdom would ultimately appear in Uruk, no such kingdom ever materialized in the city. So the prophecies about both the tenth and the eleventh kings have serious problems, but for different reasons: the first prophecy was precisely right, the second precisely wrong.

It is relatively easy for critical scholars to date *ex eventu* prophecies of this sort. One merely traces the prophetic predictions until they fail. In this case, the prophecies about the tenth king (Nebuchadnezzar II) were correct and the prophecies that followed (concerning his son) were not. For this reason, the text probably dates to the time of Nebuchadnezzar II's son, Amel-Marduk (Evil-Merodach). Why would an author compose such a text? Scholars do not know for certain, but their best guess is that the prophecy was composed during the Late Babylonian period, when a priest in Uruk took up his stylus to support a Babylonian dynasty that was favorably disposed to his city.[14] Because the text is essentially pseudoprophetic rather than genuinely prophetic, scholars often classify the Uruk Prophecy as an apocalyptic text (these frequently have pseudoprophecies) rather than as a prophetic text. It is not at all clear, however, whether we should read these pseudoprophecies as pious ruses (written with good intentions) or as outright frauds (written with deceptive intentions). The former is suggested (but not proved) by the fact that pseudoprophetic genres were well known among Mesopotamian scribes.[15]

In any case, here again we see that historical criticism does not take texts at face value. Although the Uruk Prophecy *appears* to be an authentic predictive text, most of its predictions were written after the predicted events had occurred, and its only real attempt at prophecy seems to have failed. The realistic interpretation of the text offered by Assyriologists is not merely the result of their skepticism about ancient sources. It is the result of their honest attempt to fit this strange text into its ancient Mesopotamian context.

14. For an alternative but still critical approach to the prophecy, see Jonathan A. Goldstein, "The Historical Setting of the Uruk Prophecy," *JNES* 47 (1988): 43–46.

15. For a survey of the relevant texts, see *ATSHB*, 241–45.

The Sin of Sargon

The plot of this Neo-Assyrian tale is straightforward.[16] As the story begins, we find Sennacherib, king of Assyria, noting that his own father, Sargon II (709–705 BCE), had died on the battlefield and that his body had not been properly interred. Why would the gods have permitted this indignity? Sennacherib puts this question to the gods through divination and discovers that his father had sinned against the gods by neglecting the cults of Babylon. Sennacherib quickly responds to this revelation by assuming a new posture of worship and respect toward Babylon and its chief god, Marduk. As the text concludes, Sennacherib encourages his son to continue this pro-Babylonian policy, warning Esarhaddon to persevere with this policy in the face of resistance from Assyrians, who do not care for Babylon: "Reconcile the gods of Babylonia with your [Assyrian] gods!" The historical context presumed by the texts is the eighth/seventh century, when the Neo-Assyrian Empire was ruling over the city of Babylon. The purpose of the text was obviously to support Assyria's pro-Babylonian policy in a situation where some Assyrians resisted this policy. However, Assyriologists are fairly certain that there is more to this text than meets the eye.

Although modern scholars initially read this text as an historically accurate report, it turns out that Sennacherib cannot be its historical protagonist because he was infamous in Mesopotamia for one great sin: the destruction of Babylon.[17] According to other Assyrian sources, the nation's turn toward Babylon did not take place under Sennacherib—who razed Babylon to the ground—but rather under his son Esarhaddon, who worked hard to atone for his father's sins by rebuilding Babylon and restoring its temples. It follows that this text was not composed by Sennacherib at all. It was instead a fictional piece of propaganda sponsored by Esarhaddon, whose goal was to promote a renewal of the Babylonian cults in the face of resistance from Assyria's scribal elite. Esarhaddon's strategy for bestowing legitimacy upon this turn to Babylon, and for insulating himself from blame for this pro-Babylonian policy, was to attribute the policy to his deceased father. As C. S. Lewis said, "What is new usually wins its way by disguising itself as old."[18]

Naturally, Assyriologists cannot *prove* that the Sin of Sargon was written during the time of Esarhaddon rather than during the reign of his father. Their theory is merely a strategy for explaining why other Mesopotamian sources—letters, chronicles, and annals—portray Sennacherib so differently. Making coherent sense of all of the data is a hallmark of Assyriology, and of historical criticism in general.

---

16. Text and translation: Alisdair Livingstone, *Court Poetry and Literary Miscellanea*, State Archives of Assyria 3 (Helsinki: Helsinki University Press, 1989), 77–79; Longman, *Fictional Akkadian Autobiography*, 117–18, 231–33. For discussion see *ATSHB*, 290–91.

17. Hayim Tadmor, Benno Landsberger, and Simo Parpola, "The Sin of Sargon and Sennacherib's Last Will," *State Archives of Assyria Bulletin* 3 (1989): 3–51.

18. C. S. Lewis, *Allegory of Love: A Study in Medieval Tradition* (London: Oxford University Press, 1936), 11.

The Sumerian and Lagash King Lists

Closely related to the discipline of Assyriology is Sumerology, which studies the Sumerian language and people who spoke it. The Sumerians lived in Mesopotamia before the Akkadian-speaking peoples who wrote the texts we have examined so far. Here we shall consider only two Sumerian texts.

Mesopotamian scribes frequently compiled lists of the kings who had reigned in their cities along with chronological information about how long they reigned. Two good examples are the Sumerian King List and the Lagash King List.[19] The Sumerian King List (SKL) originated around 2000 BCE. Several different editions of the text exist, revealing a complicated literary history that probably goes back to a single original composition. In its most complete form, the text includes three parts: (a) a list of kings who lived before the great flood; (b) a reference to the flood itself; and (c) a list of kings who reigned after the flood. SKL notes the length of each king's reign, but the reign lengths are often exceptionally long, particularly for the pre-flood kings. King Alalgar, for instance, supposedly reigned for 36,000 years! However, critical scholars are sure that this pre-flood portion of the list was not originally part of SKL, in part because the pre-flood list does not appear in some manuscripts of SKL, and in part because the kings mentioned in it are sometimes duplicated in the post-flood list (for example, kings Dumuzi and Enmenunna appear both before and after the flood).

According to Jacobsen's standard critical edition of the text, SKL was composed from two types of sources: date lists and legendary epics. The date lists provided the chronological backbone of the text, and the epics are reflected in brief anecdotes connected with certain kings. For example, the text not only lists King Etana but also tells us that he was "a shepherd, the one who ascended to heaven." This anecdote about Etana refers to the Etana Legend, another ancient text that we have in tablet copies. The chronological data in SKL are peculiar. Not only are the lengths of reign absurdly long, but the numbers themselves are also odd. The antediluvian chronology appears to reflect astronomical figures, while the postdiluvian dates seem to have been derived using operations from sexegesimal mathematics.[20] At any rate, the chronology provided in the early portions of SKL is anything but historically accurate information.

Why was SKL first composed? SKL presented kingship as a single succession of divinely appointed leaders that originated at the beginning of time. This scheme was entirely fictional, of course, since there were many kings in ancient Mesopotamia, and these kings often ruled at the same time in different places.

---

19. Texts and translations: Thorkild Jacobsen, *The Sumerian King List*, Assyriological Studies 11 (Chicago: University of Chicago Press, 1939); Edmond Sollberger, "The Rulers of Lagaš," *Journal of Cuneiform Studies* 21 (1967): 279–91; *ANET*, 265–67 (SKL). For discussion see *ATSHB*, 345–48.

20. "Sexegesimal" is the term for base 60 math, as opposed to the base 10 (decimal) math commonly used today. For discussion see Dwight W. Young, "A Mathematical Approach to Certain Dynastic Spans in the Sumerian King List," *JNES* 2 (1988): 123–29.

The purpose of this fiction was presumably to legitimize a specific king by painting him as the one and only authentic king. There is an ongoing debate among scholars about which Mesopotamian king was originally the focus of the list, but because the list was often reused, edited, and updated, it is no longer possible to identify him with certainty.

When the Lagash King List (LKL) was discovered, it was immediately apparent that this list was closely related to SKL. Both texts include a reference to the flood followed by a long line of post-flood kings. However, these similarities aside, LKL is peculiar for two reasons. First, although modern scholars know the names of the rulers of Lagash during this period, most of the kings in the list are entirely unknown apart from it. Second, LKL attributes extremely long reigns to the kings, not only the ancient ones, as in SKL, but also to more recent ones. What circumstances might explain these peculiarities?

Sumerologists have determined that LKL was not a real king list at all but rather a parody of SKL, constructed by adding a string of invented royal names to a list of genuine Lagashite kings. The Lagashite author probably parodied SKL because the earlier Sumerian list had failed to include the rulers of Lagash. The new text legitimized Lagashite claims to the throne by tracing kingship through Lagash rather than through the cities of Kish, Uruk, and Ur, as the author of SKL had done. This is a reasonable appraisal of the evidence and demonstrates that very similar texts can be written using quite different modes of composition.

Conclusions

I will draw three basic conclusions from this discussion of historical criticism and ancient Near Eastern texts. First, and above all, historical-critical judgments are products of academic expertise, in which intellectually gifted scholars apply their respective trades to very complex linguistic and archaeological data from the ancient world. This means, of course, that in most cases the average person is in no position to evaluate, let alone criticize, the results of critical scholarship. Such a dictum applies not only to Assyriology but also to every academic discipline, both of the sciences and the humanities. Consequently, a certain humility is warranted when those outside a scholarly discipline wish to inquire about and evaluate the tried and tested conclusions of scholars in that discipline.

Second, we are in a better position now to take note of the methods and assumptions of historical criticism, especially with regard to Assyriology and other disciplines that study texts and history. Historical critics assume that human discourse, whether verbal or textual, often turns out to be something quite other than it appears at first glance. Ancient texts are particularly rich in these ambiguous and deceptive qualities, since they were composed in genres quite different from our own and in contexts unfamiliar to us. According to historical criticism, the best way to compensate for our literary ignorance in such cases is to examine the texts with a critical eye and to attempt, as best we can, to situate the texts within the ancient world that produced them. When Assyriologists apply this critical methodology to the reading of Mesopotamian texts, the following observations result:

1. Narrative stories that have the appearance of history may be fictional, even if the characters in the story are historical figures (e.g., Gilgamesh Epic, Sin of Sargon).
2. Near Eastern texts can be the product of a very long literary process, in which various authors and editors changed the text as it passed through successive generations of readers. Moreover, historical critics are able to detect this complexity even when they have only the text in its final form (e.g., Gilgamesh Epic).
3. Although ostensibly historical and accurate, texts like the Assyrian annals and Babylonian Chronicles are shaped in various ways by the finite perspectives of the authors (who have limited sources for their research) and also by the ideological concerns of the authors (who have a bias in favor of some viewpoints and against others). For this reason, an author may have less commitment to accurate history than at first appears, and even if the author is genuinely committed to recovering and retelling the historical past, his or her effort to get the facts right will not guarantee a complete or accurate history.
4. When it comes to ancient historical narratives, some are relatively accurate (e.g., the Babylonian Chronicles) and others less so (e.g., the Assyrian annals).
5. Even genres that strike us as particularly religious and pious, such as prophetic texts, can turn out to offer pseudoprophecies instead of genuine predictions (e.g., Uruk Prophecy). In such cases, it is not clear whether we should read the texts as pious ruses, written with honorable intentions, or as pious frauds, written with deceptive motives.
6. Because many ancient texts were sponsored by the palace and temple, it was common for the texts to serve the propagandistic needs of kings or priests (e.g., Assyrian annals, Sumerian King List, Uruk Prophecy). In some cases these propagandistic writings involved the outright fabrication of "facts" in order to serve a political agenda (e.g., Uruk Prophecy, Sin of Sargon, LKL).
7. Two texts can appear very similar and yet turn out to be entirely different sorts of compositions (cf. SKL and LKL). Such generic differences are not visible on the surface but appear only as we attempt to situate these texts within their ancient contextual milieus.
8. Near Eastern texts are sometimes written by different authors, and written in different historical periods, than the texts claim or imply. While this might suggest duplicity in the ancient author, it must be remembered

that ancient authors—like their modern counterparts—sometimes used creative fiction to convey their view of reality.

According to modern biblical scholars, these eight literary patterns appear not only in Mesopotamian literature but also in the Hebrew Bible. We shall examine their evidence for this claim in the next chapter.

Third, the evidence adduced above challenges the common evangelical charge that critical scholars approach the biblical text with more skepticism than other ancient texts. Assyriologists are not at all shy about applying their critical faculties to the texts they study. If we agree with this and the above conclusions, and if we are sympathetic with the literary and historical judgments offered by Assyriologists, then we are implicitly agreeing with the utility and value of the historical-critical method. Indeed, I must confess that I do not know of any biblical scholars—even evangelical biblical scholars—who would be wholly uncomfortable with either the basic methodology of Assyriology or its conclusions about ancient Mesopotamian literature. This is because most of us, as products of the post-Enlightenment age, have already accepted the benefits of thinking things through historically and critically. I should like for this reason to make a point very clearly, and to encourage the reader to keep this point in mind for the remainder of the book. In the end, I believe that historical criticism is nothing other than reading a text in light of its context. So, though I shall continue to use expressions like "biblical criticism," "modern criticism," and "historical criticism" in the discussion that follows, it seems to me that the negative aura that often surrounds these words is unnecessary and unwarranted. For when I say historical criticism, I mean little else than "reading texts contextually."

If we have a problem with historical criticism, I suspect that it is not with historical criticism per se but rather with historical criticism as it is applied to Holy Scripture. Consequently, at the end of the day, I believe that we face two interrelated questions: (1) What are the exegetical results of an historical-critical reading of the Bible? (2) To what extent is it legitimate to read the Bible through the lens of historical criticism? I shall begin the next chapter with the first question.

3

THE PROBLEM
OF BIBLICAL CRITICISM

A Survey of the Flash Points

Introduction

The Bible is a wonderful book, the first to be printed and the best selling of all time. It enjoys this exalted status not because it is merely popular or interesting (although it is these things), nor because it has played a primary role in the spiritual formation of so many individuals and even of whole cultures (although this is true). No, the Bible is special among books because it is God's book—his very word to humanity. Here, under one cover, we find the first national histories ever written (Samuel–Kings), insightful words of sage advice (as in Proverbs), the loftiest of ethical principles (the Gospels), and a transparent portrait of the human condition, in terms of its physical suffering (as in Job), its psychological turmoil (as in Ecclesiastes), and its abject poverty (Amos). Scripture is more special still because it points us to God's great remedy for our troubled condition: Jesus Christ. So if the Bible is anything, it is certainly a book that offers divine solutions for the human soul. This is precisely why the present chapter will perhaps strike some as odd. For it will seem unwise in the best case, and impious in the worst, if we wish to speak openly about the Bible's "problems." What fool would risk asking probing and critical questions of God's holy Word?

I would like to suggest, however, that the Bible itself invites us, at least implicitly, to ask hard and critical questions of the divine Word. Let me illustrate the point by turning to that great promise that God offered to King David of Israel:

> Moreover the LORD declares to you that the LORD will make you a house. When your days are fulfilled and you lie down with your fathers, I will raise up your offspring after you, who shall come forth from your body, and I will establish his kingdom. He shall build a house for my name, and I will establish the throne of his kingdom for ever. I will be his father, and he shall be my son. When he commits iniquity, I will chasten him with the rod of men, with the stripes of the sons of men; but I will not take my steadfast love from him, as I took it from Saul, whom I put away from before you. And your house and your kingdom shall be made sure for ever before me; your throne shall be established for ever. (2 Sam. 7:11–16 RSV)

God promised David an eternal dynasty. This divine promise would seem to be straightforward and unambiguous, and it is for this reason that the exile of Judah to Babylon in the sixth century BCE—and the concomitant loss of David's throne and kingdom—came as such a shock to the people of Judah. The reaction of one astonished Jew is still preserved in Psalm 89:19–46 (RSV):

> Of old thou didst speak in a vision to thy faithful one, and say:
> "I have set the crown upon one who is mighty,
>   I have exalted one chosen from the people.
> I have found David, my servant;
>   with my holy oil I have anointed him. . . .
> My steadfast love I will keep for him for ever,
>   and my covenant will stand firm for him.
> I will establish his line for ever
>   and his throne as the days of the heavens.
> If his children forsake my law
>   and do not walk according to my ordinances,
> if they violate my statutes
>   and do not keep my commandments,
> then I will punish their transgression with the rod
>   and their iniquity with scourges;
> but I will not remove from him my steadfast love,
>   or be false to my faithfulness.
> I will not violate my covenant,
>   or alter the word that went forth from my lips.
> Once for all I have sworn by my holiness;
>   I will not lie to David.
> His line shall endure for ever,
>   his throne as long as the sun before me.
> Like the moon it shall be established for ever;
>   it shall stand firm while the skies endure." *Selah*

> But now thou hast cast off and rejected,
> > thou art full of wrath against thy anointed.
> Thou hast renounced the covenant with thy servant;
> > thou hast defiled his crown in the dust.
> Thou hast breached all his walls;
> > thou hast laid his strongholds in ruins.
> All that pass by despoil him;
> > he has become the scorn of his neighbors.
> Thou hast exalted the right hand of his foes;
> > thou hast made all his enemies rejoice.
> Yea, thou hast turned back the edge of his sword,
> > and thou hast not made him stand in battle.
> Thou hast removed the scepter from his hand,
> > and cast his throne to the ground.
> Thou hast cut short the days of his youth;
> > thou hast covered him with shame. *Selah*
> How long, O Lord? Wilt thou hide thyself for ever?
> > How long will thy wrath burn like fire?

The psalmist was intimately familiar with the Davidic promise in 2 Samuel and simply could not make good sense of what appeared to be God's broken promise. His lament eventually ended with a simple request that God would remember and restore the house of David. Then, with a disjunction so common in the Psalter's laments, the author concluded his complaint with these instructive words: "Praise be to the LORD forever! Amen and Amen" (NIV). This psalmist, whoever he was, was not averse to asking hard questions of God and of God's Word, nor was he paralyzed by his unanswered questions. So far as I can deduce from the psalm, his courage stemmed especially from his great faith, which trusted the character of God more than the apparent contradiction between the divine Word and human experience. God had a solution, and that was enough.

Now this biblical author has given us some warrant for attending closely to the problems in Scripture, whether real or apparent, and for discussing them openly and without fear. In this spirit of inquiry I would turn our attention to the problems in Scripture that have been pointed out by modern critical scholarship, and to the very problem of biblical criticism itself.

To say that modern biblical criticism is a "problem" will mean different things to different people. For many evangelicals it will mean that higher criticism is a problem because, though it is influential and widely believed, it is a rationalistic exercise that leads to erroneous and dangerous conclusions about the Bible. Biblical criticism will be a problem, not because it is true, but because so many fall under its deceptive spell. In this scenario, the task of introducing biblical criticism will be analogous to introducing atheism: we describe and expose its errors so that it can be replaced with something better. The present chapter charts a different course, however.

My purpose instead is to lay out as clearly as possible the evidence and logic behind the standard conclusions of mainstream biblical scholarship, so that readers might fairly weigh these claims in the balance of good judgment. To be sure, I am not wholly unbiased on the question. I have written this book precisely because I have already done my own weighing of the evidence and have concluded that, in many instances, the critical consensus on the Bible is essentially correct and reasonably justified. Whether the reader will reach the same conclusions I cannot say, but I hope at least to demonstrate that biblical criticism arises from a careful and thoughtful reading of the Bible rather than from reckless impiety. In certain respects I regret that we must traverse this territory. Readers unfamiliar with modern biblical criticism may find parts of the discussion unpleasant, messy, and perhaps even offensive. Yet I have the sense that many Christians ought to know something about the difficulties presented by modern scholarship. This includes not only those who teach the Bible and do serious biblical and theological research but also those who are entrusted with advancing the cause of Christian education, especially the administrators and board members of Christian colleges and universities. Ministers of the church, particularly those serving among university students or in university communities, will also face these issues sooner or later. I trust that my discussion will be of value to all such readers, even if in the end they do not agree with my conclusions.

If modern biblical criticism is to be proved right (or at least partly right) in the eyes of confessing evangelical Christians, then it must be proved right by taking the Bible seriously. So in the pages that follow, I invite readers to consider very carefully what Scripture explicitly says, and also silently implies, about the nature of its verbal discourse. On this score, one thing is clear: Scripture presents itself both as the words of God and, often, as the words of human authors. This is particularly true in the New Testament, where most of the canonical letters are presented not as God's letters but as Paul's. Similarly, the author of Luke seems aware of no author but himself:

> Inasmuch as many have undertaken to compile a narrative of the things which have been accomplished among us, just as they were delivered to us by those who from the beginning were eyewitnesses and ministers of the word, it seemed good to me also, having followed all things closely for some time past, to write an orderly account for you, most excellent Theophilus, that you may know the truth concerning the things of which you have been informed. (Luke 1:1–4 RSV)

There are, of course, good reasons for maintaining that Paul's Letters and Luke's Gospel were authored not only by men but also by God. Paul himself commended the Thessalonians for accepting his words as "the word of God" (1 Thess. 2:13). But any serious theological appraisal of biblical authorship will emphasize not only the book's divine genesis but also its human origins. To the extent that the Bible is truly a product of human authorship, this seems to imply—given the discussion in chapter 1 above—that the Bible's viewpoints will reflect the limited historical contingencies of its human authors and audience. Now it should be rather easy to find out if this expectation is correct, for it can be tested by examining closely the contents and properties of the Bible's human discourse. As we saw in the previous chapter, close readings of human discourse is what historical critics do best.

Evangelicals do not reject everything that modern critics say about the Bible. Rather, there are certain flashpoints in which modern scholarly interpretations of Scripture run afoul of traditional evangelical sensibilities. In the remainder of this chapter, I will try to elucidate the nature of this tension by examining more closely the key flashpoints that produce it. Much of our attention will be focused on the Pentateuch, not only because its five books are an important point of contention in these matters but also because the Pentateuch, being foundational for both Jews and Christians, broadens the intellectual and theological context of our discussion. It is also expedient to begin with the Pentateuch because, as Scripture's "introduction," its five books represent a common starting point for critical study of the Bible. Our discussion of the Pentateuch will be followed by a survey of similar problems that emerge when modern scholars read the Hebrew histories (in Samuel–Kings and Chronicles), Isaiah, Ezekiel, the Gospels, Daniel/Revelation, and the Pastoral Epistles (1 and 2 Timothy, Titus). This is a fairly long chapter, so I invite readers to settle in, read carefully, and consider thoughtfully. Evangelical objections to this material, which are legion, will be presented in the next chapter.

One more point before we get started. None of the perspectives that I present below are embraced by every critical scholar; in some cases even I have questions about these critical conclusions. So biblical scholarship is not something that offers us a long list of assured results. Nevertheless, as a rule, the views described below are widely held by scholars and, in many cases, are essentially matters of consensus. But more important in my opinion is that not a single view presented below fails to take the biblical evidence *very* seriously. I find this to be true even where I end up disagreeing in some measure with the standard viewpoint. Readers will need to decide for themselves whether I am right about this.

The Problem of the Pentateuch

For most of Christian history, the traditional view of the Pentateuch (inherited largely from Judaism) is that the prophet Moses composed the first five books of the Bible during the second millennium BCE. Moses wrote these books during the historical period between Israel's exodus from Egypt and his own death, just before Israel entered its promised land sometime between 1500 and 1200 BCE. According to this view, Moses's literary effort produced an accurate portrait of human and Israelite history from the creation of the universe until the rise of the Hebrew people. Traditionalists believe that this view of the Pentateuch is implied or explicitly stated by the Hebrew text, by Jewish tradition, and by the testimony of Jesus Christ himself, who referred to these books as "the books of Moses." Of course, this description of the traditional view is an ideal type and would not correspond precisely to the views of every traditional reader of the Pentateuch. Nowadays, even many conservative evangelicals would admit that things are not quite this simple. Nevertheless, on the whole, this description of the traditional viewpoint is accurate and provides a suitable foil against which we can evaluate critical readings of the Pentateuch.

Modern scholarship paints a very different portrait of the Pentateuch. According to this view, although the narratives of the Pentateuch may contain some veiled history, in its present form the Pentateuch is largely an anthology of many different genres, including not only history but also myths, legends, novellas, laws, rituals, and other ancient traditions from various times and places. If Moses existed at all, his role in composing these texts was relatively minor because the Pentateuch was written or assembled by several authors or editors who lived long after Moses. Why have modern scholars arrived at these conclusions, which differ so markedly from traditional views of the text? A complete answer to this question is beyond the scope of our discussion here, but there is adequate space to lay out the basic contours of the standard critical arguments. Let us begin with what the Pentateuch itself implies about its author.

What the Pentateuch Implies about Its Author

While conservative scholars sometimes overlook it, the Pentateuch's explicit content often implies that its author is someone other than Moses. First, the Pentateuch's account of Moses's life is written from a third-person perspective, focalized almost entirely through the eyes of someone besides Moses. Moses is unlikely, for instance, to have described himself and his own actions as follows.

> One day, when Moses had grown up, he went out to his people and looked on their burdens; and he saw an Egyptian beating a Hebrew, one of his people. (Exod. 2:11 RSV)

> And Moses wrote all the words of the LORD. (Exod. 24:4 RSV)

> Now the man Moses was very meek, more than all men that were on the face of the earth. (Num. 12:3 RSV)

Taken in the most natural way, the words here penned seem to belong not to Moses but to someone else who tells us about Moses. Of course, if we were desperate nevertheless to have Moses as the author, we could surely get past these texts. We might imagine odd scenarios in which Moses could have written about himself in this way, or we might argue that someone else added these texts after Moses finished his work. But it seems more sensible to press on with the natural implication that Moses did not pen these words.

If Moses was not the author of the Pentateuch, as these texts imply, then when was the text written, and by whom? Let us consider each part of this question. The Pentateuch offers us numerous clues about when it was written. Such a clue appears in a list of Edomite kings in Genesis 36. Readers may or may not have much interest in the list itself, but its author claims that these Edomite rulers lived "*before any king reigned over the Israelites*" (Gen. 36:31 RSV). This means, of course, that the author of Genesis 36 was living after the rise of Israel's earliest kings.[1] Because Saul and David ruled in Israel around 1000 BCE, we can conclude that the author of Genesis—or of this part of Genesis—must have lived several centuries after Moses. Such a date for the Pentateuch is also implied by Genesis 12:6 and 13:7, which tell us that in Abraham's day there were "Canaanites in the land." This comment is sensible only if the biblical author is living long after Moses, in a time when the Canaanites were no longer a problem for Israel. We can add to this evidence those instances in which the Pentateuch's author claims to have consulted written sources for his story of Moses, such as the "Book of the Wars of Yahweh" (see Num. 21:10–20). Moses would not have needed such a source, but an author writing many years after Moses would certainly have needed it. Taken together, this evidence suggests that the Pentateuch's author was not Moses but a writer who lived at some remove from the Mosaic period.

The Problem of the Pentateuch's Chronology

Another reason that scholars attribute the Pentateuch to someone other than Moses has to do with certain chronological features in the text. There are internal chronological problems in the Pentateuch that suggest it was written by more than one person, and there are external chronological problems in which the Pentateuch's portrait of history does not appear to square with what we know of ancient history. Let us begin our discussion with the internal problems.

Andrea Sacchi's *Hagar and Ishmael in the Wilderness* was painted in 1630 CE and is now hanging in the National Museum of Wales.[2] It is a beautiful portrait that brings to mind a tragic biblical scene, in which Hagar and her infant son, Ishmael, were driven by Sarah into the wilderness to face certain death. Many readers will recall the story. Hagar, unable to bear her son's suffering, placed the weeping child under a bush and moved some distance away to await his death. The Lord heard the child weeping, however, and through a miracle provided for the mother and her son.

Historical critics do not deny the tragedy and beauty of this story, nor the exquisiteness of Sacchi's painting, but they certainly notice a curious feature in the biblical narrative that stands behind Sacchi's portrait. Although the text tells us

---

1. Some evangelicals have argued that this is a scribal gloss, added by someone else long after Moses lived. This is entirely possible. But one wonders what is gained by making it a scribal gloss when the entire Pentateuch is similarly written as if the author is at some remove from Moses.

2. See K. Christiansen, *Italian Painting* (New York: Beaux Arts Editions, 1992), 143.

that Hagar physically carried her infant son into the wilderness and laid him under a bush, according to the chronology of Genesis Ishmael's age at the time would have been fourteen years plus the period of Isaac's weaning, which in antiquity would have added several more years (see Gen. 16:16; 17:1; 21:5, 8).[3] "Why," ask the critics, "does Genesis present us with an infant who is 16 or more years old?" We shall answer this question in due course, but for our present purpose it is enough to notice the difficulty.

Another internal chronological problem appears in Genesis 5, but this problem is visible only when we compare the standard Hebrew Masoretic Text (MT) with two other versions of Genesis provided by the Samaritan Pentateuch (SP) and the Greek Septuagint (LXX). When the chronological information in these three texts is compared (see table 2), a curious pattern emerges. It appears that systematic changes have been made to the texts in order to correct some kind of problem. What problem might this have been? Using textual criticism, scholars have been able to reconstruct the likely form of the original Hebrew text, and this reconstructed text reveals the difficulty that the scribes were trying to set aright.[4] In the reconstructed original text, several of the pre-flood patriarchs lived so long that they actually lived into or through the flood—an obvious impossibility (see italics). The editors of the MT and SP each solved this problem in their own way by adjusting the chronologies, and the LXX nearly fixed the problem, save Methuselah, who lived fourteen years too long.

A similar problem seems to have cropped up in the genealogy of Genesis 11, where again the chronological data appears to have been altered by the editors of the SP. In this case the difficulty is still visible in the MT and, because of that, in our English Bibles. According to Genesis 11:32, Abraham's father Terah died in Haran at the ripe old age of 205, after which Abraham received his call to the promised land in Genesis 12:1-4. However, the text also says that Terah was 70 years old when Abraham was born (Gen. 11:26) and that Abraham was 75 years old when he departed for Canaan. The problem is apparent: although according

---

3. Ancient commentators correctly recognized that Ishmael was placed upon Hagar's shoulder. This was true as early as the Septuagint (c. third century BCE) and even much later, in the comments of Origen (see Sheridan below) and in the medieval Jewish commentary of Rashi, who commented in his usual perfunctory way: "He [Abraham] placed the child [Ishmael] upon her [Hagar's] shoulder." Most modern commentators (e.g., Skinner, von Rad, Westermann) agree with these ancient readings of the text and therefore accept the chronological difficulty that escaped the attention of earlier interpreters. Evangelical commentators (e.g., Hamilton, Wenham) commonly attempt some kind of harmonization, which is to my mind ill-advised. For the relevant bibliography, see Victor P. Hamilton, *The Book of Genesis*, 2 vols., NICOT (Grand Rapids: Eerdmans, 1990–1995), 2:82; Rashi, *The Metsudah Chumash*, trans. Avrohom Davis (Hoboken, NJ: KTAV, 1991), 221; Mark Sheridan, ed., *Genesis 12–20*, Ancient Christian Commentary on Scripture, Old Testament 2 (Downers Grove, IL: InterVarsity, 2002), 96; John Skinner, *A Critical and Exegetical Commentary on Genesis*, 2nd ed., ICC (Edinburgh: T&T Clark, 1930), 322–23; Gerhard von Rad, *Genesis*, rev. ed., OTL (Philadelphia: Westminster, 1972), 233; Gordon J. Wenham, *Genesis*, 2 vols., WBC (Waco: Word, 1987–1994), 2:84; Claus Westermann, *Genesis: A Commentary*, trans. John J. Scullion, 3 vols., Continental Commentary (Minneapolis: Augsburg, 1984–1986), 2:341.

4. Ronald S. Hendel, *The Text of Genesis 1–11* (Oxford: Oxford University Press, 1998).

Table 2

		MT	SP	LXX	Archetype
Adam	b	130	130	230	130
	r	800	800	700	800
	t	930	930	930	930
	y	(1–930)	(1–930)	(1–930)	(1–930)
Seth	b	105	105	205	105
	r	807	807	707	807
	t	912	912	912	912
	y	(130–1042)	(130–1042)	(230–1142)	(130–1042)
Enosh	b	90	90	190	90
	r	815	815	715	815
	t	905	905	905	905
	y	(235–1140)	(235–1140)	(435–1340)	(235–1140)
Kenan	b	70	70	170	70
	r	840	840	740	840
	t	910	910	910	910
	y	(325–1235)	(325–1235)	(625–1535)	(325–1235)
Mehalalel	b	65	65	165	65
	r	830	830	730	830
	t	895	895	895	895
	y	(395–1290)	(395–1290)	(795–1690)	(395–1290)
Jared	b	162	62	162	62
	r	800	785	800	900
	t	962	847	962	962
	y	(460–1422)	(460–1307)	(960–1922)	(460–1422)
Enoch	b	65	65	165	65
	r	300	300	200	300
	t	365	365	365	365
	y	(622–987)	(522–887)	(1122–1487)	(522–887)
Methuselah	b	187	67	167	67
	r	782	653	802	902
	t	969	720	969	969
	y	(687–1656)	(587–1307)	(1287–2256)	(587–1556)
Lamech	b	182	53	188	88
	r	595	600	565	665
	t	777	653	753	753
	y	(874–1651)	(654–1307)	(1454–2207)	(654–1407)
Flood	y	(1656)	(1307)	(2242)	(1342)

b = age at begetting; r = remainder of life; t = total lifespan; y = year before the flood

to the narrative Terah died before Abraham left for Canaan, according to the chronology of Genesis Terah should have been very much alive at the time (since Terah's 205-year lifespan is longer than Abraham's 70 + 75 = 145 years). A partial explanation for the causes of the chronological difficulties in Genesis 5 and 11 will be offered below.

Another chronological difficulty appears with respect to Israel's sojourn in Egypt. According to Exodus 12:40, the Israelites were in Egypt for 430 years, but Genesis 15:13–16 pegs the period at 4 generations of 100 years each (= 400 years), which matches the genealogy in Exodus 6:14–25. To make matters more complicated, Paul's chronology in Galatians 3:15–17 follows the LXX in making 430 years the *combined duration* of both the patriarchal and Egyptian sojourns, that is, the period from Abraham to Moses (see Exod. 12:40). The closer one looks, the more internal chronological difficulties one finds. These internal chronological problems are difficult to explain if we postulate that the entire Pentateuch was written by a single person during a relatively short period of time. If we imagine, however, that the Pentateuch is a document that was authored by several people over a long period of time —much like the Gilgamesh Epic discussed in the previous chapter—then these chronological difficulties are not so surprising.

The difficulties presented by the Pentateuch's *internal* chronological problems are commensurate with the book's *external* chronological problems. Many of these difficulties involve anachronisms in which the ethnic and national identities mentioned in Genesis do not fit the ancient historical periods assumed by the text. For example, modern scholars are relatively sure (indeed, practically certain) that the Philistines migrated to Palestine during the twelfth century BCE and that the Arameans moved into Syria around 1000 BCE. Why then do the patriarchal stories, which ostensibly took place many centuries before these ethnic migrations, grant prominent roles to the Philistine and Aramean peoples (see Gen. 10:13, 22; chap. 20; chap. 26; 31:45–47)? Scholars conclude, quite reasonably it would seem, that this is so because the Pentateuch's author was living after the Philistine and Aramean migrations, during the first millennium BCE. Similarly, many of the nations and peoples mentioned in the genealogy of Genesis 10 date no earlier than the first millennium. The Assyrian cities mentioned in the text—cities like Nineveh and Calah—did not become significant enough to mention until the first millennium, and Sabteca, whom Genesis 10:7 remembers as a son of "Cush" (Ethiopia), is remembered by modern historians as a seventh-century Ethiopian king of Egypt's Twenty-fifth Dynasty.[5] Again and again, the evidence from the Pentateuch seems to suggest that its author was not Moses but rather someone who lived in the first millennium BCE.

The Problem of the Pentateuch's Narrative Diversity

Let us return to the chronological problem presented by Ishmael, who in Genesis 21 simultaneously appears as both an "infant" and a young man. What explanation can we offer for this inconsistency? Modern scholars are quite confident that this problem was created when two separate sources were combined by the editor of the Pentateuch. One of these sources provided the story of baby Ishmael,[6]

---

5. See Hamilton, *Genesis*, 1:337.
6. In older pentateuchal scholarship, the story in Gen. 21 was usually attributed to an author called the *Elohist* because the story refers to God as *Elohim* rather than as *Yahweh*. Scholars now realize that the Yahwist sometimes used sources that referred to God using the term *Elohim*, especially when that source had to do with

and the other source supplied the chronology that made him older. Only when these sources were knitted together did a chronological tension emerge in the narrative. Scholars believe that many of the chronological difficulties in Genesis can be attributed to the interweaving of these two (or more) sources during the book's composition.

Biblical critics have been relatively successful in differentiating these two sources, in part because the sources tend to refer to God using different names, Yahweh and Elohim.[7] But variations in the divine name would be in themselves meaningless for this purpose. What makes the name variations interesting is that they correspond with a host of other indices that reveal two parallel narratives with somewhat different views of history and theology. There are, for instance, two different creation stories in Genesis. In the Elohim version of the creation story, the animals are created before human beings (1:1–2:3), while in the Yahweh story the creation order is Adam, then animals, then Eve (2:4–2:25).[8]

These two creation stories are followed by two different genealogies. As table 3 shows, these two genealogies are actually versions of the same genealogy, one that uses the name Yahweh (chap. 4) and another that uses Elohim (chap. 5). The names in the lists are almost identical, and are in nearly the same order. The chief variation is that the version in chapter 5 has combined the Seth and Cain segments from chapter 4 into a single, linear genealogy. Each genealogy provides the transition from the respective creation story to the flood story in chapters 6–9. As a result, we have two parallel creation/genealogy narratives leading up to the flood story, the Elohim version in chapters 1 and 5 and the Yahweh version in chapters 2–4.

Do the parallel sources continue into the flood story? At first glance, the flood story itself impresses us as a single, coherent story. Nevertheless, a close inspection reveals that it too was based on two older sources that have been combined into one. Each of these stories has a distinctive beginning, chronology, and ending. In the first of these stories (the Yahweh version), Noah brought seven pairs of each clean animal onto the ark. He and the animals entered the ark seven days before

---

the origins of a person or place with an *El/Elohim* name (e.g., in this case, Ishma*el*; in Gen. 28, Beth*el*). For this reason, I would associate Gen. 21 with the Yahwist. But, whether the Yahwist or the Elohist, the story of Gen. 21 clearly does not cohere well with the chronological scheme that envelopes it.

7. As I will explain below, modern scholars refer to these two biblical authors as the Yahwist (who refers to the deity as Yahweh) and the Priestly Writer (who uses Elohim, the generic term for "god").

8. The translation offered in the NIV obscures the evidence for this problem by translating the verb "to form" (in 2:19) as a pluperfect ("had formed"), but this does not suit the immediate context, where God works to resolve Adam's solitude. Here is the errant translation of Gen. 2:18–19 from the NIV: "The LORD God said, 'It is not good for the man to be alone. I will make a helper suitable for him.' *Now the LORD God had formed* out of the ground all the beasts of the field and all the birds of the air. He brought them to the man to see what he would name them; and whatever the man called each living creature, that was its name." Compare to this the RSV translation: "Then the LORD God said, 'It is not good that the man should be alone; I will make him a helper fit for him.' *So out of the ground the LORD God formed* every beast of the field and every bird of the air, and brought them to the man to see what he would call them; and whatever the man called every living creature, that was its name."

Table 3

Gen. 4	Gen. 5
Adam	Adam
Seth	Seth
Enosh	Enosh
Cain	Kenan
Enoch	Mahalalel
Irad	Jarad
Mehujael	Enoch
Methushael	Methuselah
Lamech	Lamech

the flood began because Yahweh commanded them to do so: "Go into the ark.... Seven days from now I will send rain on the earth.... And Noah did all that the Lord commanded.... And after seven days the floodwaters came on the earth" (see 7:1-5, 10 NIV). After a flood of forty days and forty nights, Noah exited the ark and offered sacrifices to Yahweh. Yahweh then responded with a promise: "Never again will I destroy all living creatures, as I have done" (8:21 NIV). Yahweh also removed the curse that he had placed on the ground after Adam's sin in Genesis 3 (cf. 3:17; 8:21). Notice that this curse motif thematically connects the Yahwistic flood story with the Yahwistic creation-fall story in Genesis 2-3. Hence we seem to have a coherent Yahwistic story that includes three parts: creation (chaps. 2-3), genealogy (chap. 4), and flood (chaps. 6-9).

The second flood story, which refers to the Deity as Elohim, differs from the first at several points. Noah does not enter the ark seven days before the flood but rather on the same day in which the flood began: "In the six hundredth year of Noah's life, on the seventeenth day of the second month—on that day all the springs of the great deep burst forth, and the floodgates of the heavens were opened.... On that very day Noah and his sons ... entered the ark" (see 7:11, 13 NIV). Moreover, in this version of the story, Noah did not bring along seven pairs of each clean species but only a single pair of each species: "You are to bring into the ark two of all living creatures, male and female, to keep them alive with you" (6:19 NIV). That this is a second and different version of the flood story is further suggested by the fact that this story has its own conclusion, with a different promise from God to Noah. After he blesses Noah and commands him to "be fruitful and multiply, fill the earth" (9:1 RSV), God then offers this promise: "I establish my covenant with you: Never again will all life be cut off *by the waters of a flood;* never again will there be a flood to destroy the earth" (9:11 NIV, italics mine). This is a different and lesser promise than is offered in the Yahweh version, where life is protected without qualification. We should note as well that the theme of God's blessing, and his command to be fruitful and multiply, links the conclusion of the Elohim flood story to the Elohim creation story in Genesis 1. As a result, we have two primeval stories in Genesis 1-9, each including the creation, a genealogy, and the flood. The Yahweh version of this story is linked by the theme of curse, and the Elohim version is linked by the theme of blessing, fruitfulness, and multiplication. For these reasons modern scholars feel confident that two parallel sources stand behind the early chapters of Genesis. Their explanation for the features in Genesis certainly seems to merit serious consideration, even if one finally concludes that another solution is better.

Modern scholars usually associate these parallel narratives with two different authors, the *Yahwist* (J, from the German *Jahvist*) and the *Priestly Writer* (P).[9] The name given to the Yahwist is self-evident, for this author usually referred to the Deity as Yahweh (although he could of course use the generic name *Elohim* as well). As for the Priestly Writer, his designation comes from the fact that he was very interested in priestly matters related to sacrifices and rituals of the temple. He wrote not only portions of Genesis but also the tabernacle texts in Exodus 25–40, the ritual material in Numbers, and most of the priestly book of Leviticus. So our little excursion into the early chapters of Genesis is only a taste of the evidence that scholars have adduced for the existence of these two authors. As table 4 shows, were we to go on, we would find additional evidence that the parallel narratives extend through Genesis and well into the rest of the Pentateuch.

When the two narratives are compared, the unique theological features of the Yahwist and Priestly Writer stand out in relief. According to the Yahwist, people knew of the divine name early in human history (Gen. 4:26), so that the revelation to Moses in Exodus 3 was not of the name itself but rather of the name's significance, which meant "I am that I am." The Priestly Writer gives an entirely different impression. He explicitly claims that the divine name "Yahweh" was first revealed to Moses at Sinai (see Exod. 6) and that even the patriarchs knew God only as *El Shaddai* (*El* = *Elohim*). Theological differences between the Yahwist and Priestly Writer are also visible in the flood story. The Yahwist reports that seven pairs of each clean species were loaded onto Noah's ark, while the Priestly Writer had only one pair on board. The reason for this difference is transparent: the Yahwist needed the extra animals for Noah's sacrifices after the flood, while the Priestly Writer, who did not permit sacrifices before the time of Moses and the tabernacle, did not need the extra animals. The Yahwist and Priestly Writer also seem to have differed regarding the post-flood promises made by the Deity. According to the Yahwist, Yahweh promised that the cycles and seasons of human existence would never end (Gen. 8:21–22), but the Priestly Writer carefully qualified this. In his hand, the divine promise became the lesser pledge that God would never again destroy all living things *with a flood* (9:11). It is possible that the Priestly Writer did this because, unlike the Yahwist, he believed in an apocalyptic age of divine judgment and deliverance. But this is not certain.

9. For an excellent delineation of these sources in Genesis, see David M. Carr, *Reading the Fractures of Genesis: Historical and Literary Approaches* (Louisville: Westminster John Knox, 1996). For the relevant bibliography, see Kenton L. Sparks, *The Pentateuch: An Annotated Bibliography*, Institute for Biblical Research Bibliographies 1 (Grand Rapids: Baker Academic, 2002), 22–36.

Table 4

Episode/Component in Narrative	Source One: Refers to God as *Yahweh* (and *Elohim*)	Source Two: Refers to God only as *Elohim*
Creation Story	Gen. 2:4–3:24 The creation order is man, then animals, then woman; seeking to be like Yahweh is sin; the ground is cursed.	Gen. 1:1–2:3 The creation order is animals, then humanity; it is good to be like God; God says, "Be fruitful and multiply."
Genealogy from Adam to the Flood	Gen. 4 A segmented genealogy; the names occurring in this text are approximately the same, and in the same order, as in Gen. 5.	Gen. 5 A linear genealogy; the names occurring in this text are approximately the same, and in the same order, as in Gen. 4.
Beginning of Flood Story	Gen. 7:1–5, 10, 12 Noah brings seven pairs of each clean animal species, and one pair of each unclean species, onto the ark; Noah enters the ark seven days before the flood.	Gen. 6:9–22; 7:11, 13–15 Noah brings one pair of each animal species onto the ark; Noah enters the ark on the same day that the flood begins.
End of Flood Story	Gen. 8:20–22 Noah offers sacrifices (using his extra clean animals); Yahweh promises never again to destroy every living thing; Yahweh no longer curses the ground.	Gen. 8:15–19; 9:1–17 God makes a covenant never again to destroy every living thing with a flood; a rainbow becomes the symbol of this promise; God says, "Be fruitful and multiply."
Genealogy from Flood to Abraham	Gen. 10 A segmented genealogy from the flood to Abraham.	Gen. 11:10–26 A linear genealogy from the flood to Abraham.
Abrahamic Covenant	Gen. 12:1–4; 15; 18–19 Abraham promised land, progeny, and blessing; Sarah promised a son.	Gen. 17 Abraham promised land, progeny, and blessing; circumcision becomes the sign of the covenant; Sarah promised a son.
Jacob Leaves Palestine	Gen. 27:41–45; 28:10–29:1 Jacob leaves for Haran in order to escape his angry brother, Esau.	Gen. 26:34–35; 27:46–28:9 Jacob leaves for Padan-Aram in order to find a wife.

I should point out, for the sake of completeness, that biblical scholars have an ongoing debate about how to characterize the two major layers of the Pentateuch. While many scholars still believe that J and P originated as independent compositions,[10] with J being the older of the two, others believe that the Priestly layer originated not as a composition but as a late supplement that was grafted into J.[11] Both viewpoints assume that P was composed during the postexilic period of Israel's history; they merely differ on the nature of P. A third perspective on P, represented by a small but influential cadre of scholars, dates P to an earlier, preexilic

---

10. For example, E. W. Nicholson, *The Pentateuch in the Twentieth Century: The Legacy of Julius Wellhausen* (Oxford: Clarendon, 1998).

11. John Van Seters, *Prologue to History: The Yahwist as Historian in Genesis* (Louisville: Westminster John Knox, 1992); Frank Moore Cross Jr., *Canaanite Myth and Hebrew Epic* (Cambridge: Harvard University Press, 1973), 40–48.

Episode/Component in Narrative	Source One: Refers to God as *Yahweh* (and *Elohim*)	Source Two: Refers to God only as *Elohim*
Jacob Names Bethel	Gen. 28:10–22 Jacob names Bethel on his way to Haran.	Gen. 35:9–15 Jacob names Bethel after his return from Padan-Aram.
Jacob's Name Changed to Israel	Gen. 32:22–32 Yahweh changes Jacob's name to Israel after an all-night struggle at Peniel.	Gen. 35:9–15 Yahweh changes Jacob's name to Israel after his return from Padan-Aram.
Jacob Returns from Palestine	Gen. 35:1–8 Jacob returns to Bethel and builds an altar.	Gen. 31:17–18; 35:9–15, 27–29 Jacob returns to Bethel and sets up a sacred pillar.
Revelation of the Divine Name to Moses	Exod. 3* Yahweh reveals to Moses the meaning of his name, "I am that I am."	Exod. 6:2–8 God reveals to Moses his true name, Yahweh.
Water, Quail, Manna, and Rebellion in the Wilderness	Exod. 16–17 When the people complained because of their thirst, Yahweh provided water from a rock; the place was called Massah (testing) and Meribah (quarreling).	Num. 11; 20:1–13 When the people complained because of their thirst, Yahweh provided water from a rock; the place was called Meribah (quarreling), and Moses was disqualified from entering the promised land.
Administrative Help for Moses	Exod. 18:13–27 Following the advice of his father-in-law, Jethro, Moses selects leaders to help in his administration of the people of Israel.	Num. 11:10–17 Yahweh equips seventy elders to assist Moses in his administration of the people of Israel.

* The revelation of the divine name in Exod. 3 is sometimes associated with the so-called Elohist source of the Pentateuch rather than with the Yahwist. I will briefly discuss the Elohist in a moment, but regardless, the revelation of the divine name in Exod. 3 constitutes a parallel to the event in Exod. 6.

era.[12] These scholars, together with the first two groups that I have mentioned, represent the three most established viewpoints on J and P. Joining these is a new but increasingly popular perspective that views P as the first full-scale history of early Israel.[13] In this scenario the materials formerly attributed to J are regarded not as a single composition but as a collection of "non-P" Yahwistic materials joined to P in the postexilic period, after P was written. Hence the traditional pre-Priestly Yahwist disappears.

These complex debates aside, scholars remain quite certain that the first four books of the Pentateuch include two basic layers, P and J (or non-P), and that these layers probably date no earlier than the first millennium BCE. The Yahwistic

12. Avi Hurwitz, *A Linguistic Study of the Relationship between the Priestly Source and the Book of Ezekiel*, Cahiers de la Revue biblique 20 (Paris: Gabalda, 1982); Israel Knohl, *The Sanctuary of Silence: The Priestly Torah and the Holiness School* (Minneapolis: Fortress, 1995); Jacob Milgrom, *Leviticus 1–16*, AB (New York: Doubleday, 1990), 1–128; Moshe Weinfeld, *The Place of the Law in the Religion of Ancient Israel*, Vetus Testamentum Supplements 100 (Leiden: Brill, 2004).

13. Thomas B. Dozeman and Konrad Schmid, eds., *A Farewell to the Yahwist? The Composition of the Pentateuch in Recent European Interpretation*, Society of Biblical Literature Symposium Series 34 (Leiden: Brill, 2006).

materials are normally dated between the tenth and sixth centuries BCE, while the Priestly materials are normally dated to sometime after 500 BCE. Some of the reasons for these dates have already been discussed, and more evidence will be adduced along the way. But regardless of the dating schemes used, the existence of various pentateuchal sources and layers written by different authors—with somewhat different theological and historical perspectives—presents obvious difficulties for traditional Mosaic readings of the Pentateuch.

Those familiar with biblical criticism will know that the Pentateuch is often believed to contain not two but four major sources, including not only J and P but also the so-called Elohistic source (E) and Deuteronomy (D). The Elohist, who like P used the divine name *Elohim*, has increasingly faded into the background of the source discussion, not only because it is fragmentary but more importantly because E is increasingly viewed as one of J's sources. For instance, J's story of Jacob's revelation at Bethel (Gen. 28:10-28) probably used the name *Elohim* because the story was an etiology for the sacred site of Bethel (i.e., *Beth-El*, "house of El"). So the existence of an E layer in the Pentateuch remains a bone of contention.

As for the book of Deuteronomy (D), this is the next stop on our itinerary.

The Problem of Deuteronomy

According to 2 Kings 22-23, in or about 622 BCE King Josiah of Judah sponsored a renovation project to repair and improve the temple of Yahweh in Jerusalem. During these renovations a book-scroll was discovered in the temple. Those who found the book referred to it as the "Book of the Law" and the "Law of Moses," and its content can be deduced from the king's response to the book. After the scroll was read to the king, Josiah undertook a large-scale reform with three interrelated objectives: (1) to eliminate the worship of all gods except Yahweh; (2) to destroy all idols in the kingdom, whether idols of Yahweh or of other deities; and (3) to centralize the sacrificial worship of Yahweh at the Jerusalem temple, so that sacrifices at other holy places were eliminated. The threefold agenda of the reform can thus be summarized as monotheism, iconoclasm, and centralization.

It was relatively easy for modern scholars to deduce—as Jerome (342-420 CE) did many years earlier—that this description of Josiah's book fits only the biblical book of Deuteronomy.[14] It calls itself the "Book of the Law," is presented as a series of speeches given by Moses, shares the threefold agenda of Josiah's reform, and provides precise verbal parallels to the description of the reform found in 2 Kings. Additional evidence for this conclusion is found in the prophecies of Jeremiah, whose ministry began not long after Josiah's reform. Although Jeremiah referred to the law of Yahweh and quoted it often, all of his references were to Deuteronomy and none of them to the other laws in the pentateuchal books of Exodus, Leviticus, and Numbers.[15] Consequently, it appears that Deuteronomy,

---

14. See Jerome, *Against Jovinianus* 1.5 (*NPNF* 2 6:349).
15. Douglas R. Jones, *Jeremiah*, NCB (Grand Rapids: Eerdmans, 1992), 61-64, 181-82.

and Deuteronomy alone, constituted the "Law of Moses" in the days of Josiah and Jeremiah (although it may have incorporated older laws that were previously associated with Moses).

As interesting as this fact is, even more fascinating is the biblical evidence that this newly discovered lawbook had not been read, studied, or followed for most of Israel's history. The biblical account of Josiah's reform says explicitly that the book had been lost and that its regulations had not been kept "since the days of the judges who judged Israel" (2 Kings 21–23). This claim is borne out in the history of Israel itself, where we see the great prophet Samuel (c. 1000 BCE) embracing not a single location for worship, as Deuteronomy demands, but many holy sites and high places, such as Shiloh, Zuph, Bethel, Gibeah, Mizpah, and Gilgal (see 1 Sam. 9–11). Apparently, the lawbook of Deuteronomy was unknown even to Samuel, the last of Israel's great prophetic judges. Since it is very difficult to imagine how an ancient lawbook that was ignored and lost since before the temple was built suddenly turned up in the Jerusalem temple centuries later, modern scholars do not believe that Deuteronomy was merely "found" in the days of Josiah. More likely is that the book was *written* during Josiah's reign and then deposited in the temple so that the "lost" book of Moses could be discovered. This judgment is reinforced by still other evidence.

Scholars well versed in Near Eastern literature have noticed that the covenant between God and Israel in Deuteronomy is expressed in a form used in Neo-Assyrian treaties, which Assyrian overlords concluded with their vassals during the first millennium BCE.[16] Neo-Assyrian influence is visible in the basic structure of Deuteronomy,[17] in the emphasis placed on the vassal's wholehearted fidelity to the covenant (cf. Deut. 10:12; 13:3; 26:16), and especially in the curses of Deuteronomy 28, which follow the order of the Neo-Assyrian pantheon and include exact verbal parallels to the curses in Neo-Assyrian treaties.[18] The appearance of

---

16. Some years ago, it was fashionable to see close parallels between Deuteronomy and the much older second-millennium treaties of the Hittites. Scholars now find these similarities less interesting for two good reasons. First, certain features of Deuteronomy that parallel the Hittite texts, such as its historical introduction in chaps. 1–4, turn out to be later additions to the biblical book (see below). Second, and more importantly, the similarities between Deuteronomy and the later Neo-Assyrian treaties are so striking that these comparisons have simply eclipsed comparisons with the earlier Hittite treaties.

17. The basic components shared by the two texts include an introduction, treaty stipulations, and curses. For discussion see *ATSHB*, 445–47.

18. R. Frankena, "The Vassal-Treaties of Esarhaddon and the Dating of Deuteronomy," *OTS* 14 (1965): 122–54; Hans Ulrich Steymans, "Eine assyrische Vorlage für Deuteronomium 28,20–44," in *Bundesdokument und Gesetz: Studien zum Deuteronomium*, ed. Georg Braulik, Herders biblische Studien 4 (Freiburg: Herder, 1995), 119–41; Steymans, *Deuteronomium 28 und die adê zur Thronfolgeregelung Asarhaddons: Segen und Fluch im Alten Orient und in Israel*, Orbis biblicus et orientalis 145 (Freiburg: Universitätsverlag, 1995); Moshe Weinfeld, *Deuteronomy and the Deuteronomic School* (Oxford: Oxford University Press, 1972). For additional parallels between Deut. 13 and the treaties, see Weinfeld, *Deuteronomy and the Deuteronomic School*, 91–100; Paul Dion, "Deuteronomy 13: The Suppression of Alien Religious Propaganda in Israel during the Late Monarchical Era," in *Law and Ideology in Monarchic Israel*, ed. Baruch Halpern and Deborah W. Hobson, JSOTSup 124 (Sheffield: JSOT Press, 1991), 147–216.

Deuteronomy in the form of a Neo-Assyrian treaty at this historical juncture is probably not a coincidence. Up until the reign of Josiah, in whose reign the "Book of the Law" was found, Judah had been a vassal state of the Neo-Assyrian Empire. The Assyrian annals explicitly mention that Josiah's grandfather, Manasseh, had sworn an oath of loyalty to Assyria,[19] and we can reasonably assume that a copy of this treaty with Assyria—perhaps in Aramaic, but more likely in Hebrew—would have been resting in the Jerusalem temple at the time of Josiah. Given this historical context, the publication of Deuteronomy in the form of a Neo-Assyrian treaty, and the pious ruse of depositing this new text in the temple, would have been an effective way of making the religious point that Judah's covenant relationship with Yahweh was older and more important than its treaty with Assyria. Consequently, the treaty form of the book of Deuteronomy is best understood as a polemic against Neo-Assyrian oppression.[20] This does not mean, of course, that everything in the book was new and invented in the time of Josiah. Many scholars believe that the authors of Deuteronomy based their book on an older core of laws already associated with the prophet Moses. Nevertheless, as a whole, the book of Deuteronomy seems to come from the time of Josiah and is not a composition of Moses in any strict sense.

While some portions of Deuteronomy were probably older than the time of Josiah, particularly certain legal materials in the book, other portions of the book were written even later than Josiah, after Israel's exile to Babylon had occurred in 586 BCE. How do we know this? The portions in question are prophecies that predicted Israel would eventually break the terms of its covenant with Yahweh and be exiled from its land (see especially Deut. 29–31). To be sure, if we believe in the possibility of prophecy—and Christians should—then we need not perforce date these prophecies of the exile after the exile. However, there are good reasons to suppose that these prophecies do not offer genuine predictions but rather *ex eventu* predictions of the exile (such as we saw in the Mesopotamian Uruk Prophecy in chapter 2). The basis for this conclusion is as follows. Before the exile, during the time of Jeremiah, there were heated debates among Judeans about how they should respond to the Babylonians. Some Judeans, such as Jeremiah, predicted that Judah would be destroyed and exiled if it did not submit to Babylon, while other Judeans—especially those in the royal court—advised resistance against Babylon (see Jer. 20–21, 26). We have already noted that Jeremiah was very familiar with the covenant and law of Deuteronomy. If this is so, then why did Jeremiah not cite Deuteronomy's very clear exile prophecies as strong evidence for his viewpoint? Modern scholars believe that Jeremiah did not refer to Deuteronomy's exile prophecies because these prophecies did not yet exist in Jeremiah's day. Deuteronomy's predictions of the Judean exile were added to the

---

19. *ANET*, 295; see also 2 Chron. 33:11.
20. A. D. H. Mayes, "On Describing the Purpose of Deuteronomy," *Journal for the Study of the Old Testament* 58 (1993): 13–33.

book after the exile took place. These pseudoprophecies were perhaps one way to express their author's idea that God knew beforehand of Israel's infidelities (an idea that will strike us as theologically true). It is likely that some other parts of Deuteronomy were added by the same author(s) who wrote these *ex eventu* prophecies. I have in mind, most particularly, the closely related historical prologue in Deuteronomy 1–4.

For all of the reasons cited above, most biblical scholars date the book of Deuteronomy to the first millennium BCE, during the reign of Josiah. This judgment is obviously at variance with the traditional view that Moses wrote the Pentateuch during the second millennium BCE.

The Problem of the Pentateuch's Legal Diversity

Jews and Christians have for centuries ascribed the laws of the Pentateuch to Israel's traditional lawgiver, Moses, but modern scholarship has raised serious questions about this uncomplicated viewpoint.[21] Three features in the biblical laws suggest that they were written not by a single legist but rather by several different authors, or groups of authors, living at different times and in different places. First, the laws in the Pentateuch are not collected into a single code but are instead nested in several separate collections, namely, the Book of the Covenant (BC, in Exod. 20:22–23:33), the Deuteronomic Code (DC, in Deut. 12–26), the Holiness Code (HC, in Lev. 17–26), and the Priestly Code (P, primarily in Exod. 25–31, 32–40; Lev. 1–16; Numbers). This evidence suggests that we have not one but several codes stemming from different contexts and authors, an impression that is reinforced by other evidence. Second, not only do we have several blocks of law, but these blocks of law repeat the same materials. For instance, one finds repetitions of the festival laws,[22] of Sabbath rules,[23] and of that enigmatic command, "You shall not boil a kid in its mother's milk."[24] Repetitions like this would be unnecessary in a single code, but they make good sense if we imagine that the Pentateuch contains several law codes that originated in different situations. The third feature that suggests various authors have written the Hebrew laws is the presence of significant differences among the law collections. For example, the prescriptions for the altar of burnt offering differ significantly from text to text (Exod. 20:24–26 [altar of earth]; 27:1–2 [altar of wood overlaid with gold]), as do the Passover regulations given in Deuteronomy 16:7 ("boil the meat") and Exodus 12:8–9 ("roast the meat, do not boil it"). The repetitions, tensions, and differences within the laws of the

---

21. For an overview of the matter and appropriate bibliography, see John Van Seters, *The Pentateuch: A Social-Science Commentary* (Sheffield: Sheffield Academic Press, 1999); Sparks, *Pentateuch*, 75–92, 108–10, 144–49.
22. Exod. 23:14–19; 34:18–26; Lev. 23:1–44; Num. 28–29; Deut. 16:1–17.
23. Exod. 20:8–11; 31:12–17; 35:1–3; Lev. 23:3; Deut. 5:12–15.
24. Exod. 23:19; 34:26; Deut. 14:21.

Pentateuch imply that they are not the work of a single author but are instead a product of several different authors and redactors who lived in quite different situations. Consequently, biblical scholars deduce that the pentateuchal laws were traditionally "Mosaic," but certainly not literally so.

According to some scholars, with whom I agree, we are able in at least one instance to observe how a biblical author handled the changing legal scene in ancient Israel. Ezekiel was a prophet who ministered to the Jews in Mesopotamia during the early part of the Babylonian exile. This was a period of legal transition. Jews had been exiled to Babylon because they had broken the laws of Deuteronomy. At the same time, Ezekiel was beginning to cite the laws of another lawcode, the so-called Holiness Code (Lev. 17–26), for the first time in Israel's history.[25] How did Ezekiel explain the apparent failure of Deuteronomy's laws and the subsequent need for the new set of holiness laws that he was using? Here is the prophet's oracle from God in Ezekiel 20:23–26 (RSV):

> Moreover I swore to them in the wilderness that I would scatter them among the nations and disperse them through the countries, because they had not executed my ordinances, but had rejected my statutes and profaned my sabbaths, and their eyes were set on their fathers' idols. Moreover *I gave them statutes that were not good and ordinances by which they could not have life; and I defiled them through their very gifts in making them offer by fire all their first-born, that I might horrify them;* I did it that they might know that I am the LORD. (italics mine)

The last sentence explains God's view of the matter as understood by Ezekiel. Because of their sinfulness, God had provided the Israelites with "statutes that were not good" and "ordinances by which they could not live," and he did so specifically for the purpose of defiling the people. Ezekiel does not explicitly tell us that he had Deuteronomy in mind when he uttered this oracle, but in my opinion it is fairly easy to see that these were the laws in his sights.[26] Deuteronomy often uses the word pair "statutes" and "ordinances," and it permitted the profane sacrifice of firstborn animals outside the temple precinct (Deut. 12:15–25). Ezekiel and the Holiness Code viewed these sacrificial practices as acts of ritual pollution and ultimately as one cause of the exile (see Lev. 17). In essence, Ezekiel would have us understand that God intentionally gave Deuteronomy's laws to Israel in order to land them in the exile. God did so because of Israel's persistent disobedience to the good laws he had given them (see Ezek. 20:8–30). Whether and to what extent we are comfortable with Ezekiel's theological rationale on these matters is not the issue at this juncture. The important point is that not only modern scholars but also the ancient biblical authors had to deal with the changing face

---

25. Walther Zimmerli, *Ezekiel 1*, Hermeneia (Philadelphia: Fortress, 1979), 46–52.
26. Scott W. Hahn and John S. Bergsma, "What Laws Were 'Not Good'? A Canonical Approach to the Theological Problem of Ezekiel 20:25–26," *JBL* 123 (2004): 201–18.

of Israelite law. Jewish interpreters in the Second Temple period also struggled with these difficulties.[27]

The conclusion that the Pentateuch contains four basic lawcodes (BC, DC, HC, and P) is reinforced by the fact that these codes of law correspond closely with the sources that scholars have found elsewhere in the Pentateuch. The Yahwist is usually associated with BC, Deuteronomy with DC, and the Priestly Writer with both HC and P (where HC is usually considered an early precursor to P). Scholars differ in some respects on the chronological order in which the laws were written, but there is broad agreement that the Pentateuch's laws were written by several different authors over a course of many years. Although we might wonder how the ancient Israelites squared this evidence with their belief in a Mosaic law, we should remember that traditional Judaism regards not only the Pentateuch but also much later rabbinic law as Mosaic (the oral law codified as the Mishnah). The logic behind this Jewish conclusion is straightforward: all authoritative law ultimately goes back to Moses, even if its literary form and content display no visible signs of Mosaic authorship—and many visible signs of having been written by someone else.

The Problem of the Development of Israel's Religious Institutions

As in any culture, Israel's religious institutions were not static but changed over the course of the nation's long history. Many scholars are interested in reconstructing the development of these institutions, and the Pentateuch reveals more than any other biblical text the radical shifts that took place in the religious institutions of ancient Israel. Important examples of Israel's evolving religion are found in the history of Israelite sacrificial practices, of Israel's tabernacle/temple, of the ark of the covenant, and of the Israelite priesthood. Let us consider each institution in turn.

The history of Israelite sacrifices. During our discussion of the book of Deuteronomy, we noted that Josiah's seventh-century reforms sought to transfer all sacrificial activities from outlying areas to the Jerusalem temple. Before that time, even holy men like Samuel were sacrificing at many sacred sites all over the country. Careful readers of the Pentateuch will notice, furthermore, that the rituals of the Priestly Writer (P) do not argue for cult centralization, as Deuteronomy does. Rather, P assumes from its beginning that sacrifices are being done only at one site, first at the tabernacle in the wilderness and then later at the Jerusalem temple (see Exod. 25–31, 35–40; Lev. 17).[28] These developments are vividly illustrated by a comparison of our two biblical accounts of Solomon's reign. The older, preexilic

---

27. Peter E. Enns, *Inspiration and Incarnation: Evangelicals and the Problem of the Old Testament* (Grand Rapids: Baker Academic, 2005), 120–32.

28. The basic arguments were worked out long ago by Julius Wellhausen, *Prolegomena to the History of Ancient Israel* (Edinburgh: A & C Black, 1885). See also W. M. L. de Wette, *A Critical and Historical Introduction to the Canonical Scriptures of the Old Testament*, trans. Theodore Parker, 2nd ed. (Boston: Little and Brown,

account depicts Solomon sacrificing at two different places, first at the "high place" in Gibeon and then at the ark of the covenant in Jerusalem (see 1 Kings 3:1–15). However, the postexilic account in Chronicles, which reflects the influence of later Priestly thought, could not allow this. As a result, the Chronicler's account tells us that Solomon sacrificed *only* at Gibeon because the "Tent of Meeting" was there, and the Chronicler erased the record of Solomon's sacrifice in Jerusalem (2 Chron. 1:1–13). In other words, the theology of the postexilic Chronicler is precisely like that of the postexilic Priestly Writer: legitimate sacrifices could be offered at only one location, and that location was either at the tabernacle (before the temple was built) or at the temple itself. Because P did not permit any sacrifices before God provided the tabernacle at Sinai, his account of the flood story in Genesis did not include Noah's post-flood sacrifice.

Taken together, these sources allow us to express the history of Israelite sacrifice in three phases: (1) early period: Israelites sacrificed at many sacred sites; (2) Deuteronomic period: attempts were made to centralize sacrifices at the Jerusalem temple; (3) late period: sacrifice is permitted only at the Jerusalem temple. This evidence implies that the Priestly Writer, as a representative of our "late period," must have lived and worked during the postexilic period. Other evidence examined in this section will reinforce this conclusion regarding the postexilic date of P.

The history of the tabernacle and temple. Closely related to the history of Israelite sacrifice is the history of the places where sacrifices were done.[29] According to Deuteronomy, sacrifices were offered legitimately wherever one wished before Israel's settlement in the land (see Deut. 12:1–11). For this reason, the Deuteronomistic History in Samuel–Kings—which told Israel's history using Deuteronomy's theology as a guide—allowed sacrifices at various places until Solomon's temple was finally built in Jerusalem. As we have seen, P's conception of things was entirely different. According to P, God provided a portable temple in the wilderness (the tabernacle) so that Israel could sacrifice at a single place from the first moments of its covenant at Sinai until the construction of the temple in Jerusalem (see Exod. 25–31, 35–40). In his conception of the tabernacle, the Priestly Writer combined two previously separate institutions into one. While earlier sources located the "Tent of Meeting" *outside* Israel's wilderness camp (see Exod. 33:7; Num. 11:24–30) and the ark of the covenant *inside* the camp (Num. 14:44), the postexilic Priestly Writer moved the ark into the "Tent of Meeting" and then placed both at the center of the Israelite camp to create the tabernacle (Num. 2:2).[30] As we will see, this move had important implications for the development of the Israelite ark tradition.

1850). For more relevant bibliography, see Sparks, *Pentateuch*, especially 84–90, but also studies regarding the composition of the Pentateuch on pp. 22–36.

29. For the relevant bibliography, see the previous note.

30. See Menahem Haran, "The Nature of the ''Ohel Mo'edh' in Pentateuchal Sources," *Journal of Semitic Studies* 5 (1960): 50–65.

The history of the ark of the covenant. The history of the ark of the covenant parallels the history of sacrifice in certain respects and includes preexilic, exilic, and postexilic phases of the institution.[31] In its preexilic form, the ark appears to have been a simple wooden chest that contained Israel's written covenant with Yahweh (Deut. 10:1–8). Because Yahweh's presence was believed to accompany this ark, the chest was highly valued in times of war and accompanied the Israelites during military campaigns (Josh. 6; 1 Sam. 4–6). It cannot be a surprise that such a powerful icon was eventually moved by King Solomon into the Jerusalem temple. So far as we can tell, from that point onward the ark remained in Jerusalem until the Babylonian exile.

According to many scholars, a decisive moment in the ark's development appeared in the theology of the prophet Ezekiel, who worked during the era of the exile. As a priestly prophet, he was sensitive to matters of ritual purity and wondered how it was possible for God to allow Babylon to desecrate and destroy Yahweh's temple home. Ezekiel's answer was to dissociate Yahweh from the physical temple itself by averring that Yahweh could and would abandon his temple in Jerusalem before it was destroyed (Ezek. 10). In order to illustrate this point, Ezekiel fused together images of the ark, cherubim, and divine throne to fashion a movable ark that followed Yahweh's glory wherever his glory traveled (cf. Ezek. 1, 10–11, 43). Because this mobile, spiritual ark represented the genuine presence of Yahweh, it needed to be much more elaborate than the simple wooden chest still lying in the temple—and, as we see in Ezekiel's well-known vision (Ezek. 1), indeed it was.

Ezekiel's imaginary spiritual ark seems to have inspired the ark of the postexilic Priestly Writer (Exod. 25:10–22), which was much more elaborate than the simple wooden box that Israel used before the exile. The Priestly ark was a small, gold-plated, wooden chest measuring 2.5 × 1.5 × 1 cubits (about 1.25 × .75 × .5 meters). Attached to the ark were four gold rings, one on each foot, through which two staves could be placed to allow for easy transportation without human contact. The ark's lid, often called a "mercy seat," was yet more elaborate, being entirely of gold and adorned by two winged cherubim. Modern scholars wonder whether the elaborate Priestly ark was ever actually built, or whether it remained, like Ezekiel's ark, only an idea in the mind. This issue aside, however, the evidence adduced here makes it relatively easy to reconstruct the development of the ark's imagery and significance, which falls into three distinct periods: (1) the simple preexilic ark, (2) the elaborate exilic ark vision of Ezekiel, and (3) the elaborate postexilic Priestly ark.

The development of the Israelite priesthood. According to the biblical sources, in the early days of ancient Israel sacrifices were performed legitimately by any holy

---

31. For bibliography and discussion, see Kenton L. Sparks, "Ark of the Covenant," in *Dictionary of the Old Testament: Historical Books*, ed. Bill T. Arnold and H. G. M. Williamson (Downers Grove, IL: InterVarsity, 2005), 88–92.

man, regardless of his tribal affiliation—Samuel the Ephraimite is a good example (1 Sam. 7:1–11).[32] By the time of Deuteronomy, however, the priesthood was limited to men from the tribe of Levi (Deut. 17:9, 18; 18:1, 6–7; 21:5). It is not entirely clear how or why this narrowing of priestly pedigree took place, but that it took place seems quite certain. Qualifications for the priesthood narrowed still more during the exile. Ezekiel tells us that prior to the exile most of the Levitical families had defiled themselves with idolatry, leaving only one Levitical family— the Zadokites—ritually qualified to serve as priests (Ezek. 44:10–16). According to Ezekiel, the Levites could indeed *assist* the Zadokites in the temple, but they could no longer offer sacrifices themselves. Once again, this evidence will help us date the Priestly Writer of the Pentateuch. Because the Priestly Writer shared the distinction between priests and Levites that Ezekiel introduced during the exile (Exod. 40:15; Num. 16), the natural conclusion to draw is that the Priestly Writer lived during or after the exile. So the history of the Israelite priesthood can be tentatively outlined as follows: (1) the early period: holy men from various tribes performed priestly functions (see 1 Samuel); (2) the Deuteronomic period: Levites were priests (see Deuteronomy); (3) the exilic period: Zadokites were priests and Levites assisted (see Ezekiel); (4) the postexilic period: Aaronides/Zadokites were priests and Levites assisted (see the Priestly Writer). The debate about the history of the Israelite priesthood is, like so many matters of scholarship, an ongoing affair. But on this point all critical scholars agree: in antiquity there were various and contradictory understandings of the history of the priesthood, and differing opinions about which priestly groups were legitimate, and about when they were legitimate. The Pentateuch reflects these differing perspectives.

32. Here I present the standard scholarly perspective, but there is an ongoing debate about many of the details. For discussions and bibliography, see Raymond Abba, "Priests and Levites in Deuteronomy," *VT* 27 (1977): 257–67; Aelred Cody, *A History of Old Testament Priesthood*, Analecta biblica 35 (Rome: Pontifical Biblical Institute Press, 1969); Frank M. Cross, "The Priestly Houses of Early Israel," in *Canaanite Myth and Hebrew Epic* (Cambridge, MA: Harvard University Press, 1973), 195–215; John A. Emerton, "Priests and Levites in Deuteronomy: An Examination of Dr. G. E. Wright's Theory," *VT* 12 (1962): 129–38; Sparks, *Pentateuch*, 95–96; G. Ernest Wright, "The Levites in Deuteronomy," *VT* 4 (1954): 325–30; Joseph Blenkinsopp, *Sage, Priest, Prophet: Religious and Intellectual Leadership in Ancient Israel*, Library of Ancient Israel (Louisville: Westminster John Knox, 1995), 66–114; Stephen L. Cook, "Innerbiblical Interpretation in Ezekiel 44 and the History of Israel's Priesthood," *JBL* 114 (1995): 193–208; Ulrike Dahm, *Opferkult und Priestertum in Alt-Israel: Ein kultur- und religionswissenschaftlicher Beitrag*, BZAW 327 (Berlin; New York: de Gruyter, 2003); Lester L. Grabbe, *Priests, Prophets, Diviners, Sages: A Socio-Historical Study of Religious Specialists in Ancient Israel* (Valley Forge, PA: Trinity Press International, 1995); Menahem Haran, *Temples and Temple-Service in Ancient Israel* (Winona Lake, IN: Eisenbrauns, 1985); C. E. Haurer, "David and the Levites," *JSOT* 23 (1982): 33–54; Gary N. Knoppers, "Hierodules, Priests, or Janitors? The Levites in Chronicles and the History of the Israelite Priesthood," *JBL* 118 (1999): 49–72; Julia M. O'Brien, *Priest and Levite in Malachi*, SBL Dissertation Series 121 (Atlanta: Scholars, 1990); Michael S. Moore, "Role Pre-Emption in the Israelite Priesthood," *VT* 46 (1996): 316–29; Saul M. Olyan, "Zadok's Origins and the Tribal Policies of David," *JBL* 101 (1982): 177–93; J. R. Spencer, "Priestly Families (or Factions) in Samuel and Kings," in *The Pitcher Is Broken: Memorial Essays for Gösta W. Ahlström*, ed. S. W. Holloway and L. K. Handy; JSOTSup 190 (Sheffield: Sheffield Academic Press, 1995), 397–400.

In conclusion I would mention two general observations regarding Israel's religious institutions and their implications for traditional readings of the Pentateuch. First, that the Pentateuch reflects not one but several viewpoints on Israel's sacred institutions does not cohere very well with the traditional assumption that all or even most of the Pentateuch was written by Moses during the second millennium BCE. Second, when the developments in Israel's institutions are integrated into a single picture, it becomes very likely that Deuteronomy dates to the time of Josiah, and that the Priestly Writer lived and worked during the postexilic period. So even if one allows that parts of the pentateuchal tradition go back to the hoary days of Moses, significant portions of the text seem to have been composed long after Moses would have lived.

The Problem of Near Eastern Traditions in the Pentateuch

Here we meet yet another difficulty for the traditional view of the Pentateuch. When archaeologists began to unearth many thousands of clay tablets from ancient Mesopotamia, they quickly recognized that several Mesopotamian myths were uncannily similar to the biblical creation and flood stories. The Mesopotamian flood stories were particularly close to the biblical flood story, including even the well-known episode in which birds were used to confirm that the flood had ended (cf. Gen. 8:6–12; Atrahasis Epic; Gilgamesh Epic).[33] Because these Mesopotamian texts are older than the Pentateuch, the most sensible explanation for the similarities is that the pentateuchal authors borrowed some of their materials from the ancient world.

Although one need not be a scholar to recognize the obvious parallels between the biblical and Near Eastern flood stories, other parallels between biblical and Near Eastern myths are not so apparent to the average reader. Only a close look reveals that the creation story of the Priestly Writer, in Genesis 1, is very similar to the Babylonian creation myth *Enuma Elish*.[34] According to *Enuma Elish*, the high god of Babylon (Marduk) created the universe by defeating the primeval sea (*Tiamat*) in battle and by splitting her body into two parts. In this way Marduk separated the heavens from earth and provided a spatial context for the creation of the heavenly bodies and human beings. Humanity itself was the design of the wise god Ea, but this design was implemented by Marduk when he formed humanity from the blood of a rebellious demon god whom he had defeated in cosmic battle (Qingu). Once we account for the monotheism of the Priestly Writer, the similarities between *Enuma Elish* and Genesis 1 are quite striking. In

---

33. Atrahasis is the hero in one of the Akkadian flood stories. For a survey of relevant texts, translations, and discussion, see *ATSHB*, 313–14, 316–17.

34. For texts and translations of *Enuma Elish*, see René Labat, *Le poème babylonien de la création* (Paris: Adrien-Maissonneuve, 1935); *ANET*, 60–72, 501–3; *COS*, 1.111:390–402. For discussion and bibliography, see Kenton L. Sparks, "*Enūma Elish* and Priestly Mimesis: Elite Emulation in Nascent Judaism," *JBL* 126 (2007): 625–48; *ATSHB*, 314–16.

Enuma Elish Marduk defeated the waters of *Tiamat* (the sea); in Genesis God hovered over the waters of *tehom* (the sea). In *Enuma Elish* creation was effected by the splitting of *Tiamat*; in Genesis God created the space for life by separating the waters with a "firmament." In *Enuma Elish* the creation of heaven and earth was followed by the creation of the heavenly bodies and humanity, and the same counts for Genesis. In *Enuma Elish* humanity was created from the blood of a slain god, while in Genesis humanity was created in God's image. The most striking differences between the two stories arise from P's attempts to demythologize his source. Marduk was replaced by God, the goddess *Tiamat* was replaced by the impersonal waters of *tehom*, and God substituted his own image for the divine blood that Marduk used to create humanity. If there is a vestige of the old mythology in P, perhaps it appears in his brief reference to the heavenly council: "Let *us* make man in our own image."

The creation story of the Yahwist in Genesis 2 also reflects Mesopotamian influence, but in an entirely different way. The story itself is unique in the ancient world, but its motifs and themes have a strong Mesopotamian flavor.[35] The tree of life reminds us of the life-giving *haluppu* plant that was stolen from the hero of the Gilgamesh Epic by a serpent. The paradise of Eden, sustained by subterranean waters, echoes back to the subterranean waters of the primeval Dilmun paradise in Sumerian literature.[36] Even more striking is the similarity between Adam's predicament in Genesis and the troubles faced by Mesopotamia's first sage, Adapa.[37] Both stories involve the first of primeval men. In both stories the men were given dangerous knowledge by wiser beings, knowledge that ultimately caused them to face judgment from the deity. Both stories featured foods of life and death, and in both the deceived protagonist ate the wrong food (or failed to eat the right food) and so lost his chance for eternal life. Near the story's end, the god Anu lamented that the crafty god Ea had revealed to Adapa "the ways of heaven and earth," which is more than vaguely reminiscent of the "knowledge of good and evil" and "being like God" motifs in Genesis. On a related note, Adam's role in tilling and keeping the garden in post-fall Eden is reminiscent of the agricultural work assigned to humans in the Sumerian and Babylonian creation myths (cf. the Eridu Genesis, Atrahasis, etc.).[38]

The recycling of Near Eastern myths and motifs by the biblical authors raises serious questions about the traditional view that the Pentateuch provides a perfect historical portrait of human origins and early human history. Even if Moses were the author of the Pentateuch, it seems that in some cases God did not provide

---

35. Kenton L. Sparks, "The Problem of Myth in Ancient Historiography," in *Rethinking the Foundations: Historiography in the Ancient World and in the Bible: Essays in Honour of John Van Seters*, ed. Steven L. McKenzie and Thomas Römer, BZAW 294 (Berlin: de Gruyter, 2000), 269–80; John L. McKenzie, "Myth and the Old Testament," *CBQ* 21 (1959): 265–82.
36. See the myth of Enki and Ninhursag in *ANET*, 37–41; *ATSHB*, 307–9.
37. See the story of Adapa in *ANET*, 101–31; *ATSHB*, 317–19.
38. For Atrahasis see above. For the Eridu Genesis see *COS* 1.158:513–15; *ATSHB*, 310–11.

Moses with new historical data so much as with a new way of looking at old myths.[39]

The Historical Problem of the Exodus

For many Jews and Christians the exodus story is an unassailable fact of history that stands at the very center of God's dealings with his people. God created Israel by delivering them from Egypt, and that grand act of deliverance foreshadowed the defeat of evil in Christian baptism (1 Cor. 10:1–2). In spite of this theological fact, modern critical scholars have serious questions about the historicity of the exodus. The historical problems are simple and straightforward.

Although we might not expect individual persons like Abraham or Jacob to leave much archaeological or textual evidence behind, Israel's exodus from Egypt is a different matter. According to modern scholars, the Passover story depicts a death episode so large—the death of the firstborn of all Egyptian men and animals, bringing death to every household, and creating a great cry "such as there has never been, nor ever shall be again"—that this event would presumably have left deep historical footprints and ideological scars in the Egyptian tradition. Lesser catastrophes in Egyptian history, such as Egypt's battles with the Asiatic Hyksos and with the invading "Sea Peoples," left many scars in the Egyptian memory.[40] Yet there is no evidence whatever that a catastrophe of the Passover's magnitude took place anytime in second-millennium Egypt, much less during the New Kingdom period when the event ostensibly occurred. The silence of our sources regarding this event would seem to be telling evidence against the tradition's historicity. Is the story therefore pure fiction? Perhaps not.

It requires only a little imagination to see how the biblical story might dimly reflect actual events in ancient Egypt. Many of the motifs in the exodus story have an historical flavor—not in the sense of specific events but rather as recurring

---

39. For a recent, popular evangelical discussion of Near Eastern myth and its problematic relationship to the Old Testament, see Enns, *Inspiration and Incarnation*. Enns highlights the apparent difficulties spawned by Scripture's ancient literary and historical context and then provides a theological paradigm (based on Christ's incarnation) for explaining those contextual features. His primary purpose is to reorient evangelical lay readers so that they can more fully appreciate the value of Scripture's ancient context (the ancient Near Eastern and second temple Judaic contexts being examples) for our understanding of the text. Although Enns does not provide final solutions for these difficulties (that is not his purpose), his thesis that the Bible is both human and divine in its origins is a thoroughly orthodox conclusion that points us in the right direction.

40. The Hyksos ("chiefs of foreign lands") were an Asiatic people who entered Egypt during the seventeenth century BCE and took control of the Nile region, ruling Egypt until the mid-sixteenth century. Their appearance brought the Egyptian Middle Kingdom to an end and left an indelible memory on Egyptian tradition. An Egyptian family from Luxor eventually drove the Hyksos out of Egypt in 1550 BCE, ushering in the Egyptian New Kingdom. As for the Sea Peoples, these migrating groups began to arrive in the Levant via the Mediterranean Sea during the thirteenth and twelfth centuries BCE. It is believed that their migrations were prompted by some sort of ecological disaster. The Sea Peoples invaded Egypt during the late thirteenth century, with the most significant battles taking place during the twelfth-century reign of Ramses III. The Egyptians succeeded in repulsing the Sea Peoples in battles that were memorialized in various royal inscriptions.

historical patterns in ancient Egyptian history. Good examples include the motifs of Pharaoh and his Asiatic slaves, of the Egyptian oppression of Palestine, of travel and trade between Egypt and Palestine, and of the great plagues that commonly wreaked havoc in ancient Egypt.[41] These kinds of things certainly did happen. So it is quite possible that the exodus tradition is historical, at least in the sense that it summarizes as one story what were actually the repetitive patterns of life in ancient Egypt and Western Asia. But are critical scholars willing to be even more specific about the historicity of the exodus? Yes, in some cases. Some scholars suspect that the biblical story of Israel's trek into Egypt, Joseph's rise to power in Pharaoh's court, and the final expulsion of Israel from Egypt are a distorted permutation of events that transpired during the Hyksos period, when Asiatic invaders infiltrated Egypt during the seventeenth century, seized control, and then were finally expulsed from Egypt in the sixteenth century—only a few centuries before Israel first appears on the historical scene. While the association of Israel with the Hyksos might strike us as odd and speculative, it at least has the advantage of being a very ancient opinion. The Jewish historian Josephus made the identification already during the first century CE.[42] So there may indeed be historical events behind Israel's wonderful story of the lawgiver Moses and the exodus. Nevertheless, even if we grant the possibility of miracles like the Passover and the parting of the Red Sea—as thoughtful Christians should—we must admit that the expected historical evidence for these miracles is wanting. This outcome suggests that our biblical account of the exodus may have been shaped by literary embellishment and creative theological elaboration as much as by historical events.

If we must nevertheless believe in the historicity of the exodus, then our historical judgment will have to depend upon the necessity of faith rather than on the kinds of historical evidence that we would normally demand in similar situations. I will take up this matter of faith-based historical logic again, and in more detail, in chapter 9.

Concluding Remarks on the Pentateuch

Biblical scholars have not resolved all of the Pentateuch's historical problems, nor have they answered all of their literary questions. Much debate continues and much work remains to be done. Nevertheless, the present evidence, as I have outlined it, strongly suggests that the Pentateuch's narrative is more often story than history, and that its five books were composed by several different authors living in contexts at some remove from the early history of Israel. Most of this is at variance with traditional (and evangelical) approaches to the biblical text.

My discussion of the Pentateuch has been lengthy and detailed. Some readers will now know a good bit more than they knew, or perhaps wished to know,

---

41. Ronald S. Hendel, "The Exodus in Biblical Memory," *JBL* 120 (2001): 601–22.
42. See *ATSHB*, 387–88; Josephus, *Against Apion* 1.73–105, 227.

about the issues involved. Still, the discussion has been of primary importance for my theme. By giving careful attention to the Pentateuch, we have been able to witness the depth and sophistication of critical scholarship. Even if we disagree in some measure with its standard conclusions, I do not believe that we can easily deny the apparent difficulties. This is because the difficulties themselves are not the products of critical fancy so much as issues raised by a close and careful reading of the Bible itself.

Having illustrated the depth and sophistication of biblical scholarship by discussing the Pentateuch, I would now like to illustrate its breadth by surveying a number of other difficulties from both the Old and New Testaments, beginning with the Hebrew histories in Samuel–Kings and 1–2 Chronicles.

The Problem of Israelite Historiography

The Hebrew Bible contains two parallel histories of the Israelite monarchy, one in the books of Samuel–Kings and the other in 1–2 Chronicles. Traditional biblical interpretation has normally assumed that both accounts provide historically accurate portraits of Israelite history, but modern scholars are reluctant to take these historical testimonies at face value.[43] At this point, we need not wrestle with all of the difficulties. It is enough to get some idea of the basic problems.

The older of the two histories, found in Samuel–Kings, is part of a larger narrative history that includes the books of Deuteronomy, Joshua, Judges, 1–2 Samuel, and 1–2 Kings.[44] This history judges the behavior of Israel and its kings by the yardstick of Deuteronomy's laws. Israel is righteous and blessed by God when it follows the laws of Deuteronomy, but evil and subject to judgment when it disobeys these laws. Because of its relationship to Deuteronomy, modern scholars often refer to this account of Israel's history as the Deuteronomistic History (DtrH). There is nothing surprising about the Deuteronomic ideology of DtrH, but as we saw in the Assyrian annals (chapter 2), ideological biases of this sort tend to slant an author's account of the facts and may even inspire the author to invent stories that suit his purpose. This seems to have happened in DtrH. According to DtrH's account, King David replaced Saul on the throne because Saul had disqualified himself as king. What is interesting, however, is that accord-

---

43. Because 1–2 Chronicles were written after Samuel–Kings, scholarly discussions of the difference between them usually appear in books and commentaries on Chronicles. For good discussions see Yaira Amit, *History and Ideology: An Introduction to Historiography in the Hebrew Bible*, trans. Yael Lotan, Biblical Seminar 60 (Sheffield: Sheffield Academic Press, 1999), 82–98; Sara Japhet, *1 & 2 Chronicles*, OTL (Louisville: Westminster John Knox, 1993), 14–23; Isaac Kalimi, *The Reshaping of Ancient Israelite History in Chronicles* (Winona Lake, IN: Eisenbrauns, 2005); Steven L. McKenzie, *The Chronicler's Use of the Deuteronomistic History*, Harvard Semitic Monographs 33 (Atlanta: Scholars Press, 1984); H. G. M. Williamson, *1 and 2 Chronicles*, NCB (Grand Rapids: Eerdmans, 1982).

44. Note that Ruth is not included in this group; the Hebrew canonical order differs from that in our English Bibles.

ing to this history Saul disqualified himself not once but twice. In 1 Samuel 13 Saul was disqualified because he did not follow Samuel's instructions regarding sacrifices at Gilgal, and in 1 Samuel 15 Saul disqualified himself again because he broke Deuteronomy's command to completely destroy the Amalekites (Deut. 7:1–6; 13:12–18; 25:17–19). The presence of two disqualification episodes is certainly a little odd. Because of this, modern scholars suspect that the first story represents the older tradition about the rejection of Saul, while the second story represents an invention of DtrH, designed to show that Saul was disqualified not only because he was evil but also because he contravened the law of Deuteronomy. Consequently, biblical critics believe that the second story does not relate the details of an historical event. Its purpose was to express DtrH's Deuteronomic interpretation of Saul. While this judgment is not certain (few judgments are), it strikes me as quite reasonable.

There are other difficulties presented by DtrH. The historian not only introduces his own Deuteronomistic stories into the text but also seems to have used older sources that sometimes contradicted one another. A good example is found in 2 Samuel 16–17. According to this text, David appears to meet Saul *twice* for the *first time*. In the first instance (2 Sam. 16), David was a warrior-musician who soothed Saul's evil spirit with harp music and subsequently became the king's armor bearer. In the following chapter, however, David appears on the scene again, this time as a shepherd boy unaccustomed to war. When he unexpectedly defeats Goliath in mortal combat, Saul inquired of David, "Whose son are you, young man?" Now how is it that, in this second instance, Saul failed to recognize his favorite musician and chief armor bearer? Is it our modern and critical imagination, or does Saul really meet David twice for the first time? One thing that is certain is that this is not our modern imagination. The translators of the Septuagint also recognized the difficulty. They deftly corrected the problem by deleting the verses that suggested two first-time meetings of the heroes.[45] So, unless Saul was suffering from a serious case of amnesia or senility, it seems that both of these stories cannot be historical. That DtrH kept both stories means, of course, that he was not aiming to write a story that would pass our modern litmus tests for good history. As a result, although modern scholars generally suppose that the narrative in DtrH (Samuel–Kings) provides us with a pretty good window into the history of ancient Israel, they recognize as well that the historian's theological slant, and uncritical use of sources, has produced something well shy of a perfectly accurate account of Israel's past.

Now let us consider the second Hebrew history in 1–2 Chronicles. The Chronicler wrote his history of the Israelite monarchy during the postexilic period, basing

---

45. This is one of two possible scholarly judgments. Some scholars have argued instead that the Greek version is closer to the original Hebrew, meaning that the contradiction was not in the original text but resulted when something was added to the Hebrew textual tradition. The solution adopted here is more sensible, I think, since the only verses missing from the Greek were those that created the difficulties.

his account mostly on the somewhat older history found in DtrH.[46] Because of this, scholars are able to compare these synoptic histories in order to discern how the Chronicler did his work. The differences between DtrH and Chronicles are most apparent in their respective portraits of the Israelite kings. For example, although David and Solomon have serious moral and religious flaws according to DtrH (e.g., adultery, murder, idolatry), the Chronicler removed these flaws so that both kings were entirely blameless and blessed by God.[47] Thus David no longer carries off captured Philistine idols (2 Sam. 5:21); instead, he burns them (1 Chron. 14:12). Similarly, the Chronicler transformed a good king from DtrH (King Asa) into a bad king (cf. 1 Kings 15:7-24; 2 Chron. 13:1-17:1), and transformed a very bad king from DtrH (King Manasseh) into a good king (2 Kings 21:1-18; 23:26; 24:3-4; 2 Chron. 33:1-20). What would explain these odd patterns of moral and ethical transformation?

The Chronicler's understanding of history is governed by the principle of immediate retribution, in which God quickly rewards good and faithful living but promptly reprimands every act of disobedience.[48] In order to communicate this theological pattern through his history, the Chronicler frequently added, deleted, and changed the tradition that he inherited from DtrH. We can observe the Chronicler's method firsthand by returning to the examples of Asa and Manasseh. In the case of Asa, the older history in DtrH presented him as a good king but noted as well that Asa suffered from "diseased feet." Because the Chronicler subscribed to his theory of immediate retribution, Asa's health problem required a moral explanation. The Chronicler looked more closely at DtrH and found in this source an explanation for Asa's illness: Asa had enacted a political treaty with the nation of Syria (1 Kings 15:16-24). Although DtrH reflects no grave concern about this treaty, the Chronicler interpreted the treaty as an act of rebellion against God, a deed of mutiny that caused all of Asa's troubles. So good king Asa became an evil king in Chronicles.

Now in the case of Manasseh, things proceeded in precisely the opposite direction. According to DtrH, no king in Judah was as evil as Manasseh, who led the nation into idolatry and even sacrificed his own children to a foreign god. So serious were his sins that DtrH made Manasseh the primary cause of Judah's destruction and exile: "Surely this came upon Judah at the command of the LORD, to remove them out of his sight, *for the sins of Manasseh*, according to all that

---

46. This is the standard view among scholars. But readers should note that A. Graeme Auld has recently proffered a somewhat different theory, in which Deuteronomy and Chronicles look similar because each is a revision of a still earlier version of Israel's history. See A. Graeme Auld, *Kings without Privilege: David and Moses in the Story of the Bible's Kings* (Edinburgh: T&T Clark, 1994).

47. There is one important exception to this rule. The Chronicler kept the story of David's evil census because it provided an etiology for the founding of the temple's holy site (cf. 2 Sam. 24; 1 Chron. 21:1–22:1). However, the Chronicler may have attempted to reduce David's culpability by pinning part of the blame on Satan (see 1 Chron. 21:1).

48. See Raymond B. Dillard, "Reward and Punishment in Chronicles: The Theology of Immediate Retribution," *WTJ* 46 (1984): 164–72.

he had done, and also for the innocent blood that he had shed; for he filled Jerusalem with innocent blood, and the LORD would not pardon" (2 Kings 24:3 RSV). Although DtrH says explicitly that God did not forgive Manasseh or Judah for these grave sins, things are quite otherwise in Chronicles. According to the Chronicler, Manasseh eventually humbled himself and turned wholeheartedly to Yahweh, composing a beautiful penitential prayer that moved God to forgive him. The Chronicler also removed from his account every hint of DtrH's link between Manasseh's sins and Judah's destruction and exile. What triggered the Chronicler's alternative portrait of Manasseh?

Scholars surmise that the Chronicler was troubled by the fact that Manasseh—supposedly the most evil of Judah's kings—had reigned over the nation for fifty-five years, a period longer than any other king, even David or Solomon. For an evil king to reign for so long did not suit the Chronicler's doctrine of immediate retribution, so an explanation was needed. The only explanation that would make sense to the Chronicler was that Manasseh must have repented of his sins, and the Chronicler apparently found evidence to support this conclusion in the form of an ancient penitential psalm associated with Manasseh. Modern scholars believe that the psalm itself probably existed, but historically speaking we cannot have it both ways. Either Manasseh was so evil that the exile was practically caused by his sins (as DtrH would have us believe), or he was a king who repented and so was granted a long life because of God's blessing (as the Chronicler would have us believe).

If we are tempted to believe that modern scholars have imagined the differences between DtrH and Chronicles, there are yet more obvious differences between the two histories. Among the most discussed differences is the numerical information provided by the histories. Some of these numerical variations may be due to problems in the transmission of the respective texts, or to differences in the sources the authors used, but this cannot account for all of these difficulties, illustrated in table 5.[49]

Modern scholars still have many questions about the Deuteronomistic Historian and the Chronicler, but they are fairly certain—because of the evidence adduced above—that these books do not provide us with perfectly accurate histories of events as they unfolded in ancient Israel. This is not to say that the biblical historians were necessarily bad historians; it may be that they were up to something other than mere history.

The Problem of Isaiah

Like the Pentateuch, the book of Isaiah has been a perennial flashpoint in the ongoing conflict between critical and traditional readings of Scripture. According

---

49. Adapted from James Barr, *Fundamentalism* (Philadelphia: Westminster, 1978), 309-10.

Table 5

	DtrH	Chronicles
Taken by King David	1,700 horsemen, 20,000 foot soldiers (2 Sam. 8:4)	1,000 chariots, 7,000 horsemen, 20,000 foot soldiers (1 Chron. 18:4)
Ammonite Mercenaries	32,000 men (2 Sam. 10:6)	32,000 chariots, plus army of Maacah (1 Chron. 19:7)
Killed by David	700 charioteers, 40,000 horsemen (2 Sam. 10:18)	7,000 charioteers, 40,000 horsemen (1 Chron. 19:18)
Census Figures	Israel 800,000; Judah 500,000 (2 Sam. 24:9)	Israel 1,100,000; Judah 470,000 (1 Chron. 21:5)
Length of Famine	7 years (2 Sam. 24:13)	3 years (1 Chron. 21:12)
Price of Temple Site	50 shekels of silver (2 Sam. 24:24)	600 shekels of gold (1 Chron. 21:25)
Stalls for Chariot Horses	40,000 (1 Kings 4:26)	4,000 (2 Chron. 9:25)
Capacity of the Wash Basin	2,000 baths (1 Kings 7:26)	3,000 baths (2 Chron. 4:5)
Gold from Ophir	420 talents (1 Kings 9:28)	450 talents (2 Chron. 8:18)

to the traditional view, the prophet Isaiah wrote the entire book that bears his name during the eighth century BCE. The second half of this book (chaps. 40–55) is particularly impressive, for it includes astonishingly detailed predictions about the end of the Jewish exile in Babylon two centuries later, including an accurate prediction of the ultimate defeat of Babylon and of the name of the king who would deliver the Jews: Cyrus of Persia. If one believes in the possibility of genuine prophecy, then these predictions will occasion no surprise. But as one might guess, many critical scholars do not believe in miraculous prophecies. As a result, they feel quite certain that Isaiah 40–55 was composed after the exile had taken place (sixth century BCE) and not during the lifetime of Isaiah of Jerusalem (eighth century BCE).[50] But this does not mean that the critical scholars believe that the book of Isaiah is offering us pseudoprophecies made after the fact.

As it turns out, modern scholars are not entirely antagonistic to traditional views of the book of Isaiah. In recent years, they have increasingly recognized that the book of Isaiah in its final form reflects a certain editorial unity, built especially upon the theme of Yahweh as the "Holy One of Israel." Nevertheless, there are serious problems with attributing the entire book of Isaiah to a single, eighth-century prophet. Although the first thirty-nine chapters of Isaiah generally assume an eighth-century Judean audience during the lifetime of Isaiah of Jerusalem, the chapters that follow in Isaiah 40–55 presuppose that Judah's sixth-century Babylonian exile had already taken place and was now about to end.

---

50. For standard scholarly assessments of Isaiah, see Paul D. Hanson, *Isaiah 40–66*, Interpretation (Louisville: Westminster John Knox, 1995); Hans-Joachim Kraus, *Das Evangelium der unbekannten Propheten: Jesaja 40–66*, Kleine biblische Bibliothek (Neukirchen-Vluyn: Neukirchener Verlag, 1990); John D. W. Watts, *Isaiah 34–66*, WBC (Waco: Word, 1987); Claus Westermann, *Isaiah 40–66: A Commentary*, trans. David M. G. Stalker, OTL (Philadelphia: Westminster, 1969); R. N. Whybray, *Isaiah 40–66*, NCB (Grand Rapids: Eerdmans, 1981).

Hence these prophecies are neither genuine predictions of the exile nor *ex eventu* predictions, written after the fact. They are instead genuine prophecies written *to* the exiles that predicted their deliverance (Isa. 40:1–2; 44:24–28) and told them to go home: "Go forth from Babylon, flee from Chaldea, declare this with a shout of joy, proclaim it, send it forth to the end of the earth; say, 'The LORD has redeemed his servant Jacob!'" (48:20 RSV). This section of Isaiah also reflects a lively Jewish debate about the appropriateness of God using the foreign king, Cyrus, as his "messiah" for delivering Israel:

> Thus says the LORD to his *messiah*,[51] to Cyrus,
>   whose right hand I have grasped,
> to subdue nations before him
>   and ungird the loins of kings . . .
> "know that it is I, the LORD,
>   the God of Israel, who call you by your name.
> For the sake of my servant Jacob,
>   and Israel my chosen,
> I call you by your name. . . .
>
> "Woe to him [skeptical Jews] who strives with his Maker,
>   an earthen vessel with the potter!
> Does the clay say to him who fashions it, 'What are you making'?
>   or 'Your work has no handles'?
> Woe to him who says to a father, 'What are you begetting?'
>   or to a woman, 'With what are you in travail?'"
> Thus says the LORD,
>   the Holy One of Israel, and his [Cyrus's] Maker:
> "Will you question me about my children,
>   or command me concerning the work of my hands?
> I made the earth,
>   and created man upon it;
> it was my hands that stretched out the heavens,
>   and I commanded all their host.
> I have aroused him [Cyrus] in righteousness,
>   and I will make straight all his ways;
> he shall build my city
>   and set my exiles free,
> not for price or reward,"
>   says the LORD of hosts. (Isa. 45:1–13 RSV, italics mine)

It strains the imagination to believe that Isaiah addressed these theological debates about a gentile messiah some one hundred and fifty years before they took place, and that his response to those debates was copied and recopied for many years

---

51. RSV reads "his anointed," which I have rendered as "his messiah."

by scribes—and read by audiences—who could not have made heads or tales out of Isaiah's rhetoric. It is more sensible to conclude that the prophet's words did not *predict* these debates so much as *presuppose* them. It is therefore reasonable to conclude that the prophecies of Isaiah 40–55 were written during the Babylonian exile, to Jews living in the Babylonian exile. The judgment that this portion of Isaiah was written by someone other than Isaiah—called Deutero-Isaiah by scholars—is reinforced by the fact that Isaiah 1–39 mentions the prophet's name sixteen times, while the second half of the book never mentions his name.

Another important piece of evidence supports these critical conclusions. During the above discussion of Deuteronomy, I had occasion to note that the prophet Jeremiah was involved in a heated debate about how sixth-century Judah should respond to the invading Babylonians. Some Judeans advised resistance to Babylon, but Jeremiah predicted defeat and exile. Now if the second half of Isaiah had existed already for one hundred and fifty years by Jeremiah's day, as the traditional view supposes, then why did Jeremiah not cite its prophecies as foolproof evidence that Judah would be defeated by Babylon, go into exile, and then be delivered later by Cyrus of Persia? We could theorize that Jeremiah simply did not know the book of Isaiah, but that is very hard to believe. Jeremiah was a prophet living in the environs of Jerusalem, which was Judah's primary scribal and archival center. He ministered among priests and in the temple vicinity and was very familiar with another biblical book, Deuteronomy. Even the lay elders of Judah were familiar with the old southern prophets, as we see when they quote Micah's oracles in the trial of Jeremiah (Jer. 26:17–19). Because of this evidence, it seems that Jeremiah must have known the book of Isaiah.[52] That he did not cite Isaiah 40–55 in the debates about Babylon suggests that his version of Isaiah simply did not include those chapters, which were added to the book by Deutero-Isaiah only after the exile had occurred.

I have discussed Isaiah 1–55 but have not yet mentioned the book's conclusion in chapters 56–66. Modern scholars believe that the prophecies in this last portion of the book date to the *postexilic* period, so that the book of Isaiah in its final form includes prophecies from before the exile (chaps. 1–39), during the

---

52. We do not have explicit evidence that Jeremiah knew the book of Isaiah, but no scholar would seriously question that he did. Jeremiah was from a priestly family and was active in Jerusalem during the seventh and early sixth centuries BCE. He would certainly have known the prophecies of Isaiah, which had been in existence at that point for well over a century. But the prophecies of Isaiah, without chaps. 40ff., would have provided little support for Jeremiah's prediction that Jerusalem would fall (in fact, some parts of Isaiah could have been used against Jeremiah). For this reason, Jeremiah's favorite prophetic book was the old book of Hosea, which correctly prophesied the fall of the northern kingdom. By analogy, Jeremiah suggested that the south could fall as well. For a discussion of the general parallels between Jeremiah and the prophetic tradition (including Isaiah), as well as a discussion of his use of Hosea, see Jones, *Jeremiah*, esp. 41–49, 65–67. For discussions that show the dependence of Second Isaiah on Jeremiah (hence, showing that Jeremiah was written first), see Benjamin D. Sommer, "New Light on the Composition of Jeremiah," *CBQ* 61 (1999): 646–66; Shalom Paul, "Literary and Ideological Echoes of Jeremiah in Deutero-Isaiah," in *Proceedings of the 5th World Congress of Jewish Studies*, vol. 1 (Jerusalem: Hebrew University, 1969), 102–20.

exile (chaps. 40–55), and after the exile (chaps. 56–66). These three sections of Isaiah are normally referred to as Isaiah, Deutero-Isaiah, and Trito-Isaiah, or, as 1, 2, and 3 Isaiah. Why do scholars believe in Trito-Isaiah?

The case for the existence of Trito-Isaiah is perhaps not so strong as the case for Deutero-Isaiah. Scholars date the last part of Isaiah to the postexilic period for two primary reasons. First, while Deutero-Isaiah describes Israel as innocent and redeemed (40:1–2), Trito-Isaiah depicts Israel as guilty and idolatrous (see chaps. 57–59; 65:1–16). This contrast suggests a very different context for the two parts of Isaiah. Second, this last section of Isaiah talks frequently about the rebuilding of Jerusalem and the restoration of the temple and its ritual cult (56:1–8; 58:12; 60–62). All of these features suit the postexilic context, when a community of Jews was busy attempting to reconstitute itself in the land of Palestine. As I have indicated, the evidence for the existence of Trito-Isaiah is not so strong and obvious as for Deutero-Isaiah, but the mere fact that chapters 56–66 come after and are different from Deutero-Isaiah suggests that they were probably written later, during the postexilic era.

But this matter aside, my main point is this: a sober and serious reading of Isaiah will easily suggest to readers that large portions of this prophetic collection were not written by an eighth-century prophet whose name was Isaiah.

The Problem of Ezekiel's Prophecy about Tyre

The difficulty presented by the prophetic oracle in Ezekiel 26:7–21 is straightforward. In this text, prefaced with the words, "Thus says the Lord Yahweh," Ezekiel promised that Nebuchadrezzar of Babylon would utterly destroy the Phoenician city of Tyre, demolishing its walls and leaving it an uninhabited ruin, never to be rebuilt. Now modern historians are quite sure that the Babylonians accomplished no such thing, but for this knowledge they do not require their historical-critical tools and insights. Ezekiel himself admits the difficulty in 29:18–20 (RSV):

> Son of man, Nebuchadrezzar king of Babylon made his army labor hard against Tyre; every head was made bald and every shoulder was rubbed bare; yet neither he nor his army got anything from Tyre to pay for the labor that he had performed against it. Therefore thus says the Lord GOD: Behold, I will give the land of Egypt to Nebuchadrezzar king of Babylon; and he shall carry off its wealth and despoil it and plunder it; and it shall be the wages for his army. I have given him the land of Egypt as his recompense for which he labored, because they worked for me, says the Lord GOD.

According to the prophet, because Nebuchadrezzar had failed to seize the city of Tyre, God was offering as compensation the nation of Egypt. Yet here the plot thickens even more, for it appears that even this second prophecy was not fulfilled; so far as we can tell, Nebuchadrezzar failed to add Egypt to the vast Babylonian

Empire.[53] It is true that the city of Tyre was eventually destroyed in 332 BCE by Alexander the Great, and some conservative scholars appeal to these events as a solution.[54] But Alexander's conquests were long after the reign of Nebuchadrezzar and resolve neither the problem of Ezekiel's initial prophecy about Tyre, nor the problem of his subsequent prophecy about Egypt, nor the obvious tension created by the existence of modern Tyre, which is not only modern Lebanon's fourth largest city but also a city that Ezekiel said would never be rebuilt. At best it would appear that Ezekiel's prophecies were not fulfilled; at worst, they failed.

If we anticipate that all of Scripture's prophetic writers give us flawlessly accurate predictions of the future, then this text raises obvious questions and problems. One evangelical scholar, Dan Block, is refreshingly honest about the implications: "But the present prophecy [by Ezekiel about Tyre] seems to look on these developments as a failure.... Yahweh's intrusion with another prophetic message so soon after the apparent fiasco suggests that the prophet may have been agonizing over his prophetic status."[55] The potential solutions aside, it seems that our problem is not modern and historical-critical; it is a problem that Ezekiel himself faced during his own lifetime.

The Problem of the Gospels

Traditional readers of Scripture happily admit that the four canonical Gospels provide four alternative portraits of Jesus's life, but they also believe that these portraits are historically accurate and compatible. In this view, the Gospels are like the cameras of four television reporters whose stories differ only because the reporters chose to include different stories or because, when they shot the same events, they did so from different camera angles. Already in the fourth century CE (well before the advent of TV cameras) Augustine wrote a long treatise in which he carefully harmonized the apparent historical discrepancies in the four Gospels.[56] So the view that the Gospels are perfectly accurate histories (or nearly so) is traditional indeed.

Critical scholars do not believe that this traditional view does justice to the "synoptic problem"—the differences among the Synoptic Gospels (Matthew, Mark, and Luke)—nor does it take account of the more serious discrepancies between John's Gospel and the other three. The basic difficulties are as follows.[57]

---

53. For discussion see Walther Zimmerli, *Ezekiel*, trans. R. E. Clements and James D. Martin, 2 vols., Hermeneia (Philadelphia: Fortress, 1979–1983), 2:102–5, 118–21.
54. Lamar E. Cooper Sr., *Ezekiel*, NAC 17 (Nashville: Broadman & Holman, 1994), 253–54.
55. Daniel I. Block, *The Book of Ezekiel*, 2 vols., NICOT (Grand Rapids: Eerdmans, 1997–1998), 2:149.
56. Augustine, *Harmony of the Gospels* (*NPNF* 1 6:77–236).
57. For overviews and perspectives on this matter, see Robert Kysar, *John, the Maverick Gospel* (Atlanta: John Knox, 1976); Keith Nickle, *The Synoptic Gospels: Conflict and Consensus* (Atlanta: John Knox, 1980); E. P. Sanders and Margaret Davies, *Studying the Synoptic Gospels* (Philadelphia: Trinity Press International, 1989); D. Moody Smith, *John among the Gospels: The Relationship in Twentieth-Century Research* (Minneapolis: Fortress,

The three Synoptic Gospels are so similar that scholars are quite certain that one of the books served as the primary source for the other two. Mark is usually believed to be this source Gospel, although some have argued for Matthean priority.[58] At any rate, the similarities among the three Gospels cause their differences to stand out pretty clearly. One such example is found in the story of the rich young man. If we read and compare Mark's version of this story to Matthew's, striking differences appear:

> And as he [Jesus] was setting out on his journey, a man ran up and knelt before him, and asked him, "Good Teacher, what must I do to inherit eternal life?" *And Jesus said to him, "Why do you call me good? No one is good but God alone.* You know the commandments: 'Do not kill, Do not commit adultery, Do not steal, Do not bear false witness, Do not defraud, Honor your father and mother.'" (Mark 10:17–19 RSV, italics mine)

> And behold, one came up to him, saying, "Teacher, what good deed must I do, to have eternal life?" *And he said to him, "Why do you ask me about what is good? One there is who is good.* If you would enter life, keep the commandments." He said to him, "Which?" And Jesus said, "You shall not kill, You shall not commit adultery, You shall not steal, You shall not bear false witness, Honor your father and mother, and, You shall love your neighbor as yourself." (Matt. 19:16–19 RSV, italics mine)

There are several differences here, but the most significant one is found in the young man's initial question and in Jesus's response to it (highlighted by italics). In Mark, the young man addresses Jesus as "Good Teacher," and Jesus in turn questions the validity of this address. In Matthew's account, however, the adjective "good" has been moved, so that it no longer describes Jesus ("*Good* Teacher") but instead describes the sort of deeds one must do to merit eternal life ("What *good* deed must I do?"). As a result, Matthew also edited Jesus's response, replacing Mark's "Why do you call me good" with the words, "Why do you ask me about what is good?"

Most scholars believe that Mark was written first and that Matthew used Mark as one of the primary sources for his Gospel. If this is so, then it is fairly clear why Matthew changed the words he inherited from Mark. Matthew was uncomfortable with Jesus's answer to the young man ("Why do you call me good? No one is good but God alone") because it could be taken to imply that Jesus did not view himself as good or as God. Matthew changed his text to fix the problem, as even some evangelicals admit.[59]

Another Synoptic difficulty appears when we compare the birth narratives of Matthew and Luke. Most of us have pretty vivid memories of the Christmas story,

---

1992); Robert Stein, *Studying the Synoptic Gospels: Origin and Interpretation*, 2nd ed. (Grand Rapids: Baker Academic, 2001).

58. See William Farmer, *The Synoptic Problem: A Critical Analysis* (New York: Macmillan, 1964).

59. Donald A. Hagner, *Matthew 14–28*, WBC (Dallas: Word, 1995), 555.

including the trip from Nazareth to Jerusalem, the local inn with no vacancy, the manger and wise men, the trip to Egypt to escape Herod, and the family's eventual return to Nazareth. What we may not realize is that this portrait of Jesus's birth is a conflation of two quite different stories.

In Luke's Gospel, Jesus's family lives in Nazareth and must travel to Bethlehem for a Roman census. At this untimely hour, with no room in the local inn, Jesus was born in a manger. Joseph and Mary then waited forty days for the ritual period of cleansing, offered their temple sacrifices, and returned home to Nazareth. Matthew's birth story is quite different, both geographically and chronologically. Jesus's family already lived in Bethlehem when he was born, and they remained there for two years until the Magi arrived. At that point king Herod sought to kill the boy, so Jesus's family fled to Egypt, where they remained until Herod had died. Unfortunately, Herod's death did not bring the hoped-for relief because his son ruled in his stead. For this reason, upon Herod's death Joseph did not return to his home in Bethlehem but instead retreated to Nazareth.

Why are these two stories so different? We might suppose that the two Gospel authors had very different sources and so tell very different tales, but scholars believe that something more subtle is afoot. If one looks at Matthew's portrait of Jesus closely, it becomes clear that Matthew wanted to portray Jesus as a new Moses.[60] Just as Pharaoh killed the Israelite children, so Herod killed the Jewish children (Matt. 2:16–18). Just as Moses was saved from Pharaoh by being placed in the Nile, so Jesus was saved from Herod by being taken to Egypt (Matt. 2:13–15). Just as Moses exited Egypt as the savior of Israel, so Jesus exited Egypt as the savior of the world. Just as Moses fasted for forty days in the wilderness, so Jesus fasted there for forty days (Matt. 4:1–2). Just as Moses returned from his fast to deliver the law on Mount Sinai, so Jesus returned from his fast to deliver the Sermon on the Mount (Matt. 5–7). In this sermon Jesus said things like: "You have heard that it was said [by Moses], 'Eye for eye, and tooth for tooth.' But I tell you, Do not resist an evil person" (5:38–39 NIV). It is fairly clear that Matthew's Jesus was shaped not only to make him like Moses but to show that his authority superseded that of the Mosaic law. Taken together, this evidence strongly suggests that Matthew's birth account is not strictly biographical but was instead a creative composition designed to illustrate the Savior's relationship to Moses. One result was a birth narrative quite different from Luke's.

The Fourth Gospel, the Gospel of John, presents yet more serious difficulties. Not only does John contain many stories and teachings not found in the Synoptics, but these materials also reflect very different emphases.[61] The Synoptic Jesus performs his miracles in private and requests that witnesses keep the events to themselves (Mark 5:21–24, 35–43). He generally conceals his messianic identity

---

60. Dale C. Allison Jr., *The New Moses: A Matthean Typology* (Minneapolis: Fortress, 1993); Kenton L. Sparks, "Gospel as Conquest: Mosaic Typology in Matthew 28:16–20," *CBQ* 68 (2006): 251–63.

61. See Kysar, *John*; Smith, *John among the Gospels*.

and preaches about the kingdom of God rather than himself (e.g., Mark 4:1–34; 5:21–24, 35–43), publicly rebuking those who ask for miraculous proof of his identity (Matt. 12:38–42). This Synoptic Jesus contrasts sharply with John's presentation. In the Fourth Gospel Jesus frequently performs public miracles as "signs" of his messianic identity (John 20:30–31) and preaches about himself, boldly claiming his messianic identity (John 8:12–59; 10:1–31). So the portraits of Jesus's ministry in John's Gospel and in the Synoptics are very different.

John's distinctiveness comes to the fore even more in those few instances where he provides his version of a story known in the Synoptics. The passion of Christ is a good example. According to the Synoptics (see Mark 15), Jesus ate a final Passover meal with his disciples on Thursday evening, after which he was betrayed, arrested, and put on trial before the Jewish Sanhedrin and Pilate in the early morning. After he was convicted, Jesus was crucified on Friday at the "third hour" (9:00 a.m.) and suffered until he died at the "ninth hour" (3:00 p.m.).

John's description of Jesus's last few days is quite different (John 18:28–19:16). Jesus indeed ate a final meal with his disciples on Thursday evening, but it was not a Passover meal. We know this not only because John does not call it a Passover meal but also because John explicitly says that the meal occurred before the Passover (13:1–2) and explicitly identifies the following day as the "day of Preparation of Passover Week" (19:14 NIV). In fact, during Jesus's Roman trial on Friday, the Jews were not willing to enter the palace of Pilate because they wanted to remain ceremonially clean for the coming Passover meal (18:28). So John places the death of Jesus on a different day than in the Synoptics, and this is joined by yet another temporal dislocation. John's Gospel does not fix the crucifixion at the "third hour" (9:00 a.m.), as in the Synoptics, but at the "sixth hour" (noon). All of this raises the question: Why would John have Jesus crucified at noon on the day before Passover rather than at 9:00 a.m. on the day after Passover? Scholars do not have a certain answer for this question, but they do have a very sound hypothesis. In the time of Jesus, the Jews began to sacrifice the Passover lambs in the temple at noon on the day of Preparation of the Passover,[62] and John is the only Gospel that presents Jesus as "the Lamb of God, who takes away the sin of the world" (John 1:29). This identification is made more specific in John's Passion Narrative, wherein Jesus's death on the cross fulfills the requirements of the Exodus Passover law (cf. John 19:28–29, 32–36; Exod. 12:22–23, 46). For this reason, scholars suspect that John changed the day and time of Christ's death in order to present him symbolically as the Lamb of God. And this modern judgment is more than a symptom of Enlightenment-inspired skepticism. Already in his ancient commentary on John's gospel, Origen recognized so many apparent contradictions between John and the Synoptics that he finally wrote concerning

---

62. Raymond E. Brown, *The Gospel according to John*, 2 vols., AB (Garden City, NY: Doubleday, 1966–1970), 2:882–83; Joseph Bonsirven, "Hora Talmudica: La notion chronologique de Jean 19, 14, aurait-elle un sens symbolique?" *Biblica* 33 (1952): 511–15.

those gospel writers: "I do not condemn them if they sometimes dealt freely with things that to the eye of history happened differently, and change them so as to serve the mystical aims they had had in view, so as to speak of a thing which happed in a certain place, as if it had happened in another, or of what took place at a certain time, and to introduce into what was spoken in a certain way some changes of their own.... The spiritual truth was often preserved, as one might say, in the material falsehood."[63]

In a similar way, critical scholars do not deny that the canonical Gospels provide us with biographical portraits of Jesus's life, nor do they deny that in many cases these portraits are historically accurate. Because of the important differences in the accounts offered by the four Gospel writers, however, they cannot accept the traditional view that the Gospels provide us with four historically perfect accounts of what Jesus said and did. Not only were the four Gospels composed by fallible human authors using fallible human sources, but these fallible authors often took creative and symbolic liberties that precluded strictly historical concerns.

The Problem of the Pastoral Epistles

Because of their similar tone, content, and style, scholars of almost every stripe agree that the Pastorals—1 and 2 Timothy and Titus—were written by the same author. The chief difficulty presented by the books concerns who that author was. Traditional interpreters accept the Bible's ostensible claim that the books were written by Paul, while most modern scholars believe that the Pastorals are certainly not Pauline. The straightforward arguments against Pauline authorship are as follows.[64]

First, it is known that both orthodox Christians and heretics composed pseudonymous letters in Paul's name (see *3 Corinthians*; *Epistle to the Laodiceans*; *Letters to Seneca*; cf. 2 Thess. 2:2).[65] This fact in itself should alert us to the *possibility* that some of the supposed Pauline letters in the Christian canon were not actually written by Paul.

Second, the grammar and vocabulary of the Pastorals is very different than in Paul's undisputed letters. A full one-third of the words used in the Pastorals do not appear in Paul's other letters, and some of the words that do appear—such as "faith," "truth," and "Savior"—take on entirely different nuances in the Pastorals. Whereas "faith" in Paul's undisputed letters refers to one's trust in God, in the

---

63. Origen, *Commentary on John* 10:4 (*ANF* 9:383).

64. For the standard arguments on these questions, see Martin Dibelius and Hans Conzelmann, *The Pastoral Epistles*, trans. Philip Buttolph and Adela Yarbro, Hermeneia (Philadelphia: Fortress, 1972); Helmut Koester, *Introduction to the New Testament*, 2 vols. (New York: de Gruyter, 1982), 2:297–305. For a more cautious critical approach, which I will discuss below, see Luke Timothy Johnson, *The Writings of the New Testament: An Interpretation* (Minneapolis: Fortress, 1999), 423–31.

65. See J. K. Elliott, *The Apocryphal New Testament*, rev. repr. (Oxford: Clarendon, 1999), 353–54, 380–82, 543–53.

Pastorals this term is shorthand for the body of traditional Christian doctrine that we must protect and to which we must adhere. "Truth" also bears this meaning in the Pastorals. Similarly, the term "Savior" is rarely used with reference to Christ in Paul's authentic letters (see Phil. 3:20; cf. Eph. 5:23), but in the Pastorals it is often an epithet of both God and Christ. More importantly, many of the particles, conjunctions, and adverbs commonly used by Paul do not appear in the Pastorals. For many scholars, this linguistic evidence alone is more than sufficient to preclude Pauline authorship of the Pastoral Epistles.

Third, the earliest historical testimony concerning the Pastorals is unusual in comparison with the testimony for Paul's authentic letters. Whereas the indisputably authentic letters were known and accepted very early in church history, the Pastorals do not appear in $\mathfrak{P}^{46}$ and were partly rejected by Tatian.[66] This last piece of evidence is particularly important. $\mathfrak{P}^{46}$ is a codex collection of Paul's Letters that dates roughly to 200 CE.[67] Although parts of the codex are damaged, it is clear that the codex contained all of Paul's traditional letters (including even the book of Hebrews), yet it did not include the Pastorals. Now this does not mean that the Pastoral Epistles were unknown to early Christians. Polycarp alluded to them in his second-century *Epistle to the Philippians*,[68] and Tertullian refers to them in the early third century.[69] Nevertheless, the historical testimony for the authenticity of the Pastorals is not as strong as for Paul's other epistles. To be sure, this in itself does not prove the critical conclusion that the Pastorals were written pseudonymously. But when this evidence is dovetailed with other pieces of evidence, it fits well with the standard critical conclusion that the Pastoral Epistles were written somewhat later than Paul's authentic letters.

Fourth, there are historical problems with the traditional viewpoint. Paul's life as we understand it, on the basis of his epistles and the book of Acts, does not allow much room for the travel and ministry in the East assumed by the Pastorals (cf. 1 Tim. 1:3; 2 Tim. 4:21; Titus 3:14). Although some have argued that Paul was released at the end of the book of Acts and then carried out this ministry later in his life (as might be implied in *1 Clem.* 5:7), Acts itself implies that Paul never returned to the Eastern churches (see Acts 20:25; 20:38). Another historical problem is that most scholars see in the Pastorals a fairly complex hierarchy of church leadership that includes bishops, elders, and deacons. These formal offices are prominent in second-generation Christian sources like the *Didache* and the Ignatian letters, but not so much in Paul's Letters. The development of these authoritative structures probably fits a period later in the first or even early

---

66. Tatian accepted Titus but not 1 and 2 Timothy. See Dibelius and Conzelmann, *Pastoral Epistles*, 2.

67. See Bruce M. Metzger and Bart D. Ehrman, *The Text of the New Testament: Its Transmission, Corruption, and Restoration*, 4th ed. (Oxford: Oxford University Press, 2005), 54–55.

68. See Polycarp, *Letter to the Philippians* 4:1.

69. He points out that the heretic Marcion did not include them in his canon. See *Against Marcion* 5.21 (*ANF* 3:473–74).

in the second century. Such a date would also suit the gnostic heresies confronted in the Pastorals.[70]

Fifth, there seem to be some significant ethical differences between the Pastorals and the authentic Pauline Letters. As just one example we can consider the role of women in the texts. Whereas the authentic letters offer a message of gender equality (Gal. 3:28) and allow women to speak in public worship (1 Cor. 11:2–6), the Pastorals do not permit this (1 Tim. 2:11–14). It is true that one text from the authentic corpus also forbids women to teach (1 Cor. 14:34–35), but there is evidence that this text was added to 1 Corinthians by someone else.[71] One part of this evidence is textual (among the manuscripts these verses occur in different places in 1 Corinthians), and the other piece of evidence involves consistency: Why would Paul provide directions for women who prophesy in 1 Corinthians 11 and then tell them not to speak in 1 Corinthians 14? For these reasons, and for others also, many scholars believe that these verses were added to 1 Corinthians in order to align its theology more closely with the Pastorals. So there is a difference between Paul's view of women and the viewpoint of women maintained in the Pastorals. I will discuss this matter with more detail in chapter 10.

For most critical scholars the evidence considered here is more than sufficient to show that the Pastorals are pseudonymous. But at least a few critical scholars are not wholly convinced of this, Luke Timothy Johnson being a good example.[72] According to Johnson, if we set aside the critical dictum that the Pastorals were written by one author, then the case for the authenticity of each Pastoral letter will be different. In particular, he believes that 2 Timothy offers a stronger case for authenticity than either Titus or 1 Timothy. Even in the case of these last two letters, the judgment will depend upon how one handles the comparisons. To be sure, 1 Timothy is very different from Romans or Galatians, but it is perhaps not so different from Philippians. For these reasons and for a few others, Johnson is willing to say that we simply do not know who wrote the Pastoral Epistles. But of course, this is itself a critical conclusion based on an appraisal of the evidence. For it is the question of authorship itself, and not one's answer to the question, that is the real difference between the traditional view and critical scholarship. When we openly embrace the possibility that Paul did not write the Pastorals, we have already stepped into the historical-critical camp. After all, admitting that Paul might not have written the Pastorals is no more compatible with the traditional viewpoint than saying that he did not write it.

Though the evidence against Paul's authorship of the Pastorals is not as strong as the evidence against the Mosaic authorship of the Pentateuch, in the end I believe that the evidence sides strongly with those who judge the Pastorals to be pseudonymous. If we accept this, then our situation is more complex than in the

---

70. See Dibelius and Conzelmann, *Pastoral Epistles*, 2–3.
71. See Gordon D. Fee, *The First Epistle to the Corinthians*, NICNT (Grand Rapids: Eerdmans, 1987), 699–708, and the relevant discussion in chapter 10 of this volume.
72. Johnson, *Writings of the New Testament*, 431.

case of the Pentateuch, because the Pastorals make a much more explicit claim to Pauline authorship than the Pentateuch makes for Moses (cf. 1 Tim. 1:1; 2 Tim. 1:1; 4:13, 21; Titus 1). For this reason the assertion by biblical scholars that Paul did not write the Pastorals presents a special problem for traditional viewpoints, as does the scholarly claim that Paul may not have written Ephesians, Colossians, or perhaps even 2 Thessalonians.[73] Any thoroughgoing solution to the problem of biblical criticism will need to tackle the problem of pseudonymity in the New Testament, as well as in the Old.

The Problem of Daniel and Revelation

The difficulties presented by the books of Daniel and Revelation are not precisely of the same sort, but they are close enough that it is helpful to discuss the two books at the same time. Let us begin with Daniel. The book of Daniel includes two generic halves, one featuring tales about Daniel and his friends (chaps. 1–6) and the other Daniel's apocalyptic visions (chaps. 7–12). The tales present their own problems, but here we shall consider only the visions. I should warn that our discussion will seem rather detailed for the uninitiated, but this is necessary to ensure that the difficulties have been correctly understood before we attempt to provide solutions in chapters 4 and 5.

Daniel 7–12 contains four visions that predict the deliverance of the Jews from an oppressive earthly kingdom. Daniel purportedly experienced these visions during his exile in Babylon, as his people were successively ruled by the Babylonians, Medians, and Persians. Daniel predicted that these three kingdoms would be followed by a fourth kingdom, which would oppress and kill Jews until God intervened to save his people and to usher in his eternal kingdom. This, in essence, is the content of Daniel 7–12. Traditional Christian readers normally take all of this at face value and assume that Daniel was the author of the book and that he lived in the Babylonian exile during the sixth century BCE. They often regard Daniel's four kingdoms as Babylon, Medo-Persia, Greece, and Rome, so that God's kingdom appears immediately after Rome in the person of Christ and in the age of the church.

Most biblical scholars appraise the book quite differently. They are certain that Daniel's four kingdoms are Babylon, Media, Persia, and Greece, and they further aver that his apocalypses were actually composed by an anonymous author during the Greek period, when the Seleucid king Antiochus IV Epiphanes ruled Palestine (175–164 BCE). If they are correct, then the visions of Daniel are *ex eventu* prophecies, since they did not predict the historical events that transpired during the four kingdoms in question. Daniel would then be similar to other Near Eastern *ex eventu* apocalypses, such as the Uruk prophecy discussed in chapter 2. The rationale for this scholarly consensus is as follows.

---

73. See Calvin J. Roetzel, *The Letters of Paul*, 3rd ed. (Louisville: Westminster John Knox, 1991), 131–55.

Daniel's four visions (chaps. 7, 8, 9, 10–12) presuppose a sequence of four political kingdoms, which the book identifies as Babylon, Media, Persia, and Greece. The first three kingdoms are represented as a sequence of kings that includes Nebuchadnezzar and Belshazzar of Babylon, Darius the Mede, and Cyrus of Persia. The Greeks are explicitly named as the last kingdom in the angelic interpretation of chapter 8 (see 8:21–22), an identification that is made yet clearer by the detailed description of this last kingdom as a "shaggy goat," whose large horn was broken off and sprouted four smaller horns. This description is a transparent allusion to the kingdom of Alexander the Great, which was divided among his four generals after his death. The vision goes on to report that one of these little horns would abolish the daily sacrifice and desecrate the temple of the Jews, transparent allusions to Antiochus IV Epiphanes, who suppressed traditional Jewish practices and then desecrated the temple in 167 BCE (see 1 Macc. 1).

As for the prophecies themselves, scholars have noticed that each of Daniel's apocalyptic predictions is amazingly accurate and precise, so accurate that they suspect the prophecies were written after the described events had occurred. Scholars suspect this not only because so many of the predictions are right but also because, more importantly, at a certain point each of them goes awry. For example, in his first vision in chapter 7, the author predicted that God's eschatological kingdom would arrive three and one-half years ("a time, times, and half a time") after Antiochus suppressed traditional Jewish practices in 167 BCE, but we can see that this grand kingdom did not materialize. Similarly, in the second vision of Daniel 8, the author predicted that the temple would be reconsecrated 2,300 days after Antiochus desecrated it in 167 BCE, but this actually required only three years. Then in the fourth and last vision of chapters 10–12, it is predicted that the king who persecuted the Jews (i.e., Antiochus)[74] would be defeated and killed by the Egyptian Ptolemies in the land of Israel, after which the eschaton would occur (see Dan. 12:1–4).[75] However, although Jewish sources provide three different accounts of Antiochus's death, all of them agree that he died in Persia, not in Palestine as the prophecy demands (cf. 1 Macc. 6:1–17; 2 Macc. 1:14–16; 9:1–29). And, of course, we are still waiting for the full-blown eschatological kingdom predicted by the prophecy. Scholars believe that this evidence makes it very easy to date Daniel's apocalypses. One merely follows the amazingly accurate prophecies until they fail. Because the predictions of the Jewish persecutions in 167 BCE are correct, and because the final destiny of Antiochus in 164 BCE is not, it follows that the visions and their interpretations can be dated sometime between 167 and 164 BCE. From this we may conclude that the author of Daniel's apocalypses fully expected that the kingdom of God would appear during the Greek era. But indeed, it did not. We may also note that the date that critical scholars

---

74. The text explicitly warns that this king would, like Antiochus, abolish the Jewish sacrifices and desecrate the temple.

75. See John Goldingay, *Daniel*, WBC (Dallas: Word, 1989), 269–334; John J. Collins, *Daniel*, Hermeneia (Minneapolis: Fortress, 1993), 363–404.

assign to Daniel's visions is quite different from their ostensible and traditional date, which is during the sixth-century reign of Cyrus of Persia.

Biblical scholars are quick to admit, however, that at least one of Daniel's visions was fulfilled very precisely in every respect. The vision in chapter 9 predicted that Antiochus would perish within seven years of 171 BCE, which turns out to be essentially accurate, given that he died in 164 BCE. But as we might expect, critical scholars do not chalk this up to successful prophecy. Because Daniel's other accurate prophecies were authored after the fact, they suspect that this one is also an *ex eventu* composition. So, to summarize, the scholarly consensus is that Daniel contains many astonishingly accurate *ex eventu* prophecies leading up to and including events during the life of Antiochus, but most of the book's predictions from that point forward appear to have failed.

Now let us consider the book of Revelation. Because of the book's rich imagery and symbolism, modern readers often find its prophecies mysterious and impenetrable. Yet biblical scholars feel quite sure that the book's symbolism reveals more than it conceals. The book predicted that the city of "Babylon" would persecute Christians to the point of martyrdom, mainly through the agency of a great "beast" who would rule the world and force Christians to worship him under the threat of death. This terrifying beast would be the reincarnation of a previous beast (13:3; 17:8), whose "number" was 666 (see Rev. 13). Revelation offered a message of hope to Christians persecuted by this beast, promising that Christ would return, destroy the beast, and set up the eternal kingdom of God (see chaps. 18–22). This, in a nutshell, is the prophetic message of the book of Revelation.

As I said, most modern scholars believe that ancient readers of the book would have recognized easily the various symbols in its prophecies. "Babylon" was none other than Rome, not only because Rome was a city built on seven hills (Rev. 17:9) but also because early Jews and Christians often used the term "Babylon" as a code for Rome. As for the "beast" of Revelation, this was none other than the Roman emperor, who demanded worship from Christians under threat of persecution and death. This interpretation is confirmed by the author's use of the symbolic number 666, whose gematria value equals the Greek word "beast" as well as the Hebrew name for "Caesar Nero," that infamous persecutor of Christians from 64 to 68 CE.[76] More specifically, the author predicted the rise of a new Nero, whom he explicitly described as the beast "who was, and is not, and is about to ascend." This reincarnated Nero—

---

76. *Gematria* refers to the practice of adding up the numerical values of the letters in a word. This was possible because the ancients used their alphabets to represent numbers. The value of the Hebrew name for "Kaiser Nero" (*nrwn qsr*) was: nun (50) + resh (200) + waw (6) + nun (50) + qof (100) + samekh (60) + resh (200) = 666. This identification is further confirmed by the fact that some manuscripts of Revelation use the number 616 rather than 666, which would correspond to an alternate Hebrew spelling for Kaiser Nero (*nrw qsr*). For more on this feature in Revelation, see Craig R. Koester, *Revelation and the End of All Things* (Grand Rapids: Eerdmans, 2001), 132–33; Bruce M. Metzger, *Breaking the Code: Understanding the Book of Revelation* (Nashville: Abingdon, 1993), 76–77.

expected not only by Christians but by others as well[77]—would be the eighth in a series of Caesars following the first Nero (17:10–11). Emperor Domitian (81–96 CE) would have been the seventh in this eight-king sequence, suggesting that the book was written during his reign, just before the supposed appearance of the new Nero. This dating of the book suits both ancient history and early Christian tradition. Domitian seems to have renewed demands for emperor worship during his lifetime, and the earliest Christian commentators dated Revelation to the time of his reign. The obvious theological difficulty, of course, is that neither the new Nero nor God's final kingdom materialized after the passing of Domitian.

In spite of their differences, the authors of Daniel and Revelation shared a common eschatological expectation. Both authors anticipated that God's final intervention in history would free his holy people from persecution. Daniel anticipated the liberation of Jews during the Greek period, while the author of Revelation hoped for the emancipation of Christians during the Roman period. In neither case, however, did this final eschatological kingdom materialize in the predicted time frame. To be sure, this assessment of the books might seem to imply that Daniel and Revelation are nothing more than collections of failed prophecies, but modern biblical scholars do not read these books in this way. Daniel and Revelation are instead understood as apocalyptic books, whose purpose was not so much to predict the future as to encourage struggling and persecuted religious groups—Jews and Christians—with the hope of imminent deliverance by the God who loved them and whom they loved. As it turned out, however, no eschatological intervention was necessary to rid the Jews of the Seleucids, nor to rid the Christians of Rome.

The Problem of the Bible's Theological and Ethical Diversity

As we have seen, modern critiques of the Pentateuch assume that its five books reflect theological diversity on many subjects. The Pentateuch does not provide consistent judgments on such matters as who should be a priest, when sacrifices were first offered, where sacrifices should be offered, when the divine name was first known to humanity, and many other items. Overlapping with the problem of this theological diversity is the ethical diversity that appears when various strands of the Pentateuch are compared with one another and with other portions of the Bible. For the sake of illustration, let us consider how the Bible addresses the issue of slavery.

Three major blocks of pentateuchal legislation regulate the institution of slavery, including both debt slavery and chattel slavery. These laws appear in the Book of

---

77. Paul J. Achtemeier, Joel B. Green, and Marianne Meye Thompson, *Introducing the New Testament: Its Literature and Theology* (Grand Rapids: Eerdmans, 2001), 569–71; Steven J. Friesen, "Myth and Symbolic Resistance in Revelation 13," *JBL* 123 (2004): 281–313; Hans-Josef Klauck, "Do They Never Come Back? Nero Redivivus and the Apocalypse of John," *CBQ* 63 (2001): 683–98; Leonard L. Thompson, *The Book of Revelation: Apocalypse and Empire* (Oxford: Oxford University Press, 1990), 13–15.

the Covenant (Exod. 21:1–11), in the Deuteronomic Code (Deut. 15:12–18), and in the Holiness Code (Lev. 25:35–55). The laws in Exodus and Deuteronomy differ in some details but are otherwise similar in that they prescribe that Hebrew slaves who are purchased must be offered release after six years of servitude. Implicit in these laws is an ethnic distinction between Israelites and non-Israelites, since the command to release Israelite slaves implies that the offer was not extended to non-Israelites. Such an ethnic distinction certainly flies in the face of Paul's New Testament ethic, which proclaims that there is no distinction in God's eyes between Jews and gentiles (Gal. 3:28). The law in Leviticus differs from the laws in Exodus and Deuteronomy in that it improves the lot of Israelite slaves but allows for longer periods of slavery. For instance, Leviticus prohibits trade in Hebrew chattel slaves (see Lev. 25:44) and legislates that Hebrew debt slaves should be treated as hired workers rather than as slaves (25:39–43). However, it allows Israelite slaves to serve until the next Jubilee Year, which could be as much as forty-nine years and hence much longer than the seven-year span permitted in Exodus (21:2) and Deuteronomy (15:12). As we can see, the legal distinctions in the Pentateuch are often based on the ethnic or economic status of those involved, and this does not comport well with the egalitarian spirit of New Testament ethics.

A more striking ethical problem appears in the Pentateuch's legislation about the treatment of slaves. While Leviticus adjures slave owners not to treat their Hebrew debt slaves "with harshness" (Lev. 25:43), Exodus grants slave owners a great deal of latitude in their treatment of slaves: "When a man strikes his slave, male or female, with a rod and the slave dies under his hand, he shall be punished. But if the slave survives a day or two, he is not to be punished; for the slave is his money [i.e., 'property']" (Exod. 21:20–21). To be sure, the biblical legist did not explicitly advocate such extreme treatment of slaves, but he certainly maintained that slave owners could be very harsh with their slaves without fearing the specter of public jurisprudence. Only with great difficulty can we square this slave law with the ethical admonitions in the New Testament that required slave owners to treat their slaves with kindness and equity (see Eph. 6:5–9; Col. 4:1).

Yet a further ethical difficulty presents itself when we compare the Bible's explicit rulings on slavery with the ethical positions now espoused by modern Christians. Modern Christianity maintains that the owning and trading of human beings as chattel is immoral and unacceptable in the eyes of God. How is it possible that this modern theological judgment, now so putatively unassailable and certain, was not reached and preached explicitly by the biblical writers themselves, who wrote under the influence of the Holy Spirit and so presumably knew—or should have known, it seems—that slavery was an abominable practice that dishonored human bearers of the divine image?

Serious ethical difficulties of the sort that I have just described are not ubiquitous in Scripture, but there are others. One thinks, for instance, of the apparent conflict between Deuteronomy's command to kill every Canaanite—including men, women, children, and even animals—and the Gospel command to love our

THE PROBLEM OF BIBLICAL CRITICISM   121

enemies.[78] These difficulties, and others like them, bring us to the heart of the problem raised by biblical criticism. Biblical criticism suggests that the Bible does not speak with one divine voice but offers instead a range of human voices with different judgments and opinions on the same subjects. As one brave evangelical, Christopher Wright, has described it, "We are listening, not to a single voice, not even to a single choir in harmony, but to several choirs singing different songs with some protest groups jamming in the wings."[79] *At face value, Scripture does not seem to furnish us with one divine theology; it gives us numerous theologies.* Any decent solution to the problems presented by modern biblical criticism will need to explain how the Bible can be trusted as an authoritative text when it reflects diverse theological perspectives, which differ not only from one another but also from our modern theological judgments on matters like slavery.

The Problem of the Bible's Exegesis

If the foregoing discussion of biblical ethics and literature is even close to right, then it will imply something important about the context of the biblical authors. Even if their perspectives on life and faith were informed by God himself, it remains true that their ideas and perspectives were historically contingent, being radically shaped by the particular cultural settings in which they lived and worked. Modern scholars believe that this is true not only of their basic interpretations of life but also of the way that the biblical authors interpreted Scripture itself. This is especially evident in the way that New Testament authors interpreted the Old Testament.

A close examination of the biblical exegesis of Jesus, Paul, and the other New Testament writers reveals that each employed interpretive methods that were current in his own day. Here I will consider just a few examples of this phenomenon, beginning with the exegetical strategy that postbiblical Jews call *peshat* (I adopt the term here for convenience).[80] *Peshat* involved a woodenly literal reading of the biblical text. Such a reading appears in John's Gospel, when Jesus defends himself against the charge of blasphemy.[81] Jewish leaders accused him of blasphemy because he claimed to be divine. Rather than simply reaffirm his divinity, Jesus defended his claim by pointing out that Scripture itself describes human beings as "gods" in Psalm 82:6 (see John 10:31–39). It is highly unlikely, of course, that Jesus meant to suggest that his opponents shared literally in his own divinity. More

---

78. See Deut. 20:16–18; cf. Deut. 2:34; 3:6; Josh. 6:21.

79. Christopher J. H. Wright, *Old Testament Ethics for the People of God* (Downers Grove, IL: InterVarsity, 2004), 444.

80. Literal interpretation was common in the biblical period, but the use of *peshat* to designate literal exegesis appears to have arisen only in the fourth century CE. See Richard N. Longenecker, *Biblical Exegesis in the Apostolic Period*, 2nd ed. (Grand Rapids: Eerdmans, 1999), 17.

81. For this and other examples, see ibid., 14–18, 50–54.

likely is that Jesus used a *peshat* reading of the psalm to offer a disturbing critique of their fomenting anger against him. *Peshat*-like exegesis also appears in Paul's Letter to the Galatians (see Gal. 3:16). In his argument to present Christ as the fulfillment of Old Testament prophecy, the apostle points out that, according to Genesis, God promised the land of Canaan not to Abraham's *seeds* (plural) but to Abraham's *seed* (singular). This can only mean, suggests Paul, that texts like Genesis 12:7 and 13:15 point not merely to Abraham's entire family but especially to the *seed* of Abraham and, more specifically, to the seed of King David mentioned in 2 Samuel 7:12: Jesus Christ, the Davidic Messiah.[82] Of course, in the original context of Genesis it is quite clear that these texts were talking about Abraham's family, and Paul knows this.[83] That is why in Romans 4:18 he interprets the *seed* not as Christ but as Abraham's children. But the principle of *peshat* allowed Paul to capitalize on the term's two literal meanings, first as a collective noun that referred to Abraham's family and then as a singular noun that referred to the one man. It was by the hermeneutical rule of *gezerah shawah*, which I will discuss in a moment, that Paul finally connected this *seed* from Genesis with the *seed* of David promised in 2 Samuel.

Another prominent interpretive strategy in early Judaism was *pesher*, an approach used especially for interpreting the prophets.[84] It was one way of identifying the fulfillment of the prophetic words with a particular event or person. To put the matter simply, *pesher* interpretations declared "this is that," where "this" is the fulfillment of "that" prophetic word. One example of this approach comes from the ministry of Jesus himself.[85] After his final meal with the disciples, Jesus pessimistically appraised the situation with these words: "You [the disciples] will all fall away; for it is written, 'I will strike the shepherd, and the sheep will be scattered.'"[86] Now Jesus was quite right. The scattering of the sheep in Zechariah vividly illustrated the dispersion of the disciples in his hour of trial. Yet one cannot overlook the way in which Jesus (or the Gospel writers) changed the prophetic text from Zechariah, having altered its tenses, numbers, and vocabulary. "Strike the shepherds [plural]" became "strike the shepherd [singular]," and "draw out the sheep" became "the sheep will be scattered" (change of vocabulary and tense). As this example illustrates, *pesher* interpretations achieved their aim not only by drawing parallels between the prophecy and its fulfillment but also by making the parallels clearer through subtle (and not so subtle) changes to the biblical text. It

---

82. Donald H. Juel, "Interpreting Israel's Scriptures in the New Testament," in *A History of Biblical Interpretation*, vol. 1, *The Ancient Period*, ed. Alan J. Hauser and Duane F. Watson (Grand Rapids: Eerdmans, 2003), 283-303.

83. E. Earle Ellis, *Paul's Use of the Old Testament* (Grand Rapids: Baker Books, 1981), 70-71.

84. *Pesher* as an interpretive method is most closely associated with the Dead Sea Scrolls, but it appears as well in other texts and traditions. For the Dead Sea Scrolls evidence from Qumran, see Philip R. Davies, "Biblical Interpretation in the Dead Sea Scrolls," in Hauser and Watson, *Ancient Period*, 144-66.

85. See Longenecker, *Biblical Exegesis*, 54-58.

86. Mark 14:27 RSV; cf. Matt. 26:31; the quotation is from Zech. 13:7.

is a matter of some debate whether Paul and other New Testament authors used this method much, but Jesus used it on numerous occasions, as did other Jews—especially those who wrote the Dead Sea Scrolls.

Exegetical flexibility is also evident in those Jewish interpretive strategies known collectively as *midrash*.[87] Midrashic rules, such as those of Rabbi Hillel, dictated how the various texts of the Scripture could be properly related to one another.[88] For instance, according to one of those rules, *gezerah shawah* ("equal decree"), texts with the same or similar expressions, or even those that treated the same subject matter, were naturally related to one another. In the book of Romans this gave rise to what Richard Longenecker has described as Paul's "pearl stringing."[89] In a short text like Romans 3:10–18, for instance, Paul cites six Old Testament texts that bear on his theological concerns (Ps. 14; 5; 140; 10; Isa. 59; Ps. 36). Similar strings of citations occur in Romans 9:12–29; 10:18–21; 11:8–10; and 15:9–12. Early Christians also commonly used Hillel's first law, *qal wahomer* ("light and heavy"), which makes sense of two related texts—or related matters—by reasoning from an argument of lesser weight to one of greater weight. This method is often signaled by the words, "how much more." Consider the following examples from the Gospels, Paul, and the writer of Hebrews:

> If you then, who are evil, know how to give good gifts to your children, *how much more* will your Father who is in heaven give good things to those who ask him! (Matt. 7:11 RSV, italics mine)

> It is enough for the disciple to be like his teacher, and the servant like his master. If they have called the master of the house Beelzebul, *how much more* will they malign those of his household. (Matt. 10:25 RSV, italics mine)

> But if God so clothes the grass which is alive in the field today and tomorrow is thrown into the oven, *how much more* will he clothe you, O men of little faith! (Luke 12:28 RSV, italics mine)

> But the free gift is not like the trespass. For if many died through one man's trespass, *much more* have the grace of God and the free gift in the grace of that one man Jesus Christ abounded for many. (Rom. 5:15 RSV, italics mine)

> For if the sprinkling of defiled persons with the blood of goats and bulls and with the ashes of a heifer sanctifies for the purification of the flesh, *how much more* shall the blood of Christ, who through the eternal Spirit offered himself without blemish to God, purify your conscience from dead works to serve the living God. (Heb. 9:13–14 RSV, italics mine)

---

87. Gary G. Porton, "Rabbinic Midrash," in Hauser and Watson, *Ancient Period*, 198–224.
88. For Hillel's Seven Rules, see David Instone Brewer, *Techniques and Assumptions in Jewish Exegesis before 70 C.E.*, Texte und Studien zum antiken Judentum 30 (Tübingen: Mohr, 1992), 226.
89. Longenecker, *Biblical Exegesis*, 99–100.

Another example of New Testament midrash, this time from Paul, stems not from the apostle's own exegesis but from his use of older midrashic traditions. Readers will recall the biblical story of Israel's desert sojourn, told in Exodus and Numbers, in which God miraculously provided Israel with water from rocks along the way. In several midrashic texts, Jewish authorities imagined that these were not different rocks but actually a single rock, a sort of movable well that followed Israel during its desert travels.[90] Paul tells us that the movable rock was none other than Christ himself (see 1 Cor. 10:4). In doing so, Paul was extending Jewish midrash to serve a new christocentric purpose. So it is fair to say that Jesus and the New Testament writers both assumed and used midrashic methods of exegesis.

But early Jewish exegesis did not develop in a cultural vacuum. It was deeply affected by outside influences, especially by the Platonic allegories and typologies so prominent in Hellenistic interpretation. A good example appears in Paul's allegorical interpretation of Hagar and Sarah in Galatians 4.[91] Here, to support his argument that gentile Christians need not be circumcised, Paul interpreted Hagar as representing the law and Sarah as representing the promise. Scholars suspect that Paul used this allegory to counter his Judaizing opponents, who probably cited the circumcision of Hagar's son Ishmael (see Gen. 17) to support their view that gentile believers needed to observe circumcision and other Jewish rites.[92] Allegory was the convincing method of his day, so Paul used it in his argument.

Hellenistic influence is yet more prominent in the book of Hebrews.[93] The author employed Platonic exegesis ("types" and "antitypes") in order to interpret the Old Testament as a fleshly *antitype*, of which Jesus and the new covenant were the truer spiritual *types*.[94] The author even employed the Platonic technical term *antitypos* ("antitype") in his arguments (see Heb. 9:24; cf. 1 Pet. 3:21). According to this allegorical method, the Jewish high priest was a "type" corresponding to Christ, the Sabbath rest corresponded to heaven, the earthly tabernacle corresponded to a heavenly tabernacle, the Israelite animal sacrifices corresponded to Jesus's one sacrifice for all, and so forth. Similar allegorical interpretations are found in the works of Philo, a Jewish author who perhaps influenced the biblical author,[95] and also in

---

90. Peter E. Enns, "The 'Movable Well' in 1 Cor. 10:4: An Extrabiblical Tradition in an Apostolic Text," *Bulletin for Biblical Research* 6 (1996): 23-38.

91. See Juel, "Interpreting Israel's Scriptures," 289-90; Longenecker, *Biblical Exegesis*, 109-13.

92. C. K. Barrett, "The Allegory of Abraham, Sarah, and Hagar in the Argument of Galatians," in *Rechtfertigung: Festschrift für Ernst Käsemann zum 70. Geburtstag*, ed. Johannes Friedrich, Wolfgang Pohlmann, and Peter Stuhlmacher (Tübingen: Mohr, 1976), 1-16; E. D. Burton, *A Critical and Exegetical Commentary on the Epistle to the Galatians*, ICC (Edinburgh: T&T Clark, 1921), 555.

93. Luke Timothy Johnson, *Hebrews: A Commentary*, New Testament Library (Louisville: Westminster John Knox, 2006), 15-21; Craig R. Koester, *Hebrews*, AB (New York: Doubleday, 2001), 59-62, 97-100.

94. Harold W. Attridge, *The Epistle to the Hebrews*, Hermeneia (Philadelphia: Fortress, 1989), 263; Johnson, *Hebrews*, 242-43; Longenecker, *Biblical Exegesis*, 140-65.

95. See Kenneth L. Schenck, "Philo and the Epistle to the Hebrews: Ronald Williamson's Study after Thirty Years," *Studia Philonica Annual* 14 (2002): 112-35; R. McL. Wilson, *Hebrews*, NCB (Grand Rapids: Eerdmans, 1987), 22-24.

the writings of many Christian interpreters, most notably Origen (third century) and Augustine (fourth/fifth centuries).[96] It is rather easy to explain this exegetical phenomenon. Origen and Augustine, and we surmise the writer of Hebrews also, were among those deeply influenced by the Platonic philosophy and exegesis practiced in the Hellenistic world, particularly in Alexandria, Egypt. These authors read the Bible as Platonists because, apparently, they *were* Platonists—Christian Platonists, of course, but Platonists nonetheless.

To make these interpretive matters more complicated, there is good evidence that the New Testament writers not only used ancient methods of interpreting the Old Testament but sometimes presumed a different Old Testament—a different canon—than is presumed by traditional Christianity. Well-known examples of this phenomenon appear in the little book of Jude, a book so small that it has no chapter divisions at all. In Jude 9 the author refers to a dispute between the archangel Michael and Satan over the body of Moses. At issue for our purposes is not the content of the tradition but its source. Given that this dispute is nowhere described in our Old Testament, where did Jude find it? As it turns out, Jude's source is probably preserved in a fragmentary Latin manuscript.[97] I say "probably" because the ending of the text, which would have recorded the struggle over Moses's body, no longer exists. But the early fathers of the church, who also considered this question, knew that Jude's author had consulted a book called the *Assumption of Moses*.[98] Whatever this book was, the biblical author clearly took it seriously. This is because the event to which Jude refers—a struggle between an angel and Satan—could only be known to the *Assumption* through divine revelation. So we may conclude, I think, that Jude's author accepted the *Assumption of Moses* as inspired Scripture.

A similar situation arises in Jude 14–15, two verses that depend quite directly upon prophecies from the pseudepigraphic book of *1 Enoch*. The relevant texts are as follows:

> It was of these also that Enoch in the seventh generation from Adam prophesied, saying, "Behold, the Lord came with his holy myriads, to execute judgment on all, and to convict all the ungodly of all their deeds of ungodliness which they have committed in such an ungodly way, and of all the harsh things which ungodly sinners have spoken against him." (Jude 14–15 RSV)

> Behold, he will arrive with ten million of the holy ones in order to execute judgment upon all. He will destroy the wicked ones and censure all flesh on account of

---

96. Frances M. Young, "Alexandrian and Antiochene Exegesis," in *A History of Biblical Interpretation*, vol. 1, *The Ancient Tradition*, ed. Alan J. Hauser and Duane F. Watson (Grand Rapids: Eerdmans, 2003), 334–54; Richard A. Norris Jr., "Augustine and the Close of the Ancient Period of Interpretation," in Hauser and Watson, *Ancient Period*, 380–408, respectively.

97. J. Priest, "Testament of Moses," in *OTP*, 1:919–34.

98. For references in Origen, Clement of Alexandria, and other early Christian sources, see Richard J. Bauckham, *Jude, 2 Peter*, WBC (Waco: Word, 1983), 65–76.

everything that they have done, that which the sinners and wicked ones committed against him. (*1 Enoch* 1:9)[99]

Again, as in the case of the *Assumption of Moses*, it is quite natural to conclude that Jude's author accepted *1 Enoch* as a genuine book of prophecies.[100] But this presents an obvious theological difficulty, inasmuch as it brings the biblical author's viewpoint into direct conflict with the judgments of both modern scholarship and church tradition. Modern scholars are certain that the sources in question were very late pseudepigraphic compositions, falsely presented as the works of Moses and Enoch. And the church has rendered a canonical judgment that neither of these books was inspired words from God. The canonical difficulties are deeper still for evangelical Protestants, since in many instances the New Testament authors (and other early Christians) accepted as canonical those books that presently stand in the Apocrypha (and are still considered canonical by Catholicism and Orthodoxy). I will not pursue this line of inquiry any farther. It is enough to see that the New Testament authors sometimes embraced an Old Testament canon that differs from our own.

To summarize this portion of our discussion, it appears that the biblical authors used methods of Jewish and Hellenistic exegesis that most modern readers, especially modern evangelical readers, would never use or accept in our own day. This leads us back to the philosophical discussion presented in chapter 1. One implication of that discussion was that every human person is inescapably located within, and shaped by, a social and cultural context. What we have seen in this chapter so far, and especially in the present discussion, is that this was no less true of the biblical authors than of any other human beings. The biblical authors employed interpretive methods that were current in their own day, and did so simply because those were the only methods available in—and convincing to—their respective communities of faith. Paul used allegory, the author of Hebrews used typology, and Jude quoted *1 Enoch*, because these strategies were convincing to the ancient audiences of Scripture. And these strategies were convincing precisely because that was how the ancients were reading Scripture.

How *Human* Is the Biblical Perspective? Scripture's Religious and Political Propaganda

One of the most common ways to secure power in political and religious institutions is to compose literature that presents reality in a way that reinforces one's claim to authority. This can sometimes involve outright literary fabrications to

---

99. E. Isaac, "1 Enoch," in *OTP*, 1:13–14.
100. Peter H. Davids, "The Pseudepigrapha in the Catholic Epistles," in *The Pseudepigrapha and Early Biblical Interpretation*, ed. James H. Charlesworth and Craig A. Evans, Journal for the Study of the Pseudepigrapha Supplement Series 14 (Sheffield: JSOT Press, 1993), 225–45.

support one's viewpoint, or it might involve presenting history with a slant or bias that shapes the facts to suit political needs. According to most modern scholars, it seems that both types of propaganda appear in the Hebrew Bible.

Readers will recall from our earlier discussion that modern scholars have been able to reconstruct the basic features of the history of Israel's priesthood. Ezekiel 44:10–16 is the most important piece of evidence in this reconstruction. That text tells us the precise point at which the legitimate Israelite priesthood narrowed from including *all* Levites to including only *some* Levites (the Zadokites). This means that any texts that assume this narrowing probably date to the exile or afterward. Interestingly, some of the biblical texts that purport to be very old turn out to be among these late priestly texts.

Two such examples are found in Numbers 8 and 16. The first text tells the story of God's choice to give the Levites as a gift to the priests, as assistants in the daily task of ritual duty. Although this text purports to be from the Mosaic period, it presumes the distinction between priests and Levites that originated with Ezekiel during the exile. So the text actually dates to a much later period.[101] The same pattern also appears in Numbers 16, but the evidence is even stronger in this case. Here Korah the Levite and two men from the tribe of Reuben—Dathan and Abiram—strongly protest their exclusion from the priesthood. The tragic fate of these rebels is famous in the annals of divine punishment. Because of their mutinies against God's man, Moses, the ground opened up and swallowed their families. So again, the text ostensibly stems from the Mosaic period. Yet several lines of coalescing evidence suggest that the text as it stands is not that old. Not only does the story assume the exilic-era distinction between priests and Levites, but the story is itself somewhat odd. A careful reading of Numbers 16 reveals that its central characters are really Dathan and Abiram, not Korah.[102] Is it possible that the story originated as a rebellion of the Reubenites against the Levites, and that it was later edited—by adding Korah—to address Ezekiel's exclusion of most Levites from the priesthood? Is there any way to confirm this suspicion? Indeed there is.[103] The book of Deuteronomy, which modern scholars date earlier than Numbers 16, and which still assumes that all Levites are priests, knows about this story. But its allusion to the story knows only about the Reubenite rebellion of Dathan and Abiram (see Deut. 11:6). Korah and his family do not come into the picture. So all of the evidence—from Ezekiel, Deuteronomy, and Numbers—fits neatly together. For these reasons, scholars are fairly certain that these priestly texts from Numbers date to the late exilic and postexilic periods, when various

---

101. For an excellent discussion of this text as understood in the context of the history of Israel's priesthood, see Baruch A. Levine, *Numbers 1–20*, AB (Garden City, NY: Doubleday, 1993), 273–90.

102. For comments on Num. 16, see again Levine, *Numbers 1–20*, 405–32.

103. The Samaritan version of the Pentateuch attempted to fix this problem by adding "with all the men of Korah." For more on this issue, see A. D. H. Mayes, *Deuteronomy*, NCB (Grand Rapids: Eerdmans, 1981), 213; Eduard Nielsen, *Deuteronomium*, Handbuch zum Alten Testament 1/6 (Tübingen: Mohr, 1995), 122; Jeffrey H. Tigay, *Deuteronomy*, JPS Torah Commentary (Philadelphia: Jewish Publication Society, 1996), 111.

claimants struggled to secure priestly power in the wake of the temple's destruction and subsequent reconstruction. As a result, most critical scholars believe that these texts are not accurate histories of events in ancient Israel so much as later ideological texts, written as propaganda for or against various priestly groups.

Alongside this priestly propaganda, modern scholars also believe that political propaganda appears in the Old Testament. The best example is the so-called Apology of David, which appears in 1 and 2 Samuel.[104] Although the books of Samuel describe a protracted struggle for Israel's throne between the house of Saul and the house of David (see 2 Sam. 2:8–3:5), we are told that David never lifted a finger to harm his challengers from Saul's dynasty. Even the heir apparent from Saul's family, Jonathan, loved David and realized that David should be the next king. When David's military and political opponents—Saul, Jonathan, Abner, Ishbaal (or Ishbosheth)—begin to conveniently disappear one by one, we are assured again and again that David was innocent in these matters. When at last David slaughters the entire house of Saul—all seven of David's remaining competitors for the throne—we are told that David did so only because God required it (2 Sam. 21). In essence, someone wants us to believe that in every way David behaved respectfully toward his enemies from Saul's house, except when he was forced to kill them all. They also want us to see that David's opponent, Saul, was evil, impious, and rejected by God (1 Sam. 13, 15, 22, 28). The apology also defended David against the charge that he was a mercenary for the Philistines—the mortal enemies of Saul and Israel (see 1 Sam. 27, 29)—and against the charge that he sometimes killed Israelite citizens in order to seize their wives and property (1 Sam. 25). For all of these reasons, most critical scholars believe that the portrait of David found in 1 and 2 Samuel was drawn largely from political propaganda, whose design was to discredit Saul and to enhance David's claim to the throne by answering charges that he was a murderer and a traitor. This is a fairly standard view of the biblical account of David's life.

Many scholars would go even one step farther. They suspect not only that these texts are propaganda but also that David was not so innocent in these matters as the texts might suggest.[105] They suspect, for instance, that David was complicit in many of the deaths that are reported, that he was less than supportive when it came to Saul's regime, and that he fought as a Philistine mercenary against Israel. They also doubt that Saul's son, Jonathan, was as anxious to defend David's claim to the throne as the text suggests. While this dark portrait of David might strike us as problematic and even offensive at first glance, in the end it is perhaps not so different from the biblical portrait. For according to *any* reading of 2 Samuel 11, David was both an adulterer and a murderer. To add that he was also a Philistine

---

104. Kenton L. Sparks, "Propaganda," in *Dictionary of the Old Testament: Historical Books*, ed. Bill T. Arnold and H. G. M. Williamson (Downers Grove, IL: InterVarsity, 2005), 819–25; Walter Brueggemann, *First and Second Samuel*, Interpretation (Louisville: Westminster John Knox, 1990).

105. Baruch Halpern, *David's Secret Demons: Messiah, Murderer, Traitor, King* (Grand Rapids: Eerdmans, 2001); Steven L. McKenzie, *King David: A Biography* (Oxford: Oxford University Press, 2000).

mercenary, as critical scholars have done, would hardly make David less the man than he already is.

If the critics are right about the propaganda in 1–2 Samuel, then we will naturally wonder why the text relates to us the ugly matter of Uriah and Bathsheba, which can hardly have helped David's case. Scholars believe that this and a few similar exceptions to the pattern of propaganda in Samuel are best explained by the fact that the authors and editors who assembled the book lived long after the time of David. These historians probably did not know or care whether their sources were propagandistic because they were interested mainly in theological issues. In the case of David's sin against Uriah and Bathsheba, a common scholarly judgment is that this story was inserted in 2 Samuel 11 to explain why things went so poorly for David after he came to power, poor in the sense that Absalom killed another of David's sons and seized the throne from David.[106] Such a conclusion is borne out by the fact that David's life goes well before 2 Samuel 11 and terribly after it. Yet even in this troubling story, it is possible that we have an apologetic text, though its beneficiary would not have been David. A more likely beneficiary would have been David's son, Solomon. One charge that may have been raised against Solomon was that he was a son not of David but of Uriah, Bathsheba's first husband. Insofar as the biblical story made Solomon's patrimony clear, it would have served as propaganda for his claim to David's throne.[107] But even if this reading of the story turns out to be wrong, the negative portrait of David in 2 Samuel 11 only highlights the rule: much of 1–2 Samuel originated as propaganda for David's regime.

Now it seems to me that the critical case against David is circumstantial, so we can at least entertain the idea that he was innocent of the charges that his enemies leveled against him. After all, we have every reason to suppose that David's opponents sometimes lied about him. Nevertheless, to be a scholar—even a Christian scholar—means that we should consider the possibility that parts of the Bible, particularly those dealing with priestly and political power, may well have originated as pieces of ideological propaganda. The presence of this sort of material in the Bible, were we to admit it, would seem to raise serious theological questions about certain traditional preconceptions of Scripture. How can it be that God's revealed Word contains misleading Judean political propaganda? If it does, how do we put those parts of the Bible to faithful and fruitful theological uses? These are very important questions that I will attempt to answer.[108]

The Changing Face of Historical Criticism

I should say something at this point about recent developments in biblical studies as these relate to the practice of historical criticism. Nowadays one frequently

---

106. McKenzie, *King David*, 34–35.
107. Sparks, "Propaganda," 821.
108. See chap. 10, pp. 328–33.

hears pronouncements that biblical criticism is passé at best and dead at worst.[109] This claim resonates with some evangelicals who oppose historical criticism.[110] Though in my opinion these kinds of comments overstate the case, there is some truth in them. Classical historical criticism emerged during the Enlightenment and so imbibed deeply of its overconfident epistemology. But postmodernism has changed all of this. As N. T. Wright expressed it, "Nobody really believes any more the old idea that biblical scholars, equipped with neutral and objective tools and methods, provide the 'facts' about scripture which the systematic theologians can then 'interpret.'"[111] As a result, most biblical scholars now take one of two alternative paths, which correspond closely to the two branches of postmodernism I described in chapter 1.

First, a majority of scholars continue to practice modest forms of what we might call "postmodern" historical criticism.[112] By this I mean that they still try to understand the biblical materials in light of their historical contexts, in terms of things like the ancient author and audience. But this brand of postmodern criticism no longer suffers the illusion that scholarship yields the brute facts "just as they are," and it is more skeptical about—and less interested in—some of the traditional issues that have exercised scholars in the last generation. Contemporary Old Testament scholars tend to be much less interested, for instance, in reconstructing the process of the Pentateuch's composition, largely because the project strikes them as uninteresting and in some cases too speculative. Philosophically speaking, this approach reflects the influence of practical realism, a family of postmodern epistemologies (described in chapter 1) that view good scholarship as modest in its goals and as yielding results that are adequate rather than precisely accurate. In practice, this kind of scholarship does not look very different from the older brand of historical criticism. It weighs out the evidence, draws conclusions, and then decides how convincing those conclusions finally are; and it is not afraid to speak with confidence when confidence is warranted. But scholars who fully embrace this postmodern approach tend to be interested in different kinds of academic questions, and tend to be more attentive to the way in which their own perspectives affect their scholarship. Ideally, they are also more open to reconsidering their scholarly convictions in the light of new evidence or new arguments. This is the sort of direction in which I, for one, would like to see biblical scholarship head.

---

109. For two recent discussions of this issue, see James Barr, *History and Ideology in the Old Testament: Biblical Studies at the End of a Millennium* (Oxford: Oxford University Press, 2000); John J. Collins, *The Bible after Babel: Historical Criticism in a Postmodern Age* (Grand Rapids: Eerdmans, 2005).

110. V. Philips Long, "Historiography of the Old Testament," in *The Face of Old Testament Studies*, ed. David W. Baker and Bill T. Arnold (Grand Rapids: Baker Academic, 1999), 145–75; Gerald A. Klingbeil, "Historical Criticism," in *Dictionary of the Old Testament: Pentateuch*, ed. T. Desmond Alexander and David W. Baker (Downers Grove, IL: InterVarsity, 2003), 401–20.

111. N. T. Wright, *The Last Word: Beyond the Bible Wars to a New Understanding of the Authority of Scripture* (San Francisco: HarperSanFrancisco, 2005), 16.

112. See, for example, the comments by F. W. Dobbs-Allsopp, "Rethinking Historical Criticism," *BibInt* 7 (1999): 235–71.

THE PROBLEM OF BIBLICAL CRITICISM   131

The other postmodern version of biblical scholarship is represented by scholars who embrace some kind of antirealism. In this line of thought, the goal is no longer to understand the biblical text in historical terms—in terms of its original author and audience—but rather in terms of how the text plays out in the perspectives of modern readers. David J. A. Clines lays out this hermeneutical agenda: "If there are no 'right' interpretations, and no validity beyond the assent of various interest groups, biblical interpreters have to give up the goal of determinate and universally acceptable interpretations, and devote themselves to producing interpretation they can sell—in whatever mode is called for by the communities they choose to serve."[113]

An example of this approach appears in a recent article on the Song of Songs, written by Virginia Burrus and Stephen Moore.[114] At one point Burrus and Moore comment on that odd sequence in the Song, where the female protagonist is beaten in the streets (see Song 5). Though there is not the slightest evidence for it in this text, these authors conclude that one possible reading of the episode would view it as a "sado-masochistic fantasy." That this should strike anyone as fanciful will be no surprise to Burrus and Moore, who admit that it is "a blissful act of willful misreading." But this is precisely the point. Antirealist interpreters of the Bible no longer accept the theoretical constraints represented by ancient authors and contexts. Instead, these scholars revel in creative and fanciful readings of the text, even when they can sense—as Burrus and Moore evidently do—that their readings cannot suit the original situation of the biblical discourse.[115]

But Burrus and Moore are perhaps exceptional among the antirealists. I suspect that many scholars who have taken to this philosophical road do not openly admit their epistemic allegiances. The so-called biblical minimalists probably fit this bill.[116] These theorists ostensibly carry out their work by the canons of standard criticism, by which they attempt to demonstrate that most of the Old Testament narrative is very late, Hellenistic-era fiction. But because these scholars are committed to antirealism, I would suggest that their historical exercises are in form only; the standard critical rhetoric is being used to secure scholarly conclusions

---

113. David J. A. Clines, "A World Established on Water (Psalm 24): Reader-Response, Deconstruction and Bespoke Interpretation," in *The New Literary Criticism and the Hebrew Bible*, ed. J. Cheryl Exum and David J. A. Clines, JSOTSup 143 (Sheffield: Sheffield Academic Press, 1993), 87.

114. Virginia Burrus and Stephen D. Moore, "Unsafe Sex: Feminism, Pornography, and the Song of Songs," *BibInt* 11 (2003): 24–52. I was alerted to this example by John Collins in *Bible after Babel*, 16.

115. For a critique of this hermeneutical disposition, see Dobbs-Allsopp, "Rethinking Historical Criticism."

116. I have in mind the likes of scholars like Davies, Lemche, Thompson, and Whitelam. For representative works, see Philip R. Davies, *In Search of "Ancient Israel,"* JSOTSup 148 (Sheffield: Sheffield Academic Press, 1992); Niels Peter Lemche, *The Israelites in History and Tradition* (London: SPCK; Louisville: Westminster John Knox, 1998); Thomas L. Thompson, *The Mythic Past: Biblical Archaeology and the Myth of Israel* (New York: Basic, 1999); Keith W. Whitelam, *The Invention of Ancient Israel: The Silencing of Palestinian History* (New York: Routledge, 1996). For a somewhat polemical critique of minimalism, see William G. Dever, *What Did the Biblical Writers Know and When Did They Know It?* (Grand Rapids: Eerdmans, 2001), 1–40.

that were derived via antirealism. So the author and original audience do not really come into it.

At any rate, as I have said, it seems to me that any obituary for historical criticism much overstates the case. Standard biblical criticism, which attempts to understand the text of Scripture in terms of its original historical context, is still very influential in the landscape of modern biblical studies. Whether a shift of emphasis will ever appear, which moves even more in the direction of left-wing postmodernism, remains to be seen. But to my mind it is certain that such an extreme development, if it should appear, would be no friend to serious scholarship, much less to Christian theology.

Conclusions

At this point I would direct our attention again to the two initial questions with which we began. First, what are the exegetical results of an historical-critical reading of the Bible? Second, is it theologically legitimate to read the Bible through the lens of historical criticism? In this chapter we have explored the first question in some detail, with striking results. Critical readings of the Bible produce a portrait of the text that is often at odds with traditional readings of the sacred page. These readings challenge traditional views of the authorship and dating of the texts, raise serious questions about the historicity of key biblical events, aver that Scripture provides diverse and sometimes contradictory theological opinions, and in some cases even impugn the motives and insights of the Bible's human authors, who on occasion become the ostensible purveyors of failed prophecies, political ideology, and social propaganda. If the practitioners of biblical criticism are right on even a modest portion of their claims, then God's written Word certainly reflects far more humanity than traditional evangelicals might expect. This observation leads us inexorably back to our second question: Given the results of modern biblical criticism, is it legitimate to read the Bible through the lens of historical criticism in the first place? We shall begin to consider this question in the following chapter by examining the evangelical responses to modern biblical criticism.

4

"Traditional" Responses to Biblical Criticism

Introduction

The apparent tensions between critical and traditional readings of Scripture are sometimes factual and serious. When we explore these tensions and the various attempts to resolve them, it means joining a conversation that has been going on for some time. False starts and dead ends abound in this ongoing dialogue, but it seems to me that considerable progress has also been made, not only in clarifying the problems but also in outlining the kinds of solutions that are necessary. In this chapter and the next, we shall attempt to reap the benefits of this conversation by surveying both its failures and successes.

As I pointed out in the introduction, there have been three basic responses to modern biblical criticism: the traditional, constructive, and secular responses. *Traditional* responses to biblical criticism guard the authority of Scripture by rejecting biblical criticism's troublesome conclusions. In this vein of thought, biblical criticism leads to faulty conclusions because it has been wrongly done or because it is an illegitimate exercise in the first place. By way of contrast, *constructive* responses to biblical criticism accept the basic assumptions and conclusions of biblical scholarship but do not regard these as fundamentally hostile to traditional religious belief. Indeed, many constructionists believe that the standard results of biblical criticism can help develop healthier doctrines of Scripture and deeper understandings of our faith. This is why integrative responses to faith and criticism have often been dubbed *believing criticism*. I will highlight and examine a wide range of these constructive responses to biblical criticism in the following chapter. As for the *secular* response to biblical criticism, I will not consider it in any depth for an obvious reason. Its proponents regard biblical criticism as sure evidence that the Bible is nothing other than a human book. So the secular responses to modern criticism cannot provide us with any extensive resources for resolving the tensions between faith and criticism.

As the title of this chapter suggests, the subject at hand is the traditional response to biblical criticism. I have placed "traditional" in quotes because in this context the term is oxymoronic. Insofar as this response is to *modern* biblical criticism, it is perhaps most fittingly described as a "modern-traditional" perspective. And as a modern perspective, I find that it should be carefully distinguished from the traditional approaches of premodern Christian scholars referred to in chapter 1. For in many respects the scholars of the early church—men like Augustine and the other fathers—were much more open to critical conclusions than are their modern counterparts. So, while Augustine and modern conservatives certainly share a strong, traditional reflex that respects the written Word of God, they have very different tolerances for critical conclusions about Scripture. All of this will become clearer as we move along.

Traditional responses to modern biblical criticism have appeared in many Christian communities over the years, in various Protestant, Catholic, and Orthodox permutations. But the most energetic response to biblical criticism has arguably come from the fundamentalist and evangelical branches of modern Protestant Christianity, particularly in the United States. I say this not only because conservative evangelicals have been strident in their opposition to biblical criticism, but also because, unlike Catholicism and many of the Protestant traditions, evangelicalism as a whole has never fully come to terms with critical scholarship. So my special interest in the evangelical response to biblical criticism stems in part from the fact that I am an evangelical myself, and in part because it is one of the last Christian communities in the West that remains largely antagonistic toward modern biblical scholarship.

Evangelical arguments against biblical criticism vary widely in quality, ranging from simple and unsophisticated critiques that seem to hang in epistemological thin air, to more complex and nuanced critiques that should be taken more seriously. Nevertheless, in the end, I do not believe that any of these arguments resolve the essential conflict between biblical criticism and traditional readings of Scripture. So, while there is much to be valued in these conservative theological critiques of biblical criticism, one of my primary purposes in this chapter is to demonstrate that these traditional responses do not adequately resolve the theological difficulties presented by biblical criticism. The solutions lie elsewhere.

It is unfortunate that my concerns about evangelical biblical scholarship can be demonstrated only by examining and critiquing the work of several representative scholars. All of these evangelicals are people that I respect, as human beings and as fellow believers, whose love for God and the church is laudable. The critiques that I offer are only of their scholarly approaches and conclusions and not at all of the individuals themselves, whose spiritual qualities reflect a deep commitment to Christ. Though I have tried very hard to understand and fairly represent the work of these scholars, I plead in advance for grace at those points where I have failed in this important duty.

Evangelical rejections of historical criticism fall out into four main types. One of these, the first that I will discuss, is different from the others because, to my mind, its rejection of biblical criticism is *entirely justified*. I do not mean to imply that this response has correctly understood biblical criticism, for I do not believe that it has. I only mean that those who respond to historical criticism in this way have warrant for doing so. The three remaining evangelical responses to biblical criticism differ from the first because, in my opinion, they are epistemically unwarranted. Those holding these three positions either know, or should know, that their solutions are inadequate. These three mistaken solutions include (1) fideistic responses to biblical criticism, (2) philosophical responses to biblical criticism, and (3) a response that Mark Noll has aptly dubbed "critical anti-criticism."[1] The lion's share of our attention will be devoted to the last of these. But first things first.

Warranted but Erroneous Rejections of Biblical Criticism

In the days before his evangelistic ministry exploded on the world scene, Rev. Billy Graham went through a crisis of faith because of tensions he recognized between modern biblical scholarship and his traditional view of biblical authority.[2] Graham was not a biblical scholar himself, but one of his close friends, Charles Templeton, had studied in graduate school in order to resolve his doubts about Scripture's reliability. As often happens, Templeton's studies only made these doubts grow, and during the course of his relationship with Graham the two men frequently discussed the problems that Templeton was discovering in Scripture. According to Graham, the intellectual and spiritual struggles introduced by this discussion eventually brought terrific pain at the base of his skull, finally bringing him to a state of nervous tension and exhaustion. The situation came to a head in the summer of 1945, when Graham placed his Bible on a tree stump and finally put an end to the matter with this prayer: "Oh God: I cannot prove certain things, I cannot answer some of the questions Chuck Templeton is raising, some of the other people are raising, but I accept this book by faith as the Word of God."[3] Graham went on to become perhaps the greatest evangelist for the Christian gospel since the apostle Paul.

---

1. Mark A. Noll, *Between Faith and Criticism: Evangelicals, Scholarship, and the Bible in America*, 2nd ed. (Grand Rapids: Baker Books, 1991), 156–58.
2. J. Pollock, *Billy Graham: The Authorized Biography* (New York: McGraw-Hill, 1966), 53.
3. Ibid.

Even if the assertions of historical criticism are true, is it possible that Graham had *warrant* for his rejection of biblical criticism? I believe that the answer is yes. Beliefs have warrant when we have good and sufficient reasons for holding them. For instance, we can judge that ancient peoples, lacking the benefits of modern science, had warrant for their mistaken belief that the earth is flat. Conversely, those who are sufficiently versed in modern cosmology do not have warrant for believing in a flat earth. Warrant only suggests that we have good and adequate reasons for our beliefs, not that our beliefs are accurate and true. Let us return to the case of Billy Graham. All of us know that there are some things we must accept by faith. I speak here not only of God and religion but of all sorts of things that we believe. It is simply impossible for us to run around checking and proving everything that we believe, and we certainly cannot expect that the average man or woman in the church pew, presented with the tensions between critical and traditional views of the Bible, would have the time, resources, and expertise to resolve the problems. Graham was not a biblical scholar and was not much familiar with the issues and problems that confronted his friend. Consequently, it seems to me that Graham's rejection of biblical criticism was entirely warranted. Unfortunately, however, this option—a warranted rejection of biblical criticism—was not really open to Charles Templeton. As a scholar his mind could clearly see the critical problems, but his evangelical tradition insisted that the true faith would be imperiled if the problems in the Bible were real. One of the purposes of the present volume is to chart out a theological path that will allow the Charles Templetons in our world to keep their faith and their intellectual integrity at the same time.

Fideistic Refutations of Biblical Criticism

Let us consider a somewhat different interpretation of Reverend Graham's life. When Billy Graham was struggling with his questions about the Bible, he was a theologically educated rising star in evangelical ministry and was becoming a close associate of many evangelical academicians, not least his friend Templeton. Given Graham's intellectual and spiritual prominence in evangelicalism, and given that he could see the biblical difficulties sufficiently well to struggle with them to the point of intellectual and spiritual exhaustion, was it not incumbent upon Graham either to work out the problems or, at least, to accept the difficulties as real? If the answer to this question is yes, then Graham's rejection of biblical criticism was not warranted but unwarranted, because he was unwilling to test and shape the contours of his beliefs about the Bible in accordance with the reasonable observations and arguments of his friend. *Fideism*, more popularly known as "blind faith," is the term that philosophers use to refer to such instances in which religious views are held so intensely that factual realities and rational evaluation have no power to alter or affect them. Fideists certainly hold many true beliefs, but when their tightly held beliefs turn out to be false, there is no way to test them, even in cases where evidence or experience should make clear that there is something quite mistaken about their beliefs.

Almost everyone admits, at least in theory, that fideism is a serious threat to our intellectual vitality. Hence it would be nice to have ready-made diagnostic tools for recognizing and exposing fideism, but identifying fideism turns out to be a dicey business. As it is normally understood, fideism is present only when it prevents *adequately informed* individuals from altering their beliefs in light of new evidence against those beliefs. The chief difficulty, of course, is that it is essentially impossible to determine the precise tipping point at which one knows, or should know, that their beliefs stand on shaky ground. So, while we cannot help noticing and critiquing intellectual responses that seem fideistic, we should remember that only God himself can provide a sure-fire diagnosis of fideism—and we are not God! That said, we still have a responsibility to strive, as best we can, to identify instances of fideism in ourselves and in others.

Because fideism is considered intellectually unseemly by most people, it is almost never recognized by fideists themselves. Fideism is usually identified from an "outsider" (*etic*) viewpoint before it is considered—if it is considered at all—by those who are fideistic "insiders" (the *emic* viewpoint). What are the telltale signs of fideism?

1. Fideism is often indicated by *special pleading*, by those instances where the rules of evidence and rationality that we employ when examining our own faith differ substantially from the standards we employ in evaluating the religious beliefs of others. For example, although evangelicals often attempt to discredit the faith of Latter-day Saints by pointing out unfulfilled prophecies in the Book of Mormon, these same evangelicals will not entertain a similar critique of their own faith when the prophecies of Ezekiel and Daniel seem to have failed.[4] A fair assessment of Mormonism should allow Mormons the same flexibility for handling unfulfilled prophecies that evangelical Christians grant themselves.

2. Fideism is also indicated when we reject certain theories and opinions simply because these opinions belong to non-Christians or to Christians who have been supposedly "blinded" by non-Christians. The sentiment behind this apologetic move is enshrined in the saying of Saint Hilary of Poitiers: "Those situated outside the church are not able to grasp an understanding of the divine discourse."[5] Surely there is truth in this dictum, but it is simply wrong to aver that, in matters of scriptural interpretation and ancient history, every Christian opinion is superior to every non-Christian interpretation. History demonstrates quite satisfactorily that those within the church often get things wrong, and those outside often get things right.

3. A third indication of fideism appears when an unusual or unexpected amount of effort is necessary to defend our beliefs. For instance, one wonders

---

4. Gleason L. Archer, *A Survey of Old Testament Introduction*, rev. ed. (Chicago: Moody Press, 1985), 21.

5. Hilaire de Poitiers, *Sur Matthieu*, 2 vols., Sources chrétiennes 254, 258 (Paris: Cerf, 1978–1979), 1:296.

why a prominent evangelical scholar required an "encyclopedia" to resolve the apparent errors in a Bible that he claimed was free of human error.[6] Is it not possible, in light of so many difficulties, that the author's beliefs about the Bible were in some respect mistaken?

4. Perhaps the most telling indicator of fideism appears when we find ourselves believing that our own view of things is literally "what God says" while the views we oppose reflect "what human beings say." Consider this example from a fundamentalist book on biological evolution: "If the days of creation [in Genesis 1] are really 'geologic ages' of millions of years, then the gospel message is undermined at its foundation because it puts death, disease, thorns, and suffering before the Fall. This idea also shows an erroneous approach to Scripture—that the Word of God can be interpreted on the basis of the fallible theories of sinful people."[7] To be sure, the author of this statement has his finger on a potentially significant theological difficulty raised by evolution, namely, that death seems to have entered creation before the fall of humanity. Nevertheless, his understanding of the ideological conflict itself is quite erroneous. Although the author describes the situation as a quarrel between God's infallible Word and fallible human science, this is an illusion created by the assumption that his interpretation of Scripture is a perfect reflection of "what God says." In reality, however, the conflict is not between the Word of God and human science but between *fallible human interpretations of Scripture* and *fallible human interpretations of nature*. By sleight of hand, the author implicitly assumed that his own interpretation of Scripture was infallible, thereby shielding his "infallible" views from the criticisms of modern science. His fideism is perhaps emically unconscious, but it is also intellectually insidious.

Although the example just cited might strike us as unrefined and unsophisticated, this is not true of all fideistic responses to biblical criticism. A more sophisticated example of fideism is found in the theological work of Carl F. H. Henry, who is generally recognized as one of evangelicalism's founding fathers. Henry rejected the standard results of biblical criticism, but being a theologian he rarely confronted the biblical critics head-on. His primary contribution to the evangelical debate with biblical criticism was theological. He argued strenuously that the Bible does not—in fact, cannot—contain errors of any sort on any matters whatsoever.[8] Errors are logically excluded by the syllogism "God does not err, God inspired Scripture, therefore Scripture is inerrant." If the Bible contained errors, said Henry, it could not serve its authoritative role in the church because we could no longer know with certainty where the Bible speaks truly and where it does not.

Henry's arguments are thoroughly Cartesian, of course. He desires indubitable religious knowledge and fully believes that he can get it from an inerrant Bible.

---

6. Gleason L. Archer, *Encyclopedia of Bible Difficulties* (Grand Rapids: Zondervan, 1982).
7. D. Batten, ed., *The Revised and Expanded Answers Book: The 20 Most-Asked Questions about Creation, Evolution, and the Book of Genesis, Answered!* (Green Forest, AR: Master Books, 1990), 33.
8. Carl F. H. Henry, *God, Revelation, and Authority*, 5 vols. (Waco: Word, 1976–1983), 4:162–219.

How, then, does Henry handle the actual biblical features highlighted by modern critics, which seem to suggest that there are human errors in Scripture? Following the lead of B. B. Warfield, Henry argues that our doctrine of Scripture *cannot* be inductively derived from what Scripture does and how it works; we must begin instead by deductively learning what the Bible explicitly teaches about itself. If we begin at this deductive starting point, Henry believes that we will find that the Bible indeed claims to be the inspired, inerrant, and authoritative Word of God. So, although it might seem reasonable to settle the issue of inerrancy by simply looking at the Bible to see if it contains any errors, Henry believes that this approach to the problem is unjustified. Once we deductively recognize that Scripture claims or implies its own inerrancy, says Henry, we may safely assume that any critical conclusions that inductively imply error in Scripture are quite mistaken, either because of poor reasoning or because we do not have all of the data that we need to reach the correct conclusion. So much for biblical criticism.

How should we characterize Henry's response to biblical criticism? Let me say at the outset that it is entirely appropriate to embrace theological commitments and to allow those commitments to shape our view of the data we interpret. In fact, it must be so. As we saw in the previous chapter, however, the problems uncovered by biblical critics are neither minor nor insignificant. The difficulties are broad and comprehensive, a veritable avalanche of data that is far too substantial to be swept aside with the flimsy theological broom used by Henry. So far as I can tell, the only conclusion that one can draw is that Henry was unwilling to allow the biblical data itself to seriously challenge his own beliefs about the Bible. His response to biblical criticism was essentially fideistic because he used his deductive theories about the Bible as a shield to exclude inductive insights based on the Bible's actual content. While this may seem like harsh criticism for a theologian so accomplished as Henry, I believe that fideism of this sort subtly animates not only the work of Henry but also of many other evangelical responses to biblical criticism.

Before proceeding a step further, let me reiterate a point I made earlier: I am not the least troubled by the evangelical impulse to claim that the Bible is inerrant. Orthodoxy demands that God does not err, and this implies, of course, that God does not err in Scripture. But it is one thing to argue that God does not err in Scripture; it is quite another thing to argue that the human authors of Scripture did not err. Perhaps what we need is a way of understanding Scripture that paradoxically affirms inerrancy while admitting the human errors in Scripture. As we shall see, such a theological solution not only exists, but has existed for a long time.

Philosophical Critiques of Biblical Criticism

As soon as the great controversies about biblical criticism appeared at the end of the nineteenth century, fundamentalists were already attacking modern biblical criticism at its roots, claiming that the whole critical enterprise was based on naturalistic Enlightenment assumptions that were destructive to the Christian faith. Philosophical arguments of this sort are still being made against biblical criticism and tend to be fideistic, but in recent years the philosophical arguments against biblical criticism have become more sophisticated because evangelicals are adopting postmodernism's powerful critique of the Enlightenment. As the new argument goes, biblical criticism was a product of Enlightenment thinking. Now that postmodernism has revealed the fatal flaws in Enlightenment-style epistemologies, the validity of historical criticism necessarily falls with them. In order to explore these philosophical critiques of biblical criticism in more detail, I would like to consider two somewhat different examples, one from the work of Iain Provan (an evangelical biblical scholar) and the other from Alvin Plantinga (an evangelical philosopher).

The difficulty that Provan tackles is the common critical conclusion that many of the events narrated in Israel's literature—such as the Israelites' exodus from Egypt—do not pass modern tests for historicity.[9] Provan argues that these negative results are unwarranted because they stem directly from biblical criticism's excessive dedication to two errant Enlightenment assumptions: epistemic optimism and skepticism toward tradition. Biblical critics optimistically believe that they can reconstruct and narrate Israel's history *as it actually transpired*, and they further believe that this is best accomplished by assuming a very skeptical stance toward the historical value of Israel's narrative traditions. According to Provan, both the epistemic confidence (about getting Israel's history right) and the evidential suspicion (of the biblical testimony) of biblical criticism are symptoms of the Enlightenment's faulty Cartesian epistemology, an epistemology whose hallmarks are (as we may recall from chapter 1) epistemic optimism and suspicion of tradition. According to Provan, biblical critics compound these difficulties still more by placing greater confidence in the ancient textual and archaeological evidence than in the biblical text itself.

As an alternative to this Enlightenment skepticism, Provan would have us replace biblical scholarship's futile quest for an indubitable "knowledge of the past" with "faith in Israel's testimony." The key words here are *faith* and *testimony*. Provan insists that what we call historical "knowledge" is always an exercise in "faith," because our claims about history are possible only because we have placed our *faith* in the *testimony* of the historical sources that we use. In this regard, the historian studying ancient Israel should listen sympathetically to all of the relevant testimony, including not only the ancient archaeological and textual evidence but also Israel's own testimony about its past. It simply will not do, says Provan, to assume that the nonbiblical "testimonies" from Assyria and Egypt are more accurate and objective than the testimony of the biblical authors themselves.

---

9. Iain Provan, "Knowing and Believing: Faith in the Past," in *"Behind" the Text: History and Biblical Interpretation*, ed. Craig G. Bartholomew et al., SHS 4 (Grand Rapids: Zondervan, 2003), 229–66.

Provan concludes from his observations that critical scholars should give up their principled distrust of the Old Testament histories and listen to the Bible's testimony about ancient Israelite history. The result, we may presume, is that scholars will find adequate evidence for the historicity of events like Israel's miraculous deliverance from Egypt. This is precisely how things come out in Provan's jointly authored book on Israel's history.[10]

Now in principle it seems to me that Provan is undoubtedly correct. There is no such thing as perfect and unmediated access to human history. All human perceptions of the past—and of the present—are shaped by our biases and ideologies. Provan is also right to demand that the biblical evidence be given the same sort of consideration as other Near Eastern sources of information, such as the archaeological evidence and ancient textual evidence. On both of these points I agree with Provan. But there are some difficulties with his proposal. First, I find it somewhat inaccurate to claim, as Provan does, that "knowledge" is no longer knowledge but instead a variety of "faith." To be sure, Provan is correct to assert that, in our postmodern age, "knowledge" is no longer indubitable in the Enlightenment sense but is based instead on sources of information that we trust. Nevertheless, there is a great deal of difference—even for a postmodernist—between the beliefs that we hold as "certain" and those where we have lower, or at least different, confidence levels. By suggesting that every epistemic claim rests on "faith" (which is true, I think), Provan creates an impression that his faith in the testimony of Israel's historians is necessarily justified, but this does not follow.

All of us know that some historical testimonies are better than others, and that some testimonies are in fact very poor sources of history. So I would ask: Do we have warrant for supposing that Israel's historical narratives provide us with historically accurate testimony about events in ancient Israel? Provan believes that modern critical scholars have carelessly assumed that the answer is no, but it seems to me that this is not so. First, most biblical scholars accept as historical the basic outline of Israel's past as found in the books of Samuel and Kings.[11] Certainly they do not accept all of this testimony at face value, but neither do they accept in a straightforward way all of the historical testimony from Assyria, Babylonia, and Egypt. But, more to the point, where biblical scholars are skeptical about the Bible's portrait of Israel's history, this is not because scholars have carelessly *ignored* the biblical evidence but rather because they have carefully *considered* it. We saw in chapter 3, for instance, that modern scholars doubt the historicity of some parts of the Pentateuch because it provides differing accounts of the same episodes, reflects viewpoints of a time long after the putative events it narrates, and offers a sketch

---

10. Iain Provan, V. Philips Long, and Tremper Longman III, *A Biblical History of Israel* (Louisville: Westminster John Knox, 2003).

11. This is true even of fairly skeptical scholars, such as Liverani, Miller/Hayes, and Soggin. See Mario Liverani, *Israel's History and the History of Israel* (London; Oakville, CT: Equinox, 2005); J. Maxwell Miller and John H. Hayes, *A History of Ancient Israel and Judah* (Philadelphia: Westminster, 2006); J. Alberto Soggin, *A History of Ancient Israel* (Philadelphia: Westminster, 1985).

of the past that does not cohere with the extensive anthropological, linguistic, and historical evidence that we find in other sources from the ancient Near East. Moreover, modern scholars are fairly certain that the Pentateuch is not a book of historical "testimony" at all. The Pentateuch certainly contains Israelite views of history, but on the whole the Pentateuch is better understood as an anthology of Israelite laws, genealogies, folktales, myths, legends, and historical traditions. Now if the authors and editors of the Pentateuch were anthologists rather than mere historians, then it no longer pays to assume that their narratives should be taken as straightforward "testimonies" about Israel's past, as Provan insists that we do. One must first consider which portions of the Pentateuch pass as historical testimony, and then one must determine whether that testimony—based as it is on fallible sources and traditions—is likely to yield historical fruit. In the end, I would conclude that Provan's attempt to resolve the difficulties presented by biblical criticism does not take us very far, mainly because his diagnosis of the situation is mistaken in important ways.

Plantinga's philosophical critique of modern biblical criticism shares some features with the approach of Provan, particularly in its emphasis on the problems of the Enlightenment.[12] He claims that historical criticism is founded on Enlightenment assumptions that are essentially hostile to the concept of divine revelation, in either word or deed. Biblical critics operate as atheists or agnostics, who assume that faith is either out of order or should be set aside in matters of scholarship. As a result, they also set aside the authority of the Bible and such central Christian beliefs as the incarnation and virgin birth. This amounts to nothing less than the wholesale rejection of the Christian faith. Because historical criticism rests on these erroneous naturalistic assumptions, Plantinga feels that "the traditional Christian can rest easy with the claims of HBC [Historical Biblical Criticism]; she need feel no obligation, intellectual or otherwise, to modify her belief in light of its claims and alleged results."[13]

Were Plantinga's description of biblical criticism accurate, he would *perhaps* have it right. However, historical criticism does not necessarily involve purely naturalistic assumptions. A biblical scholar can believe in God, miracles, divine revelation, and the resurrection of Christ and still notice that Moses did not write most of the Pentateuch, that Isaiah was written by more than one person, that Daniel contains *ex eventu* prophecies, and that the four Gospels do not always add up historically. Since it is precisely these historical judgments about the authorship, date, and nature of the biblical books that create difficulties for the traditional viewpoint, Plantinga's arguments do not help us resolve the tensions between traditional and critical views of Scripture. On the question of biblical scholarship, Plantinga has not adequately explored the territory that

---

12. Alvin Plantinga, "Two (or More) Kinds of Scripture Scholarship," in *Warranted Christian Belief* (Oxford: Oxford University Press, 2000), 374–421. This portion of Plantinga's book also appears in Bartholomew et al., *"Behind" the Text*, 19–57.

13. Plantinga, *Warranted Christian Belief*, 418.

lies between secular biblical scholars and the uninformed Christian sitting in a church pew.

Plantinga's thesis was taken to task in rejoinders by two biblical scholars, Robert Gordon and Craig Bartholomew.[14] As a result Plantinga backed off somewhat from his critique of biblical criticism, admitting that there may be a type of biblical criticism that is legitimately Christian. But having done this, he failed to recognize the difficulty. Once he admitted that Christians can arrive legitimately at critical conclusions, he then landed right back where he was at the beginning of his paper: the church is confronted by, and must respond to, the difficulties uncovered by modern biblical criticism.

Before turning to our next topic, I would like to note the strong tendency in Provan and Plantinga—and in other philosophical critiques of historical criticism—to carry their criticisms of the Enlightenment too far.[15] Although Enlightenment-era epistemologies certainly involved many erroneous assumptions, including in many cases an unjustified skepticism toward miracles, revelation, and God, the Enlightenment was also an age of progress. Great advances in the sciences and in our knowledge of human psychology, society, literature, and history were made during the Enlightenment, and these advances have generally served as the basis for, not an impediment to, our continuing progress in the various academic disciplines. Any Christian evaluation of the Enlightenment will rightly criticize its biases against God, religion, and the supernatural, but to my mind wholesale rejections of the Enlightenment are unwarranted and unwise. What is needed instead is a nuanced way of appreciating and capitalizing on the benefits of the Enlightenment without embracing its problematic and even sinister dimensions. I have already suggested in chapter 1 that practical realism offers a way to do this.

Continuing in this vein of thought, I suggest that it is scarcely possible to maintain, as some do, that the problems highlighted by critical scholarship are the modern inventions of a faulty Enlightenment epistemology.[16] Already in the second century, Origen understood that the Gospel of John could not be historically accurate.[17] In the third century, Porphyry recognized the pseudo-prophetic nature of Daniel,[18] and at about the same time Augustine struggled to explain the profound differences between the four Gospels (see his *Harmony of the Gos-*

---

14. Craig G. Bartholomew, "*Warranted* Biblical Interpretation: Alvin Plantinga's 'Two (or More) Kinds of Scripture Scholarship'"; Robert P. Gordon, "A Warranted Version of Historical Biblical Criticism? A Response to Alvin Plantinga," in Bartholomew et al., "*Behind*" *the Text*, 58–78, 79–100, respectively.

15. See James A. Sanders, *Canon and Community: A Guide to Canonical Criticism* (Philadelphia: Fortress, 1984), xv–xvi.

16. V. Philips Long, *The Art of Biblical History*, Foundations of Contemporary Interpretation 5 (Grand Rapids: Zondervan, 1994); Provan, "Knowing and Believing."

17. Wrote Origen: "I conceive it to be impossible for those who admit nothing more than the history in their interpretation to show that these discrepant statements [between John and the Synoptics] are in harmony with each other" (*Commentary on John* 10:15 [*ANF* 9:393]).

18. These comments appear in fragments of Porphyry's treatise, "Against the Christians," which are preserved in Jerome's commentary on Daniel. See fragments 43 and 44 in Adolf von Harnack, ed. *Porphyrius, "Gegen*

pels). In the twelfth century the Jewish scholar Ibn Ezra noticed that the book of Isaiah was not written by a single prophet and that Moses did not write the entire Pentateuch.[19] In some instances the problems in Scripture were recognized even by the biblical authors themselves. When the Hebrew Chronicler saw that Goliath was killed by *both* David and Elhanan in the book of Samuel (cf. 1 Sam. 17; 2 Sam. 21:19), he solved this contradiction by having Elhanan defeat "Lahmi, *the brother of Goliath*" (1 Chron. 20:5). The Chronicler resolved the Pentateuch's contradictory Passover laws in a similar way. Exodus commanded that the Passover be "roasted, not boiled" (Exod. 12:8–9), whereas Deuteronomy commanded that it be "boiled in water" (Deut. 16:7). In Chronicles we are therefore told that the Israelites "boiled the Passover in fire" (2 Chron. 35:13a, my translation), which in the end meant nothing other than boiling the flesh in pots and jugs (35:13b).[20] Similar harmonizations appear elsewhere in Chronicles. Let us not forget also that Ezekiel himself confessed that his prophecy about Tyre did not come to pass (Ezek. 29:17–18). As these cases suggest, many of the biblical difficulties outlined in chapter 3 were already noticed long before the Enlightenment. So, while modern scholarship may indeed offer its own explanations of, and solutions for, these biblical difficulties, it manifestly did not invent the problems.

Critical Anti-Criticism: Conservative Evangelical Biblical Scholarship

So far I have described and examined three of the most common strategies for divesting historical criticism of its influence, but these are hardly the most important or effective strategies in this regard. All three suffer from the same basic weakness, namely, that they ignore the biblical data that modern critics adduce to support their critical conclusions. A more effective response to biblical criticism will necessarily engage biblical scholarship directly. In the remainder of this chapter I will attend closely to how conservative evangelical scholars attempt to do this.

One of the chief marks of conservative evangelical biblical scholarship is that it claims to accept the validity of historical criticism but limits or adapts the critical method in order to avoid or reverse the standard conclusions of modern biblical scholarship. Kenneth A. Kitchen expresses these sentiments well in his venerable defense of the Bible's accuracy and historicity:

> We do not merely advocate a return to "pre-critical" views and traditions merely for their own sake or for the sake of theological orthodoxy. Let it be clearly noted that

---

die Christen" (Berlin: Verlag der Königl. Akademie der Wissenschaften, in Kommission bei Georg Reimer, 1916), 67–74.

19. Otto Eissfeldt, *The Old Testament: An Introduction*, trans. Peter R. Ackroyd (New York: Harper & Row, 1965), 159, 304.

20. For a discussion see Michael Fishbane, *Biblical Interpretation in Ancient Israel* (Oxford: Clarendon, 1985), 134–37. Evangelical readers may wish to note that translators of the NIV bested the Chronicler with their creative solution, which was to translate Hebrew *bāšal* ("to boil") in Deut. 16 as "to roast"!

no appeal whatsoever has been made to any theological starting-point in the body of this work.... As far as the historic faith is concerned, it should have nothing to fear from any soundly-based and fair-minded intellectual investigation (anything less than this is, *ipso facto*, invalid). Its truth must stand or fall with that of Him who said, "I am the way, the truth, and the life."[21]

We might question Kitchen's Cartesian-like claim to objectivity, but the main point is clear: conservative evangelicals claim to be as interested as anyone in playing the academic game with historical-critical rules. They fully believe that the historical-critical method, *when employed properly*, will always sustain the Bible's integrity and undermine the problematic results of modern biblical criticism. This is the essence of "critical anti-criticism."[22] From whence comes this anti-critical perspective, and what scholarly results does it produce?

I have mentioned already two overlapping and closely linked modern Christian movements, fundamentalism and evangelicalism. Given that the two movements are historically and theologically related, it might be helpful to identify the most salient differences between these two identities. Fundamentalism takes its name from a series of short booklets entitled *The Fundamentals*, published in the United States between 1910 and 1915. These books expounded and defended what its writers considered to be the "fundamental" basics of Christian doctrine. The authors were committed to the inerrancy of the Bible, were generally hostile to modern theology and modern biblical criticism, and believed that those who did not share their viewpoints were not true believers.[23] This brand of fundamentalism was the taproot of modern evangelicalism.

In their efforts to confront the threat of liberal modernism in the church, academy, and society during the early twentieth century, fundamentalists sent their young men (and occasionally, women) to universities where they could be properly credentialed and suitably trained to understand and then refute the work of modern biblical critics. In many universities, however, fundamentalist perspectives were so academically unpalatable that it was almost impossible for a theologically conservative student to study the Bible and graduate with his or her religious views intact, as was evidenced, even then, by the many conservative graduate students who surrendered their faith during their pursuit of a doctoral credential. Many fundamentalists avoided these difficulties by majoring in the "safe" disciplines (textual criticism, Greek classics, and Near Eastern studies) or by studying in institutions where critical issues could be avoided (especially in conservative Jewish schools and in British universities). Nevertheless, even in these more insular circumstances, it was impossible for bright, young fundamentalist students to avoid noticing that the biblical and historical evidence created, or

---

21. Kenneth A. Kitchen, *Ancient Orient and Old Testament* (Downers Grove, IL: InterVarsity, 1966), 172–73.
22. Noll, *Between Faith and Criticism*, 156.
23. James Barr, *Fundamentalism* (Philadelphia: Westminster, 1978), 1–4.

at least seemed to create, substantial difficulties for their conservative doctrine of Scripture. As a result, while their fundamentalist forefathers tended to reject biblical criticism with anti-intellectual fideistic responses, this new generation of fundamentalists from the 1950s and 1960s—now called evangelicals—intended to use their intellectual and critical skills to prove that fundamentalism's view of the Bible was correct all along. Consequently, a common characteristic of conservative, evangelical scholarship during the twentieth century, and now at the dawn of a new century, is that it attempts to use accepted critical methodologies to demonstrate that certain conservative theological positions—such as the Bible's inerrancy and historical accuracy—fit the biblical evidence and are intellectually satisfying.

In order to explore the relative merits of this approach, I would have us look at numerous representative samples of critical anti-criticism, which to my mind fairly represent the most common strategies used by evangelical scholars to discredit modern biblical criticism. My discussion assumes some familiarity with the issues raised in chapter 3, so readers are advised to review that material before forging ahead.

Strategy One: Artificial Presentations of the Evidence

One of the strange paradoxes of conservative evangelical biblical scholarship is that conservative readers find it very convincing while critical scholars do not. Is this merely because critical scholars are biased against Scripture and faith, or are there substantive flaws in evangelical scholarship that make it unpersuasive to many experts? This is a question worth exploring, and we can begin by considering one of the chief criticisms often leveled against evangelical scholarship. Critical scholars often complain that their evangelical counterparts do not fairly represent the critical evidence in their work, especially when that evidence is apt to lead in a direction that evangelicals would not like. We can consider the merit of this critique by closely examining a few samples of evangelical scholarship, beginning with those that discuss the Pentateuch.

Let us recall that modern scholars have identified at least two parallel and sometimes conflicting versions of Israel's history in the Pentateuch. One of these histories prefers to use the name Yahweh (the Yahwist) and the other refers to the Deity as Elohim (the Priestly Writer). These conflicting sources obviously constitute a significant theological problem for traditional views of these five books, which take them as the work of a single author, Moses. It naturally follows that foremost in any traditional response to pentateuchal criticism is the task of invalidating modern scholarship's evidence for the sources in the Pentateuch. The classic maneuver for handling this difficulty, not only among traditional Christians but also among like-minded Jews, is to divide and conquer.[24] Instead

---

24. For traditional Christian scholars see Archer, *Old Testament Introduction*, 124–37; T. Desmond Alexander, *From Paradise to the Promised Land: An Introduction to the Pentateuch*, 2nd ed. (Grand Rapids: Baker

of considering the variations in the divine name (Yahweh/Elohim) and the narrative doublets at the same time (as should be done), these items are treated as if they were separate features in the text. First the use of the divine names to isolate sources is discredited, and then the doublets are discredited. By using a divide and conquer strategy, this approach sequesters these cohering pieces of evidence from one another and thus creates an artificial impression that the case for sources in the Pentateuch is more speculative than it actually is. The difficulty with this logic is that critical scholars do not base their theories of pentateuchal composition on the variations in the divine name alone, or on the doublets alone. Rather, their critical theories are founded on the coincidence of the doublets with the name variations, and on the fact that the doublets offer very different (even contradictory) portraits of the same events. I must say, for my own part, that I have yet to see an evangelical critique of pentateuchal criticism that presents the critical evidence in the coherent way that critical scholars present it. One wonders how the evidence would be overcome if it were so presented.

Another artificial presentation of the critical evidence appears in a recent evangelical treatment of the book of Isaiah. In his six-hundred-page defense of the Bible's reliability, Kitchen has confidently argued for the traditional view that the book was written by a single, eighth-century prophet.[25] As we saw in chapter 3, this traditional perspective on Isaiah differs substantially from the critical viewpoint, which regards Isaiah 40–55 as dating about 150 years after the prophet Isaiah (during the Babylonian exile) and chapters 56–66 as dating still later (after the exile). Given that Kitchen is taking his stand against critical scholars, who he claims are "stuck with nineteenth-century mind-sets," we might expect a detailed explanation and refutation of the standard scholarship. Yet this is not what Kitchen provides. Kitchen does not mention that Isaiah's name, though frequent in Isaiah 1–39, does not appear at all in Isaiah 40–55. In his discussion he also almost totally ignores the extensive critical evidence for an exilic date of Isaiah 40–55. Kitchen admits to only one instance where the biblical text seems to imply an exilic context (48:20), but this text does not finally convince him. Kitchen does not explain why this is so, but for my own part I must confess that the import of 48:20 for this matter is fairly straightforward: "Leave Babylon, flee from the Babylonians! Announce this with shouts of joy and proclaim it" (NIV). This explicit piece of the biblical

---

Academic, 2002), 19–23; Duane Garrett, *Rethinking Genesis: The Sources and Authorship of the First Book of the Pentateuch* (Grand Rapids: Baker Books, 1991), 16–22; R. K. Harrison, *Introduction to the Old Testament* (Grand Rapids: Eerdmans, 1969), 516–31; Derek Kidner, *Genesis: An Introduction and Commentary*, TOTC (Downers Grove, IL: InterVarsity, 1967), 18–22; Herbert M. Wolf, *An Introduction to the Old Testament* (Chicago: Moody Press, 1991), 67–71. For Jewish scholars see Umberto Cassuto, *The Documentary Hypothesis and the Composition of the Pentateuch*, trans. Israel Abrahams (Jerusalem: Magnes, 1961); Moses H. Segal, *The Pentateuch: Its Composition and Its Authorship and Other Biblical Studies* (Jerusalem: Magnes, 1967).

25. Kenneth A. Kitchen, *On the Reliability of the Old Testament* (Grand Rapids: Eerdmans, 2003), 378–80.

evidence is convincing not only to me but also to most modern scholars,[26] to many evangelicals,[27] and even to premodern scholars like Rabbi Ibn Ezra (twelfth century BCE).[28] Kitchen's argument would have been much stronger if he had included both a quotation and a refutation of this text, but he did not do so, nor does it seem to me that he could have succeeded. Equally problematic is that Kitchen does not address one of the most pressing problems facing his view, namely, that Jeremiah, when predicting the Babylonian exile, did not cite Isaiah's prophecies of exile and destruction in support of his claims. Though this evidence suggests that Isaiah 40–55 did not exist in the preexilic days of Jeremiah, Kitchen does not mention the problem, much less suggest a solution.

So what evidence does Kitchen adduce for his view? He first cites the manuscript evidence from the Dead Sea Scrolls, which seem to treat the book as a unity; but these texts date several hundred years after the book of Isaiah and so have no real bearing on the question of the book's original unity.[29] Second, Kitchen strongly asserts—without engaging the contrary evidence that I have mentioned—that chapters 40–55 belong to preexilic Palestine rather than exilic-era Babylon. He tells us that this conclusion is "as scholars of various stripes have been compelled to observe."[30] The impression given is that many scholars would support his conclusion, but the accompanying footnote cites only R. K. Harrison and J. A. Motyer, both fellow evangelicals, and two other scholars whose works date to 1937 and 1943. So it hardly seems fair to suggest that Kitchen's opinion is supported by "scholars of various stripes." As we have seen, if anything is true of scholarship on Isaiah, it is that most biblical scholars, including even many evangelical scholars, are prepared to date Isaiah 40–55 to the exile.

Kitchen actually seems to engage the critical evidence at only one point, on the matter of Cyrus. According to most modern scholars, when the prophet mentions the name "Cyrus" in 44:28 and 45:1, he refers specifically to the sixth-century king of Persia who would deliver the Jews from exile in Babylon. Because references to Cyrus would have been nonsense to an eighth-century audience, the reasonable

---

26. Paul D. Hanson, *Isaiah 40–66*, Interpretation (Louisville: Westminster John Knox, 1995); Hans-Joachim Kraus, *Das Evangelium der unbekannten Propheten: Jesaja 40–66*, Kleine biblische Bibliothek (Neukirchen-Vluyn: Neukirchener Verlag, 1990); Claus Westermann, *Isaiah 40–66: A Commentary*, trans. David M. G. Stalker, OTL (Philadelphia: Westminster, 1969); R. N. Whybray, *Isaiah 40–66*, NCB (Grand Rapids: Eerdmans, 1981).

27. Peter C. Craigie, *The Old Testament: Its Background, Growth, and Content* (Nashville: Abingdon, 1986); Raymond B. Dillard and Tremper Longman III, *An Introduction to the Old Testament* (Grand Rapids: Zondervan, 1994); David F. Payne, "Isaiah," in *New International Bible Commentary*, ed. F. F. Bruce (Grand Rapids: Zondervan, 1979), 714–63; John D. W. Watts, *Isaiah*, rev. ed., 2 vols., WBC (Nashville: Nelson, 2005); John Goldingay, *The Message of Isaiah 40–55: A Literary-Theological Commentary* (Edinburgh: T&T Clark, 2005). See also the procritical comments of John Halsey Wood Jr., "Oswald T. Allis and the Question of Isaianic Authorship," *JETS* 48 (2005): 249–61.

28. See Eissfeldt, *Old Testament*, 304.

29. Kitchen, *Reliability*, 378–80.

30. Ibid., 379.

implication is that Isaiah's audience knew of Cyrus and hence lived during his era, in the exilic period. So goes the standard view. Now Kitchen freely admits this apparent difficulty, but he nevertheless believes that Isaiah 40–55 dates to the eighth century *and* that it refers to the sixth-century Cyrus of Persia. His solution for this tension is straightforward. According to Kitchen, because numerous "Cyruses" were known in antiquity, it is not at all surprising that Isaiah of Jerusalem would predict Israel's deliverance by a future "Cyrus." Consequently, any references to Cyrus in Isaiah would naturally fit into both the eighth- and sixth-century contexts.

The difficulty with this thesis is twofold. First, there is no evidence whatever that any "Cyruses" reigned in the east during or around the eighth century BCE, much less that Israelites in Palestine knew about them. So Kitchen's solution on this score is little more than wishful thinking. The second and more serious difficulty is that the issue of Cyrus is only one of many problems that confront Kitchen's dating of Isaiah 40–55. It is the overall context presumed in Isaiah 40–55, not the references to Cyrus alone, that suggests an exilic era and audience. The exilic flavor of Second Isaiah is so strong that even evangelicals like J. Ridderbos who *deny* the critical viewpoint are willing to admit it:

> It is very clear that this section (to which many modern scholars restrict the appellation Deutero-Isaiah) speaks continuously of situations and events that occur long after Isaiah's time. It mentions the Babylonian exile of the Jews, the Persian king Cyrus, his conquests and victories over many nations and kings, his capture of Babylon and the subsequent release of the Jews, the Jews' return to Palestine, and the rebuilding of Jerusalem.[31]

In terms of both detail and overall import, Kitchen's arguments do not adequately present the critical evidence that favors an exilic and postexilic date for parts of Isaiah.

I fear that the same criticism applies to many evangelical treatments of the book of Daniel. To review the standard critical position, modern scholars believe that the four apocalypses in the second half of Daniel, in chapters 7–12, were *ex eventu* pseudoprophecies written during the second-century BCE reign of Antiochus IV. The prophecies can be so dated because they are almost perfect up to a certain point during that king's reign but then suddenly miss the mark. That is, the prophecies appear to be incredibly accurate before suddenly going awry. The traditional viewpoint contrasts sharply with this judgment. Daniel's prophecies are dated not to the second century but to the sixth century BCE, during the period when, according to the book, the prophet Daniel lived. How do evangelicals defend this judgment against the critical evidence?

Stephen Miller's recent commentary on Daniel is a good example of an evangelical defense.[32] Miller discusses all sorts of evidence that he believes should

---

31. J. Ridderbos, *Isaiah*, trans. John Vriend (Grand Rapids: Zondervan, 1985), 22.
32. Stephen R. Miller, *Daniel*, NAC 18 (Nashville: Broadman & Holman, 1994).

support an early dating of the book of Daniel. But if one reads him carefully, it is clear that most of the garnished evidence applies only to the Aramaic stories in the first six chapters of Daniel. This is a portion of the book that even critical scholars would consider dating earlier. What Miller does not discuss in any detail are the four (mostly) Hebrew apocalypses in chapters 7–12. It is this part of Daniel that scholars normally date very late. Further, in his treatment of the date of Daniel, he does not mention either the amazing accuracy of the prophecies in chapters 7–12 nor, more importantly, their apparent failures.[33] We discover why this is so in his detailed commentary on these portions of Daniel. Although modern scholars believe that each of the four apocalypses in chapters 7–12 ends with a reference to the Greeks and to Antiochus IV, thus pointing to the critical second-century date, Miller's analysis weaves a web of exegetical confusion. He tells us that the final kingdom of one prophecy is Rome (Dan. 7), of another the antichrist (Dan. 11–12), and of another he finally admits that it is the Greek kingdom of Antiochus IV (Dan. 8). I suspect that Miller admits to Antiochus in this last case only because the text provides an interpretation of the apocalypse that specifically identifies the last kingdom as "Greece" (8:19–22). For modern critical scholars, this piece of evidence seals the deal. If the last kingdom is specifically Greek in chapter 8, and if the description in that apocalypse and also in the others fits the reign of Antiochus IV—and it does!—then the verdict is in: all of the apocalypses date to the second-century persecutions of Antiochus IV. Yet nowhere in his commentary does Miller actually lay out the evidence for the critical position.[34] As a result, his arguments will appear convincing only to those unversed in the critical evidence.

If we may judge from these exemplars concerning the Pentateuch, Isaiah, and Daniel, evangelical scholars seem frequently to present the critical evidence either incompletely or unfairly. So the critiques commonly leveled by mainstream scholarship against evangelical scholarship in this regard certainly have some merit.

Strategy Two: Artificial Comparative Analogies

Comparisons of the Bible with ancient literature provide important touchstones for our scholarly judgments about the nature of Scripture. On this point all scholars are in full agreement. But when these comparisons are carried out by some evangelicals, there is a sense among mainstream scholars that these are not done appropriately. To explore this charge, I would turn our attention again to the problem of the Pentateuch's sources, and to an evangelical attempt to resolve that problem on the basis of comparative literature. My example comes from the work

---

33. Ibid., 22–43.
34. These same weaknesses appear in varying degrees in other evangelical treatments of Daniel. See Archer, *Old Testament Introduction*, 387–401; Joyce G. Baldwin, *Daniel: An Introduction and Commentary*, TOTC (Leicester: Inter-Varsity, 1978), 35–46; C. Hassell Bullock, *An Introduction to the Old Testament Prophetic Books* (Chicago: Moody Press, 1986), 281–92.

of Kitchen, in his venerable book, *Ancient Orient and Old Testament*. According to him, the stance of critical scholars toward the Pentateuch (and to the Bible in general) is much more skeptical than is their stance toward other ancient texts, such as those recovered from archaeological digs in Mesopotamia and Egypt. This is proved, he claims, by the fact that scholars propose complicated multisource origins for the Pentateuch but never do the same for other ancient texts. It supposedly follows that modern theories of the Pentateuch are not based on actual evidence but rather on an undue skepticism about the Bible's origins.[35]

Kitchen's analogy between the Bible and ancient texts, if true, might carry some force. But his argument falls short at two key points. First, the Near Eastern texts that Kitchen adduces to make his point against source criticism are stone inscriptions that were copied only once or perhaps only a few times. Texts of this sort are hardly comparable with the Bible, which was copied, edited, and recopied by many scribes over a very long period of time. If Kitchen had wished to draw comparative analogies that do justice to the Bible, he should have consulted Near Eastern canonical exemplars rather than monumental inscriptions. The Gilgamesh Epic, which we discussed in chapter 2, is such a canonical text, and its features are precisely like those that biblical scholars claim to find in the Pentateuch: various and sometimes contradictory narrative sources were assembled through a complex literary process that stretched over many centuries. Thus the comparative evidence does not contradict but rather supports the standard, critical views of the Pentateuch's origins.

This brings us to the second problem with Kitchen's argument. Kitchen complains that modern scholars are much more critical of the Bible than of other documents from the ancient world, but I very much doubt this. To be sure, at times in the past it was very common for scholars, anxious to undermine Scripture's authority, to search with zeal for the Bible's ostensible problems and contradictions. This was particularly true of Enlightenment-era scholars, but as a rule I do not believe that this criticism applies to modern scholarship. Assyriologists and biblical scholars are quite like-minded in the critical dispositions that they assume toward the texts that they study. This was poignantly illustrated in our discussion of Assyriology in chapter 2. Assyriologists were skeptical about the historicity of Gilgamesh and of the Mesopotamian histories, and they freely questioned the authenticity of the Uruk Prophecy and the so-called Sin of Sargon. They also had the good sense to recognize that the Lagash King List was not the authentic king list that it appeared to be. So Kitchen's characterization of the differences between Near Eastern and biblical scholarship seems inaccurate, and so too does the major thrust of his thesis.

Another artificial literary comparison appears in T. Desmond Alexander's recent introduction to the Pentateuch.[36] Alexander is taken with the ongoing

---

35. Kenneth A. Kitchen, *Ancient Orient and Old Testament* (Downers Grove, IL: InterVarsity, 1966), 117.

36. Alexander, *From Paradise*, 80–81.

debate in New Testament scholarship respecting the Synoptic problem, that is, establishing which of the Synoptic Gospels (Matthew, Mark, or Luke) was used by the others as a source. Alexander asks, "If doubts continue to exist over the composition of the Gospels [when we have the benefit of actually seeing the three different Synoptic documents], how can OT scholars with any confidence delineate correctly the sources underlying the books of the Pentateuch [when the sources are still together in one document]?"[37] Here Alexander has used comparative literature, in this case from the New Testament, to highlight the speculative nature of pentateuchal source criticism. If his parallel were legitimate he would indeed have a point, but the analogy fails on several levels.

First, just because it is difficult to isolate the sources in one document, such as the Gospel of Matthew, does not mean that sources are invisible in the Pentateuch or in other documents. If scholars could find parallel sources in Matthew, you can be sure that they would have done so. Second, Alexander misrepresents New Testament scholarship in his analysis. New Testament scholars do not find parallel sources in Matthew, but most of them agree that Mark and another hypothetical document, known to scholars as "Q," were the two primary sources used by Matthew and Luke. Because the debate about the Gospels is not as great as Alexander suggests, it follows that his argument has failed. Third, if Alexander is searching for a true Gospel parallel to the Pentateuch, a better example would be Tatian's *Diatesseron*.[38] The *Diatesseron* was composed around 150–160 CE and represents the first known effort to create a synoptic harmony of the four Gospels. It was the standard written Gospel in the Syrian churches until it gave way to the four separate Gospels during the fifth century. As a single document composed from parallel gospel sources, the *Diatesseron* would have provided a very close literary parallel to what critical scholars see in the Pentateuch.[39] I would ask this question: If modern scholars had before them only the *Diatesseron*, would they be able to deduce that the book was composed using several parallel Gospel sources? I believe that the answer to this question is yes. Scholars would quickly notice, for instance, that the *Diatesseron* includes two different and contradictory birth narratives that sit side by side. In one story Jesus's family travels to Bethlehem from Nazareth and then soon returns to Nazareth (see Luke 2), and in the other the family is from Bethlehem and lives there for several years before traveling not to Nazareth but to Egypt. Only when Herod's son blocks their return to Bethlehem does the family decide to migrate north to Nazareth (see Matt. 2). We can surmise that these two stories were not combined in the text because Tatian could not find a suitable way to do it. But Tatian's reasoning aside, my main point is that modern scholars would be able to deduce that several parallel sources stand behind his

---

37. Ibid., 80. For purposes of clarity, I have added the text in brackets.
38. See *ANF* 9:42–138.
39. David M. Carr, *Reading the Fractures of Genesis: Historical and Literary Approaches* (Louisville: Westminster John Knox, 1996), 30–39; G. F. Moore, "Tatian's *Diatessaron* and the Analysis of the Pentateuch," *JBL* 9 (1890): 201–15.

Diatesseron, even if they did not have the four Gospels sitting in front of them. The same goes for the Pentateuch.

Strategy Three: Selective and Illegitimate Appeals to Critical Scholarship

Yet another common evangelical strategy for responding to modern critics involves a selective and specious use of modern scholarship that *seems* to support the traditional, evangelical cause. The basic pattern of this argument is well illustrated in an article by Richard Schultz.[40] Schultz is alarmed that so many evangelical scholars are beginning to embrace the critical perspective that Isaiah was composed by several authors, living in vastly different time frames. He finds this paradoxical because, according to him, modern critical scholars are heading back in the traditional direction. As Schultz describes it, a growing number of scholars now "posit an intentional relationship, even an interdependence or a mutual influence, between what is popularly known as First and Second Isaiah. . . . Support for the basic unity of the canonical book has been growing steadily within non-evangelical scholarship."[41] Schultz is aware that these critical scholars would not argue for a single author of Isaiah but only, more modestly, for reading Isaiah as "one book." But this is, to his mind, a piece of evidence in support of the traditional view that the entire book of Isaiah was written essentially by one prophet.

It seems to me that this does not follow at all. As Schultz himself admits, critical scholars are saying clearly that the evidence for Isaiah's unity is not authorial but editorial. That is, there is strong evidence for numerous authors in Isaiah, but also strong evidence for an effort to editorially combine the pieces into a single book. So none of the critical evidence supports Schultz's conclusion that the whole book of Isaiah was written in the eighth century by a single prophet, and it is a mistake to suggest that it does.

Similarly specious appeals to critical scholarship appear in many evangelical treatments of the Pentateuch. In order to buttress their cases against critical source theories of the Pentateuch, evangelicals often cite the work of several critical scholars (Rolf Rendtorff, Erhard Blum, and R. N. Whybray being good examples) who have raised serious questions about pentateuchal source theories.[42] If these

---

40. Richard L. Schultz, "How Many Isaiahs Were There and What Does It Matter? Prophetic Inspiration in Recent Evangelical Scholarship," in *Evangelicals and Scripture: Tradition, Authority and Hermeneutics*, ed. Vincent Bacote, Laura C. Miguélez, and Dennis L. Okholm (Downers Grove, IL: InterVarsity, 2004), 150–70.

41. Ibid., 153–54.

42. Erhard Blum, *Die Komposition der Vätergeschichte*, Wissenschaftliche Monographien zum Alten und Neuen Testament 57 (Neukirchen-Vluyn: Neukirchener Verlag, 1984); Blum, *Studien zur Komposition des Pentateuch*, BZAW 189 (Berlin: de Gruyter, 1990); Rolf Rendtorff, *Das überlieferungsgeschichtliche Problem des Pentateuch*, BZAW 147 (Berlin: de Gruyter, 1977); translated as *The Problem of the Process of Transmission in the Pentateuch*, trans. John J. Scullion, JSOTSup 89 (Sheffield: JSOT Press, 1990); R. N. Whybray, *The Making of the Pentateuch: A Methodological Study*, JSOTSup 53 (Sheffield: JSOT Press, 1987); Whybray, *Introduction to the Pentateuch* (Grand Rapids: Eerdmans, 1995). The evangelicals include Alexander, *From Paradise*, 42–61;

scholars were actually headed in the same direction as conservative evangelicals this would be a prudent and wise point to make. But when the work of these critical scholars is carefully examined, it becomes clear that the rationale for their conclusions runs entirely counter to the traditional evangelical agenda. It is true that Rendtorff and Blum do away with the documentary sources as traditionally understood, but they replace these with a more complicated tradition process that includes many anonymous authors and editors as well as several more important tradents who substitute conceptually for the traditional Pentateuchal sources. For instance, Blum attributes the basic shape of the Pentateuch to three authors/editors who correspond closely with the traditional sigla of D, J, and P.[43] He further postulates that behind these compositions are a number of earlier written traditions that passed through various stages before these editors cast them in their present form. If the benchmark we have in mind is the traditional Mosaic view of the Pentateuch, then Rendtorff and Blum are no closer to this traditional benchmark than the standard source critics whom evangelicals wish to criticize.

Equally problematic is the citation of Whybray. It is true that Whybray attributes the whole of the Pentateuch to a single author, but he claims that this author lived very late in Jewish history—hundreds of years after Moses would have lived—and that he used many different sources that are still visible because of the tensions and contradictions among them. This sort of approach hardly serves the conservative evangelical agenda. To make matters worse, Whybray's approach is so unusual and idiosyncratic that it has been virtually ignored by mainstream pentateuchal scholarship. Properly understood, Whybray's thesis is hardly compatible with the view that a single author wrote the Pentateuch in hoary antiquity.

Enough detail. The main point is that, by citing evidence in the way that it does, evangelical scholarship sometimes gives the impression that traditional views of the Pentateuch can fit pretty comfortably within the intellectual landscape of modern biblical scholarship. Yet most biblical scholars would not recognize this portrait of the scholarship. Indeed, differences aside, nearly every stripe of scholar would agree that the Pentateuch's composition is too complex to be traced back to a single author living anywhere near the time of Moses.[44] This is true even of critical scholars like Rendtorff, Blum, and Whybray. So modern scholarship does not provide much support for the traditional viewpoint that Moses wrote the Pentateuch during the second millennium BCE, nor is it fair to imply that it does.

Garrett, *Rethinking Genesis*, 47; James K. Hoffmeier, *Israel in Egypt: The Evidence for the Authenticity of the Exodus Tradition* (New York: Oxford University Press, 1997), 7–10.

43. These three bodies of material include Deuteronomy, the Deuteronomistic Composition, and the Priestly Composition. See Blum, *Komposition der Vätergeschichte* and *Studien zur Komposition des Pentateuch*.

44. See David M. Carr, "Controversy and Convergence in Recent Studies of the Formation of the Pentateuch," *Religious Studies Review* 23 (1997): 22–31.

But let us not be too hard on evangelicals at this point, for one can hardly suppose that they are deliberately misleading readers. A more likely scenario is that evangelical scholars are so anxious to find support for their views in the scholarship that they inevitably misrepresent it. Nevertheless, one result of this tendency is that it is often difficult to get a fair sense of what is going on in biblical scholarship if one is using conservative evangelical publications to do it. Of course, these misrepresentations of the scholarship do not serve the evangelical cause very well.

Strategy Four: Lowering the Threshold for Historicity

Another perennial tension between tradition and criticism regards the historicity of the biblical narratives. The Pentateuch again provides a good example. Traditionalists take the Pentateuch as an accurate portrait of human history, while critical scholars are more skeptical about this. I am interested at this juncture in considering how evangelical scholars have engaged some of these historical issues. In order to explore this in more detail, I will turn to the work of two evangelical scholars who have tackled one of the Pentateuch's most vexing historical difficulties: the exodus.

I noted in the previous chapter that the primary historical problem with the exodus is that the expected evidence for the Passover event is wanting in Egyptian tradition. How have evangelicals handled this difficulty? The recent history of Israel by Provan, Long, and Longman simply ignores the problem and assumes the historicity of the events.[45] As for R. K. Harrison's standard Old Testament introduction of over twelve hundred pages, it offers the following one-sentence argument for the historicity of the exodus: "There is no extra-Biblical evidence relating directly to the fact of the Exodus, but it is clear that a belief so firmly rooted in the religious tradition of Israel can hardly be explained in terms other than that this stupendous liberating act of God occurred in reality."[46] One can hardly believe that this frank admission of the historical difficulties is followed by such a confident historical assertion. Are we to suppose that Harrison believes in the historicity of all ancient traditions merely on the basis of the traditions themselves? The Mesopotamians believed for many centuries that their divination literature was inspired by the gods. Would Harrison concede the point? Harrison's evidential threshold for the historicity of the exodus is so low that practically any ancient miracle report—from any major religion—would pass the test. Clearly, the exodus tradition itself is slender evidence for the historicity of an event that has left no discernible traces in the Egyptian material.

More ambitious is the recent evangelical treatment of this issue by James Hoffmeier, an Egyptologist by training.[47] Hoffmeier's volume is impressive in

---

45. Provan, Long, and Longman, *Biblical History of Israel*, 127–32.
46. R. K. Harrison, *Introduction to the Old Testament* (Grand Rapids: Eerdmans, 1969), 316.
47. Hoffmeier, *Israel in Egypt*.

its breadth and detail, as he carefully weighs the biblical and archaeological evidence in an effort to demonstrate the historical plausibility of the biblical narrative. In many respects he succeeds in showing that the exodus story fits the ancient Egyptian world in a general sort of way (and *only* in a general way), but his failure to discuss the Passover event is quite telling. The Passover is mentioned only in passing as a "supernatural" event, and Hoffmeier adduces no evidence for the historicity of what was ostensibly the most horrible episode in Egyptian history.[48] As for the nine plagues that preceded the Passover, Hoffmeier accepts Greta Hort's old theory that these were from a sequence of natural events, in which, among other things, the Nile was not literally turned to blood but looked reddish because of naturally occurring "flagellates in the floodwaters."[49] Hort's explanation lowers our expectation that the Egyptian evidence would mention the plagues because the events are now understood to be exceptional natural events rather than unequivocal sign miracles. While Hoffmeier's book certainly helps us appreciate the Egyptian flavor in the book of Exodus (not surprising given that Israel was the next-door neighbor of Egypt), it does not resolve but only underscores the most important critical problems that face evangelicals in this material.

Both Harrison and Hoffmeier admit that Egyptian evidence for a miraculous exodus is lacking, and Hoffmeier goes so far as to confess that this constitutes an evidential "dilemma."[50] Given this reality, the key issue is this: should we, or should we not, expect Egyptian evidence for the historicity of the Passover and of the other miracles in the biblical story? Kitchen's evangelical answer to this question is straightforward: "pharaohs *never* memorialize defeats on temple walls, no record of the successful exit of a large bunch of foreign slaves (with loss of a full chariot squadron) would ever have been memorialized by any king.... On these matters, once and for all, Biblicists must shed their naive attitudes and cease demanding 'evidence' that *cannot* exist."[51] So Kitchen tries to resolve the lack of evidence for the exodus and Passover by asserting that we should not expect any evidence. This argument might seem reasonable and convincing at first glance, but it strikes me as a specious way of escaping a serious difficulty.

Modern biblical scholars are savvy enough to recognize that the Egyptians would not have memorialized their defeat in a royal inscription. They "demand" no such thing. Instead, scholars suspect that calamities like the Passover and exodus—if indeed these events happened—would have been remembered in Egypt in some kind of veiled form. The Egyptians would have interpreted these defeats as victories or, this failing, they would have explained them as acts of judgment from their own gods. These two interpretive strategies appear in the Bible. Judah remembered the nearly total annihilation of the nation by King

---

48. Ibid., 149.
49. Greta Hort, "The Plagues of Egypt," *ZAW* 69 (1957): 84–103; *ZAW* 70 (1958): 48–59.
50. Harrison, *Introduction to the Old Testament*, 316; Hoffmeier, *Israel in Egypt*, 53.
51. Kitchen, *Reliability of the Old Testament*, 246.

Sennacherib of Assyria (see 2 Kings 18:13–16; Isa. 22:1–14) as a miraculous victory (2 Kings 18:17–19:37),[52] and it interpreted an obvious military defeat at the hands of Babylon as an act of Yahweh (2 Kings 24–25). Given that these strategies for interpreting "defeat" were common in the ancient world,[53] critical scholars are on the lookout for two kinds of Egyptian evidence for the Passover and exodus. They expect either an inscription that recalls Pharaoh's mighty expulsion of the Hebrews from Egypt, or some text that admits Egypt's difficulties but attributes them to one of Egypt's own gods, not to Yahweh. As it turns out, though the Egyptians have left us good evidence for two lesser "catastrophes" in their history (the Hyksos and Sea Peoples),[54] they have left us no evidence at all for the exodus or Passover.

Critical scholars anticipate that the Passover and exodus would have left behind Egyptian testimonies about these events if they had actually occurred. The silence of the Egyptian evidence on these matters is therefore an important argument against the historicity of these miracle reports. I must say, I quite agree with this expectation. While historians have no access to the supernatural miracles that would have caused the Passover, they should be able to find Egyptian evidence for this miracle's effect: the death of a whole generation of New Kingdom Egyptians. Even if Harrison and Hoffmeier believe that the historicity of the exodus is essential for the health of the Jewish and Christian faiths, there is nothing untoward with admitting honestly that the usual historical evidence does not appear to support its historicity. Perhaps the original events were much less significant historically than the Bible now remembers. And, as we shall see, one does not always require *historical-critical* evidence to believe that some events are historical; *theological* evidence also counts in our assessments of history.

Strategy Five: Red Herrings—The Misleading Use of "Test Cases"

Another common strategy for challenging critical conclusions about the Bible is to test their validity by examining selected portions of the biblical material in question. An example of this strategy appears in the work of T. Desmond Alexander, who puts modern source theories of the Pentateuch to the

---

52. See *ANET*, 287–88. For good descriptions of the destruction during Hezekiah's reign, and of the nation's recovery during the long reign of Manasseh, see Morton Cogan, *Imperialism and Religion: Assyria, Judah and Israel in the Eighth and Seventh Centuries B.C.E.*, SBLMS 19 (Missoula, MT: Scholars Press, 1974); Israel Finkelstein, "The Archaeology of the Days of Manasseh," in *Scripture and Other Artifacts: Essays on the Bible and Archaeology in Honor of Philip J. King*, ed. Michael D. Coogan, J. Cheryl Exum, and Lawrence E. Stager (Louisville: Westminster John Knox, 1994), 169–87; J. Maxwell Miller and John H. Hayes, *A History of Ancient Israel and Judah* (Philadelphia: Westminster, 1986), 353–63; J. Alberto Soggin, *A History of Ancient Israel*, trans. John Bowden (Philadelphia: Westminster, 1985), 231–41.

53. For some representative examples, see discussions of the Mesha Stela, the Erra myth, and the synchronistic history in *ATSHB*, 466–67, 319–20, 368–69, respectively.

54. See *ATSHB*, 387–88; Donald B. Redford, *Egypt, Canaan, and Israel in Ancient Times* (Princeton: Princeton University Press, 1992), 98–122, 241–56. See also chap. 3, note 37 above.

test in a chapter entitled, "The Sinai Narrative—A Test Case."[55] There is, in principle, nothing wrong with using test cases to point out the weaknesses of a theory, but when this is done, the test obviously needs to examine actual evidence for the theory to be criticized. Alexander's test case studies the Sinai pericope in Exodus 19-24 and concludes: "Our study of the Sinai narrative provides no evidence to support the existence of the sources associated with the Documentary Hypothesis." If we presume for the moment that Alexander's analysis of the text is a good one, it might seem that he has adduced significant evidence against the validity of pentateuchal source theories. But indeed, he has not. His test case fails because, as Alexander himself admits, pentateuchal source critics have always recognized that the Sinai pericope does not fall out into the orderly, straightforward sources that we find in Genesis and in other parts of the Pentateuch.[56] A proper test case for source criticism would need to consider the actual evidence for source theory, not an exception already admitted by the theory.

As it is, even if we grant the validity of Alexander's test case, the Sinai narrative would not serve his purposes. Among other things, Alexander fails to discuss a key difference between the two versions of the Ten Commandments that appear in Exodus 20 and in Deuteronomy 5. The motive for keeping the Sabbath command in Deuteronomy was to commemorate the exodus from Egypt, while the motive for the same command in Exodus was to mimic God's Sabbath rest after creation (see the Priestly Writer's creation story in Gen. 1). This is one part of the evidence for the modern scholarly distinction between the P and D sources. Also, by arbitrarily choosing to end his discussion with Exodus 24:11, Alexander manages to avoid an obvious tension with what follows in 24:12-18. If Alexander's discussion had considered 24:12-18,[57] he would have needed to explain why Moses was called up to the mountain of God in verse 12 when he was already there in verse 11, and why Moses needed to receive more laws in 25:1ff. when the laws and covenant had already been granted and ratified in 24:1-11. This and other evidence suggests that differing sources and perspectives probably play a more important role in the present shape of the Sinai pericope than Alexander argues.[58] That Alexander has discovered editorial "unity" in the text is not a surprise, given that the Sinai pericope in its final form is ipso facto a unity. But his study fails

---

55. Alexander, *From Paradise*, 62-79.

56. The traditional documentary hypothesis divided the Sinai pericope between the J and E sources, with P contributing little to the text. Because of the current debate about E (see chapter 3), and because of the suspicion that Deuteronomistic editing has also taken place in the Sinai narrative, one can see that this section of Exodus is fraught with difficulties.

57. Most scholars regard the pericope in 24:12-18 as coming from sources other than the Yahwist. Part of the text comes from P (25:15b-18), but a portion may go back to some other author/editor (24:12-15a). For a discussion on this, see Brevard S. Childs, *The Book of Exodus: A Critical, Theological Commentary*, OTL (Philadelphia: Westminster, 1974), 497-511.

58. See Thomas B. Dozeman, *God on the Mountain: A Study of Redaction, Theology, and Canon in Exodus 19-24*, SBLMS 37 (Atlanta: Scholars Press, 1989).

to demonstrate that this unity precludes the presence of sometimes discordant sources behind the text.

Problematic test cases like this appear elsewhere in Alexander's book and in many other evangelical responses to biblical criticism.[59]

Strategy Six: Misleading and Illegitimate Harmonizations

Among the most obvious difficulties for traditional readings of the Bible are those instances where Scripture provides two or more different accounts of the same incident. Parallels of this sort appear commonly in the Gospels and in the twin accounts of Israel's history in Samuel–Kings and Chronicles. These parallels often give us different but valuable information, which scholars can integrate to create more fully orbed portraits of the events in question. In other cases, however, the texts vary so much that they seem to give us entirely different and even contradictory impressions of the events they narrate. Here we will discuss two such difficulties that I have highlighted already in chapter 3, one from the Old Testament and one from the New.

Our Old Testament difficulty comes from the two accounts of King Manasseh's life, which appear in 2 Kings 21:1–18 and 2 Chronicles 33:1–20. Readers will recall that 2 Kings describes Manasseh as the most despicable king in Judean history, whose evil was so great that it caused the exile of Judah to Babylon, as well as the destruction of Jerusalem and its temple. This portrait of Manasseh is very different from that offered in Chronicles. According to the Chronicler, though Manasseh was an evil king, he eventually turned from his sins and composed a beautiful prayer of repentance. So, for the Chronicler, Manasseh's evil does not figure at all in the fall of Judah and its exile. Modern scholars believe that the differences between the two accounts of Manasseh in Kings and Chronicles are easy to explain. The Chronicler's History follows a pattern of immediate retribution, in which every good deed is promptly rewarded and every evil deed is punished.[60] Given this approach to history, the Chronicler had to explain why an evil king like Manasseh was allowed by God to rule Judah for 55 years, a period longer than any other Judean king—even longer than King David himself. The Chronicler's answer was predictable: Manasseh was allowed to enjoy a long life because he had repented of his sins.

This critical reading of Chronicles leads us directly to questions of historical accuracy. But the question at hand is not merely whether Manasseh repented. For

---

59. See Alexander's discussion of the Passover, *From Paradise*, 23–30. For other evangelicals see Kitchen, *Ancient Orient and Old Testament*, 116–20; Brian E. Kelly, "Manasseh in the Books of Kings and Chronicles (2 Kings 21:1–18; 2 Chron 33:1–20)," in *Windows into Old Testament History*, ed. V. Philips Long, David W. Baker, and Gordon J. Wenham (Grand Rapids: Eerdmans, 2002), 131–46; Erik Waaler, "A Revised Date for Pentateuchal Texts? Evidence from Ketef Hinnom," *Tyndale Bulletin* 53 (2002): 29–55.

60. See Sara Japhet, *I & II Chronicles: A Commentary*, OTL (Louisville: Westminster John Knox, 1993), 44–45; H. G. M. Williamson, *1 and 2 Chronicles*, NCB (Grand Rapids: Eerdmans, 1982), 31–33.

history writing, whether in Kings or Chronicles, goes beyond the bare listing of events that happened; it also asserts the causes of, and provides explanations for, those events. According to modern scholars, the explanations of history in Kings and Chronicles are utterly different. In the first text, Manasseh is so evil that the entire nation is punished for his sins even after his death (2 Kings 21:10–15). In the other text, Manasseh repents and has no association whatever with the fall of Judah (2 Chron. 33:12–20). These contrasting portraits of Manasseh are made more poignant by the fact that almost all scholars, even evangelical scholars, agree that the Chronicler's primary source for his history of Manasseh was none other than Kings itself.[61]

When conservative evangelicals affirm the historical accuracy of both Kings and Chronicles, they are confronted immediately by two different but related historical problems. One of these is connected to the *events* of history, and the other to the *ideology* of interpreting those events. On the event side, how can the persistent evil of Manasseh in Kings be harmonized with his repentance in Chronicles? On the ideology side, how can the consequences of Manasseh's sins in Kings be harmonized with the lack of those consequences in Chronicles? An evangelical response to these problems has recently been published by Brian Kelly.[62] Let us consider his arguments carefully.

Kelly begins by addressing the ideological side of the problem. He accentuates that, in the eyes of modern literary theory, every historical text has its own bias, ideology, or *Tendenz*. A given historical text therefore provides only one of many possible viewpoints and may be "valid and true within its own terms."[63] From this Kelly concludes that our two very different histories in Kings and Chronicles need not be interpreted as contradictory. Perhaps they are better understood as complementary accounts of history, whose differences stem not from historical errors or fictions but rather from the contrasting ideologies of their respective authors. This argument, which appeals to the insights of modern literary criticism, is an increasingly common evangelical strategy for harmonizing biblical texts with each other and with other sources of history.[64]

Now Kelly is certainly on the right track when he points out that each biblical history is not a perfect history so much as one that is "valid and true within its own terms." But there are two glaring difficulties with this as a harmonizing strategy. First, Kelly has not understood the underlying philosophy of the literary criticism that he is using. Current literary criticism is essentially postmodern, in that it views all human ideologies as finite constructions that inevitably miss the mark

---

61. A notable if idiosyncratic exception would be A. Graeme Auld, *Kings without Privilege: David and Moses in the Story of the Bible's Kings* (Edinburgh: T&T Clark, 1994).
62. Kelly, "Manasseh," 131–46.
63. Ibid., 131.
64. For similar strategies see V. Philips Long, *The Art of Biblical History*, Foundations of Contemporary Interpretation 5 (Grand Rapids: Zondervan, 1994); Provan, Long, and Longman, *Biblical History of Israel*, 36–97.

on reality itself. As a result, for these postmodern critics, even good histories will include unintentional (and perhaps even intentional) *fictions*. While this need not imply at all that Kings and Chronicles are mere tapestries of fancy, it does mean that these histories will not be perfectly accurate and compatible. Yet, so far as I can tell, Kelly does not identify a single historical contradiction between Kings and Chronicles. So the underlying philosophy of Kelly's approach contradicts his implicit but optimistic assumption that both texts are "right." Second, and I think more importantly, we must consider the more likely implication of Kelly's admission that the authors of Kings and Chronicles had different ideologies. For it is often the case that ideological differences do produce profound contradictions between two or more accounts of the past. It seems to me that the two accounts of Manasseh in the Bible are so different that this possibility, which critical scholarship embraces, should be taken more seriously by Kelly.

Continuing in this vein of thought, I would point out another difficulty with Kelly's thesis. Although he admits that the Chronicler has an ideology, he does not agree with the standard scholarly thesis—accepted even by many evangelicals—that the Chronicler's ideology is immediate retribution.[65] If this retributive theology is really a feature of Chronicles, as most scholars presume, then the standard critical view of the Chronicler's Manasseh—which has the king repent to explain his 55-year reign—is much stronger. Yet Kelly does not tell us precisely why he has rejected this standard view of the Chronicler's ideology, nor does he provide an alternative portrait of the Chronicler's ideology—although he assures us that the Chronicler has one.

How does Kelly handle the questions of historical fact? One peculiar feature of his discussion is that he hardly focuses at all on the question of whether Manasseh's repentance actually occurred. His historical interest is mainly on other features in Chronicles, particularly on whether Manasseh was ever taken captive to Mesopotamia (where the king supposedly repented) and on whether he undertook the religious reforms credited to him (after he repented). Now these are indeed interesting historical questions and are worthy of Kelly's attention. But I suspect that Kelly focuses on them precisely because they are much easier to handle than the repentance itself. But we must ask: Why, after all, did the author of Kings fail to report Manasseh's repentance? Kelly suspects that the author of Kings did not know about it, but even if he did, Kelly reasons that: "In the final form of Kings, Manasseh's sin marks the breaking point of Yahweh's patience with Judah and makes the destruction and exile inevitable.... To include an account of the punishment and restoration of Manasseh would certainly have diminished the rhetorical force of the work."[66] Indeed, Kelly is quite right. How could the author

---

65. Simon J. De Vries, *1 and 2 Chronicles*, Forms of the Old Testament Literature 11 (Grand Rapids: Eerdmans, 1989); Raymond B. Dillard, *2 Chronicles*, WBC (Waco: Word, 1987), 76–81; Rodney K. Duke, "Chronicles, Book of," in *Dictionary of the Old Testament: Historical Books*, ed. Bill T. Arnold and H. G. M. Williamson (Downers Grove, IL: InterVarsity, 2005), 161–81.

66. Kelly, "Manasseh," 140.

of Kings blame the exile on Manasseh if that king had repented so completely? But this is precisely the rub. For whether the author of Kings knew of the repentance or not, his account of the history cannot be right if Chronicles is also right. Either Manasseh repented so completely that he was not directly culpable for the fall of Judah, or he did not repent and so was culpable. As accounts of historical causation go, both cannot be wholly right (although both might be partially correct).

So far as I can tell, Kelly never actually harmonizes the most important historical contradictions between the two biblical accounts of Manasseh's life, nor, it seems to me, could he have done so. It would have been far better simply to admit that one or both accounts are not correct in all historical respects, and better still to explain this by noting that the Chronicler was perhaps more interested in theology than in history.

Now let us consider another example of historical harmonization, this time from the New Testament. In chapter 3 we noted that the last few days of Jesus's life are portrayed differently in John and in the Synoptic Gospels. According to John's Gospel, Jesus was crucified at noon on the day *before* the Passover meal, while the Synoptic Jesus was crucified earlier in the morning on the day *after* the Passover meal. Most critical scholars presume that John made this change so that Jesus was killed at the precise day and hour as the Passover lambs, which would have reinforced John's unique theological metaphor of Jesus as "the Lamb of God, who takes away the sin of the world" (John 1:29 RSV, NIV; cf. v. 36). How have conservative evangelicals handled this apparent contradiction?

Craig Blomberg handles the difficulty as follows.[67] John's audience was familiar with the oral tradition that Jesus's last meal with his disciples was a Passover meal, but John removed overt references to the Passover because he often omitted traditions that might promote "institutionalized sacramentalism." Nevertheless, according to Blomberg, if one attends to the various features in the meal, there is much in it that suits a Passover dinner; in essence, John describes a Passover meal but is careful to avoid calling it the Passover. The only difficulty that remains for Blomberg is that John places the crucifixion at the "sixth hour" (i.e., noon) rather than at the "third hour" (i.e., 9:00 a.m.), as in Mark 15:25. Blomberg theorizes that this difference arose because the crucifixion actually took place midway between these two times, so that John and Mark rounded off in different directions, one moving up to the next "watch" and the other down to the previous "watch."

How reasonable is this harmonization of the two accounts? Blomberg's theory has several difficulties. First, why did John go out of his way to dissociate Jesus's final meal from the Passover if, as Blomberg avers, John's audience already knew that the meal was a Passover rite? Did John wish them to disregard the association? What if Blomberg is wrong and John's audience did not know that the meal was a Passover rite? In this case, the standard critical reading of John emerges de facto

---

67. Craig L. Blomberg, *The Historical Reliability of John's Gospel* (Downers Grove, IL: InterVarsity, 2001).

from the text, since it is precisely the association of Jesus with the Passover lamb that John gives his audience. Second, Blomberg does not explain why John would avoid referring to the Passover in connection with the meal but then push so very hard to associate the crucifixion with the Passover, juxtaposing it in blatant fashion with the correct day and time of the slaying of the Passover lambs: "Now it was the *day of Preparation of the Passover*; it was about the *sixth hour*. He said to the Jews, 'Behold your King!'" (John 19:14 RSV). Does this verse not point, prima facie, toward the conclusion that John wanted to portray Jesus as the Passover lamb, especially when we recall that John is the only Gospel that describes Jesus using the "Lamb of God" metaphor? Third, Blomberg is wrong to assert that the Passover-like features in John's account of the Last Supper are good evidence that John intended to portray the meal as a Passover meal. This assertion falters in two different ways. On the one hand, if Jesus's last meal really was a Passover meal, as the Synoptics and most critical scholars suggest, then we should anticipate that John's account of the meal would reflect the features of a Passover rite, even if he wished to conceal these. On the other hand, if John was so careful to preserve all of these images of the Passover in his description of the meal, as Blomberg suggests, then why did John meticulously avoid explicit references to the Passover in connection with the meal? Fourth, Blomberg does not tell us how he would explain the two different time frames of Jesus's crucifixion—at the third and sixth hours—if his speculation that these are merely rounded-off figures is wrong. If John did not round off his figure but really meant what he said—the "sixth hour"—would this not strongly favor the critical theory that John has not only changed the time but also the day of Jesus's crucifixion? Fifth, and finally, Blomberg does not address one of the most glaring problems with his thesis: John's Gospel explicitly tells us that Jesus's final meal with his disciples took place "before the Passover Feast" (13:1–2 NIV). In the end, Blomberg's arguments either fail entirely or hang by the slender thread of two speculative and somewhat problematic assumptions, namely, that John's audience already knew about the Passover meal tradition and that John and Mark each rounded off their chronological data for the hour of Jesus's crucifixion—but in different directions.

Perhaps Blomberg's harmonization is possible, but I would ask: Why should Blomberg's thesis—based largely on conjecture and with so many dangling questions—be more likely than the standard critical view that John has moved the Passover Feast, so that Jesus, who is for him the "Lamb of God," dies at the day and time that the Passover lambs were slaughtered? This standard critical reading takes account of all the data and offers a good explanation for it; Blomberg's view has no hard evidence behind it and, in the end, does not solve all of the difficulties anyway. For even if Blomberg were to succeed in making John and the Synoptics "right" about the Passover, it remains true that the Synoptics go out of their way to describe the last meal as a Passover meal, while John's Gospel is everywhere at pains to insure that it is not. Given this reality, one might as well accept the critical view of the accounts.

Although E. J. Young, one of our evangelical forefathers, was often guilty of illegitimate harmonizations such as those described above, it seems to me that his words of wisdom on this subject still ring true:

> It may very well be that there are some passages which, save by strained and forced attempts, we cannot harmonize. If such is the case, by all means let us be sufficiently honest and candid to admit that we cannot harmonize the particular passages in question; for to employ strained and forced methods of harmonization is not intellectually honest. If we do employ such methods, we shall only bring upon our heads the deserved charge of intellectual dishonesty. Far better it is to admit our inability than to produce harmonization at the expense of honesty and integrity.[68]

I cannot but agree with Young's sentiment. Harmonizations so historically and rationally strained as those offered by Kelly and Blomberg cannot pass as serious scholarly readings of the biblical text, mainly because the authors present their very improbable reconstructions as if they are likely or even highly probable. If and when evangelicals feel compelled to offer up speculative harmonizations of this sort, let us confess that these harmonizations are, in fact, speculative.

Strategy Seven: Critiquing Biblical Criticism with the Biblical "Testimony"

Most modern biblical scholars believe that Moses, Isaiah, and Daniel were not the authors of the books traditionally attributed to them. The difficulty that this seems to raise is that Jesus and the New Testament writers clearly identified Moses as the author of the Pentateuch, Isaiah as the author of the second half of Isaiah, and Daniel as the author of the Daniel apocalypses. Given that Christianity must maintain the divinity and omniscience of Christ, to accept the critical denial of these authorial attributions can only mean, according to William Henry Green, to give up one's "faith in the authority and infallibility of Christ's instructions."[69] In essence, for Green and for many other conservative evangelicals living after him,[70] the deity of Christ himself rises or falls with the accuracy of his statements about Old Testament authorship.

Now Christians will want to consider seriously what Jesus and the New Testament writers said about the Old Testament. However, we should recall that creedal orthodoxy maintains that Jesus Christ is not only divine and infinite but also human and finite.[71] If the critical evidence against the traditional authorial attributions in the Old Testament is as strong as it seems to be, then it is perhaps evangelical

---

68. E. J. Young, *Thy Word Is Truth* (Grand Rapids: Eerdmans, 1957), 174.
69. William Henry Green, *The Pentateuch Vindicated from the Aspersions of Bishop Colenso* (New York: John Wiley, 1863), 19.
70. For a recent example, see Archer, *Old Testament Introduction*, 114.
71. In his discussion of Jesus's humanity and finiteness, Athanasius stressed the fact that Jesus "grew in wisdom and stature" (Luke 2:52) and that our Lord did not know when his return would come (Mark 13:32). See *Against the Arians* 3.26, 29, 42–53 (= *NPNF* 2 4:408, 416, 421).

Christology—and not critical scholarship—that needs to be carefully reconsidered. If Jesus was fully human, as orthodoxy demands, then it is likely that he learned—along with other ancient Jews—that Moses, Isaiah, and Daniel wrote their books, irrespective of factual and historical realities. Moreover, even if Jesus knew the critical fact that Moses did not pen the Pentateuch, it is hardly reasonable to assume that he would have revealed this information to his ancient audience. To the extent that Jesus drew upon his omniscience in everyday life and conversation, it would have been constantly necessary for him to pass up opportunities to tell those around him what he knew. This matter will be given more attention in chapter 7.

In connection with this discussion, I draw our attention to the little New Testament book of Jude and its use of Scripture. As I pointed out in the previous chapter, the author of Jude assumed the authority and historical accuracy of pseudepigraphic books like the *Assumption of Moses* and *1 Enoch*, and he also assumed that *1 Enoch* was penned by Enoch himself. So in this case we are more or less forced to choose between embracing *1 Enoch* as canonical or admitting that Jude mistook it for an authentic work of Enoch. The second option strikes me as far more sensible than the former. And if the inspired author of Jude got his authorship attribution wrong for *1 Enoch*, then we have no strong reason to suppose that similar New Testament attributions of authorship must be correct—even if these were offered by Jesus himself. So the putative testimony of Jesus and the Bible, while important, cannot be adduced as foolproof evidence for our judgments about who wrote the books of the Old Testament. There are good reasons to suspect that Jesus's words about these matters are not historical-critical testimonies so much as the everyday assumptions of a pious, first-century Jew. Precritical orthodoxy makes it possible, and modern critical research makes it likely, that Jesus has not told us who really wrote the Pentateuch, Isaiah, or Daniel.

Strategy Eight: Pleading Ignorance and Obfuscating the Issues

New patterns are emerging in the evangelical response to biblical criticism. One of these is the increasing tendency to insist that critical scholarship fails, not because its theories can be proved wrong, but because they are simply too speculative. In its usual form, this rejection of criticism purports to look closely at the evidence in order to discern the kinds of conclusions that the evidence really warrants. It is then determined that the evidence is so fragmentary and complex that firm conclusions, especially those of the critical consensus, are precluded. T. Desmond Alexander's introduction to the Pentateuch provides a good example.

After a lengthy introduction to the critical issues, Alexander concludes: "At this stage there is no telling how Pentateuchal studies will develop ... it is highly unlikely that biblical scholars will be able to uncover with any certainty the process by which the Pentateuch was created."[72] Alexander then goes on to address the

---

72. Alexander, *From Paradise*, 80.

problem of historicity in the Pentateuch, concluding that "the issue of historical accuracy must remain open."[73] Essentially, Alexander writes an introduction to the Pentateuch in which he manages to take no explicit positions on such basic issues as the authorship, dating, and historicity of the Pentateuch.[74] This makes the book palatable for conservatives (because it eschews the critical consensus) and also, but less so, for critical scholars (because it does not openly embrace traditional readings). In the final analysis, however, this is sleight of hand; Alexander's actual comments on the Pentateuch generally assume its antiquity and historicity.

This sort of open-ended rhetoric appears even in the more progressive and well-informed introduction to the Old Testament written by Dillard and Longman. For instance, about the Pentateuch's composition, they conclude, "the best interpretation of the data admits the presence of sources and indications of development without dogmatically delineating their scope or date. The post- and a-Mosaica [i.e., non-Mosaic parts of the Pentateuch] display the presence of glosses; the question remains their extent."[75] In other words, Dillard and Longman confess that there is non-Mosaic material in the Pentateuch and recognize that the author of the Pentateuch used sources, but they do not believe that we can determine how much Moses contributed to the Pentateuch or what sources and authors are behind it. Dillard and Longman are equally circumspect about Deuteronomy: "There is no clear consensus on most issues surrounding Deuteronomy"[76] (although it seems to me that there certainly *is* a consensus). Regarding the historicity of Jonah, they write: "it is impossible to be dogmatic either way.... The question is irrelevant to the interpretation of the book."[77] As for the book of Isaiah and the critical theory that several different prophets wrote it, Dillard and Longman conclude: "The question of the authorship of Isaiah probably should not be made a theological ... test for orthodoxy. In some respects, the end results of the debate are somewhat moot: whether written by Isaiah in the eighth century or others who applied his insights to a later time, Isaiah 40–66 clearly was addressed in large measure to the needs of the exilic community."[78] Here the authors seem to imply—but never express explicitly—that they believe the second half of Isaiah was written during or after the exile. Again and again, Dillard and Longman admirably introduce the critical problems and then proceed to suggest that the issues do not matter so much, or that the evidence does not necessarily exclude the traditional view, or

---

73. Ibid., 81.
74. Although Alexander denies that we can know much about the Pentateuch's composition, he notes—quite correctly, I think—that the Pentateuch lies within a larger exilic- or postexilic-era composition that runs from Genesis to Kings (see *From Paradise*, 83–94). This composition was created through an editorial process that joined together older sources to form the story of ancient Israel. I would only add that the evidence for this historical-critical conclusion strikes me as no stronger, and perhaps far weaker, than the evidence for the existence of postexilic P.
75. Dillard and Longman, *Introduction*, 47.
76. Ibid., 97.
77. Ibid., 392–93.
78. Ibid., 275.

that the evidence is too complex to allow any firm conclusions.[79] Although this is what they explicitly say, a careful reader will not miss that subtle impression that Dillard and Longman would be quite comfortable if most or all of the standard critical conclusions turned out to be right.

Evangelical scholars have become increasingly sophisticated in their understanding and use of modern biblical criticism, but these examples show that something unusual is afoot in the rhetoric that they use to communicate their views. Although some evangelical scholars are honest enough to confess that the Pentateuch, Isaiah, Daniel, and the Gospels present many difficulties—even admitting that the critical conclusions are *possible*—their method for handling these difficulties is often to plead ignorance. Now there is in theory nothing wrong with admitting the limitations of the evidence and of our knowledge, but why in so many instances is this agnosticism the preferable tack for forward-thinking evangelicals? I would suggest that there are, among other things, four basic reasons for this rhetorical pattern.

First, it appears to me that many evangelical biblical scholars have not yet adequately synthesized their theological commitments with critical scholarship. Scripture's difficulties are clear enough to them, but so long as it is unclear how these difficulties relate to biblical authority, these scholars will be—and perhaps should be—tentative about the critical conclusions that they embrace. Second, a number of conservative scholars, many of them ordained clergy, have pastoral hearts and so wish to shield their readers from disruptive, faith-testing bouts with cognitive dissonance. This goal may be laudable and appropriate in some circumstances, particularly in local church contexts, but as an ethos it cannot govern the production of books that profess to handle scholarly issues for academic students. A third reason for the rhetorical ambiguity of evangelical biblical scholarship is that evangelical scholars are often wedged uncomfortably between their desire to be good scholars and their desire to sell books to conservative readers. As scholars they may suspect that Moses wrote only some (or perhaps little or none) of the Pentateuch, but taking a strong and clear stand on this issue would alienate evangelical readers in droves. To put it baldly: it seems to me that serious scholarship does not sell among conservative Evangelicals. Fourth, and perhaps most importantly, there are institutional issues at stake. Many evangelicals teach in conservative schools and colleges where the administrators and board members are very suspicious of modern biblical criticism, not only because it smacks of the old and destructive liberalism but also because it seems out of touch with their

---

79. Similar issue dodging appears in the New Testament introduction written by two top evangelical scholars, Donald A. Carson and Douglas J. Moo. The book's treatment of the Gospels does not deal much with the apparent contradictions among the Synoptics, and still less with those between the Synoptics and John's Gospel. Similarly, the discussion of Revelation does not mention the standard scholarly view that its author predicted that Christ would return during the Roman period (although a careful reader might be able to piece this together from the discussion). See Donald A. Carson and Douglas J. Moo, *An Introduction to the New Testament*, 2nd ed. (Grand Rapids: Zondervan, 2005).

institution's commitment to the authority of Scripture. These conservative institutions seem more comfortable with evangelical expressions of ignorance on critical matters—such as, "we do not know how the Pentateuch was written"—than with actual, concrete theories about the Pentateuch's composition. Pleading ignorance on critical matters is about all that scholars can do if they wish to avoid publishing scholarly nonsense but desire at the same time to hold on to their teaching post. Among other things, this means that evangelicals are sometimes better and more serious scholars than their published work shows. It is my experience that many evangelical scholars, in their more candid moments, will privately confess that their views are far closer to the critical consensus than their institutions could stomach. I will devote more attention to these institutional issues in the last chapter of this book.

One final point before I conclude. Though I hesitate to say it, a good explanation for the poverty of evangelical biblical scholarship needs to include one more element. It is unfortunate (but true, I think) that some evangelical scholars are poorly trained in the critical issues of biblical scholarship, a difficulty that is in some respects inevitable. Because their views are not generally welcomed in academic settings, conservative evangelicals have always had difficulty securing advanced university degrees in biblical studies, particularly in Old Testament. As a result, evangelicals have long tended to study in programs or institutions where they are not required to face the critical issues head-on. This option has been available for a long time in evangelical institutions and in some Jewish institutions, as well as in British universities, where the system permits one to focus narrowly on one biblical topic while avoiding others. Where evangelicals have elected to study outside these more hospitable contexts, the standard solution has been to specialize in something "safe" (like textual criticism) or to sidestep the issues by studying Near Eastern literature and culture (instead of Old Testament) or the Greek classics (instead of New Testament). As a result, evangelicals who have elected to take one of these "soft" academic routes are often (though not necessarily) underinformed in matters of critical scholarship. Surprising as it may sound, it is possible to hold a PhD in biblical studies from a very reputable institution and still know very little about the evidence that critical scholars consider in their assessments of biblical literature.

Conclusions

I should point out that I do not believe for a moment that healthy theological interpretations of the biblical text necessarily require correct critical judgments about the text in question. Biblical criticism may answer many legitimate questions about the biblical text, such as who wrote it, when, and under what conditions. But the answers to these critical questions are not nonnegotiable prerequisites of all biblical interpretation. Indeed, if historical criticism were as important as that, no Christians living prior to the modern era could have read the Bible fruitfully. The idea that one must read the Bible critically, which is still popular in some circles, is no more sensible than a claim that only professional musicians can appreciate good music, or that only trained astronomers can understand anything about the moon and stars.

On the other hand, correct critical judgments *are* prerequisites for good biblical (and I would add, theological) scholarship. It seems clear to me that, for the most part, evangelical efforts to challenge the standard results of biblical criticism not only fail but often fail badly. In particular, on the whole we cannot be happy with the polemical tone and questionable strategies used by conservative evangelical scholars. Fideism, specious arguments, misconstruing evidence, strained harmonizations, leaving out evidence, special pleading, and various kinds of obscurantism are par for the course in this conservative apologetic. To be sure, no scholar's work—whether Christian or not—is entirely free of these exegetical vices. But only in the most extreme school of critical scholarship—the so-called minimalist school—does one find a use of critical faculties as warped as among very conservative Christians.[80] When bright and informed Christian scholars find it necessary to resort to these questionable strategies to preserve their views, it probably means that fundamentalism, and the evangelical tradition that still imbibes of it, are deeply committed to something erroneous, both epistemically and theologically.

Because of the strong evidence adduced by biblical criticism against the standard evangelical assumptions about Scripture, evangelical scholars are increasingly willing to reconsider how critical scholarship might be constructively integrated with an appropriately high view of Scripture's authority. For instance, many progressive evangelicals now accept that there are sources in the Pentateuch,[81] that Isaiah was authored by several prophets,[82] that Daniel includes pseudoprophecy,[83] that the Chronicler's History is partially fictional,[84] that Jonah is fictional,[85] that there are differences between John and the Synoptics that cannot be historically

---

80. The "minimalist school" includes a small but influential cadre of Old Testament scholars, especially at Sheffield and Copenhagen, who view the Old Testament narratives as very late, Hellenistic-era novels. Not only is the historicity of the Bible's account of early Israel doubted (a standard view in scholarship) but also of the entire history. For an introduction see Lester L. Grabbe, ed., *Did Moses Speak Attic? Jewish Historiography and Scripture in the Hellenistic Period*, JSOTSup 317 (Sheffield: Sheffield Academic Press, 2001); for a somewhat polemical but useful critique, see William G. Dever, *What Did the Biblical Writers Know, and When Did They Know It? What Archaeology Can Tell Us about Ancient Israel* (Grand Rapids: Eerdmans, 2001).

81. Carl E. Armerding, *The Old Testament and Criticism* (Grand Rapids: Eerdmans, 1983), 21–42; Gordon J. Wenham, *Genesis*, 2 vols., WBC (Waco: Word, 1987-1994), 1. xxxv–xlii.

82. Peter C. Craigie, *The Old Testament: Its Background, Growth, and Content* (Nashville: Abingdon, 1986), 147–57; Dillard and Longman, *Introduction*, 274–75.

83. John Goldingay, *Daniel*, WBC (Waco: Word, 1989), 274–75; Paul M. Lederach, *Daniel* (Scottsdale, PA: Herald, 1994), 23–27, 225–61.

84. Dillard, *2 Chronicles*, xviii–xix; Dillard and Longman, *Introduction*, 169–77.

85. Leslie C. Allen, *The Books of Joel, Obadiah, Jonah, and Micah*, NICOT (Grand Rapids: Eerdmans, 1976), 175–81.

harmonized,[86] and that the Pastoral Epistles were written by someone other than Paul.[87] Standard critical positions are also accepted in the ever-popular Old Testament introduction of LaSor, Hubbard, and Bush, and in two massive Scripture projects, one by Old Testament scholar John Goldingay and the other by New Testament scholar N. T. Wright.[88] I should mention as well the more popular work of Peter Enns, *Inspiration and Incarnation*, which modestly challenges evangelicals to embrace a more positive view of Scripture's historical dimensions.[89] This progressive trend among evangelicals is feeding on the growing awareness that we need not make rigid choices between traditional orthodoxy and critical readings of Scripture. Tradition can be adjusted in light of biblical criticism, and biblical criticism needs the light that shines from tradition. Consequently, progressive evangelicals are increasingly open to tertium quid solutions that constructively integrate faith and criticism. Integrative models of this sort are badly needed if we hope to address the problem described some twenty years ago by our evangelical elder, Bernard Ramm: "There is no genuine, valid working hypothesis for most evangelicals to interact with the humanity of Scripture in general and biblical criticism in particular. . . . [Evangelicals] are still under obligation to propose a program that does enable an evangelical to live creatively with evangelical theology and biblical criticism."[90] It is to this task that we now turn.

---

86. George R. Beasley-Murray, *John*, WBC (Waco: Word, 1987), xxxii–xxxvii; F. F. Bruce, *The Gospel of John* (Grand Rapids: Eerdmans, 1983), 364-65.

87. Paul J. Achtemeier, Joel B. Green, and Marianne Meye Thompson, *Introducing the New Testament: Its Literature and Theology* (Grand Rapids: Eerdmans, 2001), 461-64; David G. Meade, *Pseudonymity and Canon: An Investigation into the Relationship of Authorship and Authority in Jewish and Earliest Christian Tradition* (Grand Rapids: Eerdmans, 1987), 118-39.

88. William S. LaSor, David A. Hubbard, and Frederick W. Bush, *Old Testament Survey*, 2nd ed. (Grand Rapids: Eerdmans, 1996); John Goldingay, *Models for Scripture* (Grand Rapids: Eerdmans, 1994); Goldingay, *Models for Interpretation of Scripture* (Grand Rapids: Eerdmans, 1995); N. T. Wright, *The New Testament and the People of God*, Christian Origins and the Question of God 1 (Minneapolis: Fortress, 1992); Wright, *Jesus and the Victory of God*, Christian Origins and the Question of God 2 (Minneapolis: Fortress, 1997); Wright, *The Resurrection of the Son of God*, Christian Origins and the Question of God 3 (Minneapolis: Fortress, 2003).

89. Peter Enns, *Inspiration and Incarnation: Evangelicals and the Problem of the Old Testament* (Grand Rapids: Baker Academic, 2005).

90. Bernard Ramm, *After Fundamentalism: The Future of Evangelical Theology* (San Francisco: Harper & Row, 1983), 34.

5

Constructive Responses to Biblical Criticism

Let us take stock of the journey so far. I began in chapter 1 with a discussion of epistemology, noting that human knowledge is the genuine article but also imperfect because of our limited and fallen capacities. This observation was further extended in chapters 2 and 3, where the critical evidence demonstrated that many ancient texts—including even the Bible itself—reflect this limited and imperfect horizon. In chapter 4 we sampled numerous evangelical attempts to counter this evidence, to show that the Bible's content is, after all, much closer to perfection than critical scholars suppose. I indicated in response that this evangelical project, though often motivated by good intentions, not only fails, but fails badly. Its failure is not the result of poor biblical exegesis, although poor exegesis is certainly one of its symptoms. No—at its heart the failure stems from evangelicalism's commitment to a faulty Cartesian epistemology, to an epistemology that assumes human beings have the capacity to see the world as God sees it. This theological error is quite natural, inasmuch as it confuses *entirely adequate* human knowledge with *entirely perfect* divine knowledge. But it is an error, nonetheless.

If human knowledge could perfectly mirror God's knowledge, and if this knowledge could in turn be expressed in human language, then evangelicals would be right to assume that the Bible is likely to be a perfect book, hermetically sealed from humanity's imperfections. In reality, however, I have tried to show that the theological, philosophical, and biblical evidence all stacks up squarely against this Cartesian perspective. Human beings are finite and fallen, and the Bible's human discourse participates in this adequate but limited and imperfect economy of meaning. Now, if this is so, and if the Bible is yet the true Word of God, as Christians believe, then some sort of constructive and integrative response to biblical criticism is called for. Such a response would adequately demonstrate that biblical authority and biblical criticism are compatible partners in a Christian view of the Bible.

Because many evangelicals imagine that biblical criticism is ipso facto irreligious, they may be surprised to know that many Christian scholars and theologians, both evangelical and nonevangelical, have tried their hand at integrating criticism and faith. Some of these constructive efforts are better than others, but almost all of them offer profitable insights into the problems that we face and the kinds of solutions that will be necessary to overcome them. Many of these integrative models have their roots in the neo-orthodoxy of the early to mid-twentieth century. Neo-orthodoxy does not enjoy the best of reputations in evangelical circles, and in certain respects I share these reservations. But for the most part I think that evangelicalism's reservations about neo-orthodoxy stem largely from misunderstandings of its nature and intent. Truth be told, neo-orthodoxy was never a single unified movement with a commonly articulated set of beliefs. It is better understood as a theological attitude that expressed itself in diverse responses to the disillusionment that followed World War I. This war brought Enlightenment confidence and optimism to its knees, and with it certain aspects of the Enlightenment's natural or "liberal" religion. However, though neo-orthodoxy recognized the bankruptcy of natural religion, it also recognized that many of the Enlightenment's critical observations about Scripture were accurate. Almost all of the constructive approaches that I consider below have to some extent grown out of neo-orthodoxy's dual commitment to biblical authority and to the essential validity of biblical criticism. Though I disagree with him in various respects, it remains true that no figure looms so important in these matters as the Swiss theologian Karl Barth.

The Theological Exegesis of Karl Barth

Karl Barth was one of the most important theological minds in church history, being most remembered for the strong stand that he took against the liberal religion that he believed was sapping the orthodoxy out of the twentieth-century church. On this score he would seem to count as a friend to evangelicals. But as we shall see, unlike the fundamentalist and evangelical traditions in Europe and North America, Barth did not perceive that these theological difficulties could be so easily blamed on the rise of historical criticism and its application to the Bible. In fact, he finally pinned at least part of the blame on certain conservative strands of modern theology. I shall do my best to explain how and why Barth came to these kinds of conclusions, but I must confess that finding coherence in his work is difficult. This is in part because Barth was not always as clear as he could have been, and in part because even his clearly expressed views do not always look compatible with one another. So with this caveat in place I will press on with the discussion, beginning with Barth's view of modern biblical criticism.

Barth believed that biblical criticism was "both necessary and justified,"[1] and he expressed in the strongest possible terms that the biblical writers and the texts that they wrote had a capacity for error "even in respect of religion and theology."[2] According to Barth, this was not a modern observation but rather something known since early antiquity.[3] In Barth's view, portions of the Bible, particularly in the Old Testament, "cannot be accepted as religious and theological literature, but only as documents of secular legislation and history and practical wisdom and poetry, although the Synagogue and later the church claimed to find in them witness of revelation."[4] The biblical writers were finite and fallen human beings, and the Bible reflects their errant scientific, historical, and theological views. According to Barth, if we deny this reality we fall into a kind of heretical docetism, which wants the Bible to be divine but not human.

Barth traced the cause of our modern difficulties with the Bible to two theological errors, one that went back to early Christianity and another that magnified this error during the seventeenth century. The earliest error, which he first sees in Augustine, was a theory of biblical inspiration that attempted to protect the Bible's integrity by denying human influence in its pages. This amounted to a kind of dictation theory, in which God merely used the biblical authors as we might use an ink pen.[5] The second error appeared in the post-Reformation period when scholars like Calov and Voetius began to argue that the Bible, being God's Word and not human words, was a book in which divine and infallible truth is "necessarily diffused over all Scripture and all parts of Scripture."[6] Once the church rejected the human element in Scripture and committed itself to a docetic sort of inerrancy, it was only a matter of time—and not a long time at all—before those in the church, and especially those outside, would notice the glaring contrast between the claims of inerrancy and the obvious human errors in Scripture. For this reason, according to Barth, our path through modern biblical criticism "must carefully and consistently avoid the mistake of that orthodoxy—which is all the more dangerous because its supernaturalistic trend can make it appear advantageous. It is only at this root that the evil which broke out later can really be tackled."[7] In sum, Barth believed that the errors in Scripture became a theological

---

1. Karl Barth, *The Epistle to the Romans*, trans. Edwyn C. Hoskyns, 6th ed. (London: Oxford University Press, 1933), 6.

2. Karl Barth, *Church Dogmatics*, 4 vols. in 12, ed. G. W. Bromiley and T. F. Torrance, trans. G. T. Thomson et al. (Edinburgh: T&T Clark, 1936–1977), 1.2:50.

3. Barth, *Church Dogmatics*, 1.2:509–10.

4. Ibid., 509.

5. Ibid., 518.

6. Ibid., 524.

7. Ibid., 523.

problem primarily because Christians mistakenly embraced a docetic doctrine of inerrancy. So, while evangelicals may fancy inerrancy as a doctrinal firewall against the destructive effects of biblical criticism, Barth avers that inerrancy was actually the cause of the fire.

Many questions and objections may be rolling around in evangelical heads at this point, but the foremost questions may be along these lines. If God commits no error, as orthodoxy demands, then how is it possible for the Bible to be so utterly human as Barth suggests? How does God speak through such a human text? Let us follow Barth's logic through to its end. In Barth's view, biblical criticism was suited to explore all sorts of questions about the language and history of the text, about its original authors and audiences, and about other similar contextual questions that palpably highlight the text's complexity and finite human horizon. However, Barth strongly disagreed with historical criticism's tendency to define the focus and scope of biblical exegesis in these narrow historical terms. The proper focus of Christian exegesis was not history but theology, and the proper starting place for theological exegesis was the *final canonical form* of the Bible rather than the various hypothetical stages that the biblical books may have passed through to get there. According to Barth, when theological exegesis is done properly, it will begin with the Bible in its final form and will read it in light of the Bible's true subject matter: *God revealed in Jesus Christ*. Because the Bible is about God and not about ancient history, to use it as a source for answering critical questions about Israel's society and history is akin to reading Moby Dick as if it were a book about whales. Of course we might well learn something about whaling from Melville, but that was not Melville's purpose. In the same way the Bible's purpose is only realized fully when God speaks to the church through its words. This means, of course, that biblical criticism's "assured results" about Israelite history, whatever they may be, can never be a real impediment to God's sovereign decision to speak to his people through the Bible.

How do we hear God speak in Scripture? It is often suggested that Barth embraced a *special hermeneutic* for reading Scripture that differed from the *general hermeneutic* we employ in the reading of other books, but this portrait of Barth's approach is probably too simple.[8] Barth claimed that "there is no such thing as special hermeneutics," and he insisted that biblical and general interpretive methodologies should operate on the same assumptions, so that "biblical, theological hermeneutics is not claiming for itself a mysterious special privilege."[9] For this reason, Barth describes the proper disposition for biblical interpretation in very general terms: "I must try to hear the words of the prophets and apostles in exactly the same freedom in which I attempt to hear the words of others who speak to me or have written for me as in the main intelligible words."[10] So far, Barth's words

---

8. Thomas E. Provence, "The Sovereign Subject Matter: Hermeneutics in the *Church Dogmatics*," in *A Guide to Contemporary Hermeneutics: Major Trends in Biblical Interpretation*, ed. Donald K. McKim (Grand Rapids: Eerdmans, 1986), 241–62.

9. Barth, *Church Dogmatics*, 1.2:456, 727.

10. Ibid., 723.

do not admit a distinction between special and general hermeneutics. But this is not the end of the matter. Barth believed that healthy interpretations of the Bible could only transpire when the reader of Scripture, like the original biblical author, was illumined or inspired by the Spirit.[11] Readers of Scripture can and must pray for this inspiration, but God's decision to reveal himself rests wholly in his sovereign choice. To be sure, this biblical hermeneutic at first strikes us as a special hermeneutic, but Barth insists that his hermeneutical principle "is necessarily the principle of *all* hermeneutics."[12] In essence, Barth would say that there is a special (christological) way to interpret not only the Bible but all books. This is true because all books—in fact, all things—are only properly interpreted when they are understood in the light of God's revelation in Christ.

We have seen that Barth embraced the critical view that the Bible contains errors as well as the traditional view that the Bible is God's Word. How did Barth square these two realities? Barth believed that God adopted the words of Scripture's human authors as his own, thus making the Bible simultaneously divine and human.[13] Barth was willing to describe this transaction as divine inspiration, although he did not mean thereby a simple kind of dictation, in which the biblical authors were like stenographers. The biblical authors were men to whom God revealed himself because they submitted themselves to the Spirit. Barth put it this way: "they themselves and of themselves thought and spoke and wrote what they did think and speak and write as genuine *auctores*," but this free act "acquired this special function, was placed under the *autoritas primaria*, the lordship of God, was surrounded and controlled and impelled by the Holy Spirit, and became an attitude of obedience in virtue of its direct relationship to divine revelation—that was their *theopneustia* ['inspiration']."[14] That said, it will probably never be entirely clear whether Barth meant that God merely accepted their human speech as his own, or whether, in some sense, God provided the biblical writers with what we might call "information." The first possibility is probably closer to the truth, since Barth consistently wanted to say that the Bible provides us with a "witness" to God's revelation in Christ rather than revelation itself.

On the historical front, Barth agreed with the critical conclusion that many of the biblical narratives could not pass as modern works of history. He often attempted to solve this problem generically by describing much of the biblical narrative as saga rather than history.[15] In Barth's day *saga* was the term used by biblical scholars to express the idea that the biblical narratives, like the medieval Scandinavian sagas, were best understood as a blend of history, legend, and fiction. In practice, however, Barth's theological exegesis was rarely interested in

11. Ibid., 505–16.
12. Ibid., 468.
13. Barth, *Romans*, 1, 11–12, 16–18; Barth, *Church Dogmatics*, 1.2:505.
14. Barth, *Church Dogmatics*, 1.2:505.
15. See discussion in Garrett Green, "Myth, History, and Imagination: The Creation Narratives in Bible and Theology," *Horizons in Biblical Theology* 12 (1990): 19–38.

distinguishing the history from the fiction. His use of the saga category was very flexible. In the case of the Genesis creation narratives, Barth described these sagas as products of human imagination. The biblical authors are true witnesses to God, "*not in spite of but because* they allow their imagination to govern."[16] To put it in Barth's own words, the Genesis creation story was composed through inspired "guessing" (*sich erraten läßt*).[17] Compare this with the quite different view of one evangelical, Bruce Waltke: "In the final analysis these creation stories derive *either* from unassisted creative imagination *or* from revelation."[18] Obviously Barth did not agree that we must choose between the two. Barth also used the term *saga* in connection with biblical descriptions of Christ's resurrection, but in this case he argued that the event "is still actual and objective in space and time."[19] Barth used the terms *saga* and *legend* to describe the resurrection narratives because, in his view, miraculous historical events like the resurrection cannot be grasped using the normal methods of historical analysis, which are based on analogy (i.e., what happens in the present tells us what probably happened in the past).[20] So, although the resurrection's historicity cannot pass the usual historical tests, it happened in time and space just the same. Barth's saga genre obviously included a broad range of texts, from the historical imagination of Genesis to the objective historical fact of the resurrection.

Let us sum up Barth's work. Because Barth's theology is complicated and often leaves us with many loose ends, the debate is ongoing about how we should construe his work. Nevertheless, several features in his view of Scripture and hermeneutics are relatively clear. Regarding Scripture, Barth resolved the apparent problems raised by biblical criticism with an appeal to three factors: genre, accommodation, and divine sovereignty. (1) Genre: In some cases the "errors" we perceive in Scripture are only illusions, created when we mistakenly read Scripture's narrative sagas as books of history. When we correct this generic mistake, we eliminate some of the ostensible difficulties implied by historical criticism. (2) Accommodation: Generic adjustments do not resolve all of our difficulties with historical criticism. Even if we allow for saga in Scripture, conspicuous evidence of Scripture's limited and errant perspective remains. Barth attributes this errant human horizon to God's sovereign choice, which was (and is) to speak with us by adopting the words of finite, fallen human beings as his own, thus accommodating his divine speech to the needs of the human audience. As I will point out more clearly in chapter 7, Barth's theological emphasis on accommodation was by no means new to Christian theology. (3) Divine Sovereignty: Because God freely chooses to reveal himself through Scripture, the human errors in Scripture are not—in fact, cannot be—an

---

16. Barth, *Church Dogmatics*, 3.1:92; cf. Green, "Myth, History, and Imagination," 28–29.
17. Barth, *Church Dogmatics*, 3.1:83.
18. See Bruce K. Waltke, "Oral Tradition," in *Inerrancy and Hermeneutic: A Tradition, a Challenge, a Debate*, ed. Harvie M. Conn (Grand Rapids: Baker Books, 1988), 35, italics mine.
19. Barth, *Church Dogmatics*, 4.1:333.
20. See Karl Barth, *Karl Barth's Table Talk*, ed. John D. Godsey (Richmond: John Knox, 1963).

impediment to this sovereign act of revelation. Indeed, according to Barth, God could speak to us in any number of ways: "God may speak to us through Russian Communism, a flute concerto, a blossoming shrub, or a dead dog. We do well to listen to Him if He really does. But, unless we regard ourselves as the prophets and founders of a new Church, we cannot say that we are commissioned to pass on what we have heard as independent proclamation."[21] In Barth's view, to assume that God can speak to us only through the Bible, or only through an inerrant Bible at that, is a foolish and direct assault on God's sovereignty.

Now, to Barth's hermeneutic. About this I should like to highlight two items and then take issue with a third. First, Barth insists on a single, thoroughgoing hermeneutic that applies not only to the Bible but to all acts of interpretation. Conceptually this means that all texts, things, and persons are properly understood only when they are understood in the light of God revealed in Christ. As hermeneutical theories go, this one strikes me as conceptually more economical than the traditional Christian distinction between special and general hermeneutics. I am tempted to express my unqualified agreement with this, but there is Barthian baggage on board that I will eventually wish to discard.[22] Second, Barth's theology accentuates the spiritual dimensions of interpretation, suggesting that our disposition toward God—and especially God's disposition toward us—determine whether and how well we can understand the Bible (and everything else). This principle seems to me very sensible and much in keeping with the apostle's words, "The unspiritual man does not receive the gifts of the Spirit of God, for they are folly to him, and he is not able to understand them because they are spiritually discerned. The spiritual man judges all things, but is himself to be judged by no one" (1 Cor. 2:14–15 RSV). Any account of biblical interpretation that neglects the role of the Spirit is poor indeed. Third, I should like to take issue fairly strongly with Barth's claim that biblical critics tend to misread the Bible because they focus on the wrong subject matter. Indeed, Barth is right to contend that the Bible's proper subject matter includes God revealed in Christ, but it is hardly sensible to limit the Bible's subject matter in this way. Even if the Old Testament narrative from Genesis through Kings is about God, it is also about the history, religion, and culture of ancient Israel. If biblical critics therefore consult this material to write a history of Israel, their task is altogether legitimate (with this Barth would agree) *and* the result should not be ignored or swept under the proverbial rug by competent theologians (with this Barth might not agree). The very fact that Barth and other theologians are tempted to ignore critical reconstructions of Israel's history is evidence that this critical information is problematic for them. If

---

21. Barth, *Church Dogmatics*, 1.1:55.
22. At issue is Barth's view that interpretation requires revelation, and that the event of revelation does not depend on the interpreter but on God himself. I would prefer to say that all human beings interpret with some success, but that such interpretations will always be amiss in certain respects. One reason—but by no means the only reason—that interpretation goes awry is that the interpreter works to some extent apart from the resources of divine grace.

it is problematic in this way, then either the historical critics are wrong, or Barth's theology is lacking. Any solution to the conflict between faith and criticism needs to deal more directly with the putative problems that historical criticism creates for theological exegesis.

Heilsgeschichte and Kerygmatic Exegesis

Beginning in the 1950s and 1960s, Gerhard von Rad and several of his students, most notably Claus Westermann and Hans Walter Wolff, followed by Walter Brueggemann, undertook an exegetical project whose purpose was to combine biblical criticism with theological interpretation.[23] Good English examples of their work can be found in volumes of the journal *Interpretation* published in the 1960s and 1970s.[24] By giving careful attention to the biblical author's genre in its original context (*form criticism*), these German scholars sought to understand the author's theological response to his ancient situation and then to use the author's proclaimed message—his *kerygma*—as a source of theological insight. In essence, the practitioners of kerygmatic exegesis did not attempt to go around biblical criticism but rather depended upon it as a method for discovering the biblical author's theology. In this theological model, it does not matter whether the exodus from Egypt actually took place in history; what matters is that Israel's recitation of the event confesses a theological truth about Israel's relationship to God and about God's role as Israel's savior. The organizing principle of kerygmatic exegesis was "salvation history," better known by its German name, *Heilsgeschichte*. When the various *kerygmata* of the biblical authors were read together, they provided an account of God's unfolding redemptive actions, which led inexorably to the incarnation, resurrection, and ascension of Jesus Christ (events that kerygmatic theologians usually took seriously).

One obvious benefit of kerymatic exegesis is that, by focusing on the respective theologies of the biblical authors, it offers a theological reading of the Bible even when Scripture's ostensible historical content turns out to be either wrong or fictional in some way. But this also presents an important difficulty. For kerygmatic exegesis, focused as it is on the words of various human authors in different contexts, tends to generate not one but many different theologies. Though kerygmatic theologians usually seek to unite these diverse theologies under the rubric of *Heilsgeschichte*, the end result of this synthetic effort—best embodied

---

23. For discussion see Robert Morgan and John Barton, *Biblical Interpretation*, Oxford Bible Series (Oxford: Oxford University Press, 1988), 98–104.

24. See, for example, Walter Brueggemann, "The Kerygma of the Deuteronomistic History: Gospel for Exiles," *Int* 22 (1968): 387–402; Gerhard von Rad, "Ancient Word and Living Word: The Preaching of Deuteronomy and Our Preaching" (trans. Lloyd Gaston), *Int* 15 (1961): 3–13; Von Rad, "Typological Interpretation of the Old Testament" (trans. John Bright), *Int* 15 (1961): 174–92; Claus Westermann, "The Role of the Lament in the Theology of the Old Testament" (trans. Richard N. Soulen), *Int* 28 (1974): 20–38; Hans Walter Wolff, "The Kerygma of the Yahwist" (trans. Wilbur A. Benware), *Int* 20 (1966): 131–58.

in von Rad's *Old Testament Theology*—is little more than a history of Israel's diverse religious, historical, and cultural viewpoints.[25] It is not at all clear what theological purpose these diverse viewpoints ultimately serve. For the most part, these kerygmatic interpreters also seem to have serious reservations about the historicity of what we have called the "mighty acts" of God, excepting perhaps the Christ event itself. Their theological interest was not so much in the empirically demonstrable saving acts of God as in the kerygmatic proclamation of those ostensible acts. This trend comes to the fore in the recent work of Brueggemann, who, in his postmodern garb, comes close to the suggestion that God himself is "created" by Israel's theological rhetoric.[26]

On the other hand, I would judge that one of the real strengths of kerygmatic theology is that it highlights the theological importance of God's revealed Word as it appeared on the historical scene, at the very moment in history when it was granted through the biblical authors to their ancient audiences. Because this initial moment of inscripturation inevitably provides a trajectory for all subsequent readings of the Bible, no full-orbed reading of the Bible can afford simply to ignore the intentions, strategies, and theologies of the human authors of Scripture.

The Biblical Theology Movement

While German kerygmatic exegesis focused on the written accounts of God's actions rather than on the mighty acts themselves, its American contemporary, the biblical theology movement, placed God's mighty acts at the center of theology. Certain biblical scholars, most notably W. F. Albright, had used philology, archaeology, and literary evidence to demonstrate that the essential outline of Israel's history as presented in the Bible was correct, implying at the same time that most of the theologically important biblical events, such as the exodus, did take place.[27] Taking this as their cue, scholars in the biblical theology movement—here we may think of people like G. E. Wright and Bernard W. Anderson—argued that historical criticism could probe behind the Bible's human testimony in order to recover and understand the saving acts in which God had powerfully revealed himself, events like the exodus and resurrection.[28] In this way the results of biblical criticism were not an impediment to theology but rather a chief source of theological insight.

25. Gerhard von Rad, *Old Testament Theology*, trans. D. M. G. Stalker, 2 vols. (New York: Harper & Row, 1962–1965).

26. Walter Brueggemann, *Theology of the Old Testament: Testimony, Dispute, Advocacy* (Minneapolis: Fortress, 1997), 65–66. See also James Barr, *The Concept of Biblical Theology* (Minneapolis: Fortress, 1999), 544.

27. See W. F. Albright, *Yahweh and the Gods of Canaan: A Historical Analysis of Two Contrasting Faiths* (Garden City, NY: Doubleday, 1968); Albright, *From the Stone Age to Christianity: Monotheism and the Historical Process*, 2nd ed. (Baltimore: Johns Hopkins Press, 1957).

28. Bernard W. Anderson, *Understanding the Old Testament*, 3rd ed. (Englewood Cliffs, NJ: Prentice-Hall, 1975); G. Ernest Wright, *God Who Acts: Biblical Theology as Recital*, Studies in Biblical Theology 1/8 (London: SCM, 1952).

The biblical theology movement was billed as a response to the theological vacuity of liberal religion, a vacuity that the movement blamed, at least in part, on liberalism's rejection of biblical authority and biblical language. In a masterful 1961 critique of this movement, however, Langdon Gilkey demonstrated that its underlying epistemology was not so different from the liberalism it hoped to replace.[29] The hallmarks of natural/liberal religion are *universality* (all human beings have the same access to religious truth) and *ordinary causation* (God works through the natural order of creation). The biblical theology movement, with its emphasis on God's mighty acts, claimed to run exactly counter to this. But Gilkey noted that this contrast was an illusion. In their actual descriptions of God's great deeds, those in the biblical theology movement did not allow much room for the powerful, revelatory acts of God. Bernard Anderson, for instance, did not describe the parting of the Red Sea (or Reed Sea) as an obvious miracle but attributed it instead to "an East wind blowing over the Reed Sea."[30] In the end, asks Gilkey, is this not natural religion all over again, in which the Hebrew people, when confronted by an impressive natural phenomenon (ordinary causation), provided themselves with a theological interpretation of the experience (universality)?

Gilkey's critique of the biblical theology movement seems generally correct. Although the movement's attempt to moor theology to Scripture was admirable in its day, it seems to have unconsciously shared much of the secular epistemology of natural religion. Moreover, like its cousin, kerygmatic exegesis, the biblical theology movement suffered from a second problem. Precisely because its focus was the Bible, the movement tended to produce not one univocal theology but rather a host of differing theologies. This cannot be a surprise. As a distinctively Protestant movement that tacitly embraced the principle of *sola scriptura*, the biblical theology movement lacked the theological resources—available especially in long-standing church traditions—to integrate the Bible's diversity into a conceptual whole. This meant that the movement, already rejected or ignored by secular biblical scholars, was eventually rejected by systematic theologians.[31]

During the 1970s, the Albrightean synthesis that supported the essential historicity of the Old Testament began to disintegrate, and the biblical theology movement—which had deceived itself into believing that this history was its

---

29. Langdon Gilkey, "Cosmology, Ontology, and the Travail of Biblical Language," *Journal of Religion* 41 (1961): 194–205.

30. Here Gilkey more or less parodies in his own words those of Anderson, which appear on p. 49 of Anderson's *Understanding the Old Testament*. Anderson's actual words are as follows: The event "was not impossible in the marshy area of Lake Menzalah; in fact, it has been witnessed at other times. The miracle was that it happened at a particular time and with a particular meaning."

31. James Barr, "The Theological Case against Biblical Theology," in *Canon, Theology, and Old Testament Interpretation: Essays in Honor of Brevard S. Childs*, ed. Gene M. Tucker, David L. Petersen, and Robert R. Wilson (Philadelphia: Fortress, 1988), 3–19.

theological basis—disappeared with that synthesis.[32] The biblical theology movement is no more, but its legacy lives on in the canonical approaches of scholars like Brevard Childs.[33]

Brevard Childs: Canonical Interpretation

Drawing inspiration from the work of Karl Barth, Brevard Childs introduced canonical interpretation as a way through the impasse reached by the biblical theology movement, which could not overcome questions about the Bible's historicity or manage the theological diversity of Scripture.[34] With regard to the problem of the Bible's historicity, Childs—who studied with von Rad and was influenced by his kerygmatic exegesis—suggested that biblical scholars had committed a generic mistake by treating the Bible as a history book rather than as the theological book it was (here we hear echoes of Barth).[35] Good theology could be conveyed in any number of genres besides narrative history, as the fictional parables of Jesus show. With regard to the theological diversity of Scripture, Childs agreed that biblical criticism, focused as it is on different authors in diverse contexts, tends to produce only a cacophony of theological voices with no way to pull them together. This cacophony is not a serious problem for biblical scholars who lack theological interest, but it hardly suits the Christian pursuit of theological truth and coherence. Yet Childs does not conclude from this that biblical criticism has erred in discovering the theological diversity of Scripture. He concludes instead that healthy theology requires a larger contextual matrix in which the diversity of Scripture can be integrated properly into a theological whole. For Childs, this larger context is the biblical canon. According to him, as God's people listen to the intracanonical dialogue among the various biblical texts, we hear God's full-orbed voice and discover a theological coherence greater than the sum of the Bible's theological parts. For example, although some biblical texts might suggest that slavery is ethically permissible, *the canon as a whole*—which contains the venerable Golden Rule—will suggest that it ultimately is not. Essentially, the canon provides the theological antidote for the Bible's diversity. What we have, then, is a very sophisticated implementation of the Reformation's mantra that "Scripture interprets Scripture."

How does biblical criticism fit into this scheme? According to Childs, the historical "depth" that biblical criticism sees in the text helps us read it better. For

---

32. Note especially the important critiques of Albright by Thomas L. Thompson, *The Historicity of the Patriarchal Narratives: The Quest for the Historical Abraham*, BZAW 133 (Berlin: de Gruyter, 1974); and John Van Seters, *Abraham in History and Tradition* (New Haven: Yale University Press, 1975).
33. See Barr, *Concept of Biblical Theology*, 378–438.
34. Brevard S. Childs, *Biblical Theology in Crisis* (Philadelphia: Westminster, 1970); Childs, *Introduction to the Old Testament as Scripture* (Philadelphia: Fortress, 1979).
35. Childs, *Introduction to the Old Testament*, 39–41.

example, when we recognize that Genesis was created by combining two voices—the Yahwist and the Priestly Writer—we are able to hear the combined text with greater precision.[36] But it is the final canonical form of Genesis, and of the biblical canon as a whole, that provides the determinative literary and theological context for interpreting the significance of the two older sources. It is entirely legitimate, says Childs, for biblical scholars to take these two pentateuchal sources out of their canonical context and to use them to reconstruct Israel's religious and social history, but he cautions that "this enterprise is of a different order from the interpretation of sacred scripture which we are seeking to describe."[37] So, while Childs does not eliminate the legitimacy of biblical criticism, he tends to curb its theological importance. In practice, however, Childs's biblical interpretation includes heavy doses of historical criticism. Historical criticism is less pronounced in the theological work of Chris Seitz, a student of Childs who employs a similar, and to my mind more sophisticated, canonical approach.[38]

What difficulties does Childs's canonical interpretation present? One potential problem is that we have before us not one but several different canons, each stemming from the Jewish, Catholic, Orthodox, and Protestant traditions. But this constitutes a difficulty only insofar as each community is unsure about the limits of its own canon. The more pressing difficulty is Childs's thesis that the biblical canon provides a sufficient context for theological interpretation. Let us take slavery for an example. I pointed out in chapter 3 that our modern rejections of slavery were not founded solely on the explicit testimonies of Scripture, because both Testaments permitted the practice. But if our rejection of slavery is indeed the proper and correct course of action, and if this ethical move is not readily derived from Scripture alone, then we must conclude that Childs's canonical context, while an improvement on the cacophony of biblical voices offered by biblical critics, falls short as an adequate context for theological reflection.[39] Evidently, a still larger conceptual context is necessary for a healthy yet biblically informed theology. This is a point that I will eventually pursue at length in chapters 6 and 7.

Walter Wink: The Bankruptcy of Biblical Criticism

Like Childs, Walter Wink believes that biblical criticism offers many correct observations about the biblical text, but in doing so it is unable to accomplish its primary purpose: to use Scripture as a source for spiritual formation.[40] According

36. Ibid., 71–83.
37. Ibid., 76.
38. Christopher R. Seitz, *Figured Out: Typology and Providence in Christian Scripture* (Louisville: Westminster John Knox, 2001). See also Charles J. Scalise, *From Scripture to Theology: A Canonical Journey into Hermeneutics* (Downers Grove, IL: InterVarsity, 1996).
39. Roy F. Melugin, "Canon and Exegetical Method," in Tucker et al., *Canon, Theology, and Old Testament Interpretation*, 48–61.
40. Walter Wink, *The Bible in Human Transformation* (Philadelphia: Fortress, 1973).

to Wink, this is because the assumptions and methods of historical criticism are incommensurate with the theological intentions of the biblical text (here again, one hears echoes of Barth). Historical criticism fancies itself as an objective science and, as such, is interested only in certain kinds of historical questions. It is precisely this illusion of objectivity, with its historical focus, that voids historical criticism of its potential for theological insight. Theology must attend to all of the dimensions in human life, not only to the mind, reason, knowledge, and theory (which biblical criticism can manage) but also to the body, emotion, experience, and practice (categories that an "objective" critical approach cannot easily manage). As Wink put it, biblical critics "can describe Paul's view of grace with as much benign condescension as we adjudge the carbon date of a Qumran fragment."[41] While biblical criticism might be able to tell us when the book of Daniel was written, it will never be able to help us grow spiritually when we read Daniel.

If biblical criticism has served any vital purpose, Wink believes it was in "destroying the conservative view of biblical origins and inspiration, thereby destroying its entire ideology."[42] While this sentiment might sting evangelical ears, it is essential that we understand why Wink—and, in fact, practically all others surveyed here—expresses these kinds of sentiments. Wink views fundamentalism as intellectually bankrupt and at least as theologically dangerous as rabid liberalism. His judgment is founded on what he perceives to be fundamentalism's anti-intellectualism and its arrogant, separatist spirit toward other religious and social groups (i.e., its Pharisaical qualities). In Wink's view, although the "acid bath of criticism" served an iconoclastic function for faith by revealing the naiveté of fundamentalism, he insisted that good theology must push beyond this critical turn to what Paul Ricoeur called a "second naiveté," in which faith serves an iconoclastic function in relation to criticism.

What shall we make of Wink's observations? Evangelical readers are likely to agree with Wink—and with Barth and Childs—that reading the Bible theologically must go well beyond the historical-critical insights gleaned from academic study. To go beyond historical criticism requires that we lay aside the illusion of its objectivity and carry out our work as human beings, who empathize with the ancients of the Bible as well as with those of our own age, and who recognize that the Bible was given to us for spiritual nourishment. At the same time, Wink would have us recognize that historical criticism was valuable as a theological critique of fundamentalism, whose docetic view of Scripture, left unchecked, can breed a kind of bibliolatry that distracts us from God and Christ. Perhaps these sentiments will not resonate with some conservative Christian readers, but Wink's concern on this point seems very close to that expressed by Jesus: "You search the scriptures, because you think that in them you have eternal life; and it is they that bear witness to me; yet you refuse to come to me that you may have life" (John 5:39–40 RSV).

41. Ibid., 14.
42. Ibid., 12.

My chief difficulty with Wink's thesis is his theological critique of biblical criticism. He assumes that biblical criticism's aims should be explicitly theological, but biblical criticism—like Assyriology—is a pluralistic discipline that includes many actors with varying degrees of theological interest. As a result, the guild tends to be interested in a limited number of issues, such as when a text was written, by whom, for what purpose, and so on. There is nothing unseemly about an academic discipline whose chief interest is in asking these kinds of historical, religious, sociological, and philological questions about the Bible. One hardly needs a particular theology—or any explicit theology at all—to postulate answers for most of the straightforward questions that scholars ask of the Bible or of other ancient texts. Christians and atheists alike can offer valid critical judgments about when a biblical book seems to have been written, about how best to translate its linguistic idiom, and about what audience the book addressed. Just as Christians and atheists can share a belief in neutrons, so they can share a belief in Second Isaiah. To my mind, the differences between Christian and non-Christian views of the Bible will be most visible not in the microlevel details of critical judgment but at the macrolevel, where these critical judgments are intellectually and spiritually integrated. So, if Wink's complaint about biblical criticism applies to anyone, it would apply especially to confessing Christian scholars who never bother to integrate their critical research into a healthy, theologically informed whole.

David Steinmetz: The Return to Precritical Exegesis

As Wink has just reminded us, biblical criticism's focus on historical and sociological issues has often produced arid and sterile interpretations of the Bible. The chief cause of this, according to David Steinmetz, is that modern biblical scholarship has identified the goal of interpretation as none other than to recover the original intentions of Scripture's human authors.[43] This exegetical objective differs fairly sharply from the objectives of precritical exegesis as practiced by the church fathers and by other premodern exegetes of the church. Generally speaking, during the premodern period the church not only believed in the *literal sense* of Scripture—roughly equivalent to our idea of the human author's intention—but also in three additional senses of Scripture: the *allegorical, tropological*, and *anagogical* aspects of the text. In its classical formulation, these three levels of meaning corresponded to the three cardinal virtues of faith, love, and hope: the allegorical sense teaches what we should believe, the tropological sense teaches what we should do, and the anagogical sense points to our future hope. Here we must step carefully if we are to understand. The ancients did not believe that the literal sense was intended by the biblical author and that the other senses were merely human interpretations based on the intended literal meaning. Rather,

---

43. David C. Steinmetz, "The Superiority of Precritical Exegesis," *Theology Today* 37 (1980): 27–38.

God was the true author of Scripture, so that Scripture's threefold *sensus plenior* ("fuller sense") joined the literal sense as part of his divine intention.

The ancients found this fourfold sense of Scripture especially helpful when the literal sense of a biblical text seemed to create theological problems. Steinmetz expresses the difficulty in a way that only he can:

> How was a French parish priest in 1150 to understand Psalm 137, which bemoans captivity in Babylon, makes rude remarks about Edomites, expresses an ineradicable longing for a glimpse of Jerusalem, and pronounces a blessing on anyone who avenges the destruction of the temple by dashing Babylonian children against a rock? The priest lives in Concale, not Babylon, has no personal quarrel with Edomites, cherishes no ambition to visit Jerusalem (though he might fancy a holiday in Paris), and is expressly forbidden by Jesus to avenge himself on his enemies. Unless Psalm 137 has more than one possible meaning, it cannot be used as a prayer by the church and must be rejected as a lament belonging exclusively to the piety of ancient Israel.[44]

In such cases, the church fathers believed that Paul's dictum was apropos: "The letter kills, but the Spirit gives life" (2 Cor. 3:6 NIV). It was by the Spirit that the church could look past the problematic literal sense of Scripture to discover the healthier senses offered by allegorical, tropological, and anagogical readings. So, for the ancients, the additional levels of meaning provided an exegetical tool for resolving the apparent tensions and contradictions in Scripture. As we can see, the ancients, no less than modern readers, were sometimes troubled by the Bible's literal meanings. The fathers were undoubtedly on the right track when they realized that these difficulties would require a special hermeneutic, which fully accounted for the Bible's nature as a text written by two authors—divine and human. This is why Steinmetz has advocated a return to "pre-critical exegesis."[45]

Judged from our present vantage point, it might at first seem that this old exegetical approach opens the door to interpretive shenanigans of every sort. Can one not use allegories to make the Bible say whatever one wishes? Steinmetz admits that the allegorical readings of the fathers sometimes went too far. In his view, however, the potential for such exegetical excess is always circumscribed by the language of the Bible itself, which does not permit every reading but only a field of possible meanings. Readings that fall within this field of possibilities are valid, while idiosyncratic readings outside this field are invalid. For this reason, Steinmetz believes that a return to ancient methods of exegesis will be both safer and healthier than modern biblical criticism. What shall we make of his thesis?

Let me begin with criticisms and end with praise. Steinmetz's defense of precritical exegesis seems to need further refinement. Foremost, he does not adequately

---

44. Ibid., 29-30.
45. Ibid. For similar perspectives see Richard A. Muller and John L. Thompson, "The Significance of Precritical Exegesis: Retrospect and Prospect," in *Biblical Interpretation in the Era of the Reformation*, ed. Richard A. Muller and John L. Thompson (Grand Rapids: Eerdmans, 1996), 335-45.

explain why modern readers should accept an ancient, fourfold hermeneutic that the church fathers essentially adopted from Greek philosophy.[46] My suspicion on this point is aptly illustrated in the exegetical work of another scholar, Richard Hays. Though Hays has argued that modern Christians should employ the same exegetical methods used by the ancient authors of the New Testament,[47] his actual theological work—which is, to my mind, excellent—does not do this; he uses exegetical methods that are acceptable to modern readers.[48] The reason for this is obvious: ancient methods of exegesis are not very convincing to modern audiences. So if a case is to be made for modern uses of ancient exegesis, the argument cannot simply be "this is how it was always done." Such an argument becomes doubly weak when we realize that, indeed, this is certainly *not* how it was always done. Steinmetz fails to highlight the obvious and important point that the early church did not agree on these matters at all. Some of the old fathers, particularly of the Antiochene school, were deeply troubled by the allegories of the Alexandrian school.[49] Even the most rigorous of allegorists gave pride of place to Scripture's so-called plain meaning.[50] Under these circumstances, one wonders why we should adopt exegetical methods that have proved so foreign to both modern and ancient sensibilities.

Steinmetz's approach entails still other theoretical problems. It is too simple to suggest, as Steinmetz does, that any reading of Scripture that fits the field of possible textual meanings is legitimate. To give just one example, the words "good job" will mean one thing as sarcasm ("poor job"!) and quite another as an earnest compliment. Though the discourse surely allows for both options, both interpretations cannot be right at the same time. So it seems to me that the programmatic claim made by Steinmetz, that the biblical discourse adequately limits our allegorical imagination, needs to be fleshed out more fully. This fleshing out could be done with some success, in my opinion, but it will require heading in a somewhat different direction from what Steinmetz charts out. In his zeal to legitimize allegories, Steinmetz does not adequately explore the intriguing possibility that God speaks to the church even through its *flawed* allegorical exegesis. This is a possibility that I will consider later on, in chapter 9.

Enough of my criticism. All told, there is something profoundly true in Steinmetz's thesis. Because God speaks to his church in every age, the results of precritical exegesis *must* reflect valuable theological and exegetical insights. This should be particularly true of the early church fathers, whose responsibility it was to clarify

---

46. See Michael Burney Trapp, "Allegory, Greek," in *Oxford Classical Dictionary*, ed. Simon Hornblower and Antony Spawforth, 3rd ed. (Oxford: Oxford University Press, 1996), 64.
47. Richard B. Hays, *Echoes of Scripture in the Letters of Paul* (New Haven: Yale University Press, 1989), 154–92.
48. Richard B. Hays, *The Moral Vision of the New Testament* (San Francisco: HarperSanFrancisco, 1996).
49. Young, "Alexandrian and Antiochene Exegesis."
50. Augustine, *On Christian Doctrine* 3.1–9 (*NPNF* 1 2:556–59).

the contours of orthodoxy and to ensure that our canon of Scripture suited these contours. From a Christian perspective, the very fact that modern biblical criticism largely rejects the precritical tradition, often derisively, points to a glaring fault in its Enlightenment epistemology, a fault shared by some modernist—especially evangelical—Christians. Any healthy view of hermeneutics should attest not only to the weaknesses but also to the strengths of the church's biblical exegesis, from its earliest days to the present. I will take up this matter later in a discussion of allegorical method (see chapter 9).

Narrative Theology

It is clear enough that biblical criticism seriously disrupted the church's traditional view of biblical exegesis and theology. But why, specifically, was this the effect of historical criticism? In his landmark volume, *The Eclipse of Biblical Narrative*, Hans Frei offers a straightforward answer to this question, as well as a potential antidote for the problems.[51] According to Frei, precritical readers of Scripture assumed that the narrative world of the Bible was also their world. So, for instance, the great reformer John Calvin never doubted that the world of sixteenth-century Geneva was also the world that God created, the world where Adam and Eve once lived, the world of the great flood, and the world populated by the descendants of Noah's sons, Ham, Shem, and Japheth. So long as this seamless fabric connected the biblical text with the biblical world and the world of the contemporary reader, it was rather natural for readers of Scripture to fit their world into the biblical world. In this way, the biblical narratives served a valuable theological function by "Christianly" shaping the life of the church. Historical criticism obviously disrupted this synergetic status quo by accentuating the historical and cultural rifts that separated the ancient world from our own.

Like Barth and Wink, Frei blames the rise of historical criticism and its problems on a peculiar confluence of ideas from both radical skepticism and biblical conservatism. According to Frei, during the seventeenth and eighteenth centuries, biblicist conservatives like J. Cocceius and J. A. Bengel attempted to locate the events of their own day in the biblical narrative so that they could use the text to predict the future return of Christ. As a result, theological interests shifted from the biblical narrative itself to the actual history behind it. At about this same time, the events of biblical history were fast becoming victims of Enlightenment skepticism. By the time the critics had announced that the biblical narratives were not as historical as previously thought, everyone was believing—Christians and skeptics alike—that *objective history* was what really counted in theology (this belief is sometimes called *historicism*). Two responses ensued. On the liberal side, the biblical narratives were no longer viewed as useful accounts of God's relationship

---

51. Hans Frei, *The Eclipse of Biblical Narrative: A Study in Eighteenth and Nineteenth Century Hermeneutics* (New Haven: Yale University Press, 1974).

with Israel and the church. Its narratives became instead mere sources to be studied in the quest for modern progress and for the truths of natural religion. For advocates of natural religion, this new theological task included explaining the origins and composition of a faulty Bible, as well as the task of finding the religious value in its utterly human discourse. Conservatives headed in the opposite direction. By holding ever tighter to the Bible's historicity, their theological focus shifted from the biblical text itself to the putative referential events it narrated. As Frei put it, "All across the theological spectrum the great reversal had taken place; interpretation was a matter of fitting the biblical story into another world with another story rather than incorporating that world into the biblical story."[52] In Frei's view, neither the liberal nor conservative responses to historical criticism were truly biblical, for in neither case did the church allow itself to be determinatively shaped by the biblical story. Liberals rejected the biblical narrative, and conservatives looked behind the narrative for genuine history. Hence the "eclipse" of the biblical narrative.

How does Frei suggest that we traverse this impasse? His widely accepted solution is essentially generic. He suggests that the biblical narratives should be understood not as modern histories but as *history-like* metanarratives, whose purpose is to convey the Christian worldview. "Metanarrative"—in literal terms, the "big story"—is the grand narrative that explains how all other narratives should be understood and against which all other narratives must be judged. Metanarratives are not about the particular events they narrate but are instead about all events everywhere. If it is indeed true that the biblical stories are *history-like* and not historical—more metanarrative than narrative—then Frei says we should resist the historicist impulse to locate the meaning of the biblical narrative in its historical referent (i.e., in actual events it describes). The better and more proper way to read the biblical story is to fit our world and life into its metanarrative, so that the biblical worldview again shapes ours, just as it did in the precritical age of the church fathers. In certain respects, this move is not unlike Steinmetz's preference for precritical exegesis. Both Steinmetz and Frei believe that biblical criticism is correct in many of its historical judgments, but they also believe that it presents serious theological problems. The solution is not to dig yet deeper into the criticism but to return to older, healthier, precritical reading strategies.

According to narrativist theologians, these precritical strategies also help us resolve the problem of the Bible's theological diversity. Precritical readers took the Bible for a single story of God's redemption of humanity. If modern readers will embrace this posture anew, then we will discern from the Bible's diversity a more fundamental Christian metanarrative that absorbs its diversity. The Bible's story of the Canaanite genocide, for instance, will be understood in the light of the crucifixion story, in which the incarnate son dies for, and forgives, his enemies. Such a theological approach admits the diversity of the Bible but does not sacrifice

---

52. Ibid., 130.

unity in the process. Whether readers are prepared to embrace this approach to theology is another matter, but it seems to me that something of this sort is necessary if our thirst for theological unity is to be quenched amid the torrent waters of biblical diversity.

Though I find Frei's thesis intriguing, its key merits are accompanied by several nagging difficulties. One of these has to do with Frei's claim that the trouble with biblical criticism emerged when religious conservatives began to focus on the historicity of the events narrated in the Bible. It may well be that at a certain point conservatives became too interested in historical questions, but Frei's analysis probably makes things more complicated than they were. The reality is that most everyone in church history has believed that the biblical narratives are historically true and that their historical truth was theologically important. When historical criticism uncovered the historical problems in the Bible, and when the naturalistic philosophy of the Enlightenment rejected everything from the reality of God to the miracle of the resurrection, there were only two directions to go: give up the faith, or contend for its truth—including its historical truth. As Paul and the creeds tell us (1 Cor. 15), the Christian faith rises or falls with the historicity of the resurrection. To my mind Frei is undoubtedly right that the historicism of biblical fundamentalism is problematic, but the real difficulties rested, and continue to rest, not merely in fundamentalism but in the new insights of biblical criticism.

Another difficulty with Frei's book is his attempt to redefine the genre of biblical narrative so that it is "history-like" rather than historical. This thesis runs aground on two shoals. First, as Ricoeur correctly notices, all texts—whether history or history-like fictions—have a referential character that makes them about the world.[53] The parable of the good Samaritan, for instance, is not about a particular sequence of events in time; but it is certainly about real victims and real crimes, and about those who help—or do not help—their neighbors in distress. Because the parable can describe many times and places rather than a single time and place, its depiction of history is actually better than if it were a genuine historical report. That is, in a certain sense we could say that *parables are both historical and radically referential*. When Frei gives up the referential character of the biblical narrative, he has given up the theoretical connection between text and reality; and, if the text is not about reality, then it is hard to know why or how we should pay attention to it.

The other shoal on which Frei's generic thesis runs aground is in its utter uselessness to attack the real problem. In the eyes of modern scholarship it is now as clear as it can possibly be that the biblical writers sometimes believed that their narratives were historically accurate when they were not, and it is almost as clear that they sometimes passed off fictions as history.[54] This is the difficulty, and

---

53. Paul Ricoeur, *Essays on Biblical Interpretation*, ed. Lewis W. Mudge (Philadelphia: Fortress, 1980), 44.

54. For a discussion of the illocutionary stance of the biblical narrators and its implications for Frei's thesis, see Nathan MacDonald, "Illocutionary Stance in Hans Frei's *The Eclipse of Biblical Narrative*," in *After Pentecost:*

Frei's thesis that the Bible is history-like does not help us with it but rather uses a sleight of hand to make it disappear. The biblical historians clearly believed that much of what they wrote was historical rather than history-like, and it is equally clear that the Christian faith hinges in some serious respects on the events of history. So Frei's attempt to address these difficulties seems to leave us with several theoretical and theological loose ends.

I am also uncomfortable with the manner in which narrative theology privileges narrative genres. This generic preference stems in part from reluctance among narrative theologians to allow that propositional theological statements can be true. According to George Lindbeck, for instance, doctrinal statements like "God is a Trinity" should not be construed as true statements of ontological fact but as grammatical rules that govern our talk about God.[55] Construed in this way, doctrines are somewhat like the fences that mark off a field—in the end they tell us very little about the field itself. Narrative genres naturally suit this humble theological agenda because they portray reality's contours without making grand claims about the fundamental nature of reality.

Now it is just good theology to wonder, as Lindbeck does, about whether the doctrinal propositions of finite human beings can really correspond to the ontological nature of an infinite God. So on this point I have some sympathy with the narrative theologians. Yet Lindbeck's account of doctrine seems ultimately to sell short the theological capacity of human thought and language. If the practical realism that I have advocated in chapter 1 is right, then human beings have the capacity to speak about and understand reality in ways that usefully and adequately (but not perfectly) correspond to it. Whether we can describe our knowledge of God in this way is another matter, but the fact that we bear God's image, and have received from him the gift of language, suggests that Scripture's linguistic affirmations about God can correspond in some useful respects to the divine nature. As William Abraham has noted, we commonly accept propositions like "I am depressed" or "I am happy" as useful descriptions of human persons. Why should this not be the case respecting a God who the church has long declared is personal?[56] It seems to me that, when we assent to the doctrine that God is Trinity, we are not merely limiting the sorts of ways that we can speak about God; we are making an ontological claim about the nature of God himself, which we know precisely because God has revealed himself to us.[57] So I do not believe that we must settle for a theology that is merely grammatical and nearly apophatic.

Language and Biblical Interpretation, ed. Craig G. Bartholomew, Colin Greene, and Karl Möller, SHS 2 (Grand Rapids: Zondervan, 2001), 312–28.

55. George A. Lindbeck, *The Nature of Doctrine* (Philadelphia: Westminster, 1984).

56. William J. Abraham, *The Divine Inspiration of Holy Scripture* (Oxford: Oxford University Press, 1981), 79–80.

57. See McGrath's response to Lindbeck in Alister E. McGrath, *The Genesis of Doctrine: A Study in the Foundation of Doctrinal Criticism* (Grand Rapids: Eerdmans, 1990), 14–34.

Another reason for narrative theology's generic preference for narrative stems from a belief, now quite common in philosophy, that grand metanarratives provide the templates by which human beings understand reality.[58] The only debate nowadays is whether these metanarratives can bear truth (realists) or are merely fictions of human imagination (antirealism). It is natural, of course, to presume that narrative genres are the essential element in expressions of metanarrative, but this is perhaps to notice the bricks but not the mortar. All narratives work by presupposing certain extranarrative conceptual realities, such as justice, mercy, love, hatred, pain, pleasure, and so on. Long before my two young children embraced any sort of metanarrative, they could spot when one received more ice cream than the other. Their innate sense of justice was a prenarrative consciousness; it preceded, rather than depended upon, narrative. Injustice was given narrative expression only when my children described how it was that so much ice cream was dished out here, and not so much there. Now, I do not mean to suggest that narratives merely and only depend upon extranarrative properties. Narratives presume these properties, but they always go on to shape them and make arguments about them. For instance, the story of Jesus's crucifixion will presuppose many basic extranarrative concepts like guilt, justice, and retribution, but it will then go on to tell us something new about human sin and about God's remedy for it. Ultimately, there is no narrative that hangs in thin air. Extranarrative properties and the realia of life and events are necessary prerequisites that make the narratives work. So theological reflection should attend not only to the importance of story in expressing metanarrative but also to the extranarrative conceptual mortar that holds metanarratives together. My point is driven home by the Bible's generic diversity, which includes not only narrative stories but also psalms, proverbs, laws, rituals, letters, genealogies, prophecies, apocalypses, and many other generic types.

But it is not only the generic diversity of the Bible that challenges the narrative theologian's preference for story. A bigger problem is that there are large segments of the biblical narrative that Christians will hardly wish to "indwell" in any immediate sense. While Lindbeck might encourage the church to return to "Israel's story,"[59] major portions of that story describe the plan to exterminate the Canaanites, Israel's partial implementation of that plan, and the ultimate judgment that Israel received precisely because it had failed to complete the genocide. Many of the greatest difficulties in Western history have been spawned precisely by Christians who decided they should "indwell" this story by killing "Canaanites." It must be possible, of course, to fit this Old Testament material into a healthy Christian theology. But the path for doing so will often involve shaping the church

---

58. Narrative is especially privileged in the recent work of evangelical scholar N. T. Wright, *The New Testament and the People of God*, Christian Origins and the Question of God 1 (Minneapolis: Fortress, 1992), 31–46.

59. George A. Lindbeck, "The Story-Shaped Church: Critical Exegesis and Theological Interpretation," in *The Theological Interpretation of Scripture: Classic and Contemporary Readings*, ed. Stephen E. Fowl (Oxford: Blackwell, 1997), 39–52.

in ways that differ substantially from the templates of the biblical story, especially the earliest parts of the biblical story.

Pneumatological Solutions: The Word of God and the Spirit of God

Karl Barth believed that the Holy Spirit is an essential animating presence in the reading of Scripture, so that readers of the biblical text cannot hear God speak without it. For Barth, the Spirit's role in biblical interpretation obviated some of the historical-critical difficulties in Scripture because it brought God himself into the interpretive equation. The infinite and all-knowing God could undoubtedly speak well enough, even through the finite discourse of the Bible's human authors. For many theologians, from many different Christian traditions, this strong emphasis on the Spirit's role in biblical interpretation is more than sufficient to counterbalance the problems uncovered by historical criticism. Various evangelicals have taken to this theological path. I have in mind the likes of Bernard Ramm, Jack Rogers, Donald McKim, Dewey Beegle, and Donald Bloesch, though many others could be named.[60] What shall we make of their assertion that, as Bloesch puts it, "Theology needs to recover the paradoxical unity of Word and Spirit"? Does an emphasis on the Spirit solve our difficulties, or open up our interpretations to a dangerous kind of subjectivism?

In *Engaging Scripture*, Stephen Fowl has provided a good biblical basis for the Spirit's role in our interpretation of Scripture.[61] He calls attention to the theological debate in Jerusalem (Acts 15), where some Jewish Christians were arguing that gentile converts should be circumcised. The pro-circumcision party seemed to have the Old Testament on their side, since it explicitly required, or at least appeared to require, that all of God's people would be circumcised. Nonetheless, in the end the council determined that circumcision was not a necessary hurdle for gentile converts. The council's reasoning on this point is telling: "God, who knows the heart, showed that he accepted them by giving them the Holy Spirit, just as he did to us." So it was the Spirit's activity, and the church's willingness to "read" the Spirit, that allowed early Christians to interpret the Old Testament in this inclusive way.

Donald Bloesch follows this vein of thought. He points out that God's speech in Scripture always comes to us in and through the activity of the Spirit, so that reading Scripture is never a matter of merely rehearsing its verbal discourse. This Word-Spirit symbiosis provides a potential solution for our historical-critical difficulties, for it reminds us that God's sovereign choice to speak through Scripture

---

60. Dewey M. Beegle, *Scripture, Tradition, and Infallibility*, 2nd ed. (Ann Arbor, MI: Pettenbill, 1979); Donald G. Bloesch, *Holy Scripture: Revelation, Inspiration, and Interpretation* (Downers Grove, IL: InterVarsity, 1994); Bernard Ramm, *After Fundamentalism: The Future of Evangelical Theology* (San Francisco: Harper & Row, 1983); Jack B. Rogers and Donald K. McKim, *The Authority and Interpretation of the Bible: An Historical Approach* (New York: Harper & Row, 1979).

61. Stephen E. Fowl, *Engaging Scripture: A Model for Theological Interpretation* (Oxford: Blackwell, 1998).

could never be hindered by the humanity of the biblical author or the biblical reader. God speaks through the human text of Scripture with no more difficulty than when he speaks through a modern human evangelist who preaches the gospel. This reality, if true, raises several questions. First, if our interpretations of Scripture are always imperfect and even pretty far off the mark in some cases, then how is it that God speaks to us through our "misreading" of Scripture? Second, precisely who is it that receives this "divine illumination" when they read Scripture? Does God speak through Scripture only to those who "listen," or does God also speak to those who do not listen? To put this in concrete terms, if one woman reads John's Gospel and embraces Christ, and if her neighbor reads the same Gospel but takes it as rubbish, has God spoken to both of them? I believe that Barth, and perhaps some of these other scholars, would say no. But I, for one, am not so sure about that. We will return to this question in connection with the concepts of general revelation and natural theology, which I will discuss in chapter 8.

Catholicism and Biblical Criticism

The Catholic response to historical criticism was measured and in many respects prudent, moving from cautious enthusiasm, through a period of suspicion, to the eventual embrace of modern biblical criticism.[62] In 1893 Pope Leo XIII promulgated his encyclical letter *Providentissimus Deus*, which summoned Catholic scholars to commit themselves fully to studying the Bible using all of the linguistic, historical, and archaeological resources available to researchers. At the same time his document defended the Bible's inerrancy and reminded Catholic scholars that their work should be in keeping with the authority of the church's *Magesterium* (Rule of Faith).[63] In an effort to promote this scholarly agenda, Pope Leo's apostolic letter *Vigilantiae studiique* (1902) established the Pontifical Biblical Commission (PBC), whose purpose was to encourage Catholic scholarship while shepherding it *within* the bounds of Catholic faith.

Almost as soon as the PBC was established, however, it was called upon to address a different set of issues. The growing rise of theological liberalism was challenging many of the Catholic Church's traditional doctrines and affirmations. Between 1903 and 1914 the PBC responded to this crisis through a series of *Responsa*, published with the approval of Pope Pius X. These *Responsa* were cast as a series of questions with their corresponding answers:

> *Question:* Whether various exegetical systems that have been devised and supported under the pretense of science for the purpose of excluding the literal historical sense of the first three chapters of Genesis are grounded in solid arguments.

---

62. For English translations of the documents cited in this discussion, see Dean P. Béchard, *The Scripture Documents: An Anthology of Official Catholic Teachings* (Collegeville, MN: Liturgical Press, 2002).
63. See comments in John Goldingay, *Models for Scripture* (Grand Rapids: Eerdmans, 1994), 267.

Response: Negative.

In this representative example, which concerns Genesis, we see that the *Responsa* were decidedly negative in their appraisal of biblical criticism. Some years later this negative stance created significant confusion for Catholic biblical scholars because it seemed to conflict with official statements that were more positively disposed toward historical criticism. I have in mind the papal encyclical, *Divino afflante Spiritu*.

In comparison with the *Responsa*, Pope Pius XII's *Divino afflante Spiritu* (1943) represented an almost complete reversal of the church's position on biblical criticism. The liberal challenge to church doctrine faced earlier by Pius X had been successfully defused, and the new "threat" was a growing tendency for Catholics to set aside academic biblical study in favor of meditative or spiritual kinds of biblical interpretation.[64] In response, Pius XII called for serious biblical scholarship that would be "in full accord with the doctrine of the Church" and "satisfy the indubitable conclusions of profane sciences." This agenda showed no fear of biblical criticism and amounted to a full embrace of its methods, circumscribed only by the creedal and dogmatic orthodoxy of the Catholic Church. This creedal orthodoxy provided biblical exegetes with immense flexibility because, as Pius himself pointed out, "there are but few [biblical] texts whose sense has been defined by the authority of the Church."[65] Pius further encouraged Catholic scholars to give special attention to the study of Near Eastern history and literature, to the literary genres of expression in the ancient world and Old Testament, and to the possible presence of biblical texts that accommodated antiquated views of science and history. There was, however, an obvious tension between this positive view of biblical criticism and the earlier views enshrined in the PBC's *Responsa*. In the mid 1950s two different curial officials issued semi-official clarifications of the church's position, which stated clearly that "the interpreter of Sacred Scripture may pursue his scientific research with complete freedom and may utilize the results of these investigations, provided always that he respects the teaching authority of the Church."[66] The church's decision not to change these statements amounted to its tacit approval.

In 1993, on the hundredth anniversary of Pope Leo XIII's *Providentissimus Deus* and the fiftieth anniversary of Pius XII's *Divino afflante Spiritu*, the PBC issued an extensive document entitled "The Interpretation of the Bible in the Church." This document offers a detailed description of modern historical criticism and speaks positively about its contribution to biblical interpretation and to the Catholic Church. Pope John Paul II greeted the document with enthusiasm and congratulated the commission for its productive work. So regardless of what one thinks about historical criticism proper, it remains true that Catholicism has managed to integrate biblical criticism into its dogmatic understanding of the faith.

64. Béchard, *Scripture Documents*, 323.
65. Ibid., 132.
66. Ibid., 326–29.

How can we account for the Catholic Church's successful rapprochement with criticism? First and foremost, in its deliberations about historical criticism Catholicism has enjoyed the advantage of the Rule of Faith. This theological standard has provided clear and ancient parameters for the practice of biblical scholarship. So long as Catholic scholars remain within these parameters of orthodoxy, they are free to carry out their work with confidence and freedom. As it turns out, the boundaries of traditional creedal orthodoxy are much broader than the meticulous measures of "orthodoxy" employed in many conservative Protestant traditions. This reality has translated into more freedom for Catholic scholars because many of the standard conclusions of modern biblical criticism constitute no threat to creedal orthodoxy. The question of who authored parts of the Pentateuch or Isaiah, for instance, has little bearing on Christ's identity and redemptive work. One implication of this outcome is that the theological boundaries of Catholicism have proved healthier and truer to life than those embraced by many evangelical Protestants.

A second reason for Catholicism's successful assimilation of critical scholarship stems from its high view of the created order and of our human capacity to understand it (à la Aquinas). Early in its deliberations about historical criticism, Catholic leaders staked out their commitment to the unity of truth, to the belief that all truth is God's truth. The Catholic Church was (and is) confident that all scholarly research, when *properly done*, leads to conclusions that are compatible with the church's Rule of Faith.[67] This being so, the Catholic Church has nothing to fear from either biological theories of human evolution or literary theories of pentateuchal composition. If these scholastic theories turn out to be true, then they simply are compatible with creedal orthodoxy.

A third reason for the success of Catholic biblical criticism is experience. The Catholic Church is the recipient of a long tradition of sophisticated thinking about Scripture. Among other things, Catholic scholars have long recognized that the authors of Scripture could assume their audience's mistaken human viewpoints without occasioning divine error in the text.[68] Catholics have also attended closely to the genres of Scripture, believing that this, when thoughtfully considered, solves some of the difficulties raised by biblical criticism.[69] When one allows for a breadth of biblical genres, and for God's accommodations to the frailties of his human audiences, there remains little risk that biblical scholars will uncover difficulties that cannot be assimilated to the orthodoxy of tradition.

Fourth, and finally, the role of the Holy Spirit has played an important role in the Catholic response to biblical criticism. The Catholic Church has consistently emphasized the spiritual dimensions of biblical interpretation, accentuating both the role of the Spirit itself and the importance of the interpreter's "vigorous spiritual

---

67. Ibid., 57–58.
68. See the comments of Pius XII in Béchard, *Scripture Documents*, 116–17.
69. Ibid., 129–30, 174–75.

life."[70] In sum, it would seem that the Catholic response to biblical criticism has included many of the constructive features prominent in the other theological solutions surveyed above. If Catholicism offers something unique to the discussion, undoubtedly it would be the decisive role that it grants to creedal orthodoxy in the theological appraisal of biblical criticism. Creedal orthodoxy has a dual advantage in this regard, in terms of both antiquity and flexibility. It provides a tried and tested theological perimeter for the practice of biblical interpretation, and this perimeter rarely seems to conflict with the standard results of criticism. In my opinion, this fruitful coherence between creedal tradition and modern criticism strongly recommends the Catholic position on these issues.

The Catholic response to biblical criticism has included not only a positive assessment of modern biblical scholarship but also a fairly negative assessment of those who reject it. A suitable example appears in the PBC's recent description of biblical interpretation as practiced by evangelical fundamentalists:

> Fundamentalist interpretation starts from the principle that the Bible, being the Word of God, inspired and free from error, should be read and interpreted literally in all of its details. But by "literal interpretation" it understands a naively literalist interpretation... which excludes every effort at understanding the Bible that takes account of its historical origins and development. It is opposed, therefore, to the use of the historical-critical method, as indeed to the use of any other scientific method for the interpretation of Scripture.... The fundamentalist approach is dangerous, for it is attractive to people who look to the Bible for ready answers to the problems of life. It can deceive these people, offering them interpretations that are pious but illusory, instead of telling them that the Bible does not necessarily contain an immediate answer to each and every problem. Without saying as much in so many words, fundamentalism actually invites people to a kind of intellectual suicide. It injects into life a false certitude, for it unwittingly confuses the divine substance of the biblical message with what are in fact its human limitations.[71]

If modern biblical scholars are right about even a small number of their standard critical conclusions, then it will follow that this Catholic appraisal of evangelical fundamentalism is close to the mark. But as a criticism of fundamentalism this one pales in comparison to those offered by James Barr.

James Barr: The Bible as *an* Authoritative Tradition

For several decades now, James Barr has been a good-natured thorn in the side of conservative evangelicalism. In a series of works, including especially *Fundamentalism* and *Beyond Fundamentalism*, Barr has attempted to expose the theoretical and

---

70. Ibid., 175-76.
71. From "The Interpretation of the Bible in the Church" (1990). See Béchard, *Scripture Documents*, 273-75.

theological weaknesses of evangelicalism, and to point its conservative faith in a direction that he finds more reasonable and sensible.[72] It has been easy to suppose from this that Barr is himself on the liberal end of theology, and there is much truth in this. But at the same time, Barr has described himself as a "conservative liberal" and has recently asserted in strong terms his deep respect for theological tradition.[73] What makes him particularly interesting for our discussion is that, theoretically speaking, he stands in the margin between those who consider Scripture "the Word of God" and those who view it as merely human discourse.

Anyone familiar with Barr's work will know how difficult it can be to isolate precisely what Barr himself believes or thinks. His basic mode of scholarship is to summarize and critique the theories of other scholars rather than to state his own views. One result is that his perspectives appear only implicitly in much of his work. But we are fortunate that in a least one case Barr's ideas about the Bible and theology are more clearly expressed. I have in mind his slender but important volume, *The Scope and Authority of the Bible*.[74]

According to Barr, theology and critical biblical study are mutually informing aspects of a theological whole. Theology provides the presuppositions necessary for turning to the Bible for theological purposes, but it cannot and must not control the outcomes of biblical exegesis. Barr expressed it this way: "It is in the interest of theology that it should allow and encourage the scripture to speak freely to the church and to theology. It must be able to say something other than what current theological and interpretive fashion would have it say. But it cannot do this if theology controls the presuppositions with which it may be approached."[75] In Barr's view the Bible cannot have authority over us if, in practice, our potentially errant theological dogmas *over*determine what it can and cannot say. But as we have seen in many other cases, this critical disposition—which focuses very carefully on what the Bible actually says—tends to yield a variety of theological viewpoints rather than a single, univocal theology. At first glance this difficulty seems doubled in Barr's construal of the matter, for in his way of thinking the Bible is only a special instance of tradition, which flows from the broader and older extrabiblical traditions of Israel and the church. A schematic of this model would run like this: God → People of God → Tradition → Scripture. In this frame of reference, Scripture's authority does not depend on the purity or perfection of its discourse; it has authority because that authority "is built into the structure of Christian faith and the Christian religion."[76] As a result, Barr could say of the Bible:

---

72. James Barr, *Fundamentalism* (Philadelphia: Westminster, 1978); Barr, *Beyond Fundamentalism* (Philadelphia: Westminster, 1984).
73. James Barr, *History and Ideology in the Old Testament: Biblical Studies at the End of a Millennium* (Oxford: Oxford University Press, 2000), 180.
74. James Barr, *The Scope and Authority of the Bible* (Philadelphia: Westminster, 1980).
75. Ibid., 28.
76. Ibid., 52.

even if it is shockingly bad as literature, or quite erratic as history, or untenable as world-view,—or dubious as science if it comes to that—none of these should seriously affect the basis of its authority, though by taking them into consideration we may be helped to understand better the *nature* of that authority. But the *basis* of that authority lies in its efficacy in the faith-relation between man and God.[77]

So, though the Bible be declared poor in terms of literature, history, and science, this will have no bearing at all on its authoritative role in promoting the work of God among his people. To admit the difficulties is not an affront to Scripture's authority; it is to understand better how God uses the text as an authority in the life of the church.

Barr recognizes that conservative Christians will be deeply troubled by his approach. How is it possible to embrace biblical criticism when it openly questions the historicity of vast swaths of the biblical narrative? Is Christianity not a religion that is strongly grounded in historical events, most particularly in the death, burial, and resurrection of Christ? Barr's answer to this difficulty is straightforward:

> When people say that Christianity is dependent on historical events, in the sense that but for these events the faith would be vain, the number of events that they have in mind is quite small; and this is the difference between scripture and creeds. The passion and resurrection of Jesus Christ is the main specific historical reference in the creeds. Scripture on the other hand mentions large numbers of historical or apparently historical events, but no one supposes that all of these bear a relation to Christianity analogical to Jesus' crucifixion under Pontius Pilate or his resurrection from the dead.[78]

In Barr's opinion we do not have, nor do we need, a Bible whose narratives are essentially accurate as histories. Historicity is essential for only a small portion of the events enumerated in the Old and New Testaments. So though many parts of these two Testaments might be accurate as history, only certain parts need be so, and these essential moments in history are clearly laid out in the ecumenical creeds of the Christian tradition. This is Barr's position, which in some respects stands very close to the Catholic position on historical criticism and its theological limitations (see the previous section).

Now Barr does not systematically tell us how he would solve the other nagging problem, that is, the difficulty of discerning theological unity from the Bible's diversity. But so far as I can tell the Bible's diversity does not strike him as a serious problem. To some extent he believes that the theological diversity of Scripture can be worked out by finding the "balance" of Scripture as a whole,[79] in a process that identifies the Bible's most important principles and priorities and then

---

77. Ibid., 54.
78. Ibid., 33–34.
79. Barr, *Beyond Fundamentalism*, 111–12.

subordinates its lesser aspects to them. The priority Christians give to biblical monogamy over biblical polygamy is a good example of this. Another important element in Barr's solution for the Bible's theological diversity is the tradition of the church. Barr does not attribute any great perfection to this tradition, but its theological purview—as expressed in the ecumenical creeds—offers a more homogenized and consistent perspective than does Scripture alone. So tradition and Scripture form a hermeneutical dialectic, in which the one informs our reading and understanding of the other. Barr's only concern about this dialectic is that Scripture's voice be taken seriously as a potential critique of the tradition used to interpret it. But those familiar with Barr will know that he would add a third source of theological insight alongside Scripture and tradition.

Over the years Barr has vigorously argued that the Bible itself points us in the direction of "natural theology," whose theological insights are available through the avenues of human reason and experience.[80] Though this theology might overlap with canonical or traditional theology in various ways, to Barr's mind it retains a validity in its own right. As a result, we can rightly conclude that Barr's approach to theology involves the integration of theological resources from the Bible, tradition, and natural theology.

Though Barr may sound liberal at many points, especially to more conservative evangelicals, he claims to have fairly conservative instincts. In particular, he has always taken the message of the Bible seriously. In an age when it has become passé to speak of "biblical theology," Barr is still writing on the subject, having produced in 1999 a massive project that surveys the field and offers prospects for its future: *The Concept of Biblical Theology*. The theological result of this temperament is best illustrated in *Beyond Fundamentalism*, which bears the subtitle *Biblical Foundations for Evangelical Theology*. I have no desire and nothing to gain by painting this book as more conservative than it is. There is much in it that could be considered liberal. But in the end Barr strongly emphasizes the importance of traditional theological orthodoxy, and he asserts that modern readings of Scripture do not point us away from the church but, if anything, back into the arms of a more "catholic" type of Christianity. This is by no means a liberal conclusion, which leads to my final point.

Although Barr would not readily describe the Bible as "the Word of God" and in this sense stands decisively on the liberal end of theology, his theological destinations can tend toward the conservative end of the spectrum. This is not because he has explicitly embraced the Bible as the divine Word; it is because he has taken the Bible seriously as one important element in God's discourse with the church. From this we might conclude that, when it comes to reading the Bible theologically, one's specific doctrine of Scripture does not matter so much; what matters is whether, in the end, one actually listens to what Scripture has to say. Anyone familiar with Barr's work will know this for certain: he has always tried to pay very careful attention to the Bible.

---

80. James Barr, *Biblical Faith and Natural Theology* (Oxford: Clarendon, 1993).

Conclusions

Christian attempts to resolve the problems posed by biblical criticism provide a rich and diverse trove of insights into the nature of Scripture, biblical interpretation, and systematic theology. I have carefully noted my reservations about some aspects of the proposals that have been offered, but on the whole it seems to me that practically every school of thought brings something of value to the table. It would be impractical to summarize all that has been said, but something will be gained if I highlight several recurring themes that have emerged during the course of our survey.

1. I would begin by pointing out the obvious: there is a long-standing and intellectually vigorous tradition in scholarship that has recognized the validity of historical criticism while holding steadfastly to the belief that Scripture is God's written discourse for humanity. As a rule these scholars will admit the theological difficulties presented by critical scholarship, but none of them considers the problems insurmountable. There is general agreement that the problems are partly an illusion, created first by a lack of careful attention to the literary genres of Scripture, and second by misguided, docetic-like expectations for a perfect Bible. When these mistaken expectations are set aside, along with their modern Cartesian-like correlates, then the genuine problems that must be dealt with come into clearer focus.

2. One of those problems is fundamentally theological. It may be summed up in the question, Why is the written discourse of a perfect God less than perfect? The most common answer given in our survey is that God has chosen to speak to finite human beings through the context of our finite cultural and social horizons. As a result, he accommodates his speech to those cultural settings, imbibing as he does of our perceptual plusses and minuses. On the plus side are those points where human beings are already getting things right, and on the minus side are those perceptual deficits that God, in his wisdom, chooses to leave alone. But the net result of this divine strategy is revelation—God-given insights that take humanity a step farther in our understanding of things human, and of things divine.

3. Another problem that emerges from this discussion is not only theological but hermeneutical. How can we derive a coherent, biblically informed theology from a Bible that presents us with the diverse theological viewpoints of various human authors? On this question one finds two general words of advice. There is first the recognition that, because the Bible is diverse, good theological readings of the text will seek out the "balance" of the text as a whole. Certain themes in Scripture naturally emerge as more important and fundamental to the whole, while others finally appear less important and peripheral. The best theological judgments will be those that recognize how this balance plays out. The other word of advice is that theological interpretation should attend carefully to other things besides the Bible. Among these "other things" are the Christian tradition itself (especially its creedal traditions) and the so-called book of nature. So any

serious theological agenda will need to consider Scripture, tradition, and the natural order at the same time.

4. Now the very pursuit of a theological "balance" between Scripture, tradition, and the natural order implies that no simple one-for-one relationship needs to exist between what God has said in Scripture and what he now says through it. There is a difference, for instance, between the judgments offered in particular biblical texts (e.g., "you must be circumcised") and what the canon as a whole might say about the same matter ("you need not be circumcised"). One result of this situation is the tendency for "space" to develop between Scripture and theology, between the specific judgment of a given biblical text and the final theological judgment that we derive from that text as we integrate into the context of canon, tradition, and the natural order. An important task of those surveyed in this chapter has been to elucidate the nature of this gap. Let us take Karl Barth, Brevard Childs, and David Steinmetz as examples.

Barth would see the gap opening up between the specific instances of human discourse in Scripture and God's revelation of himself through the text to its readers. Using Barth's approach, there might be a very great difference between the original message of the Bible's discourse and the message that God chooses to speak through it at a given moment. The words of Augustine well epitomize this point:

> But any who understand a passage in the scriptures to mean something which the writer did not mean are mistaken . . . but all the same . . . if they are mistaken in a judgment which is intended to build up love . . . they are mistaken in the same sort of way as people who go astray off the road, but still proceed by rough paths to the same place as the road was taking them. God spoke the true word, in spite of the reader's error.[81]

In a similar way, Barth would allow that Christian readers can *misunderstand* the Bible's human discourse even as they properly *understand* its divinely given message of love for their neighbor. In Barth's conception of things, this is possible because of the important role that spiritual enlightenment plays in hearing the divine Word. In God's sovereignty the Spirit can say yes precisely because we mistook the text to say yes. Though Barth is undoubtedly right on this point—that God can and does speak to us even when we misunderstand the Bible—there remains a serious conceptual problem, inasmuch as Barth's theology implies a gaping vacuum between biblical words and God's Word. On Barth's account of things, one wonders why we have a Bible at all. I, for one, would much prefer a solution that befits the church's long-standing belief that the Bible *is* the Word of God, just as my words are mine—whether understood or not.

Brevard Childs has taken a somewhat different route. For him the space that opens up in our theological interpretation of Scripture is not between the human

---

81. Augustine, *On Christian Doctrine* 1.41 (*NPNF* 1 2:533).

discourse and God's sovereign Word; it is instead the space between particular instances of biblical discourse and the message of God as expressed in the biblical canon as a whole. Here the gap is suitably illustrated by the difference between a biblical text that allows for polygamy and the canonical whole that does not. This approach would seem to have certain advantages over Barth's, inasmuch as Childs ties the present Word of God more closely to his ancient canonical words. Yet it seems to me that in certain respects Childs and Barth end up in the same conceptual boat. Childs does not explain *why* there are theological gaps between pericope and canon, nor does he tackle the difficulty presented when our theology goes beyond the canon to find its footing, as in the case of slavery. So far as I can tell, Childs and Barth have not managed to close the conceptual gap between what God originally said through Scripture and what he subsequently says through those same biblical texts. They have only managed to describe the gap.

We come face-to-face with the gap again in the work of David Steinmetz. He realizes that critical readings of Scripture engender theological diversity and all of its attendant problems. As we have seen, his simple and elegant solution is to return to traditional, precritical methods of interpretation—to patristic allegories and typologies. In his view allegories provide the exegetical flexibility that is missing in modern exegesis, a flexibility that helps us resolve the apparent diversity of Scripture. Now I have already pointed out why this will not work. It will do us little good to turn to allegories in an era when few or none will be convinced by them. Allegory is not our way. At the same time, it seems to me that we cannot possibly deny that God has at times spoken to the church through those patristic allegories. So in this case we face not one but two related and problematic conceptual gaps. We have the obvious gap between what the biblical authors meant to say and what God might say through the allegories, and then we have the more subtle difficulty of allegory itself: though we might not agree with the method, good sense compels us to admit that God has actually spoken through it. These are matters that I will consider later, at the end of chapter 9.

5. Let me conclude here by turning our attention in a more focused way to the issue of biblical genre. The topic is apparently important, for every solution to the problem of biblical criticism has given some attention to this matter. Often the emphasis has been on the human genres of Scripture. If we allow for the presence in the Bible of myth, legend, saga, and allegory, for instance, we shall find that many of the Bible's difficulties disappear. The "bad science" of Genesis becomes "true myth," the "failed prophecies" of Daniel become "apocalyptic literature," and the flawed histories of Samuel–Kings become "history-like" theologies. This is the logic. At other times, however, the emphasis has been not on the human but rather on the divine genre of Scripture, on the fact that it differs from other writings because it is God's Word. The uniqueness of Scripture on this point signals a conceptual distinction between the human and divine aspects of biblical discourse. For instance, though the human author of Genesis may have intended to convey that there was a great body of water above the "firmament"

(see Gen. 1:6–8 RSV), the divine author will have intended this only in part. God intended it only insofar as, in the original discourse, he was accommodating himself to mistaken human viewpoints for the purpose of advancing his message to humanity. But God speaks this message no longer because, from our modern scientific vantage point, that accommodation is unnecessary. So modern readers can recognize the accommodation for what it is.

To summarize, attempts to synthesize biblical criticism with theology have accentuated: (a) the human genres of Scripture (some biblical errors are illusions); (b) the divine genre of Scripture (some biblical errors are accommodations to the human horizon); (c) the role of extrabiblical sources in our theology (tradition and the created order); and (d) the role of divine initiative in successful interpretations of Scripture (the Spirit's role in the reading of Bible). In the chapters that follow, I will try to run with these theses and see how far we can go in the important task of integrating faith and criticism. Chapter 6 will explore the human dimensions of biblical discourse, to be followed in chapter 7 by a discussion of Scripture's divine dimensions. Chapters 8 and 9 will focus on the contextual nature of the Bible's discourse by examining the relationship between biblical revelation and other sources of information that God has made available to human beings. In these chapters I will lay out my methodological agenda, which accentuates the "context of the whole" and its dialectical relationship to Scripture. This methodological agenda will then set the stage for the test cases discussed in chapter 10, and for my closing remarks in the concluding chapter.

6

THE GENRES
OF HUMAN DISCOURSE

I BELIEVE THAT KARL Barth was right on this point. God can and does speak to us in diverse and sometimes surprising ways, including through our reading of books. But the Bible is profoundly unique among books because it is, *in its essence*, both divine and human discourse. It is the voice of God, but also of Paul, of the evangelists, of the Israelite prophets and sages, and of countless others through whom God has given us Scripture. One of the perennial difficulties faced by interpreters has been how to relate these human voices to God's voice. A simple solution would make God's voice precisely equivalent to the human voice, but this option breaks down upon close examination. While it is certainly true, for instance, that both God and the author of Deuteronomy once forbade the eating of reptiles (Deut. 14:8), it is equally true that God is no longer saying this, or at least he is not saying it in the same way (Acts 11:4–10). Historically speaking, the church has never had much difficulty admitting that God has sometimes said one thing and then another. But it has certainly struggled with the theological implications, with the question of *how* we can discern God's voice from Scripture's diversity, and with the question of *why* God permitted the diversity in the first place. These old theological conundrums will occupy our attention over the course of the next few chapters. Our first step in exploring the relationship between the Bible's divine and human elements is to consider closely the human side of this equation. In doing so, we shall see that some of our troubles with modern biblical criticism can be resolved by attending carefully to the very human dimensions of Scripture. However, we will see as well that the humanity of Scripture is both part of the solution and a chief cause of the difficulties.

As my chapter titles indicate, I have elected to discuss the "genres of human discourse" in this chapter and "genres of divine discourse" in the next. The order of this discussion reflects my theoretical bias. Although I will eventually argue for the validity of a "special hermeneutic" when we read the Bible (special in the sense that it treats the Bible differently from other books), I strongly believe that a proper account of biblical hermeneutics should accentuate general hermeneutics, for the obvious reason that general hermeneutics is nothing other than a description and account of the way that we normally interpret texts. If we begin with general hermeneutics, we might conceivably demonstrate the validity of some special hermeneutic; but if we begin with a special hermeneutic, we have no way to show that it is valid and warranted, given that the usual way of establishing warrant is through general hermeneutics. It is by listening to the Bible's human discourse that we begin to understand how it might be understood as divine discourse. Let me illustrate the point.

According to the prescriptions in Leviticus 11:3 (NIV), Israelites could eat only mammals that "chewed the cud" and possessed a "split hoof." The literal meaning of these directions is clear enough, but we are naturally curious about why these particular criteria were used to distinguish clean and unclean animals, and we are further interested in what message the text might bear for the church. As was commonly done in the early church, Clement of Alexandria explained the text using allegory: "the split hoof is a sign of evenly balanced justice, which chews the cud of its own food of justice, the Word, which enters from without through instruction."[1] Though I am not personally persuaded by Clement's exegesis, his interpretation suitably illustrates my point about general and special hermeneutics. While one might begin with the natural way of reading Leviticus and arrive eventually at Clement's "special" allegorical hermeneutic, it is quite difficult to imagine how one could *begin* with Clement's allegory, since interpreting animal hooves as "justice" differs from our usual way of reading texts. This is why it seems right to begin in this chapter with a description of the Bible's natural human discourse before we move on in the following chapter to discuss how that human discourse can be God's Word, and the special hermeneutic that this might imply. General hermeneutics is the right place to start. Special hermeneutics, as the name implies, must follow. This does not mean that we are ignoring the divine nature of Scripture; it means instead that we are honoring God's choice, which is to provide his words in human language, through human authors, to human readers.

Genre and Verbal Discourse

Like a fingerprint, every instance of verbal discourse is unique. It reflects the distinctive marks of the speaker or writer, of his or her particular mood at that

---

1. Clement of Alexandria, *Christ, the Educator*, trans. S. P. Wood, Fathers of the Church 23 (Washington, DC: Catholic University of America Press, 1954), 257.

moment, of intended and unintended meanings, of the peculiar historical and cultural setting, of listeners and readers, of the biochemistry and psychology of the moment, and of a host of other features from the complex matrix that shapes the written and spoken word. Life, then, is a practically infinite stream of words, sentences, and paragraphs in which no two utterances are in all particulars alike. Only God himself has the capacity to juggle so many balls at once, to really know and understand each and every instance of verbal discourse in its respective uniqueness. Given these realities, how is it that finite and fallen human beings can communicate with so much apparent success, and why is it that, in the context of this success, we sometimes fail to communicate as well as we would like?

One important part of the answer is *genre*. Genre is the reason that human discourse can work well, and also, as we will see, part of the explanation for why it does not. When we speak of genres, we speak of types of discourse that are similar to one another. For instance, when we open a newspaper in search of the lead news story, we are able to distinguish it from the editorials, advertisements, obituaries, comics, and classifieds because all of these are types of articles that we have seen before. That is, in these and in all texts, genre is an essential ingredient in communication because it establishes the ground rules for dialogue shared by authors and readers (or by speakers and hearers). Just as the rules of grammar dictate how we correctly form and understand a sentence, so the rules of genre dictate how we form and understand literature. In the words of Paul Ricoeur, genre functions "to mediate between speaker and hearer by establishing a common dynamics capable of ruling both the production of discourse as a work of a certain kind and its interpretation according to rules provided by the genre."[2] In essence, we are able to understand the utterances and writings of others because their speech and literature adhere to verbal patterns that we recognize. These verbal patterns are not rigid, however, and the "rules" can be bent and even broken. This is why we are able to understand the halting, error-ridden speech of small children, and why we almost effortlessly read something like this: Teh hmaun mnid si icnrdelbie!

Let us consider the concept of genre in more detail. Because we do not—indeed, cannot—appreciate every instance of verbal discourse in all of its uniqueness, our generic strategy for dealing with verbal discourse is to guess or estimate its meaning through comparison. We have learned from experience how certain types of discourse fit into the world, so when new words come along we simply assume that they are more or less similar to words that we have read or heard before. In essence, we make sense of what is new by comparing it to what is not new. This classification of similar types of verbal discourse creates a "genre." Normally, this generic exercise is a tacit process that we carry out with great success and with little conscious effort. We are able to read new novels, newspaper articles, and poetry because we have read similar things before. Misunderstandings are nevertheless

---

2. Paul Ricoeur, "The Hermeneutical Function of Distanciation," *Philosophy Today* 17 (1973): 136.

inevitable, because our interpretations of verbal discourse ultimately involve a generic *estimate* of what others are saying rather than a foolproof reading of their mind. The reason for this difficulty is straightforward: when I use my generic sense to notice that two instances of discourse are of the same type, my natural tendency is to overlook what makes them different—and it is especially at this point, where I assume too much familiarity with the written or spoken discourse, that I misinterpret it. This error is akin to mistaking a person that I do not know for a person that I do know. Fortunately, when we interpret someone's words, we do not compare them with one genre only but also with many other genres or types of discourse that we have seen before. The result—still something of a mystery to theorists—is that human beings have the capacity to use what we know to reach beyond our own horizon to something really new to us.[3]

Given what I have said, we will at first be tempted to think that the clue to a text's genre resides in its words, but this is only partly true. Good interpretation considers not only the *locutionary* act (what is spoken or written) but also the *illocutionary* act (what the author or speaker was trying to accomplish).[4] In order to illustrate this, let us consider the following brief conversation:

Mary: "Would you like a cup of coffee?"
Sam: "That would keep me awake."

Does Sam prefer or not prefer to drink a cup of coffee? Thoughtful readers will quickly surmise that we do not know. We do not know because the conversation comes to us without an adequate context for determining his illocutionary purpose, a context that presumably would remove the ambiguity from Sam's answer. If Sam is driving a car late into the night, his words will have precisely the opposite meaning as when he is in his pajamas at bedtime. Clearly, the meaning of a text depends not merely on the words themselves but on how the words fit into the world, into the particular context—or *generic matrix*—in which, and from which, the text appeared. So the genre of a text (and hence its meanings) can never be determined by merely looking closely and carefully at its verbal discourse.

Given that human beings never understand contexts completely, this implies that we never understand instances of verbal discourse perfectly. Even when our interpretations are essentially correct, each involves subtle and inevitable elements

---

3. For comments on this problem, see Jonathan Z. Smith, *Map Is Not Territory: Studies in the History of Religions*, Studies in Judaism in Late Antiquity 23 (Leiden: Brill, 1978), 240–64, especially 242–43.

4. Some readers may hear echoes of speech-act theory at this point. Though I am not wholly committed to this theory of human discourse, I find that there is much to be learned from it. The classical expressions of speech-act theory are J. L. Austin, *How to Do Things with Words*, 2nd ed. (Cambridge, MA: Harvard University Press, 1975); John R. Searle, *Speech Acts: An Essay in the Philosophy of Language* (Cambridge: Cambridge University Press, 1969); Searle, *Expression and Meaning: Studies in the Theory of Speech Acts* (Cambridge: Cambridge University Press, 1979). For an attempt to employ this approach in biblical interpretation, see Kevin J. Vanhoozer, *Is There a Meaning in This Text?* (Grand Rapids: Zondervan, 1998).

of misinterpretation. Nevertheless, in the final analysis, our capacity for language is a beautiful thing that allows us adequately and meaningfully to share our lives and experiences with one another—*adequately, but never perfectly*. This description of genre closely parallels our philosophical discussion in chapter 1. "Genre" fits into that larger view of epistemology that I have called practical realism. Practical realism avers that human beings have the ability to understand reality in an adequate and substantive way, but never so perfectly that our interpretation could not be improved. The epistemic parallel between genre and practical realism is not an accident. Generic comparison and classification is not only an important method for interpreting texts; it is also, in the final analysis, an important tool for interpreting reality itself.[5]

Of course, all of this implies that genre provides not only the template by which we understand but also the pattern by which we write and speak. When we speak or write, we present our comments in a pattern that we suspect others will recognize and understand. It is this common dynamic—this shared experience and expectation in writers and readers, in speakers and listeners—that makes verbal discourse possible. In this generic dance, no one understands the world completely, or describes the world exactly, or interprets the words perfectly; but genuine exchanges of mind and heart certainly come to pass.

One of the chief benefits of a successful generic transaction is that the interpreter becomes aware of the author's subject matter. Because authors are finite beings, their words always concern only small parts of reality. When Melville wrote *Moby Dick*, the central concern of his work was not whaling per se so much as the effect of an obsession in Captain Ahab's life. To read *Moby Dick* as if it were a book about whales therefore misconstrues Melville's discourse. This is not to say that one could not learn something about whaling from Melville's book, nor does it mean that we should refrain from noticing when Melville gets his whaling facts wrong. Nor does it mean that we should cease asking our probing questions about what lies behind the text—questions about Melville's beliefs, personal concerns, and so forth. What it does mean, however, is that our reading of a text should attend carefully to the task of identifying the author's subject matter—the things about which the author intends to speak. When this becomes a concern in our critical readings of a text, our expectations and evaluation of that text will depend on the things that matter most. We might be right when we say "Melville doesn't

---

5. Jonathan Z. Smith put it this way: "That comparison has, at times, led us astray there can be no doubt; that comparison remains the method of scholarship is likewise beyond question" (Smith, *Map Is Not Territory*, 240–41). Though in principle I agree with Smith, I would offer this caveat. The normal generic process of comparison and contrast may have certain limits, which hinge upon the kinds of things that one is interpreting. According to Aristotle (and Aquinas, of course), although generic categories work well when it comes to interpreting *artifacts* (objects made by human beings), genre is more problematic when applied to things that exist by nature (e.g., human beings). I have neither the expertise nor the space to explore this issue presently, but given that we are dealing with texts—with artifacts—this is not a theoretical distinction that must be handled here. For Aristotle's discussion of this and related matters, see his *Metaphysics* 1032a–1045b.

know about whales," but this would surely be a petty criticism of his book. As we saw in chapter 5, Barth's theological work has accentuated the importance of subject matter in our readings of the Bible. He suggests that many of our modern difficulties with Scripture arise precisely because readers are seeking the wrong things from the biblical authors, and I believe that he is right.

Of course, the weight given to the subject matter of a text varies with the kind of text we are interpreting and also with the kind of interpretation we are undertaking. When I am reading the text of one whom I take to be an authority on some matter, then I attend very closely to its subject matter and am not much bothered by its typographical and grammatical errors, or even by its errant judgments on peripheral matters. Good readers exercise their critical faculties on the subject matter of what they read and not so much on matters peripheral to it. At the same time, it remains true that serious interpretation can, and sometimes should, go beyond the subject matter of a text. This would be the case when we use Genesis to study Hebrew grammar, or to reconstruct the history of cosmological ideas, or to study the use of sources by ancient history writers. All of these peripheral uses of Scripture are entirely legitimate. But as uses of Scripture, they are secondary and to some extent foreign to the intentions of the authors who wrote Scripture. As one biblical author expressed it, "All scripture is inspired by God and profitable for teaching, for reproof, for correction, and for training in righteousness, that the man of God may be complete, equipped for every good work" (2 Tim. 3:16–17 RSV). Insofar as modern biblical criticism puts the Bible to other kinds of uses, its conclusions may well come into apparent conflict with the aims of our theological readings of the Bible.

Genre and Interpretive Community

Before I discuss the Bible's genres in earnest, I would like to attend for a moment to the influence that culture exerts on interpretation. As we have seen, one of the hallmarks of postmodernism, in both its realist and antirealist varieties, is that it emphasizes the role of the community in shaping the viewpoint of the individual interpreter. Unlike animals, which generally become what they are through an intrinsic, purely genetic process, our species—*homo sapiens*—depends largely on *extrinsic* rather than *intrinsic* sources of information to become fully mature persons.[6] We are born human, but also *become* human. In this process of becoming, we are shaped and formed by the teaching and traditions of our families and culture. For instance, a child raised in an evangelical Christian home in Iowa will have a very different view of life than a child raised by militant, fundamentalist Muslims in Saudi Arabia. Some theorists—especially antirealists—believe that the differences between cultures are so great that the members of one culture share

---

6. Clifford Geertz, "The Growth of Culture and the Evolution of the Human Mind," in *The Interpretation of Cultures: Selected Essays* (New York: Basic Books, 1973), 55–83.

practically nothing with those of another. In essence this view holds that genuine cross-cultural communication is impossible.

Now it is surely true that cultural differences can be profound. But there are problems with this pessimistic view that human cultures are essentially disconnected social ghettos. Differences aside, every human society has been shaped by the common struggle to survive, and by the similar experiences that arise when human beings confront this struggle together. We share the physical world of rocks, trees, fire, sand, water, sun, and the night sky, and we share the human dimensions of love, hunger, hatred, fear, affection, loneliness, illness, power, and other things. The very fact that we are able to translate and learn foreign languages suggests that, whatever the intercultural problems may be, they do not constitute an impenetrable barrier to cross-cultural communication. So, while cultural worldviews undoubtedly exert a profound influence on our view of things, these cultural eyeglasses do not hopelessly segregate us from those living in other social contexts. To be sure, we do not possess the capacity for perfect intercultural communication; but we certainly do have the capacity for genuine and adequate communication between members of different cultures.

An obvious implication of the foregoing is that our interpretations of things, including the Bible, will profoundly depend upon the way that interpretation is practiced in our own culture. But it will also mean—and this is a point often overlooked—that the validity of our interpretive methods, being culturally determined, will be evaluated and appreciated differently when viewed from a different cultural perspective. The allegorical methods used by the early church fathers, for instance, will not be as compelling and convincing to us as they were to their ancient audiences. The same could be said, no doubt, of those instances in which the authors of the Bible used allegories, typologies, and Platonic methods of exegesis (see chapter 1). If this is right, then a generic look at the Bible will undoubtedly reveal that the genres of the biblical authors are not ours (or at least not wholly so), and hence certain aspects of their discourses will not be as clear and convincing to us as they might have been for their original readers. So, while modern Christians will certainly agree with the New Testament writers that Jesus Christ is the Jewish Messiah and Savior of humankind, we may not believe that allegories and Platonic exegesis are now the best ways to support this claim. We are more likely to defend Jesus's messianic identity with somewhat different philosophical and historical evidence, which in like manner is convincing to us but may not be convincing for those living a few centuries after us.

In making this point, I do not mean to suggest that the exegesis of the biblical writers was sheer fancy that modern readers may ignore. Given their intellectual and cultural contexts, the New Testament writers had plenty of warrant for their exegetical moves, and their exegetical conclusions were theologically valid. I would add as well that their allegorical and Platonic methods, which sometimes strike us as fantastic, may offer more to modern readers than we at first suppose. Nonetheless, their methods were honed for their own ancient audiences, so it will not be wise for modern Christians to slavishly replicate the exegetical methods of the biblical writers or of other early Christians.

But, to sum things up, all interpreters of Scripture—including even the biblical authors—read the Bible through the lenses of our respective cultural traditions.[7] So if we are interested in understanding what Paul was trying to say, or what other biblical authors were trying to say, then this will involve not only a linguistic translation of their words (from Greek or Hebrew or Aramaic to our language) but also a kind of cultural translation that connects their exegetical world with our own. The result will not be that we merely bring the ancient world to ours; it will mean as well that we step back into the ancient world. By imaginatively situating the biblical author in his ancient context and community, we will seek to understand what he was saying to his audience and to discern how his world was similar to, and different from, our own. The resulting images of the ancient author and audience will never be perfect, of course.[8] Nevertheless, we can anticipate the possibility of a genuine overlap of viewpoints—as Hans-Georg Gadamer has described it, a "fusing" of interpretive horizons—in which modern readers share in the perspectives of the ancient biblical author. Apart from this fusion of two somewhat different worldviews, there would be no way for us to really hear the biblical author's words, nor to accept them as ancient words that inform our modern viewpoint. For it is precisely with the human words of the Bible that biblically informed theology begins.

Analytical Genres

Genre is an essential ingredient in interpretation because it establishes the ground rules shared by authors and readers (or by speakers and hearers) when they communicate. Although our generic transactions are normally tacit, unconscious, and painless aspects of everyday conversation, the same cannot be said about reading ancient texts like the Bible. The biblical authors lived many centuries ago, in cultures and historical contexts far removed from our own. We do not have immediate access to the contexts that made those writings clear to ancient readers, nor do most of us have competence in the languages and genres that the biblical authors used. These realities can make it very difficult to understand parts of the Bible and other ancient texts. Modern scholars attempt to bridge these historical and cultural divides by studying the history and literature of the ancient world. At this point I am interested mainly in what scholars do with the ancient literature.

As we have seen, when we are confronted with a new text, we find its sense by assuming that it hangs together in a manner akin to similar texts that we have

---

7. John Goldingay, *Models for Interpretation of Scripture* (Grand Rapids: Eerdmans, 1995), 121–51.
8. Modern theorists drive home this point with concepts like the *implied author* (Paul as we imagine him, or as the Romans imagined him when reading the Epistle to Rome) and *implied readers* (the Romans as Paul imagined them when he wrote, and as we imagine them when we read).

seen before. But what shall we do if the text before us is quite unlike anything that we have ever read? What shall we do, for instance, with a text like Numbers 5:11–31, which requires a wife accused of adultery to drink "bitter water," which has been laced with dust from the tabernacle floor, and into which the ink of a written list of curses has been rinsed? What shall we do with the episode in 2 Kings 13:14–20, in which the prophet Elisha discovers God's will by watching the flight of an arrow? How shall we properly read the book of Daniel when it is the only Hebrew apocalypse we have ever seen? The scholarly solution to these difficult texts is *genre analysis*.

Modern scholars learn how to understand new kinds of texts by constructing analytical generic categories. Genres analyses are essentially exercises in comparison, in which we group together texts that have similar properties so that we can discover their common generic conventions. For instance, if I am interested in discovering how the book of Daniel works as a piece of literature, I will look for other texts from the ancient world that have similar properties, texts that include visions, dreams, angelic intermediaries, symbolic numbers, and prophecies of coming events. The texts that fit this description will together form an analytical genre. As it turns out, scholars know of numerous Near Eastern and Jewish texts that are very similar to the book of Daniel, texts assigned collectively to the analytical genre called "apocalyptic literature." As we shall see, thanks to these other apocalyptic texts, modern scholars now understand much better how to read the book of Daniel.

But let us be clear on one point. Most of us never construct analytical generic categories. When modern scholars construct these categories, they are doing in conscious and explicit ways the sorts of things that we normally do unconsciously and tacitly in our everyday listening and reading. Ancient scribes would not have needed a "genre analysis" to understand Daniel because they were already familiar with its generic character. Modern readers are not so fortunate, however. Analytical generic research provides one way that modern readers can recover and approximate the lost literary competence of the ancients. The benefits of this approach can be easily illustrated in a few concrete examples.

The Human Genres of Biblical Literature

Ancient texts often seem to be something that they are not, primarily because we read them as if they were products of modern society rather than of an ancient and sometimes alien world. It is precisely this confusion that has prompted so much tension between critical and traditional views of Scripture. My primary objectives in this portion of our discussion are to demonstrate that this generic confusion is real, and to explain how a better acquaintance with these generic realities can help us resolve our theological frictions with historical criticism. In many cases, when the biblical genres are properly compared with other exemplars from the world of ancient Israel and the early church, this analytical process reveals that our difficulties with historical criticism are properly described as illusions. Before we embark on this comparative look at the Bible's genres, however, we will first need to consider a closely related and nagging theological tension that exists between the traditional and critical viewpoints. I speak here of the problem of fiction in the Bible.

Jonah, the Parables of Jesus, and the Problem of Biblical Fiction

As we have seen, Enlightenment historicism has deeply influenced evangelical views of the Bible's genre. One consequence of this influence is that conservative evangelicals, when making generic assessments of the Bible, are strongly biased in favor of historical narrative and deeply suspicious of fictional genres like allegories, myths, legends, fables, and folktales. For many evangelicals, any hint of fiction in Job, Jonah, Daniel, 1 Kings, Acts, or in any parts of the Pentateuch or Gospels, would be theologically threatening, not only for the biblical book itself but for the Bible as a whole. Even where this angst is not wholly present in evangelicals, they often display a theoretical preference for history over fiction. Consider, for example, these thoughts from an evangelical commentary on Jonah by Douglas Stuart:

> One can appreciate the story of Jonah whether or not it represents actual historical events.... But the issue of historicity has implications beyond the formal didactic function of the narrative. If the events described in the book actually happened, the audience's existential identification with the characters and circumstances is certainly heightened. People act more surely upon what they believe to be true in fact, than merely what they consider likely in a story.[9]

I will return to these comments by Stuart in a moment. But obviously his aversion to fiction brings evangelicalism and similar historicist movements into direct conflict with modern biblical criticism, since biblical criticism increasingly claims that some or many of the Bible's "histories" are either poor histories or not historical at all. Is there a productive way to resolve the seemingly irresolvable conflict between evangelical historicism and modern biblical criticism?

First, it is undoubtedly true that modern critics are sometimes unduly skeptical of the Bible's value as an historical document. Often their skepticism regards mainly the Bible's miracles, but it sometimes goes well beyond this to a more extreme and almost rabid cynicism about everything the Bible narrates. It seems to me that the Christian faith cannot subsist in a recognizable, orthodox form if this skepticism is wholly embraced. Nevertheless, as we have seen already, it is very likely that the Bible contains more fictional literature than some evangelical readers can stomach. If we aim to take the Bible seriously as God's Word, this

---

9. Douglas Stuart, *Hosea–Jonah*, WBC (Waco: Word, 1987), 440.

leaves us with only one possible solution: perhaps fiction is a more valuable genre for conveying truth than conservative evangelicals normally suppose.

We have good biblical grounds for seeing theological value in fictional genres.[10] Although there have been many debates among scholars about the life of Jesus, on this point it would seem that all New Testament scholars agree: Jesus's favorite teaching genre was the parable. Or to put this more brashly, Jesus's preferred genre for conveying truth was fiction. How does fiction convey truth? In order to explore this question in more detail, let us consider one of Jesus's better-known parables, the story of the good Samaritan (Luke 10:30–35). Most readers will recall the tale, in which a helpless victim, robbed and beaten, was left to die on a deserted roadside. After two "holy" Jews—first a Levite and then a priest—failed to render the half-dead man assistance, a Samaritan gentleman finally saved his life.

Jesus told this fictional story in order to answer the question, Who is my neighbor? We can explore how the tale works as a vehicle of truth by imagining for a moment that the story was not a parable but an actual historical report. If the story were such a report, what would it convey? It would inform us of the impieties of two particular Jews and of a better fellow from Samaria—nothing more, and nothing less. While this might satisfy the historicist thirst for genuine history, it obviously robs the story of its rhetorical import. But taken as a parable the story becomes something else altogether. It depicts not one particular historical situation but rather all instances in which religious people fail to love their neighbor in distress. In a very concrete sense, insofar as the parable describes and applies to many historical contexts rather than just one, we can reasonably claim that parables are *more historical* than conventional historical reports. So works in fictional genres can be quite true, not only theologically but also historically.

Returning to Stuart's comments about his preference for Jonah's historicity, I would suggest at least three reasons why his logic leans in the wrong direction. First, insofar as the book of Jonah is a depiction of *reality*—of preaching the Word, of human repentance, of salvation, and of Jews who do not love their enemies— then it is very much a book of history, just as the parables of Jesus are historical. At issue is not historicity per se; the issue in Jonah, as in the parables, is how the book talks about and informs us of history. Second, we should not overlook that an essential element in the Christian gospel regards the fallen context of our human condition. Since things in our world are not as they ought to be, then we should anticipate that Scripture will include not only historical genres, which tell us what *is*, but also fictional genres, which depict what *should be*. The author of Jonah, for example, helps us to understand what our response to the repentance of others should look like—even if the penitents are our cruelest enemies. Presumably, the author could have used an actual historical incident in the story if such

---

10. See an evangelical treatment of this issue in Tremper Longman's insightful article, "Storytellers and Poets in the Bible: Can Literary Artifice Be True?" in *Inerrancy and Hermeneutic: A Tradition, a Challenge, a Debate*, ed. Harvie M. Conn (Grand Rapids: Baker Books, 1988), 137–49.

an extreme example of national repentance had existed. But with that example lacking in his knowledge of history, fiction came to the author's rhetorical rescue. As Paul Ricoeur expressed so eloquently, "We may say that history by opening us to the different, opens us to the possible, while fiction, by opening us to the unreal, opens us to the essential."[11] My third objection to Stuart regards his claim that our obedient response to God is better motivated by history than fiction. On one level I heartily agree with this sentiment, for if the events in Jonah did take place this would verify the truths affirmed in the book in a way that the fictional story could not. But of course the Christian life is much more than following God because his commands are proved true by history. If Jonah is a work of fiction, and if it is also God's Word, then I should have no more difficulty following its directives than in following the parabolic teachings of Jesus. Biblical fiction does not let us off the hook of obedience. This is because fiction is a perfectly suitable genre for conveying truth about reality—not only theological truth, but also the truths of history.

The Mimetic Genealogy in Genesis 5

During the first half of the seventeenth century, James Ussher (1581–1656) served as the Church of Ireland's archbishop of Armagh. Although he was the first scholar to carefully distinguish Ignatius's seven authentic letters from the later spurious letters, he is perhaps better known for his attempt to produce a comprehensive synthesis of all biblical, classical, and scientific chronologies. The results were published in his *Annales Veteris et Novi Testamenti* and *Chronologia sacra*, in which he concluded, among other things, that the creation of the world took place on October 22, 4004 BCE.[12] Judged from our modern perspective, Ussher's work may seem naive, for it now appears that the cosmos is quite a bit older—by cautious scientific estimates at least ten billion years old. But the bishop can hardly be blamed for his errant conclusions, because, in the absence of modern astronomical data, his primary source for early chronology was the Hebrew Bible, especially the book of Genesis. As we shall see, however, the book of Genesis is not the sort of material one should consult for accurate historical chronologies.

Let us take, for example, the genealogy of Genesis 5. This text provided the backbone for Ussher's primeval chronology. It enumerates ten generations of preflood patriarchs (from Adam to Noah) and provides chronological data about the first nine, including their ages when they first became fathers, the number of years they lived after this, and their ages at death. The lifespans of these patriarchs

---

11. Paul Ricoeur, "The Narrative Function," *Semeia* 13 (1978): 117–202, especially 117.

12. James Barr, "Why the World Was Created in 4004 B.C.: Archbishop Ussher and Biblical Chronology," *Bulletin of the John Rylands Library* 67 (1985): 575–608; Jack Finegan, *Handbook of Biblical Chronology*, rev. ed. (Peabody, MA: Hendrickson, 1998), 401–5; Jeremy Hughes, *Secrets of the Times: Myth and History in Biblical Chronology*, JSOTSup 66 (Sheffield: Sheffield Academic Press, 1990).

are particularly long, with Methuselah—the oldest man in the Bible—living 969 years. As genealogies go, this one is unusual because neither Near Eastern genealogies, nor the oral genealogies studied by modern anthropologists, normally include chronological information of this sort. How is this comparative anomaly to be explained?

Although Near Eastern genealogies do not provide chronological data, Near Eastern king lists regularly do. For instance, the Sumerian King List is very similar to the Genesis genealogy. It too provides a list of pre-flood heroes and grants them very long life spans, even longer than in Genesis (see table 6).

Table 6

Genealogy from Genesis 5				The Sumerian King List	
Name	\multicolumn{3}{l}{Ages at birth of first son, remaining years, and total}	Name	Length of reign (in years)
Adam	130	800	930	Alulim	28,800
Seth	105	807	912	Alalgar	36,000
Enosh	90	815	905	Enmenlu-Anna	43,200
Kenan	70	840	910	Enmengal-Anna	28,800
Mahalalel	65	830	895	Dumuzi	36,000
Jared	162	800	962	Ensipazi-Anna	28,800
Enoch	65	300	365	Enmedur-Anna	21,000
Methuselah	187	782	969	Ubar-Tutu	18,600
Lamech	182	595	777		
Noah	500	450	—		

Another similarity between the biblical and the Mesopotamian texts concerns the seventh person in the primeval list. The Mesopotamian king lists often stress the special importance of the seventh king (in this case Enmedur-Anna) and his wise advisor (often Utuabzu), who did not die but "ascended into heaven." Genesis 5 describes the seventh patriarch in a similar way: "Enoch walked with God; then he was no more, for God took him." This evidence suggests that the author of Genesis 5 modified a Hebrew genealogy so that it mimicked the older Mesopotamian king lists. The correctness of this reading is further confirmed by two lines of evidence. First, scholars believe that they have discovered where the author of Genesis 5 found the names he used to construct his genealogy. It turns out that the genealogy in an adjacent chapter of Genesis, chapter 4, presents almost the same names, and in almost the same order, as those in Genesis 5. The discovery of the probable source used by the author of Genesis 5 makes our mimetic theory more likely. The second piece of evidence for the theory comes from the chronological information provided by Genesis 5. The final digit of the genealogy's chronological numbers is 0, 2, 5, or 7 in all cases but one (excluding Noah, that is twenty-six out of twenty-seven;

see table 6).¹³ The probability of random data like this is on the order of 6.87 × 10⁻⁸, meaning, of course, that these numbers are not chronological in the usual sense. Indeed, a comparison of these numbers with the Near Eastern evidence suggests that in both cases—the Bible and the Sumerian King List—the numbers were derived from, or influenced by, astronomical and mathematical figures.¹⁴ In sum, Archbishop Ussher's use of the Genesis chronology did not work because his biblical source was not chronological in the sense that he had assumed. Our comparison of this genealogy with the Near Eastern king lists reveals that the bishop's quest to begin his modern chronology with creation was doomed from the start.

If the author of Genesis 5 shaped his list to make it look like a Mesopotamian king list, as seems to be the case, then why did he do so? King lists were important expressions of power and legitimacy in the Mesopotamian tradition. By placing his name at the end of such a list, the new king could enhance his status by associating himself with great kings of the past. Scholars suspect that the biblical author presented Israelite history in the form of a king list for the same purpose, namely, to express the value and significance of the Hebrew people. This was probably done at a time when Jewish identity was in some way threatened by Mesopotamian culture, perhaps during or after the Babylonian exile.

This reading of Genesis 5 is only a theory, of course. But it is a theory that makes coherent sense of the data before us and, as I will now explain, it also provides us with theological leverage. For there was a time when modern scholars spoke disparagingly of texts like the genealogy in Genesis 5, which in their critical sights became biblical examples of "bad history." As we now recognize, however, when the genre of Genesis 5 is properly understood as mimetic fiction, this critical appraisal of the Bible turns out to be unreasonable. Genesis 5 is not a piece of second-rate history; it is a truly masterful act of Israelite resistance to the arrogance of Mesopotamian culture.

The Pentateuch as Anthology

Generic research not only resolves the problem of the Pentateuch's genealogies but also helps to resolve the larger problem of the Pentateuch itself. As I have

---

13. The math is relatively simple. I exclude the sum in the right-hand column and deal only with the numbers in the first and second columns that create these sums. One then takes the probability of randomly selecting any of the four digits mentioned (i.e., ".4") and raises it to the power equivalent to the number of random selections (18). This yields $.4^{18}$ or, 6.87×10^{-8}.

14. C. J. Labuschagne, "The Life Spans of the Patriarchs," in *New Avenues in the Study of the Old Testament: A Collection of Old Testament Studies*, ed. A. S. van der Woude, *Oudtestamentische Studiën* 25 (New York: Brill, 1989), 121–27; Donald V. Etz, "The Numbers of Genesis V 3–31: A Suggested Conversion and Its Implications," *VT* 43 (1993): 171–89; Dwight W. Young, "The Influence of Babylonian Algebra on Longevity among the Antediluvians," *ZAW* 102 (1990): 321–35; Young, "A Mathematical Approach to Certain Dynastic Spans in the Sumerian King List," *JNES* 47 (1988): 123–29; Young, "On the Application of Numbers from Babylonian Mathematics to Biblical Life Spans and Epochs," *ZAW* 100 (1988): 332–61.

noted already in chapter 3, one of the implications of modern critical scholarship is that the Pentateuch contains historical narratives that contradict one another in various respects.[15] Conservative evangelicals are naturally troubled by this assertion, largely because it contradicts their belief that the Pentateuch's author wrote like a modern historian, with the purpose of giving readers an accurate account of events as they transpired on the ground in ancient Israel. If their assertion is valid, then the Pentateuch's author would appear to have been a very poor historian indeed. But one must wonder, given the diversity of the Pentateuch, whether this assumption is reasonable at all. Is the Pentateuch better understood as a history book, or as some other kind of document?

Modern scholars have been trying for a long time to explain the inherent tension between the literary unity of the Pentateuch and its generic diversity. Though it tells a kind of story, the Pentateuch is a veritable pot pourri of generic types that includes myths, legends, histories, novellas, etiologies, genealogies, king lists, itineraries, ritual descriptions, ritual prescriptions, treaties/covenants, lawcodes, census data, speeches, blessings, curses, poetry and prose, and any number of other generic types. Moreover, in many instances the Pentateuch provides us with several quite different renditions of the same events or materials. What sort of document would include so many types of genres, particularly when the genres sometimes present us with apparently contradictory views of history, law, and Israelite religion?

As usual, scholars use analytical generic comparisons to help answer this question. When they examine literature from the ancient Near East, they find that all of the major genres in the Pentateuch also appear in Near Eastern literature.[16] The texts to which I refer formed a kind of sacred canon, which the scribes copied and stored in ancient libraries. Yet in no case do all of these genres appear in a single text, as they do in the Pentateuch. In light of this comparative information, the most natural explanation for the content of the Pentateuch is that it is not a book of history so much as an anthology, in which its author (or authors) attempted to bring together Israel's ancient traditions, laws, and rituals into a single compendium or library of texts. Viewing the Pentateuch as an anthology helps us understand why it contains two or more versions of so many stories, and also why it contains so many types of genres. Its author (or compiler) was clearly more interested in preserving Israel's diverse traditions than in providing some kind of coherent book of history. Though the anthological result was unique, the basic impulse behind it—the desire to preserve cultural tradition—appears in some guise or other in every human culture, including our own.

Once we recognize the Pentateuch as the anthology that it is, it is no longer sensible to criticize its anthologist(s) for the various tensions and apparent

---

15. For the relevant literature, see Kenton L. Sparks, *The Pentateuch: An Annotated Bibliography*, Institute of Biblical Research Bibliographies 1 (Grand Rapids: Baker Academic, 2002).

16. See the various chapters of *ATSHB*.

contradictions in the text. We will never know whether the author noticed all of the difficulties that we see. But it is clear that he was not troubled by them. A complete assessment of this anthology is complicated by the fact that some of its sources were themselves already quite expansive works, whose authors were interested in tradition but also in many other things.[17] But we will not go far wrong if we suppose that the anthologist lived during or after the exile, at a time when, after the demise of the nation of Israel, it would have been increasingly important to preserve Jewish tradition.

Statutory Reformulation in Ancient and Biblical Law

Let us take a closer look at the Pentateuch, specifically, at the Pentateuch's laws. As we saw in chapter 3, the Pentateuch contains several blocks of law, which are distinguishable because (1) they are nested in different portions of Scripture, (2) they treat the same legal topics, and (3) when they treat these topics, they often do so in contradictory ways. Four law codes are usually admitted by scholars, these being the Book of the Covenant (Exod. 20:22–23:33), the Deuteronomic Code (Deut. 12–26), the Holiness Code (Lev. 17–26), and the Priestly Code (primarily in Exod. 25–31, 32–40; Lev. 1–16; Numbers). In addition to the differences among these codes, each appears to have diversity within it. These legal features obviously create serious problems for the traditional view that the Pentateuch provides us with the single, consistent legal viewpoint of one author. When the Pentateuch's laws are properly assessed in an analytical generic context, however, some of these difficulties evaporate.

Generally speaking, ancient Near Eastern law codes appear in two broad types: substantive law and nonsubstantive law. Substantive laws were, like our own, used by judges and magistrates in the actual adjudication of law in the ancient world.[18] By way of contrast, nonsubstative laws served other purposes, most often as pieces of political apologia, or as organs of socioeconomic reform, or as scholastic legal texts. Numerous features distinguish the substantive laws from their nonsubstantive counterparts, but the most striking difference is this: substantive law codes betray an ongoing pattern of legal reformulation, in which the laws were regularly edited and altered to account for new social conditions. Legal reformulation of this sort is an essential aspect of all working law because the conditions to be addressed by the law frequently change.

One result of legal reformulation is that new laws often contradict older ones, but this sort of contradiction need not involve a theological or metaphysical contradiction. Consider, for example, the Constitution of the United States. This document includes two contradictory amendments, one that proscribed

---

17. The authors who preceded the Pentateuch's final editor may have included the Yahwist, the Priestly Writer, and the author of Deuteronomy, among others. For more on these issues, see chapter 3.

18. For discussion of these matters, textual evidence from the ancient world, and an appropriate bibliography, see *ATSHB*, 417–34.

the sale of alcohol (the Eighteenth amendment) and another that permitted it (the Twenty-first amendment). There can be no doubt that the two laws contradict each other, but a thoughtful consideration of the two amendments shows that they may not reflect a fundamental contradiction. If we suppose for the moment that it is acceptable to consume alcohol, then it becomes possible to do justice to both amendments. On the one hand, because alcohol is potentially dangerous, it is perfectly reasonable to enact laws that prevent its consumption, especially if the culture in question is facing serious consequences from the misuse of alcohol. On the other hand, because alcohol consumption is not in itself a problem, it is equally appropriate to allow its sale. In this account of things, the contradiction between the Eighteenth and Twenty-first amendments is real, but it does not ultimately constitute a genuine contradiction respecting alcohol.

In light of the ancient and modern comparative data, our perspective on Hebrew law comes into clearer focus. The Pentateuch contains several different law codes because the Israelites frequently reformulated their legal traditions in order to fit them to new historical situations and social conditions. This process of statutory reformulation was as necessary and inevitable in ancient Israel as in any other culture where laws are used in adjudication. So the legal genres in the Pentateuch did not preclude but rather demanded an ongoing editorial process carried out by successive generations of legists. Though this process occasioned many tensions and differences in the various laws, we can legitimately argue that in many cases the resulting legal "contradictions" are in the deepest sense not contradictions at all.

The Chronicler's Theological History of Israel

Let us take leave of the Pentateuch and recall now our earlier discussion of the Hebrew history in 1–2 Chronicles. As we noted in chapter 3, in some cases this book's author paints a very different portrait of Israelite history than is found in the older parallel account in the books of Samuel and Kings. While David and Solomon have serious and even fatal flaws in Samuel–Kings, these kings are almost entirely blameless in Chronicles. Similarly, King Asa is righteous in Kings but turns to evil in Chronicles, while King Manasseh is evil in Kings but turns to righteousness in Chronicles. When these patterns are carefully examined, it becomes clear that the Chronicler's History is governed by the principle of "immediate retribution," in which God quickly rewards good and faithful living but promptly reprimands every act of disobedience. In order to bring this pattern to his history, the Chronicler frequently added, deleted, and changed the historical tradition that he inherited from the Deuteronomistic History. Consequently, we can reasonably conclude that it was never the Chronicler's purpose to present history as it actually transpired. His generic strategy was to depict history as it would have appeared if justice were served up in the moment-by-moment experiences of life.[19] His history is a kind of realized eschatology, in which the various characters in the story receive the consequences of their deeds in the present rather than in the afterlife.

Undoubtedly, if we are expecting the Chronicler to provide an accurate portrait of events as they actually transpired in ancient Israel, his history falls short. But in another respect the Chronicler's History is perhaps a truer picture of reality than is given in Samuel–Kings. One can easily read Samuel–Kings without gaining a clear understanding of how divine justice is actually worked out for human beings. In 2 Kings the most evil king of Judah, Manasseh, enjoyed a fifty-five-year reign—longer than any other Hebrew ruler. But this sort of outcome is never permitted in Chronicles. The Chronicler asserts that every human deed—whether good or ill—is brought into the court of God's retributive justice. This is a theological point that strongly resonates with the biblical canon as a whole, particularly with the New Testament concepts of the eschaton and final judgment. Once we realize that the Chronicler's History is theological and eschatological rather than strictly historical, it is no longer legitimate to judge his work by the canons of historical accuracy. His "history" has expressed profound theological truths, not in spite of—but because of—its so-called fictions. This will mean, of course, that the Chronicler's historical deviations from Samuel–Kings are not "errors" at all.

John's Theological Biography of Jesus Christ

To foreshadow our results here, the generic solution that I have suggested for the Chronicler's difficulties is closely akin to the solution I would propose for John's Gospel. But let us first recall the difficulties in John. As we noticed in chapter 3, the presentation of Jesus's last hours in John's Gospel differs from that found in the Synoptics. While the Synoptics have Jesus crucified at the "third hour" (i.e., about 9:00 a.m.) on the day after the Passover feast, in John's Gospel Jesus is crucified at high noon just before the Passover feast. Because John's alternate chronology places the death of Jesus at the precise day and hour that the Jews began to slaughter their Passover lambs, modern scholars strongly suspect that John has deliberately moved the day and time of Jesus's death in order to illustrate a theological point that he makes elsewhere: Jesus is the Lamb of God, who takes away the sin of the world. Some traditionalists have been deeply troubled by the historical implications of this straightforward observation and have taken great pains to counter the critical arguments for it, but their efforts have proved unsuccessful.[20] Once we account for the genre of John's Gospel, we shall see that their efforts were not only unsuccessful but also ill-advised.

---

19. For discussions of the Chronicler's theology and historical methodology, see Raymond B. Dillard, "Reward and Punishment in Chronicles: The Theology of Immediate Retribution," *WTJ* 46 (1984): 164–72; Dillard, *2 Chronicles*, WBC (Waco: Word, 1987); Sara Japhet, *I & II Chronicles*, OTL (Louisville: Westminster John Knox, 1993), 43–49; H. G. M. Williamson, *1 and 2 Chronicles*, NCB (Grand Rapids: Eerdmans, 1982), 31–33.

20. See chap. 4, pp. 160–62.

Christians remember Jesus's death as the greatest of all sacrifices, but if the Savior's crucifixion was indeed such a sacrifice, one could hardly tell from the event itself. In the eyes of ancient bystanders, Jesus's death—void of the usual ritual trappings—would have been little more than the Roman execution of a Jewish troublemaker in the backwoods province of Palestine. Only the subsequent resurrection of Jesus proved that his was an unusual death, whose significance was unlike the death of any other human being. From that point forward, early Christians sought out metaphors that could express this significance to themselves and to others. The most widely used metaphor was that of sacrifice, in which Christ's death on our behalf was compared to the animal sacrifices of the Old Testament. Christians exploited this metaphor in various ways. As we have seen already, the writer of Hebrews viewed animal sacrifices as a Platonic *type* of which Jesus's death was the genuine *antitype* (Heb. 9–10). The author of Revelation portrayed Jesus as a living lamb who sported the wounds of death (Rev. 5:6). Paul described Jesus as our "sin offering" and also as our "Passover lamb" (Rom. 8:3; 1 Cor. 5:7 NIV). Once we realize that early Christians employed sacrificial metaphors to describe their Messiah, it is no longer a surprise to notice—as we have—that John's presentation of Jesus was also shaped by sacrificial imagery, in this case by the Passover lamb theme.

Although John's description of Jesus's last hours does not conform to the actual events as closely as the Synoptics, his Gospel is perhaps closer to the theological facts of history because the death of Jesus *was* a sacrifice. By providing a theological portrait of these events, John's Gospel brings out the sacrificial significance of Jesus's death much more clearly than the more "profane" descriptions of the Synoptics. So, though John's Gospel is surely a biography of sorts, it is no slavish chronicle of events from a man's life. It is a theological Gospel that succeeds at the point where every good biography succeeds: it explains the significance and import of a person's life. When we carefully consider the genre of John's Gospel, we find that it is not a poorly researched biography, nor is it a piece of duplicitous fiction. As Origen recognized long ago, it was and is a very effective theological biography.

Daniel and Ancient Apocalypses

I noted in chapter 3 that Daniel contains a collection of several astoundingly successful prophecies in chapters 7–12. Modern scholars have noticed, however, that each of these prophecies includes not only a series of accurate predictions but also a concluding prophecy that seems to have failed. We could easily deduce from these features that the author of Daniel deceptively faked his "accurate" prophecies by composing them after the events had happened, and then tried his hand at a few genuine prophecies that eventually proved unsuccessful. Such an appraisal of Daniel would certainly raise serious theological questions about the legitimacy of Scripture. But here again genre analysis comes to our aid—but only in part.

By carefully studying a number of Near Eastern and Jewish texts that look like the book of Daniel, modern scholars have deduced that the author of Daniel was not attempting to deceive anyone with his accurate prophecies. Indeed, these prophecies were not real prophecies but *ex eventu* predictions, written by the author after the predicted events had happened. The practice of writing *ex eventu* prophecies was a well-known convention among the scribes who wrote apocalyptic literature, so we have every reason to suppose that informed members of Daniel's audience would have recognized his pseudoprophecies for what they were.[21] Undoubtedly, there would have been uninformed readers who mistook these pseudoprophecies for the genuine article, but this would not have troubled the author of Daniel and may even have been part of his intention. In some genres the effectiveness of the discourse depends upon a *generic ruse*, in which the author plays a well-intended trick on the reader in order to make some point.[22] A good example appears in 2 Samuel 12, where the prophet Nathan confronted David's adulterous affair by telling the king a fictional story, which David mistook for a genuine report. As a result, Nathan's true intention—the repentance of the king—was quickly realized. Yet the effectiveness of the prophet's parable rested precisely in his generic ruse, by which David saw guilt in the story's fictional character before seeing it in himself. Of course, in this instance the genre hits its mark only when David recognized Nathan's ruse, but in some genres the ruse has no necessary termination point. I suspect that Daniel's *ex eventu* prophecies are such texts. Although the prophecies are not genuine predictions of the future, they do express a profound theological truth: God knows what the future holds because he is in control of human history. Daniel's *ex eventu* predictions were one legitimate way of expressing the reality of God's foreknowledge and sovereignty.

But that said, the genres in Daniel do not resolve all of the book's theological difficulties. It is to that problem that I now turn.

The Full Humanity of Biblical Genres

In the examples considered so far, careful attention to the genre and subject matter of the biblical materials has solved some of the difficulties raised by modern biblical criticism. The genealogy of Genesis 5 is not bad history; it is mimetic Jewish propaganda. The Pentateuch is not a confusing blend of contradictory fictions; it is an anthology of Jewish tradition. Hebrew law is not a compendium

---

21. For an overview of the comparative texts, see *ATSHB*, 240–51; Craig A. Evans, *Ancient Texts for New Testament Studies: A Guide to the Background Literature* (Peabody, MA: Hendrickson, 2005), 29–40. For a collection of Jewish apocalyptic texts, see *OTP*, vol. 1, *Apocalyptic Literature and Testaments*.

22. I should point out that the pious ruse was not frowned upon by some of the church fathers, for whom deception depended on one's motive, whether good or bad. One thinks in this connection of Chrysostom, who feigned a "promise" to join the priesthood in order to convince his friend Basil to accept ordination. For a discussion of this and other instances, see Philip Schaff, "Prolegomena: The Life and Work of John Chrysostom," in *NPNF* 1 9:8.

of legal inconsistency; it is the result of a rational, necessary, and ongoing process of statutory reformulation. The Chronicler's History is not a pack of duplicitous lies; it is a narrative explication of retributive theology. John's Gospel is not a poor and misleading biography; it is a theological portrait of Jesus's life. Daniel's *ex eventu* prophecies are not deceptions; they are theological expressions of divine sovereignty. Again and again, in these instances and others I have not mentioned, the problem of Scripture's ostensible "errors" is resolved by generic considerations. In some quarters of progressive evangelical thought, genre has emerged as *the* solution, par excellence, for the Bible's apparent difficulties. Unfortunately, however, I suspect that the generic solutions have their limits.

Even after we have employed generic criticism to account for many of the supposed difficulties in Scripture, ample evidence remains that the biblical authors were subject to their own finitude and fallenness when they wrote Scripture. The book of Daniel is a good example. It is to my mind quite clear that the author of Daniel, like the authors of countless other Jewish apocalypses, expected the kingdom of God to appear during his own lifetime, when the Seleucid king Antiochus IV Epiphanes was killing and persecuting Jews in Palestine (second century BCE). The pressure on Jews during this period was constant and intense, and it was perfectly reasonable for suffering Jews to infer that the time of God's kingdom was near. Christians have from time to time done the same, believing that the end was near because of persecution and difficulties. Both Paul (1 Cor. 7:29) and the author of Revelation (see chapter 3 above) seem to have expected the parousia of Jesus during or not long after their own lifetimes. Although eschatological expectations of this sort are surely reasonable under difficult circumstances, these expectations clearly turned out to be incorrect. The author of Daniel's apocalypses fully expected the end to come during the Hellenistic period, but the full-blown kingdom of God did not appear during the reign of King Antiochus IV; in fact, we are still waiting for it.

We can reasonably deduce from this discussion that the author of Daniel was in some sense subject to his human finitude when he wrote the apocalypses. While this might strike us as a modern and critical perspective on the Bible, it was a possibility pondered long ago by Martin Luther. During a discussion in 1531, the great reformer mused: "I wonder whether Peter, Paul, Moses, and all the saints fully and thoroughly understood a single word of God so that they had nothing more to learn from it, for the understanding of God is beyond measure.... Who understands in all of its ramifications even the opening words, 'Our Father who art in heaven'?"[23] Though in this instance Luther was apparently comfortable with the idea that the Bible's human authors did not fully understand what they wrote, it would seem that he did not consider the possible effect of this finitude on the Bible itself. He did not consider the possibility that a *limited* human perspective

---

23. Martin Luther, *Luther's Works*, ed. Jaroslav Pelikan and Helmut T. Lehman, 55 vols. (St. Louis: Concordia; Philadelphia: Fortress, 1955–1976), 54:9.

might inevitably lead to a *mistaken* perspective. Nor did he imagine that for a biblical author, such as the author of the Daniel apocalpyses, this finite perspective might cause the author to suppose that the world's end had arrived when it had not. Though Luther did not consider that possibility, the evidence from Daniel suggests that this is indeed what happened.

But can we say more? Can we say, for instance, that the biblical authors were also fallen human beings, and that Scripture reflects this as well? Though it might at first seem reckless, I think we certainly can and even must assert that the apostles and prophets who wrote the Bible were fallen human beings. Apart from that, we would have a *real* theological problem on our hands: human beings who do not need Christ. The only question that remains, then, is whether God somehow protected or insulated their biblical words from their human fallenness. If he did so, it should be easy to recognize. Scripture would reflect a single, coherent, and consistent God-given view of morals and ethics from Genesis to Revelation. Its words would be free of the sinful vagaries of human authors and would give us the one and only universal ethic of Christ's teaching. It would mean, for instance, that Scripture would not tell us to slaughter the women and children of our enemies in a "holy war" (Deut. 2:34; 7:1–3; Josh. 1–12) and also to pray for them and love them (Prov. 25:21; Matt. 5:44); that Scripture would not allow us to beat slaves (Exod. 21:20–21) and also command us to treat them kindly (Eph. 6:9; Col. 4:1); that Scripture would not list women as the property of their husbands (Exod. 20:17) and also claim that we are all one in Christ (Gal. 3:28); that Scripture would not declare swine flesh unclean (Deut. 14:8) and also clean (Acts 9:14–15). It would mean that biblical authors would not wish emasculation upon their opponents (Gal. 5:12), or revel in the smashing of infant children against rocks (Ps. 137:9), or base their treatment of human beings on their ethnicity or race (Lev. 25:44–46). Anything less would mean that Scripture has in some sense assumed or adopted theological and ethical positions that are lower than its highest expressed ideals.[24]

The evidence seems strong that something less is indeed what we have. Scripture includes all of the unexpected features that I have just listed, even those lapses of ethical judgment endemic to the human perspective. So, though those who wrote the Bible were undoubtedly people of spirit, faith, and intelligence, and privy to divinely given insight, their discourses were by no means magical discourses, voided of human limitations and foibles. Fortunately, successful communication does not require perfect language; it requires only language that is adequate as a bearer of truth—in the case of Scripture, of God's truth.

24. Evangelicals commonly attribute some of this diversity to "progressive revelation" or to a simple contrast between the Old Testament and the New. While there is real truth in both of these solutions, as workable theological solutions they are only half-baked. That there is progressive revelation in biblical ethics, and that this difference is very pronounced between the Old and New Testaments, is clear. The real question is why a book written by God would ever assume lower ethical standards in one instance and higher standards in another. For the answer to that question, we shall have to look elsewhere—and we shall do so in chapter 7.

Conclusions

In this chapter I have attempted to illustrate how historical criticism, by helping us understand the human genres of Scripture, can provide an important theological service to the church. It helps us to understand Scripture better, and in many cases it exposes as illusion some of the Bible's ostensible errors. Now we have seen in earlier chapters that this hermeneutical strategy, which resolves the Bible's errors by an appeal to genre, is by no means new to Christian exegesis. The patristic allegories were in essence a generic solution of this sort, and I recall the very interesting hermeneutical maneuver undertaken by Origen, Chrysostom, and Jerome that explained the argument between Paul and Peter in Galatians 2 as a theatrical farce, concocted by the apostles in order to teach Jewish Christians a lesson about circumcision.[25] So the ancients were more than mere allegorists. But it remains true that the modern appeal to genre is more sophisticated than one finds in the fathers, inasmuch as our modern list of possible genres is much longer than the list used by early Christians. But the main point is clear, I hope. When we sensibly employ analytical generic categories to read Scripture, treating it as the ancient document that it is rather than as an instance of modern discourse, many of the theological difficulties implied by historical criticism are adequately resolved.

On the other hand, I have tried to show as well that this generic business turns out to be a double-edged sword. It is precisely because the Bible is genuine human discourse that it also participates in the fallible horizons of its human authors and audiences. So, whatever the divine inspiration of Scripture is or involves, it does not run roughshod over the humanity of the biblical authors in order to protect them from the limitations of their perspectives and judgments. This raises two obvious theological difficulties. First, how and why did the one true God, who does not and cannot err, speak through human discourse that includes human error? Second, how does the Bible speak as the authoritative voice of God if it includes the diverse and sometimes contradictory perspectives of its human authors? We shall consider these two important questions in the chapters that follow.

---

25. Schaff, "Prolegomena," 8.

7

The Genres
of Divine Discourse

Introduction

Christians receive the Bible as divine discourse, as God's authoritative words inscribed through human writers to human readers.[1] This much is clear. However, once we have confessed our theological commitment to Scripture as God's Word, and have declared that Scripture is also a human document, we find that our desire to hear God's voice in Scripture is complicated by two problematic features of the text. The first feature is the strangeness of Scripture's worldview. Scripture was written originally by ancient authors who communicated in literary genres quite different from our own, to audiences living in contexts, and facing concerns, that were sometimes considerably different from ours. In the previous chapter, we observed how modern biblical scholarship works to bridge the interpretive gap that stands between our world and the biblical world. Using their historical-critical tools, scholars are able to imaginatively resituate the biblical text in its ancient cultural, historical, and literary milieu, so that modern readers can listen in on what God once said to the Romans through the apostle Paul, or to Theophilus through Luke the physician, or to Israel through Ezekiel the prophet. Reading the biblical text with generic sensitivity provides us with crucial clues about what the

---

1. The present chapter represents a substantial revision of my earlier article, "The Sun Also Rises: Accommodation in Inscripturation and Interpretation," in *Evangelicals and Scripture: Tradition, Authority, and Hermeneutics*, ed. Vincent Bacote, Laura C. Miguélez, and Dennis L. Okholm (Downers Grove, IL: InterVarsity, 2004), 112-32.

ancient authors probably were, and were not, attempting to do with their words. To the extent that their ancient discourse is understood, it provides a crucial and authoritative voice in our modern theological reflection. That is, to a considerable extent historical criticism helps us resolve the first problem presented by Scripture. By bridging the historical gap between the ancient world and our own, critical scholars have helped us to understand Scripture much better and, hence, to understand God's Word better. In doing so, these scholars have also exposed more clearly the generic character of the Bible, revealing that many of Scripture's so-called errors are illusions created by our errant readings of Scripture. In this and in other respects, historical criticism has made the Bible's ancient discourse easier to understand. We could even say without blushing that historical criticism has performed invaluable theological services for the church.

Now Scripture's other problematic feature is its diversity, and it is with this problem that we will wrestle presently and in the next few chapters. The difficulty can be outlined in short order. Even if we successfully manage to understand the words of Scripture's ancient human authors, it is not at all clear that what God *has said* through those ancient authors is in every instance what God *is saying* to modern readers. For instance, while we are quite sure that God once said, "Do not eat swine flesh," we are equally sure that he no longer demands this of us. The reason, of course, is that Scripture often presents us with diverse viewpoints on the selfsame matter, respecting not only our diet but also matters of history, linguistics, ethics, theology, and religious practice. This diversity is compounded when we read Scripture alongside the ostensible results of modern historical, scientific, and social-scientific inquiry, the apparent tension between biological evolution and biblical creation being only one example. One could reasonably say that the Bible does not offer a single, well-integrated univocal theology; it offers instead numerous overlapping but nonetheless distinctive theologies!

In light of these facts, we face an obvious and perplexing theological conundrum: How can the Bible serve as the univocal and authoritative word of an inerrant God—*as divine discourse*—when this word has been passed to us through the discourse of numerous finite and fallen human beings? Some evangelicals will imagine that this is a new and unnecessary question to ask, a question prompted mainly by modern biases against God, faith, and Scripture. As we shall see, however, there is abundant evidence that this question is very old. It is old because the Bible's diversity is not an Enlightenment-era illusion but a self-evident feature of Scripture, placed in its pages according to the wisdom of God.

How has the church explained the presence of theological diversity in Scripture? How has it achieved some semblance of theological coherence on the basis of that diverse text? These two closely related questions will occupy us in this chapter and the next. I will begin here by taking up the first question.

In the course of church history, one perennial explanation for Scripture's theological diversity has been the notion of *accommodation*. Accommodation is God's adoption in inscripturation of the human audience's finite and fallen perspective. Its underlying conceptual assumption is that in many cases God does not correct our mistaken human viewpoints but merely assumes them in order to communicate with us. Although the concept has not played an important or explicit role in evangelical hermeneutics, recent developments in the "open theism" debate have brought accommodation yet again to the fore of evangelical interpretation. Open theists aver that the biblical texts that portray the Deity repenting or changing his mind are accurate depictions of the divine nature.[2] God did regret that he made humanity (Gen. 6:6), that he sent the flood (Gen. 8:21), that he was about to destroy Israel (Exod. 32:14), and that he made Saul king (1 Sam. 15:11). Traditional evangelicals argue, to the contrary, that these texts are anthropomorphic accommodations to our human viewpoint, that God is not really changing his mind when Scripture says that he is changing his mind. While I tend to agree with this traditional conclusion, many evangelicals who follow this line of thought seem not to have fully appreciated the theological implications of their position. In light of these theological developments, which presume the larger problem of Scripture's theological diversity, I would suggest along with Donald A. Carson that a restatement of accommodation "would be salutary today."[3] Our discussion of accommodation requires at the outset, however, a brief foray into the problems of human epistemology.

As we saw in chapter 1, the inflated sense of epistemic certainty by which human beings live is often well beyond the more sober estimates that our finitude and fallenness should dictate. If we could see ourselves through the eyes of the omniscient God, or even through the finite eyes of future generations, I suppose that our myopia would become clearer. I suspect, moreover, that we would be surprised to discover that some of the things about which we err are among the things that we hold with the most certainty. Of course, this is only hypothetical, for we cannot step out of our own skulls into some different and more transcendent vantage point. But perhaps we can approximate this experience by examining how Christians of the past have struggled with their finite interpretive horizons and with the fallenness of their moral perspectives. In this respect the theological debates surrounding the Copernican revolution are fascinating for students of biblical interpretation and philosophical hermeneutics.[4]

When Copernicus (1473–1543) proffered his heliocentric theory, it met with sharp resistance both within the Catholic Church and among the Reformers.[5]

---

2. See Gregory A. Boyd, *God of the Possible: A Biblical Introduction to the Open View of God* (Grand Rapids: Baker Books, 2000); John Sanders, *The God Who Risks: A Theology of Providence* (Downers Grove, IL: InterVarsity, 1998).

3. Donald A. Carson, *The Gagging of God: Christianity Confronts Pluralism* (Grand Rapids: Zondervan, 1996), 130.

4. For a dated but standard discussion, see Thomas S. Kuhn, *The Copernican Revolution* (Cambridge, MA: Harvard University Press, 1957). See also Langford's comments regarding Galileo and the church's response to him in Jerome J. Langford, *Galileo, Science, and the Church*, 2nd ed. (Ann Arbor: University of Michigan Press, 1971).

5. Early Christian interpretations of the Genesis cosmologies followed two paths. One paradigm attempted to correlate Scripture with contemporary cosmological ideas (e.g., Basil, John Philoponon of Alexandria),

The responses of Luther, Melanchthon, and Calvin are good examples. Luther (1483–1546) referred to Copernicus as an "upstart astrologer" and as a "fool [who] wishes to reverse the entire science of astronomy; but sacred Scripture tells us that Joshua commanded the sun to stand still, and not the earth."[6] Luther's associate Melanchthon (1497–1560) added these words of criticism:

> The eyes are witnesses that the heavens revolve in the space of twenty-four hours. But certain men, either from the love of novelty, or to make a display of ingenuity, have concluded that the earth moves.... Now, it is a want of honesty and decency to assert such notions publicly, and the example is pernicious. It is the part of a good mind to accept the truth as revealed by God and to acquiesce in it.[7]

Melanchthon believed that wise governments ought to "repress" the views of Copernicus because "public proclamation of absurd opinions is indecent and sets a harmful example."[8] In support of this opinion, he could cite biblical texts such as Ecclesiastes 1:5: "The sun rises and the sun goes down, and hastens to the place where it rises" (RSV).

The response of John Calvin (1509–1564) to Copernicus was a bit more complicated. His commentaries and sermons uniformly ignored the Polish astronomer, averring the traditional geocentric view at every turn, sometimes in great detail.[9] But there is a considerable debate about whether this means that Calvin should be viewed as anti-Copernican or merely as pre-Copernican. In support of the pre-Copernican view, we should note that Calvin embraced a very flexible theology of biblical inspiration that allowed for the easy assimilation of new astronomical data, as this excerpt from his Genesis commentary shows:

> Astronomers ... investigate with great labor whatever keenness of man's intellect is able to discover. Such study is certainly not to be disapproved, nor this science condemned, because some frantic persons are wont boldly to reject whatever is unknown to them.... Therefore, clever men who expend their labor upon it are

---

while the other attempted to build a cosmology on Scripture alone (e.g., the Antiochene school, i.e., Gregory of Nyssa, Chrysostom, and Diodorus of Tarsus). This second paradigm resulted in a two-story square cosmology where the first heaven was in the upper part of the lower story and the second heaven was a vaulted upper story. See the brief but insightful discussion of Clemens Scholten, "Weshalb wird die Schöpfungsgeschichte zum naturwissenschaftlichen Bericht?" *Theologische Quartalschrift* 177 (1997): 1–15.

6. Luther, *Tischreden* 1.419. English quotation from A. D. White, *A History of the Warfare of Science with Theology in Christendom*, 2 vols. (New York: Appleton, 1920), 1:126.

7. Melanchthon, *Initia Doctrinae Physicae*. English quotation from White, *Warfare*, 1:126–27.

8. See *Corpus reformatum* 4:679; 13:217.

9. For instance, see the following: John Calvin, *Commentaries on the First Book of Moses, called Genesis*, trans. John King, 2 vols. (Edinburgh: Calvin Translation Society, 1847–1850), 1:61; Calvin, *Commentary on the Book of Psalms*, trans. James Anderson, 5 vols. (Edinburgh: Calvin Translation Society, 1845–1849), 1:315; 3:186; 4:6–7, 148–49, 469; Calvin, *Commentaries on the Book of the Prophet Jeremiah and the Lamentations*, trans. John Owen, 5 vols. (Edinburgh: Calvin Translation Society, 1850–1855), 2:34; Calvin, *Two and Twentie Sermons*, trans. Thomas Stalker (London: Dawson, 1580), 99.

to be praised and those who have ability and leisure ought not to neglect work of that kind. Nor did Moses wish to withdraw us from this pursuit by omitting such things as are peculiar to the art; but because he was ordained a teacher of the unlearned and ignorant as well of the learned, he could not fulfill his office unless he descended to this more elementary method of instruction.[10]

When one views Calvin's Ptolemaic cosmology through the lens of his appreciation for astronomy, one might conclude that the reformer did not know of Copernicus, and this is precisely the conclusion that Edward Rosen has drawn.[11] But Ratner has averred to the contrary—and I tend to agree with him—that it is rather unlikely that a man of Calvin's erudition and broad interests wrote in ignorance of the important debates surrounding Copernicus.[12] Moreover, there is a tradition that Calvin once criticized the astronomer for contradicting the Bible's geocentric view, saying, "Who will venture to place the authority of Copernicus above that of the Holy Spirit?"[13] Whether Calvin ever posed this question will likely remain a mystery, but it seems probable that Calvin's lengthy discussions of Ptolemaic cosmology were pointed, at least in part, at the new system being proffered by Copernicus. Calvin, Luther, and Melanchthon are merely representative of general trends in the sixteenth century, in which clergymen feverishly searched the Bible line by line for new passages that would confirm the traditional Ptolemaic view.[14]

It is easy to see why the Reformers and others took this hard-line position against Copernicus. First, the Ptolemaic view was matched step for step by the long-standing traditions of the church. Second, the Ptolemaic view corresponded rather precisely to the usual experiences of human life—that the sun is moving and we are not. Third, as we have just seen, the geocentric view had Scripture on its side. Tradition, common sense, and the voice of Scripture joined together to create a coherent understanding of the world against which the Copernican viewpoint seemed senseless, even heretical. Ultimately, however, the Copernican viewpoint would win the day. The reason, of course, was that the scientific evidence finally coalesced into a consensus against which tradition, Scripture, and common sense could no longer prevail. Why had some of the greatest theological minds in church history failed to recognize their error? Why did they speak so maliciously and arrogantly against Copernicus, only to be, in the end, on the wrong side of the debate? *In nuce*, we could say that the Reformers suffered from finitude—hence they did not realize what they did not know—and they also suffered from moral

10. Calvin, *First Book of Moses*, 1:86–87.
11. Edward Rosen, "Calvin's Attitude toward Copernicus," *JHI* 21 (1960): 431–41; Rosen, "A Reply to Dr. Ratner," *JHI* 22 (1961): 386–88.
12. Joseph Ratner, "Some Comments on Rosen's 'Calvin's Attitude toward Copernicus,'" *JHI* 22 (1961): 382–85.
13. For a discussion of the problems with this quotation, see the articles of Rosen and Ratner.
14. Kuhn, *Copernican Revolution*, 192.

fallenness—hence their arrogant and malicious spirit. But in the case of Calvin, it is worth exploring his more measured response in some detail.

It is certainly true that Calvin and others had placed too much confidence in common sense and had either overestimated their understanding of the science or, more likely, had trusted too exclusively others who claimed to know the science. But it was the interpretation of Scripture that played a pivotal role in Calvin's perspective. At every turn of the page, he, and others like him, could show how God's Word reflected the Ptolemaic perspective over against the Copernican view. It was no coincidence that Calvin found the geocentric view in the Scriptures. Prior to Copernicus, only a few Greek philosophers—so far as we know—seriously advocated a heliocentric view.[15] In the days of ancient Israel, all of the data we have suggests that the ancients viewed the earth as a flat and level surface placed on a foundation of some sort, and that the sun moved through the sky during the day and then into the underworld each evening.[16] Such was the common understanding in antiquity, and the Scriptures simply reflect this cosmological status quo. A common evangelical answer to these observations is that Genesis—and the rest of the Old Testament with it—is not a book of science. But it would be quite strange if there were no connection between the flat earth depicted in Scripture and the ancient view that the earth was flat. Whether Scripture's cosmologies are science, myth, or something else altogether, there is little doubt that they reflect an ancient and errant viewpoint.

Although the Reformers and many others—to the misfortune of Copernicus, and especially Galileo—failed to recognize the potential role of accommodation in the astronomical debates of the time, this does not mean that Calvin was unaware, in principle, that accommodation played an important role in the Bible's description of the cosmos. The great reformer's work is well known for its rather clear enunciation of accommodation—even in his Genesis commentary.[17] For

---

15. The Greeks knew the earth was spherical by the fifth century BCE (Parmenides), and there is also evidence that a few of them toyed with the heliocentric theory (Aristarchus of Samos, c. 310–230 BCE; Archimedes, d. 212 BCE). However, it is clear that these unusual ideas were not widely known; even very educated writers, such as Thucydides, were unfamiliar with them. This explains the long-standing prominence of the geocentric view espoused by Aristotle (fourth century BCE) and Ptolemy (second century CE). For a discussion of the Greek viewpoints, see G. J. Toomer, "Astronomy," in *Oxford Classical Dictionary*, ed. Simon Hornblower and Antony Spawforth, 3rd ed. (Oxford: Oxford University Press, 1996), 196–98.

16. For a discussion of the Genesis cosmology, see Paul H. Seely, "The Geographical Meaning of 'Earth' and 'Seas' in Genesis 1:10," *WTJ* 59 (1997): 231–55. For a good example of the ancient Jewish viewpoint during the fourth through third centuries BCE, see the "Book of the Watchers" and the "Astronomical Book" in *1 Enoch*, chaps. 17–36 and 72–82, respectively. Here the earth is depicted as a flat disk with extreme edges to the east and west, and the stars and heavenly bodies are thought to pass into the heavens through portals at the extreme eastern edge of the earth.

17. For discussions of Calvin's accommodation theology, see Jon Balserak, "'The Accommodating Act Par Excellence?' An Inquiry into the Incarnation and Calvin's Understanding of Accommodation," *SJT* 55 (2002): 408–23; Ford L. Battles, "God Was Accommodating Himself to Human Capacity," *Int* 31 (1977): 19–38; David F. Wright, "Calvin's Pentateuchal Criticism: Equity, Hardness of Heart, and Divine Accommodation in the Mosaic Harmony Commentary," *Calvin Theological Journal* 21 (1986): 33–50.

instance, Calvin wrote concerning the reference to "waters above the firmament (*raqia*)" in Genesis 1:

> For, to my mind, this is a certain principle: that nothing is treated here except the visible form of the world. Whoever wishes to learn astronomy and other esoteric arts, let him go elsewhere.... Therefore, the things which he [i.e., Moses] relates, serve as the garniture of that theatre which he [i.e., God] places before our eyes. From this I conclude that the waters intended here are such as the crude and unlearned may perceive. The assertion of some, that they embrace by faith what they have read concerning the waters above the heavens, notwithstanding their ignorance of them, is not in accordance with the design of Moses. And truly a longer inquiry into a matter open and manifest is superfluous.[18]

One should not, Calvin says, believe "by faith" that there are waters above the firmament when one knows good and well that this is not the case. Genesis merely accommodates itself to the ancient view that such waters existed. Calvin similarly argued that accommodation was at work in the chronological system used to enumerate the various creation days of Genesis 1. Because the text reflects an accommodation to the ancient view of time, says Calvin, "It is useless to dispute whether this is the best and legitimate order or not."[19] In other words, for Calvin, accommodation was a useful interpretive tool because it made irrelevant in such cases any questions about the Bible's correctness.

Calvin resorted to the same kinds of explanations when, in Acts 7:14 and Hebrews 11:21, the New Testament authors appear to quote from the Greek Old Testament and, in the process, include some of its translation errors in their writings.[20] Acts 7:14 follows the Greek text of Genesis 46:17 in numbering Jacob's family as seventy-five at the beginning of the Egyptian sojourn, whereas in the Hebrew text, and also elsewhere in the Septuagint, we find that the number is seventy.[21] As for Hebrews 11:21, in that case the New Testament author followed the Septuagint, which mistook the Hebrew word for "bed" (in Gen. 47:31) as the word for "staff." Now Calvin certainly knew that the quoted texts were wrong, but he did not blame the New Testament authors. Calvin believed that in these cases Luke and Paul merely "accommodated themselves to the unlearned, who had as yet need of milk."[22]

---

18. Calvin, *First Book of Moses*, 79–80. Calvin's approach to Genesis is given more general expression in his *Institutes*: "For who is so devoid of intellect as not to understand that God, in so speaking, lisps with us as nurses are wont to do with little children? Such modes of expression, therefore, do not so much express what kind of a being God is, as accommodate the knowledge of him to our feebleness. In doing so, he must, of course, stoop far below his proper height" (John Calvin, *Institutes of the Christian Religion*, trans. Henry Beveridge, 2 vols. [London: Clarke, 1949], 1:110 [1.13.1]).

19. Calvin, *First Book of Moses*, 79–80.

20. John Calvin, *Commentary upon the Acts of the Apostles*, trans. Henry Beveridge, 2 vols. (Edinburgh: Calvin Translation Society, 1844), 1:263–64; Calvin, *Commentaries on the Epistle of Paul the Apostle to the Hebrews*, trans. John Owen (Edinburgh: Calvin Translation Society, 1853), 290–91.

21. See the LXX of Deut. 10:33.

22. Calvin, *Hebrews*, 291.

Let us be clear: Calvin always worked hard to resolve the apparent contradictions and tensions that he found in the Bible. But when this effort failed—and sometimes it did—he was not above admitting that something errant appeared in the pages of Scripture. For these kinds of difficulties, Calvin tells us that whenever it appears that the Bible speaks "falsely," this reflects an accommodation to the false views of humanity. In this sense accommodation was for Calvin what allegory was for the church fathers: a ready-made hermeneutical tool for solving the problem of diversity in the Scriptures. If Calvin's principle of accommodation is a legitimate and important aspect of Scripture's divine speech, we should anticipate that it was not some kind of radical theological innovation but a long-standing assumption about the nature of Scripture. And, indeed, this is so.

Accommodation in Early Christian Interpretation

Calvin was preceded by a long line of Bible readers who recognized the nature and necessity of accommodation in revelation and used the concept to solve the conundrums of theological diversity in Scripture.[23] Among the most important of these conundrums was that raised by Marcion, as well as by other early critics, that the Old and New Testaments ostensibly provide quite different pictures of God and his relationship to humanity. While one answer to this has always been *oikonomia*, God's salvation plan as it unfolds in various dispensations (or economies), this begs the question of why these dispensations were necessary. Church interpreters have rather consistently attributed these differences in the old and new spiritual economies to the necessity and presence of accommodation. An early example from the second century is provided by Justin, who explained to Trypho why God gave the Jews primitive rituals like Sabbath keeping, circumcision, and sacrifice:

> We also would observe the fleshly circumcision, and the Sabbaths, and in short all of your festivals, if we did not know why they were ordained, namely, because of your sins and the hardness of your hearts ... God enjoined you to keep the Sabbath and imposed on you other precepts for a sign, as I have already said, on account of your unrighteousness, and that of your fathers.[24]

Justin found confirmation of this viewpoint in Ezekiel's word that God gave the Jews "statutes that were not good" (Ezek. 20:25). But why would God do this? According to Justin, God did so because in the days of Moses the Israelites were: "wicked and ungrateful to God, and fashioned a calf in the desert. For this reason,

---

23. The spadework for my discussion in this section was provided in the excellent volume of Stephen D. Benin, *The Footprints of God: Divine Accommodation in Jewish and Christian Thought* (Albany: State University of New York Press, 1993).

24. Justin, *Dialogue with Trypho* 18, 21 (*ANF* 1:203–4); cf. discussion in Benin, *Footprints of God*, 1–4. I have modestly modernized the archaic language of *ANF* and *NPNF* quotations.

the Lord, accommodating (*harmosamenos*) Himself to those people, commanded that sacrifices be brought in his name lest you practice idolatry."[25] Justin found the dictates of Jewish law far from ideal, but they were nonetheless necessary accommodations in light of human frailty. As a result, he suggested that the various Jewish laws could be attributed to three underlying motives: (1) piety and righteousness, (2) prophetic and christological teaching, and (3) accommodation to the hardness of the human heart.[26] Irenaeus much agreed with this perspective, adding that "even in the New Testament, the apostles are found granting certain precepts in consideration of human infirmity, because of the incontinence of some, lest such persons, having grown obdurate, and despairing altogether of their salvation, should become apostates from God."[27]

Another important problem for early Christian apologists was the anthropomorphic presentation of God in the Hebrew Bible, both because this seemed to contradict other texts in the Old and New Testaments and because these anthropomorphisms reflected, in the eyes of some pagans, a rather low view of divinity. In his third-century response to the pagan philosopher Celsus, Origen of Alexandria offered this explanation for the biblical anthropomorphisms:

> Just as when we are talking to very small children we do not assume as the object of our instruction any strong understanding in them, but say what we have to say accommodating (*harmosamenos*) it to the small understanding of those whom we have before us... so the Word of God seems to have disposed the things which were written, adapting the suitable parts of his message to the capacity of his hearers and to their ultimate profit.[28]

Origen offered similar explanations for the Old Testament texts in which God seems to repent or change his mind, and pleaded accommodation extensively elsewhere in his work. His pedagogical metaphor that compares accommodation in the Scriptures to "baby talk" became standard fare in later Christian theologies. For Origen, accommodation was necessary because it was unsuitable—in fact, impossible—for an infinite God to address a fallen and sinful human audience in a manner that truly suited his own majesty. For the more spiritual and insightful reader who recognized the resulting accommodations, however, there was yet a truer and more accurate meaning of the text opened to them. In essence Origen believed that the best interpreters of Scripture were those who recognized and accounted for accommodation in the text.

In the fourth century the use of accommodation in Athanasius's (c. 296–373) work is comparable to that found in second- and third-century theologies. He

---

25. Justin, *Dialogue with Trypho* 19 (*ANF* 1:204).
26. Ibid. 44 (*ANF* 1:217).
27. Benin, *Footprints of God*, 6.
28. Origen, *Against Celsus* 4.71, in Benin, *Footprints of God*, 12; cf. *Against Celsus* 5.16 (*ANF* 4:529; cf. 550).

viewed the sacrificial system of Judaism as primitive and considered its rituals a later addition to the Mosaic law, necessary accommodations in the face of the idolatry and ignorance of the people.[29] Athanasius's work against Arianism is perhaps better known, and here accommodation was used extensively in his christological explications of the incarnation. Christ did not struggle to earn a reward as the Arians suggested; such depictions in the New Testament were accommodations to Christ's humanity and the human audience. In fact, for many ancient theologians the incarnation was not only the highest and best form of revelation but also the quintessential example of divine accommodation.

The Cappadocian fathers also embraced accommodation theology, as examples from the writings of Gregory of Nyssa (c. 330–395), Basil the Great (c. 330–379), and Gregory of Nazianzus (c. 330–390) show. For instance, Gregory of Nyssa took up Origen's "baby talk" metaphor to explain to the heretic, Eunomius, why human qualities are ascribed to God in the Scriptures:

> For as by Divine dispensation . . . like a tender mother who joins in the inarticulate utterances of her babe, [God] gives to our human nature what it is capable of receiving; and thus in the various manifestations of God to man He both adapts Himself to man and speaks in human language, and assumes wrath, and pity, and such-like emotions, so that through feelings corresponding to our own infantile life we might be led as by the hand, and lay hold of the Divine nature by means of words which His foresight has given. For that it is irreverent to imagine that God is subject to any passion such as we see in respect to pleasure, or pity, or anger, no one will deny who has thought at all about the truth of things.[30]

Basil similarly argued that much in the Old Testament was given—in accordance with divine dispensation—in accommodative language. Hence in the Old Testament the nature of divinity was frequently represented "by rough and shadowy outlines."[31] This theological imprecision prompted numerous attacks against Basil, but in his view accommodation was a necessary feature of progressive revelation, in which God revealed himself to human beings by "gradually accustoming us to see first the shadows of objects, and to look at the sun in water, to save us from dashing against the spectacle of pure unadulterated light, and being blinded."[32] The third man in the trio, Gregory of Nazianzus, addressed yet again the familiar theme among accommodationists, that the Old Testament cult reflects God's appropriation of primitive religious behavior:

> And therefore like a Tutor or Physician [God] partly removes and partly condones ancestral habits, conceding some little of what tended to pleasure, just as medical men do with their patients, that their medicine may be taken, being artfully blended

---

29. Athanasius, *Letter* 19.4 (*NPNF* 2 4:544–45); cf. Benin, *Footprints of God*, 27–28.
30. Gregory of Nyssa, *Answer to Eunomius' Second Book, NPNF* 2 5:292.
31. Basil, *De Spiritu Sancto* 14.31 (= *NPNF* 2 8:19).
32. Benin, *Footprints of God*, 33–34.

with what is nice.... For instance, the first [dispensation] cut off the idol, but left the sacrifices; the second, while it destroyed sacrifices did not forbid circumcision. Then, when once men had submitted to the curtailment, they also yielded that which had been conceded to them; in the first instance the sacrifices, in the second circumcision; and became instead of Gentiles, Jews, and instead of Jews, Christians, being beguiled into the Gospel by gradual changes.[33]

For Gregory the Hebrew sacrifices were only one step removed from the evils of idolatry and hence represented a base and fleshly element of human religion that would eventually be rejected. Nonetheless, sacrificial practices—and others like them—were condoned in revelation because of human fallenness. These examples cohere nicely with Benin's more thorough analysis of the church fathers, which revealed that the idea of accommodation took root and flourished among the fourth-century Cappadocian fathers.

We can add to this litany of fourth-century accommodationists the Antiochene voice of Chrysostom. With respect to accommodation, he is perhaps best known for his view that marriage was a divine concession (*synkatabasis*) to the more ideal state of virginity, but his treatise *The Incomprehensible Nature of God* was also rich in accommodative theology.[34] Here, like others before him, Chrysostom tackled the problem of anthropomorphism in the Old Testament. Although Isaiah 6 surely depicts God as a physical presence seated on a throne, says Chrysostom, God neither has a body nor sits on thrones. Such a revelation of God is a product of accommodation, a term that Chrysostom then proceeded to explain more precisely: "What is condescension? It is when God appears and makes himself known *not as he is*, but in the way one incapable of beholding him is able to look upon him. In this way God reveals himself proportionally to the weakness of those who behold him."[35] Here Chrysostom vividly presented the true nature of accommodation: accommodated revelation provides greater access to the divine truth by depicting some things as other than they are.

But how, in this case, did Chrysostom know that anthropomorphic presentations of God depict God as other than he is? Clearly, Chrysostom knew this because the Bible said elsewhere that God is Spirit and has no physical body; that is, accommodation became visible to Chrysostom when theological diversity appeared in Scripture. One can plainly see that in such cases accommodation becomes an indispensable aspect of interpretation, for it is the rationale that allows us to choose one text over another without charging the implied errors to God. If the diversity of Scripture is a reality, as this and other examples suggest, then we cannot help but agree with Gregory of Nyssa, who warned

33. Gregory of Nazianzus, *Orations* 5.25 (*NPNF* 2 7:325–26).
34. John Chrysostom, *On the Incomprehensible Nature of God*, trans. Paul W. Harkins, Fathers of the Church 72 (Washington, DC: Catholic University of America Press, 1984); cf. Benin, *Footprints of God*, 60–64.
35. Chrysostom, *Incomprehensible Nature of God* 3.15, trans. Benin, *Footprints of God*, 186.

that our failure to account for accommodation in the text can easily lead to theological error.[36]

From the late fourth and early fifth centuries, the North African voice of Augustine remains the strongest influence in modern theology and therefore a suitable exemplar for our inquiry. Like those who preceded him, Augustine was concerned with the apparent diversity in Scripture, especially the differences between the Old and New Testaments. Using his Platonic hermeneutic of types and antitypes, he was able to imagine a system within which the old and new dispensations were essentially alike in all respects, as he indicated in his *Retractions*: "For what is now called the Christian religion existed of old and was never absent from the beginning of the human race until Christ came in the flesh."[37] Because of this, unlike many earlier fathers, Augustine suffered no theological embarrassment from the Jewish sacrificial system:

> There are some who suppose that these visible sacrifices are suitable for other gods, but that for the one God, as he is the invisible, greatest, and best, only the invisible — the greatest and best sacrifices — are proper; and such sacrifices are the services of a pure mind and a good will. But such people evidently do not realize that the visible sacrifices are symbols of the invisible offerings, just as spoken words are the symbols of things.[38]

Even within this system of rigorous theological continuity, however, Augustine recognized that the diversity between the two Testaments required an explanation. He attributed this theological diversity to the mystery of God, and he also stressed that God was free to change his commands to human beings as he wished.[39] But, like his theological predecessors, Augustine acknowledged the role of accommodation in revelation, particularly in comparisons of the Old and New Testaments:

> If the trouble is that the moral precepts under the old law are lower and in the Gospel higher, and that therefore both cannot come from the same God, whoever thinks in this way may find difficulty in explaining how a single physician prescribes one medicine to weaker patients through his assistants, and another by himself to stronger patients, all to restore health.[40]

Augustine's use of a medical metaphor to explain accommodation constituted one of the two common paradigms used in the early church to articulate its theology of God's condescension to human beings, the other being the pedagogical meta-

---

36. Cf. Benin, *Footprints of God*, 51.
37. Quoted in ibid., 96.
38. Augustine, *City of God* 10.19 (*NPNF* 1 2:192).
39. Benin, *Footprints of God*, 101–4.
40. Augustine, *Of True Religion* 17, in *Earlier Writings*, ed. John H. S. Burleigh, Library of Christian Classics 6 (Philadelphia: Westminster, 1953), 241.

phor. These metaphors are comparable and teach the same point: God conforms his revelation to human weaknesses, to our fallenness and finitude. This theology allowed Augustine to explain how the diversity between the moral prescriptions of the two Testaments could stem from the one and consistent God. It is clear, however, that Augustine's theological effort to protect God from the charge of inconsistency was accomplished at the expense of consistency in Scripture.

The examples cited above demonstrate that accommodation is not a theological innovation but a long-standing principle of theology and revelation. It is likely that many evangelicals could follow the fathers and Calvin in applying this idea in certain instances, especially in matters of science and in the related matters of human finitude. There will be more reluctance, I suspect, to extend accommodation from science to theology and from human finitude to human fallenness. To do so might imply that Scripture rhetorically presumes the mistaken theological ideas of its human authors (or audience) and then communicates these ideas in the text. Nonetheless, I would argue that theological accommodations of this sort seem as necessary in Scripture as those of the scientific type.

Among the interpreters who have admitted accommodations to human fallenness in Scripture, we have not yet considered a very important voice:

> Now when Jesus had finished these sayings, he went away from Galilee and entered the region of Judea beyond the Jordan; and large crowds followed him, and he healed them there.
>
> And Pharisees came up to him and tested him by asking, "Is it lawful to divorce one's wife for any cause?" He answered, "Have you not read that he who made them from the beginning made them male and female, and said, 'For this reason a man shall leave his father and mother and be joined to his wife, and the two shall become one flesh'? So they are no longer two but one flesh. What therefore God has joined together, let not man put asunder." They said to him, "Why then did Moses command one to give a certificate of divorce, and to put her away?" He said to them, "For your hardness of heart Moses allowed you to divorce your wives, but from the beginning it was not so. And I say to you: whoever divorces his wife, except for unchastity, and marries another, commits adultery." (Matt. 19:1–9 RSV)

The Pharisees raised this question about divorce, no doubt, because they sensed a subtle diversity within the sacred text that they thought they could exploit to trap Jesus. Jesus addressed this diversity, like many interpreters after him, by attributing it to accommodation. In this case God had accommodated his revealed law to the cultural and ideological perspectives of the ancient Near East, which permitted divorce and which reflected the fallenness and hardness of the human heart. But Jesus pointed to another theology attested in the Scriptures, that husband and wife should permanently become one flesh. In this instance, faced with two differing biblical theologies, Jesus rejected the legal prescription that allowed divorce in favor of the creation ordinance that forbade it. In the language of our modern discussion, I would argue that Jesus not only allowed for, but explicitly testified to, Scripture's theological and ethical accommodations to fallen humanity. So if we were at first surprised by the accommodation theology of the church fathers, we need be no longer; indeed, their accommodation theology was apparently in some measure derived from this Gospel text.[41]

As for the Reformers, I cannot say whether Calvin's view of accommodation was influenced by Matthew 19, it being unclear whether he regarded that text as accommodation. Nevertheless, Jon Balserak has pointed out that Calvin did allow for accommodations to human sinfulness in Scripture.[42] One example is Calvin's treatment of Genesis 19, in which God granted Lot's request to move to a different location than God at first selected:

> Some [interpreters] ignorantly argue from this expression that Lot's prayer was pleasing to God, because he assented to his request and gave him what he sought. For it is no new thing for the Lord sometimes to grant, as an indulgence, what he nevertheless does not approve. And he now indulges Lot, but in such a way that he soon afterwards corrects his folly. Meanwhile, however, since God so kindly and gently bears with the evil wishes of his own people, what will he not do for us if our prayers are regulated according to the pure direction of his Spirit, and are drawn from his word?[43]

As we can see, Calvin does more than allow for God's accommodations to human evil; he actually suggests that we should take pastoral comfort from it!

Accommodation in Contemporary Theology

As we saw in chapter 4, accommodation has played an implicit or explicit role in many modern attempts to solve the difficulties raised by biblical criticism. Nowhere has the discussion of accommodation been pursued more clearly and vigorously than in the philosophical work of Nicholas Wolterstorff, *Divine Discourse*.[44] Wolterstorff argues that God speaks in the Scriptures by appropriating the human inscriptions of the biblical authors as his own. God in essence says of Paul and the other writers of Scripture, "He speaks for me." This approach has the advantage of allowing for special revelation—God truly speaks—while at the same time it can attribute the diversity of Scripture to the diverse perspectives of the human authors. For this reason, says Wolterstorff, interpretation requires a first

---

41. For brief but fascinating discussions of this text, see Tertullian, *On Monogamy* 14 (*ANF* 4:70–71); Chrysostom, *Homily on Matthew* 17.4 (*NPNF* 1 10:118–19). For an evangelical rejection of this viewpoint, which argues that Jesus's pronouncement did not trump or set aside the Mosaic legislation, see Roger D. Congdon, "Did Jesus Sustain the Law in Matthew 5?" *Bibliotheca sacra* 135 (1978): 117–25.
42. Balserak, "Accommodating Act," 416.
43. Calvin, *First Book of Moses*, 1:511.
44. Nicholas Wolterstorff, *Divine Discourse: Philosophical Reflections on the Claim That God Speaks* (Cambridge: Cambridge University Press, 1995).

and second hermeneutic. In the first instance our focus is on the text and what it says. In the second instance our focus is on what God intends to say through the text. How do we distinguish the two?

> We do our interpreting for divine discourse with convictions in two hands: in one hand, our convictions as to the stance and content of the appropriated discourse and the meanings of the sentences used; in the other, our convictions concerning the probabilities and improbabilities of what God would have been intending to say by appropriating this particular discourse-by-inscription.[45]

While the complexity and depth of Wolterstorff's arguments are perhaps new in comparison to earlier patristic discussions, in the essentials Wolterstorff reflects much of what we see in the church fathers. For Wolterstorff, there can be a substantial distinction between what God ultimately says through all combinations of special and natural revelation and what he has said in discrete instances to particular audiences. Or, to put this in straightforward terms, there are things that God has said in the past that he no longer says in the present. God has said, "Do not eat swine flesh," but he says it no longer. God has said, "Kill the gentiles in Canaan," but he says it no longer. God has said, "Eye for an eye," but he says it no longer. God has said, "Offer sacrifices at the temple," but he says it no longer. God has said, "You may own slaves," but he says it no longer. This list could be extended considerably, and with little difficulty. Wolterstorff's point is this: Good biblical interpretation attends carefully not only to what God has said in discrete instances through his human authors in Scripture but also to whether God is still saying the same thing with that discourse or whether he would have us understand his discourse differently in light of other things that he has told us. Whenever God's Word in particular instances of Scripture is at variance with what seems to be the case within the larger context of his speech to us, this difference may reflect God's appropriation in Scripture of the fallen and finite perspectives of the human author and audience.[46]

As readers may have deduced from the previous discussion, I am suggesting that accommodation is necessary on two related levels. First, accommodation is necessary because the utter transcendence of God can be expressed to the finitude of humanity only through condescension to our perspective. There is simply no way to transfer God's infinite perception of reality into a finite human mind. Second, accommodation is a necessary feature of revelation when this is mediated to us through the finitude and fallenness of a human author. My assertion on

---

45. Ibid., 204.
46. This construal of Scripture and biblical interpretation is subtly but significantly different from what one finds on the very conservative end of the evangelical spectrum, where J. I. Packer assumes that what the human authors of Scripture "were consciously expressing... is what God *says*" (J. I. Packer, "Understanding the Bible: Evangelical Hermeneutics," in *Honouring the Written Word of God*, Collected Shorter Writings of J. I. Packer, vol. 3 [Carlisle: Paternoster, 1999], 153, italics mine).

this point is lent additional support by recent developments in hermeneutics and postmodern philosophy (see chapter 1), which show that the finite and partially fictive horizons of human understanding always color our viewpoints, even when we can rightly say that our viewpoints are generally correct. As a result, although we are right to assert that the biblical authors were privy to special revelation in a way that we are not, and that the texts that they wrote are God's inspired Word, these authors were nonetheless subject, like all of us, to their own finite and fallen interpretive horizons. That this is the case is strongly suggested by the literary, historical, ethical, and theological diversity in Scripture that scholars have documented a thousand times over.

Now we need to address several potential misunderstandings of accommodation at this point. First, some readers will imagine that "accommodation" is merely a cipher for "error," but this is certainly not the case. Because human beings tend to have a fairly adequate grasp on reality, God's adoption of the human viewpoint embraces not only our epistemic failures but also our epistemic successes. So, while accommodation indeed implies the presence of errant human viewpoints in the biblical text, it also implies the presence of *accurate* human viewpoints in the text—in the case of Scripture, of human viewpoints informed by divine insight.

Second, even in those instances where we recognize that God has accommodated his Word to our false or finite viewpoints, this will not always mean that we can or should move beyond those words. My point is easily illustrated by comparing biblical cosmologies with biblical Christology. In the case of the cosmologies, we are able to recognize the Bible's accommodations to ancient cosmology because modern astronomy provides us with a visibly better alternative. We can move beyond Scripture because we have access to information that goes beyond Scripture. But Christology is a different matter altogether. Though it has long been admitted that Jesus Christ was an accommodation to our human horizon, in which God appeared to us "*not as he is*, but in the way one incapable of beholding him is able to look upon him,"[47] our access to things beyond the incarnation is fairly limited. We cannot go into the heavens in order to see some other "real" Jesus Christ. So, while we are quite sure that the infinite God has accommodated himself to us in the finitude of Jesus, we will have to be satisfied with that accommodation and with any mysteries that this leaves dangling before our eyes. If there is one difference between orthodox Christology and its two heretical counterparts, adoptionism and docetism, it would be that the two heresies attempted to push beyond the limits of what God has revealed in his incarnate Son. Jesus appeared to us as both human and divine, and we cannot push much beyond this in our effort to understand the Second Person of the Trinity.

Third, and finally, the foregoing discussion might create the impression that ancient scholars (like the church fathers and Reformers) and modern scholars (like Wolterstorff, G. C. Berkouwer, and John Goldingay) have embraced the

---

47. Chrysostom, *Incomprehensible Nature of God* 3.15, in Benin, *Footprints of God*, 186.

same ideas about accommodation, but there are indeed subtle differences between the ancient and modern versions of accommodation.[48] In order to illustrate the differences, let us return to Calvin's Genesis commentary. As we have seen, Calvin believed that the cosmology of Genesis was accommodated to the errant views of its ancient and uneducated audience, but Calvin certainly did not believe that all Scripture was accommodated to humanity in this way. Instead, he believed that accommodation applied only in certain discrete cases, where it was difficult to avoid the conclusion that Scripture seemed to speak falsely. Moreover, in such instances Calvin did not believe that accommodation was the work of God alone. In the case of Genesis, for instance, Calvin imagined that the truths of the cosmos were divinely revealed to Moses, so that Moses became a colluding partner with God in the accommodation. This account of accommodation (which would suit Augustine as well, I think)[49] removed not only God's error but also the human author's error from Scripture, since both God and Moses were now understood as wisely conforming their speech to the views of a mistaken human audience. Such a maneuver was inevitable for Calvin, who believed that "if the expositor reveals the mind of the [human] writer, he is revealing the mind of the Spirit."[50]

This is where modern proponents of accommodation take a different route. Though they are as interested as anyone else in allaying impressions of divine error in Scripture, they are uncomfortable with slavishly equating the mind of God with the mind of the human author, and have no fixation whatever on rescuing the Bible's human authors from error. After all, the epistemic limits that necessitated accommodation for Scripture's human audience would have applied to the human author as well. From this they surmise that God has accommodated his discourse to us, not by instructing the human author to express things simply, but by adopting the simple viewpoints of that human author, whose perspectives, personality, vocabulary, and literary competence were well suited to the ancient audience of Scripture.

Though this is the modern view of accommodation, I should point out that it was not wholly foreign to the ancient fathers. In his opening lecture on John's Gospel, Augustine provided a description of the evangelist's limited insights:

> I would venture to say, my brothers, that perhaps John himself spoke of the matter not as it is, but even he, only as he was able. For it was a man that spoke of God. Inspired indeed by God, but still a man. Because he was inspired he said something;

---

48. See G. C. Berkouwer, *Holy Scripture*, trans. and ed. Jack B. Rogers (Grand Rapids: Eerdmans, 1975), 176–77; John Goldingay, *Models for Scripture* (Grand Rapids: Eerdmans, 1994), 341–45; Wolterstorff, *Divine Discourse*.

49. Wayne Spear correctly understands that inerrancy was very important to Augustine but fails to recognize that, for Augustine, this did not exclude the possibility that God might accommodate his discourse to human error. See Wayne R. Spear, "Augustine's Doctrine of Biblical Infallibility," in *Inerrancy and the Church*, ed. John D. Hannah (Chicago: Moody Press, 1984), 37–65.

50. Quotation from T. H. L. Parker, *Calvin's New Testament Commentaries* (London: SCM, 1971), 59.

if he had not been inspired, he would have said nothing. But because he was a man inspired, he spoke not the whole, but what a man could, he spoke.[51]

Though divine insights surely pass from God to a human in the act of revelation, Augustine tells us that those insights can go no farther than the man himself can bear. Judged in the light of modern hermeneutical theory, this understanding of revelation corresponds closely to the perspectives of practical realism (see chapter 1), which avers that genuine exchanges of meaning are possible (in this case, between God and the human author of Scripture) but never perfect (because the human author's finite and fallen interpretive horizons prevent this). In this account of things, Scripture's words are truly informed by and convey revealed truths from God, but these truths were received by and communicated through the finite, fallen horizon of a human author.

Another, closely related difference separates ancient and modern approaches to accommodation. The church fathers understood the event of accommodation as a necessary aspect of God's plan to progressively unveil his truths, and himself, to humanity. While there is undoubtedly something to this idea, commonly known as "progressive revelation," modern theologians would want to carefully nuance our understanding of this progressive process.[52] Goldingay points out, for instance, that it is a mistake to understand progressive revelation as a straight line, as if we can assume that revelation moves inexorably from basic theology in the Old Testament to more advanced concepts in the New Testament.[53] The height of divine revelation was and is in Jesus Christ himself, who came to humanity in an historical context that lay chronologically *between* the two Testaments.

There are also various instances in which the more advanced theological concepts seem to appear before those that are less advanced. One thinks here of the fact that Paul allowed women to prophesy and to speak in tongues in the church (1 Cor. 11:5; 14:1–33), whereas the author of the Pastorals, writing later in Paul's name, required silence of women (1 Tim. 2:11–15).[54] Though Paul's ideas on this matter are certainly more forward thinking than those expressed in 1 Timothy, there was a tendency in the early church to follow the dictates of the latter. This is apparently why a later editor added the little gloss in 1 Corinthians 14:34–35 that forbade women to speak in church.[55] The editor wished to bring 1 Corinthians into

---

51. Augustine, *Homilies on the Gospel of John* 1.1 (*NPNF* 1 7:7).

52. I should mention that I disagree with Edgar V. McKnight, who argues that progressive revelation depends conceptually upon Enlightenment notions of "progress." It seems to me that if God does reveal himself to us in written, historically contingent textual installments, then the result will be progressive. That is, to say that revelation is progressive is merely to notice how revelation necessarily works. See his comments in *Postmodern Use of the Bible: The Emergence of Reader-Oriented Criticism* (Nashville: Abingdon, 1988), 67–69.

53. Goldingay, *Models for Scripture*, 341–42.

54. See Martin Dibelius and Hans Conzelmann, *The Pastoral Epistles*, trans. Philip Buttolph and Adela Yarbro, Hermeneia (Philadelphia: Fortress, 1972), 47–49.

55. See the appropriate sections of Hans Conzelmann, *1 Corinthians: A Commentary*, trans. James W. Leitch, Hermeneia (Philadelphia: Fortress, 1975); Gordon D. Fee, *The First Epistle to the Corinthians*, NICNT

theological conformity with 1 Timothy, as even some evangelicals will admit.[56] In my opinion this is only one of many instances in which the church should adopt as its rule of faith not what was last said in the process of inscripturation but that which seems to incarnate Scripture's highest ideals: "There is neither Jew nor Greek, there is neither slave nor free, there is neither male nor female; for you are all one in Christ Jesus" (Gal. 3:28 RSV). In the next few chapters I will discuss in more detail how interpretive and theological decisions like this should be made. Where I appeal to "progressive revelation" in that discussion, I have in mind the more nuanced, modern understanding of this concept.

But returning again to the specific matter of accommodation, I may summarize the differences between ancient and modern views of accommodation as follows. The ancients viewed accommodation as an exceptional feature in Scripture, which appears only in specific instances and by the joint agency of God and the human writer. By way of contrast, modern theologies view all of Scripture as accommodated, not merely to the human audience but also to the biblical authors themselves. God accomplished this end by adopting the words and viewpoints of the human authors as his own, so that Scripture's human authors unwittingly participated in the divine act of accommodation. As it turns out, this modern description of accommodation comports nicely with the common evangelical notion that Scripture has been communicated to us through the vocabulary, style, and personality of its human authors.[57] It will not comport so easily, I fear, with some other aspects of popular evangelical theology.

Evangelical Objections to Accommodation

Where evangelicals adhere strictly to certain conceptions of inerrancy, which disallow even the slightest human errors in the biblical text, this will oblige them in principle (or so it would seem) to reject the conceptual validity of accommodation altogether. This is because, as I have pointed out, accommodation is theologically necessary only if we believe that errors appear in Scripture. Indeed, very conservative evangelicals wholly reject the theological viability of accommodation. At this point I would like to examine some of these evangelical arguments against

---

(Grand Rapids: Eerdmans, 1987); Richard B. Hays, *First Corinthians*, Interpretation (Louisville: Westminster John Knox, 1997); Hans-Josef Klauck, *1 Korintherbrief*, NEchtB (Würzburg: Echter Verlag, 1984); Wolfgang Schrage, *Der erste Brief an die Korinther*, EKKNT, 3 vols. (Neukirchen-Vluyn: Neukirchener Verlag, 1991–1999); Christoph Senft, *La première épitre de saint Paul aux Corinthiens*, 2nd rev. ed., CNT (Geneva: Labor et Fides, 1990); August Strobel, *Der erste Brief an die Korinther*, ZBK (Zurich: Theologischer Verlag, 1989).

56. Fee, *First Corinthians*, 699–708. Also open to the idea is Craig S. Keener, *1–2 Corinthians*, New Cambridge Bible Commentary (Cambridge: Cambridge University Press, 2005), 117–18.

57. Article 8 of the Chicago Statement on Biblical Inerrancy reads as follows: "We affirm that God in His Work of inspiration utilized the distinctive personalities and literary styles of the writers whom He had chosen and prepared. We deny that God, in causing these writers to use the very words that He chose, overrode their personalities."

accommodation and take stock of their validity. I have chosen in this regard to look closely at the arguments against accommodation that appear in the systematic theology of Wayne Grudem, and also at the arguments offered in the older but more massive theological work of our evangelical patriarch, Carl F. H. Henry. We shall also consider certain theological affirmations that appear in the Chicago Statement on Biblical Hermeneutics.

Let us begin with Grudem's work. He mounts two basic arguments against the theological legitimacy of accommodation. His resistance to the idea stems mainly from a concern about the doctrines of God and biblical inerrancy. Let us consider each argument in turn. Grudem's first objection to accommodation runs like this:

> Those who hold this position [accommodation] argue that it would have been very difficult for the biblical writers to communicate with the people of their time if they had tried to correct all the false historical and scientific information believed by their contemporaries. Those who hold this position would not argue that the points where the Bible affirms false information are numerous, or even that these places are the main points of any particular section of Scripture. Rather, they would say that when the biblical writers were attempting to make a larger point, they sometimes incidentally affirmed some falsehood believed by the people of their time.
>
> To this objection to inerrancy it can be replied, first, that God is Lord of human language who can use human language to communicate perfectly without having to affirm any false ideas that may have been held by people during the time of the writing of Scripture. This objection to inerrancy essentially denies God's effective lordship over human language.[58]

I am tempted to quibble with Grudem's characterization of accommodation, but for the sake of the discussion I will let it stand. The more important matter is that Grudem's objection does not address the biblical evidence for accommodation; he objects to accommodation by tracing its implications to a faulty theological conclusion. Expressed straightforwardly, he believes that Scripture cannot accommodate human error because this would imply that God is not sovereign over human language.

Now at first glance it might seem easy to counter this argument. One could point out that God is sovereign not only over human language but over humanity itself. And if God is sovereign even over sinful humanity, then he could equally be sovereign over a Bible that accommodates error. So Grudem's argument about God's sovereignty turns out to be nothing more than a red herring. But I suspect that Grudem's objections are more nuanced than this. What Grudem appears to assume is that God exercises his sovereignty differently in the two cases of humanity and biblical inspiration. God's sovereignty is exercised in the first instance by permitting human sin, and in the second instance by inerrantly writing the truth.

---

58. Wayne Grudem, *Systematic Theology: An Introduction to Biblical Doctrine* (Grand Rapids: Zondervan, 1994), 97–98.

From this Grudem reasons: If the inerrant God of the universe has accommodated his words to humanity's errors, then it follows that he must; and if he must, then the limits of human language have forced him to do so. Hence God is not sovereign over human language. I believe that this is his argument in a nutshell.

In my opinion Grudem's argument fails because he has not given sufficient thought to the nature of human language. Though it is true that our capacity for language was created by God, the languages themselves are human creations. Any reflection on the history and nature of living languages will confirm this. As human creations, these languages reflect the finite and errant parsings of reality by human beings. These linguistic parsings of life are not wholly wrong, but neither are they perfect. Consequently, we may conclude that God, *in his sovereignty*, has not only permitted human beings to create languages but has chosen to speak to us through those humanly created languages. God's choice to speak to us in this way is *his* choice. To question his wisdom in doing so is to strike at the heart of God's sovereignty. In essence, because he presupposes what God must do, Grudem fails to consider the possibility that God has spoken to us though the errant medium of human language because that is how finite human beings communicate.

Grudem's second objection to accommodation is potentially more serious. As we have seen, a central claim of accommodation is that God, in order to communicate more effectively, has intentionally adopted errant human viewpoints and tacitly affirmed them in the Bible's discourse. According to Grudem, this can mean only one thing: that God has lied to humanity. So accommodation, if true, would not only threaten our view of God's character but might also carry an unnerving ethical message: human beings should follow God's example by "lying" in order to enhance our communication to others. Does Grudem's argument hold water? I do not think so. None of the early fathers, nor the later Reformers, considered accommodation to be a divine lie. They understood quite clearly that all speech from one with greater knowledge to one with less knowledge requires some sort of accommodation, if for no other reason than that the lesser mind *cannot* understand the full reality as it is understood by one greater. For instance, when small children ask what clouds are, the answer that we will give—if we know anything at all about relative humidity and dew point—will inevitably fall far short of the meteorological details in our head. We shall hopefully advance their knowledge of clouds, but we will privately recognize the subtle misinformation that our simplified explanation entails. This misinformation will have to stand until their minds mature and become capable of understanding a fuller, more detailed answer. So it seems to me that Grudem's two arguments against accommodation are inadequate rebuttals of the church's long-standing appreciation of this venerable theological concept.

Carl Henry's arguments against accommodation are of a different sort.[59] His first stop is Calvin. As we have seen, many take Calvin's doctrine of accommoda-

---

59. Carl F. H. Henry, *God, Revelation, and Authority*, 6 vols. (Waco: Word, 1976–1983), 4:375–78.

tion to imply that the reformer found errors in Scripture. Henry wishes to allay this belief, apparently because he recognizes the authority and influence of Calvin in evangelical circles:

> Where Calvin goes further, and declares the biblical forms of speaking to "not so much express what God is like, as accommodate the knowledge of him to our slight capacity" (*Institutes*, I, xiii, 1) or that God's method was "to represent himself to us, not as he is in himself but as he seems to us" (*Institutes*, I, xvii, 13), we should carefully note that Calvin is here dealing with anthropomorphic representations, and that in no case does Calvin imply that scriptural teaching is fallacious.[60]

Henry here asserts that Calvin's doctrine does not "imply" the presence of human error in Scripture. But is this not precisely the rub? Whether Calvin's doctrine allowed for human error in the Bible is a matter of judgment, since the issue is not only what Calvin explicitly says but also what his work implies. Indeed, Calvin never says anything quite like "Scripture errs."[61] For him this would have been tantamount to hoisting errors upon God. But as we have seen already in his Genesis commentary, Calvin nonetheless recognized the presence of errant human viewpoints in Scripture. When confronted with these viewpoints, he did not refer to them as "errors" but attributed them instead to accommodation. This does not mean that the reformer failed to notice the errors. It means instead that his first theological priority was to demonstrate that God's discourse does not err when its rhetoric assumes some errant human viewpoint. As I have pointed out already, this was the only move available to Calvin because he did not conceptually distinguish between the human and divine authors of Scripture. Modern advocates of accommodation recognize this subtle distinction and so can say with a straight face that God's discourse in Scripture does not err when it accommodates human discourse that does.

But back to the main point. Henry's effort to enlist the support of Calvin for his viewpoint ultimately fails, mainly because Henry has failed to understand the subtleties of Calvin's thought on accommodation. What Calvin believed does not suit Henry's theology, nor similar theologies that aver "accommodation to

---

60. Ibid., 4:376.

61. Some have asserted that Calvin attributed mistakes and errors to the biblical authors, the case of Matt. 27:9 being a commonly cited example. As readers may know, that Gospel text errantly attributes a quotation from the prophet Zechariah to the prophet Jeremiah. Concerning this evidence, Calvin writes: "The passage itself plainly shows that the name of Jeremiah has been put down by mistake, instead of Zechariah, for in Jeremiah we find nothing of this sort, not any thing that even approaches it" (John Calvin, *Commentary on a Harmony of the Evangelists*, trans. William Pringle, 3 vols. [Edinburgh: Calvin Translation Society, 1845–1846], 3:272). While this might appear to be an admission by Calvin that the biblical authors erred, James I. Packer has cogently argued that here Calvin is probably blaming the difficulty on those scribes who copied the Bible rather than the biblical authors themselves. For additional comments, see John T. McNeill, "The Significance of the Word of God for Calvin," *Church History* 28 (1959): 131–46; James I. Packer, "John Calvin and the Inerrancy of Holy Scripture," in *Inerrancy and the Church*, ed. John D. Hannah (Chicago: Moody Press, 1984), 143–88.

error... is incompatible with inerrancy."[62] While errant viewpoints in the Bible are not God's error for Calvin, they must be God's errors for Henry. [63] Hence in Henry's opinion there can be no accommodations to human error.

Another of Henry's objections to accommodation is that, when taken to imply error, accommodation undermines the authority of Scripture. In this part of his discussion Henry cites with some concern the evangelical work of E. J. Carnell, James Orr, and E. F. Harrison. All three of these scholars have argued that, though the Bible is inerrant, its authors sometimes depended upon errant historical sources when writing their historical narratives. These three scholars reasoned that, in such cases, God did not err but merely accommodated himself to those finite human records. Their logic on this point stands very close to that of the church fathers and Calvin. Now Henry does not choose to counter this thesis directly but instead quotes with approval the objections expressed by another evangelical, Millard Erickson. According to Erickson, if inspiration guarantees only the inerrant copying of errant sources, then "one can only be sure of accuracy where he knows that direct revelation is involved or where he has some independent way of checking the correctness of the underlying sources.... This position is an unstable one, and would tend to logically move toward... admission of historical errors in the text."[64] Henry then follows Erickson's comment with his own: "To affirm the errancy of the text but to insist on the divine authority and reliability of the Bible requires one to impose upon the notion of biblical authority 'the death of a thousand qualifications.'"[65] It is fairly easy to recognize in Henry's words, and in the words that he cites from Erickson, the key issue that animates their objection to accommodation. These evangelicals deeply thirst for incorrigible, theological certainty, and the admission that God has accommodated human errors in the Bible would make this kind of certainty inaccessible. So Henry reasons that accommodations to human error simply cannot exist in Scripture. End of argument.

Now Henry's objection seems to fail at three key points. First, I do not believe that his notion of Cartesian-style certainty is accessible to human beings, however much we may wish things were otherwise. We can be dead certain—and dead wrong. Once the onus of that Cartesian quest is lifted from our evangelical shoulders, we shall be able to get along with much less anxiety because we, who know so little, have placed our trust in the God who knows all. The second difficulty with Henry's objection is closely related to the first. Let us note carefully the seemingly innocuous but obvious fact that *all* human beings form judgments that are certain, and routinely do so on the basis of much less evidence than a supposedly inerrant Bible. If this observation is right—and I think it must be—then

---

62. Paul D. Feinberg, "A Response to Adequacy of Language and Accommodation," in *Hermeneutics, Inerrancy, and the Bible: Papers from ICBI Summit II*, ed. Earl D. Radmacher and Robert D. Preus (Grand Rapids: Zondervan, 1984), 389.
63. Henry, *God, Revelation, and Authority*, 4:192.
64. Quoted from ibid., 180.
65. Ibid., 181.

it cannot be correct to assert, as Henry does, that theological certainty requires an inerrant source of theological truth. Human beings often form and embrace theological judgments as certain; the fact that these certain judgments can be wrong proves my point, I think. A third difficulty with Henry's argument stems from the biblical testimony itself. On numerous occasions the Bible establishes authorities that are errant and human, the authority of a government over its citizens being a good example. If God can establish pagan governments as authorities over his people, how much more could he decree that a Bible, written by fallible but truly inspired authors, is authoritative for the church? The implication of my question is clear: neither authority nor theological certainty requires "inerrancy" in the fundamentalistic sense of the word. Thus, to my mind, none of the arguments posed by Henry, or by Grudem, succeeds in countering the church's traditional affirmation that accommodation played a role in inscripturation and hence should play an important role in our biblical interpretation.

A somewhat different argument against accommodation is offered in the Chicago Statement on Biblical Hermeneutics (1982),[66] which sought to provide a hermeneutic in keeping with its evangelical notion of inerrancy. The denial offered in article 2 reads: "We deny that the humble, human form of Scripture entails errancy any more than the humanity of Christ, even in His humiliation, entails sin." The spirit of the argument is clear. If the human nature of the incarnate Word entailed no sin or error in Christ, then it follows that the same is true of God's written Word in Scripture. Scripture's discourse will therefore be free from the influences of human sin and error. Now no serious Christian will want to resist this thesis in every respect. The Bible is God's Word, and we will want to formulate a description of the Bible's inspiration and inscripturation that precludes divine errors in either the process or its result. So, even though I will eventually disagree with the Chicago Statement on this point, I want to say that there are healthy theological impulses behind it. But there are also some unhealthy impulses, and that has resulted in an argument that fails on two important counts.

First, the christological argument fails because, though Jesus was indeed sinless, he was also human and finite.[67] He would have erred in the usual way that other people err because of their finite perspectives. He misremembered this event or that, and mistook this person for someone else, and thought—like everyone else—

---

66. See Radmacher and Preus, *Hermeneutics, Inerrancy, and the Bible*, 881–87.

67. There is no serious debate among theologians about whether Jesus took on the finitude of human intellect. What is hotly debated, however, is whether and in what way he took on our fallen humanity. The Roman Catholics, Eastern Orthodox, and some Protestants affirm that Jesus did indeed take on our fallen human nature (cf. Rom. 8:3). For discussions see Aquinas, *Summa Theologica*, pt. 3, q. 14, art. 2, in *The Summa Theologica*, 5 vols. (Allen, TX: Christian Classics, 1981), 4:2096–97; Karl Barth, *Church Dogmatics*, ed. G. W. Bromiley and T. F. Torrance, trans. G. T. Thomson et al., 4 vols. in 12 (Edinburgh: T&T Clark, 1936–1977), 1.2:152; Oliver Crisp, "Did Christ Have a Fallen Human Nature?" *International Journal of Systematic Theology* 6 (2004): 270–88; Bishop Kallistos Ware, *The Orthodox Way* (Crestwood, NY: St. Vladimir's Seminary Press, 1995), 67–87; Thomas Weinandy, *In the Likeness of Sinful Flesh: An Essay on the Humanity of Jesus* (Edinburgh: T&T Clark, 1993).

that the sun was literally rising. To err in these ways simply goes with the human territory. These errors are not sins, nor even black marks against our humanity. They stem from the design of God, which God has declared to be "very good." As a result, the christological analogy cited in the Chicago Statement seems to be a good one, but it sends us in a direction opposite to what the statement's framers supposed. The finite, human form of Jesus tells us that Scripture's authors and their discourse will be finite and human.

The other point at which the statement's argument fails regards its use of christological categories to formulate a doctrine of Scripture. Its authors wish to draw a very precise theological parallel between the incarnate Word of Christ (which is free of human sin) and the written words of Scripture (which would also be free from human sin). The controlling assumption seems to be that we should say about the written Word whatever we say about Jesus Christ. Now such an equation might make sense at first glance, but it does not bear close scrutiny. There is certainly long-standing precedent in church history for drawing a close conceptual analogy between Christ and Scripture. These analogies are explicitly suggested by their common status as the Word of God, each being divine and human.[68] Nevertheless, the parallel is not precise in all respects. The joining of humanity and divinity in Scripture is of a different sort than in the hypostatic union of deity and humanity in Christ. The Son incarnate brings humanity and divinity together into one person, whereas the Scriptures speak divine revelation through the perspectives of finite and fallen human authors. Scripture's humanity is perhaps better illustrated through an adoptionistic metaphor (God has adopted the human author's words as his own) than through a christological metaphor (where the human Word *is* God). Such a distinction would theoretically highlight the substantive difference between God's *written Word* and the *incarnate Word* to which that written Word testifies (see John 5:39). At any rate, if there is going to be an argument that frees the personalities, ideas, and temperaments of Scripture's human authors from fallenness and finitude, it will need to take a very different path. The christological analogy ends before it can serve as an objection to the implications of accommodation.

Some readers will want to aver, nonetheless, that God could with great ease protect his written Word from the influences of its finite and fallen human authors. Perhaps this is so, but it is not necessarily so. We are wise to hesitate before we say what God can and cannot do, but we can certainly say that God *cannot* sin. Could we say as well that God *cannot* make Moses and Paul infinite, or make them sinless apart from the parousia? I will not answer my own question, as I only point to a possibility. But the possibility itself raises serious questions about the theory that God somehow shielded the Bible from human foibles. At any rate, perhaps the really interesting question is not *could* God but *did* God protect the Bible from

---

68. For a recent treatment of the issue, see Telford Work, *Living and Active: Scripture in the Economy of Salvation* (Grand Rapids: Eerdmans, 2002).

the foibles of its human authors? In response to this question, I would point out that God does not perfect us morally when we become Christians. We know this because we can recognize the continuing effects of sin in our own lives and in the lives of others. Perhaps God *could* perfect our behaviors upon conversion, but he evidently does not. In the same way, even if we admit that God *could* rid his book of its fallible human elements, we must press forward to consider whether the evidence suggests that this is what he has actually done. The theological and ideological diversity of Scripture suggests that God has done no such thing. The Bible is at the same time God's written Word and a genuinely human book. Because it is a book from God to humanity, it entails many accommodations to our humanity—accommodations to our finitude, as well as to our fallenness.

If church tradition is right about the conceptual necessity of accommodation in biblical revelation, then we should expect that even very committed inerrantists will have stumbled into using accommodation to explain the Bible's features. This is, of course, what has often happened. Two such examples can be cited from the work of Gleason Archer. Archer was a dean among conservative evangelical Old Testament scholars and a staunch defender of biblical inerrancy. He wrote an entire encyclopedia to prove that the Bible's "difficulties" are in no case real errors. Nevertheless, like all interpreters, he found it necessary to explain those instances in which Scripture reflects a faulty perspective. Such an instance appears in Acts 7:42-43, when Stephen's sermon quotes a defective Greek version of Amos 5:25-27 rather than the original Hebrew.[69] Archer and his coauthor Gregory Chirichigno resolve the difficulty as follows:

> It should be remembered that Stephen is closely following the wording of the LXX [Greek translation] here, for the simple reason that he is addressing an audience composed both of Palestinian Jews (who would have access to the Proto-masoretic Hebrew text) and of Diaspora Jews, whose knowledge of Amos would be largely confined to the LXX. It would have been inappropriate for him at that point to explain to his hearers that the LXX had used the wrong spelling of the name of the idol; it was only important to emphasize that even in the days of the Exodus their forefathers had already fallen into a clandestine idolatry.[70]

Although Archer does not use the word "accommodation" in this context, it is clear that accommodation provides the conceptual scaffold for his explanation of the text's error. There is indeed a "wrong spelling" in Stephen's speech, but this error does not concern the biblical author's purpose and so it is theologically irrelevant.

---

69. I would note that I am not the least troubled by the "difficulties" presented in these examples. My only point is that Archer appeals to accommodation to solve the problems that he perceives, not that the problems should be taken as seriously as he takes them.

70. Gleason L. Archer and Gregory Chirichigno, *Old Testament Quotations in the New Testament* (Chicago: Moody Press, 1983), xxx.

Archer makes a similar argument when confronted by Leviticus 11:5–6, a text that errantly includes rabbits among the animals that ruminate. Archer freely admits that this is an error, but he goes on to explain why this error appears in Scripture:

> We need to remember that this list of forbidden animals was intended as a practical guide for the ordinary Israelite as he was in the wild looking for food. He might conclude from the sideways movement of the jaws [of the rabbit] that these animals ruminated like larger cattle; and since they fed on the same kind of grass and herbs, they might well be eligible for human consumption. Thus it was necessary to point out that they did not have hooves at all and therefore could not meet the requirements for clean food.[71]

Here again it is accommodation that serves as the explanation for the text's error. The ancient Israelites mistakenly assumed that rabbits ruminate because of their jaw movement. God did not correct this error but rather accommodated it, primarily because his purpose was to define what should be eaten, not to provide a list of animals that chew cud. The implication of these two examples could not be clearer: the Bible contains errors, but, according to Archer, these errors are irrelevant accommodations to the human perspective. Whether Archer would explicitly agree with Calvin's approach to accommodation I cannot say. But pragmatically speaking, Archer's conceptual solution for the errors in Scripture is very close to what Calvin offered several centuries earlier. In sum, I believe that Archer has admitted the human error in Scripture without realizing that he has done so. And he has done so because Scripture does accommodate human error in its discourse.

Accommodation: Questions and Answers for Evangelicals

Not a few evangelical readers will be relieved to discover that accommodation is a valuable and ancient theological resource for explaining the very human dimensions of Scripture. Others will be more troubled by what has been said, most likely because of its potential implications for their view of Scripture and theology. Given that I am an evangelical myself, and a former fundamentalist, it is fairly easy to imagine what might make some readers suspicious. In what follows I should like, if I can, to anticipate and allay some of these suspicions and concerns, and to explain why accommodation is conceptually compatible with a robust, evangelical faith.

Foremost, in matters of accommodation something is apparently lost in our doctrine of Scripture because accommodation introduces error into God's text. Indeed, at first glance this may seem to be the case; but I do not believe that it

---

71. Gleason L. Archer, *Encyclopedia of Bible Difficulties* (Grand Rapids: Zondervan, 1982), 126.

really is the case. The doctrine of accommodation as presented here, and as often understood by interpreters through church history, does not *introduce* human error into Scripture. Rather, accommodation is the *explanation* for the errors that are already in the text. Conceptually, accommodation is entirely unnecessary if one denies the errors in Scripture, but it is absolutely *essential* if one admits the errors. Why so? Because it is only when we admit the errors that the need arises to explain why these appear in the divine speech of an infinite and perfect God. Accommodation tells us that any errant views in Scripture stem, not from the character of our perfect God, but from his adoption in revelation of the finite and fallen perspectives of his human audience. This explanation is an effort to answer the charge that God speaks errantly in the Scriptures, and the voices of accommodationists from the first century to the present are on this point unanimous: God does not err in the Bible when he accommodates the errant views of Scripture's human audiences. To repeat: accommodation does not introduce errors into Scripture; it is instead a theological explanation for the presence of human errors in Scripture.

Does this mean that the term *inerrancy* should lose its theological currency? In order to explore this question, I would like to turn again to the theology of Calvin. Calvin firmly believed that God could not err and that, by implication, God's utterances in Scripture are "inerrant." How, then, could he explain that the Scriptures sometimes reflect errant human viewpoints? Calvin concluded that "the Holy Spirit would rather speak childishly than unintelligibly to the humble and unlearned," and from this he reasoned that God does not err when he accommodates his speech to humanity, thereby adopting the errant viewpoints of his human audience.[72] In essence, Calvin paradoxically believed in inerrancy but allowed for errant viewpoints in Scripture.[73] On this score I quite agree with Calvin and could sign my name to the list of those who argue, in a similar way, that inerrancy is a theologically important—and indeed, ancient—concept implied by the nature and character of God. On the other hand, fundamentalistic notions of inerrancy that deny the influence of flawed human perspectives in the text are bound to be found wanting, not only because of theological and philosophical necessity (finite human perspectives are never inerrant) but also because the theological diversity of Scripture is so transparent. To attribute error to God is surely heresy, but to deny the errant human elements in Scripture may verge on a kind of docetism.

A second objection that some evangelicals might raise is interpretive. If we admit that errant human perspectives sometimes appear in the pages of Scripture, does

---

72. John Calvin, *Commentary on the Book of Psalms*, trans. James Anderson, 5 vols. (Edinburgh: Calvin Translation Society, 1845–1849), 5:184.

73. This is precisely why Calvin is enlisted to support the view of both evangelical errantists and inerrantists. On the one hand, Calvin was absolutely opposed to the notion that the human authors ever erred intentionally or in ethical and theological matters. On the other hand, he was not at all troubled by unintentional errors that stemmed from slips of memory or limited human knowledge. See Jack B. Rogers and Donald K. McKim, *The Authority and Interpretation of the Bible: An Historical Approach* (New York: Harper & Row, 1979), 109–14.

this not imply that our biblical interpretations lack something solid upon which to find theological traction? What prevents Scripture from becoming a wax nose that one shapes and molds as one wishes? Could one not eliminate the testimony of any biblical text that one chooses simply by labeling it "accommodation"? I will answer this objection at length in the next few chapters, but at this point let me offer a brief and straightforward response to the question. Every serious reader of the Bible manages to pursue theological coherence by strategically picking and choosing the texts that speak with greatest clarity and authority. We set aside one text that allows us to beat slaves (Exod. 21:20) out of deference for another that enjoins us to love others as we love ourselves (Lev. 19:18; cf. Luke 6:27). We subordinate the texts in which God changes his mind or has a physical body to those texts that present God as immutable and impassible. In doing so, we are navigating in an implicit and sometimes unconscious way through the very real diversity of Scripture. It follows that Scripture's theological diversity is already implicit in all theological approaches to the biblical text, even in very conservative evangelical approaches. *Accommodation is simply an explicit theological rationale for what we already do.* It explains why the biblical texts that we subordinate as less complete or less accurate—such as those that permit slavery and those in which God changes his mind—ended up in God's Word. These texts are, as tradition has suggested, God's rhetorical accommodations to our human context and viewpoint. For the serious student of God's Word, this reality does not make the Scriptures a wax nose, because the ultimate goal of interpretation is to hear God's voice, not to make God say what we wish he would say. Nevertheless, it is undoubtedly true that some readers of Scripture will employ accommodation as yet another ploy for evading the authoritative reach of God into human affairs. This reality is unfortunate and even tragic, but there are no hermeneutical formulas that can prevent it. Admitting the humanity of Scripture's authors does not negate the objective and authoritative voice of Scripture, but it does mean that Scripture's authoritative words are best understood when we fully account for the humanity of its authors. Our readings of Scripture therefore find their theological traction in a God who never errs rather than in human authors who do.

A third and related question that some evangelicals will now have is this: If Scripture reflects various human viewpoints rather than a single inerrant viewpoint, how does one achieve any kind of certainty in matters of theology? This question is entirely understandable when one comes at things from a Cartesian perspective, but it rests upon several assumptions that do not pass muster. First, the question more or less implies that biblical inerrancy will guarantee good and indubitable interpretations of Scripture, but this is clearly not the case. One needs to recall only that among committed inerrantists we will find those who believe in "predestination" and "free will," in "premillennial" and "postmillennial" eschatology, in "infant baptism" and "believer's baptism," and in "elder rule" and "congregational rule." On almost every important interpretive question in every biblical book, we find a wide variety of "inerrantist" readings. So it is clear that inerrancy does not guarantee a correct reading of Scripture, nor does it prevent all sorts of exegetical tomfoolery.

The other problematic assumption in this "certainty" question is that its demand for theological certainty arises from a faulty Cartesian philosophy. So long as we mistakenly suppose that human beings need and can achieve this kind of absolute certainty, we will always believe that incorrigible certainty is both necessary and available in a book written by God. As I have endeavored to make clear in the foregoing discussion, however, I believe that these Cartesian demands and expectations are fundamentally flawed. Human beings can certainly enjoy a useful and adequate grasp on the truth, but with the possible exception of simple claims like "the fire truck is red," this grasp will never be incorrigibly free of error. It is perhaps more than a little myopic to demand inerrant theological knowledge from the same God who has allowed most of humanity to live and die without any Bible at all. If the Bible really is the Word of God, and if it offers us adequate theological insights through the finite and flawed lenses of human authors, then let us conclude that we are still in a far, far better position, theologically speaking, than most of those who have ever lived. Once we have dispensed of our Cartesian thirst to see reality precisely as God sees it, we will no longer be too concerned by the epistemic condition that has always confronted human beings: whether in matters of theology or in other matters, we simply cannot share God's perfect, divine knowledge. In the end, we must make our human theological judgments and live by them; it is ultimately for God to decide whether we have made those judgments wisely (see 1 Cor. 4:1–4). But this much seems certain: if we are in the habit of twisting Scripture to make it fit our theological agendas, or to make it suit our sinful purposes, then we shall hurt ourselves and others in the process—and for this, God will certainly hold us responsible (cf. James 3:1; 2 Pet. 3:16).

Conclusions

The theological diversity in the Scripture constitutes an important challenge for its interpreters. Among the tools that can help us negotiate these issues is accommodation, which has enjoyed a long and venerable history in the theology and hermeneutics of the church. Its loss to evangelical interpreters is perhaps, as Roland Frye has suggested, "one of the gravest calamities in the intellectual history of Christianity."[74] Accommodation is theologically and philosophically necessary, carries a long-standing historical pedigree, and can help us provide better answers for many of the problems we face in the sacred text. Insofar as they have helped us recognize this, the historical critics have done us an invaluable theological

---

74. Roland M. Frye, "A Literary Perspective for the Criticism of the Gospels," in *Jesus and Man's Hope*, ed. Donald G. Miller and Dikran Y. Hadidian, 2 vols. (Pittsburgh: Pittsburgh Theological Seminary Press, 1970–71), 2:193–221, especially 204.

service.[75] By laying bare the docetic tendencies in some evangelical doctrines of Scripture, they have compelled us take its diverse voices more seriously, and to work more diligently and cautiously to discern the voice of God from them. To be sure, the explicit recognition of theological diversity in the Scriptures might at first appear as a theological dusk, a setting sun on evangelical hermeneutics. But the sun also rises, for accommodation is among the important interpretive principles that can help us negotiate this diversity while holding, at the same time, to the authentic and special revelation given to us in God's Word. Accommodation is not a threat to evangelical theology; it is, as the church fathers have told us, God's wise *oikonomia*, by which he leads human beings back to himself.

---

75. See James D. Smart, "The Theological Significance of Historical Criticism," in *The Authoritative Word: Essays on the Nature of Scripture*, ed. Donald K. McKim (Grand Rapids: Eerdmans, 1983), 227–37.

8

The Context of the Whole and Biblical Interpretation

The "God's-Eye" View and Human Interpretation

Our discussion in the last two chapters has focused on the generic character of the biblical text. My purpose was to explain how the text functions simultaneously as both human and divine discourse, and also to elucidate the subtle relationship that prevails between those two levels of verbal discourse. But even if the foregoing discussion was successful to some extent, I am aware that it has raised many important issues and questions. I do not intend to take up and answer all of those questions. But in the chapters that follow, I will try to address some of the issues that strike me as most pressing. One of those issues regards the role that Scripture's context plays in our interpretation of its discourse. In this chapter and the next, I would like to look carefully at the nature of that context, in terms of both its breadth and its detail.

Good readings of the Bible depend on successful generic engagements with the text, engagements in which we fit the textual discourse into its context. This act of contextual fit is always dialectical, inasmuch as the benefit goes both ways. The context helps us make sense of the text, and the text in turn helps us make better sense of the context. If this is right, then the best interpreter of the Bible will be one who best understands both the textual and the contextual elements.

Now on this point all Christians will agree: the only complete master of these textual and contextual elements is God himself. Given that this is so, it is sometimes imagined—at least among religious people—that the proper aim of interpretation is to see things as God sees them: perfectly! I see nothing wrong with this goal if we take it as a kind of shorthand for "seeing things rightly," but as a statement of bald fact it cannot be right. The Bible reminds us at certain points that God's view of things is not available to human interpreters. "Oh, the depth of the riches of the wisdom and knowledge of God," said the apostle, "How unsearchable his judgments, and his paths beyond tracing out! Who has known the mind of the Lord?" (Rom. 11:33 NIV). Job learned the same lesson. When the suffering patriarch challenged the equity of divine justice, God responded in a storm: "Who is this that darkens my counsel with words without knowledge? Brace yourself like a man; I will question you, and you shall answer me. Where were you when I laid the earth's foundation?" (Job 38:1–3 NIV). These and other biblical texts highlight the great gulf that separates God's perspective from our own.

Although this "God's-eye" view of things is not available to us, the Bible suggests that it is theologically important to recognize and appreciate that such a pristine view exists, and that it differs from our own. Perhaps this awareness enhances our adoration of God, or inspires our faith in Christ, or engenders Christian humility. One could think of many such benefits. But the one thing that the God's-eye view cannot be is a proper yardstick for measuring the aims and objectives of human inquiry. It would be the height of arrogance to suspect that we might see things precisely as God sees them. That is why, in the end, even the righteous Job confessed his ignorance and then repented in dust and ashes (Job 42:3, 6).

So God's knowledge (if we may call it that) is greater than ours, in both nature and scope. But apart from this declaration, can we put our finger in some way on the fundamental reasons for the disparity between divine and human knowledge? Perhaps we can. One point that I have accentuated again and again in our discussion is the dependent relationship between *text* and *context*. Interpretations of a text are not merely interpretations of words on a page so much as hermeneutical acts in which we coherently fit those words into a context that makes them intelligible. For instance, if I scribble the word *bear* on a notepad, you will have no way of knowing whether I am referring to a big furry thing or to what Jesus has called us to do with our cross. Meaning is inferred successfully only when there is sufficient context in which to fit the text before us. Now as we have seen, modern hermeneutics has stressed that all human interpretation—not only of texts, but of life itself—follows this sort of circular path that seeks coherence between parts and the whole. We understand facts, experiences, and texts by fitting them into the world, and we understand the world in light of those myriad facts, experiences, and texts. If this is indeed how interpretation works, then it is very easy to see why God's knowledge differs from our own.

God enjoys a divine vantage point from which all things appear as a coherent whole. His understanding is complete because he alone knows every individual thing as well as the infinite context of other things, and other verities, into which it fits. This divine vantage point provides an exhaustive understanding of the created order and of whatever stands behind and beyond it: God's own eternal and infinite trinitarian identity. That is, God alone knows the "context of the whole." By comparison, our finite perspective is surely narrow and myopic. Our knowledge and understanding of the created order is fairly limited—and it is even more limited when the subject of inquiry is God's nature and character. So God's view of things will always best our own, because his knowledge is immediate and infinite while ours is the lesser product of a finite and warped hermeneutical circle.

I believe that this brings the proper goal and nature of human interpretation into clearer focus. Human interpretation should seek to understand things *only insofar as the Creator has declared this possible and appropriate for his finite creatures*. On the one hand, this will mean that our perspective and understanding will always fall well short of God's. On the other hand, it will mean that when we get things right, our understanding of them is in some measure *like* God's (although certainly not *equal* to God's). In these comments readers may hear yet again echoes of the practical realism that I advocated in chapter 1. Practical realism contends that human interpretations are never *perfectly right* but that they can surely be *adequately right*. As an account of human epistemology, this takes seriously the difference between divine and human knowledge; it does not merely assert the difference but to some extent explains the nature of the difference. Because of this, practical realism—when it has been seasoned with faith—has sure implications for how we should pursue knowledge. It will mean that the best interpretations of anything will be those that approximate the divine viewpoint by seeing those things in the context of the whole, in that grand context where each interpreted thing makes sense. Our hermeneutical task is to pursue an understanding of this grand context, while circumscribing that pursuit by the limits that God has placed on human inquiry. I am free, for instance, to pursue an understanding of the archaeological record of ancient Israel, but I should not do so by illegally pilfering its artifacts. I am free to explore the created order, but I should not explore firsthand the sexual habits of anyone but my spouse. Human inquiry faces many divine limits, including not only the limits that we *cannot* surmount but also those that we *should not* transgress.

The Context of the Whole: The Created Order and Special Revelation

Thus, to the extent that it is possible and admissible, our goal in human inquiry is to understand the context of the whole. Traditional Christian theology usually distinguishes between two basic sources from which human beings gain an understanding of this grand context. One of these sources is the created order. Observation of and experience in the created order informs us not only about nature and humanity but also about God. Theologians usually describe the theological content that we derive from our experiences in and with the created order as *general revelation*, a subject that I will shortly consider in more detail.

Interpretation of the created order is complicated by three factors. First, there is the problem that the created order, though finite, is practically infinite from our finite human perspective. So, while there is much that we can know, there is undoubtedly much that we will never know. Second, from a Christian point of view, the natural order suffers from the consequences of human sin (cf. Gen. 3:14-19; Rom. 8:19-22), so that what is "true" of nature is not always what ought to be true. Consider the smile of a child whose body is ridden with terminal cancer, in an awkward image that joins natural beauty with nature gone amok. In this case, good interpretation will distinguish between what nature should be (the smile) and what it should not be (the cancer). Distinctions like this are made not only by Christians but by just about everyone—including even those without religion. As a result, certain features in the natural order, such as homosexuality, are very difficult to interpret. Is homosexuality a naturally predetermined sexual preference, and even if it is, should it be? This brings us at once to a third and closely related difficulty with interpreting the natural order: it includes human beings. Humanity is certainly part of the natural order, but human thoughts and behaviors are human creations rather than divine creations like the sun, moon, stars, trees, and animals. As a result, the products of human endeavor—our traditions, our philosophies, our art and literature, our technology, and our acts and deeds—are best understood as special cases *within* the created order. Whether our human creations are good or bad, beautiful or ugly, wise or foolish, true to the created order or flying in the face of it, is one of the judgments that interpreters must make.

Now as I have mentioned already, creation is a bearer of (or, at least, a catalyst for) general revelation. Theologians usually distinguish pretty rigidly between the general revelation received through creation and our other major source of theological insight, God's *special revelation* in the Bible and in the person of Jesus Christ.[1] These two sources of insight—creation and special revelation—together constitute the total of what human beings can know about the context of the whole. At this point I would like to explore the relationship between creation and special revelation more closely, for there is much to learn from doing so.

If it is true that the meaning of God's written Word depends so much on the larger context in which it was written and subsists, then it stands to reason that the best interpretations of Scripture will be those that best understand that larger context—the created order. This will mean, for instance, that the best readings of the early chapters of Genesis will be from scholars who are informed not only about theology and the nuances of ancient Israelite literature but also about matters of modern science and cosmology. The whole of the created order, including the whole of human observations and theories about it, provides the ideal context for biblical interpretation. If this is so, then it would seem that in some

---

1. Let me point out in passing that "special revelation" should not be conceptually limited to what we have received through the Bible and the incarnation. God can and has revealed himself specially to many people apart from the *explicit* witness of Scripture and Christ. That this is so seems to be confirmed by Scripture itself, which often depicts God speaking to men and women.

respect God's divine speech in creation *precedes* his written words, for creation is the larger context that makes his written words intelligible. *It is not only the Bible but also creation itself that speaks a "word" from God.* This assertion not only makes reasonable sense but also is given biblical expression. The psalmist writes in Psalm 19:1–6 (NIV):

> The heavens declare the glory of God;
> the skies proclaim the work of his hands.
> Day after day they pour forth speech;
> night after night they display knowledge.
> There is no speech or language
> where their voice is not heard.
> Their voice goes out into all the earth,
> their words to the ends of the world.
>
> In the heavens he has pitched a tent for the sun,
> which is like a bridegroom coming forth from his pavilion,
> like a champion rejoicing to run his course.
> It rises at one end of the heavens
> and makes its circuit to the other;
> nothing is hidden from its heat.

Surely it is metaphor to describe the created order as "word," but the metaphor is not so different from one that makes Jesus Christ "the Word." Creation speaks God's "word," and its "voice" is heard by all humanity. Implicit in this theology of creation is that the created order was *made to be known*; it discloses itself to us.[2] In this sense, all that we come to know through the created order can be understood as revealed truth. Readers may know that this line of thought brings us inexorably to the sticky matter of natural revelation and natural theology. How much theology can human beings know apart from God's special revelation in the written Bible and the incarnate Son?

Some Christian traditions conceive of creation's word in fairly modest terms.[3] It amounts to little more than a voice that teaches human beings of God's existence and the rudiments of his holiness. This view of natural revelation takes its cue from Paul's comment in Romans that the created order reveals God's "eternal power" and "divine nature." Human beings hear and understand this word, but then reject it without excuse (see Rom. 1:19–21; cf. 2:14–15). As a result, the most that can be said is that "there is a possibility of some knowledge of divine truth outside the special revelation."[4] Now this account of things is certainly true as far as it goes, but I suspect that the scope of natural theology will be defined

---

2. See Colin E. Gunton, *A Brief Theology of Revelation* (Edinburgh: T&T Clark, 1995), 20–63.

3. Wayne Grudem, *Systematic Theology: An Introduction to Biblical Doctrine* (Grand Rapids: Zondervan, 1994), 121–24.

4. Millard J. Erickson, *Christian Theology* (Grand Rapids: Baker Academic, 1985), 173.

too narrowly if we attend *carelessly* to what Paul has said about it in Romans. It is careless, for instance, to read Romans 1 without reading an important text that probably inspired Paul's ideas about idolatry:

> For all men who were ignorant of God were foolish by nature; and they were unable from the good things that are seen to know him who exists, nor did they recognize the craftsman while paying heed to his works; but they supposed that either fire or wind or swift air, or the circle of the stars, or turbulent water, or the luminaries of heaven were the gods that rule the world. If through delight in the beauty of these things men assumed them to be gods, let them know how much better than these is their Lord, for the author of beauty created them. And if men were amazed at their power and working, let them perceive from them how much more powerful is he who formed them. For from the greatness and beauty of created things comes a corresponding perception of their Creator. *Yet these men are little to be blamed, for perhaps they go astray while seeking God and desiring to find him.* For as they live among his works they keep searching, and they trust in what they see, because the things that are seen are beautiful. *Yet again, not even they are to be excused*; for if they had the power to know so much that they could investigate the world, how did they fail to find sooner the Lord of these things? (Wis. 13:1-9 RSV, italics mine)

As we can see, this text from Paul's Greek Bible—which included the apocryphal Wisdom of Solomon—juxtaposes two somewhat different impressions of natural revelation, one pessimistic and the other optimistic.[5] Pessimistically, human beings are in the dark and without excuse; but optimistically, their idolatry can be understood as groping or seeking after God, and as an expression of their desire to find him. In Romans 1 Paul focuses mainly on the pessimistic side of natural revelation, though the optimistic viewpoint is not wholly absent. In particular, while the Wisdom of Solomon claims that the gentiles have no knowledge of God (Wis. 13:1), Paul seems to move optimistically beyond this assessment when he claims that the gentiles "knew God" (Rom. 1:21).[6]

This "brighter side" of Paul's natural theology appears even more starkly in the apostle's Mars Hill sermon, which he delivered to Greek philosophers in Athens. There Paul suggests that the Greeks have a habit of worshiping the true God in ignorance (the "unknown God" of Acts 17). He then goes on to say that God has "made from one every nation of men to live on all the face of the earth, having determined allotted periods and the boundaries of their habitation, that

---

5. On the close connection between Rom. 1 and the Wisdom of Solomon, see Joseph A. Fitzmyer, *Romans*, AB (New York: Doubleday, 1993), 272; Luke Timothy Johnson, *Reading Romans: A Literary and Theological Commentary* (Macon, GA: Smyth & Helwys, 2001), 32-33; Douglas J. Moo, *The Epistle to the Romans*, NICNT (Grand Rapids: Eerdmans, 1996), 125.

6. See Hans Bietenhard, "Natürliche Gotteserkenntnis der Heiden? Eine Erwägung zu Rom. 1," *Theologische Zeitschrift* 12 (1956): 275-88. Though I agree with Bietenhard that Paul's view of natural theology may at this point outstrip that offered by Wisdom, I quite disagree with his claim that natural theology was foreign to early Judaism.

they should seek God, in the hope that they might feel after him and find him. Yet he is not far from each one of us, for 'In him we live and move and have our being'; as even some of your poets have said, 'For we are indeed his offspring'" (Acts 17:26–28 RSV). That Paul would say this, and quote with approval the theological insights of pagan philosophers,[7] surely yields a "high view" of natural theology in comparison with the "low view" supposedly implied by Romans. It is precisely because of Scripture's apparent diversity on this point—its pessimism and optimism about natural theology—that the spiritual status and destiny of "those who have not heard the gospel" is a matter of so much discussion. That issue is not something that I wish to resolve at this point, except to say that the Bible itself already implies that people of faith (such as Abraham and Moses) can be saved through Christ apart from an explicit knowledge of Christ. But that discussion is for another time. My main point is that, according to the New Testament, pagans seem to know more about God than merely that he exists.

None of this should surprise us. Creation's word provides the fundamental context for understanding all of special revelation, including both the written and incarnate Word. We should therefore anticipate that the Bible will make something more of natural revelation and natural theology than we see in Romans 1 and Acts 17, and I find that it surely does. There is an important corpus of biblical literature whose source of insight is the word of creation. I have in mind the Wisdom corpus of the Old Testament, which includes especially the books of Proverbs, Job, Ecclesiastes, Song of Songs, and certain psalms (as well as other parts of the Bible).[8] Although the theoretical foundations of biblical wisdom are implied at many points in this corpus, they are explicitly laid out in the prologue of the book of Proverbs (Prov. 1–9). Here we discover that Wisdom was the first of God's created works, brought into existence before the oceans, waters, mountains, hills, and dust from which humanity was made (8:22–29). Before anything was made, Wisdom was the "craftsman" (8:20) who stood at God's side during creation: "By wisdom the LORD laid the earth's foundations, by understanding he set the heavens in place; by his knowledge the deeps were divided, and the clouds let dew drop" (3:19–21 NIV).[9] The theological implications are profound. If the created order reflects the pattern of God's wisdom,

---

7. Paul quotes the stoic philosopher Arataus and perhaps Epimenides of Crete. For discussion see Joseph A. Fitzmyer, *The Acts of the Apostles*, AB (New York: Doubleday, 1998), 610–11; William Neil, *The Acts of the Apostles*, NCB (Grand Rapids: Eerdmans, 1981), 191.

8. For good introductions to the wisdom tradition of ancient Israel, see Richard J. Clifford, *The Wisdom Literature* (Nashville: Abingdon, 1998); James L. Crenshaw, *Old Testament Wisdom: An Introduction* (Atlanta: John Knox, 1981); Roland E. Murphy, *The Tree of Life: An Exploration of Biblical Wisdom Literature*, millennium supplement ed. (Grand Rapids: Eerdmans, 2002); *ATSHB*, 56–83; Gerhard von Rad, *Wisdom in Israel*, trans. James D. Martin (Nashville: Abingdon, 1972).

9. The Hebrew word translated as "craftsman" in 8:20 is *'āmôn*. It occurs only once in the Bible and so its meaning is much debated. Recent work suggests that it should be understood as a close cognate of the Akkadian term *ummānu*, a "scholar" who served in the royal courts of Mesopotamia. Following this line of thought, Wisdom served as God's wise consultant (*'āmôn*) just as Mesopotamian wise men served their kings. For a

then one can learn something of God's wisdom by observing the created order. Creation reveals not only God's existence but also God's wisdom. Of course, the editor of Proverbs is adamant that our pursuit of wisdom will be incomplete if we scrutinize creation apart from religious affections. From the outset he declares that "the fear of the LORD is the beginning of knowledge" (Prov. 1:7 NIV). No conscientious Jew or Christian would dispute this. But it does raise an interesting question. What of those who observe creation without the benefit of affections for God? Do the inquiries of nonbelievers result in the discovery of divine wisdom?

I do not believe that we can too quickly assume that those outside Judaism and Christianity have no fear of God. As I have pointed out already, Paul was willing to say that all human beings have known God (Rom. 1:21) and that their consciences serve as a guide to judge human action (2:15); he also admitted the legitimacy of the pagan search for God, and affirmed the modest theological wisdom in their philosophy (Acts 17). It is with this New Testament evidence in mind that we can consider the important Old Testament evidence, which appears in the wisdom tradition, especially in the book of Proverbs.

Israelite wisdom was produced by a particular class of Israelite leaders, one of three groups highlighted in the prophecies of Jeremiah. Jeremiah refers to the *priests* who teach the law, the *prophets* who speak God's word, and the *sages* who offer wise counsel (see Jer. 18:18). It was that last group, the sages, who produced the book of Proverbs and the other wisdom books. Among other things, we know that these sages were well versed not only in the Hebrew tradition but also in foreign wisdom traditions. This is implied by 1 Kings 4:30, which compares Solomon's wisdom with the wisdom of the East and of Egypt, and also by the presence of foreign wisdom in the Israelite tradition, such as we have in Proverbs 30 (the wisdom of Agur) and Proverbs 31:1–9 (the wisdom of King Lemuel).[10] I would like to proceed by highlighting another instance in which Proverbs draws upon foreign wisdom.

Proverbs 22:17–23:14 bears the anonymous title, "Sayings of the Wise." Can we discern anything more about the source of this anonymous wisdom? Scholars well versed in ancient literature think so. They recognized long ago that there are striking similarities between this part of Proverbs and the "thirty chapters" that appear in the Egyptian Instruction of Amenemope.[11] Proverbs also describes its content as "thirty sayings," and it includes wisdom that mirrors very closely the Instruction of Amenemope (see table 7).[12]

---

fuller discussion of the issue, see Richard J. Clifford, *Proverbs: A Commentary*, OTL (Louisville: Westminster John Knox, 1999), 23–28, 99–101.

10. Clifford, *Proverbs*, 260–71.

11. For translations see *ANET*, 421–25; *COS*, 1.47:115–22.

12. See John A. Emerton, "The Teaching of Amenemope and Proverbs xxii 17–xxiv 22: Further Reflections on a Long-standing Problem," *VT* 51 (2001): 431–65; Paul Overland, "Structure in *The Wisdom of Amenemope* and Proverbs," in *"Go to the Land I Will Show You": Studies in Honor of Dwight W. Young*, ed. Joseph E. Coleson

Table 7

Proverbs	Amenemope
22:17	III.9-10
22:18	III.11-16
22:20	XXVII.7-10
22:21	I.5-6
22:22	IV.4-5
22:24	XI.13-14
22:25	XI.15-18; XIII.8-9
22:28	VII.12-13
22:29	XXVII.16-17
23:1-3	XXIII.13-18
23:4-5	IX.14-X.5
23:6-7	XIV.5-10
23:8	XIV.17-18
23:9	XXII.11-12
23:10-11	VII.12-19; VIII.9-10

The editor of Proverbs apparently found words of authentic wisdom in the Egyptian text and so included them in his collection of wisdom. This move was theologically possible for him because all human beings, including Egyptians, can observe the realities of the created order and draw divine wisdom from it. Although the Egyptian author did not know of Yahweh, the biblical editor explicitly identified his Egyptian wisdom as Yahweh's wisdom (22:19). All truth is God's truth, no matter who recognizes it.

How much good theology informed the author of the Egyptian instructions mentioned above? Egyptian wisdom instructions, such as those of Amenemope, were considered expressions of the principle of *maat*.[13] According to Egyptian thinking, the creator god ordered his creation according to this principle, which was a kind of retributive justice in which righteous acts were ultimately blessed and evil finally punished. *Maat* is well illustrated by a popular spell/vignette combination that appears in the Egyptian Book of the Dead, a ritual guidebook that helped dead Egyptians advance to a blessed afterlife. The vignette, known as the "Judgment of the Dead" (Book of the Dead 125), depicts the heart of a deceased man being weighed in the balance opposite the justice and order of *maat*.[14] In the

---

and Victor H. Matthews (Winona Lake, IN: Eisenbrauns, 1996), 275-91; Diethard Römheld, *Wege der Weisheit: Die Lehren Amenemopes und Proverbien 22:17-24:22*, BZAW 184 (Berlin: de Gruyter, 1989).

13. See Jan Assmann, *Ma'at: Gerechtigkeit und Unsterblichkeit im alten Ägypten* (Munich: Beck, 1990); Assmann, *The Mind of Egypt: History and Meaning in the Time of the Pharaohs*, trans. Andrew Jenkins (New York: Metropolitan Books, 2002), 135-68.

14. See E. A. W. Budge, *The Book of the Dead: The Papyrus of Ani in the British Museum. The Egyptian Text with Interlinear Transliteration and Translation* (London: British Museum, 1895).

texts that accompany this scene, the deceased identifies himself with the god of the afterlife, Osiris, and denies his sins in what amounts to a negative confession (i.e., "I have done nothing wrong, excepting minor faults"). The crocodile Apophis flanks the scene, ready to consume the heart if it fails the divine tribunal.

I am not suggesting that this Egyptian account of the afterlife parallels in all respects the personal eschatology offered in Christian theology. Christians believe that salvation is by grace through faith in Christ and that it cannot be earned by mere human merit. This is certainly not the Egyptian viewpoint. Nevertheless, as a basic portrait of human destiny, these Egyptian traditions, which date considerably earlier than the Old Testament, offer a much fuller picture of the afterlife than anything that appears in the Hebrew canon. Christians could easily find points of agreement with this Egyptian theology, particularly in regard to the divine order of creation, justice, mercy, and the final judgment. Christians could also agree that there is a correlation between how one lives and the quality of one's afterlife. Given these realities, one is compelled to admit that certain aspects of Egyptian theology were true. One is further compelled to admit that a good bit of natural theology can be derived from the careful observation of human experiences and the created order. By this I do not mean to suggest that the natural person, unaided by God's grace, can step into salvation by his or her own insights and efforts. That would be a heresy of the Pelagian sort.[15] No, I am making the more modest claim that human beings have a natural capacity to understand things about God. This is a very different thing from saying that human beings have the natural capacity to respond appropriately to God.

Though my perspective on this issue by no means depends on it, I believe that it is vividly underscored by Paul's words in Romans 7:13–25, which describe a natural mind that can recognize what is true but cannot live accordingly. This is, at least, how I and many others now read it. Because there is a long-standing debate about how to interpret this passage, and because I believe that it is valuable for our discussion, I will quote the text and then discuss it in some detail.

> Did that which is good, then, become death to me? By no means! But in order that sin might be recognized as sin, it produced death in me through what was good, so that through the commandment sin might become utterly sinful. We know that the law is spiritual; but I am unspiritual, *sold as a slave* to sin. I do not understand what I do. For what I want to do I do not do, but what I hate I do. And if I do what I do not want to do, I agree that the law is good. As it is, it is no longer I myself who do it, but it is sin living in me. I know that nothing good lives in me, that is, in my sinful nature. For *I have the desire to do what is good, but I cannot carry it out.*

---

15. Pelagius (c. 360–420) was a British monk whose views the church eventually branded as heretical. He maintained that human beings have the natural capacity, apart from divine grace, to do meritorious deeds and respond to God appropriately. His chief opponent in this theological debate was Augustine, who maintained the orthodox view that divine grace is necessary for a proper human response to God. See "Pelagianism," *ODCC*, 1248–49.

For what I do is not the good I want to do; no, the evil I do not want to do—this I keep on doing. Now if I do what I do not want to do, it is no longer I who do it, but it is sin living in me that does it. So I find this law at work: When I want to do good, evil is right there with me. For in my inner being I delight in God's law; but I see another law at work in the members of my body, waging war against the *law of my mind* and *making me a prisoner of the law of sin* at work within my members. What a wretched man I am! Who will rescue me from this body of death? Thanks be to God—through Jesus Christ our Lord! So then, *I myself in my mind am a slave to God's law*, but *in the sinful nature a slave to the law of sin*. (NIV, italics mine)

Informed readers will know that Christians have interpreted this text in two entirely different ways. According to one perspective Paul here describes his spiritual struggle as a redeemed believer, and according to the other he describes his failures as a Jew living under the law. For the sake of convenience, let us simply refer to these options as the "Christian" and "Jewish" views of Romans 7:13–25.

The first perspective is most common among Protestants in the Reformed tradition, who essentially follow the judgment of Augustine.[16] In this way of thinking, Romans 7:13–25 describes Paul's struggle to live a holy Christian life. The primary reasons for this conclusion are straightforward. First, Paul's words are cast in the first person, present tense at a point when he was himself a Christian. This naturally suggests that this text describes his Christian experience. Second, Paul asserts his full-blown desire to follow God's law. If human nature is entirely depraved (as Christian tradition demands), and if this is further understood to preclude any natural desire to do what is right (as Reformed theology believes), then it would seem that these words could be uttered truthfully only by a genuine Christian. Third, the spiritual struggle described in Romans 7 seems very similar to the struggle with sin that Paul describes in Galatians 5:16–26, a text that is undoubtedly about Christian living. So goes the logic of the Reformed viewpoint.

The other view of Romans 7 is prominent among the church fathers[17] and in the Arminian wing of the Protestant churches.[18] It is therefore the older and more traditional view of the text. According to this view Romans 7 cannot describe

---

16. See, for example, the old commentary of Calvin, *Commentaries on the Epistle of Paul the Apostle to the Romans*, trans. John Owen (Grand Rapids: Eerdmans, 1947), 257–75; and the modern commentary of C. E. B. Cranfield, *A Critical and Exegetical Commentary on the Epistle to the Romans*, 2 vols., ICC (Edinburgh: T&T Clark, 1975–1979), 1:356–70.

17. Among the fathers one finds this interpretation in Irenaeus, Tertullian, Origen, Cyprian, Chrysostom, Basil, Theodoret, Cyril of Alexandria, Ambrose, Jerome, and in other early Christian commentaries. As I have mentioned, the notable exception is Augustine, who at first followed the traditional viewpoint but then shifted his position in response to the Pelagian heresy. For a survey of the patristic views, see Arminius (next footnote) as well as Gerald Bray, ed., *Romans*, Ancient Christian Commentary on Scripture, New Testament 6 (Downers Grove, IL: InterVarsity, 1998), 189–99.

18. For examples of the Arminian view of Rom. 7, see James Arminius, *The Works of James Arminius*, trans. James Nichols and William Nichols, 3 vols. (London: Longman, Hurst, Rees, Orme, Brown, and Green, 1825–1875), 2:488–683; John Wesley, *The Works of John Wesley*, 12 vols. (London: Wesleyan Methodist Book Room, 1872), 5:105–7; 9:296–98.

Paul's Christian experience because its describes him as a "slave to sin" and depicts him as lacking the capacity to do good or to resist evil. Here is no struggle between spirit and flesh that can be won, as in Galatians; we have instead a Jewish conflict between the mind and flesh that cannot be won. This is the traditional argument. Let me say from the outset that I find that this older, more traditional view far outpaces Reformed readings of the text. When the rhetorical purposes and strategies of Paul are carefully noted, and when the text is thoughtfully considered in light of what comes before and after it in Romans 6 and 8, and in comparison with Galatians 5, there is no room left for the view that Paul here describes his Christian experience. My argument is as follows.

We should begin by observing that early Christian interpreters were almost unanimous in reading Romans 7:13–25 as a description of Jewish experience under the law. This in itself is strong evidence in favor of the Jewish view over the Christian view. Another point in favor of the Jewish view is found in the two questions that Paul addresses in chapter 7. It is apparent from Paul's rhetoric in Romans that he was responding to objections that some in Rome (particularly Jewish Christians) had to his gospel. Paul explicitly notes their two questions: "Is the law sin?" (v. 7), and "Did that which is good [the law], then, become death to me?" (v. 13). These were very sensible questions given Paul's gospel and its far-flung reputation. Paul was teaching that salvation was by faith rather than by works of God's law. Did this mean that God's law was a bad thing? Paul deals with the first question in verses 7–12, and with the second question in the text cited above (vv. 13–25). Let us refer to these as the first and second panels of Paul's argument.

To the first question, "Is the law sin?" Paul responded with a resounding "Certainly not!" But Paul did not stop there. He went on to explain in theological detail how it was that the law exposed the sins of Jews living under its authority. According to Paul, the law is a kind of moral thermometer that measures the righteousness of those subject to it. When applied to the Jews, it reveals that they are, in fact, sinners deserving of death. It follows, then, that the commandments of the law are good even though they result in a death sentence. Now most every commentator will admit that this first panel of Romans 7 describes the experience of Jews living under the law.[19] The key interpretive question, then, is whether the second panel that follows in verses 13–25 continues to address the same situation addressed in verses 7–12.

Indeed, the second panel seems clearly to continue the line of thought introduced in the first panel. If the law reveals sin and results in a death sentence (as claimed in vv. 7–12), then the second Roman question naturally follows: "Did that which is good, then, become death to me?" Paul's answer to this question is like his answer to the first. He offers an emphatic "By no means!" and then goes on to explain this in more detail. What should interest us at this point is that

---

19. Though there is debate about whether Paul here describes his own experience as a Jew or rhetorically describes the lot of all Jews who live under the law.

Paul's detailed explanation begins in the *past tense* (v. 13) before abruptly shifting to the *present tense*. Let's look at his words closely:

> [**Verse 13. Question:**] Did that which is good, then, become death to me? By no means! [**Past tense:**] But in order that sin might be recognized as sin, it produced death in me through what was good, so that through the commandment sin might become utterly sinful. [**Verse 14. Present tense:**] We know that the law is spiritual; but I am unspiritual, sold as a slave to sin.

If we accept the Reformed view that verse 14 describes a Christian, then we are forced to admit that Paul addresses the Jewish experience in verse 13 (*past tense*) and then suddenly shifts topics to describe the Christian struggle with sin in verse 14 (*present tense*). Most ancient interpreters of this text, and many modern ones, do not think that this is the best way to understand the shift in tense. Rather, they understand that in verse 14 Paul is continuing with the same argument as in verse 13, but does so by assuming the persona of a Jew living under the law. The purpose of this argument would then be to illustrate how it is that the law is good even though it leads to a death sentence for those living under it. If this is what Paul was doing, then we should find that Paul's rhetoric will try to juxtapose the goodness of the law with the sin that it exposes, and we should find as well that the person described in verses 14–25 will certainly not be like the Christian that Paul vividly describes in Romans 6 and 8. This is, I think, precisely what we find.

Paul's argument is straightforward. The mind of a Jew living under the law can recognize the law's goodness and even embrace the goal of observing its statutes, but that same Jew will find at every turn that achieving this goal is mere chimera. The good things commanded by the law are left undone, and the many evils it proscribes are constantly done. The Jewish conscience can see what is good and right (the law), but the sinful flesh prevents him from living it out. As a result, says Paul, "I myself in my mind am a slave to God's law, but in the sinful nature a slave to the law of sin." Interpreters who take the Christian view of Romans 7 will make this last text out as a parallel to Galatians 5, in which Paul describes the Christian struggle between Spirit and flesh. Only a Christian mind, it is assumed, could be a "slave to God's law." But if one reads Paul's discussion in Romans 6 and 8, then it becomes clear that Christians can never be the things that Paul describes here, neither "slave to sin" nor "slave to the law."

Paul says clearly in chapter 6 that Christians are "no longer slaves to sin" and that they have in fact been "freed from sin" (6:6–7, 18). The old self was crucified so that "the body of sin might be done away with" (6:6). He then goes on to warn that "you are slaves to the one whom you obey—whether you are slaves to sin, which leads to death, or to obedience, which leads to righteousness" (6:16). He says the same sort of thing in Romans 8. "You, however, are controlled not by the sinful nature but by the Spirit, *if* the Spirit of God lives in you" (8:9 NIV, italics mine). "If you live according to the sinful nature, you will die; but if by the Spirit you put to death the misdeeds of the body, you will live" (8:13 NIV). One could add many more quotations of this sort, but in the end Paul's slavery metaphor is crystal clear: if a person is a slave to sin and lives according to the sinful flesh, that person does not have the Spirit and will not inherit eternal life.

The other phrase in 7:25, "slave to the law," cannot be applied to Christians either. According to Paul, Christians are no longer under the law (6:14–15) and have in fact "died to the law" (7:4). He illustrates this principle at length by using a marriage metaphor, in which he points out that the married woman is no longer bound to her husband when he dies (7:1–6). In the same way, says Paul, we have died with Christ to the law and are therefore released from it.

In sum, the entire context of Romans 6–8 renders a "Christian" reading of 7:13–25 very dubious. This point is driven home by Paul's comment in 8:7, which describes an unbelieving mind that "does not submit to God's law, nor can it do so" (NIV). This is precisely the sort of hapless fellow described in 7:14–25, where Paul, taking on the persona of a Jew under the law, vividly describes how sin controls him and prevents him from keeping the demands of the law. Such a person desperately needs a mind that has been spiritually renewed (12:2), which not only recognizes but also submits to God's truth (8:5–8).

To sum up, with what has emerged as the standard view among scholars, 7:14–25 does not describe a Christian's tussle with sin.[20] It describes a Jew (or, by extension, an unbelieving gentile) whose mind can see that the law is good but whose sinful nature prevents obedience to that law. So the law is good (the mind can see that), but it also produces a death sentence (because of the sinful flesh). Paul has answered the Roman questions about his gospel, and his answers benefit our inquiry as well.

Numerous implications follow from the foregoing discussion of biblical wisdom, Egyptian literature, and Romans 7. I wish to highlight only a few of these. First, if we were to envision human inquiry as the task of putting together a grand puzzle, then it turns out that the vast majority of the pieces that we need for the puzzle come from observing the created order—from creation's "voice"—rather than from sources that we might describe as special revelation. Christ, and the biblical witness to him, are perhaps the most significant and important pieces in this grand puzzle, but they are intelligible precisely because of their fit into the larger created order. The better we order the pieces gleaned from the created order, the better we understand how the incarnate Word and the written Word fit into that puzzle. Conversely, the better we understand Christ and Scripture,

---

20. See W. G. Kümmel, *Römer 7 und die Bekehrung des Paulus* (Leipzig: Hinrichs, 1929); C. D. Myers Jr., "Romans, Epistle to the," *ABD* 5:816–30; Krister Stendahl, "The Apostle Paul and the Introspective Conscience of the West," *Harvard Theological Review* 56 (1963): 199–215; Stephen Westerholm, *Perspectives Old and New on Paul: The "Lutheran" Paul and His Critics* (Grand Rapids: Eerdmans, 2004), 14–45; John Ziesler, *Paul's Letter to the Romans* (Philadelphia: Trinity Press International, 1989). For an example of recent evangelical moves in this direction, see Douglas J. Moo, *The Epistle to the Romans*, NICNT (Grand Rapids: Eerdmans, 1996), 441–67.

the better we can reorder and reconfigure the puzzle as a whole. Here again we meet the hermeneutical circle, this time in a dialectic between the larger context of creation and the more modest but weighty content of special revelation.

This hermeneutical circle brings us to my second point. It is not sensible to envision general and special revelation as entirely distinct categories, as if one were hermetically sealed from the other. General revelation (such as we see in Egyptian wisdom) holds true and can for this reason be absorbed fruitfully into the special revelation of Scripture. At the same time, insofar as special revelation *is* revelation, it has entered into and become part of the created order. Jesus walked this earth as a human being, and the Bible contains the words of flesh-and-blood human authors. My primary point, then, is that there are vital connections between general and special revelation, so that we should not carelessly pit our perception of nature against our perception of Scripture, as was done long ago in the case of Copernicus and as is still done in many evangelical critiques of biological evolution. This mistaken move assumes that in any apparent conflict between human perception (science) and the Bible, the Bible wins hands down. Things would be so easy if this were the case. In reality, however, the conflicts at hand are not between "human science" and "God's Word" so much as between human interpretations of creation (science) and human interpretations of Scripture (biblical interpretation). Serious Christians will want to carefully consider *both* of these voices in the effort to hear what God is finally saying to humanity. In the case of Copernicus, it seems that God's word in creation properly trumped his word in Scripture because the latter had been accommodated to an ancient and partially mistaken view of the cosmos. I would venture that the mounting scientific evidence in favor of biological evolution presents us with a similar situation.[21]

A third implication of our discussion is that the content of general revelation, which comes to us in and through our experiences with the created order, clearly tells us something more than "God exists." Ancient Egyptian theology, for instance, had a fairly advanced and in some respects accurate portrait of things native to Christian belief. To be sure, certain dimensions of Egyptian theology were lacking and just plain wrong, as could be said of other non-Christian religions (and to some extent even of our own theologies). Nevertheless, what we have seen here is that the special revelation of Scripture is intelligible precisely because it speaks to a world where human beings are already familiar with a vast array of issues and concepts that are essentially theological. One cannot understand the first few chapters of Genesis, for instance, unless one is already familiar with concepts of deity, the divinely created order, good and evil, sin, retributive

---

21. Concerning this point, I would simply suggest the following materials: Niels Henrik Gregersen and J. Wentzel van Huyssteen, *Rethinking Theology and Science: Six Models for the Current Dialogue* (Grand Rapids: Eerdmans, 1998); Ted Peters and Martinez Hewlett, *Evolution from Creation to New Creation: Conflict, Conversation, and Convergence* (Nashville: Abingdon, 2003); David L. Wilcox, *God and Evolution: A Faith-Based Understanding* (Valley Forge, PA: Judson, 2004).

justice, authority, mercy, and any number of other theological insights. So we will not go far wrong if we say that Scripture functions not so much by giving us new theology as by ordering, correcting, and extending the natural theology that we already possess.

A fourth implication of this discussion, which I place last for emphasis, is that Christians will need to pay much closer attention to the insights and perspectives of those outside the church. If an ancient Egyptian author can offer wisdom so true that the biblical authors adopted that word as their own, then it follows that truth—even theological truth—might be found almost anywhere. The issue here is not whether those living outside the visible church might be saved. That is a matter worth discussing, but it is not my point here. The question at hand is whether those outside the church can understand anything truly, and whether the church would therefore benefit by listening to them. I am arguing that the answer to this question is an unequivocal yes! This answer should not be a surprise, for the church has long maintained that human beings are recipients of a universal common grace from God, which includes not only God's general care for them but also an "actual grace" that allows the unchurched to do good deeds.[22] Calvin went so far as to say that God sometimes extends special revelation to unbelievers, in a grace that is insufficient for salvation but quite adequate for their understanding of God. In this sense, the created order does not passively speak the truth to humanity; it is God who has "shown it to them" (Rom. 1:19).[23] Whether we should follow Wesley and the other Arminians by making this act of grace "prevenient," and hence sufficient to restore a universal ability to respond spiritually to God, is another matter that I will not tackle here.

But I have certainly taken a position on two other venerable and closely related theological debates, one very old and the other more recent. The first debate is epitomized by the contrasting opinions of two brilliant church fathers, Tertullian and Augustine. Tertullian quipped, "What does Jerusalem have to do with Athens?"[24] To which Augustine eventually responded, "Let us plunder the Egyptians."[25] The first father warned Christians to steer clear of "pagan" scholarship; the second counseled the opposite course: let us learn what we can from wise unbelievers. Though Tertullian's comment is not without its merits, on the main question I have sided with Augustine, and for good reason. Only by duplicity can we deny the many benefits that Christians have reaped from the erudition of unbelievers. Let us give credit where it is due.

---

22. See "Grace," *ODCC*, 697–98.

23. Said Calvin: "God himself, to prevent any man from pretending ignorance, has endowed all men with some idea of his Godhead, *the memory of which he constantly renews and occasionally enlarges*, that all to a man, may be condemned by their own conscience when they neither worship him nor consecrate their lives to his service" (*Institutes*, 1:43 [1.3.1], italics mine).

24. Tertullian, *On Prescription Against Heretics* 7 (= *ANF* 3:246). I have been told anecdotally that Tertullian was sometimes more sanguine about pagan scholarship, but in this case his viewpoint could not be clearer.

25. Augustine, *Reply to Faustus the Manichaean* 23.71 (= *NPNF* 1 4:299–300).

I have also taken sides in the modern debate, made prominent by Barth and Brunner, about whether "natural theology" is possible.[26] On this question, I strongly believe that non-Christians can offer insights—even profound insights—about theology. So on this point I would side with Brunner against Barth. However, I am implying at the same time that any solutions to this theoretical debate cannot be easily applied in our analyses of discrete, concrete situations. We cannot know, for instance, whether the valuable wisdom of the Egyptian sages stemmed from the insights of their natural God-given capacities or from some additional, special work of God's grace. Christian orthodoxy, with its dual emphasis on the universal fall and common grace, makes either option a possibility. In the final analysis, this will mean that conscientious Christians should never accept an opinion simply because many Christians hold it, nor should they reject out of hand the opinions expressed by non-Christians. Religious litmus tests of this sort cannot substitute for the exercise of reasonable and thoughtful judgment.

Conclusions

The main themes of this chapter are organically related to the chapter that follows, so I will save the bulk of my summary for later. Here I will reiterate a few points. My primary purpose in this chapter has been to accentuate and elucidate the vital connection between the Bible and the created order. One point of connection is contextual. Like all texts, the Bible is understood only insofar as we properly relate it to the context that makes it intelligible. Insofar as the Bible is written to address human beings—created beings living in the created order—to that same extent our understanding of Scripture hinges on a proper understanding of creation. Given that this is true, our interpretation of the Bible requires that we attend carefully to God's "word" in nature and his "word" in Scripture. Hebrew and Greek grammar count in our theology, but so do the insights of anthropology, astronomy, biology, chemistry, history, literature, physics, psychology, philosophy, sociology, and other academic disciplines. To err by neglecting any of this can produce poor biblical interpretations and hence poor theology. As N. T. Wright has so ably expressed it, we honor biblical authority by "being attentive to context, to sense, and to wider knowledge of all sorts."[27]

Perhaps we can make good on Wright's wise charge if we remember this: God needn't reveal to us anything that we can figure out for ourselves. So, for instance, there was no reason for God to tell us in Genesis how he made the cosmos, how

---

26. See their debate in Emil Brunner and Karl Barth, *Natural Theology*, trans. Peter Fraenkel (London: Bles, 1946). For discussions see Trevor A. Hart, *Regarding Karl Barth: Toward a Reading of His Theology* (Downers Grove, IL: InterVarsity, 1999), 139–72; Joan E. O'Donovan, "Man in the Image of God: The Disagreement between Barth and Brunner Reconsidered," *SJT* 39 (1986): 433–59.

27. N. T. Wright, *The Last Word: Beyond the Bible Wars to a New Understanding of the Authority of Scripture* (San Francisco: HarperSanFrancisco, 2005), 119.

he made life and humanity, or how long that process required if he has already given us the hermeneutical tools to find answers to those questions. Consequently, our study of the created order through the academic disciplines should not be opposed to Scripture but understood instead as one of the ways that God actually speaks to us. God tells us through our pursuit of the biological sciences how life developed; he tells us through Scripture that he's the one responsible for that biological miracle.

Another point of connection between the Bible and the created order regards our insight into realms divine. Though it is true that the Bible is a book that reveals to us the things of God, we have seen that even here its message depends to some extent on the created order. By God's design, the creation points beyond itself, so that theological verities can be understood to a surprising extent even by those who have never seen a Bible. One can find even among unbelievers a belief in God's existence and an awareness of good and evil, wisdom and folly, retributive justice and judgment, and the need for divine grace. Whether these things are only understood but never acted upon properly is another matter, but it is clear that those without Christ or the Bible certainly do understand theological concepts.

One implication of this observation is that Christians should take the insights of non-Christians more seriously than we sometimes do. Just as the author of Proverbs was wise to adopt the wisdom of an Egyptian text, in the same way we are wise to embrace the truth in whatever way that God brings it to us. If an Egyptian scholar can get religious truths right, then we should not be at all surprised if a secular biblical scholar has gotten it right when he or she says that the Pentateuch was written by several authors, or that Second Isaiah dates to the exile, or that the book of Jonah is a story rather than history.

But this matter aside, concerning the main theme of this chapter, the "Context of the Whole," we have only begun to scratch the surface. It is time that we look at this grand context in more detail.

9

Negotiating the Context of the Whole

Choices, Scripture, and Traditions

The purpose of this chapter is to consider in more detail the context of the whole, which I discussed in the previous chapter. There I suggested that *ideal* readings of Scripture will understand its words in dialectical relation to the context of the whole. While this might well be the ideal approach, it is hardly possible or practical. I have just returned from a jaunt to the impressive library at the University of Pennsylvania, a research facility that contains several million separate volumes written by many men and women who have lived over the course of many centuries. Although this library and its books constitute only a small part of the "context of the whole," I could not in one lifetime either read all of those books or understand them. Even less could I pass competent judgments on which books are right and which are not. This observation has obvious and profound implications for how we ought to understand interpretation. It will first mean that, though our view of things is profoundly finite, *most of what we need to know* about the context of the whole is ready at hand. The very experience of living life, and of acclimating to our native traditions, infuses us with a tacit understanding of the world and of how we fit into it. The importance of this tacit knowledge for human beings has been accentuated especially in the epistemological work of Michael Polanyi, for whom very little of what we know has been explicitly and consciously pursued.[1] Most of our knowledge "happens to us," so to speak. On this point Polanyi is undoubtedly correct. On the other hand, Scripture has made it abundantly clear that human beings have fiduciary responsibilities to pursue wisdom in an explicit and conscientious way. What I would like to discuss at this point is how we can make good on this fiduciary role.

If we are confronted by a practically infinite menu of voices, and if our explicit pursuit of knowledge requires that we listen to at least some of them, then one part of interpretation involves making wise choices about the voices that we will heed and those we will ignore. The choices to be made in this regard will vary from person to person, depending on the particular task at hand. If I am a biologist, I will likely spend more time reading biological research than the Wall Street Journal. If I am struggling to raise my children, I will likely want to inquire about the virtues and strategies that make for good parenting, and I will need to make wise choices about which sources to consult as I do. Perhaps I will seek advice from other parents, or from notable experts, or from books written by experts. But whatever my particular station in life may be, and whatever duties may accrue to that station, filling that role will require again and again that I must discharge my fiduciary responsibilities as an interpreter by deciding which issues I should be informed about, which books I should read, which authorities I should trust, which friends I should listen to, and so forth. Now, if I am a Christian, one voice will be truly indispensable for me: the voice of God. It is through hearing and obeying this voice above all others that Christians become knitted together with Christ and his body. God's voice is, in theory, the one voice that every Christian wishes to hear and understand.

Taking up the "voice of God" as our theme could quickly land us in a theological quagmire, since Christians differ at many points about what constitutes and what does not constitute, a "word" from God. I would prefer to sidestep that debate by focusing on the public word of God rather than his private words. Let me say quite candidly that I do believe that God has spoken and still speaks private words of direction and insight to individuals. Whether these words are mediated through reason, conscience, or a miraculous voice—or some combination of these—is another matter, but as private words these cannot be binding upon the Christian community at large. What *is* binding on the church is the public word of God, which includes the voices of creation, Scripture, and the incarnation itself. All differences aside, Christians agree across the board that these voices disclose God to us through the ministry of the Holy Spirit. As I have pointed out, nonbelievers can also read, perceive, and understand these divine words to some extent, sometimes to a great extent, but apart from divine grace they cannot respond to God's words as they should.

Although I have enumerated several sources of the divine word (creation, Scripture, Christ), the Christian effort to hear God's voice has generally focused

---

1. Michael Polanyi, *The Tacit Dimension* (Garden City, NY: Anchor Books, 1967).

on Scripture itself. This is because something from creation's voice is already tacitly understood, and also because much of what we understand of the incarnate Word, and of our common experience with Christ, is mediated to us through the words of Scripture. So Christians of every stripe give the voice of Scripture a privileged and authoritative place in their thinking. Now I have argued already that listening to this voice inevitably involves listening to the human authors of Scripture. If I wish to understand what God is saying through the book of Romans, then I will have to begin with the written verbal discourse of the apostle Paul. There is simply no other way to begin. In making this point I am obviously standing firmly in the camp of historical criticism, with its emphasis on interpreting texts in relation to their human authors and contexts. But it is precisely this historical-critical posture that has prompted so many theological difficulties in the first place, for it almost forces us to confront the genuine diversity of the Bible's theological terrain. Can historical criticism legitimate itself by pointing us to an exit from the ostensible dilemma that it has created? I believe that it can, at least in part.

If we are to pursue theological coherence on the basis of Scripture's theological diversity, then we will need a larger context in which those diverse perspectives can be adjudicated. As I pointed out in chapter 5, many Christian theorists identify this larger context as the canon of Scripture itself. In this vein of thought, the canonical shape of the Bible provides the key to its theological interpretation. If the Bible commanded its ancient readers to kill their enemies and also to love them, then Scripture's canonical shape will suggest to us that one of these commands should take priority over the other. In this case, priority will naturally fall to the New Testament's love command rather than to the Old Testament's command that all Canaanites be killed. Now I quite agree with this sort of judgment, but what is sometimes overlooked is that historical criticism—if practiced correctly—provides a basis for this theological maneuver, which moves from the individual books of Scripture to the canon as a whole. In doing so, historical criticism also directs us beyond the Bible to the larger context of the Christian tradition. Let me explain.

On any *historical* account, the human author of the Christian canon was the church.[2] Early Christian leaders, confronted by heresies and theological debates, sought to alleviate some of these difficulties by promulgating the authoritative canon of Scripture. This collection of books was formed around the nucleus of the older Jewish canon by adding to it a variety of early Christian writings that were deemed apostolic in origin and orthodox in theological perspective. If we wish to know what the church intended to say through this canon, then we shall have to attend (in good historical-critical fashion) to the ancient context of the church and to the sorts of things that its leaders believed in those early days. Tak-

---

2. See Lee M. McDonald, *The Formation of the Christian Biblical Canon*, rev. and expanded ed. (Peabody, MA: Hendrickson, 1995); Bruce M. Metzger, *The Canon of the New Testament: Its Origin, Development, and Significance* (Oxford: Clarendon, 1987).

ing this historical and theological step is not terribly difficult. Many early Christian texts are ready at hand, including numerous documents in which the church formally summarized the tenets of orthodox Christian belief. I speak here of the patristic sources and also of the great creeds and declarations made in the church's early ecumenical councils. The church fathers and the earliest of the ecumenical councils help us understand the criteria of orthodoxy that were applied during the canonical process (c. 100–400 CE) and so reveal to us something important about the meaning of the Christian canon. These sources tell us what the church intended to say with the canon.[3] Certainly the early fathers of the church suffered from many personal faults, and as Abelard made clear long ago,[4] their theologies contradicted one another in many respects. Also by establishing Scripture as the locus of canonical authority, these leaders ostensibly placed themselves and the traditions of the church under the authority of the canonical text. So the Protestant emphasis on the primacy of Scripture is secured rather than undermined by history and tradition. Nevertheless, it remains true that the fathers of the church were the direct recipients of the oral apostolic tradition and were much closer than we to both the apostles and the context in which the New Testament books were composed and canonized. When we understand their assertions of creedal orthodoxy, we see in explicit terms the theological boundaries that produced the contours of the Christian canon. So, to express this in historical-critical terms, *the church is to canon as Paul is to the Romans epistle*.

My historical defense of the creeds and their significance raises an obvious question. Have I not admitted that the creeds are historically contingent documents, like the books of the canon itself? If the trouble is that historically contingent documents give us diverse theology, then does it not follow that the creeds land us in the very problem that the canon itself presents? This objection is, of course, partially true. Creeds or not, we face theological diversity that needs to be hashed out. Nevertheless, there is something about the creeds that sets them apart from Scripture itself, and it is this difference that makes their contribution to theology so important. The purpose of a creed, generically speaking, is to summarize and clarify the contours and boundaries of theology as reflected in the canon as a whole. Scripture itself does not provide anything quite like this genre, which is why Christians have often found it necessary to compose creeds and catechisms to guide our interpretations of Scripture. So, both historically and generically, the creeds have a special place in our handling of Scripture. For this reason serious readers of Scripture should lean heavily, and with confidence, upon the creedal traditions of the church and upon the patristic sources that help us understand them. This is all the more true when we recall that the creeds were *ecumenical* documents, composed by the church as a whole rather than by

---

3. See "Oecumenical Councils," *ODCC*, 1175.
4. See Peter Abelard, *Sic et Non* (1120 CE). For a modern critical edition, see Peter Abailard, *Sic et Non: A Critical Edition*, ed. Blanche B. Boyer and Richard McKeon, 2 vols. (Chicago: University of Chicago Press, 1976).

peripheral splinter groups. That the Holy Spirit was active in these ecumenical contexts goes without saying.[5]

The Catholic and Eastern Orthodox branches of the church have always maintained that healthy scriptural interpretation depends upon the traditional insights of creedal orthodoxy. Protestant Christianity has tended, as its name implies, to either reject or greatly minimize tradition's importance, largely because the Bible itself is thought to provide an adequate theological guide for differentiating orthodoxy from heresy. Experience has proved otherwise, however. The religious landscape in the West, especially in North America, has long been dotted with heretical cults, whose leaders have practiced a kind of biblical exegesis that is entirely unmoored from the church's theological tradition.[6] Indeed, if one reads the Biblical canon apart from the insights of the early Christians who canonized it, then heresy of some sort will almost surely result. The only reason that the great Protestant traditions have remained orthodox is that their early leaders valued the great traditions, especially the creeds and early fathers. Nonetheless, it is surprising how many Protestants clergy turn out to be *materially* heretical (though not necessarily *formally* heretical) when they are quizzed on the theological details of something like Christology.[7]

So my point is this. When we interpret any text, there is a kind of critical contextual mass that is necessary to get its most basic and salient points. In the case of Scripture, this critical contextual mass includes not just the canon itself but also the great traditions of the church. The importance of tradition is a theological reality that is now embraced even by many Protestants, who increasingly define their identity in terms of traditional creedal orthodoxy (what C. S. Lewis called "mere Christianity") rather than in terms that differentiate them wholly from Catholicism or Eastern Orthodoxy.[8] These ecumenical sentiments are now boldly expressed in consultations like "Evangelicals and Catholics Together," and in recent titles like *Is the Reformation Over?* and *Nicene Christianity*.[9] By pointing

---

5. For a recent theological appraisal of the creeds in terms of their function and value, see John Webster, "Confession and Confessions," in *Nicene Christianity: The Future for a New Ecumenism*, ed. Christopher R. Seitz (Grand Rapids: Brazos, 2001), 119-31.

6. Robert S. Ellwood Jr., *Religious and Spiritual Groups in Modern America* (Englewood Cliffs, NJ: Prentice-Hall, 1973), 61-69; Winthrop S. Hudson, *Religion in America: An Historical Account of the Development of American Religious Life*, 4th ed. (New York: Macmillan, 1987), especially 179-87, 324-26; Mark A. Noll, *A History of Christianity in the United States and Canada* (Grand Rapids: Eerdmans, 1992), 185, 195-97, 464-66.

7. The church has historically distinguished between heresies that are innocently and naively embraced (material heresies) and those that are consciously professed (formal heresies). Obviously, formal heresy has been considered more grave and serious than material heresy. See "Heresy," *ODCC*, 758-59.

8. The trailblazer among evangelicals was Thomas Oden, whose programmatic work was *Agenda for Theology* (San Francisco: Harper & Row, 1979). For an updated edition of this book, see Oden, *After Modernity ... What? Agenda for Theology* (Grand Rapids: Zondervan, 1992).

9. See James J. Buckley and David S. Yeago, "A Catholic and Evangelical Theology?" in *Knowing the Triune God: The Work of the Spirit in the Practices of the Church*, ed. James J. Buckley and David S. Yeago (Grand Rapids: Eerdmans, 2001), 1-20; Scot McKnight, "From Wheaton to Rome: Why Evangelicals Become

this out, I have no interest in carelessly bashing the Reformation. The Reformation offered an important path of correction for the church, not only for the Reformed branches of the church but also for Catholicism, where the Counter-Reformation had many positive benefits. Eastern Orthodoxy has much to learn from the Reformation as well. Nevertheless, present developments between Catholics and Protestants suggest that the church is taking important steps toward answering the prayer of Jesus that his people would be one (John 17:20–21).

Explicit in the foregoing discussion is a serious critique of Protestant preoccupations with *sola scriptura*.[10] That much is clear. Less clear perhaps is that our discussion also implies a critique of Protestant confidence in Scripture's perspicuity, in the idea that the Bible's words and expressions are clear and easy to understand. This belief was an essential tenet in the Protestant rejection of Catholic tradition, for the Catholic Church held that the Bible could not be safely interpreted apart from the church's traditional magisterium. Protestants retorted that Scripture could stand alone because the meaning of God's written discourse was utterly lucid. Now I should like very much to side with the Protestants on this point, to say that anyone who reads the Bible can learn a great deal from it and also hear God's voice through it. I have known many unchurched people who, sitting alone in a hotel room, with Gideon Bible in hand, have recognized their need for Christ and called upon him for help. They understood the clear words of Scripture and responded appropriately. So there is something perspicuous about Scripture. On the other hand, in the end I do not believe that things are altogether simple when it comes to reading the Bible and doing theology. Although I have no formal medical training, I can confidently remove a splinter from my young daughter's finger, or treat her minor wounds to prevent infection. At the same time, it would be sheer folly for me to cut through her skull to remove a cancerous brain tumor, or to select and administer powerful antibiotics to quell her pneumonia. I believe that this description of medical competence crudely parallels biblical interpretation. The Bible is fairly straightforward if one puts its discourse to simple uses, but if one wishes to interpret certain parts of the Bible (like Joshua, Leviticus, or Romans), or to do serious theology or ethics using the Bible, then things can become complicated very quickly. A sophomore university theology student recently visited my office, excited to explain to me his new theory of the atonement. He deduced that God has forgiven our sins because, through his experience in the incarnation,

---

Roman Catholic," *JETS* 45 (2002): 451–72; Mark A. Noll and Carolyn Nystrom, *Is the Reformation Over? An Evangelical Assessment of Contemporary Roman Catholicism* (Grand Rapids: Baker Academic, 2005); Seitz, *Nicene Christianity*; Geoffrey Wainwright, *Is the Reformation Over? Catholics and Protestants at the Turn of the Millennia* (Milwaukee: Marquette University Press, 2000); D. H. Williams, *Evangelicals and Tradition: The Formative Influence of the Early Church* (Grand Rapids: Baker Academic, 2005).

10. The evangelical critique of *sola scriptura* is already in full swing. For example, see A. N. S. Lane, "Sola scriptura? Making Sense of a Post-Reformation Slogan," in *A Pathway into the Holy Scripture*, ed. P. E. Satterthwaite and D. F. Wright (Grand Rapids: Eerdmans, 1994), 299–313; Keith A. Mathison, *The Shape of Sola Scriptura* (Moscow, ID: Canon, 2001); Williams, *Evangelicals and Tradition*, 96–102.

God discovered just how difficult temptation can be. My point is therefore clear. Leave the heavy-duty theology to the theologians, not to the sophomores. The "priesthood of all believers," whatever it may mean, does not mean that everyone is equally suited to interpret Scripture theologically.

But let us return to our main theme in this part of the discussion. Given that we live in a large and complex world, we must make wise choices about the sources that we will consult in our pursuit of truth and light. Though Christians should recognize the importance of just about everything in the context of the whole, in the final analysis two sources of insight are vital to healthy theological reflection: Scripture, and the Christian tradition that contextually elucidates its meaning and significance. For this reason, anyone who aspires to interpret the Bible competently will at the same time aspire to become familiar with the theological traditions of the church. I have in mind, of course, the theological work of the early fathers, but I would add to this the whole tradition of theological reflection in Catholicism, Orthodoxy, and the Reformation.

Moving "beyond" the Bible and Christian Tradition: Interdisciplinary and Multicultural Theology

When we accentuate the role of church tradition in biblical interpretation, we are beginning to interpret Scripture by moving beyond it, by listening to and considering voices outside Scripture that can help bring clarity to our reading of Scripture. But in the final analysis the traditions of the church are no less human than Scripture itself, and this will inevitably mean that even the formidable combination of Scripture and tradition is not in itself a foolproof guide to the truth. The cases of Copernicus and Galileo demonstrate as much. Although Scripture, church tradition, and even common sense seemed lined up against those much-maligned astronomers, in the end the scientists were right and the theology was wrong. The scientists turned out to be right because they attended not only to Scripture and tradition but also to the voice of God's creation, which was for them loud and clear.

Copernicus and Galileo heeded creation's voice by applying the mathematical and scientific tools of astronomy, and their rational capacities, to the cosmos that lay before them. Once they realized that the earth moved about the sun, it followed that Scripture and church tradition were either wrong or had been seriously misunderstood. Conflicts of this sort arise not only in astronomy but in every academic discipline, as the advances in biology, chemistry, physics, psychology, political science, history, philosophy, and literature challenge long-held assumptions about the Bible's message and Christian tradition. If the church is seeking a healthy way to manage these conflicts, we could do no better than to examine how we finally managed to marry the science of Copernicus and Galileo with the theology of the church.

The marriage was not as difficult as the courtship. Although Copernicus and particularly Galileo faced fairly strong opposition to their views, their heliocentric theories were eventually accepted by astronomers and theologians alike. What brought about the change of mind? Human rationality tries to make sense of the world by ordering all that is before it into a coherent whole. Once it became clear that the astronomers were right, then coherence required an adjustment to the church's belief that the Ptolemaic (geocentric) system was the biblical system. One solution, attempted by some Christians, tried to show that the Bible had been teaching a heliocentric viewpoint all along. This exegetical move, originally attempted by Galileo himself, was ingenious but did not satisfy most inquiring minds. The other solution admitted that Scripture reflected a finite human viewpoint and then proceeded to explain why God's Word would do so. As we saw in the previous chapter, the church's traditional explanation for this difficulty was accommodation: that God had adopted the finite views of humanity in his discourse with us. Accepting this account of divine discourse means that the Bible's word is not the last word on any and every issue that is at hand. In the end, the healthiest way to interpret Scripture, and to do theology, is to listen to all that God has to say through creation, Scripture, and tradition and then to apply our rational capacity to these voices, so that we might discover the best and most coherent way to understand what God is finally saying to us. There is a sense, then, in which the best readings of Scripture, and the best work in theology, will carefully consider the larger context that lies beyond Scripture, not only because this context makes Scripture intelligible, but also because, in some instances, this larger context offers new insights that were unknown to the biblical authors.

Theology that moves "beyond the Bible" might sound pretty ominous to some conservative evangelical ears, but a little reflection on the matter reveals that this move is inevitable. The Bible is certainly a big book, but as the sum total of God's written discourse to humanity it is surely a fairly modest tome. That God intended us to move beyond the Bible in our search for insight is suggested by this reticence, as well as by Scripture's diversity (which implies that we have more theological work to do) and by its emphasis on creation's voice and on the wisdom tradition that listens to it (which implies that we have more to learn). Situated within this larger interpretive context, theological reflection becomes a more complex undertaking than is traditionally conceived, for it must consider a much broader range of materials than the Bible and systematic theology. In the context of the whole, *everything is theological*—even the proverbial "price of tea in China." Among other things, this means that human inquiry can never be construed as a task of individual insight. No individual can master all of the disciplines of learning, and this becomes truer still as each discipline advances in the extent and complexity of what it knows. Human inquiry is better practiced as a communal activity, as an interdisciplinary effort undertaken by the entire human community. Christians, as the recipients of Scripture, salvation, and the Spirit, naturally have something special to offer in this ongoing pursuit of human understanding. But we are by no means the only ones who have something to offer.

The communal nature of human inquiry has been accentuated especially in the work of the Russian literary theorist Mikhail Bakhtin.[11] Bakhtin would have us understand the advance of human knowledge as a conversation that includes many different voices and perspectives, which together give us a better portrait of the whole than is available from any one person. Implicit in this approach is not only the interdisciplinarity but also the multicultural nature of human inquiry. Each culture, each social class within each culture, and each gender within each culture offer experiences and perspectives that contribute something unique to our perspective of the whole. As an example, I have before me a book entitled *Introduction to Biblical Christianity from an African Perspective*.[12] Chapters that appear in this African theology book include "The Saints and the Spirit World," "The Origin of Evil and the Strategies of Satan," "Spiritual Warfare," and "Ancestors, Magic, and Divination." The material covered in these chapters would add substantial insight to comparable Western theologies, whose systematic categories often allow no space for these quite biblical topics.[13] "Spiritual warfare" drops through the cracks of a Western theological grid like water through a screen. My primary point is that the best readings of Scripture, and the best of theological thinking, will draw upon many theological and ideological perspectives—from Asian theologies, African theologies, African-American theologies, Indian theologies, Islamic theologies, Latin-American theologies, Marxist ideologies, feminist theologies, liberation theologies, and gay and lesbian theologies. For the thoughtful inquirer, there is no quarter of human experience that will fail to yield some fruits of truth. So, although it may often be difficult to do so in practice, we should make every effort—and seize every opportunity—to inform our theologies from the widest swaths of human insight.

Ideal communities of Christian learning require that Christian scholars attend not only to their own disciplines but also to the touchstones of Scripture and Christian tradition, to the many other disciplines, and to the many other cultures that inform us about the created order. At the same time, Christian scholars will have to take up the onus of making their research and insights as accessible as possible to those outside their respective disciplines. To the extent that we are successful in creating a truly interdisciplinary community, to that same extent the Christian community will be one that is well suited for the task of hearing and obeying God's voice.[14] In this approach to human inquiry,

11. Mikhail Bakhtin, *The Dialogic Imagination*, ed. Michael Holquist, trans. Caryl Emerson and Michael Holquist (Austin: University of Texas Press, 1981); Michael Holquist, *Dialogism: Bakhtin and His World* (New York: Routledge, 1990).

12. Wilbur O'Donovan Jr., *Introduction to Biblical Christianity from an African Perspective* (Ilorin, Nigeria: Nigeria Evangelical Fellowship, 1992).

13. Notable exceptions appear in some charismatic theologies.

14. Joel B. Green, "Scripture and Theology: Uniting the Two So Long Divided," in *Between Two Horizons: Spanning New Testament Studies and Systematic Theology*, ed. Joel B. Green and Max Turner (Grand Rapids: Eerdmans, 2000), 23–43.

the best interpretations will be those that make the best sense of the context of the whole.

Biblical Authority in Theology beyond the Bible

Let us suppose that, as I have suggested, the Bible sometimes accommodates the errant views of its human authors and audiences, and that our search for the truth on some issues will therefore require that we move beyond the Bible for better insights. If we suppose that these propositions are right, where does that leave biblical authority? How can the Bible serve as the authoritative Word of God when we are busy trumping its voice with voices from "beyond the Bible"? This is a reasonable and important question that any serious Christian should raise at this point.

Let me begin to consider this issue by noting a solution that I do not much like. One way of making the theological space for a move beyond the Bible is to limit or circumscribe the domain to which the Bible's authority applies. Doctrinal statements are worded, for example, so that the Bible's authority does not hold in all matters but only when it comes to "faith and practice." Defining the Bible's authority in this way is fairly common in progressive theological circles, where the Bible's antiquated views of the cosmos and of other scientific matters seem to run afoul of modern sensibility. In such cases we are supposedly free to go beyond the Bible's "science" because Scripture's authority does not extend to these matters.

My reservations about this move are twofold. First, I find that Scripture makes fairly straightforward claims about matters of science, particularly in the cosmological portraits of Genesis. These texts find their closest ancient parallels in scientific texts from Egypt and Mesopotamia.[15] So I would prefer to say that the Bible speaks authoritatively even on scientific matters like cosmology, but that it does so through the accommodated viewpoint of the human author of Genesis. Genesis is not modern science, but it might well be ancient science.

The other reservation that I have, and this may be the more important of the two, is that I do not believe that the world of our experience can be neatly divided into distinct domains, such as the domains of "faith" and "science." That God created the cosmos is, for instance, a matter of concern for both faith and science. Recent work in the philosophy of science has demonstrated to the satisfaction of most theorists that science, no less than the other human branches of inquiry, depends upon tradition and faith.[16] If this is right, then it will mean that we must move beyond the Bible not only in matters of science but also in matters that we would associate more closely with faith and theology. Nevertheless, it seems to

---

15. See *ATSHB*, 305–41.
16. Thomas S. Kuhn, *The Structure of Scientific Revolutions*, 3rd ed. (Chicago: University of Chicago Press, 1996); Michael Polanyi, *Scientific Thought and Social Reality* (New York: International Universities Press, 1974).

me that the Bible can serve as the final and authoritative Word of God even when our theology moves beyond its explicit words.

Moving beyond the Bible's theology does not amount to ignoring the Bible. When we move beyond the Bible in order to claim something that it has not said, or to say something that seems to contradict it, or at least parts of it, this will in every case be vouchsafed by the fact that some parts of the Bible already point us in this new direction. There will be biblical *trajectories* that are already heading in the direction that we believe we ought to go with our theology. In many cases these trajectories are essentially eschatological, in that they either anticipate or participate in the redemptive order to come, whose beachhead was the resurrection of Christ and whose final fulfillment will be the resurrection of the church and the judgment of the world.[17] According to Kevin Giles and William Webb, Christian responses to slavery provide a good example.[18]

Christians eventually recognized that this social institution had two important strikes against it. It was not demanded by God, and it was among the most oppressive of human institutions. But it took a long time for the church to arrive at this conclusion. One reason for the delay was, of course, the content of the Bible itself. In both the Old and New Testaments, the institutions of slavery were regulated rather than prohibited. The treatment of slaves permitted by the Old Testament was particularly harsh, since corporal beatings were expressly permitted by Hebrew law: "If a man beats his male or female slave with a rod and the slave dies as a direct result, he must be punished, but he is not to be punished if the slave gets up after a day or two, since the slave is his property" (Exod. 21:20–21 NIV). As I pointed out in chapter 3, ethnic distinctions were made in the slave laws, so that foreign slaves were treated more harshly (so Leviticus) and were denied the six-year manumissions offered to Hebrew slaves (at least, in the case of debt slavery). Of course, the Old Testament also offered images of hope for suffering slaves, most notably in the exodus narrative. One cannot but wonder at the fact that Israel's emancipation from that enslavement carried so little import for its laws.

At any rate, the lot of slaves seems to have improved somewhat in the New Testament, where slave owners were enjoined to treat their slaves with kindness (Eph. 6:9; Col. 4:1) and where, in at least one instance, a slave owner was asked to release his slave because of the gospel (see Philemon). It is only in this last case that we begin to see the firstfruits of Paul's words from Galatians: "There is neither Jew nor Greek, slave nor free, male nor female, for you are all one in Christ Jesus" (Gal. 3:28 NIV). But in no instance does Scripture demand the general manumission

---

17. For recent examples of this approach, see Ray S. Anderson, *The Shape of Practical Theology: Empowering Ministry with Theological Praxis* (Downers Grove, IL: InterVarsity, 2001); Oliver O'Donovan, *Resurrection and Moral Order: An Outline for Evangelical Ethics*, 2nd ed. (Grand Rapids: Eerdmans, 1994); William J. Webb, *Slaves, Women, and Homosexuals: Exploring the Hermeneutics of Cultural Analysis* (Downers Grove, IL: InterVarsity, 2001).

18. Kevin Giles, *The Trinity and Subordinationism: The Doctrine of God and the Contemporary Gender Debate* (Downers Grove, IL: InterVarsity, 2002), 215–50; Webb, *Slaves, Women, and Homosexuals*.

of slaves. I suspect that Paul and the other early Christians developed no agenda for social reform because of their expectation that Christ would soon return. But that matter aside, given the Bible's explicit content, we cannot be surprised that the church fathers and almost all other premodern Christians supported the institution of slavery. Included in this list of supporters are the likes of Clement of Alexandria, Origen, Chrysostom, Augustine, Aquinas, Luther, Calvin, and the Puritans.[19] After all, if one wished to follow strictly the voice of biblical theology—and most of the ancients did—then slavery would have to stand.

In the case of American slavery, many eighteenth- and nineteenth-century evangelicals supported the institution, especially in the South. But Northern evangelicals tended to think differently on the matter. As a result, Protestant denominations all across the board were splitting along North-South lines over the issue of slavery.[20] The geographical distribution of the two opposing views was of course not a function of Scripture; the driving force was not exegesis but economics, for Southern culture was hopelessly dependent on slaves. Nowhere was this expressed more clearly than in Georgia, when the prominent evangelical, George Whitefield, fought *to bring* slavery to his state: "Georgia never ... will be a flourishing province without negroes."[21] Or, as the title of one pro-slavery book expressed it, "Cotton Is King."[22] As a result, Southern pastors and biblical scholars labored feverishly to demonstrate that Scripture fully and firmly supported slavery—and their task was made easier by Scripture itself.

It will at first seem that the men who took this position were callous to the plight of slaves, but this is to misunderstand their theological position—at least in the case of those who were ethically sensitive. This "sensitive" pro-slavery posture is well illustrated in the work of an evangelical, Charles Hodge:

> The grand mistake, as we apprehend, of those who maintain that slaveholding is itself a crime, is, that they do not discriminate between slaveholding in itself considered, and its accessories at any particular time or place. Because masters may treat their slaves unjustly, or governments make oppressive laws in relation to them, is no more valid argument against the lawfulness of slaveholding, than the abuse of parental authority.... We may admit all those laws which forbid the instruction of slaves; which interfere with their marital or parental rights; which subject them to the insults and oppressions of whites, to be in the highest degree unjust, without at all

---

19. See Giles, *Trinity and Subordinationism*, 219–20.
20. William Warren Sweet, *The Story of Religion in America* (New York: Harper, 1950), 285–326; Katie Geneva Cannon, "Slave Ideology and Biblical Interpretation," in *The Postmodern Bible Reader*, ed. David Jobling, Tina Pippin, and Ronald Schleifer (Oxford: Blackwell, 2001), 195–204.
21. Edward A. Johnson, *A School History of the Negro Race in America, from 1619 to 1890: With a Short Introduction as to the Origin of the Race; also a Short Sketch of Liberia* (Raleigh: Edwards & Broughton, 1890), 44; cf. Allan Gallay, "The Origins of Slaveholders' Paternalism: George Whitefield, the Bryan Family, and the Great Awakening in the South," *Journal of Southern History* 53 (1987): 369–94.
22. E. N. Elliott, ed., *Cotton Is King and Pro-Slavery Arguments* (Augusta, GA: Pritchard, Abbott & Loomis, 1860).

admitting that slaveholding itself is a crime. Slavery may exist without any of these concomitants.[23]

Hodge's argument is crystal clear. Authority in the home, be it of parent over child or master over slave, presents the Christian with no ethical problems, so long as that authority is exercised according to the biblical mandate to love and care for others. In taking this position, Hodge was merely taking the apparent biblical position, which allowed for slavery but demanded love for one's neighbor.

Those who opposed slavery had a harder road to go when it came to the Bible. At the front of the class was John Wesley, whose critiques of slavery inspired the abolitionist work of William Wilberforce in England and also of American abolitionists.[24] What is interesting about Wesley's rhetoric is that his written deliberations on slavery hardly use Scripture at all. He mainly describes the gross cruelties of slavery and takes the evil of the institution as self-evident: "Did the Creator intend that the noblest of creatures in the visible world should live such a life as this?"[25] Where Scripture is cited by Wesley, it is usually to remind readers that they will be judged according to the treatment of their fellows: "Is there a God? You know there is. Is he a just God? Then there must be a state of retribution; a state wherein the just God will reward every man according to his works."[26] Although Wesley himself would not have described his theological strategy in these words, it is fairly easy to see what he has done. He has ignored those texts that seem to legitimize slavery and trumped them with texts that call upon Christians to love their fellows and to treat them with dignity and respect, such as "do unto others as you'd have done to you."[27] The same can be said about the rhetoric of Wilberforce and other abolitionists.[28] Given their theological context, this was the proper exegetical course for the abolitionists to follow—they followed the voice of the Spirit. But a renewed appreciation for the role of accommodation in revelation, and for the resulting importance of a trajectory theology that moves beyond the Bible, helps us situate their work into a still healthier theological context.

Some modern evangelicals, particularly those of a more conservative stripe, have elected to tackle head-on the slavery texts that Wesley ignored. But their purpose is not to resist slavery but rather to demonstrate that the Bible's acceptance of slavery involves not the slightest conflict with Christian ethics. The net result of this maneuver lands them fairly close to the nineteenth-century pro-

23. For the pro-slavery work of Charles Hodge, see Elliott, *Cotton Is King*, 822–77. The above citation is from p. 850.
24. John Wesley, *The Works of John Wesley*, 12 vols. (London: Wesleyan Methodist Book Room, 1872), 11:59–79. On the influence of Wesley on others, see Giles, *Trinity and Subordinationism*, 236–37.
25. Wesley, *Works*, 11:68.
26. Ibid., 11:76–77.
27. Ibid., 11:77.
28. See William Wilberforce, *A Practical View of the Prevailing Religious System of Professed Christians in the Higher and Middle Classes of This Country Contrasted with Real Christianity* (London: Cadell & Davies, 1797).

slavery arguments of Charles Hodge. Let us consider the arguments of Robert W. Yarbrough as an example.[29] Yarbrough admits that slavery in the Old South was a "great evil," but he seeks to distinguish the institutions of American slavery from the slavery addressed in the Bible. According to Yarbrough, slavery in the biblical period was more like modern employment than cruel Southern slavery. For this reason, he tells us, "While it is true that the biblical world . . . was far from utopian, it is not as easy as Giles [an advocate of the trajectory approach] imagines to demonstrate the inherently higher moral ground of modernity in the area of social relations." Essentially, Yarbrough is arguing—or at least seems to be arguing—that perpetuation of slavery by the biblical authors is wholly compatible with our modern theological sensibilities.

Now it seems to me that Yarbrough's thesis fails on several counts. First, the issue at hand is not whether the ancient world was more or less moral than modern society. I take it at face value that our modern society has its share of vices. The real comparative issue is not morality per se but slavery in particular, and on this score the personal freedoms offered in the modern West easily best the world of antiquity.

Second, anyone familiar with slavery in the ancient Near East, or in the Greco-Roman world, will know that ancient varieties of slavery were every bit as cruel and depersonalizing as slavery in the American South.[30] During the well-documented Roman period, slaves were mere bodies, to be used according to the whims of their owners. They were presented naked for inspection to prospective buyers and were often branded upon purchase. Attractive women and boys were especially prized for there service in hetero- and homosexual gratification. This was particularly true when their owners wished to engage in sexual activities that their spouses found unsavory, or where their owners wished to rent out their sexual services. Slaves were constant victims of physical and emotional deprivation, and of extreme corporal punishment. According to Roman law, the legal testimonies of slaves had to be verified under torture. All this is not to mention the generally destructive effect that Roman slavery had upon the affected families. It is true that Roman-era slavery sometimes provided comfortable and prosperous lives for slaves, and that most slaves were eventually released, usually by age 30 or so. But I believe that Yarbrough is wrong, and also unwise, when he accentuates the parallels between modern employment and ancient slavery. The two things are entirely different at precisely the most important points. Consequently, it is an empty and fruitless endeavor to "save" the Bible from its endorsement of slavery.

---

29. Robert W. Yarbrough, "The Hermeneutics of 1 Timothy 2:9–15," in *Women in the Church: A Fresh Analysis of 1 Timothy 2:9–15*, ed. Andreas J. Köstenberger, Thomas R. Schreiner, and H. Scott Baldwin (Grand Rapids: Baker Academic, 1995), 155–96.

30. S. Scott Bartchy, *Mallon Chrēsai: First-Century Slavery and the Interpretation of 1 Corinthians 7:21*, SBLDS 11 (Missoula, MT: Scholars Press, 1973); Bartchy, "Slavery (Greco-Roman)," *ABD* 6:65–73; Moses I. Finley, *Ancient Slavery and Modern Ideology* (London: Chatto & Windus, 1980); Jennifer A. Glancy, *Slavery in Early Christianity* (Oxford: Oxford University Press, 2002).

The biblical authors lived in a day when slavery was an accepted social institution, and in many cases they displayed only the most rudimentary tendencies to swim against that social current.

Third, and finally, Yarbrough fails to recognize the full import of Christian theology for the institution of slavery. If human tendencies are as sinful as the Bible suggests, then it is dangerous to perpetuate an institution in which masters own slaves and exert total control over their destinies. Christians rejected slavery because it proved to be an intractable ethical problem, and we do well to avoid that old quagmire, which still exists in some quarters of the modern world. No biblical text applies so clearly to this question as the Golden Rule: "Do unto others as you would have them do unto you." If I prefer freedom, then I should prefer it for my neighbor as well.

In the final analysis, a good theological assessment of the Bible's view of slavery needs to follow contours that are something like what I am laying out in this book. As we move from the Old to the New Testament, we can discern a positive trajectory in the status granted to slaves. While the Old Testament allows for rather cruel treatment of slaves, the New Testament regulates this more narrowly by calling for their humane treatment and even for their freedom in certain cases. This positive trajectory should be read in the light of other New Testament developments, such as the New Testament command to love our neighbors and to do for others as we would have them do for us. The New Testament also includes texts that minimize ethnic, gender, and social distinctions, such as its assertion in Galatians 3:28 that there is neither "slave nor free . . . we are all one in Christ." When our rational capacities are applied to these texts, the only way to make good sense of them is to head in the direction of manumitting slaves. During the eighteenth and nineteenth centuries, Christians were prodded in this direction by the Enlightenment and its emphasis on human dignity and individual freedom. So, ultimately, the decision to reject slavery resulted from a combination of theological reflection and Enlightenment insight.[31] If for no other reason than this, Christians can be thankful for the Enlightenment, for it helped us to recognize the theological and ethical trajectories in the Bible that were heading toward and hence legitimizing manumission. By fighting for the freedom of slaves, Christian abolitionists were merely completing what Scripture had left partly undone. So when the abolitionists trumped the words of Scripture, we may legitimately say that Scripture invited them to do so. There is a biblical way to go beyond the Bible.

Can we confirm the legitimacy of this "trajectory" approach by citing a compelling example of the practice *within* Scripture itself? I believe that we can. One of the more serious debates in primitive Christianity regarded the relationship between gentile Christians and biblical law. There were at that time many Jewish Christians who believed, apparently with the sanction of Scripture, that circumcision and the ritual law were perpetual requirements of covenant life for Jews and

---

31. Giles, *Trinity and Subordinationism*, 235–36.

gentiles alike. For the permanence of circumcision and its application to gentile proselytes, these "Judaizers" could cite the following text:

> Then God said to Abraham, "As for you, you must keep my covenant, *you and your descendants after you for the generations to come.* This is my covenant with you and your descendants after you, the covenant you are to keep: Every male among you shall be circumcised. You are to undergo circumcision, and it will be the sign of the covenant between me and you. *For the generations to come* every male among you who is eight days old must be circumcised, including *those born in your household or bought with money from a foreigner—those who are not your offspring. Whether born in your household or bought with your money, they must be circumcised.* My covenant in your flesh is to be an *everlasting covenant.* Any uncircumcised male, who has not been circumcised in the flesh, will be cut off from his people; he has broken my covenant." (Gen. 17:9–14 NIV, italics mine)

Equally clear, or so it seemed, was that the priestly cult and its rituals were permanent ordinances of God, as this and other biblical texts suggested:

> Bring Aaron and his sons to the entrance to the Tent of Meeting and wash them with water. Then dress Aaron in the sacred garments, anoint him and consecrate him so he may serve me as priest. Bring his sons and dress them in tunics. Anoint them just as you anointed their father, so they may serve me as priests. Their anointing will be to *a priesthood that will continue for all generations to come.*" (Exod. 40:12–15 NIV, italics mine)

Now in spite of this strong (seemingly water-tight!) biblical evidence to the contrary, we know that the early church eventually rejected this Jewish reading of the Old Testament, opting instead for a more inclusive and less restrictive doctrine. Churches would welcome gentile believers and would not require them to follow Jewish law. This official position, agreed upon at the earliest ecumenical council in Jerusalem (see Acts 15), was founded on two fundamental bases: the biblical text and human experience.[32] Regarding the biblical text, the pro-gentile movement could cite texts like Amos 9:11–12, which predicted that gentiles would eventually be numbered among God's people. We may presume as well that Paul, who attended the meetings, cited the biblical evidence that God had counted Abraham as righteous *before* he was circumcised and *before* the law of Moses (cf. Gen. 15; Gal. 3:6–25). Such was the biblical evidence. As for experience, the pro-gentile movement could highlight two different types of evidence for their viewpoint. They could point to the Jewish experience that living under the law was a burden so intolerable that it implied that salvation must be by grace through faith (Acts 15:10–11; cf. Rom. 7:14–25). They could also cite the church's experience that uncircumcised gentile believers had received the Holy Spirit (Acts 15:8, 12; cf.

---

32. For a good discussion of the role of experience in theological reflection, see Alister E. McGrath, *Christian Theology: An Introduction*, 2nd ed. (Oxford: Blackwell, 1997), 223–32.

Gal. 3:1–5). After weighing this evidence against the Judaizing viewpoint, the church made its choice in favor of what has become Christian orthodoxy.

For the present purpose of our discussion, it is significant to recall that the church's only canonical text during this Jewish/gentile controversy was the Old Testament. It was a text that confronted the church with two quite different theological viewpoints on the gentile question, and only after much discussion did the church finally decide to go beyond the Bible in rendering a conclusive (and in some respects, surprising) judgment. So far as I can tell, if we were to judge the matter solely on the basis of the Old Testament, the case for the Jewish viewpoint seems much stronger. Hardly anything in the Old Testament suggests that Israel's "eternal" rites would pass away or that gentiles would be exempted from those rites. Consequently, it seems to me that if there was anything that tipped the scale in favor of the pro-gentile party, it was undoubtedly the church's experience that gentiles were receiving and experiencing life in the Spirit. This experiential evidence will not seem very convincing to Cartesian-minded evangelicals who are thirsty for indubitable theological conclusions, but it was undoubtedly quite important evidence for the pre-Cartesian church.

In sum, I would argue that the Bible teaches us to go beyond the Bible, and that it implicitly shows us how. Good theology must consider all of the canonical viewpoints, however diverse they might be, and then evaluate these together through the witness of God's Spirit. This spiritual reading of Scripture is possible because "the word of God is living and active, sharper than any two-edged sword" (Heb. 4:12 RSV). Thus, paradoxical though it might seem, I would argue that trumping the Bible in this way is thoroughly biblical; it is the Bible itself that forces us to wrestle with its diversity.

When we legitimately trump the Bible with newer insights, as the church did in the case of circumcision, and as was eventually done in the case of Galileo's astronomy and in the case of slavery, we should recognize at once that this need not involve disrespect for the Word of God. In the best of circumstances, trumping Scripture is evidence that God is still speaking to his church and that the church is still listening to God. It is only when the Bible's voice is twisted and contorted to suit our theological fancies and social conveniences that this becomes an act of rebellion rather than an act of submission. It will not always be easy to distinguish in a given case whether our theology is submitting or rebelling, or whether it represents some combination of these two opposing responses to God. But of this we can be sure: we shall be held accountable when we represent God as saying something that we know, or should know, that he is not saying. This admonition is especially fitting for those who are charged with teaching the Word of God to the church of God (James 3:1).

I must say, however, that even if we are very careful, the work of recognizing and characterizing biblical trajectories can be tricky business. This is largely because there seem to be different kinds of theological trajectories in Scripture. The safest and simplest trajectories are those drawn from the Bible's explicit testimony. Here we might recall the words of Jesus in his Sermon on the Mount: "You have heard that it was said, 'Eye for eye, and tooth for tooth.' But I tell you, Do not resist an evil person" (Matt. 5:38–39 NIV). This is a clear theological trajectory that runs from Moses to Jesus, from Old Testament to New; few would question its legitimacy. Another kind of trajectory is illustrated by the early church's debates over circumcision. In this case, if it were a matter of sheer magnitude and majority voice, the Old Testament evidence would have been soundly on the side of the Judaizers. But Scripture's minority voice had a deeper logic. Its pro-gentile viewpoint could assimilate circumcision more easily than the pro-circumcision party could assimilate the biblical evidence regarding salvation for the gentiles and Abraham's right standing with God prior to circumcision. It was the structure of rationality that indicated the correctness of the minority evidence, and this was further confirmed by the church's experience with the Spirit. A third sort of trajectory allows us to benefit from the insights of modern science. In this case it is not a matter of noticing that the Bible is gradually guiding us toward the insights of Copernicus, Newton, Darwin, or Einstein. It is instead a matter of recognizing that the Bible's primary subject matter is not scientific in the modern sense, even where it reflects ancient views of the cosmos. This generic observation about Scripture allows us to accept a trajectory that runs from Genesis to Copernicus without isolating an explicit trajectory within the Bible itself. A fourth kind of trajectory, if we should call it a trajectory, might be indicated when Scripture's diversity lacks vector or direction. In the case of church governance, for instance, one might argue that the Bible presents us with several different methods for selecting church leaders and for exercising leadership. Some of these methods are congregational and others episcopal; some are egalitarian and others less so. As a result, the Bible does not provide a single approach to governance so much as a menu of political options that suit different situations and contexts. Wisdom is not pursued by melding together all of these texts into one, still less by assuming that one political solution is essentially better than the others. No, in this case we would exercise wisdom by choosing the political solution that best suits our context or predicament.

There are undoubtedly other kinds of biblical trajectories, but these examples give us some idea of the variety that might be involved. The main point is that there are indeed biblical trajectories that point us beyond the explicit voice of certain texts within Scripture, and in some cases beyond the explicit voice of Scripture as a whole.

Moving beyond the Bible in our theological inquiry is by no means conceptually new to Christian scholarship, but it is somewhat novel in evangelical circles. I have already mentioned the work of Kevin Giles and William Webb, two theologians who have embraced the trajectory approach.[33] Another recent evangelical champion of trajectory theology is British New Testament scholar I. Howard Marshall,

---

33. See also R. T. France, *Women in the Church's Ministry: A Test-Case for Biblical Hermeneutics* (Carlisle: Paternoster, 1995).

who has accentuated this theme in a book that is suitably titled, *Beyond the Bible: Moving from Scripture to Theology*.[34] I will not try to summarize Marshall's approach in detail because, if I have understood him correctly, his approach to theological inquiry—and to the Bible's role in it—is fairly close to my own. What I would like to do instead is to consider the criticisms that have been leveled against his book by Kevin Vanhoozer, an evangelical theologian whose objections are included as an appendix in Marshall's book.

Vanhoozer describes a number of theological options for going beyond the Bible and then provides his own view of the subject. Rather than summarize his arguments in detail, I will simply enumerate (and respond to) what seem to be his primary concerns and objections respecting the approach of Marshall and similar approaches to theology. One theological outcome that Vanhoozer wishes to avoid is the implication that Scripture sometimes reflects errant moral judgments, particularly in the harsher portions of the Old Testament. Vanhoozer is not at all keen, for instance, on Marshall's argument that the Canaanite genocide, or the biblical slave laws, or the imprecatory psalms, reflect sub-Christian ethical viewpoints:

> Marshall wants Christians to get "beyond genocide." So do I. But I am not prepared to say that God's judgment of the world, or of the nations, is "intrinsically wrong" if it involves killing people.... Unless we are prepared to jettison significant portions of the Old Testament ... this way of going beyond Scripture has more of Marcion than of Marshall about it. For it really is not about numbers. If Marshall is to be consistent, he should say that God does not have a right to take a single life.[35]

I see several problems with Vanhoozer's objection. To begin with, there is a complex relationship between God taking a life and Israelites killing Canaanites, just as there is a complex relationship between God taking a life and Europeans killing Native Americans, or between God taking a life and Crusaders killing Muslims. Is it only in Israel's case that divine sanction legitimizes the extermination of pagans? Or is it more likely that the biblical text has simply assumed standard but erroneous Near Eastern ideas about the relationship between ethnicity, religion, and war? Theologically speaking, the latter possibility seems more likely to me than the former.[36] The Israelite massacre of Canaanites is no more compatible with a gospel of love than was European imperialism or the Crusades. The real difference, if there is one, is that European Christians committed their atrocities

---

34. I. Howard Marshall, *Beyond the Bible: Moving from Scripture to Theology* (Grand Rapids: Baker Academic, 2004).

35. Kevin J. Vanhoozer, "Into the Great 'Beyond': A Theologian's Response to the Marshall Plan," in I. Howard Marshall, *Beyond the Bible: Moving from Scripture to Theology* (Grand Rapids: Baker Academic, 2004), 85.

36. Hebrew *ḥērem* ("ban") theology appears quite prominently in the Mesha Stela, a ninth-century inscription of Israel's Moabite neighbors. See *ATSHB*, 466–67.

while basking in the light of the gospel, whereas the Israelites lived in a time before that light had shined. At any rate, it seems theologically reasonable to conclude that the systematic killing of pagan enemies *simply because they are pagans*—and this is certainly the basic logic of Deuteronomy—is not compatible with the gospel of love. If Vanhoozer wishes to get beyond genocide, then he will have to take a longer theological step than he seems willing to take. But it is a step that Marshall is quite willing to take.

As for Vanhoozer's assertion that Marshall's approach is Marcion-like, I think that this criticism of Marshall is shy of the mark. Marcion rejected the Old Testament and its God altogether, whereas Marshall—like the New Testament writers—has fully embraced the Old Testament and then pursued creative and thoughtful ways to assimilate its voice to the gospel message. In my opinion Marshall's approach is much closer to that of the apostles and early church fathers than to Marcion's exegesis; if anyone in this discussion is leaning in a heretical direction, I would suggest that it is Vanhoozer, inasmuch as his desire to rid the Bible of its human foibles leans in a docetic direction. But to my mind the real difficulty with Vanhoozer's objection is that it simply does not come to grips with the profound ethical and theological diversity in the canon. In my opinion, if there is a basic and fundamental theological division emerging among evangelical scholars at this juncture in history, it is the division between those like Marshall who recognize this diversity, and those like Vanhoozer who more or less want to deny it.

Another objection of Vanhoozer to Marshall's thesis involves his belief that Marshall has applied to the Bible certain interpretive criteria that are foreign or external to it. For instance, Marshall's method, like my own, wants to give careful attention to the presence of theological trajectories in the Bible, which indicate the direction in which biblical revelation is moving on particular issues. Vanhoozer's objection goes like this: "Can one decide what counts as redemptive movement without *pretending* to stand at the end of the process, without *claiming to know* what kind of eschatological world the Spirit is creating? Can one go beyond Scripture via the redemptive trajectory approach and at the same time *prevent one's own view of the trajectory from lording it over the text?*"[37]

Again, I see several difficulties with this objection. First, Vanhoozer's initial question attributes to Marshall two quite different claims and then wrongly assumes that they are of the same type. There is a great deal of difference between "pretending" and "claiming to know." I certainly do not believe that Marshall would "claim to know" in any absolute sense what kind of eschatological world God is creating. As for "pretending," that is a different matter that calls for more attention. If we take "pretend" to mean "imagine," then I believe that Marshall would not be much troubled by the characterization. Trajectory theology attends to the direction of biblical theology and then uses good sense to imagine or extrapolate where

---

37. Vanhoozer, "Into the Great 'Beyond,'" 91, italics mine.

that trajectory is heading. Logical inductions of this sort are essential to human reasoning, not only when we go "beyond the Bible" but in all theories, which by their very nature extend beyond the data they seek to explain. The application of good sense to the Bible's theological trajectories does not produce foolproof theological knowledge, of course. But it can and often does yield wise and fruitful theological judgments.

As we can see, Vanhoozer is very suspicious of this theological method, which he describes as "lording it over" the Bible. But for an obvious reason, this criticism of trajectory theology simply will not stick. Whether one is doing trajectory theology or not, the interpreter of Scripture *always* decides what the Bible is saying, and in doing so applies his or her ideological and theological assumptions in an act of interpretive judgment. While these assumptions can be impediments to good interpretation, they are also, as Gadamer has pointed out, the necessary ground from which we read and understand. One might call this "lording it over" a text, but I would prefer to say that it is nothing other than the act of interpretation itself, in which the reader renders a judgment about what a text says and how its significance should be construed. If "lording it over" the biblical text ever occurs—and I believe that it often does—then it will come to pass not in the act of reading itself but when the reader has stopped listening to the text and proceeds, in an act of eisegetical violence, to infuse it with meanings that are foreign to it. But Vanhoozer knows all of this, so his objections are perhaps in a different direction.

I suspect that his real objection is that trajectory theology, by its very nature, purports to offer theological judgments that are superior to those offered in some texts of Scripture. It is this theological maneuver that he describes as "lording it over" the biblical text. Now Vanhoozer's objection would perhaps have traction if his were a proper description of trajectory theology, but trajectory theology does not purport to trump Scripture with a human viewpoint. It makes instead a more modest claim. It claims that Scripture has implicitly invited us to take a theological step beyond the written word by listening to God's living voice, which includes not only Scripture but also the voices of creation, tradition, and the Spirit. The necessity of this theological step is implied by the Bible's theological diversity itself, which is sure evidence that the church always has more theological work to do. In sum, taking biblical authority seriously does not preclude—but indeed requires—that we follow Scripture's theological trajectories to their apparent conclusions.

One final point on Marshall's monograph. Although Vanhoozer offers numerous and pointed criticisms of his book, in the end he affirms that Marshall's work is within the orbit of evangelical theology. Moreover, Vanhoozer confesses that the church must discover a theological approach that can go beyond the Bible *biblically*. This task is perhaps the most important theological challenge that faces contemporary evangelical theology.

Biblical Theology and the Christian Metanarrative

Here, on the heels of my discussion of biblical authority, is a fitting place to briefly consider the concept of "biblical theology." I am not referring to the modern biblical theology movement discussed in chapter 5 but rather to the older type of biblical theology as envisioned many years ago by J. P. Gabler, which understood biblical theology in terms of its contrast with systematic theology.[38] The problem that confronted Gabler and other biblical scholars in the eighteenth century was their perception that dogmatic theology tended to demand or exclude certain readings of Scripture, so that Scripture could no longer speak with authority in the church. Gabler provided no concrete examples of the problem in his lecture on the matter, but I suspect that he had in mind those occasions where biblical scholars find one thing (a contradiction between two or more of the Gospels) and theologians want to find something else (no contradictions). Gabler's objective, at least ostensibly, was to liberate biblical scholarship from the constraints of dogmatic and systematic theology, so that the Bible could finally "speak for itself." This project has taken on a particular character in modern evangelical circles, however. Whereas Gabler's biblical theology was quite comfortable with the Bible's theological diversity, in its modern evangelical incarnation biblical theology has normally assumed that the biblical books, in spite of their superficial differences, present us with a single and univocal theological viewpoint that can be analytically reconstructed by organizing the Bible's content into a conceptual whole.[39] In this model of theology there are no genuine conflicts or tensions within the Bible, nor between the Bible and other things. Scripture speaks with one clear voice, and its voice is nothing other than its explicit content. If and when we must go beyond this explicit content to consider theological questions and issues exterior to it, this is considered an operation of systematic or dogmatic theology rather than of biblical theology. As such, these "higher" levels of theology—systematic and dogmatic—do not hold the same sort of authority as biblical theology. Dogmatic theology can err, but the Bible's theology—properly understood—will never err. For this reason, one finds evangelicals who can insist that "our proclamation of the gospel [should] be a subset of biblical theology."[40]

---

38. J. P. Gabler, "De justo descrimine theologiae biblicae et dogmaticae regundisque recte ultriusque finibus," *Kleinere Theologische Schriften* 2 (1831): 179–98 (English translation: "An Oration on the Proper Distinction between Biblical and Dogmatic Theology and the Specific Objectives of Each," trans. John Sandys-Wunsch and Laurence Eldredge, in *The Flowering of Old Testament Theology*, ed. Ben C. Ollenburger, Elmer A. Martens, and Gerhard Hasel [Winona Lake, IN: Eisenbrauns, 1992], 489–502). For a modern assessment of Gabler's work, see John Sandys-Wunsch and Laurence Eldredge, "J. P. Gabler and the Distinction between Biblical and Dogmatic Theology: Translation, Commentary, and Discussion of His Originality," *SJT* 33 (1980): 133–58.

39. For example, see Walter C. Kaiser Jr., *Toward an Old Testament Theology* (Grand Rapids: Zondervan, 1978).

40. Donald A. Carson, *The Gagging of God: Christianity Confronts Pluralism* (Grand Rapids: Zondervan, 1996), 502.

This is, at least, a common evangelical understanding of the relationship between biblical and systematic theology.

If biblical theology is defined in this rigid fashion, then my arguments in this book have called into question the whole notion of biblical theology. As biblical scholars have shown us, the Bible does not contain a single coherent theology but rather numerous theologies that sometimes stand in tension or even in contradiction with one another. This being so, it is no longer possible to envision biblical theology in the way that very conservative evangelicals construe it. To my mind, a better way to construe biblical theology is presented in the work of Rolf Knierim. In light of the Bible's theological diversity, Knierim has argued that biblical theology is a kind of systematic theology, since it must discern a logical coherence and consistency within a canonical collection that is neither entirely coherent nor perfectly consistent:[41] "We must be able to discern theologically legitimate priorities. We must ask which theology or theological aspect or notion governs others, and which is relative to, dependent upon, or governed by others. Ultimately, we must ask whether there is one aspect that dominates all others, is therefore fundamental, and must be understood as the criterion for the validity of all others."[42] The nature of Knierim's theological operation can be illustrated by our experiences with dreams. When we have them, our dreams feel genuinely real and authentic. This is precisely why we are so relieved to discover that our nightmares are "only dreams," and why we are so disappointed when our best dreams turn out to be illusions. But, whether they are good or bad, the interesting question raised by our dreams is this: If our dream experiences are so tangible and realistic, how is it that we can distinguish so easily between reality and dream worlds?

We are able to distinguish dreams from reality because one serves as the context for the other. Our dreams can be explained in light of the larger experience of human life, but our life experiences cannot be fitted into the diverse and disjointed world of our dreams. One context is more basic than the other and hence serves as the baseline for interpreting the other. Now Knierim's approach to biblical theology is something like this. When we read the Bible thoughtfully, we will be able to discern that it contains certain primary or basic theological principles that provide the larger context for interpreting the Bible's diverse theologies. We need not concern ourselves with what these basic criteria might be for Knierim. It is enough to see that biblical theology can succeed by using the Bible's basic principles as a template for ordering its theological diversity. We will have to make wise judgments about what these basic principles seem to be, and how the other materials in Scripture might be ordered on their basis.

While Knierim's approach to biblical theology strikes me as very profitable, I suspect that his analysis of biblical theology sells the Bible's unity short. Unity

---

41. Incidentally, this theoretical posture parallels very closely the approach and method originally proffered by J. P. Gabler in his biblical theology project.

42. Rolf P. Knierim, *The Task of Old Testament Theology: Method and Cases* (Grand Rapids: Eerdmans, 1995), 9.

and diversity are not mutually exclusive qualities. A circle of theologians with different and even contradictory perspectives can often find room for substantial theological agreement. In the same way, it seems to me that Scripture's diversity can be fruitfully understood as the foreground of a larger unity that lies behind it. As a case in point, I and many others believe that the basic shape of the Christian canon displays a strong narrative character, a story line about the progress of redemption that begins with creation in Genesis and ends with recreation in Revelation.[43] So in spite of the Bible's obvious diversity, there is a genuine sense in which it reads like a single book and tells a single story. It is this biblical story—with Christ and his work at its conceptual center, as the clue to history—that shapes our Christian thought about reality and theology.[44] To take this line of thought a step farther, insofar as the biblical story is *God's account of human history*, it is what modern theorists call a *metanarrative*. A metanarrative is an attempt to explain the significance and destiny of human history by telling a story. It purports to be the grand story by which all other stories and claims about reality are to be judged. Of course, every culture, society, and religion has its metanarrative or metanarratives, but Christians believe that the Bible, as an account of God's project in history, is the true story that reveals where these others stories get things right or wrong. I believe that this is right, so far as it goes. But the matter needs to be considered in more detail.

Metanarratives are viewed with suspicion these days. It was Jean-François Lyotard, the French philosopher, who finally summed up the spirit of left-wing postmodernism on this matter.[45] For Lyotard, and for deconstructionists of his ilk, metanarratives are dangerous because, as totalizing projects, they quickly become agendas of control and oppression, which seek to stamp out every element of diversity in the quest for one grand unity. One could think here of the Nazi metanarrative, or of the great conflict in our own day between the metanarratives of Islamic fundamentalism and globalization (global economic growth).[46] Insofar as Christianity's metanarrative is understood in this frame of reference, its gospel will hardly pass for "good news." Now I will freely admit that Christian mission has often been clothed with an oppressive agenda, of the sort that Lyotard and others fear so much. But our study of Scripture has revealed, I think, that the Christian faith, *when biblically construed*, steers a healthy path between open-ended

---

43. Craig G. Bartholomew and Michael W. Goheen, *The Drama of Scripture: Finding Our Place in the Biblical Story* (Grand Rapids: Baker Academic, 2004); Richard Bauckham, "Reading Scripture as a Coherent Story," in *The Art of Reading Scripture*, ed. Ellen F. Davis and Richard B. Hays (Grand Rapids: Eerdmans, 2003), 38–53; Raymond Van Leeuwen, "Reading the Bible Whole in a Culture of Divided Hearts," *Ex Auditu* 19 (2003): 1–21; N. T. Wright, *The New Testament and the People of God*, Christian Origins and the Question of God 1 (Minneapolis: Fortress, 1992).

44. Lesslie Newbigin, *The Gospel in a Pluralist Society* (Grand Rapids: Eerdmans, 1989), 103–15.

45. Jean-François Lyotard, *The Postmodern Condition: A Report on Knowledge*, trans. Geoff Bennington and Brian Massumi (Minneapolis: University of Minnesota Press, 1984).

46. Richard Bauckham, *Bible and Mission: Christian Witness in a Postmodern World* (Grand Rapids: Baker Academic, 2003), 1–11.

relativisim and tyrannical totalitarianism. The Bible's unity is real but partial, and certainly not final. Its materials are diverse and untidy, so that Richard Bauckham can rightly say, "There are too many fragments that seem to lead nowhere and too many that seem to point in opposite directions."[47] Consequently, it is to our theological detriment that we "finish" our biblical metanarrative, as if we had finally arrived at a proper summary of it. So, though our theological work will certainly need to presuppose such a metanarrative, we will always presuppose that it is something partial that we are still working to fully grasp. I have argued that to do this properly, we will have to read the Bible dialectically against the context of the whole. This context includes not only the canon of Scripture itself but also the voices of creation, tradition, and the Spirit, as well as the facts of history, language, and culture. No book or story is self-contained and hermetically sealed from the concrete realities that make its discourse sensible.

The Spiritual and Psychological Health of the Interpreter

If interpretation involves "listening to the Spirit," then good interpretation depends to some extent on the spiritual and psychological health of the interpreter. In the context of the present discussion, however, the spiritual dimensions of biblical interpretation should be approached with prudence and caution. This is not because I wish to deny a vital connection between spiritual health and good theology. Such a relationship surely exists. If caution is in order, it is because very conservative Christians have sometimes unfairly blamed the "problems" of biblical criticism on the spiritual weakness of biblical critics. The conservative argument usually goes something like this: "Biblical critics are not Christians, and, as Paul has said, 'The man without the Spirit does not accept the things that come from the Spirit of God, for they are foolishness to him, and he cannot understand them, because they are spiritually discerned' (1 Cor. 2:14 NIV)." End of argument. According to this line of thought, the critics err because they do not share our faith assumptions and/or because they lack the resources of the Holy Spirit.[48] So we may safely ignore their pagan version of "scholarship."

If there is one perspective that I am challenging in this book, it is the fideistic perspective embodied in the argument that I have just described. While I do not doubt for a minute that the spiritual dimensions of biblical interpretation are of grave importance, this argument against biblical criticism is specious for two important reasons. First, many thoughtful, confessing Christians appreciate the

---

47. Ibid., 93.
48. See Fred H. Klooster, "The Role of the Holy Spirit in the Hermeneutic Process," Wilber T. Dayton, "A Response to the Role of the Holy Spirit in the Hermeneutic Process," and Art Lindsley, "A Response to the Role of the Holy Spirit in the Hermeneutic Process," in *Hermeneutics, Inerrancy, and the Bible: Papers from ICBI Summit II*, ed. Earl D. Radmacher and Robert D. Preus (Grand Rapids: Zondervan, 1984), 451–72, 475–84, 487–92, respectively.

robust character of modern biblical scholarship. So there is adequate evidence that those with the appropriate "spiritual qualifications" are endorsing and practicing historical criticism. Second, this fundamentalist argument against "secular knowledge" is based upon a serious misreading of Paul. As I argued earlier in this chapter in my discussion of Romans 7:13–25, the linchpin of Paul's argument in Romans is that fallen human beings can indeed understand the truth of God in some sense. He is even willing to say that they "clearly" see and understand God's "divine nature" (Rom. 1:20 NIV). That is Paul's position, and if that is his position, then our reading of 1 Corinthians 2:14 will probably need to go in a different direction than that followed by some fundamentalists. The text will not mean that one needs great spiritual insight in order to understand the historical and social context of the Bible and its verbal discourse. It will mean instead that one needs spiritual insight in order to *believe* and *obey* the Spirit's discourse in Scripture. So Paul's words in 1 Corinthians certainly have profound implications for a Christian understanding of interpretation, but not the implications that the fundamentalist arguments against biblical criticism think they have.

Let me clarify Paul's point by following his rhetoric in 1 Corinthians a bit further, focusing as I do on the implications of his words for the task of biblical interpretation. His words in a slightly larger context read as follows:

> We have not received the spirit of the world but the Spirit who is from God, that we may understand what God has freely given us. This is what we speak, not in words taught us by human wisdom but in words taught by the Spirit, expressing spiritual truths in spiritual words. The man without the Spirit does not accept the things that come from the Spirit of God, for they are foolishness to him, and he cannot understand them, because they are spiritually discerned. (1 Cor. 2:12–14 NIV)

For Paul, the words of Scripture reflect the Spirit's wisdom about truth and God. Regarded in this way, these words can be received and believed only by those who have God's Spirit. When we read this simple and straightforward passage in the light of Paul's discourse in Romans, we can surmise that the interpretation of Scripture—if we wish to *understand* Scripture faithfully—involves at least two fundamental steps. We must first render a judgment about what the discourse says, and then pass judgment on it. By this I mean that we must first assess the meaning of words themselves and then decide whether we find them true, wise, and helpful, or merely fanciful and foolish. This is, incidentally, the same two-step process that we use for interpreting any piece of discourse: first we understand it, then we decide whether we agree with it. Though I do not believe that Paul in 1 Corinthians was contemplating consciously the two-step hermeneutic that I have just described, in 1 Corinthians he does seem to have in mind what I have called the second interpretive step. He is telling us that readers who lack the Spirit's illumination cannot properly assess the significance and import of biblical discourse. To use the terms of this book, we might say that critical scholarship can clear the first hurdle of biblical interpretation (it can understand what Paul said), but it cannot clear the second hurdle (understanding what to do about it).

At first glance this will mean that Christian readers of Scripture enjoy a significant advantage over non-Christian readers. Though there is some truth in this, even profound truth in it, as a simple assertion it is not always true,[49] because, as is painfully obvious, Christian readers of Scripture often fail on both steps of biblical interpretation. We fail to understand what the Bible says, and we fail to assess the truth and significance of its verbal discourse for Christian living. When we fail on this second point, on the spiritual assessment of the discourse, this is precisely because we are not yet spiritually prepared to embrace the words that we have understood. Perhaps we are so controlled by financial insecurities that we fail to "give cheerfully." Or perhaps we are so habitually angry that we do not embody those beautiful spiritual fruits, "love, joy, peace, patience, and kindness." Or perhaps we are so self-absorbed that we consistently use people as tools to fulfill our wishes. Or perhaps we so fear for our safety that we ignore God's call to "go and make disciples of all nations." It is only in the context of our union with Christ, and of our faith experience with him—in prayer and service—that we become men and women who not only hear but also believe and follow God in these matters.

This point was often made by the church's early fathers. Gregory of Nazianzus declared that scriptural study "is permitted only to those who have been examined, and are past masters in meditation, and who have been previously purified in body and soul, or at the very least are being purified."[50] Athanasius said something similar: "Anyone who wishes to understand the mind of the sacred writers must first cleanse his own life, and approach the saints by copying their deeds."[51] The connection between spiritual life and exegesis was very close for the fathers because they knew, as does the evangelical James I. Packer, that *"one can know a great deal about God without much knowledge of Him."*[52] There is no substitute in biblical interpretation for knowing God intimately and personally. So there is no full-orbed interpretation of Scripture until, by the Spirit, the words of the text have become our Christian praxis, the actual doing of what God has called us to do.

Sensitivity to the Spirit's voice is even more important if the Bible's theology is as diverse as I am suggesting. It is one thing to follow Scripture when it consistently tells me to worship Yahweh and reject idol worship. It is quite another thing to follow Scripture's lead when I am confronted by contradictory discourses like "kill the Canaanites" and "love your enemies," or "beat your slaves" and "treat slaves

---

49. See I. Howard Marshall, "The Holy Spirit and the Interpretation of Scripture," in *Rightly Divided: Readings in Biblical Hermeneutics*, ed. Roy B. Zuck (Grand Rapids: Kregel, 1996), 66–74.

50. "The First Theological Oration," quoted from Christopher A. Hall, *Reading Scripture with the Church Fathers* (Downers Grove, IL: InterVarsity, 1998), 41–42.

51. "On the Incarnation," quoted from Hall, *Reading Scripture*, 41.

52. James I. Packer, *Knowing God* (Downers Grove, IL: InterVarsity, 1973), 21.

kindly," or "circumcise" and "don't circumcise." As I have noted already, the early church was able to discern a theological path through this diversity by following the Spirit's lead. The same must be true for us. Prayer, worship, and sacrament are the amniotic fluids of full-orbed theological reflection. They are spiritual activities that we undertake *as* individuals and *in* communities, and they put us in touch with God's voice. But we should remind ourselves, lest we forget, that "piety and faithfulness are no guarantee of truth."[53] In the end, there are no substitutes for good critical skills, nor for a healthy relationship with God.

Of course, healthy interpretations of Scripture require not only spiritual but also psychological wholeness, though the two elements cannot be wholly separated from each other. As Calvin has argued, "Without knowledge of self there is no knowledge of God," and "Without knowledge of God there is no knowledge of self."[54] This connection has been admitted even by fairly secular theorists like Carl Jung, who said that "every psychological problem is ultimately a matter of religion."[55] When our psychological difficulties are of the spiritual sort, then one aspect of our psychological healing will be our spiritual healing. At the same time, the interventions necessary to allay these difficulties will sometimes be psychological rather than merely theological. This is truer still when our psychological difficulties cannot be traced to any spiritual causes. Medications may be necessary, as well as in-depth analyses of personal experiences, of relationships, and of feelings and beliefs about self, others, and God. These interventions are carried out by competent professionals, who have been adequately trained in the appropriate pharmacology and in the art and science of human psychology. As for me, I am neither a psychologist nor the son of a psychologist, so I will not go very far with this. My primary point is that our psychological difficulties, whether they are minor neurotic fears or more serious varieties of psychosis, exert a profound influence on our interpretation of Scripture. This influence appears not only in our reading of Scripture's discourse but also in our appropriation of the message that we read. For this reason, interpreters of Scripture have the responsibility to care for their souls by attending to their spiritual and psychological health. Whole persons, who are spiritually and psychologically healthy and emotionally mature, make the best interpreters of Scripture. Reading Scripture in the context of the whole involves a correct interpretation of the self as well as of Scripture and the created order.

The subject of psychological health in interpretation is uniquely poignant for evangelicalism because of the movement's fundamentalist roots and its persistently close relationship with fundamentalism.[56] Several studies have demonstrated that

---

53. John Goldingay, *Models for Scripture* (Grand Rapids: Eerdmans, 1994), 312.
54. John Calvin, *Institutes of the Christian Religion*, trans. Henry Beveridge, 2 vols. (London: J. Clarke, 1949), 1:37–39; see also Jens Zimmermann, *Recovering Theological Hermeneutics: An Incarnational-Trinitarian Theory of Interpretation* (Grand Rapids: Baker Academic, 2004), 29–36.
55. Thomas Moore, *Care of the Soul* (New York: HarperCollins, 1992), xii.
56. Mark A. Noll, *The Scandal of the Evangelical Mind* (Grand Rapids: Eerdmans, 1994), 137; George M. Marsden, *Understanding Fundamentalism and Evangelicalism* (Grand Rapids: Eerdmans, 1991).

Christian fundamentalism is one of many religious fundamentalisms that have emerged in response to the modern age.[57] One can as easily speak of Islamic, Jewish, Hindu, Sikh, and even Marxist fundamentalisms. It goes too far to say that these fundamentalisms reflect mental illness, but neither are they the products of psychological wholeness.[58] At its heart, each of these movements views modernism as a threat to the stability of culture and to the predictability of life. Fundamentalists yearn for a world in which all is fixed and certain. For this reason they militantly eschew anything and anyone that introduces doubt, uncertainty, or ambiguity into their worldview. This ideology puts fundamentalism into direct conflict with modernism because modernity is the product of a world gone international and intercultural. But modernity is not the creator of pluralism, as fundamentalists often suppose. Modernity's pluralism is instead the inevitable consequence of human diversity—and it is contact with this diversity, and its "pollution," that fundamentalism fears.

Fundamentalism's response to modernism is a kind of ideological paranoia that features two interrelated defensive strategies. First, every fundamentalism secures the uniqueness of its worldview by claiming access to an inerrant text or authority that provides perfect knowledge. This assertion not only secures the validity of the community's beliefs but also ensures that the beliefs of outsiders are in error. Nothing is more important to a fundamentalist than being right and being sure of it. Fundamentalism's second defensive strategy erects a thick cultural wall between the community and those outside it. The primary purpose of this wall is to prevent contact with opposing views that might challenge or raise too much doubt about the community's worldview. As a rule, this barrier is constructed by forbidding or greatly discouraging the study of materials that come from those outside the fundamentalist guild. For instance, while Christian fundamentalists are quite likely to read descriptions of modern evolutionary theory that have been written by other fundamentalists, they would rarely study a book that was written by an evolutionist, or study evolutionary biology in a university setting. For most fundamentalists, such pursuits would be a waste of time at best, and downright dangerous at worst.

The nature of fundamentalism's intellectual insularity is made clearer by turning again to the concept of the hermeneutical circle. As we have seen, human beings make sense of reality by relating the whole to the parts and the parts to the whole. So there is an inevitable circularity in all human thinking. In fundamentalism, however, this circularity takes the form of a vicious circle, which we would commonly describe as circular reasoning. It is not that circularity itself is a problem;

---

57. Richard T. Antoun, *Understanding Fundamentalism: Christian, Islamic, and Jewish Movements* (Walnut Creek, CA: Altamira, 2001); Norman J. Cohen, ed., *The Fundamentalist Phenomenon: A View from Within; A Response from Without* (Grand Rapids: Eerdmans, 1990); Martin E. Marty and R. Scott Appleby, *Fundamentalisms Comprehended* (Chicago: University of Chicago Press, 1995).

58. Mortimer Ostow, "The Fundamentalism Phenomenon: A Psychological Perspective," in Cohen, *Fundamentalist Phenomenon*, 99–125.

as I have pointed out, all human thought has this circular or spiral property. No, the difficulty in circular reasoning is that it includes far fewer pieces of reality than it should. It juggles a few balls successfully when there are many other balls that should be juggled. Fundamentalists attempt to perpetuate this illusion of hermeneutical success by denying the existence of the extra balls. But so long as Christian fundamentalists live in the real world, they will face an almost constant barrage of evidence that does not fit their view of things—evidence that the universe is very old, that evolution is true, that languages were not created at the tower of Babel, that there was no worldwide flood, and so forth. This is a list that could be easily extended. It is pitiful and even painful to watch as naive fundamentalist students nervously and fearfully traverse their first university Bible classes, flailing desperately to keep their heads above the water in a sea of evidence that neither they, nor their parents and pastors, suspected could exist. At the same time, it is truly exciting to see thoughtful and healthy Christian students, fully committed to the theological orthodoxies of the Christian tradition, who are able to traverse those same seas with a spirit of enthusiasm for discovery. Fundamentalism fears the evidence that challenges its views; healthy Christian orthodoxy revels in the evidence, since it believes that all evidence, properly understood, will lead to a healthier view of life and faith.

In the final analysis, Christian fundamentalism may indeed share many basic commitments with traditional Christian orthodoxy,[59] but as a religious ideology its temperaments are often intellectually and psychologically unhealthy. In certain respects, its adherents perpetuate the very obsession that stood behind original sin: an obsession for God's perfect knowledge, and for the totalitizing power that supposedly comes with it. A far better theological route will be satisfied with the God-ordained limitations on human intellect and perception. Christians should have no fear of mystery.[60]

Reason, Faith, and Mystery

This route leads to my next point and back to the primary theme of this chapter: the context of the whole and its proper role in biblical interpretation. Christian theology requires that, as best we can, we should attend to this broad context—including creation, Scripture, and the Christian tradition—and that we should properly order our gleanings from these sources into the most coherent whole

---

59. Jaroslav Pelikan, "Fundamentalism and/or Orthodoxy? Toward an Understanding of the Fundamentalist Phenomenon," in Cohen, *Fundamentalist Phenomenon*, 3–21.

60. But all of this said, the existence and perpetuation of fundamentalism is probably inevitable. In a famous landmark study of human perception and interpretation, Bruner and Postman demonstrated that the temperaments of fundamentalism—a thirst for stability and resistance to ambiguity—occur more strongly in a modest but significant portion of the population. See J. S. Bruner and L. Postman. "On the Perception of Incongruity: A Paradigm," *Journal of Personality* 18 (1949): 206–23.

that is possible. But on what basis shall we order these diverse materials? I would suggest that it is easy to answer this question. As in any other pursuit of understanding, we use our wits—our rational capacities—to make coherent sense of what we see. There is no other way to do it. Interpretation is nothing other than a search for rational coherence, an attempt to understand how the parts fit the whole and how the whole relates to the many parts. That is how interpretation works. Nevertheless, my straightforward description of the process does not make the process easy. It can be very difficult to determine how we should properly construe the relationship between the voices of Scripture, tradition, and the created order. To make matters more complicated, my emphasis on the rationality of interpretation raises several important issues and questions.

First, we should note that there is an ongoing debate about the extent to which our rational capacities were casualties of Adam's fall. According to medieval theologian Thomas Aquinas and those of his ilk (called "Thomists"), human reason was not wholly marred by the fall and so provides an essential tool for seeing things rightly in a postlapsarian world. To put the matter crudely, Aquinas would say that reason prepares us for faith in Christ, inasmuch as it can supply certain foundations for our faith, such as a belief in God. Catholic theologians commonly embrace this Thomist perspective, but some Protestants—particularly of the more conservative stripe—view Thomism as offering an incomplete understanding of the fall's consequences. On their analysis of history (let us take Carl Henry's view as an example), it was Aquinas's recklessly high view of human reason that opened the door for natural or philosophical theology apart from biblical revelation; this in turn bred the theological liberalism of the modern and postmodern age.[61] Such is the essence of this debate about human reason.

Now regarding these non-Thomist concerns, I wish to point out two things and then draw several conclusions. First, one of the fundamental assertions of Thomist theology is the concept of dual agency, the belief that every successful exercise of reason by human agents takes place in the context of divine agency. This will mean that, for Aquinas, there is no success in our natural theology apart from the workings of divine providence. The proper exercise of our reason is *always* aided by God.[62] My second point is that Aquinas has expressed very clearly in the *Summa* that the theological successes of reason, whatever they may be, are incomplete apart from the special revelation that by grace has been given to us in Scripture and through Christ.[63] If one follows these points carefully, then it becomes clear that the crucial distinction between Thomists and non-Thomists does not concern reason per se. Rather, the real difference regards

---

61. For a critique of Aquinas, see Carl F. H. Henry, *God, Revelation, and Authority*, 6 vols. (Waco: Word, 1976–1983), 1:184–85.

62. A. N. Williams, "Argument to Bliss: The Epistemology of the *Summa Theologiae*," *Modern Theology* 20 (2004): 505–26.

63. Thomas Aquinas, *Summa Theologica*, pt. 1, q. 75–89; pt. 1.2, q. 82–85, in *The Summa Theologica*, 5 vols. (Allen, TX: Christian Classics, 1981), 1:363–458; 2:956–71.

their concepts of agency. But the matter of agency aside, the charge often leveled against Aquinas—that he had denied the fall of our rational capacities—stems from a careless reading of Aquinas. He believed that our rational capacities were disordered by the fall, and for that reason he believed, like Henry and everyone else, that we will get some things right and some things wrong. So, in the final analysis, I do not believe that one's position on Thomism necessarily affects our present discussion of hermeneutics.

These deliberations on human reason inevitably bring to mind that age-old discussion of the relationship between reason and faith. Scripture teaches often that we should have faith in God rather than in the vagaries of human wisdom. "Lean not on your own understanding," says the sage of Proverbs (3:5 NIV). But where is the room for faith in a worldview so rationally ordered as I have described above? This is an important and reasonable question, so I shall try to answer it, albeit in a perfunctory way.

We cannot begin to think rationally without believing something beforehand. Every use of rationality therefore depends upon and operates by some set of faith assumptions. For the Christian, these faith assumptions cause us to see things that unbelievers will not see, and this will mean that our rationality must juggle balls that others do not have to juggle. If I recognize by faith that God exists and that he will serve as the final judge of human action, then in my ethical reflection I will have to consider a number of things that an unbeliever can happily (if naively and unfortunately) ignore. A chief difficulty of course is that our faith, no less than our rational judgment, can be mistaken. This suggests that faith and reason subsist within a kind of mutual dialectic, where beliefs pass muster because they help reason to make better sense of things, and reason stands ready to question faith when new or better faith commitments might be more sensible. This faith-reason dialectic highlights two possible noetic pathologies. In the case of *fideism*, we hold so tightly to our concept of "the faith" that strong rational evidence against its claims are ignored; in the other, which usually goes by the name of *rationalism*, we trust our reason to the exclusion of necessary faith commitments, in what amounts to doubting the goodness and faithfulness of God. Sound Christian thinking therefore depends upon a healthy equilibrium between faith and reason, an equilibrium that avoids the errant extremes of fideism and rationalism.

Fideism has crossed our path already in chapter 4, so I have nothing else to say about it at this point. There is, however, something more to discuss about the problem of rationalism. One feature of human rationality is that it has the ability to recognize its own limits. We are able to notice when we cannot figure out something. Our ability to notice this rational limit is imperfect and can sometimes fail, but it is indeed a capacity that we possess. Rational*ism* is essentially a failure to use this capacity. It is a misplaced trust in our rational abilities, whose chief symptom is a tendency to push our rational exercises beyond their useful limit. The problem is fairly easy to illustrate. One perennial theological debate centers on the apparent tension between God's sovereignty and human freedom. Is God so sovereign over the human will that our decisions are never really free (the classic Reformed position), or do human beings possess a God-given freedom of the will (the classic Arminian position)? The Reformed viewpoint is based especially on Romans 9, and on similar texts like Proverbs 21:1 and Ephesians 1:11, which describe God as predetermining our spiritual destinies and as controlling our human decisions by either hardening or softening our wills toward himself. From this it is deduced that all biblical texts dealing with the human will describe wills that are under God's sovereign control and hence wills that are not free. As for the Arminian view, it is based on many other texts (the vast majority of the Bible) that imply that God invites all to respond to him (John 3:16–17), that he wishes for us to respond to him (2 Pet. 3:9), that he takes no pleasure when we do not (Ezek. 18:23), and that we are responsible for our choices. "What sort of choice does God offer," reason the Arminians, "if human beings lack the free capacity to respond appropriately?" From this some deduce that God does not sovereignly predestine our spiritual destinies.

What shall we make of this theological debate, in which both sides seem to have Scripture on their side? May I respectfully suggest that we cannot do justice to the Bible's account of things unless we conclude that there is something profoundly true about both of these positions. God is sovereign over the human soul, and human beings choose freely. I would agree that these twin propositions seem inherently contradictory and that, if both are true, our attempts to see how they cohere will end in a rational cul-de-sac. This cul-de-sac is precisely what has troubled both Reformed and Arminian theologians, and it is precisely why each tradition has felt compelled to make a choice and leave the other view in the dust. I believe that this way of construing the situation, as if we had come to a fork in the theological road, is not the best way to understand our theological predicament. A better approach would accentuate that *mystery* is an important ingredient in any healthy theology.[64] We are free to assert that God is sovereign and that humans are free, and to confess at the same time that we do not have a rational resolution for how both assertions can be true. *Antinomy* is the technical name for such rational conflicts, where we find it necessary to embrace two conflicting principles as true because each seems valid and necessary. This is now a well-known move in modern physics, where scientists recognize the inherent tension between the reigning theories of general relativity (the physics of big things) and quantum mechanics (the physics of very small things). Perhaps the new string theories will one day resolve this tension, but until they do, modern

---

64. I note in passing that I am no more satisfied with the "middle knowledge" approach, espoused especially by William Lane Craig, than with either of the two more traditional solutions I mention here. In the end, as Basinger has pointed out, Craig's thesis lands him back in the Calvinist camp, since God merely manipulates circumstances to control "free" exercises of the human will. See William Lane Craig, "Middle Knowledge: A Calvinist-Arminian Rapprochement?" in *The Grace of God, the Will of Man*, ed. Clark H. Pinnock (Grand Rapids: Zondervan, 1989), 141–64; David Basinger, "Divine Control and Human Freedom: Is Middle Knowledge the Answer?" *JETS* 36 (1993): 55–64.

physicists seem prepared to embrace the antinomy. Theologians could probably benefit by following this scientific lead. It is no accident that Paul concludes his long discourse on Israel and predestination with this humble benediction:

> Oh, the depth of the riches of the wisdom and knowledge of God! How unsearchable his judgments, and his paths beyond tracing out! "Who has known the mind of the Lord? Or who has been his counselor?" "Who has ever given to God, that God should repay him?" For from him and through him and to him are all things. To him be the glory forever! Amen. (Rom. 11:33–36 NIV)

Should we conclude from this text that Paul himself did not understand how God's sovereignty and human freedom could be true at the same time? I think that we can, particularly if we attend to the historical evidence from ancient Judaism. In the Wisdom of Ben Sirah, a Jewish text dating to the second century BCE, the author asserts quite explicitly both that human beings have "free choice" (15:14) and that their destinies are determined by God, who like a clay potter "appointed their different ways," some for blessing and others for a curse (33:10–13). The description of God's sovereignty here is so close to the description in Romans 9 that scholars are quite sure that Paul's ideas about predestination were in some respect influenced by Ben Sirah's theology;[65] this conclusion is made more likely by the fact that Paul's Bible, the Greek Septuagint, contained Ben Sirah. If Paul agreed with Ben Sirah's portrait of God as a clay potter who determines human destinies, then he may well have believed the other assertion of Ben Sirah: that human beings have free will. In the world of ancient Judaism, and I suspect for the apostle as well, true wisdom did not choose between the two alternatives.

The role of mystery in theology was accentuated in two well-received books in the 1990s,[66] and two of my university colleagues—Steven Boyer and Christopher Hall—will soon add another. What all of these scholars wish to emphasize is that modern theology, with its desire to dot every *i* and cross every *t*, tends to "domesticate transcendence" (so Placher).[67] I suspect that a better approach to theology would make ample space for mystery by resisting the temptation to reach final closure in our systematic theologies. Sometimes this will involve embracing mysterious antinomies, and in other instances it will require genuine confessions of ignorance: "We simply do not know." Good theology appreciates the inevitable distinction between the infinite scope of divine knowledge and the very limited

---

65. James D. G. Dunn, *Romans*, 2 vols., WBC (Dallas: Word, 1988), 2:559, 565; Robert Jewett, *Romans: A Commentary,* Hermeneia (Minneapolis: Fortress, 2007), 594; John Piper, *The Justification of God: An Exegetical and Theological Study of Romans 9:1–23* (Grand Rapids: Baker Academic, 1983), 176; E. Elizabeth Johnson, *The Function of Apocalyptic and Wisdom Traditions in Romans 9–11*, SBLDS 109 (Atlanta: Scholars Press, 1989), 149.

66. Andrew Louth, *Discerning the Mystery: An Essay on the Nature of Theology* (Oxford: Clarendon, 1990); William C. Placher, *The Domestication of Transcendence* (Louisville: Westminster John Knox, 1996).

67. Placher, *Domestication of Transcendence.*

scope of human knowledge (Job 1–3, 38–41). The only caveat that I would offer on this point is that we should avoid appealing to mystery too carelessly, since the very notion of theology implies that we can indeed say something true about God (and about other things). Certain contemporary evangelical movements, such as the so-called emerging church, sometimes seem to make too much of mystery and not enough of valid theology.[68]

Miracles, History, and Historical Criticism

At this point I am nearing the end of my conceptual portrait of interpretation as it should be practiced in the context of the whole. As I do, it is fitting that we finally address the perennial and sometimes perplexing conflict that has long raged between historical criticism and the church's belief in miracles. Can the Christian scholar affirm the miracles of the Bible and at the same time practice historical criticism, an approach to the biblical text that almost always seems to deny that miracles have occurred?

It is true that many biblical scholars doubt the historicity of the Bible's miracles. When it comes to the history of ideas one rarely gets to the bottom of things, but if we are seeking the origins of modern skepticism about miracles—a skepticism that has for a long time dominated historical criticism—then we could do no better than to begin with David Hume's famous essay "On Miracles."[69] It was this little essay from 1748 that asserted what many modern scholars now believe: thoughtful, rational human beings have no business believing in miracles. Hume's influence can be traced in many directions. One thinks, for instance, of that well-known essay by F. H. Bradley, which attempted to distill, clarify, and extend the application of Hume's ideas to the emerging practice of historical criticism.[70] But by far the most influential advocate of Hume in biblical and theological studies was Ernst Troeltsch (1865–1923), whose work will provide the touchstone for my discussion.[71] In certain respects Troeltsch's arguments are outdated, for there have been many subsequent discussions in modern philosophy—discussions about causation, natural law, and personal agency—that have raised questions about some of his

---

68. For a prominent example of the movement's literature, see Brian D. McLaren, *A Generous Orthodoxy* (El Cajon, CA: Youth Specialties, 2004). For a somewhat misguided introduction to the movement, see Donald A. Carson, *Becoming Conversant with the Emerging Church* (Grand Rapids: Zondervan, 2005).

69. The essay appears in numerous anthologies and, of course, in David Hume, *An Enquiry concerning Human Understanding* (1748; repr. Oxford: Oxford University Press, 2000).

70. See "The Presuppositions of Critical History," which first appeared in 1874. For publication see F. H. Bradley, *Collected Essays*, 2 vols. (Oxford: Clarendon, 1935), 1:5–70.

71. Ernst Troeltsch, "Über historische und dogmatische Methode in der Theologie," in *Gesammelte Schriften*, 4 vols. (Tübingen: Mohr, 1913), 2:729–53; Troeltsch, "Historiography," in *Encyclopaedia of Religion and Ethics*, ed. James Hastings, 13 vols. (Edinburgh: T&T Clark, 1925), 6:716–23. For discussion see John J. Collins, "Is Critical Biblical Theology Possible?" in *The Hebrew Bible and Its Interpreters*, ed. William H. Propp, Baruch Halpern, and David Noel Freedman (Winona Lake, IN: Eisenbrauns, 1990), 1–17.

fundamental methodological assumptions. But many theologians and biblical scholars continue to find the basic thrust of his arguments persuasive.[72]

According to Troeltsch, our historical research should be carried out on the basis of three fundamental principles: (1) methodological doubt, (2) the principle of analogy, and (3) the principle of correlation. Let us consider each in turn. We came face-to-face with Troeltsch's first principle, methodological doubt, in our discussion of Descartes. This approach to historical inquiry assumes a critical stance toward the historical sources, so that the sources are not trusted until they are properly interrogated and considered. In certain respects this seems a fairly decent principle to employ, especially if one is a Christian historian. For on our faith-based account of things, we should anticipate that historical sources created by finite human beings will often deviate from accurate history. At the same time, in the previous chapters I have tried to show that full-blown methodological doubt is impossible. We simply cannot doubt every word of historical testimony and keep our sanity, still less escape our subjective presuppositions when we make historical judgments. So if we care at all about history, at some point we must inevitably trust historical testimony. Moreover, I believe that we have good reasons for doing so. As was brought out so well in the Common Sense philosophy of Thomas Reid, it is the very nature of human testimony—of a claim about the historical past—that it is more often true than not.[73] Lies are common enough, but in the final analysis lies are exceptions to the moral rule, else human life would be far more chaotic than it is. One can of course be too optimistic in these matters, by failing to take seriously the fallibilities of eyewitness perception or by overlooking the complex vagaries of testimony and tradition. C. A. J. Coady's excellent study of "testimony" has critiqued Reid at precisely these points.[74] But in the end Coady joins Reid in taking human testimony seriously. On these bases I would maintain that, though Troeltsch is undoubtedly right about the importance of examining the sources critically, he is mistaken to suggest that we can carry out our historical quests with complete objectivity, and equally mistaken to aver that we must always assume a skeptical posture toward our sources. "Cautious optimism" strikes me as far more sensible than "critical pessimism." But as Coady has suggested, we must always contend with the possibility that the sources in question are historically very poor, either because the testimony itself draws upon poor sources, or because the testimony is unduly influenced by errant ideologies, or because it turns out to be a pack of lies.

But let us imagine that Troeltsch will allow this concession, and that we can begin our historical inquiries by cautiously trusting rather than doubting historical testimony. Even if this were so, when we turn to the Bible we would immediately

---

72. Troeltsch's influence on these scholars has often been indirect, coming as it does from disciples like Van A. Harvey, *The Historian and the Believer* (New York: Macmillan, 1966).

73. For discussion see Nicholas Wolterstorff, *Thomas Reid and the Story of Epistemology* (Cambridge: Cambridge University Press, 2001), 163–84.

74. C. A. J. Coady, *Testimony: A Philosophical Study* (Oxford: Clarendon, 1992), 120–29.

trip over Troeltsch's second principle of historical research. According to Troeltsch, historical knowledge is possible because the events of human history are governed by certain patterns. We may assume, for instance, that the so-called laws of nature at work in our own day were those at work in the recent past and in antiquity. It is on this very principle, the principle of historical analogy, that most of us doubt or discount the miracle stories offered by the non-Christian religions. Troeltsch wholly agrees with this logic but then wants to press the point home: if we do well to doubt the miracles of India on this principle, are we not obliged as well to doubt the miracles of Scripture? I must confess that the rationale behind this question strikes me as fairly clear and sensible, for any who are honest—including believing Christians—will admit that the principle of historical analogy generally governs our conduct in everyday life and in our scholarly work. As one evangelical philosopher, C. Stephen Evans, expressed it:

> there is a sense in which a moderate version of this methodological naturalism might be acceptable to the believer in miracles. The believer in miracles does not wish to endorse gullible superstition. She may agree that miracles are strange and surprising things, and, particularly if she is inclined to think that genuine miracles are highly unusual... she will agree that some degree of initial skepticism is reasonable when faced with miracle claims.[75]

Consequently, if we wish to defend our belief in the historicity of biblical miracles, then we will need to explain why the tacit, naturalistic assumptions that influence our everyday historical judgments are more or less set aside in the case of the biblical miracles. I will return to this theme in a moment.

The third principle that governs Troeltsch's historical inquiry, the principle of correlation, asserts that the various phenomena of history are interrelated events, so that every event of history inevitably participates in the historical sequence of cause and effect. Consequently, if events are truly historical, then they will fit into the historical landscape as we have it. Historical events will have anterior events that lead up to them, as well as posterior events that proceed from them. Here again, I suspect that we evangelicals are more or less forced by our own habits to agree with Troeltsch. For in our everyday life as well as in our serious research, we assume—like everyone else—that our experiences fit more or less neatly into the sequence of historical events. If my car keys are missing, my immediate response is to reconstruct the moments leading up to and following their disappearance. I do not suspect that the keys were taken by demons, or by angels. Historical research is impossible without the principle of correlation. But this is precisely the problem with miracles. For it is the very nature of the case that miracles are not caused by antecedent *historical* events. Their cause is not a product of human agency or of natural events; their immediate cause is divine agency, which moves into history

---

75. C. Stephen Evans, *The Historical Christ and the Jesus of Faith: The Incarnational Narrative as History* (Oxford: Clarendon, 1996), 159.

from without. This will necessarily mean that in at least some respects miracles will defy the usual arguments and evidence that we use to reconstruct history. If the body of our friend is missing from the grave, then our first assumption will undoubtedly be that someone moved it (principle of analogy), and our second assumption will be that an investigation of circumstances anterior and posterior to the body's disappearance will lead to its recovery (principle of correlation).

Here is the difficulty for the believer. Although we can plainly see that much good sense attaches to Troeltsch's historical principles, so much so that we tacitly and even explicitly employ those principles in everyday life, these very principles are finally at odds with the fundamentals of Christian orthodoxy. Christian orthodoxy rests on a miracle: that God supernaturally entered human history in the person of Jesus Christ, and that Jesus Christ miraculously rose from the dead and ascended into heaven. This being so, the task at hand is either to demonstrate that our Christian commitments are not an exception to the rule, or to show why the Christian exception should be accepted when other exceptions are not.

Perhaps we can begin to address this difficulty by distinguishing two different types of miracles that appear in Scripture. Let us call them *providential miracles* and *sign miracles*. In the former God providentially guides the events of history behind the scenes, as he does in the stories of Ruth and Esther.[76] God is not mentioned in the book of Esther, and is hardly mentioned in Ruth. But we know that he is there in the story—everywhere. If one ventures through life by faith, as those women did, then one will see that God is at work in life's circumstances on behalf of those he loves. This is the first kind of miracle. The other sort of miracle provides an overt sign of God's supernatural power. I refer to these as "sign miracles" because they are not concealed within the events of history but occur—like the miracles of Elisha and Jesus—as obvious evidence that God's hand has moved in history. It is this second type of miracle, which Troeltschians will very much doubt, that interests me at this point. I wish to demonstrate that a belief in the historicity of sign miracles is very sensible, and to explain how we can make reasonable judgments about which of the biblical miracles actually occurred in history.

I will begin with this observation: Human traditions from every time, place, and culture bear testimonies of miraculous events. Though conservative Christians tend to assume that these are false testimonies, this assumption, while possibly true, strikes me as tenuous.[77] If God is the creator and lover of all human beings,

---

76. Whether this is accomplished through God's providential design of the natural order or through some kind of supernatural "intervention" into that order is an important question, but in the end it has little bearing on my main point here, which concerns the more visible, "special acts" of God.

77. Note in this connection the comment of Barnabas Lindars: "There are in fact two reasons why many scholars are very cautious about miracle stories. The first is theological.... The second reason is historical. The religious literature of the ancient world is full of miracle stories, and we cannot believe them all. It is not open to a scholar to decide that, just because he is a believing Christian, he will accept all the Gospel miracles at their face value, but at the same time he will repudiate miracles attributed to Isis. All such accounts have to be scrutinized with equal detachment" ("Jesus Risen: Bodily Resurrection but No Empty Tomb," *Theology* 89 [1986]: 90-91).

then there is little reason to suppose that he has reserved his miracles solely for Jews and Christians. The Bible itself depicts God as speaking directly to the first murderer, Cain (Gen. 4), and implies that both Melchizedek and Jethro, as non-Israelite priests of the true God, were privy to divine revelation (see Gen. 14; Exod. 3). Also, some modern missiologists and theologians will cite evidence that God has performed miracles among the nations prior to the arrival of Christian missionaries.[78] Whether this is certainly so, I cannot say. But if God by common grace sends rain upon unbelievers, it is perhaps by such grace that he blesses them in other ways—even by miracles. The universal scope of miracle testimonies gives us one reason to suspect that miracles, while exceptional, do occur.

Now miracles are possible only if there is a sacred or divine realm that could break in on the world of our existence. Is there any evidence that such a supernatural realm exists? Indeed, the human perception that there is another dimension of reality, to some extent distinct from our own, is a widespread phenomenon. Any student of religion knows this.[79] One must assume, I think, the existence of such a "sacred realm" to make any sense of our experience with human categories like "goodness" and "justice." I can illustrate my point by considering the alternative, as expressed in the playful but dark words of Friedrich Nietzsche:

> Once upon a time, on a little star in a distant corner of the universe, clever little animals invented for themselves proud words, like truth and goodness. But soon enough the little star cooled, and the little animals had to die and with them their proud words. But the universe, never missing a step, drew another breath and moved on, dancing its cosmic dance across endless skies.[80]

Perhaps Nietzsche was right, and Hitler will never pay for brutally killing and torturing millions of Jews and others. But is this the most sensible hypothesis, that justice is merely an evolutionary illusion thrown up by an impersonal cosmos? Or does this evidence, like the other religious evidence, point us to a sacred realm beyond our own, where the reality of justice is finally grounded in divine judgment? I cannot prove that God exists, nor will I try. I can only say that, as hypotheses go, the hypothesis that a sacred realm exists, and that it will eventually intervene in human life, offers a better account—dare I say, a far better account—

---

78. Don Richardson, *Eternity in Their Hearts*, rev. ed. (Ventura, CA: Regal Books, 1981); David K. Clark, "Miracles in the World Religions," in *In Defense of Miracles: A Comprehensive Case for God's Action in History*, ed. R. Douglas Geivett and Gary R. Habermas (Downers Grove, IL: InterVarsity, 1997), 199–213.

79. As expressed in very different ways by Mircea Eliade, *A History of Religious Ideas*, trans. Willard R. Trask, 3 vols. (Chicago: University of Chicago Press, 1978–1985); Rudolph Otto, *The Idea of the Holy*, trans. John W. Harvey (London: Oxford University Press, 1923); Immanuel Kant, *Critique of Practical Reason*, trans. and ed. Mary Gregor (Cambridge: Cambridge University Press, 1997).

80. As quoted by John D. Caputo, *Philosophy and Theology* (Nashville: Abingdon, 2006), 1. Original quotation in Friedrich Nietzsche, *Philosophy and Truth: Selections from Nietzsche's Notebooks of the Early 1870s*, trans. and ed. Daniel Breazeale (Atlantic Highlands, NJ: Humanities Press International, 1979), 79.

of the evidence than any secular account can. Miracles may be few or none, but the structure of reality does not seem to preclude miracles.[81]

But this does not resolve all of the problems raised by Troeltsch. According to his logic, even if a miracle occurred, it would not be amenable to historical inquiry because miracles defy the historical principles of methodological doubt, analogy, and coherence. Historians can offer reconstructions of what *probably happened*, yet it is the very nature of the case that miracles are *never* probable events. Indeed, to the extent that history is understood as constrained by natural laws, to that same extent miracles become not only improbable but, pushed to the limits, impossible. Can any arguments be adduced against this Troeltschian logic?

Troeltsch seems right on this basic point: miracles have no anterior historical events that cause them. They are not part of the causal chain in the same way that normal historical events are. In saying this, I do not mean to suggest at all that the contextual events leading up to a supposed miracle are irrelevant in our historical assessment of that miracle testimony. In the case of the resurrection, for instance, it might be very important if we concluded that Jesus believed in a theology of resurrection and predicted his resurrection before it occurred. But as for the resurrection itself, Troeltsch is correct when he asserts that this event did not flow from the natural order of previous historical events.

Yet Troeltsch seems to have overlooked something in his analysis of miracles: once they occur, miracles certainly produce posterior historical effects. As a result, although we will not be able to adduce evidence for the *immediate* anterior cause of a miracle like the resurrection, we might be able to adduce evidence for its posterior effects. In the case of the resurrection these effects would include confusion about the fate of Jesus's body, testimonies that he was seen alive, and evidence that these postresurrection appearances deeply affected the lives of those who claimed to see him.[82] Whether this evidence is finally convincing is not the point. My only point is that genuine miracles leave historical effects in their wake, just as a dropped stone leaves emanations on the surface of water. Because these effects are historical effects, they are also amenable to the usual tests of analogy and coherence, albeit with a twist. Given that all miracles are exceptional, any testimonies about them would have to be judged not only on the usual analogies but also on creative analogies. For instance, in the case of resurrections from the dead, we will have to imagine how human beings would respond if their dead friend came back to life. When this creative analogy has been added to the template that we use to make our historical judgments, then we are in a better position to assess the historical evidence for the miracle in question. In sum, I believe that we live in a world where miracles might occur,

---

81. For good evangelical discussions of this issue, see Evans, *Historical Christ*, 137–202; Alvin Plantinga, *Warranted Christian Belief* (Oxford: Oxford University Press, 2000).

82. For a recent defense of the prominent role that eyewitness testimony played in the Gospel accounts of Jesus's life and resurrection, see Richard Bauckham, *Jesus and the Eyewitnesses: The Gospels as Eyewitness Testimony* (Grand Rapids: Eerdmans, 2006).

and in a world where—if they do occur—the historical evidence for them could be thoughtfully considered.

But in this instance the other shoe falls. Although it is my opinion that Christ's resurrection has left significant historical emanations in its wake, many other events in Scripture—even some important events like the Passover and exodus—leave us gawking at peaceful, undisturbed waters (see chapter 3). Where are the emanations in Egyptian history from these catastrophic events? I, for one, cannot find them, even though I very much wish that I could. In such cases, how should thoughtful Christians pass judgment on the historicity of the biblical narratives?

First, historical inquiry of the type we are discussing here has scarcely been possible for most of human history, and remains a fairly restricted possibility even in our own day. Very few people have the expertise in the ancient sources to "test" the historicity of the biblical narratives. The faith of almost everyone who has ever believed the gospel has rested on little else than testimonies—especially biblical testimonies—about the miracles of Jesus and his resurrection. Enlightenment-style historical research, with its fixation of "evidence," has not come into it.[83] Given that this is so, it is worth asking why so many have believed this gospel testimony. To my mind, one part of the explanation is that people are very different. Some persons are simply more interested in and sensitive to matters of religious faith than others. We need not get into why this is so at this point; it is enough to take note of it. Another explanation for the propensity of so many to believe the Christian miracle is that there is something about the gospel story itself—about the coming of God in the flesh, his love for us, his sacrifice for us, and his resurrection—that resonates as true in the human soul. As C. S. Lewis put it, "I believe in Christianity as I believe that the sun has risen: not only because I see it, but because by it I see everything else."[84] Perhaps we believe in the Bible's miracles precisely because they are miracles of the right sort, not because they rest upon historical "evidence." So critical historiography does not hold all of the cards when it comes to making judgments about history.

Second, I think it important to recall that the church has always made room for the possibility that some biblical narratives are not strictly historical. Origen interpreted the story of Adam and Eve's fall as an allegory,[85] and Augustine did something similar with the six days of creation, which he took not only as "literal" days but also as an explanation for what God did at one moment in time.[86] Allegorical moves of this sort have been fairly common in church history, especially when reading the Bible as history presented serious theological problems. I will shortly discuss what I think about these allegories. But right or not, the allegories suggest that I am not on thin ice when I assert that Scripture has preserved not only

---

83. For comments along these lines, see Evans, *Historical Christ*, 185–86.
84. C. S. Lewis, *The Weight of Glory and Other Addresses* (New York: Macmillan, 1965), 92.
85. Origen, *The Philocalia of Origen*, trans. G. Lewis (Edinburgh: T&T Clark, 1911), 18–19.
86. Augustine, *The Literal Meaning of Genesis*, trans. John Hammond Taylor, 2 vols., Ancient Christian Writers 41–42 (New York: Paulist Press, 1982), 1:141–45.

stories about what God has actually done but also popular stories about what God *could* have done. So the ancient testimony of the church gives us no good reason to suppose, let alone demand, that every miracle story in the Bible is historical. At the same time, allowing that this is so cannot mean that any and every miracle story in the Bible is some type of allegory or parable. Since its earliest days, the church has also recognized and maintained that the validity of Christian faith depends upon the historicity of some events, including certain miracles. Among these necessary historical events are Christ's virgin birth, his crucifixion, his resurrection, and his ascension. The historicity of these events seems to be nonnegotiable for a fully coherent Christian theology, being defined as such by creedal orthodoxy and also by Scripture itself (cf. 1 Cor. 15; the Nicene Creed).

This leads to my third point. One difficulty faced by modern Christians is that, in some cases, these truly essential historical events not only lack historical evidence but seem to have some evidence against them. Let us take as one example the virgin conception. Although we might adduce substantial historical evidence for the resurrection of Christ, the historical evidence for his birth by a virgin seems fairly thin. Paul does not mention it, nor do two of the four Gospels, including the earliest Gospel, Mark. Under these circumstances, it is easy to imagine that the virgin birth of Jesus was, like the immaculate conception of Mary, a later theological deduction of the early church rather than part of the primitive Christian testimony. If this is right (and it need not be, except for my illustration), then the birth narratives of Matthew and Luke—which include the virgin birth—would represent the final stages of early Christian reflection on Jesus's divine identity, just as the pseudepigraphic *Gospel of James*—which provides an account of Mary's immaculate conception—was a product of the church's reflection on Mary's identity.[87] In other words, were we to judge these matters strictly by modern standards of historical inquiry, we might find good reasons for doubting the historicity of events like the virgin birth and immaculate conception. But of course there is no reason at all that the church should consider these matters *only* in terms of modern historiography. The theological reflection of the church on the persons of Jesus and Mary also counts as evidence in our historical equations. Whether this reflection was soon or long after those holy births is beside the point, since the cogency of a theological deduction hardly depends on historical proximity to the contemplated event. As a result, Protestants believe in one of these birth miracles, and Catholics in both, because these events are understood as necessary in their respective visions of orthodoxy. In these cases the theological evidence of faith and creedal orthodoxy serve a vital role in our historical judgment. We believe in miracles, like the virgin birth, not because they are supported by so much historical-critical evidence, but because they are theologically reasonable and necessary. The only caveat that I would offer on this point is that our theo-

---

87. For the text in translation, see David R. Cartlidge and David L. Dungan, *Documents for the Study of the Gospels* (Philadelphia: Fortress, 1980), 107–17.

logical judgment on these matters can be wrong just as easily as our historical judgment. For instance, some fundamentalists will wish to maintain—on the basis of theology—that all or most of the Bible's narratives must be historical and also wholly free of human error. To this I would respond that neither the evidence of Scripture and history nor the theological judgments of the church through the ages support such an extreme conclusion.

Given that we are in this territory, perhaps it is prudent to discuss at this point which of the events in the biblical story are "theologically necessary." Must Noah's flood be history? The tower of Babel? The lives of Abraham and Jacob? The exodus and Passover? Paul's miraculous deliverance from prison? First, I would note that when the question of biblical historicity is raised, it is often expressed in Boolean terms, as if we must say that the exodus either took place or did not. But what if the exodus is *partly* historical? What if God did deliver a cadre of slaves from Egypt, but in an event of less grandeur and power than the Bible now describes? Or what if Jesus performed only *some* of the miracles attributed to him in the Bible, while others are fictional traditions spawned by his genuine miracles? Or what if Jesus did rise again, but Matthew has his story wrong because he reports only one angel at the grave instead of two, as Luke has told us? My point is that, when it comes to biblical history, it is quite reasonable to suppose that some of the biblical traditions are partly but not wholly accurate as historical sources.[88] This is precisely why it becomes important to inquire not only about which traditions are historical but also about which aspects or parts of each tradition must be historical.

During the modern era, the body of necessary history in the Bible has tended to be much larger for Protestant evangelicals than for the Catholic tradition, where "there are but few texts whose sense has been defined by the authority of the Church."[89] I must say that I tend to side with the Catholics on this point, in part because some of the Bible's most important stories seem to lack historical evidence or to have evidence against them. One result is that the urgency of this matter is not so great for me as for some evangelicals, since I do not believe that a wrong judgment about the historicity of something like the plagues in Egypt, or Paul's prison stay at Philippi, would be so grave as denying a central doctrine like the virgin birth. Even in this last case, getting the theology wrong might not be a disaster. Evangelicals have long had deep respect and admiration for the life and ministry of Dietrich Bonhoeffer—most not knowing that he very much doubted that Mary was a virgin.[90] For these reasons I am happy at this

---

88. For a fascinating illustration of the partial nature of historical representation, see the various lithographic depictions of Abraham Lincoln's last hours in Harold Holzer and Frank J. Williams, *Lincoln's Deathbed in Art and Memory: The "Rubber Room" Phenomenon* (Gettysburg: Thomas Publications, 1998).

89. See the comments of Pius XII in Dean P. Béchard, *The Scripture Documents: An Anthology of Official Catholic Teachings* (Collegeville, MN: Liturgical Press, 2002), 132.

90. See Dietrich Bonhoeffer, *Christ the Center*, trans. E. H. Robertson (San Francisco: Harper & Row, 1978), 102–5. For discussion see Andreas Pangritz, *Karl Barth in the Theology of Dietrich Bonhoeffer* (Grand Rapids: Eerdmans, 2000), 106–14.

point to avoid that old quagmire regarding the Bible's historicity, except to say that I would affirm in the strongest possible way the historicity of those events that are affirmed in the creeds of the church. I consider the Bible's historicity an issue of real importance at the theological center but of less importance in the margins.

But questions of "essential" history notwithstanding, I believe that my basic point in this discussion still holds. Although some and perhaps many of Scripture's narratives are not strictly historical in all respects, there are narratives in Scripture—some of them about miracles—whose historicity is essential to the validity and cogency of the creedal faith. Consequently, in any given case, our judgments on the Bible's historicity will have to weigh not only the relevant contextual evidence but also the philosophical and theological evidence, including especially the theological traditions of the church. One consequence of this approach is that we will sometimes accept the historicity of an event even when it does not pass our everyday litmus tests for history. As historical methodologies go, this one will not suit Troeltsch's Enlightenment era project, but it is certainly a fitting approach to history for one who believes that God is, and that he can and has intervened in history. So, as the Christian philosopher Alvin Plantinga has made clear, Troeltschian-styled historical criticism is ultimately incompatible with an orthodox-styled Christian faith.[91] But the defects in Troeltsch's historical project have little to do with the kind of historical criticism—"*believing* criticism"—that I am advocating in this book.

Excursus: The Problem and Promise of Allegory

As I pointed out in chapter 5, one of the more popular *modern* solutions to the problem of biblical criticism has been a return to the *ancient* allegories. If the criticism uncovers contradictions that we do not like, or theological perspectives that we find wanting, then we will simply allegorize the text so that its stormiest waves are concealed by a sea of symbolism. According to this theological rationale, if allegories were good enough for Augustine, then they are good enough for the church. Though I have already explained some of the problems with this approach in chapter 5, I promised then, and on several other occasions, to provide a fuller account of my opinion on the matter. Here I will make good on those promises.[92]

As many readers know, this patristic hermeneutic has been a favorite whipping boy of modern interpreters, being regularly criticized over the years because of its speculative and sometimes reckless character. I have no interest in turning back the clock so that we can simply return to the patristic allegories, as Steinmetz and some others have suggested. But I am interested in presenting a more nuanced

---

91. Plantinga, *Warranted Christian Belief*, 374–421.
92. See chap. 5; chap. 6; chap. 9.

approach to allegory, which recognizes not only its weaknesses but also its strengths and benefits. In my opinion there is much to learn by doing so.

The critics of allegory tend to assume that the act of interpretation can lead to only two possible results. Interpretations are either right or wrong. But our discussion of practical realism in chapter 1 has challenged this assumption by revealing that successful interpretation lies instead on a continuum that runs from better to worse. When judged on this kind of scale, the patristic allegories fare much better. For example, the church fathers usually interpreted the Song of Songs as an allegory about Christ's love for the church.[93] Let us suppose that the fathers were wrong on this point because the Song's human author had in mind not some spiritual meaning about the church but rather the physical intimacy between a man and woman. If all of this is true, is there nothing to say except that the fathers were wrong about the Song?

Although the fathers probably erred in interpreting the Song's *human discourse* as a book about Christ and the church, I do not believe that their reading erred so much when it comes to the Bible's *divine discourse*. Let me explain. Anyone familiar with Scripture knows that several times it draws a close parallel between God's relationship with his people and the marital intimacy that obtains between husbands and wives. The relationship drawn is so close that we can reasonably conclude that marriage was in some measure created to serve this metaphor. If this is so, it would seem that the fathers were precisely right when they drew out images of divine love from the Song's portrait of human love. This would be true even if the Song's human author envisioned nothing of the sort. So, while patristic interpretations of the Song were not perfect, their allegories were at least partly right. I shall draw out the valuable implications of this observation in a moment.

Now let us consider the patristic allegories from a slightly different angle, continuing with the Song of Songs as our example. One of the reasons that the fathers interpreted the Song allegorically was that its overt and provocative images of human sexuality made them uncomfortable. Such interpretive reflexes were endemic to patristic exegesis. Whenever the fathers were troubled by the straightforward implications of Scripture, their favorite solution was to turn the text into a symbol of something else. Origen expressed it this way:

> If, for instance, we are asked about the daughters of Lot and their apparent unlawful intercourse with their father, or about the two wives of Abraham, or the two sisters who were married to Jacob, or the two handmaids who increased the number of his sons, what else can we reply than that these are sacraments and figures of spiritual things, but that we are ignorant of their precise nature?[94]

---

93. See Marvin H. Pope, *Song of Songs*, AB (Garden City, NY: Doubleday, 1977), e.g., 112–32; Richard A. Norris Jr., trans. and ed., *The Song of Songs: Interpreted by Early Christian and Medieval Commentators* (Grand Rapids: Eerdmans, 2003).

94. *On First Principles* 4.1.9 (*ANF* 4:357).

As this example illustrates, the theological impulse behind the allegories was a desire to resolve the apparent contradictions between basic Christian teachings (in this case, on monogamy) and the biblical texts that seemed to contradict them (in this case, the polygamy of the patriarchs). This theological maneuver required a set of implicit or explicit interpretive priorities, so that one theological viewpoint in Scripture could take precedence over others. Nowhere was such a principle more clearly expressed than in Augustine, whose basic principle for interpretation gave priority to the love of God and neighbor. "Whoever thinks that he understands the Holy Scriptures," said Augustine, "but puts such an interpretation upon them as does not tend to build up this two-fold love of God and our neighbor, does not yet understand them as he ought."[95] Because the literal meaning of some biblical texts obviously contradicted this love principle, Augustine offered a solution: "Whatever there is in the word of God that cannot, when taken literally, be referred either to purity of life or soundness of doctrine, you may set down as figurative. Purity of life has reference to the love of God and one's neighbor; soundness of doctrine to the knowledge of God and one's neighbor."[96] Augustine's exegetical strategy is crystal clear. The fundamental principle of Scripture is love, and anything that appears to contradict this principle is an allegory. An example of this principle in action appears in Augustine's commentary on Psalm 137. The psalm's last two verses read, "O daughter of Babylon, doomed to destruction, happy is he who repays you for what you have done to us—*he who seizes your infants and dashes them against the rocks*" (NIV, italics mine). What will one committed to the gospel of God's love do with this horrifying image of judgment? Augustine's solution is ingenious, if strained. The "little ones of Babylon," he tells us, are not literal children but rather "evil desires at their birth," nascent lusts that we must conquer before they grow troublesome.[97] Perhaps we will not buy into this allegorical solution, or into others proffered by Augustine and the fathers. But I believe that modern readers have much to learn from the patristic model of biblical interpretation.

First, patristic exegesis bears important implications for how we should approach the exegetical work of others. As we have seen in the allegories, interpretations of the Bible are not merely right or wrong but range from better to worse. This means that our purpose in reading biblical and theological commentary cannot be merely to criticize error but also to look with charity for where the readings offered might be correct and fruitful. This posture is possible because the correctness of a biblical interpretation does not rest in a *perfect* correspondence between the views of the exegete and the biblical author. It rests instead in the overlap—the common ground—that obtains between these views. Let us take patristic interpretations of the Song of Songs as an example. Regarding the Song, we can reasonably and biblically argue for a God-given ontological connection

---

95. *On Christian Doctrine* 1.36 (*NPNF* 1 2:533).
96. *On Christian Doctrine* 3.10 (*NPNF* 1 2:561).
97. *Commentary on Psalm 137* (*NPNF* 1 8:630–32).

between the physical intimacy of men and women, which the Song's human author probably had in mind, and the spiritual intimacy between Christ and the church, which the fathers took as the Song's theme. So the patristic allegories were partly right. This is no coincidence. Allegories are always drawn out of the text because the reader has recognized certain metaphorical connections between one thing and another, in the case of the Song, between human love and divine love. The metaphors that we see are admittedly subject to error, but they almost always hit upon some dimension of genuine similarity—else we would not have noticed them in the first place. If we take this principle to heart, then we shall be able to better appreciate the exegetical work of the fathers, and of others, even if we find that their exegetical methods and interpretations err in certain respects.

The second point that I wish to make about the patristic allegories regards their purpose. Allegory was an essential tool in the patristic effort to navigate the Bible's theological diversity. To be sure, the fathers sometimes employed fanciful or creative exegesis to resolve the tensions in Scripture, and for that we might criticize them. But the final result of their allegories was often the proper result, in that they effectively interpreted the Bible's problem texts in light of its highest theological principles, such as loving God and neighbor. This suggests that scriptural interpretations should not be judged merely on their formal exegetical successes but also by their final theological results. Even if the patristic allegories were sheer fancy, the theological instinct to resolve the Bible's tensions, and to do so by stressing some theological themes rather than others, was the proper—I would say, "spirit-led"—instinct. Is there a sensible way for us to follow this patristic lead?

If modern exegesis is going to benefit by emulating the exegesis of the early fathers, it will not be by merely imitating their allegories. Allegorical interpretation may have been current and acceptable in antiquity, and for that reason the fathers—and in some instances, the biblical authors—were wise to use it. But as an approach to Scripture, it is not an exegetical method that will convince many readers in our own day. What we must discern is how these patristic methods can nevertheless profitably inform and challenge our modern exegetical viewpoints. Our first observation along these lines is that the theological impulse behind the patristic allegories was—and to my mind, still is—fundamental to the theological interpretation of Scripture. Allegories provided a way to discern what was good and right in a problematic biblical text. We have already noted how Augustine interpreted the slaughter of infants in Psalm 137 as the slaughter of evil desires. In doing so, he preserved an account of God's all-out assault on evil while disarming the text of its apparent brutality. Now the same sort of theological sifting can be accomplished without allegory. For instance, while modern exegetes will not wish to use the Old Testament's Canaanite genocide as a behavior for Christians to imitate, we can still discern—if we are willing to look carefully—a significant connection between God's command to destroy the Canaanites and the Bible's other theological priorities, which include a determined effort to eradicate sin and sinful influences from the life of the church. So there *is* something of genuine theological value in the Old Testament conquest account, even if we embrace not the whole text but only aspects of it. Now this modern reading of the Old Testament is by no means an allegory, but its exegetical result is precisely like that of an allegory. Certain dimensions of the text are preserved, while others are set aside.

In the example that I have just provided, the chief difference between the modern approach and the patristic allegories is in the explanations behind their respective theological maneuvers. The patristic move was essentially generic: the genre of the biblical text is an allegory, so we shall simply read it differently. Modern readers also use genre to resolve some of the Bible's theological tensions, but in the genocide example the solution is not the text's human genre. Modern readers will simply admit that the Canaanite genocide means what is says, and that what it says is ultimately at odds with other texts in the Bible, especially those that teach us to love and pray for our enemies. But this modern move obviously requires a theological explanation that goes beyond the text's human genre, and I have already laid out what the solution might be. The tensions between New Testament love and Old Testament genocide may be explained by the divine genre of Scripture, by the fact that God accommodated ancient Israelite notions of ethnicity and warfare when he spoke to Israel in the Old Testament. The church fathers would not have made this theological move in their interpretation of Joshua's conquest (although Augustine came close), but, as we have seen, they certainly believed that accommodation played a significant role in biblical revelation and therefore in biblical interpretation.

To summarize, we may say that the fathers used genre (allegory) and accommodation to manage the Bible's theological diversity. Modern Christians should do the same, but our generic analysis of the text will be more sophisticated than resorting to simple allegories, and our appeal to accommodation will be necessary more often, given that we live in a time when many of Scripture's accommodations have become clearer to us. As men and women, we are certainly no better than the ancient fathers and are probably worse off in many respects, but our modern vantage point does afford us certain advantages of perspective. All I am saying is that our approach to Scripture should capitalize on those advantages.

Conclusions

The thesis of this and the previous chapter is fairly simple. The best interpretations of Scripture are those that read Scripture in relationship to its context, and that context is not merely Scripture's immediate context—the worlds of David, Solomon, Jesus, and Paul—but the context of the whole, which comprises both the created order and any special revelation that God has provided to humanity. God's Word is the final authority in this approach, but listening to his Word is complicated by several factors. Scripture is not the only word that God has spoken.

He has spoken as well in Christ and in the created order, and he continues to speak to the church by his Spirit. This would present no problems if these sources of revelation spoke an entirely consistent and coherent message, but this is not the case. God has elected to present his written discourses to humanity at discrete points in history, and at each of these points he has accommodated his voice to the finite and fallen horizons of his human audience. As a result, God's Word has not been passed to us as a single, univocal voice but as a series of disparate and sometimes contradictory installments, whose final significance must be spiritually discerned by listening—with the Spirit's help—to that full range of God's discourses. By reason and spiritual wisdom, the church is able to discover from these diverse voices the unique voice of God for us today. Theological interpretation is a process that hears God's univocal *Word* by listening to his many *words*.

Some evangelicals will be alarmed by this approach to Scripture and theology, but what I am advocating is not so different from what evangelicals already do when they interpret Scripture. Even though evangelicals often deny the diversity of Scripture, the theological diversity within evangelicalism is a good and ready indicator of Scripture's truer nature. Some evangelicals are premillennialists, others amillennialists; some are Arminians, others Calvinists; some evolutionists, others creationists; some require head coverings for women, others do not; some believe that Romans 7 describes a Christian, others that it describes a pagan; some believe in capital punishment, others find it murder. I could of course go on and on with this exercise, but the point is by now evident. It is hardly conceivable that evangelicals could assent to so many differing and contradictory viewpoints if the Bible spoke as clearly and univocally as we are wont to suppose. Like all Christians, evangelicals must navigate the Bible's diversity by either ignoring certain problem texts or by subordinating them to other texts that strike them as more sensible. Even very conservative evangelicals are sometimes forced by the facts either to admit Scripture's errors or to explain them using accommodation. I have provided examples of this pattern already in chapter 7, to which we can add Goldingay's observations about the theological work of men like Luther, Calvin, Wesley, Matthew Henry, and Charles Hodge.[98] So my proposals in this book are, in principle, not so far from the actual practice of evangelicals, and still closer to the exegetical and theological flexibility exhibited in the work of the early fathers of the church. Nevertheless, it remains true that my conceptual portrait of biblical interpretation, and of biblical authority, is very different from that espoused by very conservative evangelicals. Let me try to explain the difference.

Evangelicals often perceive Scripture as a kind of lens through which one looks at life. Those without the Bible see the world wrongly, while those who look at things through the lens of Scripture see it rightly. Though I would not wish to say that this description of things is entirely mistaken, it seems to me that it overlooks subtle but important dimensions of the interpretive event. The lens metaphor fails

---

98. Goldingay, *Models for Scripture*, 261–65.

in certain respects because it imagines the Bible as an instrument insulated from the world observed through it. In reality, however, the meaning of Scripture, as of all texts, is dependent upon its cultural and historical context. So, if the Bible were a lens, the very lens itself would be altered by the things one looks at using it. Evangelicals would prefer to understand the biblical lens as nothing other than a clear glass that brings things into proper focus, but in many instances the Bible is anything but clear, and the proper theological focus comes not from Scripture alone but from contextual things that are external to it. Such was the case when modern science bested biblical portraits of the cosmos.

To my mind a better metaphor for expressing the nature of biblical authority should begin by imagining the Bible as one part of the complex web of reality. Like all texts, Scripture depends upon this contextual web to make its words intelligible, but those biblical words then cast their light back upon the web so that all of its parts can come into a newer, Christian perspective. In this metaphor the Bible is like a good virus that gradually spreads and infuses its wisdom into the entire network of our worldview. At the same time, the insights and realities of the web continually improve our understanding of Scripture. The result is not so much a biblical worldview as a biblically informed worldview. The advantage of this web metaphor is that it takes biblical authority seriously without trapping us when the Bible speaks less clearly, or even incorrectly, in comparison with other God-ordained voices in the web.

To some readers this weblike approach to biblical authority may seem to open up a veritable Pandora's box, which removes every biblical constraint on our theological reflection. It is in response to this concern that I have presented and defended pragmatic realism as an account of epistemology; it allows for the validity of human knowledge and biblical authority while making appropriate room for the inevitable dialectic between Scripture and other sources of knowledge and insight. My task in the following chapter is to demonstrate how this approach works in our theological use of Scripture.

10

BIBLICAL CRITICISM AND CHRISTIAN THEOLOGY

A Few Examples

Given the many claims that I have made regarding the Bible and its interpretation, and its proper use in theology, it is fitting that I should illustrate how my approach fleshes out in actual readings of the Bible. But the space limitations of a book being what they are, the examples that follow should be regarded not as full-blown theological inquiries but as mere samples of how I would practice theology that is grounded in, but sometimes moves beyond, the Bible. I have only the slightest interest in convincing readers to accept my critical readings of the text and the resulting theological judgments that I offer. More important in my opinion is that readers will see that the approach to Scripture that I have advocated takes biblical authority very seriously, and that it need not lead to open-ended, cut-to-fit theology. That sort of theology is precisely what I wish to avoid.

The discussion to follow includes three samples of biblical interpretation. The first two, which are briefer, will tackle problems that I have highlighted in earlier discussions of biblical criticism. One of these will explore the historical problems associated with the biblical account of King David's life, and the other will explore the problems presented by biblical apocalyptic literature, in the books of Daniel and Revelation. The third sample, which addresses the present theological debate about gender and authority, will be considerably longer than the first two. I offer it as a more thoroughgoing example of my approach to Scripture.

But even here the discussion remains an example, and does not do full justice to the topic at hand.

The Story of David in the Books of Samuel

I have already pointed out that, as a rule, modern scholars believe that the biblical story of David in 1–2 Samuel portrays the king as other than he actually was (see chapter 3). The rupture between history and tradition is detected especially in those events that relate to David's claim to the Israelite throne. Let us consider the biblical tradition first. According to that tradition:

1. David was a reluctant king who deeply respected the regime of his predecessor, King Saul. Though Saul himself became jealous of David and routinely sought to kill his younger Judean rival, David never reciprocated, even though he had many opportunities to do so.
2. Because of Saul's misplaced rage against him, David was more or less compelled to seek refuge among Saul's Philistine enemies, for whom David and his band of men served as mercenaries. But the tradition makes clear that David's support for Philistia against Israel was a ruse; he never actually fought against Israel but only claimed to do so.
3. We are further told that David enjoyed the support of Jonathan, Saul's son and heir-apparent. Jonathan became David's fast friend and so covertly protected David from his belligerent father.
4. The tradition relates to us a long series of deaths that profited David's new regime. Those murdered or killed included not only men from Saul's house and military apparatus but also opponents from David's own family, such as Absalom. Though these convenient deaths benefited David and were often carried out by his supporters, the tradition uniformly maintains that David was never complicit in these deaths. David was not there at the time, or did not give the orders, or was deeply saddened by the news. The single exception to this rule appears when David was compelled by divine command to kill what was left of the entire ruling family of Saul.
5. David's claim to the throne is further supported by the tradition's strong emphasis on his divine election. We are informed of the many impieties that led to Saul's disqualification from kingship, and also of David's piety and of God's choice to put him on the throne.

Hence we may summarize the biblical tradition about David's rise to power this way: Violent war marked the transition from Saul's regime to the kingdom of David, resulting in many losses on both sides, especially on Saul's side. Though David was himself a great warrior and rose to fame because of his victories over Israel's enemies, he lifted nary a finger to secure the throne for himself. His rise to power was essentially the work of his supporters and of God, who eliminated the threat from Saul and put David on the throne without David's help or even his sanction. So goes the biblical tradition.

Now, many scholars believe that when it comes to David, the tradition tells only half of the story.[1] There was indeed violent war and conflict between Saul of Benjamin and the house of David to the south, but the David of history was a darker figure than the David of tradition. Though the tradition is at pains to show that David was wholly innocent in the many deaths that secured his power, and that he was never a turncoat Philistine mercenary, it is hard to imagine that all of this activity in support of David went down without his imprimatur. It is difficult to accept, for instance, that David's slaughter of Saul's household near the end of his life, which is cast in the tradition as an act of necessary piety, was anything other than a politically motivated attempt to secure the Israelite throne for his son. What we have in 1–2 Samuel, then, is not a completely accurate account of what transpired but a propagandistc version of the events, designed to garner support for David by denying the charges against him: that he was a ruthless and narcissistic serial killer, and a traitor to the cause of Israel.

This scholarly portrait of David is dark indeed and may go too far. But even if it does, I think that the evidence still sides with a David much darker than the tradition depicts. We could guess as much on the basis of several dark moments in David's life that the text does record for us, such as his cruelty toward Moab (systematically killing two-thirds of its captured soldiers), his cruelty toward the Ammonites (burning them in brick kilns), his hatred for the blind and lame (who were excluded from Jerusalem), and of course his acts of adultery and murder in the matter of Bathsheba and Uriah.[2] That these were genuine black marks on David's life is suggested by the fact that the Chronicler's more positive portrait of David's life simply leaves them out.[3] The theological question before us, then, is what to do with this critical reconstruction of David's life, and with its implication that the biblical story of David is based in some measure on a pack of propagandistic lies. Once again, I find that the critics can help us resolve some of the problems that the criticism has created.

My first critical observation regards the historian who authored the books of Samuel. Like all historians, he did his work by consulting whatever sources were available to him. Probably these included both oral and written sources,

---

1. See, for example, Baruch Halpern, *David's Secret Demons: Messiah, Murderer, Traitor, King* (Grand Rapids: Eerdmans, 2001); Steven L. McKenzie, *King David: A Biography* (Oxford: Oxford University Press, 2000); Kenton L. Sparks, "Propaganda," in *Dictionary of the Old Testament: Historical Books*, ed. Bill T. Arnold and H. G. M. Williamson (Downers Grove, IL: InterVarsity, 2005), 819–25.

2. For the relevant texts see 2 Sam. 8:2 (on Moab); 12:31 (on Ammon); 5:6–8 (on the lame and blind); 11:2–12:24 (Bathsheba and Uriah).

3. In the case of Bathsheba and Uriah, the Chronicler excluded the entire narrative context. In the other three cases the Chronicler simply edited his source to remove the implication of David's cruelty. See 1 Chron. 18:2 (on Moab); 20:3 (on Ammon); 11:6 (on the lame and blind).

though modern scholars suspect that textual evidence was the rule for the author of Samuel. There is an ongoing debate about the nature of the books of Samuel and about when and in what place the author lived. The more common viewpoint would identify him as the so-called Deuteronomistic Historian, who composed the books of Samuel as one installment in a longer history that ran from Joshua through 2 Kings, thus including Joshua, Judges, 1–2 Samuel, and 1–2 Kings. The name of this historian—the *Deuteronomistic* Historian—stems from the fact that his history measured the behaviors of Israel and its kings by employing the law of Deuteronomy as a yardstick. Some scholars date the first edition of this history to the preexilic period, and others to the exilic period. But either way, the author of the Deuteronomistic History lived several centuries after the time of King David.

If this standard account of the biblical literature is right, then it will mean that the historian who composed the books of Samuel had nothing to do with the Davidic propaganda his books now contain. Like any good historian, he consulted sources for his work, which in this case were apparently fairly ancient sources. But he had no way of knowing that these sources were chock-full of royal propaganda. His was an era when that old propaganda was already at home in popular memory. David was remembered as a man of God, whose heroic and pious deeds had ushered in the golden age of early Israel. Consequently, even if the sources behind our story of David were once composed by duplicitous agents of the king, we could legitimately presume that the biblical author was in no way culpable for these duplicities. That is, given the human genre of David's story, we could say with a straight face that the biblical author did not err.

A second insight of the critics might also serve our theological agenda. As I have said, the critics regard the stories of Saul and David as largely composed of political propaganda, whose original design was to win popular support for the rise of David to power and prominence. In saying this, scholars mean to indicate that the sources depict David as a better man, perhaps a much better man, than he actually was. But notice what this means. On the one hand, it will mean that as historians we will be cautious and critical in our use of the testimony in Samuel. We will not assume that the text gives us precisely what happened in the days of Saul and David; we will read the text against the grain. This is the historical implication. But on the other hand, there is an obvious theological implication. Insofar as the story of David portrays an ideal David, his example becomes a source of moral instruction. It was with this David of tradition, who loved and protected the man who tried to kill him, that the ancient Israelites fell in love. And no wonder, for the David of the Bible, more than any other character in the Old Testament, epitomizes the gospel directive that we should love our enemies. So we have the very human and sinful David of history, as well as the principled and righteous David of tradition. If we hope to offer a full-orbed theology of the text, both of these Davids must ultimately figure in our appraisal of 1–2 Samuel.

Given that this is the case, allow me to offer a third observation, which is at the same time both critical and theological. According to the apostle Paul, one aspect of our love for others involves a kind of idealization in which we overlook the bad and embrace the good in others. "Love," he says, "is patient... is not easily angered... keeps no record of wrongs... always trusts... and always hopes." This is precisely why genuine love "never fails" (1 Cor. 13:4–8 NIV). Given that this portrait of love is central to holy living, one wonders whether critical scholars are being fair when they paint David as darkly as they sometimes do, and when they point a finger of unbridled judgment at the propagandists who worked on his behalf.[4] I do not mean to imply that the critics are wrong about David and his scribal henchmen; I mean to suggest instead that by describing only David's dark side, the critics may well have told only part of his story.

When I consider the insightful and valuable biographies of David by Baruch Halpern and Steven McKenzie (and even, to some extent, my own article on David), their critical histories of his life seem to overlook several matters not merely of theology but of historical criticism.[5] Let me mention just a few of these. To begin, while both scholars are quite willing to critique David's personality and moral character, there is very little attention given to the fact that moral flaws can be expected in his opponents as well. We can reasonably presume, for instance, that David's enemies sometimes proffered lies about him, to which David's propaganda was merely a natural response. So David was perhaps not quite as bad as we might suppose. Moreover, to continue in this vein of thought, these critical biographies tend to overlook a strong witness in the tradition regarding David's piety. David was a poet and a musician, who exercised his gifts by composing worship songs for God. Though I would by no means recommend that we accept this traditional portrait of the king uncritically, it is doubtful in my opinion that this softer side of David was invented out of whole cloth. That critical scholars overlook this aspect of David's life in their biographies is evidence that conservative evangelicals are not wholly wrong when they complain, as they often do, that the critics tend to be more negative than is necessary in their appraisals of the Bible and its authors. In some measure I would trace this negative posture to an understandable but problematic tendency among modern scholars to carry out their work apart from important religious affections, such as the love that we ought to have for those we write about and describe. Whether the subject of our inquiry is David or some other ancient person or author, a better posture toward our biographical subjects will expect and look for the positive side of that person and of their life and message. This is to some extent what love is all about.

This brings to mind a closely related matter: all persons deserve to be judged in the context of their times. This may strike us as a theological assertion, but

---

4. For comments on the role of love in our epistemology and hermeneutics, see P. J. Watson, "After Postmodernism: Perspectivism, a Christian Epistemology of Love, and the Ideological Surround," *Journal of Psychology and Theology* 32 (2004): 248–61.

5. Halpern, *David's Secret Demons*; McKenzie, *King David*; Sparks, "Propaganda."

surely it is a matter of historical criticism, not merely of theology and ethics, to take the changing ebbs and tides of morality seriously. When we speak of Luther and Calvin, and offer evaluations of them as men, we are wise to make allowances for the moral conventions in play during their lifetimes. We are wise to grant that Luther was a man of genuine piety and love for God, even though he was anti-Semitic to an extent that would turn the stomach of the Lutherans that I know.[6] In the same way, we will judge that Calvin was a man of faith and intelligence who, in an (understandable?) error of judgment, supported the execution of the heretic Michael Servetus.[7] Considering Luther and Calvin in this way is simultaneously a matter of historical criticism *and* faith. It is of criticism because it recognizes the contextual differences that prevail between morality as judged in antiquity and in our own day; and it is of faith because, ultimately, love provides the foundation for that patience which we extend when others act wrongly out of ignorance. As Jesus expressed it, "Father, forgive them, for they do not know what they are doing" (Luke 23:34 NIV; cf. Acts 17:30).

The implication for our portrait of David is straightforward. Even if we grant that the critics are right about him, a fully Christian evaluation of his life will be somewhat different from the standard critical portrait. David lived in a world where every day his life was threatened by enemies and where enemies could arise even from within his own family. Paranoia easily ruled in that sort of world, and political calculus routinely assumed that it was necessary to kill one's enemies and to cover up the deed with lies. I am not suggesting that David, if he did these things, acted in faith and holiness. I am suggesting only that he would not be culpable for these acts in the same way that we would be if, knowing the gospel more fully, we did the same sorts of things.

We will never know this side of heaven just how close the ideal David of tradition was to the David of history. I suppose that we can hope for the best. But even the best possible David was a really sinful man, in need of grace like everyone else. When we juxtapose the historical and traditional images of David, the resulting tension is theologically important, for it points us toward that person in whom the ideal and the historical finally meet. I speak, of course, of Jesus the Messiah. But respecting David himself, the question is not whether the biblical David is the David of history; the question is whether the David described in Scripture is good and holy. And in most respects he is good and holy—as we should be. So there is not a reason in the world why the good David of tradition cannot be preached in our churches, even as the darker David of history is critically reconstructed in our scholarship. But that critical reconstruction should include the proper religious affections for David, affections of love that the critics do not always exercise. In

---

6. Martin Luther, *Luther's Works*, ed. Jaroslav Pelikan and Helmut T. Lehman, 55 vols. (St. Louis: Concordia; Philadelphia: Fortress, 1955-1976), 47:123-306.

7. J. Friedman, "Servetus, Michael," *The Oxford Encyclopedia of the Reformation*, ed. Hans Joachim Hillerbrand, 4 vols. (Oxford: Oxford University Press, 1996), 4:48-49.

Christ the image of David is redeemed; in part because we love David as a soul redeemed, and in part because Christ himself is the ideal David. In sum, I would say this of the Bible's Davidic propaganda: the propagandists intended it for evil, but God intended it for good (cf. Gen. 50:20).

The Imminent Eschaton in Daniel and Revelation

What shall we do when the prophecies of Scripture seem to miss their mark? In the cases of Daniel and Revelation, the difficulty that we face is this: the author of each book believed that the full-blown kingdom of God would appear in his own day. The author of the Daniel apocalypses anticipated this during the reign of Antiochus IV Epiphanes, in the second century BCE; and the author of Revelation expected the return of Christ during the Roman period, during the first-century reign of Caesar Domitian. That this is so, and the evidence for it, I have already explained in earlier parts of the discussion (see chapter 3). Here our question is theological: what shall we make of this phenomenon, and how shall we make good use of these texts in the life of the church?

I would suggest that, in certain respects, the phenomenon of biblical apocalyptic is not really so different from the phenomenon of biblical cosmology. In the area of cosmology, we have seen that the biblical authors simply assumed that the whole earth was flat because, viewed from their limited vantage point, the part of the world they could see seemed flat. They quite reasonably inferred from this that the earth in its entirety was flat, in an understandable error of judgment that neither we nor God would hold against them. Now this is very close to the problem we face in biblical apocalyptic. The authors of Daniel and Revelation lived within finite horizons, historical horizons that were dominated by violent, foreign rulers who persecuted the people of God.[8] Given their prophetic sense that the end of time would arise in such a time of universal turmoil, it is not at all surprising that they expected the end to come at any moment.

We can better appreciate the effects of this horizon by looking at the ministries of Paul and Jesus. Readers may recall that in 1 Corinthians Paul advised his readers to forego marriage because "the time is short" (1 Cor. 7:29 NIV). Believing that Jesus would soon return, Paul thought it wiser for Christians to invest their remaining days in God's service. Even to the married, Paul advised that those with spouses should act "as if they had none." Why did Paul arrive at this conclusion? It seems that early Christians closely connected the return of Christ with the evangelization of the world. As Matthew's Gospel expressed it, "And this gospel of the kingdom will be preached throughout the whole world, as a testimony to all nations; and then the end will come" (Matt. 24:14 RSV). Now we know from Paul's letter to Rome, written not long after 1 Corinthians, that the apostle

---

8. John J. Collins, *Daniel*, Hermeneia (Minneapolis: Fortress, 1993), 62–65; George R. Beasley-Murray, *The Book of Revelation*, NCB (Grand Rapids: Eerdmans, 1981), 38.

was planning a trip to Spain. By the standards of the ancient world, Spain was essentially the end of the world, at least if one was heading west. From this we may reasonably conclude that Paul expected the return of Christ, at least in part, because he understood that the end of the church's gospel mission was at hand. Apparently Paul did not know about Australia, nor did God tell him about it.

But what of Jesus? Did he too anticipate an imminent eschatological kingdom? We might infer as much from Matthew 24:34, where on the heels of his description of the eschaton, Jesus told his audience, "this generation will not pass away till all these things take place" (RSV). At the same time, we should not overlook his response to the disciples when they questioned him about God's eschatological schedule. To those questions, Jesus responded that "of that day or that hour no one knows, not even the angels in heaven, *nor the Son*, but only the Father" (Mark 13:32 RSV). That is, when pointedly asked about when the end would come, Jesus resolutely claimed that *he, the Son, did not know*. Given that even the Son was in the dark on this matter, it will no longer surprise us that the authors of Daniel and Revelation, and also Paul, mistakenly anticipated that the eschaton would unfold within or not long after their own lifetimes. If the eschatology of Jesus differed from these biblical authors, it was perhaps not so much in terms of what he knew about the eschaton; it was rather in his deeper awareness that God's plan for the parousia is truly a mystery, a hidden moment that "the Father has set by his own authority," as Jesus is later reported to say (Acts 1:7 NIV). From this we should conclude that Jesus, insofar as we are considering his human nature, simply did not know when the end would come.

If all of this is right, then how shall we properly use Daniel and Revelation in our historical and theological deliberations? On the one hand, as historically minded critics of early Jewish and Christian literature, we certainly do well to observe how these two texts fit into their historical contexts, and to notice that their respective authors anticipated an invasion of God's kingdom in their own day. By attending carefully to this and to other aspects of Daniel and Revelation, and by comparing these two texts to other ancient texts, we are able to reconstruct—with modest success—the development of eschatological ideas in the ancient Judeo-Christian context.[9] This evidence reveals that for a long time Israelites and Jews did not see the need for an eschatological kingdom of God. They believed that divine justice was already worked out within the bounds of normal history, so that good deeds were rewarded and evil deeds were punished. Some Israelites believed that this worked out rigidly, on a moment-by-moment basis (see 1–2 Chronicles; Job's friends; Ben Sirah), whereas others believed that it was over the scope of one's whole life that complete justice was discernible (1–2 Kings; Job). But on the whole, the sources tell us that this is how people thought.

---

9. For reconstructions of the development of Jewish and Christian apocalyptic thought, see John J. Collins, *The Apocalyptic Imagination: An Introduction to Jewish Apocalyptic Literature*, 2nd ed. (Grand Rapids: Eerdmans, 1998); Paul D. Hanson, *The Dawn of Apocalyptic*, rev. ed. (Philadelphia: Fortress, 1979); D. S. Russell, *The Method and Message of Jewish Apocalpytic: 200 BC–AD 100*, OTL (Philadelphia: Westminster, 1964).

At a certain point, however, some Jews began to doubt that this approach to justice offered a complete explanation for life's experiences. The author of Ecclesiastes, for instance, noticed that good people sometimes die young while evil people enjoy long lives (Eccles. 7:15). Other Jews began to wonder how God's great promises to Israel, such as a secure homeland ruled by a wonderful Davidic king, could come about in a world that was dominated by powerful foreign kings, such as the kings of Babylon, Persia, and Greece (and eventually Rome). As a result, Jews began to draw the conclusion that their hopes and dreams for freedom, and for divine justice, could be achieved and fulfilled only in a decisive act of God, whereby the Deity broke in on history to create something entirely new: the kingdom of God. This new viewpoint, which appeared rather late in Israel's history, is ensconced in numerous Jewish apocalypses and is vividly expressed in the books of Daniel and Revelation.[10] To miss this point is to miss a fascinating page in the history of theological ideas and, in turn, to overlook the manner in which God uses history, and human experience, to progressively unveil new theological insights to his people. His sovereign choice to sanction these eschatological ideas is expressed in the canonical process, whereby the books of Daniel and Revelation were finally recognized as authoritative and hence canonical for the Jews (in the case of Daniel) and for Christians (in the case of both books).

This brings us to the question of theology. That Daniel and Revelation are authoritative goes without saying. But have I not said plainly that the authors of Daniel and Revelation, and also Paul, got it wrong when they expected God's kingdom to appear in their own lifetimes? If they did get that wrong, what can we say?

It is indeed true, I think, that on this particular point the biblical authors got the eschatology wrong. But by now it should be clear that God's choice to accommodate these errant eschatological expectations in his Word should be no more troubling, in fact certainly less troubling, than his accommodation to genocide in the book of Deuteronomy. Moreover, as I have emphasized several times, the accommodation of error in a biblical text does not in the slightest mean that the text is wholly wrong and has nothing to offer us. What these texts offer is both explicit and implicit. Explicitly, the books of Daniel and Revelation provide indispensable insights into the nature of history, and into God's final solution for our human predicament. More than any other witnesses, these books help us to understand the cosmic battle that now rages between God's goodness and the forces of evil, and to understand that this great conflict will end only with God's final intervention in human history. Revelation, in particular, provides a powerful portrait of how those last days might look. Though the things envisioned by its author did not come to pass in the days of Rome, as he expected, we do well to

---

10. For a collection of Jewish apocalyptic literature, see *OTP*, vol. 1, *Apocalyptic Literature and Testaments*. For an overview of the materials, see Craig A. Evans, *Ancient Texts for New Testament Studies: A Guide to the Background Literature* (Peabody, MA: Hendrickson, 2005), 29–40.

remember that the eschaton will one day come to pass. For this reason, let none of us accept the beast's mark, which in the context of first-century Rome was an invisible mark borne by those who defected the faith (i.e., those who worshiped the emperor). When the end finally comes, John tells us plainly that God can see whether we are bearers of that mark (Rev. 13:16–18) or of the Lamb's seal (Rev. 14:1). This is an explicit message of Daniel and Revelation to the church.

As for the implicit messages in these books, I would like to highlight two. First, we should not overlook the significance of this fact: on two different occasions the persecutions leveled at God's people were so severe that the biblical authors thought the end was upon them. This very negative expectation of history is found in other books of the Bible as well. In Matthew, for instance, the disciples were told that "all men will hate you" (Matt. 10:22 NIV). In John's Gospel, too, we are warned that the world will hate Christians because it hates our Savior (John 15:19). These are, of course, very dark portraits of the relationship that obtains between the people of God and the world. Other texts in the canon, and also what we know from history itself, suggest that this adversarial pattern need not hold in every moment or era of history. When the author of Hebrews advised Christians to "strive for peace with all men" (Heb. 12:14 RSV), he evidently thought that this aim was to some extent possible. Who can deny that from the time of Constantine onward, we can see many instances—sometimes enduring instances—in which world governments have been hospitable to Christianity? When this reality is juxtaposed with the words of Daniel and Revelation, the implicit message of Scripture seems wholly clear: though the people of God live in a world that will sometimes be hospitable to faith, it is not and has never been an anomaly when we face persecutions of the most extreme kind. When we face those fiery moments of testing, it is by our faith in God, and by our hope in the coming kingdom, that we are able to keep the faith firmly until the end. Whether our final deliverance from the ordeal comes in the form of our resurrection after death, or in the form of Christ's return before it, does not matter so much. What matters most is that Christ will eventually return to take us home.

The other implicit message of Daniel and Revelation involves God's choice to accommodate in those books the errant expectation that the kingdom was more imminent than it actually was. Among other things, this means that neither we nor others are out of line if, at some point, we begin to surmise from the "signs" that the approach of God's kingdom is close at hand. Perhaps we will be wrong on this point, and we should remember that. But there is nothing unseemly about forming such an opinion. For the most part, it cannot hurt to live as if the return of Christ will be tomorrow. At the same time, the fact that the authors of Daniel and Revelation got their predictions wrong provides an implicit warning against eschatological sensationalism. Though Paul expected the kingdom in his own lifetime, he admonished the Thessalonians to work hard and earn a living while they awaited Christ's return (1 Thess. 4:11; 2 Thess. 3:6–12). We should heed both sides of the biblical admonition. That is, we are wise on the one hand to avoid that error which neglects the coming kingdom and does little or nothing of eternal value. We are wise on the other hand to steer clear of that error which so much embraces the kingdom that nothing of earthly good is done. True Christian wisdom is to know how to live in this world while keeping one's eye, at the same time, on what comes next. For Christ will indeed come again.

Gender, Authority, and Theology

I would like to conclude my deliberations in this chapter by considering a particular cluster of theological problems relating to gender and authority. As most readers know, there is an ongoing debate within the evangelical church about the traditional roles of men and women. The two basic positions on this question are commonly referred to as the "complementarian" and the "egalitarian" positions. Complementarians believe that Scripture supports the full equality of men and women, but they further believe that Scripture assigns to each gender a set of different, but complementary, roles in the home and in the church. Roles of authority, they would say, have been assigned to men. So the husband is the proper authority in the home, and, as a corollary of this, men are the proper authorities in the church. Egalitarians head in a different direction. Agreeing with the complementarians that Scripture affirms the full equality of men and women, they take what they see to be the next logical step: they conclude that husbands and wives share authority in the home, and they further maintain that women can be ordained as leaders in the church.

Thoughtful egalitarians will admit what every complementarian is quick to point out: that the Bible contains numerous texts that are patriarchal in orientation. But we have seen already in the previous chapter that on occasion the church has gone beyond the explicit discourse of Scripture when formulating its theological and ethical viewpoints. The chief example was slavery, though other examples could be adduced as well. The question at hand in our modern setting is whether, in the matter of women and their role in the home and in the church, we should move beyond the explicit teaching of Scripture—which is often patriarchal—in order to support an egalitarian view of gender that admits women for ordination and that regards husbands and wives as sharing equal authority in the home. But before I embark on the particulars of that discussion, a preliminary issue requires some attention. I refer to the debate about "hierarchy."

In recent years, it has become increasingly popular to argue that social hierarchies, in which some people exercise authority over others, are inherently evil structures in which those with power oppress those without it. This being so, it is assumed that all authority structures—such as the traditional patriarchal structures that give husbands authority in the home—should become the targets of our Christian polemic. Hierarchy reflects the fallen world order, so it is thought, and Christians must replace that fallen order with an egalitarian society that treats all people as equals. This is the argument.

While all of this might ring true for those schooled in enlightened democratic ideals, from a theological perspective there is at least one obvious difficulty with this line of thought. According to many theologians, both ancient and modern, when we speak of the Father and the Son, this relationship implies a kind of subordination, in which the Son, though *fully divine and equal to the Father*, is hierarchically "ordered below" or "ordered under" the Father.[11] Advocates of this position can cite evidence for their position from both Scripture and tradition. As for Scripture, Paul wrote: "Now I want you to realize that the head of every man is Christ, and the head of the woman is man, and the head of Christ is God" (1 Cor. 11:3 NIV). This would ostensibly suggest that Christ's authority over men is somehow analogous to God's authority over Christ. As for tradition, we find that God the Father is described as "the beginning of the whole divinity" (Augustine), "the source" of Son and Spirit (Gregory of Nazianzus), the "cause of the Son" (John of Damascus), "the principle of the Son" (Aquinas), and the "origin of the Son and Spirit" (Calvin).[12] Such is the evidence for this hierarchical view of the Trinity's order. If this view of the Trinity is correct, then it becomes very difficult to argue that human hierarchies are inherently evil; indeed, it becomes more likely that hierarchies are good things.

Those who take the other side of this debate, such as Kevin Giles, say that we cannot have it both ways.[13] We cannot say that the Father and Son are equal and also affirm that their order is asymmetrical. It is the nature of the case that asymmetrical order involves an implicit Arianism, that old heresy—also called "subordinationsim"—which denied the full divinity of Christ. To support this conclusion, Giles, and others who proffer a symmetrical view of the Trinity's order, often appeal to the very theologian who took up arms against Arius and the Arians, Athanasius.[14] Giles cites a number of texts from Athanasius in which that great father of the church asserted that the Son's subordination to the Father was a temporal result of the incarnation: "Now the scope and character of Holy Scripture, as we have often said, is this: it contains a double account of the Savior; that he was ever God and is the Son, being the Father's *Logos* and Radiance and Wisdom, and that afterwards for us he took the flesh of a virgin. . . . This scope is to be found through inspired Scripture."[15] From this and similar texts, some argue that the mutual divinity of the Father and Son, and their full equality, preclude any talk about hierarchical order in the Trinity. For Giles, there is simply no

---

11. In this discussion I draw generously from the unpublished paper of my Eastern University colleague, Dr. Steven Boyer, "Articulating Order: Orthodox Trinitarianism and Subordination."

12. These citations are taken directly from Boyer's article. The appropriate references, also from Boyer, include the following: Augustine, *On the Trinity* 4.29; Gregory of Nazianzus, *Oration (On Holy Baptism)* 40.43; John of Damascus, *Orthodox Faith* 1.8; Aquinas, *Summa Theologica*, pt. 1, q. 33–34; Calvin, *Institutes*, 1.13.20.

13. Kevin Giles, *The Trinity and Subordinationism: The Doctrine of God and the Contemporary Gender Debate* (Downers Grove, IL: InterVarsity, 2002).

14. Ibid., 33–41.

15. *Against the Arians* 3.26, 29 (= *NPNF* 2 4:407–9).

theological room for saying that the Son stands in any respect "under" the Father's authority. Where the Bible portrays Jesus as submitting to the Father's authority, this is not an image of the *immanent* Trinity (the eternal ontological relationship between Father and Son) but of the *economic* Trinity (the Trinity as it appears in the temporal dimension of the incarnation). So for Giles and those like-minded, the relationships in the Trinity are fully symmetrical and egalitarian, and the same should count for redeemed human relationships. This is the egalitarian logic.

Now on this matter the traditional view seems to have almost all of the good cards in its hand. Scripture describes the relationship between the Father and Son in hierarchical terms, and tradition does as well. Even Athanasius, the chief opponent of subordinationism, freely admits that an asymmetrical order obtains between the Father and Son:

> Jesus has said "was given unto Me," and "I received," and "were delivered to Me," only to show that He is not the Father, but the Father's Word, and the Eternal Son, who because of His likeness to the Father, has eternally what He has from Him, and because He is the Son, has from the Father what He has eternally. Moreover ... "was given" and "were delivered," and the like, do not impair the Godhead of the Son, but rather show Him to be truly Son.... For the Savior Himself says, "As the Father hath life in Himself, so hath He given also to the Son to have life in Himself." Now from the words "hath given," He signifies that He is not the Father; but in saying "so," He shows the Son's natural likeness and propriety towards the Father.... Then is the Word faithful, and all things which He says that He has received, He has always, yet has from the Father; and the Father indeed not from any, but the Son from the Father.[16]

As I have noted already, Giles has cited Athanasius in an entirely different way, in support of symmetrical order. Shall we conclude that Athanasius has equivocated? I think not. It seems to me that Giles has simply misread Athanasius. Athanasius was not the opponent of asymmetrical order in the Trinity but rather of asymmetries that made the Son unequal to the Father. Giles apparently finds it impossible to imagine that both equality and ordered asymmetry can cohere in the Trinity, but it seems to me that neither Athanasius nor the fathers shared his logic. To make matters still clearer, Steven Boyer reminds us that the Bible speaks about hierarchical asymmetries not only respecting the Trinity but also regarding numerous human relationships. Humanity is said to have authority over the natural order, governments over citizens, church leaders over congregants, parents over children, and husbands over wives. Many similar examples could of course be cited. So, in the end, I think that the overall picture supports the legitimacy of asymmetrical hierarchies in the Godhead and in human societies.

Perhaps our theological perspective on these questions can be broadened by asking why these hierarchies exist at all. According to Boyer, the shorthand answer

---

16. *Against the Arians* 3.36.

to this question is that hierarchy "contributes to beauty, joy, and life." That is, when authoritative hierarchies are ideally construed and lived out, submission to authority is a beautiful thing that expresses something of the very nature of the Holy Trinity. The difficulties with hierarchy arise only when its structures are transmogrified by human sin, so that human authority is exercised in evil acts of oppression, tyranny, and cruelty. Unfortunately, such abuses of power are quite common, so it cannot be a surprise that the impulse to rid our world of hierarchies altogether is very strong in some quarters. This is undoubtedly the reality that fuels the rhetoric of Giles and of others who view all hierarchies as evil. But this perspective on hierarchy paints with a brush that is too broad. Even though the biblical authors were profoundly aware of the problem of sin, they certainly espoused hierarchies in human relationships, and they also tell us why. In the case of government authority, for instance, we are told to submit to its authority because the government is "God's servant to do you good" (Rom. 13:1-5 NIV). Government officials serve this role by rewarding behaviors that promote social order and by punishing behaviors that are destructive. So political hierarchies are a good thing. Of course, Scripture also speaks of governments that run amok and so become the object of God's wrath (Isa. 10:5-19; Rev. 18), but in every case where this is so, Scripture tells us that these authorities were removed from their post because of their oppressive and tyrannical behavior. In sum, while Christians should recognize the potential threats created by hierarchical authority structures and work to remove these if and when they become unduly oppressive, these liberating priorities should be counterbalanced by a theological appreciation for the important role that hierarchies play in promoting and preserving social order. So, with respect to the preliminary matter of hierarchy, I do not believe that we can legitimately exclude hierarchies of authority from our deliberations about gender theology. Hierarchy is not evil; it is at least necessary—and perhaps even beautiful.

With this in mind let us turn again to the subject at hand, which is the theological debate about gender and authority. My purpose going forward is to focus more narrowly on Scripture, and on what it has to say about this debate. According to Mary Stewart Van Leeuwen, an avowed advocate of the egalitarian position (and one of my valued colleagues here at Eastern University), the use of Scripture in the gender debate has often degenerated into a game of "proof-text poker," in which each side of the discussion plays its favorite Scripture cards. Traditionalists cite texts like Genesis 3:16, Ephesians 5:22, 1 Corinthians 11:3-10, and Titus 2:4-5; while egalitarians cite texts like Genesis 1:26-28, Job 42:15, Acts 2:17-19, and Galatians 3:28.[17] Rhetorically speaking, this leaves us with the impression that the Bible is somewhat ambiguous on the issues, leaving an open door for

---

17. Mary Stewart Van Leeuwen, "Is Equal Regard in the Bible?" in *Does Christianity Teach Male Headship? The Equal-Regard Marriage and Its Critics*, ed. David Blankenhorn, Don Browning, and Mary Stewart Van Leeuwen (Grand Rapids: Eerdmans, 2004), 13-22.

Van Leeuwen's more nuanced theological discussion in *Gender and Grace*.[18] But as Maggie Gallagher, another egalitarian, has noted, this proof-text rhetoric is somewhat misleading.[19] The content of these biblical texts reveals that, in the game of proof-text poker, the traditionalists have a far stronger hand than the egalitarians. Whereas the traditionalist verses speak very directly and specifically to the issue at hand ("wives, submit yourselves to your own husbands, as to the Lord"), the egalitarian texts often seem strained to the breaking point. The text that Van Leeuwen cites from Job provides a good example: "Nowhere in all the land were there found women as beautiful as Job's daughters, and their father granted them an inheritance along with their brothers" (Job 42:15 NIV). If anything, this last text probably supports the traditional viewpoint, since it is Job—and not his wife—who has the authority to distribute the family inheritance. A brief survey of the relevant texts reveals just how strong the traditional, complementarian argument seems to be:

> To the woman he said, "I will greatly multiply your pain in childbearing; in pain you shall bring forth children, yet your desire shall be for your husband, and he shall rule over you." (Gen. 3:16 RSV)

> Wives, be subject to your husbands, as to the Lord. For the husband is the head of the wife as Christ is the head of the church, his body, and is himself its Savior. As the church is subject to Christ, so let wives also be subject in everything to their husbands. Husbands, love your wives, as Christ loved the church and gave himself up for her, that he might sanctify her, having cleansed her by the washing of water with the word, that he might present the church to himself in splendor, without spot or wrinkle or any such thing, that she might be holy and without blemish. Even so husbands should love their wives as their own bodies. He who loves his wife loves himself. (Eph. 5:22–28 RSV)

> But I want you to understand that the head of every man is Christ, the head of a woman is her husband, and the head of Christ is God. Any man who prays or prophesies with his head covered dishonors his head, but any woman who prays or prophesies with her head unveiled dishonors her head—it is the same as if her head were shaven. For if a woman will not veil herself, then she should cut off her hair; but if it is disgraceful for a woman to be shorn or shaven, let her wear a veil. For a man ought not to cover his head, since he is the image and glory of God; but woman is the glory of man. For man was not made from woman, but woman from man. Neither was man created for woman, but woman for man. For this reason, and because of the angels, the woman ought to have a sign of authority on her head. (1 Cor. 11:3–10 RSV)

---

18. Mary Stewart Van Leeuwen, *Gender and Grace: Love, Work, and Parenting in a Changing World* (Downers Grove, IL: InterVarsity, 1990).

19. Maggie Gallagher, "Reflections on Headship," in Blankenhorn, Browning, and Van Leeuwen, *Does Christianity Teach Male Headship?* 111–25.

Let a woman learn in silence with all submissiveness. I permit no woman to teach or to have authority over men; she is to keep silent. For Adam was formed first, then Eve; and Adam was not deceived, but the woman was deceived and became a transgressor. Yet woman will be saved through bearing children, if she continues in faith and love and holiness, with modesty. (1 Tim. 2:11–15 RSV)

And so train the young women to love their husbands and children, to be sensible, chaste, domestic, kind, and submissive to their husbands, that the word of God may not be discredited. (Titus 2:4–5 RSV)

Likewise you wives, be submissive to your husbands, so that some, though they do not obey the word, may be won without a word by the behavior of their wives, when they see your reverent and chaste behavior. Let not yours be the outward adorning with braiding of hair, decoration of gold, and wearing of fine clothing, but let it be the hidden person of the heart with the imperishable jewel of a gentle and quiet spirit, which in God's sight is very precious. So once the holy women who hoped in God used to adorn themselves and were submissive to their husbands, as Sarah obeyed Abraham, calling him lord. And you are now her children if you do right and let nothing terrify you. (1 Pet. 3:1–6 RSV)

The biblical evidence in support of the traditional viewpoint spans the canon from creation to the General Epistles, and the resulting perspective is remarkably consistent. But we have seen that the same consistency marks the biblical view of slavery. So we can with good reason ask: In spite of the Bible's general consistency on this issue, does Scripture provide us with a theological trajectory, in which the relationship between men and women moves in an egalitarian direction? I believe that it does.

As one moves from the Old to the New Testament, a biblical trajectory in the direction of gender equality seems fairly clear. Almost every sentence of the Old Testament is focalized through male eyes, and what is said from that viewpoint nearly always suits male preferences. This is especially true in the laws of the Old Testament. In matters of marriage, divorce, and inheritance, men enjoy many advantages over women—not to mention the flexibility associated with polygamy.[20] Even in the Ten Commandments—a text purportedly written by the finger of God himself—women are listed among the properties of their husbands.[21] Both before and after marriage, it is the women—and not the men—who are subjects of close scrutiny in matters of sexual fidelity.[22] In the case of rape, it is the father, not the daughter, who is paid for the "damage"—while the raped

---

20. Marriage: Exod. 20:17; 21:10–11; Num. 30:1–16; cf. Josh. 15:16; Hos. 2:1–3, 10; Jer. 13:20–27; Ezek. 16:32–42; 23:22–30. Divorce: Deut. 20:10–14; 22:1–4, 19, 29; 24:1–4. Inheritance: Deut. 20:10–14; 21:16–17; Num. 27:5–8; 31:1–9.

21. Exod. 20:17; cf. Deut. 5:21; Judg. 5:30.

22. Virginity: Gen. 19:18; 24:16; Num. 31:35; Deut. 22:13–14. Adultery: Exod. 22:16–17; Lev. 20:10; Num. 5:11–31; Deut. 22:22–24.

woman must marry the rapist.[23] In many respects, Old Testament law breathes the air of patriarchalism.

The status of women in these Israelite laws contrasts rather sharply with the status of women in many New Testament texts. But on these issues the New Testament has a diversity of its own, particularly within that corpus of letters that we associate with Paul. Egalitarians often cite Paul's Letter to the Galatians ("all are one in Christ") as evidence for their equal-regard agenda, whereas complementarians appeal to texts like 1 Timothy 2:11–15 and 1 Corinthians 14:34–35, two texts that forbid women to speak in church. Although one complementarian has argued that Paul's "contradictions" on this matter are illusions of a sort,[24] critical scholars have offered another, I think better, explanation for the apparent discrepancy. As a rule, the critics do not believe that Paul wrote either of the texts that demand silence from women. The Pastoral Epistles were composed by someone who wrote in Paul's name,[25] and the little text in 1 Corinthians 14:34–35 was added to the epistle by someone else after Paul wrote the rest of 1 Corinthians.[26] If we set aside these two texts, then the true egalitarian spirit of Paul comes shining through. Contrary to the judgments in 1 Timothy and 1 Corinthians 14:34–35, Paul permitted women both to prophesy and to speak in tongues in the public worship services (see 1 Cor. 12; 14). That he allowed them to prophesy is especially relevant to our discussion, since prophesying was nothing less than delivering the words of God to the church in a public setting—very close to what we might

23. Deut. 22:28–29.
24. Harold O. J. Brown, "The New Testament against Itself: 1 Timothy 2:9–15 and the 'Breakthrough' of Galatians 3:28," in *Women in the Church: A Fresh Analysis of 1 Timothy 2:9–15*, ed. Andreas J. Köstenberger, Thomas R. Schreiner, and H. Scott Baldwin (Grand Rapids: Baker Academic, 1995), 197–208.
25. See my discussion in chapter 3.
26. The basic arguments are as follows: (1) 1 Cor. 14:34–35 fits awkwardly into the context of Paul's rhetoric in 1 Cor. 14 (see especially Gordon D. Fee, *The First Epistle to the Corinthians*, NICNT [Grand Rapids: Eerdmans, 1987], 699–708). (2) These two verses (vv. 34–35) appear in different places in our manuscript evidence, sometimes between 14:33 and 14:35 and sometimes at the end of the chapter. This suggests that they may reflect later additions to the text. (3) These verses contradict Paul's argument elsewhere in 1 Corinthians, where it is assumed that women do speak in church (e.g., 1 Cor. 11:2–6). (4) These verses contradict the egalitarian spirit of Paul's other epistles, such as we see in Gal. 3:28. For discussions of the text-critical and literary evidence, see Philip B. Payne, "MS. 88 as Evidence for a Text without 1 Cor. 14:34–35," *New Testament Studies* 44 (1998): 152–58; Payne, "The Originality of Text-Critical Symbols in Codex Vaticanus," *Novum Testamentum* 42 (2000): 105–13; Payne, "The Text-Critical Function of the Umlauts in Vaticanus, with Special Attention to 1 Corinthians 14.34–35: A Response to J. Edward Miller," *JSNT* 27 (2004): 105–12; J. Edward Miller, "Some Observations on the Text-Critical Function of the Umlauts in Vaticanus, with Special Attention to 1 Corinthians 14.34–35," *JSNT* 26 (2003): 217–36. See also the appropriate sections of Hans Conzelmann, *1 Corinthians: A Commentary*, trans. James W. Leitch, Hermeneia (Philadelphia: Fortress, 1975); Fee, *First Epistle to the Corinthians*; Richard B. Hays, *First Corinthians*, Interpretation (Louisville: Westminster John Knox, 1997); Hans-Josef Klauck, *1 Korintherbrief*, NEchtB (Würzburg: Echter Verlag, 1984); Wolfgang Schrage, *Der erste Brief an die Korinther*, EKKNT, 3 vols. (Neukirchen-Vluyn: Neukirchener Verlag, 1991–1999); Christoph Senft, *La première épître de saint Paul aux Corinthiens*, 2nd rev. ed., CNT (Geneva: Labor et Fides, 1990); August Strobel, *Der erste Brief an die Korinther*, ZBK (Zurich: Theologischer Verlag, 1989).

call preaching.[27] That Paul extended these freedoms to both men and women was undoubtedly an expression of his deep conviction about the gospel, that "there is neither Jew nor Greek, there is neither slave nor free, there is neither male nor female; for you are all one in Christ Jesus" (Gal. 3:28 RSV). Once we admit that this egalitarian voice appears in the New Testament,[28] and according to the apocryphal *Acts of Paul* that it took hold in the early church,[29] then we are in a position to take more seriously some of the other texts that point in egalitarian directions. In Judges 4–5, for instance, we find that God himself chooses Deborah as Israel's judge. To be sure, Deborah was not an ordained pastor. But in terms of leadership and authority, hers was certainly a higher post than the author of 1 Timothy would allow, given that he proscribed female authority over men (see 1 Tim. 2:11–15). And regarding the Bible's egalitarian spirit, we cannot overlook that little text in Romans 16:7, which Eldon Epp has helped us to read properly: "Greet *Andronicus* [masculine] and *Junia* [feminine], my relatives who were in prison with me; they are prominent among the apostles, and they were in Christ before I was" (NRSV).[30] So far as we can tell, here at the end of Romans Paul appears to identify Junia as a female apostle. So, whatever else we may say, it is certain that the New Testament tends to soften, and in some cases almost eliminates, the one-sided authority of men over women. As a result, the expectation of mutuality placed on husbands in marriage is more specific and far-reaching than anything one finds in the Old Testament:

> Husbands, love your wives, as Christ loved the church and gave himself up for her, that he might sanctify her, having cleansed her by the washing of water with the word, that he might present the church to himself in splendor, without spot or wrinkle or any such thing, that she might be holy and without blemish. Even so husbands should love their wives as their own bodies. He who loves his wife loves himself. (Eph. 5:25–28 RSV)

Nothing in the Old Testament even comes close to this portrait of mutual submission in marriage, excepting perhaps—in the most cryptic way—the Song of Songs. So the Bible as a whole is certainly far more egalitarian than the Old Testament alone. Perhaps it is Jesus himself who pursues this egalitarian vision to its eschatological end: "When the dead rise, they will neither marry nor be given

---

27. Fee, *First Corinthians*, 595–96.
28. See also Acts 2:17–18 (citing Joel 2:28–29); Acts 21:9.
29. In this apocryphal text, which dates c. 200 CE, Paul directs a young female convert, Thecla, to "go and teach the word of God" (*Acts of Paul* 41). This text may have bearing on our text-critical judgment concerning 1 Cor. 14:34–35. As I have pointed out, many scholars believe that these verses were not originally in the letter. Given that the author of the *Acts of Paul* took 1 Cor. 7 very seriously (by preferring singleness to married life), his approval of female teaching might suggest that his 1 Corinthians *Vorlage* did not include 14:34–35. I will soon take up this matter in a short article. For a translation of the *Acts of Paul*, see J. K. Elliott, *The Apocryphal New Testament*, rev. repr. (Oxford: Clarendon, 1999), 350–88.
30. Eldon Jay Epp, *Junia: The First Woman Apostle* (Minneapolis: Fortress, 2005).

in marriage; they will be like the angels in heaven" (Mark 12:25 NIV). If this comment by our Lord is taken at face value, or even close to face value, then the Bible's eschatological trajectory points beyond a restoration of the created order to a quite different eschatological reordering of creation. Jesus's words could provide a strong argument in support of the egalitarian position, and I am surprised that equal-regard scholars do not make more of them. At any rate, we may safely say that the biblical trajectories regarding gender are analogous to those that prevail respecting slavery: in matters of gender, the Bible is pointing us away from extreme male-female asymmetries and toward gender equality.

But trajectory theology is interested not only in the direction of the biblical trajectories but also in their magnitude. How far is the trajectory telling us to go? To give just one example, if Jesus means quite literally in Mark 12 that, in the eschaton, there will be no marriages, then why should we delay the fulfillment of that great vision? Why not eliminate marriage once and for all? One part of the answer, I think, is that we are called to live out that eschatological vision within a created order that is not yet suited to the new order. So marriage remains an important part of the Christian vision. In some respects, then, the Bible's trajectory toward gender equality goes no further than Genesis 1:27: a husband and wife who together bear the divine image. It is time for us to look closely at this text from Genesis.

It is truly paradoxical that some of the most important biblical texts in the egalitarian arsenal are those that the author of 1 Timothy uses *against* the ordination of women. I speak of Genesis 1:27 and 3:16. How do egalitarians read these two texts? According to them, the first text presents the first human couple in a way that highlights their full equality. God's image is borne by neither gender alone but rather by male and female together: "So God created man in his own image, in the image of God he created him; male and female he created them" (RSV, NIV). According to egalitarians, we could hardly ask for a more vivid image of gender equality. So the original design of creation was egalitarian in spirit. That this is the case is reinforced, they tell us, by the dramatic shift in gender relations that followed the "fall" of the man and woman in Genesis 3:16: "I will greatly increase your pains in childbearing; with pain you will give birth to children. *Your desire will be for your husband, and he will rule over you*" (NIV, italics mine).

Equal-regard theologians explain these two texts from Genesis in a fairly consistent way. First, they insist that, according to Genesis 1, the husband and wife were created as full equals, and that no authority structures prevailed in their perfect, primordial marriage. Second, equal-regard advocates point out that the patriarchal authority structures, so prevalent in human society, seem to be a consequence of the fall rather than a divinely intended feature of the created order. Third, egalitarians strongly aver that in Genesis 3:16, God did not *prescribe* the proper order of marriage ("your husband will rule over you") but merely *describes* how marital relationships would succumb to the disorder of a fallen world. If this reading of Genesis is accurate, then it is very important for the egalitarian argument. It will mean that patriarchal authority was not an intention of God either before or after the fall, and it will further mean that patriarchal authority is itself an expression of our fallen humanity. By all means, if we join these exegetical observations about the creation with the theological trajectory that we have already seen in Scripture, then male headship in the family and church is something to be rid of as soon as possible.

But frankly, I do not believe that this reading of Genesis does the text justice. Although Genesis 1 describes the male and female as full equals who jointly bear the divine image, there is no a priori reason to suppose that this is an expression of pure asymmetrical egalitarianism, especially when this text is situated properly within its biblical and theological context. That the woman was made from man to be his helper, and that he twice names her (Gen. 2:23; 3:20), as he does the animals (2:20), suggests his priority and thus authority over her—just as 1 Timothy 2:11–15 and 1 Corinthians 11:5–10 indicate.[31]

As for Genesis 3:16, despite egalitarian objections, it remains very likely that the subordination of Eve to Adam is a *prescription* from God rather than a mere *description* of the fall's natural consequences. As many scholars have noted, God's judgments upon the serpent, woman, and man in Genesis 3:14–19 are cast in the form of his legal judgments against them.[32] In the case of the serpent and the man there is no question that God has punished each by pronouncing curses, first upon the serpent itself (3:14–15) and then upon the ground that Adam tills (3:17–19). These are not mere consequences of sin; they are divine judgments followed by divine acts, as we are told explicitly in 8:21 (it was God who cursed the ground). On the basis of the judgments received by both the serpent and Adam, we should anticipate that Eve's punishment was also by divine prescription. And this was certainly so. God explicitly tells the woman in 3:16, "*I* will increase your pain in childbearing; in pain you will birth children. And your desire will be for your husband, but he will rule over you" (my translation). It was the decree and action of God, and not merely the fall of humanity itself, that produced the hierarchies so endemic to human families and society. The tendency to think otherwise about 3:16 sometimes arises when the clause "he will rule over you" is interpreted more negatively, as in, "he will dominate you."[33] If this translation were accurate then perhaps we would have cause to rethink the text, but there is no reason to render the phrase so negatively, as if God had done something in the first half of 3:16 that indirectly led to men oppressing women in the second half of the verse. The Hebrew term *māšal*, "to rule," is standard political language for royal power over one's subjects (e.g., Ps. 8:7). Whether the exercise of this authority

---

31. Gordon J. Wenham, *Genesis*, 2 vols., WBC (Waco: Word, 1987–1994), 1:81.
32. Gerhard von Rad, *Genesis*, rev. ed., OTL (Philadelphia: Westminster, 1972), 92–93; Claus Westermann, *Genesis*, trans. John J. Scullion, 3 vols., Continental Commentary (Minneapolis: Augsburg, 1984–1986), 1:193.
33. Victor P. Hamilton, *The Book of Genesis*, 2 vols., NICOT (Grand Rapids: Eerdmans, 1990–1995), 1:201-2.

is sinful depends on the one wielding it, but it remains true enough that women lost ground in the post-fall economy of power. Genesis 3:16 does not explicitly tell us why God instituted this hierarchical structure, but we can surmise that the issue was authority. Just as human societies require divinely appointed authorities to promote order and stability, so too there is a corresponding need for authority and order in the family.

Now it is not merely the Old Testament but also the New Testament that explicitly tells us that these asymmetries were part of the created marital order. In a text that has import for our interpretation of both Genesis 1:27 and 3:16, the author of 1 Timothy says:

> Let a woman learn in silence with all submissiveness. I permit no woman to teach or to have authority over men; she is to keep silent. For Adam was formed first, then Eve; and Adam was not deceived, but the woman was deceived and became a transgressor. Yet woman will be saved through bearing children, if she continues in faith and love and holiness, with modesty. (1 Tim. 2:11–15 RSV)

Egalitarians do not much like this text and tend to ignore it or strategically marginalize it. Linda Belleville's response is a good example: "The simple fact is that this is the lone New Testament reference to Adam's seniority. If it defines the pecking order of men and women, why does it surface only here?"[34] Of course, Belleville here begs the question and ignores important biblical evidence. First Timothy does not speak for itself; it depends upon a reading of Genesis that, in my opinion, can withstand close scrutiny. So we have two biblical texts—not one New Testament text—that assert Adam's authority. Moreover, we have seen already that many biblical texts either assert or imply male headship in the home and church, even in the New Testament. So, while Belleville is technically correct to say that "this is the lone New Testament reference to *Adam's* seniority," good theology requires that this text be read in light of the many other biblical texts that highlight male authority in the home and church.

Belleville's egalitarian treatment of this very important text from 1 Timothy is far inferior to that offered by a cadre of complementarian scholars, who have recently thrown their support behind a more patriarchal interpretation of the text.[35] A considerable mass of convincing exegetical, theological, and historical evidence supports this traditional reading, as is admitted even by egalitarians like William Webb.[36] Webb can admit this because, unlike Belleville, he feels no compulsion to make 1 Timothy say something that it clearly does not say. Webb

---

34. Linda L. Belleville, *Women Leaders and the Church: Three Crucial Questions* (Grand Rapids: Baker Academic, 2000), 170.

35. Andreas J. Köstenberger, Thomas R. Schreiner, and H. Scott Baldwin, eds., *Women in the Church: A Fresh Analysis of 1 Timothy 2:9–15* (Grand Rapids: Baker Academic, 1995).

36. William J. Webb, *Slaves, Women, and Homosexuals: Exploring the Hermeneutics of Cultural Analysis* (Downers Grove, IL: InterVarsity, 2001).

believes that 1 Timothy reflects the antiquated cultural views of Christians whose theologies had not yet assimilated some of Scripture's richer and deeper theological perspectives. So, although the author of 1 Timothy may have believed that male authority was grounded in the order of creation, Webb believes that Scripture as a whole would have us reach a different, egalitarian conclusion.

Having taken this stand, however, Webb confesses that he has some reservations about his theological conclusions. In a chapter entitled, "What If I Am Wrong," he suggests that the options before us might include not only his approach, which he dubs "complementary egalitarianism," but also a more modest traditional approach that he calls "ultra-soft patriarchy."[37] Why does Webb hesitate on this point? My guess is that 1 Timothy presents him with a special problem. As we have seen, one of the most common egalitarian arguments for moving beyond Scripture's explicit viewpoint is that the very shape of the created order beckons us to do so. The difficulty in this case is that 1 Timothy 2:11–15 would seem to preclude this theological move, for its inner logic, which depends on a patriarchal reading of the creation story in Genesis 1–3, contradicts any argument that uses the created order as the foundation for an egalitarian agenda. In the end, if one wishes to do serious exegesis and to come out as an egalitarian, there is only one direction to go: one will have to follow in the footsteps of Paul Jewett, an evangelical who finally concluded that, on the matter of the subordination of women, texts like 1 Timothy 2:11–15 are simply out of step with the canonical voice and theological trajectory of Scripture as a whole.[38] To do otherwise would be akin to arguing that the laws in Leviticus 11:7 and Deuteronomy 14:8 do not allow us to eat pork. In such cases, I think it is far better to simply admit that some individual texts in Scripture do stand in tension with what we judge to be the final voice of Scripture.

Because I teach in a university where the egalitarian perspective dominates the institutional discourse, it would serve my advantage to follow Jewett's lead on this issue. And given that I have made the same sort of theological move in the case of slavery, it is not the principle of the thing that would prevent me from doing so. The real difficulty is that, when it comes to gender and theology, the biblical, theological, and historical evidence for a traditional view of male authority in the home is very strong. At the same time, like any conscientious reader of the New Testament, I also notice the subtle and not so subtle biblical trajectories that soften the hard edges of male authority. It is in light of this biblical evidence that I would like to lay out what are at this point my own theological convictions regarding gender in the home and church.

Authority and equality do not seem to be mutually exclusive categories. Neither the perfect asymmetrical equality of the Father and Son, nor the perfect

---

37. Ibid., 236–44.

38. Paul K. Jewett, *Man as Male and Female: A Study in Sexual Relationships from a Theological Point of View* (Grand Rapids: Eerdmans, 1975).

asymmetrical equality of husband and wife, need entail any sort of difficulty or disappointment for the subordinates in those relationships. These hierarchical relationships are characterized by mutual love and respect, and by a continuous act of self-giving that moves in both directions, from the one to the other. Egalitarians who assume that equality and authority are mutually exclusive categories have succumbed to an interpretive myopia, which cannot get beyond the oppressive examples of authority present in human society. Scripture gives us every reason to believe that authority need not be oppressive. It suggests that husbands have been entrusted with authority over their families, and that this authority, when properly ordered and expressed as an act of self-giving, will bring joy to their wives and families. It is this sort of mutuality that was lost at the fall, and that Christ calls us to restore. No one expresses this portrait of Christian mutuality more vividly than Paul, whose comments reflect both the authority of the husband as well as the new spirit of mutual submission that has appeared in Christ:

> Any man who prays or prophesies with his head covered dishonors his head, but any woman who prays or prophesies with her head unveiled dishonors her head—it is the same as if her head were shaven. For if a woman will not veil herself, then she should cut off her hair; but if it is disgraceful for a woman to be shorn or shaven, let her wear a veil. For a man ought not to cover his head, since he is the image and glory of God; but woman is the glory of man. For man was not made from woman, but woman from man. Neither was man created for woman, but woman for man. That is why a woman ought to have a veil on her head, because of the angels. *Nevertheless, in the Lord woman is not independent of man nor man of woman*; for as woman was made from man, so man is now born of woman. And all things are from God. (1 Cor. 11:4-12 RSV, italics mine)[39]

As the italicized phrase shows, Paul seems to be struggling to situate the male-female relationship into the context of the gospel, trying to see how marital hierarchies might work "in the Lord." That Paul would attend to this theological issue can be no surprise given his programmatic statement in Galatians 3:28, that in Christ there is neither "male nor female" because we are all one in Christ.

But even as God has acted in Christ to reverse the consequences of the fall, he has also introduced certain structures into human society to quell the threats of disorder and human sin. One thinks here of the law's stipulations and consequences,

39. In the immediate context of 1 Cor. 11, Paul ponders the matter of head coverings for women in light of the authority structures of the cosmos. For the most part, modern Christians take Paul's judgment on the matter—that women must cover their heads when they prophesy—to depend on a specific cultural situation that no longer pertains to us. Nevertheless, as I mentioned above (pp. 338-40), the matter of gender and authority comes into play here; I mentioned as well that though the text tends toward a patriarchal view (woman was taken from man), Paul immediately softens this perspective by citing the dependence of men on women. It seems to me that he was still struggling to work out the implications of his egalitarian gospel for a patriarchal world. This is no surprise, given that in this very letter Paul distinguishes his own judgment on practical matters from the "word of the Lord" itself (see 1 Cor. 7:25, 40).

of human governments, of the husband's authority over the family, and of parental authority over children. To be sure, these structures are baser solutions to human conflict than redeemed living. I say this because it is inherently simpler, if less satisfying, to submit to authority than to find the space for mutual love, submission, and agreement. As a result, when divinely ordained authorities must exercise their authority to tame the disharmonies of society or marriage, this is always evidence that someone has failed to live out the gospel. The offending party in such cases could be the authority as easily as the one subject to it, but I suspect that, more often than not, these kinds of conflict reflect guilt on both sides of the authority equation. But insofar as redeemed persons truly live by the Spirit, these bald *assertions* of authority become unnecessary because our human differences are resolved through mutual submission. As Paul has told us, the Spirit-filled believer has no need for the law (Rom. 8:1–4), nor does the Spirit-filled marriage require that husbands "rule" over their wives in exercises of authority (implied by Gen. 3:16). However, when our human disagreements succumb to the influence of sin—be it in the church, in the home, or in regard to our neighbor—Scripture calls us, for the sake of order, to submit our wills and behaviors to the preferences of others. This is the lot of men as well as women, since all of us live to some extent under the aegis of God-ordained authorities. While we will not always appreciate how those authorities exercise the prerogatives of their power, it is certain that those authorities often produce great benefits for human persons.

In light of what I have just said, the proper aim of Christian marriage is to incarnate the vision of mutual love and submission that is so vividly described in Ephesians 5 and in similar biblical texts. Whenever a husband overtly exercises his authority to bring order to the home, and even more when he has become so tyrannical and oppressive that the marriage itself is threatened, these instances of family conflict represent genuine defeats in the quest to create marital relationships that taste of Genesis 1 and of the coming kingdom. But so long as there is human sin, the divine decree that husbands shall have authority in the home still stands and is still needed. Modern feminism has played an important role in curtailing the tyranny and oppression caused by sinful twists of this male authority, but insofar as feminism wishes to remove these domestic authority structures altogether, it is surely a movement that runs out of bounds. As some egalitarians now admit, it may be that extreme expressions of feminism have unwittingly contributed to the family crisis so prevalent in the United States.[40] Preferable would be a softer feminism, one that recognizes the genuine beauty of a "love that submits" and of a "love that leads by serving"; this sort of mutual love reflects the inner beauty of the Trinity—especially the beauty of the Son as he submits to his Father.

---

40. J. W. Miller, *Biblical Faith and Fathering* (New York: Paulist Press, 1989); Miller, "The Problem of Men, Reconsidered," in Blankenhorn, Browning, and Van Leeuwen, *Does Christianity Teach Male Headship?* 65–73; John Witte Jr., "Male Headship: Reform of the Protestant Tradition," in Blankenhorn, Browning, and Van Leeuwen, *Does Christianity Teach Male Headship?* 28–39.

Now how does male authority in the domestic context relate to life in the church? Can we safely presume that women must remain under the authority of men in the church as in the home? Can women serve as pastors or leaders in the church? My answers to these questions are perhaps not what one might expect. I would like to pursue these questions by returning yet again to the crucial text from 1 Timothy and its reading of Genesis. As we have noted, the author of 1 Timothy does not "permit a woman to teach or to have authority over a man," and he does so on the basis of the created order and the consequences of the fall. The theological basis for his conclusion seems sound and very nearly beyond question, since his patriarchal viewpoint is supported by Genesis, by large swaths of the biblical metanarrative, and by the Christian tradition itself. So the *foundation* of the author's argument is secure. But I am not at all sure that his *conclusion* is ultimately secure.[41]

As I have already pointed out, several biblical texts gainsay the ruling that women should remain "silent" and should not teach or have authority over men. Paul's Letters presume that women speak in church and even that they "prophesy," which was a fairly significant theological activity, whatever it may have entailed (1 Cor. 11:1–16). We know as well that women were prophets in the Old Testament (Exod. 15:20; 2 Kings 22:14), and that Deborah the prophetess was selected by God to lead the people of Israel (Judg. 4–5). I see no easy way to dovetail these texts with the ruling delivered in 1 Timothy, which is based on a particular understanding of the created order itself. For this reason a sensible canonical approach will have to choose between the two perspectives, and it seems best to say that 1 Timothy reflects a cultural accommodation that is behind the theological curve in comparison with the more egalitarian texts of the Bible, such as Galatians 3:28.[42] At the very least, one will have to admit that God makes exceptions to the patriarchal rules when it comes to women in leadership, and this fact is perhaps all that one needs to begin a theological case for the ordination of women.

Equally important from my own theological vantage point is that the ordination of women does not create the "crisis of authority" that would appear if we adopt an egalitarian vision of marriage. My comment requires an explanation. As

---

41. As I have stated previously, I doubt that Paul authored the Pastoral Epistles. Nevertheless, the idea that this author has reached a questionable conclusion regarding women in the church comports well with comments made by Paul, in which the apostle intimates a lack of certainty about his teaching. Paul tells us that he was unsure how many people he had baptized (1 Cor. 1:14–16), unclear about the details of God's plan for Israel (Rom. 11:33–36), and drew on his own thoughts when he had no word from God (1 Cor. 7:10, 25). We should note as well Paul's discussion of predestination, which couches his explanation of the doctrine in speculative "what ifs" (Rom. 9:22–23).

42. Note the following comment from Van Leeuwen: "Just as Paul does not call for the sudden overturning by Christians of slavery as an institution, but undermines it from within by urging both slaves and masters to treat each other as brothers in Christ, so too for the sake of social order and successful evangelism he advises the recipients of his letters to play along with some of the local norms of patriarchy even as he proclaims that in Christ 'There is no longer Jew or Greek, there is no longer slave or free, there is no longer male and female; for all of you are one in Jesus Christ' (Gal. 3:28)" ("Is Equal Regard in the Bible?" 21).

I have said already, purely egalitarian marriages do not admit that divinely ordered authority is necessary to resolve the inevitable conflicts that arise between husbands and wives. We can surely applaud the impulse behind this utopian vision, but it seems to me that it does not suit the real world in which we live. When fallen people live together, conflict and irreconcilable differences are inevitable. When these differences arise in marriage—or in society as a whole—the divinely ordained means of preserving order is the exercise of authority and submission to it. Because egalitarians essentially demand mutuality in marriage, they lack the theological resources to confront irreconcilable differences between husband and wife. This engenders a crisis of authority that can threaten the health of the marriage and the stability of the home.

I do not believe that the same can be said regarding women in church leadership. Although many churches require that leaders be male, these leaders are never selected on the simple basis of gender. Indeed, church leaders are usually appointed by other church authorities or are selected by committees or congregations, often by some kind of vote. As is easy to see, this selection process could include women without occasioning any crisis of authority at all. Women would be duly selected and would simply take their assigned place in church leadership. This puts the issue of women in leadership on very different footing than the issue of women in the home. Whereas the husband's authority in the home is foundational for the stability of the family and hence of society, the same is not the case regarding women in church leadership. It follows that the issue of female leadership in the church is not as theologically pressing as some believe, perhaps no more pressing or important than the church's perennial debates about eschatology, or about free will and predestination. Even if ordaining women errs wide of God's "perfect plan," the error and its consequences may be little more—or even far less than—what is reaped when we ordain male pastors with poor preaching skills. The result may not be ideal, but it would certainly not be tragic.

Given this reality, and the Bible's very positive trajectory toward gender equality, and the notable exceptions that Scripture makes for women in leadership, I am prepared to accept a larger role for women in church leadership than church tradition has heretofore permitted. Many gifted women are ready to lead our churches, and we should not stand in their way so long as Scripture reflects at least some ambiguity on the issue. So, while I deeply respect the theological conclusions of those who think otherwise, the ordination of women to the ministry seems to me entirely suitable as Christian practice.

Conclusions

In this chapter I have attempted to illustrate how theology might look if Scripture is read and interpreted in the manner that I have laid out in previous chapters. In spite of my open-ended approach, which allows for the accommodation of error in Scripture and for going beyond Scripture in our theology, and in spite of my epistemology that denies the epistemic certainty so many evangelicals crave, it seems to me that the final theological product is fairly close to the standard conclusions of church tradition. I have concluded that the life of King David, as depicted in Scripture, provides an example that is worthy of our emulation. I have embraced the message of Daniel and Revelation, that because a kingdom is still to come in which all will be set aright, we should live in light of that coming kingdom. On the matter of gender and theology, I have concluded that the traditional authority of the husband in the family, these days so much under attack in society and in some corners of the church, is securely founded in Scripture. On all of these matters, it seems to me that I have come down precisely at the place where so many conservative evangelicals, Catholics, and Eastern Orthodox are already standing. I have arrived at these positions not only while accepting the standard critical conclusions but, in some cases, *because* of those critical conclusions.

But to be fair and clear, it remains true, I think, that at two fundamental points my approach to Scripture parts ways with very conservative evangelicalism. First, more so than many evangelicals, I have allowed Scripture itself to set the agenda for my theology of Scripture. If the return of Christ did not come to pass in the first century, as Paul and the author of Revelation anticipated, then so be it: such is the Word of God. If Scripture tells us on the one hand that women cannot speak in church, and on the other hand that they may prophesy there, then so be it: such is the Word of God. In like manner, if Scripture tells us that women cannot have authority over men, and if at the same time God has chosen Deborah to lead Israel, then so be it: such is the Word of God. And if such is the Word of God—that it is diverse in its messages—then our theological work will sometimes involve judgments about which of God's diverse messages to Israel and the church should set the final precedent in our theology. In the case of ordaining women to the ministry, I have argued that the minority voice of Scripture should take that final precedent. Admitting the diversity in Scripture, and taking seriously its minority voice, is surely one way in which my approach differs from standard evangelical practice.

The other way in which I depart from the usual evangelical approach to Scripture is in regard to the "peripheral use" of Scripture. By this I mean the use of Scripture as a source of insight into matters that are peripheral to the intentions of the biblical author. Such is the case when we reconstruct a modern biography of David's life from the sources in 1–2 Samuel. The biblical sources were based on an uncritical use of ancient propaganda, which painted David's life in the most positive and ideal light. This suited the author's purpose, which was to show that right living leads to blessing and that vice leads to trouble. That is precisely how it comes out in the biblical story of David. But the agenda of modern biography differs from this ancient theological agenda. What matters most in modern biography is not whether retributive theology is true. What matters most is what David actually did. So it should not be a surprise that these very different agendas have produced correspondingly different portraits of David. Nor, to extrapolate from this, should it surprise us that biblical criticism—which constantly puts the Bible to peripheral uses—often comes into conflict with theology. I would suggest that these conflicts are often illusions, inasmuch as they are created by an errant assumption that the biblical authors are doing something that they are not really doing. To criticize the biblical author's account of David on historical grounds is like criticizing Melville's *Moby Dick* because it has its whaling tactics wrong. We must always be careful to attend to the genres of biblical literature, and to take note of the ways in which those genres are foreign to our modern research agendas.

Again, though I admit that there are differences between my approach and what often passes as a traditional, evangelical approach to Scripture, I would reiterate that the theological conclusions I have reached in this chapter are largely in keeping with the long-standing traditions of the church. The obvious point that I wish to highlight is that, if we take biblical authority seriously when we practice biblical criticism, then the criticism need not lead to the kinds of problematic theological conclusions that so many conservative evangelicals expect. I believe that the biblical criticism rightly feared by conservative Christians is of a very different sort. It is a biblical criticism that admits Scripture's authority in word but not in deed. Where this brand of criticism is practiced, concepts like "trajectory," "accommodation," and "going beyond Scripture" become theoretical licenses for making the Bible say whatever we wish it to say. No better example exists than the work of Gotthold Lessing, for whom accommodation became a ready tool for rejecting everything he disliked about Scripture.[43] When this is how biblical interpretation is done, the church might as well not have a Bible at all.

I have suggested that *believing criticism* provides a different and better theological path, which steers clear of the problems created by traditional fundamentalism on the one hand and by secular biblical criticism on the other. The importance of my project rests in its attempt to assimilate the useful methods and reasonably assured results of biblical criticism to a healthy Christian faith. Although this task will not seem of pressing importance for many evangelicals, its importance for evangelical biblical scholars cannot be overestimated. If evangelicals are to join other Christians in representing Christ in the broader academy, then it will be absolutely necessary for them to be honest—sometimes painfully honest—about the biblical and historical evidence, and about the direction in which this evidence points. To do anything less will be careless at best and duplicitous at worst, and I must say that much of what passes as evangelical scholarship is both. The purpose of this book is to preserve a place at the evangelical table for genuine critical study of the Bible, and it is presently unclear whether such a place will finally be achieved, at least in some quarters. How and to what extent should modern biblical criticism be embraced in the life of the church? That is the question I consider in the concluding chapter.

---

43. Gotthold E. Lessing, *The Education of the Human Race* (London: Paul, Trench, Trubner, 1896).

Conclusions

Biblical Criticism
and Christian Institutions

Many of the standard critical conclusions about the Bible turn out to be true. Though evangelical Christians often believe that these conclusions necessarily contradict the faith and contravene the authority of Scripture, I have suggested that this is a mistaken perception, which stems from an intellectual marriage that unevenly yokes the very orthodox doctrine of inerrancy with Enlightenment modernism. That God speaks inerrantly, and that he therefore speaks inerrantly in Scripture, cannot be doubted by any orthodox Christian. But when this doctrine is affirmed in the context of Enlightenment modernism, the result is not only that God is inerrant; the result must be that the human beings who wrote the Bible offer us indubitable and incorrigible knowledge, wholly free from the foibles of human error. This version of inerrancy is mistaken, for it wrongly assumes that the human grasp on the truth—especially important religious truths—can and even must be perfect and absolute. Never is it considered that the Bible might offer us revelation that is wholly *adequate* but imperfect discourse, which is subject to the usual limitation of human understanding and at the same time useful "for teaching, for reproof, for correction, and for training in righteousness" (2 Tim. 3:16 RSV). This possibility is not considered because Enlightenment thinking thirsts for incorrigible knowledge, and also because many evangelicals believe that to admit the errant human elements in Scripture would amount to the heresy of saying that God is not perfect.

I have suggested *believing criticism* as another way to construe the situation, which is able at the same time to trust the Bible as our authority and to admit and even to appreciate the insights of biblical scholarship. At its core, believing criticism rests upon the close conceptual relationship that obtains between two views of human knowledge, namely, the ancient Christian view and the postmodern, practical realist view. Both of these traditions recommend an epistemic humility that flies in the face of the Enlightenment's epistemic optimism. The agreement is no accident, for it appears that practical realism is in some measure a rediscovery of what the Bible and the Christian tradition have long said about the nature and limits of human knowledge. This is not to say that men like Augustine and Gadamer agree in every respect; it is rather to say that when it comes to epistemology, Gadamer is in important ways much closer to Augustine than is an evangelical like Carl F. H. Henry. As a result, a practical realist like myself now feels comfortable saying what very conservative evangelicals do not wish to say: that the church fathers were right to affirm that the Bible accommodates human error in its pages. By admitting this, the fathers—and later Christians like Calvin—were not denying inerrancy. Rather they were affirming inerrancy, insofar as accommodation was their explanation for why the human errors in Scripture are by no means the errors of God. Properly understood, those "errors" become one element in the wise—one could even say perfect—discourse of an infinite God who speaks to very finite people. This approach to the Bible certainly affirms the orthodox doctrine of divine inerrancy; but it also means that the Bible cannot be the straightforward source of indubitable and incorrigible knowledge that Enlightenment-style evangelicals wish it to be. To the extent that the Bible is properly interpreted as a canonical document, and in the light of the Christian tradition and created order, it offers us the wholly adequate Word of God. But it does not offer, and in fact warns that we cannot and should not have, perfect, God-like knowledge. Consequently, that the critics have uncovered human errors in Scripture should not be a surprise, nor must it become an intractable theological problem. Insofar as we recognize this, I would suggest that our theology will be much healthier. For once we admit that the Bible, as divine discourse, is accommodated to various human viewpoints and contexts, then we will listen with more care to all that it says, and make better, more informed theological judgments.

At the outset of my work, and at several points along the way, I have promised to discuss the institutional dimensions of the problem presented by biblical criticism. At this point I will make good on that promise.

Biblical Criticism and the Local Church

It does not take long before the newer biblical studies students in my university begin to ask the question: Why does the church talk so little about the critical issues raised by biblical scholarship? Their question is animated by a kind of righteous indignation, as if they are the victims of a grand conspiracy that has hidden the truth from a mindless flock. Nearly all of these students attend or work in evangelical churches, and they are initially anxious to bring their "critical insights" about the Bible to bear on their ministries and congregations. I remember those feelings well. So I understand why my students are frustrated by my response to their question, which usually goes something like this.

Because all human knowledge is contextual, it is quite possible for "true facts" to be falsely and even harmfully understood. Consider again the example of Copernicus. In the days of his new cosmology, there were many different responses to his astronomical evidence. Some rejected it as heretical and preposterous, while others bought the idea and made room for it in their faith. But we can imagine as well that things were not always so simple. Undoubtedly there were also those who, convinced by his evidence, believed that the conflict between faith and science was so severe that it could never be fully resolved. When this was so, the only option left was to jettison the faith in favor of astronomy. Retrospectively we easily see that this theological move was a genuine tragedy because it was simply unnecessary. But it certainly looked necessary, and for that reason the "truth" was destructive.

Christians of many persuasions will agree that critical scholarship has often had destructive effects when it is brought into the pulpits and classrooms of the local church. I have made this point already at the outset of our discussion,[1] and I make it here again for emphasis. Now the reason for this is not as simple as it might first appear. To be sure, certain kinds of historical criticism—in the Troeltschian style—are simply antithetical to the Christian faith. Basic doctrines like the vicarious atonement of Christ and his resurrection and ascension have no place in this skeptical kind of criticism, so we cannot be surprised at all by its destructive effects. But not all historical criticism is so opposed to Christian doctrine. As we have seen, many confessing believers—who embrace the fundamentals of creedal orthodoxy—will also admit that many of the standard conclusions of biblical criticism are right. This is because the evidence for these critical conclusions is far stronger than for the traditional alternatives. But if the critical conclusions are right, then why are they so destructive to the faith?

The correct observations of biblical criticism are often destructive for precisely the same reasons that the astronomy of Copernicus could be destructive. When a "true fact" is interpreted in the wrong context, its implications and significance will be wrongly understood. While it is quite possible for faith to persist if Moses did not write the Pentateuch (for our salvation can hardly depend on such a judgment), this possibility is greatly diminished if our faith errantly depends upon, or is closely connected with, the Pentateuch's Mosaic origins. As a result, in most cases it will be irresponsible for the leader or minister of the church to teach the standard results of biblical criticism when they know, or should know, that the implications of those facts will be misunderstood by their congregations. The best advice that I have seen in this regard is still the ancient advice of Augustine: "For

---

1. See p. 21.

there are some passages which are not understood in their proper force, or are understood with great difficulty... and these should never be brought before the people at all, or only on rare occasions when there is some urgent reason."[2]

What would constitute an "urgent reason"[3] for broaching a difficult subject like historical criticism with the local church, and under what conditions is it wise to do so? Let me address the last part of the question first. As a rule of thumb, it is unwise to bring up any complex issue in the church unless there is a corresponding likelihood that the issue can be properly contextualized for the intellectual consumption of rank-and-file believers. Theological paradigms that combine biblical authority and divine inerrancy with an admission of the Bible's human errors are fairly sophisticated, involving a basic competency in epistemology, generic theory, church history and tradition, and the subtle relationship that prevails between the Bible's divine and human discourse. To the extent that men and women in the pew are either unable or unwilling to juggle these kinds of issues, to that same extent it is unwise to bring the problems of biblical criticism to their attention. But as Augustine has pointed out, there can be urgent reasons that force our hand in such decisions. Simply because we would prefer to avoid a problem does not mean that we can. There will be individuals within the church, for instance, who see through the veneer of Sunday morning lay theology to the deeper problems and questions that lay behind it. For these church members, the problems of the Bible are already in play—so they will be greatly relieved to learn some of the things that we have discussed in this book. I am presently involved in numerous private conversations with lay evangelicals who are struggling with the intellectual dimensions of their faith. My conversations with these Christians are honest and wide open—the kinds of conversations that I would rarely initiate from the pulpit of a local church.

But of course, Aquinas reminds us that in some cases these difficult theological issues are thrust upon the Christian laity in the course of life, by circumstances wholly beyond their control.[4] These public matters, he tells us, will have to be addressed not only for those who are theologically astute but also for those he describes as "simpleminded." For example, I suspect that this is increasingly the case with respect to biological evolution, since in every direction, from elementary school to university, Christian students are being confronted by the scientific evidence for this theory. For this reason evangelicals are discussing the problems

---

2. Augustine, *On Christian Doctrine* 4.9.23 (*NPNF* 1 2:581); for similar comments see Aquinas, *Summa Theologica*, pt. 2.2, art. 7, in *Summa Theologica*, 5 vols. (Allen, TX: Christian Classics, 1981), 3:1212. For similar ideas expressed by Basil and Gregory of Nyssa, see Stephen D. Benin, *The Footprints of God: Divine Accommodation in Jewish and Christian Thought* (Albany: State University of New York Press, 1993), 31–33.

3. This is not an elitist strategy, though it might appear so at first glance. Augustine merely recognizes that most lay Christians are no more equipped to do serious theology, philosophy, and biblical exegesis than to engage in other scholarly pursuits, such as classical literature, genetics, and astrophysics. To be sure, lay expertise in biblical and theological studies, and in philosophy, is certainly possible, particularly in our modern era. But such expertise remains an exception that proves the rule.

4. *Summa Theologica*, pt. 2.2, art. 7.

of Genesis and modern science with increasing frequency. The magnitude of evangelical movement on this issue was illustrated recently in my own very evangelical church, when the science teacher from a local Christian school taught our adult Sunday school class that both creation and theistic evolution were viable Christian alternatives. In doing so, he clearly presented the scientific evidence that could favor evolution, and he also cited those Christian scholars of the past—like Origen, Augustine, and Calvin—who have warned Christians to avoid using Genesis as a science book. I suspect that some ten years ago this teacher would have been run out of the church on a rail, but in this case very few members of the class were troubled by his assertions. Whether the members of this Sunday school class realized it or not, I suspect that they were witnessing the nascent stages of the evangelical church's acceptance of evolution.[5] Perhaps, in a few decades or so, evangelical Christians will be no more troubled by the apparent "conflict" between Genesis and evolution than by the conflict between Genesis and Copernicus. The result will not be an unbiblical liberalism so much as a Christian movement that has come to grips with scientific reality.

I would venture, however, that the issue of Genesis and evolution is something of an exception. Most of the problems and questions raised by biblical criticism should be discussed somewhere other than in local church settings. But this does not mean that the pastors and teachers in local churches should not learn about biblical criticism, nor does it mean that their preaching and teaching should go on as if biblical criticism never existed. Allow me to suggest several examples. First, because of our new appreciation for postmodern epistemology and its import for reading texts like the Bible, evangelicals will want to assume a humbler posture in our preaching and teaching. Because our interpretations of the Bible and our theological formulations can be dead wrong, we will be wise to reserve our most confident preaching rhetoric for those moments when we have the strongest sense of urgency and certainty. Nowhere is this new spirit of epistemic humility incarnated more intentionally than in the so-called Emerging Church (EC), so closely associated with names like Brian McLaren, Spencer Burke, and Dan Kimball.[6] Although ECers sometimes carry this cautious style of epistemology a bit too far (by denying "certainty" as a valid and important epistemic experience),[7] conservative evangelicals can learn a great deal from this trendy evangelical movement.

---

5. Numerous evangelical churches have more or less embraced evolutionary theory, or at least accepted it as a scientific option. But at this juncture in history I suspect that the vast majority of evangelical churches either reject or are very suspicious of the theory.

6. Spencer Burke, *Making Sense of Church: Eavesdropping on Emerging Conversations about God, Community, and Culture* (Grand Rapids: Zondervan, 2003); Dan Kimball, *The Emerging Church: Vintage Christianity for New Generations* (Grand Rapids: Zondervan, 2003); Brian D. McLaren, *A Generous Orthodoxy* (El Cajon, CA: Youth Specialties, 2004); McLaren, *A New Kind of Christian: A Tale of Two Friends on a Spiritual Journey* (San Francisco: Jossey-Bass, 2001).

7. This point is made by Donald A. Carson, in what is otherwise a fairly misguided critique of *Becoming Conversant with the Emerging Church* (Grand Rapids: Zondervan, 2005).

More specifically, when it comes to biblical exegesis and theology, informed pastors and teachers will wisely avoid numerous errors. They should certainly avoid any rhetoric that hitches the Christian faith to a fundamentalistic notion of biblical inerrancy. It will be enough to teach that God does not err in Scripture and to show, by how we work, live, and do our theology, that we take the Bible seriously as the authoritative Word of God. But to insist on an inerrant Bible in a naive sense, which denies the full humanity of Scripture, will only paint the evangelical church and Christian scholarship into a corner—the same corner in which the Catholic Church now stands because of its claim to ecclesial infallibility.[8] As we have seen, infallibility and inerrancy are not the necessary ingredients of authority. If they were, then no human authorities would be possible—and it is precisely the Bible that tells us to obey human authorities.

Pastors and teachers well versed in biblical criticism will also do their exegetical and theological work in a style that differs from that of their underinformed counterparts. They will know better than to insist that the six days of creation are literal, or that we should spend our hard-earned cash searching for Noah's ark, or that human languages originated at the tower of Babel. They will also avoid creating elaborate strategies for harmonizing the four Gospel accounts, or for producing grand eschatologies that interpret Daniel and Revelation as if they were prophetic videotapes of the end times. Most importantly, they will know that good theology cannot be derived from one or a few biblical texts, even when the meaning of those texts seems fairly lucid and obvious. Good theology will require instead that we listen to God's voice as he has spoken to us in the wholeness of canon, tradition, and creation. So it seems to me that the church on the corner has much to gain from modern biblical criticism, even if it will not and should not talk much about certain problematic details of modern scholarship. In the final analysis, our judgments about what should be discussed in the local church, and how it should be discussed, are matters of wisdom and spiritual insight. In such matters God has promised wisdom to those who ask (James 1:5). So ask we should.

Though I have been speaking about the problems of biblical criticism, I should like to reiterate that the church has also garnered substantial benefits from historical-critical study. Modern pastors and teachers, for instance, are in a better exegetical position than their ancient counterparts because they know a great deal more about the Near Eastern, Greco-Roman, and Judaic backgrounds of the Bible; about Pharisees, Sadducees, and the Sanhedrin; about the best ways to translate the Bible's Hebrew, Aramaic, and Greek; and about many other things. God's discourse is understood best when situated in its ancient context, and that is possible only because of historical criticism. So Christians of many persuasions owe scholars a word of thanks.

---

8. For a discussion of Roman Catholic efforts to address this difficulty, see Robert L. Saucy, "Recent Roman Catholic Theology," in *Challenges to Inerrancy: A Theological Response*, ed. Gordon R. Lewis and Bruce Demarest (Chicago: Moody Press, 1984), 215–46.

Biblical Criticism and the Christian Academy

Our discussion so far raises an important question. If the problems of modern biblical criticism should be generally excluded from the discourse of the local church, then in what context will Christians ponder these weighty theological matters? I would like to explore this question by turning our attention to an entirely different topic: Christian missions. The Magna Carta of the Protestant missionary movement was William Carey's little monograph with the big title, *An Enquiry into the Obligations of Christians to Use Means for the Conversion of the Heathen*.[9] In this book Carey argued for the legitimacy of what Ralph Winter has called the "modalities" and "sodalities" of the church. Modalities are those organs of the church—such as local congregations—to which every Christian either belongs or should belong. They represent the fundamental structures of the church. Sodalities contrast with modalities insofar as participation in them is not a requirement or expectation of all believers. These are special structures of the church, in which some of its members participate in order to carry out certain tasks or purposes that are the responsibility of the whole church. Carey made his argument in order to legitimize the use of special agencies (sodalities) for sponsoring and promoting world missions. He thought that this was a necessary strategy for world evangelization because para-church structures were proving to be more flexible and effective in carrying out world evangelization than the oft-fossilized local church seemed to be. Ralph Winter has extended Carey's argument by showing that the church has a long history of such specialized sodalities, which serve the needs of the church by promoting renewal and by focusing on particular tasks that the church is called to carry out.[10] From an historical perspective, some of the most important sodalities of the church have been its academic sodalities—its monasteries, schools, and universities.

The argument for academic sodalities in the church is supported not only by experience and tradition but also by the Bible itself. Here again we see the import of the Old Testament's wisdom tradition, which was produced by the scholars of ancient Israel. Their function was to promote Israel's standard wisdom (see Proverbs) as well as to interrogate that wisdom, to probe its theoretical foundations for loose ends, untested assumptions, and new or unanswered questions (see Job, Ecclesiastes). In the New Testament as well, a great deal of the material was composed by those with theological and philosophical training (Paul and the author of Hebrews) or with skills in the art of historiography (Luke–Acts). Like their counterparts who wrote our Old Testament wisdom, the New Testament writers were charged with the task of reflecting critically about the Bible's connection with Christ and his work. So we have many *biblical* reasons for accepting

---

9. William Carey, *An Enquiry into the Obligations of Christians to Use Means for the Conversion of the Heathen* (Leicester: Printed and sold by Ann Ireland, 1792).

10. Ralph D. Winter, "The Two Structures of God's Redemptive Mission," in *Perspectives on the World Christian Movement*, ed. Ralph D. Winter and Steven C. Hawthorne (Pasadena: William Carey Library, 1981), 178–90.

the importance of academic sodalities within the church. In saying this, I do not mean to imply that modalities like the local church serve no role in thinking critically about tradition. It is ultimately the church proper—and not merely its academic sodalities—that is responsible for perpetuating its theological traditions and also for rethinking and reformulating those traditions in light of new insights and experiences. What I wish to point out, however, is that the duty of interrogating tradition is not evenly distributed between the church's local modalities and academic sodalities. Local churches tend to focus more attention on the perpetuation of the Christian tradition and on its practical application, while Christian scholars and academic institutions normally undertake the lion's share of critical reflection on the tradition and its theoretical implications. The primary advantage of this role distinction, and its concomitant balance of responsibility, is that rank-and-file church members are better insulated from the potentially destructive effects of intense academic inquiry and debate.

One implication of this role division is that Christian scholars and academic institutions will be more open to outside influences than their nonacademic counterparts in local church settings. If the church were a living cell, then its cell membrane—which determines what gets in and what finally stays out—would be its spiritually vital academic organs. These academic organs provide the liminal intellectual space between the church and the world, a place where both wheat and chaff are welcomed for sifting. This is the place where Christian scholars search the context of the whole for the ripe wheat of truth and wisdom, for those insights and resources that will be of value for a healthy Christian perspective on reality. So, while local churches would never add a Muslim to their pastoral staff—and for good reason—a Christian university might legitimately hire a Muslim to teach Islam to its students. After all, if one wishes to learn the truth about how Muslims perceive the world, there can be no better source than a Muslim. But in a Christian university the Islamic perspective will not be the end of the matter; it will be one perspective among many that must be integrated into a fuller Christian understanding of the world and of the church's mission to the world.

At this point I would like to continue with my discussion of Christian higher education, but I would remind readers that Christian colleges and universities are a fairly small piece of the church's academic pie. Many Christian scholars interface with the intellectual world by serving in secular and public universities, and by active participation in the broader academy and society. I will come back to this issue presently. My immediate interest, however, is in how Christian academic institutions should manage the liminal space that they are called to provide between the church and the vastness of humanity and its staggering diversity.

In *Conceiving the Christian College*, Duane Litfin has pointed out that there are essentially two different models for managing this liminal space, the *umbrella model* and the *systemic model*.[11] The umbrella model places a higher value on ideo-

---

11. Duane Litfin, *Conceiving the Christian College* (Grand Rapids: Eerdmans, 2004).

logical and theological diversity. It would not require that all faculty members of a Christian institution be confessing Christians but would instead foster the institution's religious identity by preserving a critical mass of convinced Christians in the administration and on the faculty. The upside of this model is that it allows the widest possible space for Christian contact with the context of the whole. The obvious downside of this model is that the diversity might get out of hand and threaten the institution's Christian commitments over time. Few would contest that this downside has become a reality in many umbrella institutions. By comparison, systemic-model institutions value ideological conformity over diversity. Every faculty member is required to believe and embrace a doctrinal statement that outlines the most important and essential elements of the Christian faith as these are understood by the institution. It is in his role as president of Wheaton College that Litfin espouses this second approach, although he does not by this suggest that the umbrella model is inherently problematic. According to Litfin, both models have their legitimate place.

Anyone familiar with Christian higher education will know that evangelical institutions tend to prefer the systemic model, largely because the umbrella model seems to invite heresy in the front door. Perhaps this is true, but we should not forget that the systemic model also has its Achilles' heal. Let me illustrate this by quoting Litfin:

> The noetic effects of sin, of course, cut both ways—that is, they affect our understanding of both revelation and the world [i.e., creation]. But they do not affect the two equally. In our attempts to understand both God's word and God's works it is revelation that takes precedence, for faith is the precondition for the right use of reason. This is why, to use the Church's ancient language, it is a committed faith in Jesus Christ that seeks understanding, not a committed understanding that seeks how it may somehow cut its faith to fit.[12]

If I have understood Litfin correctly, he argues that our sin affects our interpretation of Scripture less than our interpretation of the natural world. As a result, whenever the two things seem to conflict—as in the case of Genesis and evolution—Litfin would have us side with faith. Now anyone who has followed my discussion in this book will know that I do not agree at all with Litfin's conceptual understanding of revelation and creation, or of faith and reason. We cannot so easily pit "revelation" against "creation," because, as we have seen, creation itself also speaks for God. Moreover, it is certainly a mistake to assert that the noetic effects of sin are greater when we interpret creation than when we interpret Scripture. If anything, the stronger biblical case could be made in the opposite direction, since, according to Paul (Rom. 1), creation's voice is understood by all human beings whereas this is not the case for God's special words of revelation (see Rom. 7). Litfin's philosophical foundations illustrate a serious problem that emerges in

12. Ibid., 205–6.

many systemic models of higher Christian education. The model often seeks to protect the institution's Christian orthodoxy by erecting a doctrinal firewall, whose purpose is to keep out everything that seems to contradict parts of the biblical discourse. While this commitment to Scripture's authority is commendable, it wrongly assumes that Scripture is essentially or entirely free of human error and that God has nothing else to say, through either creation or the Spirit, that might modify our perspective on the Bible's discourse. The net effect is sometimes a kind of pseudoscholarship, in which biologists can no longer believe in evolution and biblical scholars can no longer believe in three Isaiahs or in a non-Mosaic Pentateuch. Let me say quite candidly that I agree with Litfin's contention that divine revelation trumps human insight. The difficulty is that it is not always clear how our sources of divine insight—Scripture, tradition, and the created order—come together to speak for God. Pressed to its logical conclusion, Litfin's "Scripture-first" approach might imply that we can legitimately return to trading in slaves or to the Bible's flat-earth cosmology. That his institution does not teach or espouse these biblical viewpoints only shows that Litfin's account of Christian academics does not describe reality.

Nathan Hatch, now president of an umbrella-style institution (Wake Forest University), seems to have his finger on a fundamental problem that plagues many evangelical colleges and universities. Evangelicalism is a movement with strong populist and democratic roots, in which theological reflection and intellectual inquiry are believed to go no deeper than the capacities of the average person in the church pew. This often means that "uncomfortable complexity is flattened out, that issues are resolved by a simple choice of alternatives, and that fine distinctions are lost in the din of ideological battle. In these camps there is little fear that further reduction of content for popular consumption could at times involve downright falsification."[13] Evangelical colleges and universities often play to the tune of these uninformed constituencies, either because they agree with those constituencies or merely because they wish to attract their tuition dollars. When populist or pecuniary concerns govern scholarship, the whole Christian academic enterprise is in jeopardy. Breadth of audience is substituted for depth of insight, and the pursuit of truth has become hostage to theological viewpoints that would fit nicely into any child's Sunday school curriculum. There is no room in this populism for a sophisticated or nuanced doctrine of Scripture, even though that is precisely what is sorely needed in an academic setting.

If the systemic model of Christian higher education is to be effective in promoting academic inquiry and Christian learning, it will need to lean more in the direction of ideological freedom and less in the direction of restrictive popular sentiments. For this reason, Anthony Diekema, former president of Calvin College, has argued strenuously that the faculties, administrations, and boards of

---

13. Nathan O. Hatch, "Christian Thinking in a Time of Academic Turmoil," in *Faithful Learning and the Christian Scholarly Vocation*, ed. Douglas V. Henry and Bob R. Agee (Grand Rapids: Eerdmans, 2003), 91.

Christian colleges and universities should become fanatics and zealots for "academic freedom." Academic freedom is "the fundamental right in the academy to pursue truth."[14] It is absolutely necessary because any institution that really cares about and teaches the truth—and Christian colleges certainly should—will also take seriously their responsibility to test and challenge the validity of the truths being taught. Paradoxically, progress often begins with *deviance*. The task of interrogating accepted traditions and dogmas is a risky business and creates obvious ideological tensions, especially when the matters at hand are theological. But, according to Diekema, these tensions are healthy and inevitable features in a serious academic setting.

The resulting tensions within the institution, as well as between the institution and its supposed constituencies, can be mishandled quite easily by well-meaning college administrators. Diekema has well expressed the potential difficulty and it consequences:

> Nothing is more destructive to the maintenance of morale in a faculty than the "chilling effect" that comes with the use of college authority to restrain or censor. Indeed, I believe that the most devastating threats to academic freedom come not from outside or from blatant tyranny but rather from well-meaning persons who have little or no understanding of the long-range negative effect of their actions to inhibit the essential freedoms of the academy. Well-meant but misguided concerns for the fact that the academy's freedom can or may offend some group or individual can have lethal effects on the long-term health of a college or university. When offensiveness is used as grounds for suppression, it opens the road to widespread censorship and restraint because almost everything of consequence in the life of the mind will be offensive to someone.[15]

How much damage is really done when this sort of administrative censorship is practiced? Here I would turn our attention once again to the insightful article by Nathan Hatch. Hatch believes that the forces of populist censorship often do more harm than good. Rather than stem the tide of liberalism, suppressions of academic freedom actually "accelerate the forces of secularization within our own [Christian] institutions."[16] He gives as an example the recent resurgence of populist fundamentalism in Southern Baptist seminaries and schools. It is precisely this sort of ill-guided fundamentalist populism that has driven so many other institutions—such as Duke, Emory, and Southern Methodist University—further away from their traditional Christian roots. After all, judged from any serious academic standpoint, fundamentalism will seem much more dangerous than open-minded liberalism. In order to allay this outcome, the administrations of systemic-model institutions should provide faculty members with the widest

---

14. Anthony J. Diekema, *Academic Freedom and Christian Scholarship* (Grand Rapids: Eerdmans, 2000), 7.
15. Ibid., 33–34.
16. Hatch, "Christian Thinking," 92.

possible latitude in their academic work, intervening with questions only when there is broad agreement within the institution that questions are in order, and only when those questions are triggered by an obvious breach of clearly defined parameters.

I have spoken here about the general institutional effects of academic censorship, but we should not overlook the damage it can do to individual scholars. The well-known case of Edward Carnell (1919–1967) is an extreme example.[17] Carnell was raised in a conservative, fundamentalist household where the Christian faith was taught and lived out. He studied at Wheaton College and Westminster Theological Seminary—both evangelical institutions—and then finished his education with two doctorates, one at Harvard and the other at Boston University. His personal goal was to present a philosophically and rationally consistent defense of the gospel that would both buttress the historic faith and challenge the modernist attacks against the faith. In the 1950s and 1960s, Carnell rose to prominence in evangelicalism. He published award-winning books, was tapped as president of Fuller Theological Seminary, and became one of evangelicalism's most prominent representatives in the world of mainstream theology. While all would seem to have been right with Carnell's world, a more detailed examination of his life reveals a chronic and sometimes incapacitating struggle with psychological and emotional stability. He frequented the offices of psychiatrists, suffered numerous emotional breakdowns, and submitted himself regularly to controversial electroshock therapies. What was the source of Carnell's struggle?

Although there is seldom a single, simple cause for psychological difficulties, a careful examination of the facts suggests that an important element of the problem was cognitive dissonance. Carnell's intensive and meticulous study of philosophy, theology, and Scripture had gradually uncovered problems that seemed incompatible with conventional evangelical ideas about the Bible, especially with the doctrine of inerrancy. This presented Carnell with obvious difficulties, since his entire life and identity were firmly situated within an evangelical world that was not very enthused about his new ideas. Although Carnell's public persona continued to reflect an evangelical identity, inside he struggled with the cognitive dissonance between the evangelical identity he wanted to preserve and his private theological perspectives, as this personal letter shows:

> One of my difficulties is that I have sort of painted myself into a corner. . . . The upshot is that I end up (so it seems) being liberal in the eyes of the literalists [who read the Bible literally], and a literalist in the eyes of those who have joined the mad race for [theological] relevance. Sometimes I wish I could go to the Isle of Patmos for about fifteen years and meditate, study, and pray.[18]

---

17. Rudolph Nelson, *The Making and Unmaking of an Evangelical Mind: The Case of Edward Carnell* (Cambridge: Cambridge University Press, 1987).

18. Ibid., 205.

This ideological dissonance was more than a product of internal struggles, however. After his tenure as president at Fuller Theological Seminary, Carnell resumed his role as a professor at Fuller. His publications, which probed and tested the limits of some evangelical ideas, met with increasing criticism. Even the generally supportive Fuller board chairman, Harold J. Ockenga, warned Carnell that others were describing him as "lost to the evangelical cause." Ockenga also urged Carnell to submit his publications to colleagues for evaluation prior to their publication. Ockenga's message was clear: although he privately supported Carnell, he also wanted Carnell to avoid publishing materials that were a threat to the more conservative, fundamentalist elements of Fuller's constituency. At this stage in his life (c. 1961–1967), the emotional struggles of Carnell intensified and, according to his psychiatrist, "he was often angry at the rigidity of creedal and moral codes in which he was trapped by his connection with Fuller Theological Seminary."[19] The various pressures took a heavy toll on Carnell, who was at that point using various medications to control his emotional problems.

In April of 1967, Carnell was found dead in his Oakland hotel room, just before he was scheduled to present a conference lecture. He was the victim of a barbiturate overdose, which the coroner labeled as "either accidental or suicidal." Whether directly or indirectly, it appears that the combination of emotional depression, intensive cognitive dissonance, and external pressures from criticism were finally Carnell's undoing. If my sense is right, Carnell is not alone. Many evangelical theologians and biblical scholars now find themselves in a place similar to Carnell's, inasmuch as they recognize that their carefully considered, private scholarly conclusions no longer fit into the old fundamentalistic wineskins demanded by their institutions. Whether these institutions will have the courage to reconsider the wisdom of allowing populist ideas to dictate their commitments, as is now being done by several evangelical seminaries, is another question. Regardless, it is my contention that healthy academic environments can be fostered and preserved in systemic, doctrinally driven evangelical institutions only if those institutions are rigorous—truly rigorous—in defending the academic freedom of their faculty members, even when doing so flies in the face of external, populist constituencies.

Can the umbrella model of higher Christian education best the narrow ideological tendencies of its systemic kin? Umbrella institutions seem to have contributed far more to our academic progress in almost every field of study—including biblical studies—than their more conservative, systemic counterparts. This is perhaps because systemic institutions tend to be more interested in protecting tradition than in advancing it. But in matters of faith, the advantages seem to flow in the other direction. In many cases the faculties of religion and theology in umbrella institutions no longer espouse any serious expressions of Christian orthodoxy, in matters of either theological substance or moral standards. The deity of Christ

19. Ibid., 117.

and his resurrection are out; abortion, homosexuality, and extramarital sex are in. As a result, conservative onlookers commonly argue that there is necessarily an inverse relationship between "open scholarship" and faith commitments. As this logic goes, the more a Christian institution fosters wide-open scholarship, the further it will drift from Christianity.

Now one can hardly be blamed for drawing this straightforward conclusion, but I, for one, am not so sure that this analysis gets to the heart of the matter. More likely is that, in any Christian institution, there will be "conservatives" and "liberals" who are threatened by each other, the one threatened by potential heresies and the other threatened by charges of heresy. When these tensions are not handled well—and they seldom are—they inevitably result in winners and losers. Conservatives tend to have the upper hand in systemic-model institutions, whereas liberals have the advantage in umbrella-model institutions. If this is how things generally play out, then it is too simple to declare that umbrella institutions simply "go liberal." More likely is that liberal institutions are driven in that direction by overzealous conservative elements within the institution or its constituencies.

There are no easy solutions for these perennial difficulties. I wonder whether we might fruitfully combine the systemic and umbrella models in one academic institution. But that discussion is for another time.

So far my focus has been on systemic and umbrella Christian institutions, but the venue of Christian scholarship is not limited to the work being done in Christian colleges and universities. Many confessing believers serve in secular and public universities, and participate actively in the academy and contribute to the intellectual life of the church. Academic freedom is as important for these scholars as for their counterparts in Christian institutions, but concerns in this regard will be of a different sort in their more secular settings. Secular institutions are in principle not much troubled by confessional religious commitments, but they tend to be very troubled *if* these religious commitments are perceived to affect one's scholarship. As a result, there can sometimes be a strong implicit and even explicit opposition to scholars who write anything about theology, or who follow the contours of faith when interpreting Scripture.[20] But the responsibilities of these scholars are no different than those in Christian institutions: they must faithfully discharge their duty to seek the truth and to present the resulting insights to those it can benefit. By all means, this will require that biblical scholars serving in nonparochial institutions should nourish their minds and souls in spiritually vital contexts, in both the life of the local church and in the larger Christian academic community. Their academic counterparts in Christian institutions can contribute to this cause by initiating and preserving healthy relationships with those serving in more secular institutions.

20. George M. Marsden, *The Outrageous Idea of Christian Scholarship* (Oxford: Oxford University Press, 1997); George M. Marsden and B. J. Longfield, eds., *The Secularization of the Academy* (Oxford: Oxford University Press, 1992).

Rapprochement between the Church and the Christian Academy

It would be relatively easy to preserve the neat distinction that I have made between local church modalities and academic sodalities if these were not parts of the one church. But Christian academic institutions exist to serve the church, and as long as this is true, we should anticipate that some degree of conflict will persist between open-minded scholarship and populist lay theology. Where modern biblical criticism is taught in Christian colleges, the conflict often arises at Thanksgiving, as excited freshman Bible students describe the "myths of Genesis" to their parents over a turkey dinner. The parental response usually ranges from bewilderment to anger, and almost always results in at least a nascent distrust of Christian academics. Other conflicts crop up when students schooled in biblical criticism become pastors and teachers in the local church. Congregations are told from their pulpits that the creation days of Genesis are not literal, that the flood did not occur, that there is little historical evidence for the exodus, that Nineveh did not respond to Jonah's preaching, that the four Gospels sometimes contradict one another, and that the author of Revelation missed on his prediction of Christ's return. These critical conclusions are passed on without any serious consideration of genre, of theological import, or of the rhetorical nuances that could build a bridge of understanding rather than a wall of offense. Presented in this way, these critical judgments are at best half-truths, and in the absence of a proper intellectual context they are downright false—at least as they are understood in the pew. A natural result is that well-meaning but uninformed opponents of biblical criticism will stir up populist sentiments against Christian scholars and institutions that are supposedly trading in this destructive, critical ideology. When these populist movements "win," the Christian academy loses—and ultimately, so does the church.

One might argue that Christian academics deserve to lose under these circumstances, and perhaps there is some truth in this. But the verdict assumes that those who teach are wholly or largely responsible for the choices made by their adult students. Knowledge is seductive, and young people fresh out of college or seminary often find it very difficult to manage wisely the new things that they know about the Bible. So even after they have been carefully and dutifully warned about the potentially negative effects of biblical criticism, these same students will proceed to teach biblical criticism in the local church as if it were water for the thirsty—to the utter dismay of both the local church and the seminary that trained them to be there. Given that this is so often the case, why not simply do away with biblical criticism altogether?

One reason that we cannot do this is the great charge, given to the church, that it must respond to ideas that seem to threaten the truth of the gospel. As Paul expressed it, "We demolish arguments and every pretension that sets itself up against the knowledge of God, and we take captive every thought to make it obedient to Christ" (2 Cor. 10:5 NIV). Because biblical criticism has often set itself up as an opponent to our knowledge of God, it becomes the task of Christian scholarship to show how the criticism can be made captive to the faith. As it turns out, the best solutions will not deny everything about the criticism, as is done in many traditional responses to it. That is a sort of scholastic alchemy that we must by all means avoid. The solution instead seems to be that the criticism must be understood in a very different way, so that its results become a genuine affirmation of Christian orthodoxy. God has spoken to us in human language, through the human viewpoints of human authors. In doing so he has fulfilled two fundamental expectations of theological orthodoxy: he has not erred, but his human authors sometimes did.

Another related reason that we cannot be rid of the criticism is that it stems from the Bible itself. As Robert Gordon has expressed it, "some of the impetus for Historical Biblical Criticism comes from the Bible itself, and from the questions that it prompts in the mind of the attentive reader."[21] There will always be attentive readers in the church. The trick is that the church must learn how to manage the diversity created by those who read Scripture very carefully, as scholars do, and those who read it with less care and so overlook the problems. Just as we must manage our cultural, ethnic, economic, and theological diversity, so too must we manage our intellectual diversity, not only as this relates to raw intelligence but also as it relates to education. So long as inquiring Christians study the Bible in great detail, by giving thoughtful attention to ancient history and to what the text actually says, the problems that we have encountered in our discussion of biblical criticism will simply pop up again and again, no matter how much we might wish them away. This is because the Bible's difficulties are not illusions but perennial questions that come up as each generation of Christian scholarship takes its turn at the church's academic helm. The sooner that this scholarly activity is accepted by and assimilated to a healthy and conservative orthodoxy, as has been accomplished in Catholicism, the sooner we shall put the perennial conflict between church and scholar behind us. Complete rapprochement on these issues will undoubtedly have to await the eschaton, but this does not mean that we cannot and should not work toward it now.

To achieve such a rapprochement will require that academic institutions become more sensitive to the needs of the local church, and it will also require that the church's nonacademic leadership—its pastors, elders, school administrators, and board members—become more cognizant of the genuine problems that biblical scholars face in their academic work. For many of these leaders, critical biblical scholarship will be accepted only when a new paradigm explains how the criticism can fit into a life of faith. This book was written to advance that cause, and I hope and pray that in some small way it will succeed in doing so.

---

21. Robert P. Gordon, "A Warranted Version of Historical Biblical Criticism?" in *"Behind" the Text: History and Biblical Interpretation*, ed. Craig G. Bartholomew et al., SHS 4 (Grand Rapids: Zondervan, 2003), 88.

CONCLUSIONS

A Final Word on Evangelical Biblical Scholarship

The evangelical scholars that I know are wonderful people, and in many cases their scholarship is excellent. But it is my opinion that in some cases the scholarship is either partially or wholly soured by a mistaken belief that the biblical authors cannot have meant or said certain things that the authors did, in fact, say or mean. To the extent that my assessment of things is right, then the admonition of Augustine is fitting: "it is a disgraceful and dangerous thing for an infidel to hear a Christian, presumably giving the meaning of Holy Scripture, talking nonsense on these topics; and we should take all means to prevent such an embarrassing situation, in which people show up vast ignorance in a Christian and laugh it to scorn."[22] Augustine's words are strong, of course. But I suspect that we have come to the point where strong words are needed.

If evangelical biblical scholars wish to offer the Lord the very best of our academic wares, then our approach to Scripture and style of scholarship will certainly do more than simply mime the secular academy; but if the academy must criticize our scholarship, let it be because it rejects our Lord, not because our historical and exegetical judgments are poor or even silly. Even if we are convinced that biblical inerrancy extends not only to the Bible's divine author but also to its human authors, this does not necessitate that the actual evidence will point in that direction. Because evidence can be incomplete and even misleading—and all of us know this—let us admit when the historical, literary, and linguistic evidence stacks up against traditional viewpoints like the Mosaic Pentateuch. In the game of scholarship, that is what it means to play fair. But it seems to me that evangelicals have a well-deserved reputation for not playing fair.

If I were to use a cosmological metaphor to describe conservative evangelical scholarship, I would not describe it as "flat-earth" scholarship. That would be too strong and unfair. Perhaps a more accurate metaphor would be "Ptolemaic." Ptolemaic cosmologies were very sophisticated, having concocted a complex epicyclic theory to explain solar motion in the sky. Even though the theory mistakenly supposed that the sun moved about the earth, the theory worked tolerably well as a description and prediction of the sun's movements. Moreover, the complex elegance of the theory seemed altogether fitting for the genius of God.

The Christian scientists who followed Ptolemy's lead were very bright and in certain respects successful in their cosmological research, but they were generally unwilling to accept the views of Copernicus and resisted them until the accumulating evidence simply caved in on everyone. May I respectfully say to evangelical biblical scholars: the evidence has been caving in on us for some time. Though we rightly affirm that God does not err in Scripture, it is no longer sensible—on either historical or theological grounds—to marry that great doctrine of inerrancy to a docetic view of the Bible, which imagines that its discourse was hermetically

---

22. Augustine, *The Literal Meaning of Genesis*, trans. J. H. Taylor, 2 vols. (New York: Paulist Press, 1982), 1:42–43.

sealed from the diversity of human ideas and viewpoints. The time has come for us to confess that our imaginative harmonizations and theories to the contrary are no less illusory than the Ptolemaic epicycles. The lordship of Christ requires that we not fear the truth; it is, after all, the truth that sets us free. Let us bring an end to the "scandal of the evangelical mind."[23]

What I am suggesting is not really new to evangelicalism, nor even to fundamentalism. Although he was a contributor to *The Fundamentals*, our evangelical forefather, James Orr, warned long ago that it is quite dangerous to transfer our faith in the God who does not err to human authors who do: "One may plead, indeed, for 'a supernatural providential guidance' which has for its aim to exclude all, even the least, error or discrepancy in statement.... But this is a violent assumption which there is nothing in the Bible really to support. It is perilous, therefore, to seek to pin down faith to it as a matter of vital importance."[24] How "violent" and "perilous" is this theological path? The litany of souls who have surrendered their faith in academia tells the tale. While these apostasies might be chalked up to the deceptive influences of Enlightenment rationalism and post-Enlightenment relativism, I believe that the evangelical tradition is equally culpable. Too often it has equipped its students with a view of Scripture that could never endure rigorous academic scrutiny. Sometimes the result has been half-baked theology, poor scholarship, and a fragile faith that can survive only by closing its eyes to the God-given evidence in Scripture, tradition, and the created order. A more robust faith would chart a different course, one that is at the same time critical in its disposition and wholly committed to the theological and ethical demands of Christian orthodoxy.

In the spirit of that orthodoxy, I will conclude our deliberations with this wisdom-filled prayer from Charles Wesley:

> Would to God that all the party names and unscriptural phrases and forms which have divided the Christian world were forgot, and that we might all agree to sit down together as humble, loving disciples, at the feet of our common Master, to hear His word, to imbibe His Spirit, and to transcribe His life in our own![25]

---

23. Mark A. Noll, *The Scandal of the Evangelical Mind* (Grand Rapids: Eerdmans, 1994).
24. James Orr, *Revelation and Inspiration* (New York: Scribner's, 1910), 213-14.
25. Cited in Wilber T. Dayton, "Infallibility, Wesley, and British Wesleyanism," in *Inerrancy and the Church*, ed. John D. Hannah (Chicago: Moody Press, 1984), 244.

Bibliography

Abailard, Peter. *Sic et Non: A Critical Edition.* Edited by B. B. Boyer and R. McKeon. Chicago: University of Chicago Press, 1976.

Abba, Raymond. "Priests and Levites in Deuteronomy." *VT* 27 (1977): 257–67.

Abraham, William J. *The Divine Inspiration of Holy Scripture.* Oxford: Oxford University Press, 1981.

Achtemeier, Paul J., Joel B. Green, and Marianne Meye Thompson. *Introducing the New Testament: Its Literature and Theology.* Grand Rapids: Eerdmans, 2001.

Albright, William F. *From the Stone Age to Christianity: Monotheism and the Historical Process.* 2nd ed. Baltimore: Johns Hopkins Press, 1957.

———. *Yahweh and the Gods of Canaan: A Historical Analysis of Two Contrasting Faiths.* Garden City, NY: Doubleday, 1968.

Alexander, T. Desmond. *From Paradise to the Promised Land: An Introduction to the Pentateuch.* 2nd ed. Grand Rapids: Baker Academic, 2002.

Allen, Leslie C. *The Books of Joel, Obadiah, Jonah, and Micah.* NICOT. Grand Rapids: Eerdmans, 1976.

Allison, Dale C., Jr. *The New Moses: A Matthean Typology.* Minneapolis: Fortress, 1993.

Amit, Yaira. *History and Ideology: An Introduction to Historiography in the Hebrew Bible.* Translated by Yael Lotan. Biblical Seminar 60. Sheffield: Sheffield Academic Press, 1999.

Anderson, Bernard W. *Understanding the Old Testament.* 3rd ed. Englewood Cliffs, NJ: Prentice-Hall, 1975.

Anderson, Ray S. *The Shape of Practical Theology: Empowering Ministry with Theological Praxis.* Downers Grove, IL: InterVarsity, 2001.

Antoun, Richard T. *Understanding Fundamentalism: Christian, Islamic, and Jewish Movements.* Walnut Creek, CA: Altamira, 2001.

Aquinas, St. Thomas. *Questions on the Soul.* Translated by James H. Robb. Milwaukee: Marquette University Press, 1984.

———. *The Summa Theologica.* 5 vols. Allen, TX: Christian Classics, 1981.

Archer, Gleason L. *Encyclopedia of Bible Difficulties.* Grand Rapids: Zondervan, 1982.

———. *A Survey of Old Testament Introduction.* Rev. ed. Chicago: Moody Press, 1985.

Archer, Gleason L., and Gregory Chirichigno. *Old Testament Quotations in the New Testament.* Chicago: Moody Press, 1983.

Armerding, Carl E. *The Old Testament and Criticism.* Grand Rapids: Eerdmans, 1983.

Arminius, James. *The Works of James Arminius.* Translated by J. Nichols and W. Nichols. 3 vols. London: Longman, Hurst, Rees, Orme, Brown, and Green, 1825–1875.

Assmann, Jan. *Ma'at: Gerechtigkeit und Unsterblichkeit im alten Ägypten.* Munich: Beck, 1990.

———. *The Mind of Egypt: History and Meaning in the Time of the Pharaohs.* Translated by Andrew Jenkins. New York: Metropolitan Books, 2002.

Attridge, Harold W. *The Epistle to the Hebrews*. Hermeneia. Philadelphia: Fortress, 1989.

Audi, Robert. *Epistemology: A Contemporary Introduction to the Theory of Knowledge*. New York: Routledge, 1998.

Augustine. *City of God, On Christian Doctrine*. NPNF 1 2. Repr. Peabody, MA: Hendrickson, 1994.

———. *Earlier Writings*. Edited by John H. S. Burleigh. Library of Christian Classics 6. Philadelphia: Westminster, 1953.

———. *Expositions of the Book of Psalms*. NPNF 1 8. Repr. Peabody, MA: Hendrickson, 1994.

———. *The Literal Meaning of Genesis*. Translated by John Hammond Taylor. 2 vols. Ancient Christian Writers 41–42. New York: Paulist Press, 1982.

Auld, A. Graeme. *Kings without Privilege: David and Moses in the Story of the Bible's Kings*. Edinburgh: T&T Clark, 1994.

Austin, J. L. *How to Do Things with Words*. 2nd ed. Cambridge: Harvard University Press, 1975.

Bakhtin, Mikhail. *The Dialogic Imagination*. Edited by Michael Holquist. Translated by Caryl Emerson and Michael Holquist. Austin: University of Texas Press, 1981.

Baldwin, Joyce G. *Daniel: An Introduction and Commentary*. TOTC. Leicester: Inter-Varsity, 1978.

Balserak, Jon. "'The Accommodating Act Par Excellence?' An Inquiry into the Incarnation and Calvin's Understanding of Accommodation." *SJT* 55 (2002): 408–23.

Barr, James. *Beyond Fundamentalism*. Philadelphia: Westminster, 1984.

———. *Biblical Faith and Natural Theology*. Oxford: Clarendon, 1993.

———. *The Concept of Biblical Theology*. Minneapolis: Fortress, 1999.

———. *Fundamentalism*. Philadelphia: Westminster, 1978.

———. *History and Ideology in the Old Testament: Biblical Studies at the End of a Millennium*. Oxford: Oxford University Press, 2000.

———. *The Scope and Authority of the Bible*. Philadelphia: Westminster, 1980.

———. "The Theological Case against Biblical Theology." In *Canon, Theology, and Old Testament Interpretation: Essays in Honor of Brevard S. Childs*, edited by Gene M. Tucker, David L. Petersen, and Robert R. Wilson, 3–19. Philadelphia: Fortress, 1988.

———. "Why the World Was Created in 4004 B.C.: Archbishop Ussher and Biblical Chronology." *Bulletin of the John Rylands Library* 67 (1985): 575–608.

Barrett, C. K. "The Allegory of Abraham, Sarah, and Hagar in the Argument of Galatians." In *Rechtfertigung: Festschrift für Ernst Käsemann zum 70. Geburtstag*, edited by Johannes Friedrich, Wolfgang Pöhlmann, and Peter Stuhlmacher, 1–16. Göttingen: Vandenhoeck & Ruprecht, 1976.

Bartchy, S. Scott. *Mallon Chrēsai: First-Century Slavery and the Interpretation of 1 Corinthians 7:21*. SBLDS 11. Missoula, MT: Scholars Press, 1973.

———. "Slavery, Greco-Roman." In *ABD* 6:65–73.

Barth, Karl. *Church Dogmatics*. Edited by Geoffrey W. Bromiley and Thomas F. Torrance. Translated by G. T. Thomson et al. 4 vols. in 12. Edinburgh: T&T Clark, 1936–1977.

———. *The Epistle to the Romans*. Translated by Edwyn C. Hoskyns. 6th ed. London: Oxford University Press, 1933.

———. *Karl Barth's Table Talk*. Edited by John D. Godsey. Richmond: John Knox, 1963.

Bartholomew, Craig G., C. Stephen Evans, Mary Healy, and Murray Rae, eds. *"Behind" the Text: History and Biblical Interpretation*. SHS 4. Grand Rapids: Zondervan, 2003.

Bartholomew, Craig G., and Michael W. Goheen. *The Drama of Scripture: Finding Our Place in the Biblical Story*. Grand Rapids: Baker Academic, 2004.

Bartholomew, Craig G., Colin Green, and Karl Möller, eds. *Renewing Biblical Interpretation*. SHS 1. Grand Rapids: Zondervan, 2000.

Basinger, David. "Divine Control and Human Freedom: Is Middle Knowledge the Answer?" *JETS* 36 (1993): 55–64.

Batten, D., ed. *The Revised and Expanded Answers Book: The 20 Most-Asked Questions about Creation, Evolution, and the Book of Genesis, Answered!* Green Forest, AR: Master Books, 1990.

Battles, Ford L. "God Was Accommodating Himself to Human Capacity." *Interpretation* 31 (1977): 19–38.

Bauckham, Richard. *Bible and Mission: Christian Witness in a Postmodern World*. Grand Rapids: Baker Academic, 2003.

———. *Jesus and the Eyewitnesses: The Gospels as Eyewitness Testimony.* Grand Rapids: Eerdmans, 2006.

———. "Reading Scripture as a Coherent Story." In *The Art of Reading Scripture*, edited by Ellen F. Davis and Richard B. Hays, 38–53. Grand Rapids: Eerdmans, 2003.

Beasley-Murray, George R. *The Book of Revelation.* NCB. Grand Rapids: Eerdmans, 1981.

———. *John.* WBC. Waco: Word, 1987.

Beaulieu, Paul-Alain. "The Historical Background of the Uruk Prophecy." In *The Tablet and the Scroll: Near Eastern Studies in Honor of William W. Hallo*, edited by Mark E. Cohen, Daniel C. Snell, and David B. Weisberg, 41–52. Bethesda, MD: CDL, 1993.

Béchard, D. P. *The Scripture Documents: An Anthology of Official Catholic Teachings.* Collegeville, MN: Liturgical Press, 2002.

Beegle, Dewey M. *Scripture, Tradition, and Infallibility.* 2nd ed. Ann Arbor: Pettenbill, 1979.

Belleville, Linda L. *Women Leaders and the Church: Three Crucial Questions.* Grand Rapids: Baker Academic, 2000.

Benin, Stephen D. *The Footprints of God: Divine Accommodation in Jewish and Christian Thought.* Albany: State University of New York Press, 1993.

Berkouwer, G. C. *Holy Scripture.* Translated and edited by Jack B. Rogers. Grand Rapids: Eerdmans, 1975.

Bietenhard, Hans. "Natürliche Gotteserkenntnis der Heiden? Eine Erwägung zu Rom 1." *Theologische Zeitschrift* 12 (1956): 275–88.

Blenkinsopp, Joseph. *Sage, Priest, Prophet: Religious and Intellectual Leadership in Ancient Israel.* Library of Ancient Israel. Louisville: Westminster John Knox, 1995.

Block, Daniel I. *The Book of Ezekiel.* 2 vols. NICOT. Grand Rapids: Eerdmans, 1997–1998.

Bloesch, Donald G. *Holy Scripture: Revelation, Inspiration, and Interpretation.* Downers Grove, IL: InterVarsity, 1994.

Blomberg, Craig L. "Gospels, Historical Reliability." In *Dictionary of Jesus and the Gospels*, edited by Joel B. Green and Scot McKnight, 291–97. Downers Grove, IL: InterVarsity, 1992.

———. *The Historical Reliability of John's Gospel.* Downers Grove, IL: InterVarsity, 2001.

Blum, Erhard. *Die Komposition der Vätergeschichte.* Wissenschaftliche Monographien zum Alten und Neuen Testament 57. Neukirchen-Vluyn: Neukirchener Verlag, 1984.

———. *Studien zur Komposition des Pentateuch.* BZAW 189. Berlin: de Gruyter, 1990.

Bonhoeffer, Dietrich. *Christ the Center.* Translated by E. H. Robertson. San Francisco: Harper & Row, 1978.

Bonsirven, Joseph. "Hora Talmudica: La notion chronologique de Jean 19, 14, aurait-elle un sens symbolique?" *Biblica* 33 (1952): 511–15.

Boyd, Gregory A. *God of the Possible: A Biblical Introduction to the Open View of God.* Grand Rapids: Baker Books, 2000.

Boyer, Steven. "Articulating Order: Orthodox Trinitarianism and Subordination." Unpublished paper.

Bradley, F. H. *Collected Essays.* 2 vols. Oxford: Clarendon, 1935.

Bray, Gerald, ed. *Romans.* Ancient Christian Commentary on Scripture, New Testament 6. Downers Grove, IL: InterVarsity, 1998.

Brettler, Mark Zvi. "Biblical Literature as Politics: The Case of Samuel." In *Religion and Politics in the Ancient Near East*, edited by A. Berlin, 71–92. Bethesda: University Press of Maryland, 1996.

———. *The Creation of History in Ancient Israel.* New York: Routledge, 1995.

Brewer, David Instone. *Techniques and Assumptions in Jewish Exegesis before 70 C.E.* Texte und Studien zum antiken Judentum 30. Tübingen: Mohr, 1992.

Brinkman, J. A. "The Babylonian Chronicle Revisited." In *Lingering over Words: Studies in Ancient Near Eastern Literature in Honor of William L. Moran*, edited by Tzvi Abusch, John Huehnergard, and Piotr Steinkeller, 73–104. Harvard Semitic Studies 37. Atlanta: Scholars Press, 1990.

Brown, Harold O. J. "The New Testament against Itself: 1 Timothy 2:9–15 and the 'Breakthrough' of Galatians 3:28." In *Women in the Church: A Fresh Analysis of 1 Timothy 2:9–15*, edited by Andreas J. Köstenberger, Thomas R. Schreiner, and H. Scott Baldwin, 197–208. Grand Rapids: Baker Academic, 1995.

Brown, Raymond E. *The Gospel according to John.* 2 vols. AB. Garden City, NY: Doubleday, 1966–1970.

Bruce, F. F. *The Gospel of John.* Grand Rapids: Eerdmans, 1983.

———. *Tradition: Old and New.* Grand Rapids: Zondervan, 1970.

———. "The Tyndale Fellowship for Biblical Research." *Evangelical Quarterly* 19 (1947): 51–62.

Brueggemann, Walter. *First and Second Samuel.* Interpretation. Louisville: Westminster John Knox, 1990.

———. "The Kerygma of the Deuteronomstic History: Gospel for Exiles." *Int* 22 (1968): 387–402.

———. *Theology of the Old Testament: Testimony, Dispute, Advocacy.* Minneapolis: Fortress, 1997.

Bruner, J. S., and L. Postman. "On the Perception of Incongruity: A Paradigm." *Journal of Personality* 18 (1949): 206–23.

Brunner, Emil, and Karl Barth. *Natural Theology.* Translated by Peter Fraenkel. London: Bles, 1946.

Buckley, James J., and David S. Yeago. "A Catholic and Evangelical Theology?" In *Knowing the Triune God: The Work of the Spirit in the Practices of the Church,* edited by James J. Buckley and David S. Yeago, 1–20. Grand Rapids: Eerdmans, 2001.

Bullock, C. Hassell. *An Introduction to the Old Testament.* Chicago: Moody Press, 1986.

Burke, Spencer. *Making Sense of Church: Eavesdropping on Emerging Conversations about God, Community, and Culture.* Grand Rapids: Zondervan, 2003.

Burrus, Virginia, and Stephen D. Moore. "Unsafe Sex: Feminism, Pornography, and the Song of Songs." *BibInt* 11 (2003): 24–52.

Burton, E. D. *A Critical and Exegetical Commentary on the Epistle to the Galatians.* ICC. Edinburgh: T&T Clark, 1921.

Calvin, John. *Commentaries on the Book of the Prophet Jeremiah and the Lamentations.* Translated by John Owen. 5 vols. Edinburgh: Calvin Translation Society, 1850–1855.

———. *Commentaries on the Epistle of Paul the Apostle to the Hebrews.* Translated by John Owen. Edinburgh: Calvin Translation Society, 1853.

———. *Commentaries on the Epistle of Paul the Apostle to the Romans.* Translated by John Owen. Repr. Grand Rapids: Eerdmans, 1947.

———. *Commentaries on the Epistles of Paul to the Galatians and Ephesians.* Translated by William Pringle. Edinburgh: Calvin Translation Society, 1854.

———. *Commentaries on the First Book of Moses, Called Genesis.* Translated by John King. 2 vols. Edinburgh: Calvin Translation Society, 1847–1850.

———. *Commentary on the Book of Psalms.* Translated by James Anderson. 5 vols. Edinburgh: Calvin Translation Society, 1845–1849.

———. *Commentary on a Harmony of the Evangelists.* Translated by William Pringle. 3 vols. Edinburgh: Calvin Translation Society, 1845–1846.

———. *Commentary upon the Acts of the Apostles.* Translated by Henry Beveridge. 2 vols. Edinburgh: Calvin Translation Society, 1844.

———. *Institutes of the Christian Religion.* Translated by Henry Beveridge. 2 vols. London: Clarke, 1949.

———. *Two and Twentie Sermons.* Translated by Thomas Stocker. London: T. Dawson, 1580.

Campbell, Alexander, and Robert Owen. *Debate on the Evidences of Christianity.* London: R. Groombridge, 1839.

Cannon, Katie Geneva. "Slave Ideology and Biblical Interpretation." In *The Postmodern Bible Reader,* edited by David Jobling, Tina Pippin, and Ronald Schleifer, 195–204. Oxford: Blackwell, 2001.

Caputo, John D. *Philosophy and Theology.* Nashville: Abingdon, 2006.

Carey, William. *An Enquiry into the Obligations of Christians to Use Means for the Conversion of the Heathen.* Leicester: Printed and sold by Ann Ireland, 1792.

Carlyle, Thomas. *Critical and Miscellaneous Essays.* Edited by H. D. Traill. 5 vols. Works of Thomas Carlyle 26–30. New York: Scribner's, 1904.

Carr, David M. "Controversy and Convergence in Recent Studies of the Formation of the Pentateuch." *Religious Studies Review* 23 (1997): 22–31.

———. *Reading the Fractures of Genesis: Historical and Literary Approaches.* Louisville: Westminster John Knox, 1996.

Carson, Donald A. *Becoming Conversant with the Emerging Church.* Grand Rapids: Zondervan, 2005.

———. *The Gagging of God: Christianity Confronts Pluralism.* Grand Rapids: Zondervan, 1996.

Carson, Donald A., and Douglas J. Moo. *An Introduction to the New Testament.* 2nd ed. Grand Rapids: Zondervan, 2005.

Cartlidge, David R., and David L. Dungan. *Documents for the Study of the Gospels*. Philadelphia: Fortress, 1980.

Cassuto, Umberto. *The Documentary Hypothesis and the Composition of the Pentateuch*. Translated by Israel Abrahams. Jerusalem: Magnes, 1941.

Charlesworth, James H., ed. *The Old Testament Pseudepigrapha*. 2 vols. Garden City, NY: Doubleday, 1983–1985.

Childs, Brevard S. *Biblical Theology in Crisis*. Philadelphia: Westminster, 1970.

———. *The Book of Exodus: A Critical, Theological Commentary*. OTL. Philadelphia: Westminster, 1974.

———. *Introduction to the Old Testament as Scripture*. Philadelphia: Fortress, 1979.

Chisholm, Roderick M. *Theory of Knowledge*. 3rd ed. Englewood Cliffs, NJ: Prentice-Hall, 1989.

Christiansen, K. *Italian Painting*. New York: Beaux Arts Editions, 1992.

Chrysostom, John. *On the Incomprehensible Nature of God*. Translated by Paul W. Harkins. Fathers of the Church 72. Washington, DC: Catholic University of America Press, 1984.

Clark, David K. "Miracles in the World Religions." In *In Defense of Miracles: A Comprehensive Case for God's Action in History*, edited by R. Douglas Geivett and Gary R. Habermas, 199–213. Downers Grove, IL: InterVarsity, 1997.

Clifford, Richard J. *Proverbs: A Commentary*. OTL. Louisville: Westminster John Knox, 1999.

———. *The Wisdom Literature*. Nashville: Abingdon, 1998.

Clines, David J. A. "A World Established on Water (Psalm 24): Reader-Response, Deconstruction, and Bespoke Interpretation." In *The New Literary Criticism and the Hebrew Bible*, edited by J. Cheryl Exum and David J. A. Clines, 79–90. JSOTSup 143. Sheffield: Sheffield Academic Press, 1993.

Coady, C. A. J. *Testimony: A Philosophical Study*. Oxford: Clarendon, 1992.

Cody, Aelred. *A History of Old Testament Priesthood*. Analecta biblica 35. Rome: Pontifical Biblical Institute Press, 1969.

Cogan, Morton. *Imperialism and Religion: Assyria, Judah and Israel in the Eighth and Seventh Centuries B.C.E.* SBLMS 19. Missoula, MT: Scholars Press, 1974.

Cohen, Norman J., ed. *The Fundamentalist Phenomenon: A View from Within; A Response from Without*. Grand Rapids: Eerdmans, 1990.

Collins, John J. *The Apocalyptic Imagination: An Introduction to Jewish Apocalyptic Literature*. 2nd ed. Grand Rapids: Eerdmans, 1998.

———. *The Bible after Babel: Historical Criticism in a Postmodern Age*. Grand Rapids: Eerdmans, 2005.

———. *Daniel*. Hermeneia. Minneapolis: Fortress, 1993.

———. "Is Critical Biblical Theology Possible?" In *The Hebrew Bible and Its Interpreters*, edited by William H. Propp, Baruch Halpern, and David Noel Freedman, 1–17. Winona Lake, IN: Eisenbrauns, 1990.

Congdon, Roger D. "Did Jesus Sustain the Law in Matthew 5?" *Bibliotheca sacra* 135 (1978): 117–25.

Conzelmann, Hans. *1 Corinthians: A Commentary*. Translated by James W. Leitch. Hermeneia. Philadelphia: Fortress, 1975.

Cook, Stephen L. "Innerbiblical Interpretation in Ezekiel 44 and the History of Israel's Priesthood." *JBL* 114 (1995): 193–208.

Cooper, Lamar E., Sr. *Ezekiel*. NAC 17. Nashville: Broadman & Holman, 1994.

Craig, William Lane. "Middle Knowledge: A Calvinist-Arminian Rapprochement?" In *The Grace of God, the Will of Man*, edited by Clark H. Pinnock, 141–64. Grand Rapids: Zondervan, 1989.

Craig, William Lane, and J. P. Moreland. *Philosophical Foundations for a Christian Worldview*. Downers Grove, IL: InterVarsity, 2003.

Craigie, Peter C. *The Old Testament: Its Background, Growth, and Content*. Nashville: Abingdon, 1986.

Cranfield, C. E. B. *A Critical and Exegetical Commentary on the Epistle to the Romans*. 2 vols. ICC. Edinburgh: T&T Clark, 1975–1979.

Crenshaw, James L. *Old Testament Wisdom: An Introduction*. Atlanta: John Knox, 1981.

Crisp, Oliver. "Did Christ Have a Fallen Human Nature?" *International Journal of Systematic Theology* 6 (2004): 270–88.

Cross, F. L., and E. A. Livingstone, eds. *Oxford Dictionary of the Christian Church*. 3rd ed. Oxford: Oxford University Press, 1997.

Cross, Frank Moore, Jr., *Canaanite Myth and Hebrew Epic*. Cambridge: Harvard University Press, 1973.

Dahm, Ulrike. *Opferkult und Priestertum in Alt-Israel: Ein kultur- und religionswissenschaftlicher Beitrag*. BZAW 327. Berlin; New York: de Gruyter, 2003.

Davids, Peter H. "The Pseudepigrapha in the Catholic Epistles." In *The Pseudepigrapha and Early Biblical Interpretation*, edited by James H. Charlesworth and Craig A. Evans, 228–45. Journal for the Study of the Pseudepigrapha Supplement Series 14. Sheffield: JSOT Press, 1993.

Davies, Philip R. "Biblical Interpretation in the Dead Sea Scrolls." In *A History of Biblical Interpretation*. Vol. 1, *The Ancient Period*, edited by Alan J. Hauser and Duane F. Watson, 144–66. Grand Rapids: Eerdmans, 2003.

———. *In Search of "Ancient Israel."* JSOTSup 148. Sheffield: Sheffield Academic Press, 1992.

De Vries, Simon J. *1 and 2 Chronicles*. Forms of the Old Testament Literature 11. Grand Rapids: Eerdmans, 1989.

Derrida, Jacques. *Deconstruction in a Nutshell: A Conversation with Jacques Derrida*. Edited by John D. Caputo. New York: Fordham University Press, 1997.

———. *Writing and Difference*. Translated by Alan Bass. Chicago: University of Chicago Press, 1978.

Descartes, René. *Discourse on Method and The Meditations*. Translated by F. E. Sutcliffe. New York: Penguin, 1968.

Dever, William G. *What Did the Biblical Writers Know, and When Did They Know It? What Archaeology Can Tell Us about Ancient Israel*. Grand Rapids: Eerdmans, 2001.

Dibelius, Martin, and Hans Conzelmann. *The Pastoral Epistles*. Translated by Philip Buttolph and Adela Yarbro. Hermeneia. Philadelphia: Fortress, 1972.

Diekema, Anthony J. *Academic Freedom and Christian Scholarship*. Grand Rapids: Eerdmans, 2000.

Dillard, Raymond B. "Reward and Punishment in Chronicles: The Theology of Immediate Retribution." *WTJ* 46 (1984): 164–72.

———. *2 Chronicles*. WBC. Waco: Word, 1987.

Dillard, Raymond B., and Tremper Longman III. *An Introduction to the Old Testament*. Grand Rapids: Zondervan, 1994.

Dion, Paul. "Deuteronomy 13: The Suppression of Alien Religious Propaganda in Israel during the Late Monarchical Era." In *Law and Ideology in Monarchic Israel*, edited by Baruch Halpern and Deborah W. Hobson, 147–216. JSOTSup 124. Sheffield: JSOT Press, 1991.

Dobbs-Allsopp, F. W. "Rethinking Historical Criticism." *BibInt* 7 (1999): 235–71.

Dorrien, G. *The Remaking of Evangelical Theology*. Louisville: Westminster John Knox, 1998.

Dozeman, Thomas B. *God on the Mountain: A Study of Redaction, Theology, and Canon in Exodus 19–24*. SBLMS 37. Atlanta: Scholars Press, 1989.

Dozeman, Thomas B., and Konrad Schmid, eds. *A Farewell to the Yahwist? The Composition of the Pentateuch in Recent European Interpretation*. Society of Biblical Literature Symposium Series 34. Leiden: Brill, 2006.

Duke, Rodney K. "Chronicles, Book of." In *Dictionary of the Old Testament: Historical Books*, edited by Bill T. Arnold and H. G. M. Williamson, 161–81. Downers Grove, IL: InterVarsity, 2005.

Dunn, James D. G. *Romans*. 2 vols. WBC. Dallas: Word, 1988.

Eissfeldt, Otto. *The Old Testament: An Introduction*. Translated by Peter R. Ackroyd. New York: Harper & Row, 1965.

Eliade, Mircea. *A History of Religious Ideas*. Translated by Willard R. Trask. 3 vols. Chicago: University of Chicago Press, 1978–1985.

Elliott, E. N., ed. *Cotton Is King and Pro-Slavery Arguments*. Augusta, GA: Pritchard, Abbott & Loomis, 1860.

Elliott, J. K. *The Apocryphal New Testament*. Rev. repr. Oxford: Clarendon, 1999.

Ellis, E. Earle. *Paul's Use of the Old Testament*. Grand Rapids: Baker Books, 1981.

Ellwood, Robert S., Jr. *Religious and Spiritual Groups in Modern America*. Englewood Cliffs, NJ: Prentice-Hall, 1973.

Emerton, John A. "Priests and Levites in Deuteronomy: An Examination of Dr. G. E. Wright's Theory." *VT* 12 (1962): 129–38.

———. "The Teaching of Amenemope and Proverbs xxii 17–xxiv 22: Further Reflections on a Longstanding Problem." *VT* 51 (2001): 431–65.

Enns, Peter E. "Apostolic Hermeneutics and an Evangelical Doctrine of Scripture: Moving Beyond a Modernist Impasse." *WTJ* 65 (2003): 263–87.

———. *Inspiration and Incarnation: Evangelicals and the Problem of the Old Testament.* Grand Rapids: Baker Academic, 2005.

———. "The 'Movable Well' in 1 Cor 10:4: An Extrabiblical Tradition in an Apostolic Text." *Bulletin for Biblical Research* 6 (1996): 23–38.

Epp, Eldon Jay. *Junia: The First Woman Apostle.* Minneapolis: Fortress, 2005.

Erickson, Millard J. *Christian Theology.* Grand Rapids: Baker Academic, 1985.

———. *Postmodernizing the Faith: Evangelical Responses to the Challenge of Postmodernism.* Grand Rapids: Baker Academic, 1998.

Etz, Donald V. "The Numbers of Genesis V 3–31: A Suggested Conversion and Its Implications." *VT* 43 (1993): 171–89.

Evans, C. Stephen. *The Historical Christ and the Jesus of Faith: The Incarnational Narrative as History.* Oxford: Clarendon, 1996.

Evans, Craig A. *Ancient Texts for New Testament Studies: A Guide to the Background Literature.* Peabody, MA: Hendrickson, 2005.

———. *From Prophecy to Testament: The Function of the Old Testament in the New.* Peabody, MA: Hendrickson, 2004.

Exum, J. Cheryl, and David J. A. Clines, eds. *The New Literary Criticism and the Hebrew Bible.* JSOTSup 143. Sheffield: Sheffield Academic Press, 1993.

Farmer, William. *The Synoptic Problem: A Critical Analysis.* New York: Macmillan, 1964.

Fee, Gordon D. *The First Epistle to the Corinthians.* NICNT. Grand Rapids: Eerdmans, 1987.

Feinberg, Paul D. "A Response to Adequacy of Language and Accommodation." In *Hermeneutics, Inerrancy, and the Bible*, edited by Earl D. Radmacher and Robert D. Preus, 379–89. Grand Rapids: Zondervan, 1984.

Finegan, Jack. *Handbook of Biblical Chronology.* Rev. ed. Peabody, MA: Hendrickson, 1998.

Finkelstein, Israel. "The Archaeology of the Days of Manasseh." In *Scripture and Other Artifacts: Essays on the Bible and Archaeology in Honor of Philip J. King*, edited by Michael D. Coogan, J. Cheryl Exum, and Lawrence E. Stager, 169–87. Louisville: Westminster John Knox, 1994.

Finley, Moses I. *Ancient Slavery and Modern Ideology.* London: Chatto & Windus, 1980.

Finocchiaro, Maurice A. *Retrying Galileo, 1633–1992.* Berkeley: University of California Press, 2005.

Fishbane, Michael. *Biblical Interpretation in Ancient Israel.* Oxford: Clarendon, 1985.

Fitzmyer, Joseph A. *The Acts of the Apostles.* AB. New York: Doubleday, 1998.

———. *Romans.* AB. New York: Doubleday, 1993.

Fowl, Stephen E. *Engaging Scripture: A Model for Theological Interpretation.* Oxford: Blackwell, 1998.

France, R. T. *Women in the Church's Ministry: A Test-Case for Biblical Hermeneutics.* Carlisle: Paternoster, 1995.

Frankena, R. "The Vassal-Treaties of Esarhaddon and the Dating of Deuteronomy." *OTS* 14 (1965): 122–54.

Frei, Hans. *The Eclipse of Biblical Narrative: A Study in Eighteenth and Nineteenth Century Hermeneutics.* New Haven: Yale University Press, 1974.

Friedman, J. "Servetus, Michael." In *The Oxford Encyclopedia of the Reformation*, edited by Hans Joachim Hillerbrand, 4:48–49. 4 vols. Oxford: Oxford University Press, 1996.

Friesen, Steven J. "Myth and Symbolic Resistance in Revelation 13." *JBL* 123 (2004): 281–313.

Frye, Roland M. "A Literary Perspective for the Criticism of the Gospels." In *Jesus and Man's Hope*, edited by Donald G. Miller and Dikran Y. Hadidian, 2:193–221. 2 vols. Pittsburgh: Pittsburgh Theological Seminary Press, 1971.

Gabler, J. P. "De justo discriminie theologiae biblicae et dogmaticae regundisque recte ultriusque finibus." *Kleinere Theologische Schriften* 2 (1831): 179–98.

Gadamer, Hans-Georg. *Truth and Method.* Translated by Joel Weisenheimer and Donald G. Marshall. 2nd rev. ed. New York: Continuum, 1989.

Gallagher, Maggie. "Reflections on Headship." In *Does Christianity Teach Male Headship? The Equal-Regard Marriage and Its Critics*, edited by David Blankenhorn, Don Browning, and Mary Stewart Van Leeuwen, 111–25. Grand Rapids: Eerdmans, 2004.

Gallay, Allan. "The Origins of Slaveholders' Paternalism: George Whitefield, the Bryan Family, and the Great Awakening in the South." *Journal of Southern History* 53 (1987): 369–94.

Garrett, Duane. *Rethinking Genesis: The Sources and Authorship of the First Book of the Pentateuch.* Grand Rapids: Baker Books, 1991.

Gay, Peter. *The Enlightenment: An Interpretation*. 2 vols. New York: Norton, 1966–1969.

Geertz, Clifford. *The Interpretation of Culture: Selected Essays*. New York: Basic Books, 1973.

George, A. R. *The Babylonian Gilgamesh Epic: Introduction, Critical Edition, and Cuneiform Texts*. 2 vols. Oxford: Oxford University Press, 2003.

Giles, Kevin. *The Trinity and Subordinationism: The Doctrine of God and the Contemporary Gender Debate*. Downers Grove, IL: InterVarsity, 2002.

Gilkey, Langdon. "Cosmology, Ontology, and the Travail of Biblical Language." *Journal of Religion* 41 (1961): 194–205.

Ginzburg, Carlo. "Lorenzo Valla on the 'Donation of Constantine.'" In *Carlo Ginzburg, History, Rhetoric, and Proof*, 54–70. Hanover: University Press of New England, 1999.

Glancy, Jennifer A. *Slavery in Early Christianity*. Oxford: Oxford University Press, 2002.

Goldingay, John. *Daniel*. WBC. Waco: Word, 1989.

———. *The Message of Isaiah 40–55: A Literary-Theological Commentary*. Edinburgh: T&T Clark, 2005.

———. *Models for Interpretation of Scripture*. Grand Rapids: Eerdmans, 1995.

———. *Models for Scripture*. Grand Rapids: Eerdmans, 1994.

Goldstein, Jonathan A. "The Historical Setting of the Uruk Prophecy." *JNES* 47 (1988): 43–46.

Gordon, Robert P. "A Warranted Version of Historical Biblical Criticism?" In *"Behind" the Text: History and Biblical Interpretation*, edited by Craig G. Bartholomew et al., 79–91. SHS 4. Grand Rapids: Zondervan, 2003.

Grabbe, Lester L., ed. *Did Moses Speak Attic? Jewish Historiography and Scripture in the Hellenistic Period*. JSOTSup 317. Sheffield: Sheffield Academic Press, 2001.

———. *Priests, Prophets, Diviners, Sages: A Socio-Historical Study of Religious Specialists in Ancient Israel*. Valley Forge, PA: Trinity Press International, 1995.

Grayson, A. K. *Assyrian and Babylonian Chronicles*. Locust Valley, NY: J. J. Augustin, 1975.

Green, Garrett. "Myth, History, and Imagination: The Creation Narratives in Bible and Theology." *Horizons in Biblical Theology* 12 (1990): 19–38.

Green, Joel B. "Scripture and Theology: Uniting the Two So Long Divided." In *Between Two Horizons: Spanning New Testament Studies and Systematic Theology*, edited by Joel B. Green and Max Turner, 23–43. Grand Rapids: Eerdmans, 2000.

Green, William Henry. *The Pentateuch Vindicated from the Aspersions of Bishop Colenso*. New York: John Wiley, 1863.

Greenfield, J. C., and B. Porten. *The Bisitun Inscription of Darius the Great, Aramaic Version*. London: Lund Humphries, 1982.

Grudem, Wayne. *Systematic Theology: An Introduction to Biblical Doctrine*. Grand Rapids: Zondervan, 1994.

Gundry, Robert H. *Matthew: A Commentary on His Handbook for a Mixed Church Under Persecution*. 2nd ed. Grand Rapids: Eerdmans, 1993.

Gunton, Colin E. *A Brief Theology of Revelation*. Edinburgh: T&T Clark, 1995.

Gutting, Gary. *Foucault: A Very Short Introduction*. Oxford: Oxford University Press, 2005.

Hagner, Donald A. *Matthew 14–28*. WBC. Dallas: Word, 1995.

Hahn, Scott W., and John S. Bergsma. "What Laws Were 'Not Good'? A Canonical Approach to the Theological Problem of Ezekiel 20:25–26." *JBL* 123 (2004): 201–18.

Hall, Christopher A. *Learning Theology with the Church Fathers*. Downers Grove, IL: InterVarsity, 2002.

———. *Reading Scripture with the Church Fathers*. Downers Grove, IL: InterVarsity, 1998.

Hallo, W. W., ed. *The Context of Scripture*. 3 vols. Leiden: Brill, 1997–2002.

Halpern, Baruch. *David's Secret Demons: Messiah, Murderer, Traitor, King*. Grand Rapids: Eerdmans, 2001.

Hamilton, James E. "Academic Orthodoxy and the Arminianizing of American Theology." *Wesleyan Theological Journal* 9 (1974): 52–59.

———. "Epistemology and Theology in American Methodism." *Wesleyan Theological Journal* 10 (1975): 70–79.

Hamilton, Victor P. *The Book of Genesis*. 2 vols. NICOT. Grand Rapids: Eerdmans, 1990–1995.

———. *Handbook on the Pentateuch*. Grand Rapids: Baker Academic, 1982.

Hanson, Paul D. *The Dawn of Apocalyptic.* Rev. ed. Philadelphia: Fortress, 1979.

———. *Isaiah 40–66.* Interpretation. Louisville: John Knox, 1995.

Haran, Menahem. "The Nature of the "Ohel Mo'edh' in Pentateuchal Sources." *Journal of Semitic Studies* 5 (1960): 50–65.

———. *Temples and Temple-Service in Ancient Israel.* Winona Lake, IN: Eisenbrauns, 1985.

Harnack, Adolf von, ed. *Porphyrius, "Gegen die Christen."* Berlin: Verlag der Königl. Akademie der Wissenschaften, in Kommission bei Georg Reimer, 1916.

Harrisville, Roy A., and Walter Sundberg. *The Bible in Modern Culture: Theology and Historical-Critical Method from Spinoza to Käsemann.* Grand Rapids: Eerdmans, 1995.

Hart, Trevor A. *Regarding Karl Barth: Toward a Reading of His Theology.* Downers Grove, IL: InterVarsity, 1999.

Harvey, Van A. *The Historian and the Believer.* New York: Macmillan, 1966.

Hatch, Nathan O. "Christian Thinking in a Time of Academic Turmoil." In *Faithful Learning and the Christian Scholarly Vocation*, edited by Douglas V. Henry and Bob R. Agee, 87–100. Grand Rapids: Eerdmans, 2003.

Haurer, C. E. "David and the Levites." *JSOT* 23 (1982): 33–54.

Hauser, Alan J., and Duane F. Watson, eds. *A History of Biblical Interpretation.* Vol. 1, *The Ancient Period.* Grand Rapids: Eerdmans, 2003.

Hays, Richard B. *Echoes of Scripture in the Letters of Paul.* New Haven: Yale University Press, 1989.

———. *First Corinthians.* Interpretation. Louisville: Westminster John Knox, 1997.

———. *The Moral Vision of the New Testament.* San Francisco: HarperSanFrancisco, 1996.

Hegel, G. W. F. *Phenomenology of Spirit.* Translated by A. V. Miller. Oxford: Oxford University Press, 1977.

Hendel, Ronald S. "The Exodus in Biblical Memory." *JBL* 120 (2001): 601–22.

———. *The Text of Genesis 1–11.* Oxford: Oxford University Press, 1998.

Henry, Carl F. H. *God, Revelation, and Authority.* 6 vols. Waco: Word, 1976–1983.

Henry, Douglas V., and Bob R. Agee, eds. *Faithful Learning and the Christian Scholarly Vocation.* Grand Rapids: Eerdmans, 2003.

Hoffmeier, James K. *Israel in Egypt: The Evidence for the Authenticity of the Exodus Tradition.* New York: Oxford University Press, 1997.

Holmes, A. F. *Building the Christian Academy.* Grand Rapids: Eerdmans, 2001.

Holquist, Michael. *Dialogism: Bakhtin and His World.* New York: Routledge, 1990.

Holzer, Harold, and Frank J. Williams. *Lincoln's Deathbed in Art and Memory: The "Rubber Room" Phenomenon.* Gettysburg: Thomas Publications, 1998.

Hort, Greta. "The Plagues of Egypt." *ZAW* 69 (1957): 84–103; *ZAW* 70 (1958): 48–59.

Houghton, Walter E. *The Victorian Frame of Mind, 1830–1870.* New Haven: Yale University Press, 1957.

Hudson, Winthrop S. *Religion in America: An Historical Account of the Development of American Religious Life.* 4th ed. New York: Macmillan, 1987.

Hughes, Jeremy. *Secrets of the Times: Myth and History in Biblical Chronology.* JSOTSup 66. Sheffield: Sheffield Academic Press, 1990.

Hughes, R. T. "The Christian Faith and the Life of the Mind." In *Faithful Learning and the Christian Scholarly Vocation*, edited by Douglas V. Henry and Bob R. Agee, 3–25. Grand Rapids: Eerdmans, 2003.

Hume, David. *An Enquiry concerning Human Understanding.* 1748. Repr. Oxford: Oxford University Press, 2000.

———. *A Treatise on Human Nature.* Edited by D. G. C. Macnabb. London: Collins, 1962.

Hunger, Hermann, and Stephen A. Kaufman. "A New Akkadian Prophecy Text." *JAOS* 95 (1975): 371–75.

Hurwitz, Avi. *A Linguistic Study of the Relationship between the Priestly Source and the Book of Ezekiel.* Cahiers de la Revue biblique 20. Paris: Gabalda, 1982.

Jacobsen, Thorkild. *The Sumerian King List.* Assyriological Studies 11. Chicago: University of Chicago Press, 1939.

Japhet, Sara. *1 and 2 Chronicles.* OTL. Louisville: Westminster John Knox, 1993.

Jerome. *Against Jovinianus.* In *NPNF* 2 6:346–416. Repr. Peabody, MA: Hendrickson, 1994.

Jewett, Paul K. *Man as Male and Female: A Study in Sexual Relationships from a Theological Point of View.* Grand Rapids: Eerdmans, 1975.

Jewett, Robert. *Romans: A Commentary.* Hermeneia. Minneapolis: Fortress, 2007.

Johnson, E. Elizabeth. *The Function of Apocalyptic and Wisdom Traditions in Romans 9–11.* SBLDS 109. Atlanta: Scholars Press, 1989.

Johnson, Edward A. *A School History of the Negro Race in America, from 1619 to 1890: With a Short Introduction as to the Origin of the Race. Also a Short Sketch of Liberia.* Raleigh: Edwards & Broughton, 1890.

Johnson, Luke Timothy. *Hebrews: A Commentary.* New Testament Library. Louisville: Westminster John Knox, 2006.

———. *Reading Romans: A Literary and Theological Commentary.* Macon, GA: Smyth & Helwys, 2001.

———. *The Writings of the New Testament: An Interpretation.* Minneapolis: Fortress, 1999.

Jones, Douglas R. *Jeremiah.* NCB. Grand Rapids: Eerdmans, 1992.

Juel, Donald H. "Interpreting Israel's Scriptures in the New Testament." In *A History of Biblical Interpretation.* Vol. 1, *The Ancient Period*, edited by Alan J. Hauser and Duane F. Watson, 283–303. Grand Rapids: Eerdmans, 2003.

Kaiser, Walter C., Jr. "The Single Intent of Scripture." In *Rightly Divided: Readings in Biblical Hermeneutics*, edited by Roy B. Zuck, 158–70. Grand Rapids: Kregel, 1996.

———. *Toward an Old Testament Theology.* Grand Rapids: Zondervan, 1978.

Kalimi, Isaac. *The Reshaping of Ancient Israelite History in Chronicles.* Winona Lake, IN: Eisenbrauns, 2005.

Kant, Immanuel. *Critique of Practical Reason.* Translated and edited by Mary Gregor. Cambridge: Cambridge University Press, 1997.

———. *Critique of Pure Reason.* Translated by N. K. Smith. New York: St. Martin's Press, 1965.

Kelly, Brian E. "Manasseh in the Books of Kings and Chronicles (2 Kings 21:1–18; 2 Chron 33:1–20)." In *Windows into Old Testament History*, edited by V. Philips Long, David W. Baker, and Gordon J. Wenham, 131–46. Grand Rapids: Eerdmans, 2002.

Kidner, Derek. *Genesis: An Introduction and Commentary.* TOTC. Downers Grove, IL: InterVarsity, 1967.

Kimball, Dan. *The Emerging Church: Vintage Christianity for New Generations.* Grand Rapids: Zondervan, 2003.

Kitchen, Kenneth A. *Ancient Orient and Old Testament.* Downers Grove, IL: InterVarsity, 1966.

———. *On the Reliability of the Old Testament.* Grand Rapids: Eerdmans, 2003.

Klauck, Hans-Josef. "Do They Never Come Back? *Nero Redivivus* and the Apocalypse of John." *CBQ* 63 (2001): 683–98.

———. *1 Korintherbrief.* NEchtB. Würzburg: Echter Verlag, 1984.

Knierim, Rolf P. *The Task of Old Testament Theology: Method and Cases.* Grand Rapids: Eerdmans, 1995.

Knohl, Israel. *The Sanctuary of Silence: The Priestly Torah and the Holiness School.* Minneapolis: Fortress, 1995.

Knoppers, Gary N. "Hierodules, Priests, or Janitors? The Levites in Chronicles and the History of the Israelite Priesthood." *JBL* 118 (1999): 49–72.

Koester, Craig R. *Hebrews.* AB. New York: Doubleday, 2001.

———. *Revelation and the End of All Things.* Grand Rapids: Eerdmans, 2001.

Koester, Helmut. *Introduction to the New Testament.* 2 vols. Berlin: de Gruyter, 1982.

Köstenberger, Andreas J., Thomas R. Schreiner, and H. Scott Baldwin, eds. *Women in the Church: A Fresh Analysis of 1 Timothy 2:9–15.* Grand Rapids: Baker Academic, 1995.

Kraus, Hans-Joachim. *Das Evangelium der unbekannten Propheten: Jesaja 40–66.* Kleine biblische Bibliothek. Neukirchen-Vluyn: Neukirchener Verlag, 1990.

Krusche, Werner. *Das Wirken des Heiligen Geistes nach Calvin.* Göttingen: Vandenhoeck & Ruprecht, 1957.

Kuhn, Thomas S. *The Copernican Revolution.* Cambridge, MA: Harvard University Press, 1957.

———. *The Structure of Scientific Revolutions.* 3rd ed. Chicago: University of Chicago Press, 1996.

Kümmel, W. G. *Römer 7 und die Bekehrung des Paulus.* Leipzig: Hinrichs, 1929.

Kysar, Robert. *John, the Maverick Gospel.* Atlanta: John Knox, 1976.

Labat, René. *Le poème babylonien de la création.* Paris: Adrien-Maissonneuve, 1935.

Labuschagne, C. J. "The Life Spans of the Patriarchs." In *New Avenues in the Study of the Old Testament: A Collection of Old Testament Studies,* edited by A. S. van der Woude, 121–27. Oudtestamentische Studiën 25. New York: Brill, 1989.

Lane, A. N. S. "*Sola scriptura?* Making Sense of a Post-Reformation Slogan." In *A Pathway into the Holy Scripture,* edited by P. E. Satterthwaite and D. F. Wright, 299–313. Grand Rapids: Eerdmans, 1994.

Langford, Jerome J. *Galileo, Science, and the Church.* 2nd ed. Ann Arbor: University of Michigan Press, 1971.

LaSor, William Sanford, David Allen Hubbard, and Frederick W. Bush. *Old Testament Survey.* 2nd ed. Grand Rapids: Eerdmans, 1996.

Lederach, Paul M. *Daniel.* Scottsdale, PA: Herald, 1994.

Lehrer, Keith. *Thomas Reid.* London: Routledge, 1989.

Lemche, Niels Peter. *The Israelites in History and Tradition.* London: SPCK; Louisville: Westminster John Knox, 1998.

Lessing, Gotthold E. *The Education of the Human Race.* London: Paul, Trench, Trubner, 1896.

———. *Lessing's Theological Writings.* Translated by Henry Chadwick. Stanford: Stanford University Press, 1956.

Levenson, Jon D. *The Hebrew Bible, the Old Testament, and Historical Criticism: Jews and Christians in Biblical Studies.* Louisville: Westminster John Knox, 1993.

Levine, Baruch A. *Numbers 1–20.* AB. Garden City, NY: Doubleday, 1993.

Lewis, C. S. *Allegory of Love: A Study in Medieval Tradition.* London: Oxford University Press, 1936.

———. *The Weight of Glory and Other Addresses.* New York: Macmillan, 1965.

Lindars, Barnabas. "Jesus Risen: Bodily Resurrection but No Empty Tomb." *Theology* 89 (1986): 90–96.

Lindbeck, George A. *The Nature of Doctrine.* Philadelphia: Westminster, 1984.

———. "The Story-Shaped Church: Critical Exegesis and Theological Interpretation." In *The Theological Interpretation of Scripture: Classic and Contemporary Readings,* edited by Stephen E. Fowl, 39–52. Oxford: Blackwell, 1997.

Lindsell, Harold. *The Battle for the Bible.* Grand Rapids: Zondervan, 1976.

Lints, Richard. *The Fabric of Theology: A Prolegomenon to Evangelical Theology.* Grand Rapids: Eerdmans, 1993.

Litfin, Duane. *Conceiving the Christian College.* Grand Rapids: Eerdmans, 2004.

Liverani, Mario. *Israel's History and the History of Israel.* London; Oakville, CT: Equinox, 2005.

Livingstone, Alisdair. *Court Poetry and Literary Miscellanea.* State Archives of Assyria 3. Helsinki: Helsinki University Press, 1989.

Long, V. Philips. *The Art of Biblical History.* Foundations of Contemporary Interpretation 5. Grand Rapids: Zondervan, 1994.

———. "Historiography of the Old Testament." In *The Face of Old Testament Studies,* edited by David W. Baker and Bill T. Arnold, 145–75. Grand Rapids: Baker Academic, 1999.

Longenecker, Richard N. *Biblical Exegesis in the Apostolic Period.* 2nd ed. Grand Rapids: Eerdmans, 1999.

Longman, Tremper, III. *Fictional Akkadian Autobiography: A Generic and Comparative Study.* Winona Lake, IN: Eisenbrauns, 1991.

———. "Storytellers and Poets in the Bible: Can Literary Artifice Be True?" In *Inerrancy and Hermeneutic: A Tradition, a Challenge, a Debate,* edited by Harvie M. Conn, 137–49. Grand Rapids: Baker Books, 1988.

Louth, Andrew. *Discerning the Mystery: An Essay on the Nature of Theology.* Oxford: Clarendon, 1990.

Luther, Martin. *Luther's Works.* Edited by Jaroslav Pelikan and Helmut T. Lehman. 55 vols. St. Louis: Concordia; Philadelphia: Fortress, 1955–1976.

Lyotard, Jean-François. *The Postmodern Condition: A Report on Knowledge.* Translated by Geoff Bennington and Brian Massumi. Minneapolis: University of Minnesota Press, 1984.

MacDonald, Nathan B. "Illocutionary Stance in Hans Frei's *The Eclipse of Biblical Narrative.*" In *After Pentecost: Language and Biblical Interpretation,* edited by Craig Bartholomew, Colin Greene, and Karl Möller, 312–28. SHS 2. Grand Rapids: Zondervan, 2001.

MacIntyre, Alisdair C. *Whose Justice? Which Rationality?* Notre Dame: University of Notre Dame Press, 1988.

Malachowski, Alan. *Richard Rorty*. Princeton: Princeton University Press, 2002.

Marsden, George M. *The Outrageous Idea of Christian Scholarship*. Oxford: Oxford University Press, 1997.

———. *Understanding Fundamentalism and Evangelicalism*. Grand Rapids: Eerdmans, 1991.

Marsden, George M., and B. J. Longfield, eds. *The Secularization of the Academy*. Oxford: Oxford University Press, 1992.

Marshall, I. Howard. *Beyond the Bible: Moving from Scripture to Theology*. Grand Rapids: Baker Academic, 2004.

———. "The Holy Spirit and the Interpretation of Scripture." In *Rightly Divided: Readings in Biblical Hermeneutics*, edited by Roy B. Zuck, 66–74. Grand Rapids: Kregel, 1996.

Marty, Martin E., and R. Scott Appleby. *Fundamentalisms Comprehended*. Chicago: University of Chicago Press, 1995.

Mathison, Keith A. *The Shape of Sola Scriptura*. Moscow, ID: Canon, 2001.

Mayes, A. D. H. *Deuteronomy*. NCB. Grand Rapids: Eerdmans, 1981.

———. "On Describing the Purpose of Deuteronomy." *Journal for the Study of the Old Testament* 58 (1993): 13–33.

McDonald, Lee M. *The Formation of the Christian Biblical Canon*. Rev. and expanded ed. Peabody, MA: Hendrickson, 1995.

McGrath, Alister E. *Christian Theology: An Introduction*. 2nd ed. Oxford: Blackwell, 1997.

———. *The Genesis of Doctrine: A Study in the Foundation of Doctrinal Criticism*. Grand Rapids: Eerdmans, 1990.

McKenzie, Steven L. *The Chronicler's Use of the Deuteronomistic History*. Harvard Semitic Monographs 33. Atlanta: Scholars Press, 1984.

———. *King David: A Biography*. Oxford: Oxford University Press, 2000.

McKnight, Edgar V. *Postmodern Use of the Bible: The Emergence of Reader-Oriented Criticism*. Nashville: Abingdon, 1988.

McKnight, Scot. "From Wheaton to Rome: Why Evangelicals Become Roman Catholic." *JETS* 45 (2002): 451–72.

McLaren, Brian D. *A Generous Orthodoxy*. El Cajon, CA: Youth Specialties, 2004.

———. *A New Kind of Christian: A Tale of Two Friends on a Spiritual Journey*. San Francisco: Jossey-Bass, 2001.

McNeill, John T. "The Significance of the Word of God for Calvin." *Church History* 28 (1959): 131–46.

Meade, David G. *Pseudonymity and Canon: An Investigation into the Relationship of Authorship and Authority in Jewish and Earliest Christian Tradition*. Grand Rapids: Eerdmans, 1987.

Melugin, Roy F. "Canon and Exegetical Method." In *Canon, Theology, and Old Testament Interpretation: Essays in Honor of Brevard S. Childs*, edited by Gene M. Tucker, David L. Petersen, and Robert R. Wilson, 48–61. Philadelphia: Fortress, 1988.

Metzger, Bruce M. *Breaking the Code: Understanding the Book of Revelation*. Nashville: Abingdon, 1993.

———. *The Canon of the New Testament: Its Origin, Development, and Significance*. Oxford: Clarendon, 1987.

Metzger, Bruce M., and Bart D. Ehrman. *The Text of the New Testament: Its Transmission, Corruption, and Restoration*. 4th ed. Oxford: Oxford University Press, 2005.

Milgrom, Jacob. *Leviticus 1–16*. AB. New York: Doubleday, 1990.

Miller, J. Edward. "Some Observations on the Text-Critical Function of the Umlauts in Vaticanus, with Special Attention to 1 Corinthians 14.34–35." *JSNT* 26 (2003): 217–36.

Miller, J. Maxwell, and John H. Hayes. *A History of Ancient Israel and Judah*. Philadelphia: Westminster, 1986.

Miller, J. W. *Biblical Faith and Fathering*. New York: Paulist Press, 1989.

———. "The Problem of Men, Reconsidered." In *Does Christianity Teach Male Headship? The Equal-Regard Marriage and Its Critics*, edited by David Blankenhorn, Don Browning, and Mary Stewart Van Leeuwen, 65–73. Grand Rapids: Eerdmans, 2004.

Miller, Stephen R. *Daniel*. NAC 18. Nashville: Broadman & Holman, 1994.

Mitchell, Margaret M. "Pauline Accommodation and 'Condescension' (συγκατάβασις): 1 Cor 9:13-23 and the History of Influence." In *Paul Beyond the Judaism/Hellenism Divide*, edited by T. Engberg-Pedersen, 197–214. Louisville: Westminster John Knox, 2001.

Moo, Douglas J. *The Epistle to the Romans*. NICNT. Grand Rapids: Eerdmans, 1996.

Moore, G. F. "Tatian's *Diatessaron* and the Analysis of the Pentateuch." *JBL* 9 (1890): 201–15.

Moore, Michael S. "Role Pre-Emption in the Israelite Priesthood." *VT* 46 (1996): 316–29.

Moore, Thomas. *Care of the Soul*. New York: HarperCollins, 1992.

Moreland, J. P. "Truth, Contemporary Philosophy, and the Postmodern Turn." *JETS* 48 (2005): 77–88.

Morgan, Robert, and John Barton. *Biblical Interpretation*. Oxford Bible Series. Oxford: Oxford University Press, 1988.

Morris, Leon. *The Gospel according to John*. NICNT. Grand Rapids: Eerdmans, 1971.

Muller, Richard A., and John L. Thompson. "The Significance of Precritical Exegesis: Retrospect and Prospect." In *Biblical Interpretation in the Era of the Reformation*, edited by Richard Muller and John L. Thompson, 335–45. Grand Rapids: Eerdmans, 1996.

Murphy, Roland E. *The Tree of Life: An Exploration of Biblical Wisdom Literature*. Millennium supplement ed. Grand Rapids: Eerdmans, 2002.

Myers, C. D., Jr. "Romans, Epistle to the." In *ABD* 5:816–30.

Neil, William. *The Acts of the Apostles*. NCB. Grand Rapids: Eerdmans, 1981.

Nelson, Rudolph. *The Making and Unmaking of an Evangelical Mind: The Case of Edward Carnell*. Cambridge: Cambridge University Press, 1987.

Newbigin, Lesslie. *The Gospel in a Pluralist Society*. Grand Rapids: Eerdmans, 1989.

———. *Proper Confidence: Faith, Doubt, and Certainty in Christian Discipleship*. Grand Rapids: Eerdmans, 1995.

Newman, John Henry. *A Grammar of Assent*. Garden City, NY: Doubleday, 1955.

———. *The Idea of a University*. 3rd ed. London: Pickering, 1873.

Nicholson, E. W. *The Pentateuch in the Twentieth Century: The Legacy of Julius Wellhausen*. Oxford: Clarendon, 1998.

Nickle, Keith. *The Synoptic Gospels: Conflict and Consensus*. Atlanta: John Knox, 1980.

Nielsen, Eduard. *Deuteronomium*. Handbuch zum Alten Testament. Tübingen: Mohr, 1995.

Nietzsche, Friedrich. *Ecce Homo*. Translated by R. J. Hollingdale. London: Penguin, 1992.

———. *Philosophy and Truth: Selections from Nietzsche's Notebooks of the Early 1870s*. Translated and edited by Daniel Breazeale. Atlantic Highlands, NJ: Humanities Press International, 1979.

———. *The Will to Power*. Translated by Walter Kaufman and R. J. Hollingdale. New York: Vintage, 1967.

Noll, Mark A. *Between Faith and Criticism: Evangelicals, Scholarship, and the Bible in America*. 2nd ed. Grand Rapids: Baker Books, 1991.

———. *A History of Christianity in the United States and Canada*. Grand Rapids: Eerdmans, 1992.

———. *The Scandal of the Evangelical Mind*. Grand Rapids: Eerdmans, 1994.

Noll, Mark A., and Carol Nystrom. *Is the Reformation Over? An Evangelical Assessment of Contemporary Roman Catholicism*. Grand Rapids: Baker Academic, 2005.

Norris, Richard A., Jr. "Augustine and the Close of the Ancient Period of Interpretation." In *A History of Biblical Interpretation*. Vol. 1: *The Ancient Period*, edited by Alan J. Hauser and Duane F. Watson, 380–408. Grand Rapids: Eerdmans, 2003.

———, translator and editor. *The Song of Songs: Interpreted by Early Christian and Medieval Commentators*. Grand Rapids: Eerdmans, 2003.

O'Brien, Julia M. *Priest and Levite in Malachi*. SBL Dissertation Series 121. Atlanta: Scholars Press, 1990.

Oden, Thomas C. *After Modernity... What? Agenda for Theology*. Grand Rapids: Zondervan, 1992.

———. *Agenda for Theology*. San Francisco: Harper & Row, 1979.

O'Donovan, Joan E. "Man in the Image of God: The Disagreement between Barth and Brunner Reconsidered." *SJT* 39 (1986): 433–59.

O'Donovan, Oliver. *Resurrection and Moral Order: An Outline for Evangelical Ethics*. 2nd ed. Grand Rapids: Eerdmans, 1994.

O'Donovan, Wilbur, Jr. *Introduction to Biblical Christianity from an African Perspective*. Ilorin, Nigeria: Nigeria Evangelical Fellowship, 1992.

Ollenburger, Ben C., Elmer A. Martens, and Gerhard Hasel, eds. *The Flowering of Old Testament Theology*. Winona Lake, IN: Eisenbrauns, 1992.

Olyan, Saul M. "Zadok's Origins and the Tribal Policies of David." *JBL* 101 (1982): 177–93.

Origen. *The Philocalia of Origen*. Translated by G. Lewis. Edinburgh: T&T Clark, 1911.

Orr, James. *Revelation and Inspiration*. New York: Scribner's, 1910.

Osborne, Grant R. *The Hermeneutical Spiral*. Downers Grove, IL: InterVarsity, 1991.

Ostow, Mortimer. "The Fundamentalism Phenomenon: A Psychological Perspective." In *The Fundamentalist Phenomenon: A View from Within; A Response from Without*, edited by Norman J. Cohen, 99–125. Grand Rapids: Eerdmans, 1990.

Otto, Rudolph. *The Idea of the Holy*. Translated by John W. Harvey. London: Oxford University Press, 1923.

Overland, Paul. "Structure in *The Wisdom of Amenemope* and Proverbs." In *"Go to the Land I Will Show You": Studies in Honor of Dwight W. Young*, edited by Joseph E. Coleson and Victor H. Matthews, 275–91. Winona Lake, IN: Eisenbrauns, 1996.

Packer, James I. *Fundamentalism and the World of God*. Grand Rapids: Eerdmans, 1958.

———. "John Calvin and the Inerrancy of Holy Scripture." In *Inerrancy and the Church*, edited by John D. Hannah, 143–88. Chicago: Moody Press, 1984.

———. *Knowing God*. Downers Grove, IL: InterVarsity, 1973.

———. "Understanding the Bible: Evangelical Hermeneutics." In *Honouring the Written Word of God*, 147–60. Collected Shorter Writings of J. I. Packer 3. Carlisle: Paternoster, 1999.

Pangritz, Andreas. *Karl Barth in the Theology of Dietrich Bonhoeffer*. Grand Rapids: Eerdmans, 2000.

Parker, T. H. L. *Calvin's New Testament Commentaries*. London: SCM, 1971.

Patterson, Sue. *Realist Christian Theology in a Postmodern Age*. Cambridge: Cambridge University Press, 1999.

Paul, Shalom. "Literary and Ideological Echoes of Jeremiah in Deutero-Isaiah." In *Proceedings of the 5th World Congress of Jewish Studies*. Vol. 1, pages 102–20. Jerusalem: Hebrew University, 1969.

Payne, David F. "Isaiah." In *New International Bible Commentary*, edited by F. F. Bruce, 714–63. Grand Rapids: Zondervan, 1979.

Payne, Philip B. "The Fallacy of Equating Meaning with the Human Author's Intention." *JETS* 20 (1977): 243–52.

———. "MS. 88 as Evidence for a Text without 1 Cor 14:34–35." *New Testament Studies* 44 (1998): 152–58.

———. "The Originality of Text-Critical Symbols in Codex Vaticanus." *Novum Testamentum* 42 (2000): 105–13.

———. "The Text-Critical Function of the Umlauts in Vaticanus, with Special Attention to 1 Corinthians 14.34–35: A Response to J. Edward Miller." *JSNT* 27 (2004): 105–12.

Pelikan, Jaroslav. "Fundamentalism and/or Orthodoxy? Toward an Understanding of the Fundamentalist Phenomenon." In *The Fundamentalist Phenomenon: A View from Within; A Response from Without*, edited by Norman J. Cohen, 3–21. Grand Rapids: Eerdmans, 1990.

———. *The Idea of a University: A Reexamination*. New Haven: Yale University Press, 1992.

Peters, Ted, and Martinez Hewlett. *Evolution from Creation to New Creation: Conflict, Conversation, and Convergence*. Nashville: Abingdon, 2003.

Piper, John. *The Justification of God: An Exegetical and Theological Study of Romans 9:1–23*. Grand Rapids: Baker Academic, 1983.

Placher, William C. *The Domestication of Transcendence*. Louisville: Westminster John Knox, 1996.

Plantinga, Alvin. "Two (or More) Kinds of Scripture Scholarship." In *"Behind" the Text: History and Biblical Interpretation*, edited by Craig G. Bartholomew et al., 19–57. SHS 4. Grand Rapids: Zondervan, 2003.

———. *Warranted Christian Belief*. Oxford: Oxford University Press, 2000.

Plantinga, Cornelius, Jr. *Engaging God's Word: A Christian Vision of Faith, Learning, and Living*. Grand Rapids: Eerdmans, 2002.

Polanyi, Michael. *Knowing and Being*. Chicago: University of Chicago Press, 1969.

———. *Scientific Thought and Social Reality*. New York: International Universities Press, 1974.

———. *The Tacit Dimension*. Garden City, NY: Anchor Books, 1967.

Pollock, J. *Billy Graham: The Authorized Biography.* New York: McGraw-Hill, 1966.

Pope, Marvin H. *Song of Songs.* AB. Garden City, NY: Doubleday, 1977.

Popper, Karl. *The Open Society and Its Enemies.* 2 vols. London: Routledge, 1945.

———. *The Poverty of Historicism.* 1957. Repr. London: Routledge, 1993.

Porton, Gary G. "Rabbinic Midrash." In *A History of Biblical Interpretation.* Vol. 1: *The Ancient Period,* edited by Alan J. Hauser and Duane F. Watson, 198–224. Grand Rapids: Eerdmans, 2003.

Poythress, Vern S. "Language and Accommodation." In *Hermeneutics, Inerrancy, and the Bible,* edited by Earl D. Radmacher and Robert D. Preus, 351–76. Grand Rapids: Zondervan, 1984.

Preus, Robert D. "Luther and Biblical Infallibility." In *Inerrancy and the Church,* edited by John D. Hannah, 99–142. Chicago: Moody Press, 1984.

Pritchard, J. B., ed. *Ancient Near Eastern Texts Relating to the Old Testament.* 3rd ed. Princeton: Princeton University Press, 1969.

Propp, Vladimir. *Morphology of the Folktale.* Translated by Laurence Scott. Bloomington: Indiana University Press, 1958.

Provan, Iain. "Knowing and Believing: Faith in the Past." In *"Behind" the Text: History and Biblical Interpretation,* edited by Craig G. Bartholomew et al., 229–66. SHS 4. Grand Rapids: Zondervan, 2003.

Provan, Iain, V. Philips Long, and Tremper Longman III. *A Biblical History of Israel.* Louisville: Westminster John Knox, 2003.

Provence, Thomas E. "The Sovereign Subject Matter: Hermeneutics in the *Church Dogmatics.*" In *A Guide to Contemporary Hermeneutics: Major Trends in Biblical Interpretation,* edited by Donald K. McKim, 241–62. Grand Rapids: Eerdmans, 1986.

Rad, Gerhard von. "Ancient Word and Living Word: The Preaching of Deuteronomy and Our Preaching." Translated by Lloyd Gaston. *Int* 15 (1961): 3–13.

———. *Genesis.* Rev. ed. OTL. Philadelphia: Westminster, 1972.

———. "Typological Interpretation of the Old Testament." Translated by John Bright. *Int* 15 (1961): 174–92. Repr. in *Essays on Old Testament Hermeneutics,* edited by Claus Westermann, 17–39. Atlanta: John Knox, 1963.

———. *Wisdom in Israel.* Translated by James D. Martin. Nashville: Abingdon, 1972.

Radmacher, Earl D., and Robert D. Preus, eds. *Hermeneutics, Inerrancy, and the Bible: Papers from ICBI Summit II.* Grand Rapids: Zondervan, 1984.

Ramm, Bernard. *After Fundamentalism: The Future of Evangelical Theology.* San Francisco: Harper & Row, 1983.

Rashi. *The Metsudah Chumash.* Translated by Avroham Davis. Hoboken, NJ: KTAV, 1991.

Ratner, Joseph. "Some Comments on Rosen's 'Calvin's Attitude toward Copernicus.'" *JHI* 22 (1961): 382–85.

Rawlinson, Henry C. *The Persian Cuneiform Inscription at Behistun Decyphered and Translated.* London: J. W. Parker, 1847.

Redford, Donald B. *Egypt, Canaan, and Israel in Ancient Times.* Princeton: Princeton University Press, 1992.

Reid, Thomas. *Essays on the Intellectual Powers of Man.* Edited by D. R. Brookes and K. Haakonssen. University Park: Pennsylvania State University Press, 2002.

———. *Thomas Reid's Inquiry and Essays.* Edited by K. Lehrer and R. E. Beanblossom. Indianapolis: Bobbs-Merrill, 1975.

Rendtoff, Rolf. *The Problem of the Process of Transmission in the Pentateuch.* Translated by John J. Scullion. JSOTSup 89. Sheffield: JSOT Press, 1990.

———. *Das überlieferungsgeschichtliche Problem des Pentateuch.* BZAW 147. Berlin: de Gruyter, 1977.

Richardson, Don. *Eternity in Their Hearts.* Rev. ed. Ventura, CA: Regal, 1981.

Ricoeur, Paul. *Essays on Biblical Interpretation.* Edited by Lewis W. Mudge. Philadelphia: Fortress, 1980.

———. "The Hermeneutical Function of Distanciation." *Philosophy Today* 17 (1973): 129–41.

———. *Interpretation Theory: Discourse and the Surplus of Meaning.* Fort Worth: Texas Christian University Press, 1976.

———. "The Narrative Function." *Semeia* 13 (1978): 117–202.

———. *The Rule of Metaphor: The Creation of Meaning in Language.* Translated by Robert Czerny. 1977. Repr. New York: Routledge, 2003.

Ridderbos, J. *Isaiah.* Translated by John Vriend. Grand Rapids: Zondervan, 1985.

Roetzel, Calvin J. *The Letters of Paul*. 3rd ed. Louisville: Westminster John Knox, 1991.

Rogers, Jack B., and Donald K. McKim. *The Authority and Interpretation of the Bible: An Historical Approach*. New York: Harper & Row, 1979.

Rogers, R. W. *A History of Babylonia and Assyria*. 6th ed. New York: Abingdon, 1915.

Römheld, Diethard. *Wege der Weisheit: Die Lehren Amenemopes und Proverbien 22:17–24:22*. BZAW 184. Berlin: de Gruyter, 1989.

Rorty, Richard. *Philosophy and the Mirror of Nature*. Princeton: Princeton University Press, 1979.

Rosen, Edward. "Calvin's Attitude Toward Copernicus." *JHI* 21 (1960): 431–41.

———. "A Reply to Dr. Ratner." *JHI* 22 (1961): 386–88.

Russell, D. S. *The Method and Message of Jewish Apocalyptic: 200 BC–AD 100*. OTL. Philadelphia: Westminster, 1964.

Sanders, E. P., and Margaret Davies. *Studying the Synoptic Gospels*. Philadelphia: Trinity Press International, 1989.

Sanders, James A. *Canon and Community: A Guide to Canonical Criticism*. Philadelphia: Fortress, 1984.

Sanders, John. *The God Who Risks: A Theology of Providence*. Downers Grove, IL: InterVarsity, 1998.

Sandys-Wunsch, John, and Laurence Eldredge. "J. P. Gabler and the Distinction between Biblical and Dogmatic Theology: Translation, Commentary, and Discussion of His Originality." *SJT* 33 (1980): 133–58.

Santillana, Giorgio de. *The Crime of Galileo*. Chicago: University of Chicago Press, 1955.

Saucy, Robert L. "Recent Roman Catholic Theology." In *Challenges to Inerrancy: A Theological Response*, edited by Gordon R. Lewis and Bruce Demarest, 215–46. Chicago: Moody Press, 1984.

Saussure, Ferdinand de. *Course in General Linguistics*. New York: McGraw-Hill, 1959.

Scalise, Charles J. *From Scripture to Theology: A Canonical Journey into Hermeneutics*. Downers Grove, IL: InterVarsity, 1996.

Schaff, Philip. "Prolegomena: The Life and Work of John Chrysostom." In *NPNF* 1 9:3–23. Peabody, MA: Hendrickson, 1994.

Schenck, Kenneth L. "Philo and the Epistle to the Hebrews: Ronald Williamson's Study After Thirty Years." *Studia Philonica Annual* 14 (2002): 112–35.

Schleiermacher, Friedrich. *The Christian Faith*. New York: Harper & Row, 1963.

———. *Hermeneutics: The Handwritten Manuscripts*. Translated by J. Duke and J. Frostman. American Academy of Religion Texts and Translation Series 1. Missoula, MT: Scholars Press, 1977.

Schmitt, R. *The Bisitun Inscriptions of Darius the Great, Old Persian Text*. London: Lund Humphries, 1991.

Scholten, Clemens. "Weshalb wird die Schöpfungsgeschichte zum naturwissenschaftlichen Bericht?" *Theologische Quartalschrift* 177 (1997): 1–15.

Schrage, Wolfgang. *Der erste Brief an die Korinther*. 3 vols. EKKNT. Neukirchen-Vluyn: Neukirchener Verlag, 1991–1999.

Schultz, Richard L. "How Many Isaiahs Were There and What Does It Matter?" In *Evangelicals and Scripture: Tradition, Authority, and Hermeneutics*, edited by Vincent E. Bacote, Laura C. Miguélez, and Dennis L. Okholm, 150–70. Downers Grove, IL: InterVarsity, 2004.

Schuster, Marguerite. *The Fall and Sin: What We Have Become as Sinners*. Grand Rapids: Eerdmans, 2004.

Scott, Leland H. "The Message of American Methodism." In *The History of American Methodism*, edited by Emory Stevens Bucke, 1:291–359. 3 vols. New York: Abingdon, 1964.

Searle, John R. *Expression and Meaning: Studies in the Theory of Speech Acts*. Cambridge: Cambridge University Press, 1979.

———. *Speech Acts: An Essay in the Philosophy of Language*. Cambridge: Cambridge University Press, 1969.

Seely, Paul H. "The Geographical Meaning of 'Earth' and 'Seas' in Genesis 1:10." *WTJ* 59 (1997): 231–55.

Segal, Moses H. *The Pentateuch: Its Composition and Its Authorship and Other Biblical Studies*. Jerusalem: Magnes, 1967.

Seitz, Christopher R. *Figured Out: Typology and Providence in Christian Scripture*. Louisville: Westminster John Knox, 2001.

———. *Nicene Christianity: The Future for a New Ecumenism*. Grand Rapids: Brazos, 2001.

BIBLIOGRAPHY

Senft, Christoph. *La première épitre de saint Paul aux Corinthiens*. 2nd rev. ed. CNT. Geneva: Labor et Fides, 1990.

Sheridan, Mark, ed. *Genesis 12–20*. Ancient Christian Commentary on Scripture, Old Testament 2. Downers Grove, IL: InterVarsity, 2002.

Shils, Edward. "Tradition." *Comparative Studies in Society and History* 13 (1971): 122–59.

Skinner, John. *A Critical and Exegetical Commentary on the Book of Genesis*. 2nd ed. ICC. Edinburgh: T&T Clark, 1930.

Smart, James D. "The Theological Significance of Historical Criticism." In *The Authoritative Word: Essays on the Nature of Scripture*, edited by Donald K. McKim, 227–37. Grand Rapids: Eerdmans, 1983.

Smith, D. Moody. *John among the Gospels: The Relationship in Twentieth-Century Research*. Minneapolis: Fortress, 1992.

Smith, James K. A. *The Fall of Interpretation: Philosophical Foundations for a Creational Hermeneutics*. Downers Grove, IL: InterVarsity, 2000.

Smith, Jonathan Z. *Map Is Not Territory: Studies in the History of Religions*. Studies in Judaism in Late Antiquity 23. Leiden: Brill, 1978.

Soggin, J. Alberto. *A History of Ancient Israel*. Translated by John Bowden. Philadelphia: Westminster, 1985.

Sollberger, Edmond. "The Rulers of Lagaš." *Journal of Cuneiform Studies* 21 (1967): 279–91.

Sommer, Benjamin D. "New Light on the Composition of Jeremiah." *CBQ* 61 (1999): 646–66.

Sparks, Kenton L. *Ancient Texts for the Study of the Hebrew Bible: A Guide to the Background Literature*. Peabody, MA: Hendrickson, 2005.

———. "Ark of the Covenant." In *Dictionary of the Old Testament: Historical Books*, edited by Bill T. Arnold and H. G. M. Williamson, 88–92. Downers Grove, IL: InterVarsity, 2005.

———. "*Enūma Elish* and Priestly Mimesis: Elite Emulation in Nascent Judaism." *JBL* 126 (2007): 625–48.

———. "Gospel as Conquest: Mosaic Typology in Matthew 28:16–20." *CBQ* 68 (2006): 651–63.

———. *The Pentateuch: An Annotated Bibliography*. Institute of Biblical Research Bibliographies 1. Grand Rapids: Baker Academic, 2002.

———. "The Problem of Myth in Ancient Historiography." In *Rethinking the Foundations: Historiography in the Ancient World and in the Bible: Essays in Honour of John Van Seters*, edited by Steven L. McKenzie and Thomas Römer, 269–80. BZAW 294. Berlin: de Gruyter, 2000.

———. "Propaganda." In *Dictionary of the Old Testament: Historical Books*, edited by Bill T. Arnold and H. G. M. Williamson, 819–25. Downers Grove, IL: InterVarsity, 2005.

———. "The Sun Also Rises: Accommodation in Inscripturation and Interpretation." In *Evangelicals and Scripture: Tradition, Authority, and Hermeneutics*, edited by Vincent Bacote, Laura C. Miguélez, and Dennis L. Okholm, 112–32. Downers Grove, IL: InterVarsity, 2004.

Spear, Wayne R. "Augustine's Doctrine of Biblical Infallibility." In *Inerrancy and the Church*, edited by John D. Hannah, 37–65. Chicago: Moody Press, 1984.

Spencer, J. R. "Priestly Families (or Factions) in Samuel and Kings." In *The Pitcher Is Broken: Memorial Essays for Gösta W. Ahlström*, edited by S. W. Holloway and L. K. Handy, 397–400. JSOTSup 190. Sheffield: Sheffield Academic Press, 1995.

Stein, Robert. *Studying the Synoptic Gospels: Origin and Interpretation*. 2nd ed. Grand Rapids: Baker Academic, 2001.

Steinmetz, David C. "The Superiority of Precritical Exegesis." *Theology Today* 37 (1980): 27–38.

Stendahl, Krister. "The Apostle Paul and the Introspective Conscience of the West." *Harvard Theological Review* 56 (1963): 199–215.

Steymans, Hans Ulrich. "Eine assyrische Vorlage für Deuteronomium 28,20–44." In *Bundesdokument und Gesetz: Studien zum Deuteronomium*, edited by Georg Braulik, 119–41. Herders biblische Studien 4. Freiburg: Herder, 1995.

———. *Deuteronomium 28 und die adê zur Thronfolgeregelung Asarhaddons: Segen und Fluch im Alten Orient und in Israel*. Orbis biblicus et orientalis 145. Freiburg: Universitätsverlag, 1995.

Strobel, August. *Der erste Brief an die Korinther*. ZBK. Zurich: Theologischer Verlag, 1989.

Stuart, Douglas. *Hosea–Jonah*. WBC. Waco: Word, 1987.

Stuhlmacher, Peter. *Historical Criticism and Theological Interpretation*. Philadelphia: Fortress, 1977.

Sundberg, Walter. "The Social Effect of Biblical Criticism." In *Renewing Biblical Interpretation*, edited by Craig Bartholomew, Colin Greene, and Karl

Möller, 66–81. SHS 1. Grand Rapids: Zondervan, 2000.

Sweet, William Warren. *The Story of Religion in America*. New York: Harper, 1950.

Tadmor, Hayim. "Autobiographical Apology in the Royal Assyrian Literature." In *History, Historiography, and Interpretation: Studies in Biblical and Cuneiform Literatures*, edited by Hayim Tadmor and Moshe Weinfeld, 36–57. Jerusalem: Magnes, 1983.

Tadmor, Hayim, Benno Landsberger, and Simo Parpola. "The Sin of Sargon and Sennacherib's Last Will." *State Archives of Assyria Bulletin* 3 (1989): 3–51.

Taylor, Charles. "Overcoming Epistemology." In *After Philosophy: End or Transformation?* edited by Kenneth Baynes, James Bohman, and Thomas McCarthy, 464–88. Cambridge: Massachusetts Institute of Technology Press, 1987.

Thompson, Thomas L. *The Mythic Past: Biblical Archaeology and the Myth of Israel*. New York: Basic Books, 1999.

Tigay, Jeffrey H. *Deuteronomy*. JPS Torah Commentary. Philadelphia: Jewish Publication Society, 1996.

———. *The Evolution of the Gilgamesh Epic*. Philadelphia: University of Pennsylvania Press, 1982.

Toomer, G. J. "Astronomy." In *The Oxford Classical Dictionary*, edited by Simon Hornblower and Antony Spawforth, 196–98. 3rd ed. Oxford: Oxford University Press, 1996.

Torrance, T. F. *Reality and Scientific Theology*. Edinburgh: Scottish Academic Press, 1982.

———. *Theological Science*. Oxford: Oxford University Press, 1969.

Troeltsch, Ernest. "Historiography." In *Encyclopaedia of Religion and Ethics*, edited by James Hastings, 6:716–23. 13 vols. Edinburgh: T&T Clark, 1925.

———. "Über historische und dogmatische Methode in der Theologie." In *Gesammelte Schriften*, 2:729–53. 4 vols. Tübingen: Mohr, 1913.

Van Leeuwen, Mary Stewart. *Gender and Grace: Love, Work, and Parenting in a Changing World*. Downers Grove, IL: InterVarsity, 1990.

———. "Is Equal Regard in the Bible?" In *Does Christianity Teach Male Headship? The Equal-Regard Marriage and Its Critics*, edited by David Blankenhorn, Don Browning, and Mary Stewart Van Leeuwen, 13–22. Grand Rapids: Eerdmans, 2004.

Van Leeuwen, Raymond C. "Reading the Bible Whole in a Culture of Divided Hearts." *Ex Auditu* 19 (2003): 1–21.

Van Seters, John. *The Pentateuch: A Social-Science Commentary*. Sheffield: Sheffield Academic Press, 1999.

———. *Prologue to History: The Yahwist as Historian in Genesis*. Louisville: Westminster John Knox, 1992.

Van Til, Cornelius. *A Christian Theory of Knowledge*. Philadelphia: Presbyterian & Reformed Publishing, 1969.

Vanhoozer, Kevin J. "Into the Great 'Beyond': A Theologian's Response to the Marshall Plan." In I. Howard Marshall. *Beyond the Bible: Moving from Scripture to Theology*, pages 81–95. Grand Rapids: Baker Academic, 2004.

———. *Is There a Meaning in This Text?* Grand Rapids: Zondervan, 1998.

Voightlander, E. von. *The Bisitun Inscription of Darius the Great, Babylonian Version*. London: Lund Humphries, 1978.

Waaler, Erik. "A Revised Date for Pentateuchal Texts? Evidence from Ketef Hinnom." *Tyndale Bulletin* 53 (2002): 29–55.

Wainwright, Geoffrey. *Is the Reformation Over? Catholics and Protestants at the Turn of the Millennia*. Milwaukee: Marquette University Press, 2000.

Waltke, Bruce K. "Oral Tradition." In *Inerrancy and Hermeneutic: A Tradition, a Challenge, a Debate*, edited by Harvie M. Conn, 117–35. Grand Rapids: Baker Books, 1988.

Ware, Kallistos. *The Orthodox Way*. Crestwood, NY: St. Vladimir's Seminary Press, 1995.

Watson, P. J. "After Postmodernism: Perspectivism, a Christian Epistemology of Love, and the Ideological Surround." *Journal of Psychology and Theology* 32 (2004): 248–61.

Watts, John D. W. *Isaiah*. 2 vols. WBC. Waco: Word, 1985–1987. Rev. ed. Nashville: Nelson, 2005.

Webb, William J. *Slaves, Women, and Homosexuals: Exploring the Hermeneutics of Cultural Analysis*. Downers Grove, IL: InterVarsity, 2001.

Webster, John. "Confession and Confessions." In *Nicene Christianity: The Future for a New Ecumenism*, edited by Christopher R. Seitz, 119–31. Grand Rapids: Brazos, 2001.

Weinandy, Thomas. *In the Likeness of Sinful Flesh: An Essay on the Humanity of Jesus.* Edinburgh: T&T Clark, 1993.

Weinfeld, Moshe. *Deuteronomy and the Deuteronomic School.* Oxford: Oxford University Press, 1972.

———. *The Place of the Law in the Religion of Ancient Israel.* Vetus Testamentum Supplements 100. Leiden: Brill, 2004.

Weiss, James Michael. "Renaissance." In *The Oxford Encyclopedia of the Reformation*, edited by Hans Joachim Hillerbrand, 3:418–21. 4 vols. Oxford: Oxford University Press, 1996.

Wellhausen, Julius. *Prolegomena to the History of Ancient Israel.* Edinburgh: A & C Black, 1885.

Wenham, Gordon J. *Genesis.* 2 vols. WBC. Waco: Word, 1987–1994.

Wesley, John. *The Works of John Wesley.* 12 vols. London: Wesleyan Methodist Book Room, 1872.

Westerholm, Stephen. *Perspectives Old and New On Paul: The "Lutheran" Paul and His Critics.* Grand Rapids: Eerdmans, 2004.

Westermann, Claus. *Genesis.* Translated by John J. Scullion. 3 vols. Continental Commentary. Minneapolis: Augsburg, 1984–1986.

———. *Isaiah 40–66: A Commentary.* Translated by David M. G. Stalker. OTL. Philadelphia: Westminster, 1969.

———. "The Role of the Lament in the Theology of the Old Testament." Translated by Richard N. Soulen. *Int* 28 (1974): 20–38. Repr. in Claus Westermann, *Praise and Lament in the Psalms*, 259–80. Atlanta: John Knox, 1981.

Wette, W. M. L. de. *A Critical and Historical Introduction to the Canonical Scriptures of the Old Testament.* Translated by Theodore Parker. 2nd ed. Boston: Little and Brown, 1850.

White, A. D. *A History of the Warfare of Science with Theology in Christendom.* 2 vols. New York: Appleton, 1920.

Whitelam, Keith W. *The Invention of Ancient Israel: The Silencing of Palestinian History.* New York: Routledge, 1996.

Whybray, R. N. *Introduction to the Pentateuch.* Grand Rapids: Eerdmans, 1995.

———. *Isaiah 40–66.* NCB. Grand Rapids: Eerdmans, 1981.

———. *The Making of the Pentateuch: A Methodological Study.* JSOTSup 53. Sheffield: JSOT Press, 1987.

Wilberforce, William. *A Practical View of the Prevailing Religious System of Professed Christians in the Higher and Middle Classes of This Country Contrasted with Real Christianity.* London: Cadell & Davies, 1797.

Wilcox, David L. *God and Evolution: A Faith-Based Understanding.* Valley Forge, PA: Judson, 2004.

Willard, Dallas. *Logic and the Objectivity of Knowledge: A Study in Husserl's Early Philosophy.* Athens: Ohio University Press, 1984.

Williams, A. N. "Argument to Bliss: The Epistemology of the *Summa Theologiae*." *Modern Theology* 20 (2004): 505–26.

Williams, D. H. *Evangelicals and Tradition: The Formative Influence of the Early Church.* Grand Rapids: Baker Academic, 2005.

Williamson, H. G. M. *1 and 2 Chronicles.* NCB. Grand Rapids: Eerdmans, 1982.

Wilson, R. McL. *Hebrews.* NCB. Grand Rapids: Eerdmans, 1987.

Wink, Walter. *The Bible in Human Transformation.* Philadelphia: Fortress, 1973.

Winter, Ralph D. "The Two Structures of God's Redemptive Mission." In *Perspectives on the World Christian Movement: A Reader*, edited by Ralph D. Winter and Steven C. Hawthorne, 178–90. Pasadena: William Carey Library, 1981.

Witte, John, Jr. "Male Headship: Reform of the Protestant Tradition." In *Does Christianity Teach Male Headship? The Equal-Regard Marriage and Its Critics*, edited by David Blankenhorn, Don Browning, and Mary Stewart Van Leeuwen, 28–39. Grand Rapids: Eerdmans, 2004.

Wolf, Herbert M. *An Introduction to the Old Testament.* Chicago: Moody Press, 1991.

Wolff, Hans Walter. "The Kerygma of the Yahwist." Translated by Wilbur A. Benware. *Int* 20 (1966): 131–58. Repr. in Walter Brueggemann and Hans Walter Wolff, *The Vitality of Old Testament Traditions*, 41–66. 2nd ed. Atlanta: John Knox, 1982.

Wolff, Hope Nash. "Gilgamesh, Enkidu, and the Heroic Life." *JAOS* 89 (1969): 392–98.

Wolterstorff, Nicholas. *Divine Discourse: Philosophical Reflections on the Claim that God Speaks.* Cambridge: Cambridge University Press, 1995.

———. *Thomas Reid and the Story of Epistemology.* Cambridge: Cambridge University Press, 2001.

Wood, John Halsey, Jr. "Oswald T. Allis and the Question of Isaianic Authorship." *JETS* 48 (2005): 249-61.

Work, Telford. *Living and Active: Scripture in the Economy of Salvation*. Grand Rapids: Eerdmans, 2002.

Wright, Christopher J. H. *Old Testament Ethics for the People of God*. Downers Grove, IL: InterVarsity, 2004.

Wright, David F. "Calvin's Pentateuchal Criticism: Equity, Hardness of Heart, and Divine Accommodation in the Mosaic Harmony Commentary." *Calvin Theological Journal* 21 (1986): 33-50.

Wright, G. Ernest. *God Who Acts: Biblical Theology as Recital*. Studies in Biblical Theology 1/8. London: SCM, 1952.

———. "The Levites in Deuteronomy." *VT* 4 (1954): 325-30.

Wright, N. T. *Jesus and the Victory of God*. Christian Origins and the Question of God 2. Minneapolis: Fortress, 1997.

———. *The Last Word: Beyond the Bible Wars to a New Understanding of the Authority of Scripture*. San Francisco: HarperSanFrancisco, 2005.

———. *The New Testament and the People of God*. Christian Origins and the Question of God 1. Minneapolis: Fortress, 1992.

———. *The Resurrection of the Son of God*. Christian Origins and the Question of God 3. Minneapolis: Fortress, 2003.

Yarbrough, Robert W. "The Hermeneutics of 1 Timothy 2:9-15." In *Women in the Church: A Fresh Analysis of 1 Timothy 2:9-15*, edited by Andreas J. Köstenberger, Thomas R. Schreiner, and H. Scott Baldwin, 155-96. Grand Rapids: Baker Academic, 1995.

Yarchin, William. *History of Biblical Interpretation: A Reader*. Peabody, MA: Hendrickson, 2004.

Young, Dwight W. "The Influence of Babylonian Algebra on Longevity among the Antediluvians." *ZAW* 102 (1990): 321-35.

———. "A Mathematical Approach to Certain Dynastic Spans in the Sumerian King List." *JNES* 2 (1988): 123-29.

———. "On the Application of Numbers from Babylonian Mathematics to Biblical Life Spans and Epochs." *ZAW* 100 (1988): 332-61.

Young, E. J. *Thy Word Is Truth*. Grand Rapids: Eerdmans, 1957.

Young, Frances M. "Alexandrian and Antiochene Exegesis." In *A History of Biblical Interpretation*. Vol. 1: *The Ancient Period*, edited by Alan J. Hauser and Duane F. Watson, 334-54. Grand Rapids: Eerdmans, 2003.

———. *The Making of the Creeds*. London: SCM, 1991.

Ziesler, John. *Paul's Letter to the Romans*. Philadelphia: Trinity Press International, 1989.

Zimmerli, Walther. *Ezekiel*. Vol. 1. Translated by Ronald E. Clements and James D. Martin. Hermeneia. Philadelphia: Fortress, 1979.

Zimmermann, Jens. *Recovering Theological Hermeneutics: An Incarnational-Trinitarian Theory of Interpretation*. Grand Rapids: Baker Academic, 2004.

Scripture and Ancient Sources Index

Genesis

1   12, 83, 84, 97, 138, 158, 235, 347, 352
1–3   350
1–9   84
1:1–2:3   83, 86
1:6–8   203
1:26–28   342
1:27   347, 349
1:27–28   50
2   98
2–3   84
2–4   83
2:4–2:25   83
2:4–3:24   86
2:18–19   83n8
2:19   83n8
2:20   348
2:23   348
3:5   49
3:14–15   348
3:14–19   264, 348
3:16   342, 343, 347, 348, 349, 352
3:17   84
3:17–19   348
3:20   348
3:22   49
4   83, 84, 86, 217, 317
4:26   85
5   80, 81, 83, 84, 86, 216–218, 224
6–9   83, 84
6:6   231
6:9–22   86
6:19   84
7:1–5   84, 86
7:10   84, 86
7:11   84, 86
7:12   86
7:13   84
7:13–15   86
8:6–12   97
8:15–19   86
8:20–22   86
8:21   84, 231, 348
8:21–22   85
9:1   84
9:1–17   86
9:6   50
9:11   84, 85
10   86
10:7   82
10:13   82
10:22   82
11   80, 81
11:10–26   86
11:26   80
11:32   80
12:1–4   80, 86
12:6   79
12:7   122
13:7   79
13:15   122
14   317
15   86, 294
15:13–16   82
16:16   80
17   86, 124
17:1   80
17:9–14   294
18–19   86
19   242
19:18   344n22
20   82
21   82, 82n6, 83n6
21:5   80
21:8   80
24:16   344n22
26   82
26:34–35   86
27:41–45   86
27:46–28:9   86
28   83n6
28:10–22   87
28:10–29:1   86
31:17–18   87
31:45–47   82
32:22–32   87
35:1–8   87
35:9–15   87
35:27–29   87
36   79
36:31   79
46:17   235
47:31   235
50:20   335

Exodus

2:11   78
3   85, 87, 317
6   85, 87
6:2-8   87
6:3   11
6:14-25   82
12:8-9   91, 144
12:22-23   112
12:40   81, 82
12:46   112
15:20   353
16-17   87
18:13-27   87
19-24   158
20   158
20:8-11   91n23
20:17   226, 344n20, 344n21
20:22-23:33   91, 220
20:24-26   91
21:1-11   120
21:2   120
21:10-11   344n20
21:20   257
21:20-21   120, 226, 289
22:16-17   344n22
23:14-19   91n22
23:19   91n24
24:1-11   158
24:4   78
24:11   158
24:12-15a   158n57
24:12-18   158, 158n57
25-31   91, 93, 94, 220
25-40   85
25:1   158
25:10-22   95
25:15b-18   158n57
27:1-2   91
31:12-17   91n23
32-40   91, 220
32:14   231
33:7   94
34:18-26   91n22
34:26   91n24
35-40   93, 94
35:1-3   91n23
40:12-15   294
40:15   96

Leviticus

1-16   91, 220
11:3   206
11:5-6   255
11:7   350
17   92, 93
17-26   91, 92, 220
19:18   257
20:10   344n22
23:1-44   91n22
23:3   91n23
25:35-55   120
25:39-43   120
25:43   120
25:44   120
25:44-46   226

Numbers

2:2   94
5:11-31   213, 344n22
8   127
11   87
11:10-17   87
11:24-30   94
12:3   78
14:44   94
16   96, 127
20:1-13   87
21:10-20   79
27:5-8   344n20
28-29   91n22
30:1-16   344n20
31:1-9   344n20
31:35   344n22

Deuteronomy

1-4   89n16, 91
2:34   121n78, 226
3:6   121n78
5   158
5:12-15   91n23
5:21   344n21
7:1-3   226
7:1-6   102
10:1-8   95
10:12   89
10:33   235n21
11:6   127
12-26   91, 220
12:1-11   94

12:15-25   92
13   89n18
13:3   89
13:12-18   102
14:8   205, 226, 350
14:21   91n24
15:12   120
15:12-18   120
16   144n20
16:1-17   91n22
16:7   91, 144
17:9   96
17:18   96
18:1   96
18:6-7   96
20:10-14   344n20
20:16-18   121n78
21:5   96
21:16-17   344n20
22:1-4   344n20
22:13-14   344n22
22:19   344n20
22:22-24   344n22
22:28-29   345n23
22:29   344n20
24:1-4   344n20
25:17-19   102
26:16   89
28   89
29-31   90

Joshua

1-12   226
6   95
6:21   121n78
15:16   344n20

Judges

4-5   346, 353
5:30   344n21

1 Samuel

4-6   95
7:1-11   96
9-11   89
13   102, 128
15   102, 128
15:11   231
17   144

Scripture and Ancient Sources Index

22   128
25   128
27   128
28   128
29   128

2 Samuel

2:8–3:5   128
5:6–8   331n2
5:21   103
7:11–16   74
7:12   122
8:2   331n2
8:4   105
10:6   105
10:18   105
11   128, 129
11:2–12:24   331n2
12   224
12:31   331n2
16   102
16–17   102
21   128
21:19   144
24   103n47
24:9   105
24:13   105
24:24   105

1 Kings

1:1–4   28
3:1–15   94
4:26   105
4:30   268
7:26   105
9:28   105
15:7–24   103
15:16–24   103

2 Kings

13:14–20   213
18:13–16   157
18:17–19:37   157
21–23   89
21:1–18   103, 159
21:10–15   160
22–23   88
22:14   353
23:26   103

24–25   157
24:3   104
24:3–4   103

1 Chronicles

11:6   331n3
14:12   103
18:2   331n3
18:4   105
19:7   105
19:18   105
20:3   331n3
20:5   144
21:1   103n47
21:1–22:1   103n47
21:5   105
21:12   105
21:25   105

2 Chronicles

1:1–13   94
4:5   105
8:18   105
9:25   105
13:1–17:1   103
33:1–20   103, 159
33:11   90n19
33:12–20   160
35:13a   144
35:13b   144

Job

1–3   313
38–41   313
38:1–3   262
42:3   262
42:6   262
42:15   342, 343

Psalms

5   123
8:7   348
10   123
14   123
19:1–6   265
36   123
71:6   48
82:6   121
89:19–46   74–75

131:2   49
137   185, 324, 325
137:9   226
138:8–9   28
140   123

Proverbs

1–9   267
1:7   268
3:5   310
3:19–21   267
4:5–9   28
8:20   267, 267n9
8:22–29   267
21:1   311
22:17   269
22:17–23:14   268
22:18   269
22:19   269
22:20   269
22:21   269
22:22   269
22:24   269
22:25   269
22:28   269
22:29   269
23:1–3   269
23:4–5   269
23:6–7   269
23:8   269
23:9   269
23:10–11   269
25:21   226
30   268
31:1–9   268

Ecclesiastes

1:5   232
7:15   337

Song of Solomon

5   131

Isaiah

1–39   107
1–55   107
6   239
10:5–19   342
22:1–14   157

40–55   105, 107, 108, 147, 148, 149
40–66   166
40:1–2   106, 108
43:8   50
44:24–28   106
44:28   148
45:1   148
45:1–13   106
48:20   106, 147
56–66   107, 108, 147
56:1–8   108
57–59   108
58:12   108
59   123
60–62   108
65:1–16   108

Jeremiah
13:20–27   344n20
18:18   268
20–21   90
26   90
26:17–19   107

Ezekiel
1   95
10   95
10–11   95
16:32–42   344n20
18:23   311
20:8–30   92
20:23–26   92
20:25   236
23:22–30   344n20
26:7–21   108
29:17–18   144
29:18–20   108
43   95
44:10–16   96, 127

Daniel
1–6   116
7   117, 150
7–12   116, 149, 150, 223
8   117, 150
8:19–22   150
8:21–22   117
9   117, 118

10–12   117
11–12   150
12:1–4   117

Hosea
2:1–3   344n20
2:10   344n20

Joel
2:28–29   346n28

Amos
5:25–27   254
9:11–12   294

Zechariah
13:7   122n86

1 Enoch
1:9   125–126
17–36   234n16
72–82   234n16

1 Maccabees
1   117
6:1–17   117

2 Maccabees
1:14–16   117
9:1–29   117

Wisdom of Ben Sirah
15:14   312
33:10–13   312

Wisdom of Solomon
13:1   266
13:1–9   266

Matthew
2   152
2:13–15   111
2:16–18   111
4:1–2   111

5–7   111
5:38–39   111, 296
5:44   226
7:11   123
10:22   338
10:25   123
12:38–42   112
19   242
19:1–9   241
19:16–19   110
24:14   335
24:34   336
26:31   122n86
27:9   250n61

Mark
4:1–34   112
5:21–24   111, 112
5:35–43   111, 112
8:18   50
10:17–19   110
12:25   347
13:32   164n71, 336
14:27   122n86
15   112
15:25   162

Luke
1:1–4   76
2   152
2:52   164n71
6:27   257
10:30–35   215
12:28   123
23:34   334

John
1:29   112, 162
1:36   162
3:16–17   311
5:39   253
5:39–40   183
8:12–59   112
10:1–31   112
10:31–39   121
13:1–2   112, 163
15:19   338
17:20–21   284
18:28   112

Scripture and Ancient Sources Index 399

18:28–19:16 112
19:14 112, 163
19:28–29 112
19:32–36 112
20:30–31 112

Acts

1:7 336
2:17–18 346n28
2:17–19 342
7:14 235
7:42–43 254
9:14–15 226
11:4–10 205
15 192, 294
15:8 294
15:10–11 294
15:12 294
17 266, 267, 268
17:26–28 267
17:30 50, 334
20:25 114
20:38 114
21:9 346n28

Romans

1 266, 266n5, 267, 365
1:4 32n22
1:19 276
1:19–21 265
1:20 304
1:21 266, 268
2:14–15 265
2:15 268
3:10–18 123
4:18 122
5:15 123
6 272, 273
6–8 274
6:6 273
6:6–7 273
6:14–15 274
6:16 273
6:18 273
7 271, 273, 274, 327, 365
7:1–6 274
7:4 274
7:7 272
7:7–12 272
7:13 272, 273

7:13–25 270, 271, 272, 274, 304
7:14 273
7:14–25 274, 294
7:25 274
8 272, 273
8:1–4 352
8:3 223, 252n67
8:5–8 274
8:7 274
8:9 273
8:13 274
8:19–22 264
9 311
9:12–29 123
9:22–23 353n41
10:18–21 123
11:8–10 123
11:33 262
11:33–36 312, 353n41
12:2 274
13:1–5 342
15:9–12 123
16:7 346

1 Corinthians

1:6 32n22
1:14–16 353n41
2:12 32n22
2:12–14 304
2:14 303, 304
2:14–15 177
4:1–4 258
4:4 50
5:7 223
7 346n29
7:10 353n41
7:25 351n39, 353n41
7:29 225, 335
7:40 351n39
10:1–2 99
10:4 124
11 115, 351n39
11:1–16 353
11:2–6 115, 345n26
11:3 340
11:3–10 342, 343
11:4–12 351
11:5 246
11:5–10 348
12 345

13:4–8 333
13:12 50
14 115, 345, 345n26
14:1–33 246
14:33 345n26
14:34–35 115, 246, 345, 345n26, 346n29
14:35 48, 345n26
15 189, 320

2 Corinthians

3:6 185
10:5 371

Galatians

3:1–5 295
3:6–25 294
3:15–17 82
3:16 122
3:28 115, 120, 226, 247, 289, 293, 342, 345n26, 346, 351, 353, 353n42
4 124
4:21–31 30
5 272, 273
5:12 226
5:16–26 271

Ephesians

1:4 32n22
1:11 311
5 352
5:22 342
5:22–28 343
5:23 114
5:25–28 346
6:5–9 120
6:9 226, 289

Philippians

3:20 114

Colossians

4:1 120, 226, 289

1 Thessalonians

2:13 76
4:11 338

2 Thessalonians
2:2 113
3:6–12 338

1 Timothy
1:1 116
1:3 114
2:11–14 115
2:11–15 246, 344, 345, 346, 348, 349, 350

2 Timothy
1:1 116
3:16 357
3:16–17 210
4:13 116
4:21 114, 116

Titus
1 116
2:4–5 342, 344
3:14 114

Hebrews
4:12 295
9–10 223
9:13–14 123
9:24 124
11:21 235
12:14 338

James
1:5 362
3:1 258, 295
3:9 50

1 Peter
3:1–6 344
3:21 124

2 Peter
3:9 311
3:16 258

Jude
9 125
14–15 125

Revelation
5:6 223
13 118
13:3 118
13:16–18 338
14:1 338
17:8 118
17:9 118
17:10–11 119
18 342
18–22 118

Author Index

Abba, Raymond 96n32
Abelard, Peter 282n4
Abraham, William J. 190, 190n56
Achtemeier, Paul J. 119n77, 170n87
Albright, W. F. 179, 179n27, 181n32
Alexander, T. Desmond 146n24, 151, 151n36, 152, 153n42, 157, 158, 158n55, 159, 159n59, 165, 165n72, 166, 166n74
Allen, Leslie C. 169n85
Allison, Dale C., Jr. 111n60
Ambrose 271n17
Amit, Yaira 101n43
Anderson, Bernard W. 179, 179n28, 180, 180n30
Anderson, Ray S. 289n17
Antoun, Richard T. 307n57
Appleby, R. Scott 307n57
Aquinas, Thomas 27, 29, 29n12, 29n13, 29n14, 30, 55, 195, 209n5, 252n67, 290, 309, 309n61, 309n63, 310, 340, 340n12, 360, 360n2
Archer, Gleason L. 137n4, 138n6, 146n24, 150n34, 164n70, 254, 254n69, 254n70, 255, 255n71
Ariminius, James 271n17, 271n18
Aristotle 209n5
Arius 340
Armerding, Carl E. 169n81
Assmann, Jan 269n13
Athanasius 237, 238, 238n29, 340, 341
Attridge, Harold W. 124n94
Augustine 13, 27, 27n7, 28, 28n8, 29, 32, 42n48, 51n64, 52, 53, 55, 109n56, 125, 134, 143, 173, 186n50, 201, 201n81, 240, 240n38, 240n40, 245, 245n49, 246, 246n51, 270n15, 271, 271n17, 276, 276n25, 290, 319, 319n86, 322, 324, 325, 326, 340, 340n12, 358, 359, 360, 360n2, 360n3, 361, 373, 373n22
Auld, A. Graeme 103n46, 160n61
Austin, J. L. 208n4

Bakhtin, Mikhail 287, 287n11
Baldwin, Joyce G. 150n34
Balserak, Jon 234n17, 242, 242n42
Barr, James 104n49, 130n109, 145n23, 179n26, 180n31, 181n33, 196–199, 197n72, 197n73, 197n74, 198n79, 199n80, 216n12
Barrett, C. K. 124n92
Bartchy, S. Scott 292n30
Barth, Karl 172–178, 181, 183, 187, 192, 201, 202, 205, 210, 252n67, 277, 277n26
Bartholomew, Craig G. 142n12, 143, 143n14, 302n43
Barton, John 21n5, 178n23
Basil the Great 224n22, 231n5, 238, 238n31, 271n17, 360n2
Basinger, David 311n64
Batten, D. 138n7
Battles, Ford L. 234n17
Bauckham, Richard J. 125n98, 302n43, 302n46, 303, 318n82
Beasley-Murray, George R. 170n86, 335n8
Beaulieu, Paul-Alain 66n13
Béchard, Dean P. 193n62, 194n64, 195n68, 321n89
Beegle, Dewey M. 192, 192n60
Belleville, Linda L. 349, 349n34
Bengel, J. A. 187

401

Benin, Stephen D. 27n6, 236n23, 236n24, 237n27, 237n28, 238n29, 238n32, 239, 239n34, 239n35, 240n36, 240n39, 244n47, 360n2
Bergsma, John S. 92n26
Berkouwer, G. C. 244, 245n48
Bietenhard, Hans 266n6
Blenkinsopp, Joseph 96n32
Block, Daniel I. 109, 109n55
Bloesch, Donald G. 192, 192n60
Blomberg, Craig L. 162, 162n67, 163, 164
Blum, Erhard 153, 153n42, 154, 154n43
Bonhoeffer, Dietrich 321, 321n90
Bonsirven, Joseph 112n62
Boyd, Gregory A. 231n2
Boyer, Steven 312, 340n11, 340n12, 341
Bradley, F. H. 313, 313n70
Bray, Gerald 271n17
Brewer, David Instone 123n88
Brinkman, J. A. 65n11
Brown, Harold O. 345n24
Brown, Raymond E. 112n62
Bruce, F. F. 20, 20n2, 170n86
Brueggemann, Walter 128n104, 178, 178n24, 179n26
Bruner, J. S. 308n60
Brunner, Emil 277, 277n26
Buckley, James J. 283n9
Budge, E. A. W. 269n14
Bullock, C. Hassell 150n34
Burke, Spencer 361, 361n6
Burrus, Virginia 131, 131n114
Burson, D. D. 18 [illegible]
Bush, Frederick W. 170, 170n88

Calvin, John 31, 31n17, 32, 32n22, 35, 52, 53, 55, 187, 232, 232n9, 233, 233n10, 234, 234n17, 235, 235n18, 235n19, 235n20, 235n22, 236, 241, 242, 242n43, 245, 249, 250, 250n61, 251, 255, 256, 256n72, 256n73, 271n16, 276, 276n23, 290, 306, 306n54, 327, 334, 340, 340n12, 358, 361
Calvo 173
Campbell, Alexander 13, 14
Cannon, Katie Geneva 290n20
Caputo, John D. 42n48, 53n66, 317n80
Carey, William 363, 363n9
Carlyle, Thomas 34, 34n26, 34n27
Carnell, Edward J. 251, 368–369
Carr, David M. 85n9, 152n39, 154n44
Carson, Donald A. 167n79, 231, 231n3, 300n40, 313n68, 361n7
Cartlidge, David R. 320n87

Cassuto, Umberto 147n24
Celsus 237
Childs, Brevard S. 158n57, 181n34, 183, 201, 202
Chirichigno, Gregory 254, 254n70
Chisholm, Roderick M. 39n43
Christiansen, K. 79n2
Clark, David K. 317n78
Clement of Alexandria 125n98, 206, 206n1, 290
Clifford, Richard J. 267n8, 268n9, 268n10
Clines, David J. A. 131, 131n113
Coady, C. A. J. 314, 314n74
Cocceius, J. 187
Cody, Aelred 96n32
Cogan, Morton 157n52
Cohen, Norman J. 307n57
Collins, John J. 117n75, 130n109, 131n114, 313n71, 335n8, 336n9
Congdon, Roger D. 242n41
Conzelmann, Hans 113n64, 114n66, 115n70, 246n54, 246n55, 345n26
Cook, Stephen L. 96n32
Cooper, Lamar E. 109n54
Copernicus 17, 18, 231, 232, 233, 234, 275, 285, 296, 359, 361, 373
Craig, William Lane 46, 46n60, 51, 311n64
Craigie, Peter C. 148n27, 169n82
Cranford, C. E. B. 271n16
Crenshaw, James L. 267n8
Crisp, Oliver 252n67
Cross, Frank Moore, Jr. 86n11, 96n32
Cyprian 271n17
Cyril of Alexandria 271n17

Dahm, Ulrike 96n32
Darwin, Charles 296
Davids, Peter H. 126n100
Davies, Margaret 109n57
Davies, Philip R. 122n84, 131n116
Dayton, Wilber T. 303n48, 374n25
De Vries, Simon J. 161n65
Derrida, Jacques 26, 26n1, 41n46, 42, 42n48
Descartes, René 33, 33n23, 36, 40, 50, 314
Dever, William G. 131n116, 169n80
Dibelius, Martin 113n64, 114n66, 115n70, 246n54
Diekema, Anthony J. 366–367, 367n14
Dillard, Raymond B. 12, 103n48, 148n27, 161n65, 166, 166n75, 167, 169n82, 169n84, 222n19
Diodorus of Tarsus 232n5
Dion, Paul 89n18
Dobbs-Allsopp, F. W. 130n112, 131n115
Dozeman, Thomas B. 87n13, 158n58

Author Index

Duke, Rodney K. 161n65
Dungan, David L. 320n87
Dunn, James D. G. 312n65

Ehrman, Bart D. 114n67
Eichhorn, J. G. 34
Einstein, Albert 296
Eissfeldt, Otto 144n19, 148n28
Eldredge, Laurence 300n38
Eliade, Mircea 317n79
Elliott, E. N. 290n22, 291n23
Elliott, J. K. 113n65, 346n29
Ellis, E. Earle 122n83
Ellwood, Robert S., Jr. 283n6
Emerton, John A. 96n32, 268n12
Enns, Peter E. 93n27, 99n39, 124n90, 170, 170n89
Epp, Eldon Jay 346, 346n30
Erickson, Millard J. 251, 265n4
Etz, Donald V. 218n14
Eunomius 238
Evans, C. Stephen 315, 318n81, 319n83
Evans, Craig A. 224n21, 337n10
Ezra, Ibn 144, 148

Farmer, William 110n58
Fee, Gordon D. 115n71, 246n55, 247n56, 345n26, 346n27
Feinberg, Paul D. 43n49, 251n62
Fichte, J. G. 37n36
Finegan, Jack 216n12
Finkelstein, Israel 157n52
Finley, Moses I. 292n30
Finocchiaro, Maurice A. 17n1
Fishbane, Michael 144n20
Fitzmyer, Joseph A. 266n5, 267n7
Foucault, Michael 42, 42n47
Fowl, Stephen E. 192, 192n61
Fox-Talbot, W. H. 59
France, R. T. 296n33
Frankena, R. 89n18
Frei, Hans 187n51
Friedman, J. 35n29, 334n7
Friesen, Steven J. 119n77
Frye, Roland M. 258, 258n74

Gabler, J. P. 300, 300n38, 301n41
Gadamer, Hans-Georg 43, 43n50, 53, 358
Galileo 17, 18, 21, 23, 234, 285
Gallagher, Maggie 343, 343n19
Gallay, Allan 290n21
Garrett, Duane 147n24, 154n42
Gay, Peter 35n30

Geertz, Clifford 210n6
George, A. R. 60n3
Giles, Kevin 289, 289n18, 290n19, 291n24, 293n31, 296, 340n13, 342
Gilkey, Langdon 180, 180n29, 180n30
Ginzburg, Carlo 22n7
Glancy, Jennifer A. 292n30
Goheen, Michael W. 302n43
Goldingay, John 117n75, 148n27, 169n83, 170, 170n88, 193n63, 212n7, 244, 245n48, 246, 246n53, 306n53, 327
Goldstein, Jonathan A. 67n14
Gordon, Robert P. 143, 143n14, 372, 372n21
Grabbe, Lester L. 96n32, 169n80
Graham, Billy 135, 136
Grayson, A. K. 64n10
Green, Garrett 175n15, 176n16
Green, Joel B. 119n77, 170n87, 287n14
Green, William Henry 164, 164n69
Greenfield, J. C. 58n1
Gregersen, Niels Henrik 275n21
Gregory of Nazianzus 238, 239, 239n33, 305, 340, 340n12
Gregory of Nyssa 232n5, 238, 238n30, 239, 360n2
Gregory the Great 28, 28n10
Grudem, Wayne 248n58, 252, 265n3
Gunton, Colin E. 265n2
Gutting, Gary 42n47

Hagner, Donald A. 110n59
Hahn, Scott W. 92n26
Hall, Christopher A. 27n5, 305n51, 305n50, 312
Halpern, Baruch 128n105, 331n1, 333, 333n5
Hamilton, James E. 36n33, 44n53
Hamilton, Victor P. 80n3, 82n5, 348n33
Hanson, Paul D. 105n50, 148n26, 336n9
Haran, Menahem 94n30, 96n32
Harnack, Adolf von 143n18
Harrison, E. F. 251
Harrison, R. K. 147n24, 148, 155, 155n46, 156, 156n50, 157
Harrisville, Roy A. 21n4
Hart, Trevor A. 277n26
Harvey, Van A. 314n72
Hatch, Nathan O. 366, 366n13, 367, 367n16
Haurer, C. E. 96n32
Hayes, John H. 141n11, 157n52
Hays, Richard B. 186, 186n47, 186n48, 247n55, 345n26
Hegel, G. W. F. 34, 37n36, 39, 39n41, 39n42, 40
Hendel, Ronald S. 80n4, 100n41

Henry, Carl F. H. 138, 138n8, 139, 248, 249n59, 251n63, 309, 310, 358
Henry, Matthew 327
Herder, J. G. 34
Hewlett, Martinez 275n21
Hilary of Poitiers 137, 137n5
Hincks, E. 59
Hodge, Charles 290–291, 291n23, 292, 327
Hoffmeier, James K. 154n42, 155, 155n47, 156, 156n50, 157
Holquist, Michael 287n11
Holzer, Harold 321n88
Hort, Greta 156, 156n49
Houghton, Walter E. 34n26
Hubbard, David A. 170, 170n88
Hudson, Winthrop S. 283n6
Hughes, Jeremy 216n12
Hume, David 35, 36, 36n31, 37, 313, 313n69
Hunger, Hermann 66n12, 66n13
Hurwitz, Avi 87n12
Huyssteen, J. Wentzel van 275n21

Ignatius 216
Irenaeus 271n17
Isaac, E. 126n99

Jacobsen, Thorkild 69, 69n19
Japhet, Sara 101n43, 159n60, 222n19
Jastrow, Marcus 60
Jerome 28, 28n9, 88n14, 143n18, 227, 271n17
Jewett, Paul K. 350, 350n38
Jewett, Robert 312n65
John Chrysostom 27n5, 224n22, 227, 232n5, 239, 239n34, 239n35, 242n41, 244n47, 271n17, 290
John of Damascus 340, 340n12
John Paul II, Pope 194
John Philoponon of Alexandria 231n5
Johnson, E. Elizabeth 312n65
Johnson, Edward A. 290n21
Johnson, Luke Timothy 113n64, 115, 115n72, 124n93, 124n94, 266n5
Jones, Douglas R. 88n15, 107n52
Josephus 100n42
Juel, Donald H. 122n82, 124n91
Justin Martyr 236, 236n24, 237n25

Kaiser, Walter C., Jr. 44n51, 300n39
Kalimi, Isaac 101n43
Kant, Immanuel 36, 37, 37n35, 37n37, 38, 39, 40, 317n79
Kaufman, Stephen A. 66n12, 66n13

Keener, Craig S. 247n56
Kelly, Brian E. 159n59, 160, 160n62, 161, 161n66, 162, 164
Kidner, Derek 147n24
Kimball, Dan 361, 361n6
Kitchen, Kenneth A. 11, 12, 144, 145, 145n21, 147, 147n25, 148, 148n29, 149, 151, 151n35, 156, 156n51, 159n59
Klauck, Hans-Josef 119n77, 247n55, 345n26
Klingbeil, Gerald A. 130n110
Klooster, Fred H. 303n48
Knierim, Rolf P. 301, 301n42
Knohl, Israel 87n12
Knoppers, Gary N. 96n32
Koester, Craig R. 118n76, 124n93
Koester, Helmut 113n64
Köstenberger, Andreas J. 349n35
Kraus, Hans-Joachim 105n50, 148n26
Krusche, Werner 32n22
Kuhn, Thomas S. 231n4, 233n14, 288n16
Kümmel, W. G. 274n20
Kysar, Robert 109n57, 111n61

Labat, René 97n34
Labuschagne, C. J. 218n14
Landsberger, Benno 68n17
Lane, A. N. S. 284n10
Langford, Jerome J. 17n1, 231n4
LaSor, William S. 170, 170n88
Lederach, Paul M. 169n83
Lehrer, Keith 36n32
Lemche, Niels Peter 131n116
Leo XIII, Pope 193, 194
Lessing, Gotthold E. 34, 35n28, 356, 356n43
Levinas, Emmanuel 41n46
Levine, Baruch A. 127n101, 127n102
Lewis, C. S. 68, 68n18, 283, 319, 319n84
Lewis, G. C. 59
Lindars, Barnabas 316
Lindbeck, George A. 190, 190n55, 190n57, 191, 191n59
Lindsley, Art 303n48
Lints, Richard 45, 45n56, 46, 46n59, 51
Litfin, Duane 364n11
Liverani, Mario 141n11
Livingstone, Alisdair 68n16
Long, V. Philips 130n110, 141n10, 143n16, 155, 155n45, 160n64
Longenecker, Richard N. 121n80, 122n85, 123, 123n89, 124n91, 124n94
Longfield, B. J. 370n20

Author Index

Longman, Tremper, III 66n12, 68n16, 141n10, 148n27, 155, 155n45, 160n64, 166, 166n75, 167, 169n82, 169n84, 215n10
Louth, Andrew 312n66
Luckenbill, D. D. 63n7
Luther, Martin 22, 31, 31n16, 31n17, 32, 52, 53, 225, 225n23, 232, 232n6, 233, 290, 327, 334, 334n6
Lyotard, Jean-François 302, 302n45

MacDonald, Nathan 189n54
MacIntyre, Alisdair C. 43, 43n50
Malachowski, Alan 42n47
Marcion 114n69, 236
Marsden, George M. 306n56, 370n20
Marshall, I. Howard 296, 297n34, 298, 305n49
Marty, Martin E. 307n57
Mathison, Keith A. 284n10
Mayes, A. D. H. 90n20, 127n103
McConnel, Tim 36n33, 44n53
McDonald, Lee M. 281n2
McGrath, Alister E. 190n57, 294n32
McKenzie, John L. 98n35
McKenzie, Steven L. 101n43, 128n105, 129n106, 331n1, 333, 333n5
McKim, Donald K. 192, 192n60, 256n73
McKnight, Edgar V. 246n52
McKnight, Scot 283n9
McLaren, Brian D. 313n68, 361, 361n6
McNeill, John T. 250n61
Meade, David G. 170n87
Melanchthon 232, 232n7, 233
Melugin, Roy F. 182n39
Melville, Herman 174, 209
Metzger, Bruce M. 114n67, 118n76, 281n2
Milgrom, Jacob 87n12
Miller, J. Edward 345n26
Miller, J. Maxwell 141n11, 150, 157n52
Miller, J. W. 352n40
Miller, Stephen R. 149, 149n32
Moo, Douglas J. 167n79, 266n5, 274n20
Moore, G. F. 152n39
Moore, Michael S. 96n32
Moore, Stephen D. 131, 131n114
Moore, Thomas 306n55
Moreland, J. P. 46, 46n60, 47, 47n61, 51
Morgan, Robert 21n5, 178n23
Motyer, J. A. 148
Muller, Richard A. 185n45
Murphy, Roland E. 267n8
Myers, C. D., Jr. 274n20

Neil, William 267n7
Nelson, Rudolph 368n17
Newbigin, Lesslie 54n68, 302n44
Newman, John Henry 54, 54n67
Newton, Isaac 296
Nicholson, E. W. 86n10
Nickle, Keith 109n57
Nielsen, Eduard 127n103
Nietzsche, Friedrich 39, 40, 40n44, 40n45, 54, 317, 317n80
Noll, Mark A. 13n1, 135, 135n1, 145n22, 283n6, 284n9, 306n56, 374n23
Norris, Richard A., Jr. 125n96, 323n93
Nystrom, Carolyn 284n9

O'Brien, Julia M. 96n32
O'Donovan, Joan E. 277n26
O'Donovan, Oliver 289n17
O'Donovan, Wilbur, Jr. 287n12
Ockenga, Harold J. 369
Oden, Thomas 283n8
Olyan, Saul M. 96n32
Oppert, J. 59
Origen of Alexandria 27n7, 80n3, 113n63, 125, 125n98, 143, 143n17, 223, 227, 237, 237n28, 238, 271n17, 290, 319, 319n85, 323, 361
Orr, James 13, 251, 374, 374n24
Osborne, Grant R. 39n40
Ostow, Mortimer 307n58
Otto, Rudolph 317n79
Overland, Paul 268n12
Owen, Robert 13

Packer, James I. 243n46, 250n61, 305, 305n52
Pangritz, Andreas 321n90
Parker, T. H. L. 245n50
Parpola, Simo 68n17
Paul, Shalom 107n52
Payne, David F. 148n27
Payne, Philip B. 44n52, 345n26
Pelagius 270n15
Pelikan, Jaroslav 308n59
Peters, Ted 275n21
Philo 124
Piper, John 312n65
Pius X, Pope 193, 194
Pius XII, Pope 194, 195n68, 321n89
Placher, William C. 312n66, 312n67
Plantinga, Alvin 140, 142, 142n12, 142n13, 143, 318, 322, 322n91
Polanyi, Michael 26, 26n3, 43, 43n50, 279, 280n1, 288n16

Pollock, J. 135n2
Polycarp 114, 114n68
Pope, Marvin H. 323n93
Popper, Karl 34n25
Porphyry 143, 143n18
Porten, B. 58n1
Porton, Gary G. 123n87
Postman, L. 308n60
Preus, Robert D. 252n66
Priest, J. 125n97
Provan, Iain 140, 140n9, 141, 141n10, 142, 143, 143n16, 155, 155n45, 160n64
Provence, Thomas E. 174n8
Ptolemy 373

Rad, Gerhard von 80n3, 178, 178n24, 179, 179n25, 181, 267n8, 348n32
Radmacher, Earl D. 252n66
Ramm, Bernard 170, 170n90, 192, 192n60
Rashi 80n3
Ratner, Joseph 233, 233n12, 233n13
Rawlinson, Henry C. 59, 59n2
Redford, Donald B. 157n54
Reid, Thomas 36, 36n32, 44, 314
Reimarus, Hermann 33
Renan, J.-E. 59
Rendtorff, Rolf 153, 153n42, 154
Richardson, Don 317n78
Ricoeur, Paul 43, 43n50, 183, 189, 189n53, 207, 207n2, 216, 216n11
Ridderbos, J. 149, 149n31
Roetzel, Calvin J. 116n73
Rogers, Jack B. 192, 192n60, 256n73
Rogers, R. W. 59n2
Römheld, Diethard 269n12
Rorty, Richard 42, 42n47
Rosen, Edward 233, 233n11, 233n13
Russell, D. S. 336n9

Sacchi, Andrea 79
Sanders, E. P. 109n57
Sanders, James A. 21n4, 143n15
Sanders, John 231n2
Sandys-Wunsch, John 300n38
Santillana, Giorgio de 17n1
Saucy, Robert L. 362n8
Scalise, Charles J. 182n38
Schaff, Philip 224n22
Schelling, F. W. J. 37n36
Schenck, Kenneth L. 124n95
Schleiermacher, Friedrich 38, 38n38, 38n39
Schmid, Konrad 87n13

Schmitt, Richard L. 58n1
Scholten, Clemens 232n5
Schrage, Wolfgang 247n55, 345n26
Schultz, Richard L. 20, 20n3, 153, 153n40
Schuster, Marguerite 50n63
Scott, Leland H. 36n33, 44n53
Searle, John R. 208n4
Seely, Paul 234n16
Segal, Moses H. 147n24
Seitz, Christopher R. 182, 182n38, 284n9
Semler, J. S. 33
Senft, Christoph 247n55, 345n26
Servetus, Michael 35, 334
Sheridan, Mark 80n3
Shils, Edward 26n2
Simon, Richard 33
Skinner, John 80n3
Smith, D. Moody 109n57, 111n61
Smith, James K. A. 46n59, 49n62
Smith, Jonathan Z. 208n3, 209n5
Soggin, J. Alberto 141n11, 157n52
Sollberger, Edmond 69n19
Sommer, Benjamin D. 107n52
Sparks, Kenton L. 85n9, 94n28, 95n31, 96n32, 97n34, 98n35, 111n60, 128n104, 129n107, 219n15, 229n1, 331n1, 333n5
Spear, Wayne 245n49
Spencer, J. R. 96n32
Spinoza, Baruch 33
Stein, Robert 110n57
Steinmetz, David C. 184n43, 188, 201, 202, 322
Stendahl, Krister 274n20
Steymans, Hans Ulrich 89n18
Strobel, August 247n55, 345n26
Stuart, Douglas 214, 214n9, 215, 216
Sundberg, Walter 21n4
Sweet, William Warren 290n20

Tadmor, Hayim 64n9, 68n17
Tatian 114, 114n66, 152
Taylor, Charles 43, 43n50
Templeton, Charles 135, 136
Tertullian 114, 242n41, 271n17, 276, 276n24
Theodore of Mopsuestia 28, 28n11
Theodoret of Cyrus 28, 28n11, 271n17
Thompson, John L. 185n45
Thompson, Leonard L. 119n77
Thompson, Marianne Meye 119n77, 170n87
Thompson, Thomas L. 131n116, 181n32
Tigay, Jeffrey H. 61n4, 127n103
Toomer, G. J. 234n15
Torrance, T. F. 43, 43n50, 44

Author Index

Trapp, Michael Burney 186n46
Troeltsch, Ernst 313, 313n71, 314, 315, 318, 322
Trypho 236

Ussher, James 216

Valla, Lorenzo 22
Van Leeuwen, Mary Stewart 342n17, 343n18, 353n42
Van Leeuwen, Raymond 302n43
Van Seters, John 11, 86n11, 91n21, 181n32
Van Til, Cornelius 45, 45n54, 45n55, 46
Vanhoozer, Kevin J. 55n69, 208n4, 297, 297n35, 298, 298n37
Voetius 173
Voightlander, E. von 58n1

Waaler, Erik 159n59
Wainwright, Geoffrey 284n9
Waltke, Bruce K. 176n18
Ware, Kallistos 252n67
Warfield, B. B. 139
Watson, P. J. 333n4
Watts, John D. W. 105n50, 148n27
Webb, William J. 289, 289n17, 289n18, 296, 349n36
Webster, John 283n5
Weinandy, Thomas 252n67
Weinfeld, Moshe 87n12, 89n18
Weiss, James Michael 30n15
Wellhausen, Julius 93n28
Wenham, Gordon J. 80n3, 169n81, 348n31
Wesley, Charles 374
Wesley, John 271n18, 276, 291, 291n24, 291n25, 327
Westerholm, Stephen 274n20
Westermann, Claus 80n3, 105n50, 148n26, 178, 178n24, 348n32
Wette, W. M. L. de 93n28
White, A. D. 232n6, 232n7

Whitefield, George 290
Whitelam, Keith W. 131n116
Whybray, R. N. 105n50, 148n26, 153, 153n42, 154
Wilberforce, William 291, 291n28
Wilcox, David L. 275
Williams, A. N. 309n62
Williams, D. H. 284n9, 284n10
Williams, Frank J. 321n88
Williamson, H. G. M. 101n43, 159n60, 222n19
Wilson, R. McL. 124n95
Wink, Walter 182n40, 187
Winter, Ralph D. 363, 363n10
Witte, John, Jr. 352n40
Wolf, Herbert M. 147n24
Wolff, Hans Walter 178, 178n24
Wolff, Hope Nash 61n6
Wolterstorff, Nicholas 36n32, 37, 37n34, 43, 43n50, 44, 242, 242n44, 243, 244, 245n48, 314n73
Wood, John Halsey, Jr. 148n27
Work, Telford 253n68
Wright, Christopher J. H. 121, 121n79
Wright, David F. 234n17
Wright, G. Ernest 96n32, 179, 179n28
Wright, N. T. 130, 130n111, 170, 170n88, 191n58, 277, 277n27, 302n43

Yarbrough, Robert W. 292, 292n29, 293
Yarchin, William 28n10, 28n11
Yeago, David S. 283n9
Young, Dwight W. 69n20, 218n14
Young, E. J. 164, 164n68
Young, Frances M. 125n96, 186n49

Ziesler, John 274n20
Zimmerli, Walther 92n25, 109n53
Zimmermann, Jens 38n38, 41n46, 51n64, 53, 53n65, 306n54
Zwingli, Ulrich 31

Subject Index

Abraham, William, 190
academic freedom, 367
accommodation
    Calvin and, 230–36
    in contemporary theology, 242–47
    in early Christian interpretation, 236–42
    evangelical objections to, 247–58
    See also inerrancy, of Bible
Acts of Paul, 346
Adam and Eve, 49
agency, dual, 309–10
Akkadian, 60
Albright, W. F., 179
Alexander, T. Desmond, 151–52, 157–58, 165–66
allegory, in biblical exegesis, 27–28, 29–30, 31, 124, 184–87, 319–20, 322–26
Ancient Orient and Old Testament (Kitchen), 151
Anderson, Bernard, 180
Annales Beteris et Novi Testamenti (Ussher), 216
anthologies, as genre, 218–20
anti-intellectualism, 183
antinomy, 311–12
Antiochus IV Epiphanes, 116–17, 149
antirealism, 40–42, 131–32
apocalypses, ancient, 223–24
Apocrypha, 126
Apology of David, 128–29
Aquinas, Thomas, 29–30, 309
Archer, Gleason, 254–55
Aristotle, 29
ark of the covenant, 95
Arminians, 311
Asa, 103

Assumption of Moses, 125, 165
Assyrian annals, 63–66
Assyriology
    critical disposition of, 151
    Gilgamesh Epic, 60–63
    Mesopotamian historiography, 63–66, 218
    origins of, 58–60
    Sin of Sardon, 68
    Uruk Prophecy, 66–67
Athanasius, 237–38, 305, 340–41
Augustine, 28, 125, 143, 173, 240–41, 276, 319, 324, 360
authority and gender equality, 339–54
authorship, biblical. *See* human beings, finitude of

Babylon, 116–17
Babylonian Chronicle Series, 63–66
Babylonian "infants," 28
Bakhtin, Mikhail, 287
Barr, James, 196–99
Barth, Karl, 172–78, 192, 201, 277
Bartholomew, Craig, 143
Basil the Great, 238
Bathsheba, 129
Belleville, Linda, 349
Beyond Fundamentalism (Barr), 199
Bible
    authority, in extra-biblical theology, 288–99
    and created order, 277–78
    Enlightenment and, 34
    exegesis within, 121–26
    as God's voice, 280–81
    Hellenistic influences, 124–25

409

historicity of, 175–76, 181, 187–92, 198
inerrancy of, 55, 138, 173–74, 225–26, 256, 357, 358, 362, 373–74 (*See also* accommodation)
Luther on nature of, 31n17
prooftexting, 48
religious and political propaganda in, 126–29
as saga, 175–76
secularization of, 18–19
theological and ethical diversity, 119–21, 181, 230–31
theological reading of, 183–84
and truth, 17–18, 29, 31
See also interpretation, biblical
biblical theology movement, 179–81
biography, theological, 222–23
Bisitun, Mount, 59–60
Bloesch, Donald, 192–93
Blomberg, Craig, 162–63
"The Bondage of the Will" (Luther), 31n17
Bonhoeffer, Dietrich, 321
Book of the Covenant, 91, 220
Book of the Dead, Egyptian, 269–70
Brunner, Emil, 277
Burrus, Virginia, 131

Calvin, John, 31, 32–33, 35, 187, 334
and accommodation, 232–36, 242, 245, 250, 256
Campbell, Alexander, 13–14
Canaanites, 79
canon, 125–26, 182, 281–82
Cappadocian fathers, 238
Carey, William, 363
Carlyle, Thomas, 34
Carnell, Edward, 368–69
Carnell, E. J., 251
Carson, Donald A., 167n79, 231
Cartesian realism, 33, 42
cause and effect, 36
certainty, epistemic, 53–54, 231, 258
Chicago Statement on Biblical Hermeneutics, 252
Childs, Brevard, 181–82, 201–2
Christian epistemology, 47–54
Christology. *See* Jesus Christ
1–2 Chronicles, 94, 101–4, 159–60, 221–22
Chronologia sacra (Ussher), 216
Chrysostom, 239–40
church, authority and criticism, 18–21, 27, 31
circumcision, 192, 294–95
Clement of Alexandria, 206
Clines, David J. A., 131
Coady, C. A. J., 314
Common Sense realism, 36–37, 44, 314
Conceiving the Christian College (Litfin), 364–65

Constantine, 22
constructive response, to biblical criticism. *See* evangelical biblical scholarship—constructive responses of
context, in discourse, 208–9
Copernicus, Nicolaus, 17, 231–34, 285–86
cosmology, 33
Craig, William Lane, 46, 311n64
created order. *See* revelation, general *vs.* special
creation narratives, 83, 97–98, 176, 348
creedal traditions, 282–83
criticism
believing, 20, 133–34, 322, 356, 357–58
biblical (*See* historical criticism, biblical; interpretation, biblical)
higher (*See* historical criticism, biblical)
Critique of Practical Reason (Kant), 37–38
Critique of Pure Reason (Kant), 37
culture, and interpretive community, 210–12
cuneiform languages. *See* Assyriology
Cyrus of Persia, 105, 106, 148–49

Daniel, 116–18, 119, 149–50, 164–65, 223–24, 335–39
Darius, 58
David, 101–3, 330–35, 355–56
Abishag and, 28
apology of, 128–29
Davidic promise, 74–75
Deborah, 346, 353
deconstruction, 41–42
Derrida, Jacques, 42
Descartes, René, 33, 314
De Spiritu et Anima, 29–30
Deuteronomic Code, 91, 220
Deuteronomic History (DtrH), 101–4, 332
Deuteronomy. *See also* Pentateuch
critical interpretation, 88–91
Deuteronomy source (D), 88
Diatesseron (Tatian), 152–53
Diekema, Anthony, 366–67
Dillard, Ray, 12, 166–67
Divine Discourse (Wolterstorff), 242
Divino afflante Spiritu (Leo XIII), 194
Domitian, 119
Donation of Constantine, 22–23
doubt, methodological, 314
dual agency, 309–10

Eastern Orthodoxy, 284
The Eclipse of Biblical Narrative (Frei), 187–92
Egypt, ancient, 99–100, 269–70
Eichhorn, J. G., 34

Subject Index

Elamite, 60
Elohistic source (E), 88, 158n56
Emerging Church (EC), 361
empiricism, 33–34
Engaging Scripture (Fowl), 192
Enlightenment, 33–39, 140–43
Enns, Peter, 170
1 Enoch, 125–26, 165
An Enquiry into the Obligations of Christians to Use Means for the Conversion of the Heathen (Carey), 363
Enuma Elish, 97–98
epistemic optimism, 39, 140–42, 231
epistemology
    Christian, 47–54
    in modern period, 30–39
    in postmodern period, 39–55
    in premodern period, 26–30
Epistles, Pastoral, 113–16
Epistle to the Philippians (Polycarp), 114
Erickson, Millard, 251
Esarhaddon Apology, 64
eschatology
    in Daniel and Revelation, 119, 335–39
    Egyptian, 270
    of Jesus, 336
    of Paul, 335–36
evangelical biblical scholarship—constructive responses of
    about, 18–21, 171–72, 200–203
    Barth's theological exegesis, 172–78
    biblical theology movement, 179–81
    canonical interpretation, 181–82
    Catholic responses, 193–96
    James Barr, 196–99
    kerygmatic exegesis, 178–79
    narrative theology, 187–92
    pneumatological solutions, 192–93
    Steinmetz's precritical exegesis, 184–87
    Wink's theological exegesis, 182–84
evangelical biblical scholarship—traditional responses of
    about, 12–13
    appeals to critical scholarship, 153–55
    artificial comparative analogies, 150–53
    artificial presentations of evidence, 146–50
    citing biblical "testimony," 164–65
    critical anti-criticism, 144–46
    ignorance and obfuscation, 165–68
    lowering historicity threshold, 155–57
    misleading and illegitimate harmonizations, 159–64
    misleading use of "test cases," 157–59
    objections to accommodation, 247–58
evangelicalism, American
    about, 20
    criticism and local church activities, 358–62
    epistemological position of, 51–54
    evangelical scholarship, 12–13, 168
evangelical responses to biblical criticism
    about, 134–35
    in the Academy, 363–72
    conservative evangelical biblical scholarship, 144–70, 373–74
    fideism, 136–39
    philosophical critiques, 139–44
    warranted but erroneous rejections of, 135–36
evolution, 361
Exodus
    critical interpretation of, 99–100, 154–55
    Sinai narrative, 158
    sources, 11
    See also Pentateuch
Ezekiel, 92, 95, 108–9

faith, and reason, 310–11
fall, of man, 309
fiction, as biblical genre, 212–14
fictions, as genre, 214–16
fideism (blind faith), 135–39, 310
flood narratives, 83–85, 97
Foucault, Michael, 42
Fowl, Stephen, 192
Frei, Hans, 187–92
fundamentalism, 145, 306–8, 367
Fundamentals, The, 145

Gadamer, Hans-Georg, 43, 53, 358
Galileo Galilei, 17, 285–86
Gematria, 118n76
Gender and Grace (Van Leeuwen), 343
gender equality, and theology, 339–54
genealogy, as biblical genre, 216–18
Genesis
    Calvin's approach to, 235
    and epistemology, 49–51
    genealogy in, 216–18
    reality and imagination, 176
    sources, 11
    See also Pentateuch
genres
    of biblical literature
        about, 213–14
        ancient apocalypses, 223–24
        anthology, 218–20
        fictions, 214–16

mimetic genealogy, 216–18
statutory reformulation, 220–21
theological biography, 222–23
theological history, 221–22
of human discourse
  about, 205–6, 227
  analytical genres, 212–13
  fallibility of, 224–26
  genres of biblical literature, 213–24
  and interpretive community, 210–12
  verbal discourse, 206–10
of writing, 34
gezerah shawah, 122
Giles, Kevin, 340–41
Gilgamesh Epic, 60–63, 151
Gilkey, Langdon, 180
God
  divine image, 50–51
  divine name, 83, 147
  divine speech, 192–93
  dual agency, 309–10
  God's-eye view, 261–62
  voice of God (word), 280–81, 304
good Samaritan, parable of, 213
Gordon, Robert, 143
Gospels, Synoptic. *See* synoptic problem
grace, and interpretation, 45
Graham, Billy, 135–36
Grammar of Assent, A (Newman), 54
Greece, 116–17
Green, William Henry, 164
Gregory of Nazianzus, 238–39, 305
Gregory of Nyssa, 238
Gregory the Great, 28
Grudem, Wayne, 248–49

Hagar and Ishmael, 79–80
Hagar and Ishmael in the Wilderness (Sacchi), 79
Halpern, Baruch, 333
Harrison, E. F., 251
Harrison, R. K., 155
Hatch, Nathan, 366, 367
Hays, Richard, 186
Hebrews, 124–25
Hegel, G. W. F., 34, 39
Heilsgeschichte, 178–79
heliocentrism, 17, 231–35
Henry, Carl F. H., 138–39, 249–52, 358
Herder, J. G., 34
heresy, 283n7
hermeneutics
  general, 25–26, 177, 206, 210–12
  hermeneutical circle, 38–39, 275, 307–8

in modern period, 30–39
in postmodern period, 39–55
in premodern period, 26–30
hierarchical authority, 339–54
higher education, Christian, 363–72
Hilary of Poitiers, 137
historical analogy, 315
historical consciousness, 23, 30
historical correlation, 315–16
historical criticism, biblical
  about, 73–77, 132
  applied to Mesopotamian ancient texts, 62–63, 65–67, 70–72
  assumptions of, 57–58
  benefits of, 362
  example of, 22–23
  influence of, 21–22, 358–62
  and miracles, 313–22
  recent developments, 129–32
  responses to, 18–21
historicism, 34, 140–41, 187
historiography
  Israelite, 101–4, 154–57, 177–78, 221–22
  Mesopotamian, 63–66
history, theological, 221–22
Hodge, Charles, 292
Hoffmeier, James, 155–56
Holiness Code, 91, 220
Holy Spirit, 195–96
human beings, finitude of, 49–50, 225–26, 241, 252, 374
Hume, David, 35–38, 313
Hyksos, 99n40

Ibn Ezra, 144, 148
idealism, 37
image, divine, 50–51
implied authors/readers, 212n8
incarnation, 53
inerrancy, of Bible
  accommodation as explanation for, 256
  Barth on, 173–74
  and evangelical scholarship, 373–74
  Henry on, 138
  human nature of, 55, 225–26, 357, 358
  and lay audience, 362
Inspiration and Incarnation (Enns), 170
Instruction of Amenemope, 268
interpretation, biblical. *See also* evangelical biblical scholarship—constructive responses of; evangelical biblical scholarship—traditional responses of

Subject Index

and allegory, 27–28, 29–30, 31, 124, 184–87, 319–20, 322–26
authority and extra-biblical theology, 288–99
and the Christian academy, 363–72
and Christian theology, 329–54
church traditions and, 283–85
divine *vs.* human knowledge, 261–62
early interpretive stances, 27–28
general *vs.* special revelation, 263–78
goal of, 262, 263
interdisciplinary and multicultural, 285–88
interpreter's spiritual and psychological health, 303–8
introduction to, 73–77
and local church, 358–62
and miracles, 313–22
in modern period, 30–39
in postmodern period, 39–55
in premodern period, 26–30
reason, faith, and mystery in, 308–13
text and context, 262–63
"The Interpretation of the Bible in the Church" (PBC), 194
interpretive community, and culture, 210–12
Introduction to Biblical Christianity from an African Perspective (O'Donovan), 287
Introduction to the New Testament, An (Carson and Moo), 167n79
Irenaeus, 237
Isaiah, 104–8, 147–49, 153, 164–65
Ishmael, 79–80, 82–83
Israel, sojourn in Egypt, 81–82
Israelite historiography, 101–4, 141, 154–57, 177–78, 221–22

Jeremiah, 90–91, 107, 148, 268
Jerome, 28
Jesus Christ
and accommodation, 241–42, 244
authority and infallibility, 164–65
birth narrative, 110–11, 320
crucifixion, 162–63
eschatology of, 336
exegesis methods of, 121–22
finitude and sin of, 252–53
in John's gospel account, 112
passion story, 112
John, Gospel of, 111–12, 162–63, 222–23
Johnson, Luke Timothy, 115
Jonah, 214–16
Josiah, 89–90
Judah, 107
Jude, 125

Justin, 236–37

Kant, Immanuel, 36, 37–38
Kelly, Brian, 160–62
kerygmatic exegesis, 178–79
Kings, 101–4, 222
Kitchen, Kenneth A., 11–12, 144, 147–48, 150–51
knowledge
and action, 305–6
and faith, 140–41
human *vs.* divine, 27, 30, 171–72, 262–63
nature of human inquiry, 287–88
Korah, 127–28

Lagash King List, 69–70
Lamb of God, Jesus as, 112, 162–63, 222–23
language, 40, 249
Law of Moses. *See* Deuteronomy
legal diversity, in Pentateuch, 91–93, 220–21
Leo XIII, 193
Lessing, Gotthold, 34–35
Levinas, Emmanuel, 41n46
Levites, 96, 127
Lindbeck, George, 190
Lints, Richard, 45–46
Litfin, Duane, 364–66
Longman, Tremper, III, 166–67
Luke, Gospel of, 152
Luther, Martin, 31–32, 232, 334
Lyotard, Jean-François, 302

MacIntyre, Alisdair, 43
Manasseh, 103–4, 159–60
Marduk, 97–98
Mark, Gospel of, 110
marriage, 347, 354
Matthew, Gospel of, 110, 111, 152
McKenzie, Steven, 333
meaning, intended, 44
Media, 116–17
Meditations, The (Descartes), 33
Melanchthon, 232
Mesopotamia. *See* Assyriology
middle knowledge approach, 311n64
Miller, Stephen, 149–50
minimalist school, 169n80
miracles, skepticism and, 214, 313–22
"On Miracles" (Hume), 313
mission work, Christian, 363–70
Moo, Douglas J., 167n79
Moore, Stephen, 131
morality, 40
Moreland, J. P., 46, 47

Moses, 78–79, 164–65
myths, Mesopotamian, in Pentateuch, 97–99

name, divine, 83, 147
Nebuchadnezzar II, 67
Nebuchadrezzar, 108–9
Neo-Assyrian treaty language, 89–90
Nero, Caesar, 118–19
Newman, John Henry, 54
Nietzsche, Friedrich, 39–40
Numbers, 127–28. *See also* Pentateuch

Old Persian, 60
Old Testament canon, 125–26, 182
Old Testament Theology (von Rad), 179
open theism, 231
ordination, of women, 339
Origen, 125, 143, 237, 319
Orr, James, 251, 374

pantheism, 38n39
papal authority, 31
parables, 189, 214–16
Passion Narrative, 112
Passover narrative, 155–57
Pastoral Epistles, 113–16, 353n41
patriarchalism, 344–45
Paul
  eschatology of, 335–36
  natural theology, 265–68, 270–72
  and Pastoral Epistles, 113–16, 345, 353n41
  predestination, 312
  status of women, 345, 351, 353nn41–42
Pentateuch
  as anthology, 218–20
  authorship, 78–79
  chronology, 80–82
  critical interpretation of, 77–78, 100–101
  Deuteronomy, 88–91
  Exodus, 99–100
  Israel's religious institutions, 93–97
  legal diversity, 91–93, 220–21
  narrative diversity, 82–88, 146–47, 151
  Near Eastern traditions in, 97–99
  slavery in, 120
  sources, 11, 85–88, 153–54
  traditional *vs.* historical-critical readings, 18–20, 165–66
perception and reality, 36–37
persecutions, of faithful, 338
Persia, 116–17
peshat, 121–22
pesher, 122–23

Philistines, 128
Philo, 124
philology, 29–30
philosophical inquiry, secular, 29
Pius XII, 194
Plantinga, Alvin, 142–43
Platonic exegesis, 124–25
Platonism, 27, 125
Polanyi, Michael, 43, 279–80
Polycarp, 114
Pontifical Biblical Commission, 193–96
Porphyry, 143
postmodernism, 39–55
practical realism, 40, 42–44, 52–53, 263
presuppositionalism, 44–45
preunderstanding, 42
priesthood, Israelite, 95–96, 127
Priestly Code, 91, 220
Priestly Writer source (P), 85–88, 93, 97–98, 146–47
progressive revelation, 246
prooftexting, 48
propositional school, 46–47
Protestantism, 34, 284
Provan, Iain, 140–42, 143
Proverbs, 268
providential miracles, 316
Providentissimus Deus (Leo XIII), 193

Rad, Gerhard von, 178–79
rationalism, 310–11
rationality. *See* reason, human
Rawlinson, Henry C., 59
reason, human, 32, 35–36, 40, 309–10
Recovering Theological Hermeneutics (Zimmerman), 53
reductionism, 52
Reformation, 31–33, 284
Reid, Thomas, 36–37, 44, 314
Reimarus, Hermann, 33
religion, and the Enlightenment, 35
Renaissance, 30–33
Revelation, Book of, 118–19, 335–39
revelation, general *vs.* special, 263–78
rich young man, parable of, 110
Ricoeur, Paul, 43
Ridderbos, J., 149
Roman Catholic Church, 31, 193–96, 284
Rome, 118–19
Rorty, Richard, 42
Ruth, 316

Subject Index

sacrificial activity, Israelite, 93–94
saga, 175–76
Samuel, 101–4, 128–29, 222, 330–35
Saul, 101–2, 128
Schleiermacher, Friedrich, 38
scholarship, biblical. *See* historical criticism, biblical; interpretation, biblical
Schultz, Richard, 153
science, 231–34, 285–86, 288
Scope and Authority of the Bible, The (Barr), 197
Scripture. *See* Bible
secular response, to biblical criticism, 18–21
Semler, J. S., 33
Sennacherib, 68
sign miracles, 316
Simon, Richard, 33
Sin of Sardon, 68
slavery, 119–20, 289–93, 344
Smith, Jonathan Z., 209n5
Solomon, 103, 129
Song of Songs, 131, 323, 324–25
soteriology, 32–33
special pleading, 137
speech, divine, 192–93. *See also* accommodation
speech-act theory, 208n4
Spinoza, Baruch, 33
statutory reformulation, genre, 220–21
Steinmetz, David, 184–87, 202
Stuart, Douglas, 213–14
subordinationism, 340–41
Sumerian King List, 69–70, 217
Summa Theologica (Aquinas), 29, 309
synoptic problem, 109–13, 143–44, 152, 162–63, 222–23

tabernacle and temple, 94
tacit knowledge, 26
Tatian, 152–53
Taylor, Charles, 43
Templeton, Charles, 135
Tertullian, 276
Theodore of Mopsuestia, 28
Theodoret of Cyrus, 28
theology
 and gender equality, 339–54
 interdisciplinary and multicultural, 285–88
 narrative, 187–92
 natural, 199, 265–68, 270–72
Thirty Years' War, 35
Thomists, 309

1–2 Timothy, 113–16, 349–50
Titus, 113–16
Torrance, T. F., 43–44
tradition, skepticism of, 26, 30, 140
traditional response, to biblical criticism. *See* evangelical biblical scholarship—traditional responses of
Trinity, the, 340–41
Troeltsch, Ernst, 313–18
truth
 in Cartesian realism, 42
 correspondence theory of, 46
 and knowledge, 33–34
 propositionalist, 46–47
 and Scripture, 17–18, 29, 31
 theological, 269, 276
 See also inerrancy, of Bible
Tyre, 108–9

Ur, 61
Uriah, and Bathsheba, 129
Uruk Prophecy, 66–67
Ussher, James, 216

Van Leeuwen, Mary Stewart, 342–43
Van Seters, John, 11
Van Til, Cornelius, 44, 46
Vigilantiae studiique (Leo XIII), 193

Waltke, Bruce, 176
Webb, William, 349–50
Wesley, John, 291
Westermann, Claus, 178–79
Whitefield, George, 290
Whybray, R. N., 154
will to power, 39–40
Wink, Walter, 182–84
Wisdom of Ben Sira, 312
Wolff, Hans Walter, 178–79
Wolterstorff, Nicholas, 43–44, 242–43
women, 115, 339–54
Wright, Christopher, 121

Yahwist source (J), 85–88, 98, 146–47, 158
Yarborough, Robert W., 292
Young, E. J., 164

Zadokites, 96, 127
zeitgeist, 39
Zimmerman, Jens, 53

Made in the USA
Middletown, DE
06 May 2021